Direct Energy Conversion
third edition

STANLEY W. ANGRIST

Professor of Mechanical Engineering
Carnegie-Mellon University

NORTHWEST COMMUNITY COLLEGE

Allyn and Bacon, Inc.   Boston   London   Sydney   Toronto

This book is part of the
ALLYN AND BACON SERIES IN MECHANICAL
ENGINEERING AND APPLIED MECHANICS
Consulting Editor: Frank Kreith
University of Colorado

Library of Congress Cataloging in Publication Data

Angrist, Stanley W
    Direct energy conversion.

    Includes bibliographical references.
    1. Direct energy conversion.
TK2896.A6   1977   621.312'4   76-28391
ISBN 0-205-05581-8
Second printing . . . May, 1977

Contents

CONTENTS

Preface

This edition of *Direct Energy Conversion* intends to reflect how the book has been used by faculty members teaching from the first two editions during the past ten years. Most instructors have elected to stress the fundamentals of the five major methods of direct energy conversion, that is, thermoelectricity, photovoltaics, thermionics, magnetohydrodynamics, and fuel cells and have elected to omit the material in Chapter 2 on irreversible thermodynamics. Because of their usual choice of material and because irreversible thermo-dynamics is not required to understand any of the balance of the book, Chapter 2 has been moved in its entirety into Appendix D. It will thus be available to instructors who wish to continue to include it in their courses.

The new Chapter 2 is a rather comprehensive review of various methods of energy storage. After several years of teaching direct energy conversion I felt a strong need to point out to students how various energy storage methods could be teamed up with different direct energy conversion methods to create unique power-producing systems. Energy storage systems that might be used in central-station power plants or in automotive applications are given special attention.

Chapter 9 which is a catalog of little known effects and devices has been updated to reflect changes in their state-of-the-art. While this material is in-teresting, it is, of course, not required for understanding the major effects or devices.

The entire text, excluding Appendix D, can be covered in a single-semester course that meets three times a week if a little judicious editing of material is done. A two-quarter course on direct energy conversion should provide ample time to cover all of the text material including Appendix D.

I take pleasure in acknowledging the careful reading of the entire manu-script by Professor George T. Hankins of Wright State University. Professor Hankins may take credit for several useful changes which improved the text significantly, in my judgment. I will, of course, bear the usual responsibilities for any errors or mistakes that appear herein.

I would also like to acknowledge the encouragement of Professor Frank Kreith, University of Colorado, the Consulting Editor on the Allyn and Bacon series in Mechanical Engineering and Applied Mechanics, who first came up with the idea for a new edition. His valuable criticism is appreciated.

My editor, Harvey Pantzis, pushed, pulled, tugged, bellowed, and, finally, bullied me into completing this revision. In retrospect, I sincerely appreciate his efforts.

Ms. E. Jean Stiles again had the unenviable task of turning what anyone else would classify as illegible waste paper into a finished and very readable manuscript. She not only did this task with speed and efficiency, but also with good cheer that never faltered.

STANLEY W. ANGRIST
Pittsburgh, Pennsylvania

View of a 25-kilowatt photovoltaic array in extended position designed and built at Lockheed for the NASA Space Station. This 30-ft (9.1-m) by 100-ft (30.5-m) array supplies one-fourth of the total space station power of 100 kilowatts. This array is made up of a lightweight, flexible, Kapton substrate incorporating a printed circuit. The array has an area density of only 1.95 kg/m² (0.4 lb/ft²) compared with a typical value for rigid arrays of 4.86 kg/m² (1.0 lb/ft²). Photo courtesy of Lockheed Missiles and Space Company, Inc.

1 Direct Energy Conversion: Past, Present, and Future

Surely the 1970's will be remembered as the age in which the ways we think about and use energy underwent a profound change. This was the decade that brought an end to a century of cheap energy. No doubt we will look back on that century with some nostalgia as an uncomplicated time when we could all be energy wastrels. Individual nostalgia is a harmless exercise in daydreaming, but nostalgia on a national scale has no place in the debate on energy policies that will affect the economic stability and national security of the United States for years to come. The tendency to look back at the decades of cheap energy simply misleads the public into believing that cheap energy will return and ignores the truths which characterize our real situation. Frank Zarb [1], the head of the Federal Energy Administration in 1975, presented these truths and the reasons why they must be confronted in order to deal effectively with real world conditions. The truths relevant to our subject are as follows:

The energy crisis is real. As a nation we became accustomed to cheap energy. We ignored our own resources such as coal and relied instead on unstable foreign sources. The era of cheap energy is over. We must reduce our consumption of foreign oil and produce energy from our own resources.

For years the United States had surplus domestic oil capacity and American-based companies dominated the international trade in petroleum. In those days cheap energy made productive economic sense. The United States, which easily withstood three embargoes before 1973, is no longer the world's leading oil producer—it is now other nations which control the oil export trade.

OPEC is not going to go away. The Organization of Petroleum Exporting Countries (OPEC), the business agent of the controlling oil-producing nations, is a cohesive international bloc in business to maximize profits. It is a monopoly that has cornered the market—that's us—and while it may leak a little from time to time, it will not fly apart soon. To count on its collapse is to flirt with delusion of the highest order.

There is no easy way out. The only course that we can follow to extricate ourselves from utter dependence on OPEC is to establish a policy that reduces our reliance on imported oil by making our consumption more efficient and supplying more of our own needs. We must recognize fully the unpleasant fact that energy is costly to produce, and that means energy is valuable. The *only* successful means our society has yet developed to measure the actual value of a commodity is its real price.

In plain language then: if we allow price to reflect the economic facts of energy—that it is scarce and valuable—then consumers, both industry and individuals, will begin to react to reality. They will begin to use energy efficiently in the home, in the factory, and on the road.

Constructing a government-controlled system will only exacerbate our dependence on unreliable energy sources. The establishment of controls or an allocation system would propose—unknowingly or otherwise—an expensive nightmare made all the more frightening by the government's tendency to give at least equal weight to political as well as economic profit in making decisions.

Energy and the environment can coexist. Energy independence requires that we use all of our energy sources—coal, nuclear power, oil shale, and additional oil and natural gas from Alaska's North Slope and the outer continental shelf. We can develop those resources and still preserve our environment if apparently conflicting interests will sit down and discuss objectives rather than polarizing and politicizing the issues.

The American people can handle the truth. The entire premise of democratic government is that the people can reason their way to the right decisions and make hard choices that self-government requires. We must tell the public the truth about our energy problem and its solution and stop making political promises of cheaper energy that cannot be delivered.

Like it or not—and clearly most of the people living in the United States do like it—we have created a high-energy society that demands more energy in more remote places. We now demand energy on a satellite orbiting Mars 50 million miles away and on a deep-sea exploration vehicle five thousand feet below the surface of the Pacific Ocean. Engineers in the coming years are going to be expected to be able to supply energy for more and more esoteric uses, as well as to be able to wring significant amounts of energy from sources that have been largely ignored—the sun, the winds, and the tides. This book is written with the goal of trying to help engineers find solutions to some of those vexing problems.

The development of society in the past two centuries has been characterized by the progressive substitution of machine power for muscle power. Much of that machine power, at least in the last seventy years, has been desired and used in the form of electricity. At present, man generates the bulk of his electricity by two methods: (1) he burns fossil fuel to convert water into steam and then expands the steam through a turbine which in turn powers a generator; or (2) he forces water flowing from a lake or river to fall down a channel at the bottom of which the water's kinetic energy is made to turn a hydraulic turbine that in turn powers a generator. Neither of these traditional methods lends itself very readily to supplying power to satellites in orbit about Mars or other remote locations. Furthermore, man is also beginning to realize that the earth's fossil fuel supply is finite, its water power restricted to a few geographical areas, and that he must start now to look for new methods of converting thermal, radiant, and mechanical energy to electricity.

The new methods are the ones that will be considered in this book. Their chief advantage over the traditional methods is that they convert energy to electricity using fewer intermediate steps—in many cases bypassing the intermediate steps altogether. It might be more accurate, in fact, to describe the subject of this book as "new forms of energy conversion," except that common usage has already given it the name direct energy conversion. The chief disadvantage of the new methods is that few of them have achieved efficiencies that approach those of the more traditional methods.

Much of the subject matter contained in this text might well be classified as applied thermodynamics. However, it will be observed by the reader that simply applying the principles of thermodynamics to these devices is not sufficient to gain an understanding of the principles by which they operate. Certainly, thermodynamics is *one* of the key building blocks necessary to achieve a reasonable level of competence in the subject, but a true mastery of the fundamentals cannot be gained without at least a rudimentary understanding of the basic principles of quantum mechanics, the solid state, transport theory, and electromagnetics. Wherever possible, the necessary background in these topics has been provided; however, where space limitations have prevented the going into extensive detail, references have been provided (denoted by numbers in brackets) that will enable the reader to fill in the necessary material.

Before beginning consideration of the myriad processes and generators that make up this subject, the stage will be set by discussing the beginnings of direct energy conversion, the energy sources from which the devices must be powered, the fundamental limitations on energy conversion, and the power needs that direct conversion will fill. A few remarks about the units used in the rest of the book conclude this chapter.

1.1 EARLY WORK IN DIRECT CONVERSION

Without a doubt one of the first direct conversion devices that man had knowledge of was the electric eel (Fig. 1-1). So far man has not been able to duplicate the eel's ability to convert directly chemical energy to high voltage electrical energy. The electric eel is characterized by its lethal high voltage discharge; almost without exception most of man's direct conversion devices are noted for their low voltage.

FIG. 1-1. A unique direct energy converter found in nature is the electric eel. This eel delivers what would be a lethal 600-volt zap to the metal rod being held down in the tank. Photograph courtesy of the Westinghouse Research Laboratories.

However interesting nature's contributions to direct conversion may be, we must devote most of our attention to man's activities in this area. Therefore at the beginning of each chapter a brief historical introduction will be given to the material that will be studied therein. These will include discussions of some of the more important workers and contributions that brought the field to its present state. In this section, however, we will examine the field of energy conversion from a broader perspective while we look at the more or less simultaneous developments going on in different modes of energy conversion. We will not give many details here, but will rather sketch what was going on in specific areas at a given time.

It is hard to say exactly when the first steps in direct conversion were taken. As early as 1802, Humphrey Davy suggested that the chemical energy released when coal is oxidized might be converted directly into electricity. Though he did not succeed in building one, his suggestion certainly contained the germ of the idea on which fuel cells are based. There is no doubt, however, in the case of Thomas Johann Seebeck's discovery in 1821 of the effect that bears his name. His discovery of the fact that a junction of dissimilar metals upon which a temperature difference had been imposed could deliver an electric current was a remarkable one in several respects. Perhaps the most interesting consequence of his finding was that he failed to interpret it correctly: he thought he had showed that he could produce a magnetic field by means of a temperature difference. Seebeck examined a great many materials, including some metal oxides and minerals. Among these were materials now called semiconductors, with which, had he used them to build a generator, he could have produced electricity with an efficiency of about 3 percent. This compared favorably with steam engines of the day and far exceeded the performance of the weak electrostatic generators of that time.

Thirteen years later, Jean Peltier discovered that the passage of an electric current through a junction of two different conductors could produce heating or cooling at that junction, depending on the direction of the current. He too failed to understand the meaning of his discovery, simply ascribing his observations to the fact that Ohm's law may be disobeyed by very small currents. In 1838 Emil Lenz explained Peltier's work correctly; no one thought of using Peltier's discovery as a means of refrigeration for over seventy years.

Meanwhile Michael Faraday, a blacksmith's son who began his scientific career as a bottle washer at the Royal Institution, performed one of the earliest experiments in what we now call magnetohydrodynamics: in 1831, he moved mercury contained in a glass tube through the poles of a magnet and detected a voltage rise perpendicular to the direction of the magnetic field and the motion of the mercury. Two years later Faraday made contributions to the principles of electrochemistry that aided in the studies subsequently made on fuel cells.

Faraday also noted, in 1834, that the resistance of silver sulfide went down as the temperature went up—a characteristic that is now sometimes associated with semiconductors. This trait was at variance with the behavior of other conductors with which he worked. Faraday was unquestionably a prolific worker in the area of direct conversion.

The year 1839 saw several fundamental developments in the area of direct conversion. Edmond Becquerel, in one of the earliest uses of light as a primary source of energy, noted that a voltage could be developed when light was directed onto one of the electrodes in an electrolyte solution. That same year the English chemist, William Grove, constructed a battery (we would now call it a fuel cell) in which the water-forming reaction of hydrogen and oxygen generated an electric current. His cell used platinum electrodes in contact with dilute sulfuric acid. Twenty-six of his devices hooked in series produced sufficient power to decompose water back into oxygen and hydrogen.

In the middle of the eighteenth century Charles DuFay had noted that the space in the vicinity of a red-hot body is a conductor of electricity. It was not until 1853, however, when Edmond Becquerel turned his attention to the subject that a theoretical explanation for what DuFay had observed was presented. Three years later the versatile Lord Kelvin (William Thomson), who made contributions in the areas of electrical theory and solar radiation as well as thermodynamics, found the relationship that exists between the Seebeck and Peltier effects. He did this by separating the effects into those that he considered reversible (the Seebeck and Peltier) and those which he considered irreversible (the I^2R heating and ordinary thermal conduction). He also found that a conductor carrying an electric current in a temperature gradient experiences a lateral heat transfer that is dependent on the nature of the material; this phenomenon is known today as the *Thomson effect.*

In 1873 Willoughby Smith discovered that light could reduce the electrical resistance of a circuit element made of selenium, thus beginning the study of photoconductivity; this property is now recognized as one found in certain semiconductors. One year later F. Braun discovered that lead sulfide and certain of the iron pyrites could be used as rectifiers. In 1877 W. G. Adams and R. E. Day also conducted experiments with selenium, noting that light could produce a voltage across a solid. In 1879 William Crookes considered the unusual properties of matter in discharge tubes and suggested that this material be considered as a "fourth state of matter" after the solid, liquid, and gaseous states. That same year, E. H. Hall reported the effect that today carries his name in which a voltage appears perpendicular to an applied current in a solid located in a magnetic field.

Not long after Hall's work, two British chemists, L. Mond and C. Langer, developed a device they actually called a fuel cell; their device had an output of about six amperes per square foot. The successful development of the electric generator at about the same time overshadowed their effort and fuel cells dropped from the scene until the 1940's.

One of the first attempts to exploit the properties of semiconductors was made by Alexander Graham Bell in 1880 with a device he called a "photophone." Bell devised a valve with which a voice could modulate a beam of light; in this device the receiver was fabricated from a piece of selenium.

Two years later, the next step in understanding the phenomenon of thermionic emission was taken when Elster and Geitel reported on the work they had done with a sealed tube containing two electrodes, one that could be heated and one that could be cooled. In 1883 Thomas Alva Edison, in one of his numerous patents, disclosed that he had chanced upon thermionic emission and proposed a voltmeter that could utilize this effect. A true understanding of the nature of the negative charge carriers emitted by an incandescent conductor in a vacuum was not discovered until 1879, when J. J. Thomson found that their ratio of charge to mass agreed, within the limits of experimental uncertainty, with the value he found for electrons; he made measurements of the deflection of a beam of charged particles subject to crossed magnetic and electric fields.

In 1904 J. C. Bose took out a patent that made use of the rectifying properties of semiconductors to build a detector for use in a radio receiver. Altenkirch in 1909 and 1911 derived the basic theory for thermoelectric refrigerators and generators. He also noted at that time what properties would be needed to make the devices practical.

Arnold Sommerfeld derived equations for the motion of electrons in a solid in 1928 by applying the principles of the then-infant science of quantum mechanics. Three years later A. H. Wilson, also using quantum mechanics, gave a satisfactory definition of a semiconductor. It was during this same period that increased use was made of selenium rectifiers and other materials that exhibited the properties we now associate with semiconductors.

In 1933 Langmuir had achieved considerable insight into the phenomena of plasma and thermionic emission. In a more applied vein, such workers as B. Karlovitz, C. Petersen, and E. Rupp made attempts to construct gaseous magnetohydrodynamic generators. Their attempts, made in the years from the late twenties to the early forties, failed chiefly because they could not attain a sufficient degree of ionization in the working fluid.

Shortly after the end of World War II there were breakthroughs in nearly all areas of direct energy conversion due to a series of technological advances. The following are only a few of the highlights. In 1948 H. B. Callen, as part of a doctoral thesis at the Massachusetts Institute of Technology, derived all of the relations between the thermoelectric and thermomagnetic coefficients by means of the Onsager reciprocal relations of irreversible thermodynamics. In 1949 one of the most dramatic demonstrations of what semiconductors could achieve was announced by workers then at the Bell Telephone Laboratories; for their work on the discovery of transistor action W. Shockley, J. Bardeen, and W. H. Brattain later received the Nobel prize. One year later A. F. Joffe, a Russian physicist, began publishing his work on the use of semiconductors in thermoelectric elements. All during the fifties Joffe and his co-workers continued to announce advances in the development of thermoelectric materials and applications for thermoelectric devices.

The year 1954 was particularly fruitful, witnessing the development of a high-pressure fuel cell by F. T. Bacon in England, the construction of a silicon solar cell with an efficiency of 6 percent by workers at the Bell Telephone and RCA Laboratories, and the announcement by Maria Telkes of a solar thermoelectric generator with an overall conversion efficiency of 3.5 percent. In 1956 G. N. Hatsopoulos completed his doctoral thesis on the successful design and operation of a close-spaced thermionic generator, and in 1958 H. J. Goldsmid, A. R. Sheard, and D. A. Wright published the results of their work on the development of a very promising thermoelectric material, bismuth telluride.

During and since the period of time just described, the level of research and development activity has remained very high. We will describe some of the more recent work as we go into the details of each mode of conversion in later chapters.

1.2 THE PRIMARY ENERGY SOURCES

The design of an energy converter is based to a large extent on the type of energy with which it starts. One of the main reasons for studying direct energy conversion is to seek out new and better ways to convert our present forms of primary energy to electricity. We are interested in doing this because much of the energy that the world uses today in its conversion devices is exhaustible; some of our primary energy sources might even become quite scarce in our lifetime. In this section, therefore, we shall examine the primary energy sources of the world and how they are being used at present.

To place our discussion in perspective let us take a brief look at how man has been spending energy to date and at the rate at which he is expected to spend it in the future. For this discussion we shall use a very large energy unit in order to keep to a minimum the writing out of large numbers. This unit of energy is called the Q and is defined as being equal to 10^{18} Btu (2.93×10^{14} kWh). It is roughly the amount of energy which would be required to bring Lake Michigan to a boil.

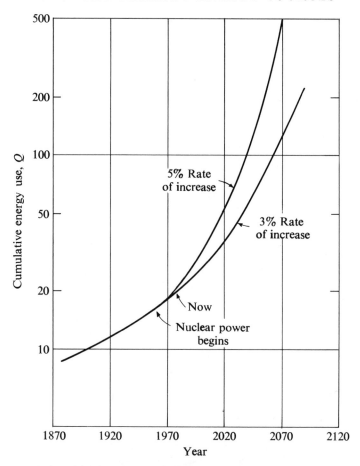

FIG. 1-2. Probable world cumulative energy demands during the last 100 and the next 100 years. The energy demand is given in units of Q defined as 10^{18} Btu. The probable energy demand is shown for two rates of increase: 3 percent and 5 percent.

About 18 Q has been used during the last 2000 years, but half of this was used in the past 100 years. Even with the increasing demands for energy that took place after the Industrial Revolution, the world in 1850 was only spending about 0.01 Q per year. By 1977 the rate was about 0.24 Q per year —a 24-fold increase in 127 years, during which time the world's population only tripled. If we take into account increasing industrialization and population growth, by the year 2070 the world will have spent between 120 Q estimated at a 3 percent rate of increase, and 460 Q at a 5 percent rate of increase as shown in Fig. 1-2.

The United States accounts for about 34 percent (estimated to be 0.083 Q in 1977) of the world's energy expenditure with only 6 percent of the world's population. Since the United States has industrialized rapidly during the last 100 years, it is interesting to see how it has changed and will change the way it spends its energy. Figure 1-3 shows this change, starting with the year 1800 and projecting the changes to the year 2050. We may break down the information given in Fig. 1-3 further by noting that in 1966 only about 21 percent of the energy supplied to the ultimate consumer was supplied as electrical energy. Interestingly enough, an equal amount was supplied to the consumer as fuel for internal combustion engines.

The world is obtaining its energy from the sources [4] shown in Fig. 1-4. While about 34 percent of its needs were met by coal in 1968, it is interesting to note that coal supplied 56 percent of the world's energy needs only 18 years earlier. The shift in reliance from coal to petroleum and natural gas has been massive. As shown in Fig. 1-5, the shift in supply sources for the United States is even more dramatic: coal supplied 78 percent of our energy in 1920 but dropped to only 18 percent in 1973, while petroleum and natural gas combined to supply 77 percent of our energy needs in 1973.

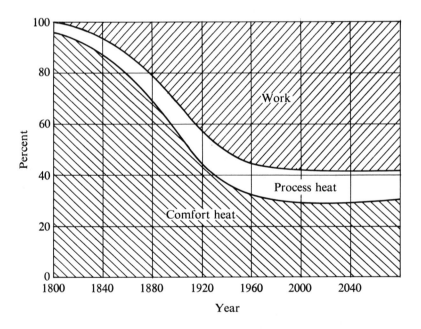

FIG. 1-3. The projection of the relative proportions of three components of the energy system to the year 2050 for the United States. After Putnam [2] with permission.

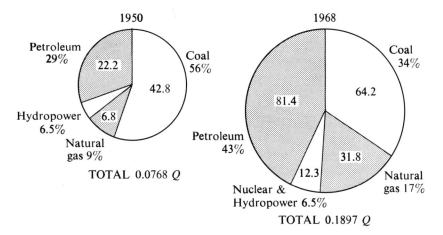

FIG. 1-4. Sources of world energy supply in 1950 and 1968. After Ref. [4].

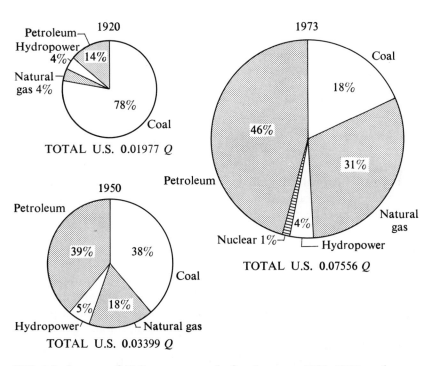

FIG. 1-5. Sources of U.S. energy supply for the years 1920, 1950, and 1973. After Ref. [4].

It is convenient to classify the world's energy sources into two main groups, called *energy capital* and *energy income*. Energy capital consists of fossil fuels, including coal, oil, and natural gas, that were created several hundred million years ago. In effect they represent solar energy that was stored in the form of chemical energy by the action of living organisms. Energy storage of this type is no longer taking place at a rate and on a scale to be of interest to man before he becomes extinct. Thus we must conclude that sooner or later all the fossil fuel in the world will be used up. Nuclear fuels such as are used in fission reactions must also be included among our capital reserves of energy, since they too are finite. Breeder reactors will be able to extend nuclear fuel supplies, but they must still be considered exhaustible.

Energy income refers to resources that are being continuously replenished and renewed. These include sources such as the wind, the tides, rivers, natural steam, and vegetable and animal wastes. Of course, ultimately most of this energy can be traced back to the sun, no less than the fossil fuels. For example, solar energy falling on the earth's atmosphere causes local temperature gradients that induce the convection currents we call the wind. The sun's heat also evaporates from the oceans water that is subsequently returned to the land as rain; the rain returns to the oceans via rivers. The sun's energy also causes the growth of plant life, and thus of animal life, since the latter basically depends on plant life.

Looking at Fig. 1-4 again, we see that more than 88 percent of the world's present energy needs are supplied from capital reserves. The question to be answered is: How long can we continue to live on our capital? At the *current* rate of consumption, conventional fossil fuels are believed to be sufficient for another 500 years. However, as we have already mentioned, the demand for energy under the pressure of increasing industrialization and population growth would reduce that estimate by *at least* a factor of five. In the next several sections we shall examine the reserve potential of the various forms of energy in the light of predicted energy needs.

1.2.1 Fossil fuels. Because fossil fuels are distributed very unevenly around the world, some countries will feel their shortage before others; there is little doubt that with time the shortage will become worldwide. Just when that time will come is not easy to pinpoint. The prediction involves geological and engineering judgments on quantities of coal, oil and gas that lie buried beneath the surface of the earth, estimates on improvements in the technology of recovery methods, projection of future energy needs of various parts of the economy, and last but certainly not least, high-power (no pun intended) politics. Needless to add, the history of the "science" of projected energy needs and reserves is littered with the remains of obsolete guesses, some of which have turned out to be spectacularly wrong. However, aside from digging up the first twelve miles of the earth's surface from pole to pole, there is no absolutely certain way to predict fossil fuel reserves.

To protect the U.S. oil industry's economic position in the domestic oil market and to prevent over-reliance on foreign oil—subject to cutoff in time of international strife—oil import quotas were established by President Eisenhower in 1959 and maintained until 1973. During the 1960's, despite quotas on imported oil—some would say because of the quotas—the nation's comfortable position with respect to its oil needs began to deteriorate. Exploration declined and major new oil finds were limited to a few offshore areas and the North Slope of Alaska. Offshore leasing was held up for 17 months in the wake of the Santa Barbara oil spill as environmental concerns emerged. Since 1970, oil imports have supplied our growth needs in oil.

Oil imports have tripled since 1960. By 1975, 35 percent of total oil demand was imported, one-third in the form of residual fuel oil. Traditionally, the bulk of U.S. petroleum imports has come from Venezuela and Canada, with smaller amounts coming from the Middle East, North Africa, Nigeria, and Indonesia. However, in recent years about one-third of our imports (12 percent of our total oil consumption) has been coming from Arab nations.

The Ford Foundation study cited earlier [4] provides some of the most recent data on world and U.S. energy supplies by source. Their estimates are presented in Tables 1-1 and 1-2.

The data is broken down by the geological terms "reserves," "recoverable resources," and "remaining resource base." "Reserve" estimates are based on detailed geological evidence, usually obtained through drilling, while the other estimates reflect less detailed knowledge and more geological inference. All of these estimates are based on assumptions about technology and economics. In general, the size of the last two estimates will increase over time as technology improves or prices increase.

In Table 1-1 it may be seen that U.S. petroleum reserves are only about nine times 1973 consumption and about one-half of the cumulative production that has taken place in the United States. In stark contrast is the fact that world petroleum reserves are more than twice the cumulative world production to date.

The estimation of gas reserves is also an uncertain business. Experts appearing as witnesses before the Federal Power Commission, which by law sets the rates on interstate gas, have presented estimates on natural gas reserves that differ from each other by as much as a factor of four. Natural gas reserves in the United States are estimated to be about 13 times 1973 consumption with reserves equal to about three-fourths of cumulative production. World reserves are estimated to be about three times cumulative production. In recent years industrial purchasers of natural gas who operate under interruptable contracts have experienced more and more interruptions as supplies have fallen beneath current demand.

TABLE 1-1. MAJOR ENERGY RESOURCES, U.S. †

	1973 consumption (Q)	Cumulative production (Q)	Reserves (Q)	Recoverable resources (Q)	Remaining resource base (Q)
Petroleum	0.0347	0.605	0.302	2.910	16.790
Shale oil	—	—	0.465	N/A	975.
Tar sands	—	—	—	N/A	0.168
Natural gas	0.0236	0.405	0.3	2.470	6.8
Coal	0.0135	0.810	4.110	14.6	64.
Strippable coal	N/A	N/A	0.925	2.6	2.6
Low-sulfur coal	N/A	N/A	2.390	N/A	38.200
Uranium					
Used in light-water reactors	0.00085	0.002	0.228	0.6	3.2
Used in breeders	—	—	17.7	47.	2×10^5
Thorium used in breeders	—	—	4.2	17.5	570.
Hydropower	0.0029	—	—	0.0058‡	—

N/A not available

† All values given in units of $Q = 10^{18}$ Btu. See text for definition of recoverable resources and remaining resource base. After Ref. [4].

‡ Ultimate capability

14

TABLE 1-2. MAJOR ENERGY RESOURCES, WORLD†

	Cumulative production (Q)	Reserves (Q)	Recoverable resources (Q)	Remaining resource base (Q)
Petroleum	1.550	3.68	14.40	60
Shale oil	—	1.10	N/A	12,000
Tar sands	0.0006	1.00	2.15	N/A
Natural gas	0.670	1.86	15.80	32
Coal	3.340	N/A	N/A	340
Uranium				
Used in				
light-water				
reactors	N/A	0.510	0.990	6.5×10^5
Used in				
breeders	—	40	77	6×10^8
Thorium used				
in breeders	—	22	66	N/A

† All values given in units of $Q = 10^{18}$ Btu. See text for definition of recoverable resources and remaining resource base. After Ref. [4].

Two of the chief problems in making estimates of coal reserves are determining the maximum thickness of coal that can be mined economically and determining the maximum depth at which economic mining can take place. Coal has, in recent years, been the stepchild of the energy industries. The shift from coal-fired steam locomotives to diesel engines eliminated a major market. At the same time, home coal furnaces were scrapped in favor of oil, gas, or electricity. Production of coal dropped 36 percent between 1947 and 1962—a blow from which the industry is only now beginning to recover. Labor problems and poor working conditions have plagued the coal industry. Rising labor costs and the increased costs of safety equipment have encouraged mining companies to turn increasingly to surface mining, which produces three times the coal output of an underground mine with the same number of man-hours.

Even a cursory reexamination of Table 1-1 reveals that the United States has huge reserves of coal. If one assumes that only half of our coal reserves are recoverable, then our coal supplies would last 150 years at 1973's rate of consumption. This tremendous energy reserve has been the driving force behind the campaign to develop economical methods of producing synthetic natural gas and solvent-refined liquids from coal.

Even with the uncertainties associated with the forecasting of fossil fuel reserves, the examination of future estimates of energy resources is interesting and instructive. Keep in mind that the estimates presented in

Tables 1-1 and 1-2 for the United States and the world were computed by standard geological and engineering techniques, but they are still far from being certain.

How long will this tremendous reservoir of energy from the past last us? The answer to this question depends on several factors. Consider first, the U.S. reserves which amount to 5.177 Q. Assuming that demand remains at the 1973 level of 0.072 Q and ignoring the contribution of hydropower, one finds that our fossil fuel reserves would last 72 years. But if one assumes that U.S. demand for fossil fuels will increase at an annual rate of 3 percent, then our fossil fuel reserves would last only about 42 years. If one assumes that ultimately we will be able to use half of the energy listed under "recoverable resources"—some 9.99 Q—then our fossil energy reserves would last about 60 years (again at a 3 percent growth rate). Both of these calculations ignore the role of imports in meeting our energy needs.

A similar calculation can be made for the world. Assuming a constant world energy consumption rate of 0.24 Q per year and coal reserves equal to 211 Q, one finds that the world's fossil fuel energy reserves would last about 900 years. However, assuming a 4 percent annual growth rate for energy, then one finds that fossil fuel reserves (not recoverable resources) would last about 90 years.

To lengthen the time before our fossil fuels are all used, it will be necessary to:

(1) find vast new reservoirs of fossil fuel not already included in our projections;

(2) reduce our energy consumption;

(3) develop other energy sources.

The most probable outcome will be some combination of these three options.

1.2.2   Nuclear fuels. Nuclear fuels must also be counted as energy capital even though the energy stored in them is certainly substantial. At present, the low temperature reactors which have been put into service obtain only a small fraction of the latent energy in the nuclear fuel. However, it should be noted that the unfissioned fuel can be reprocessed and then returned to a reactor. Estimates on the future energy available from nuclear fuels are extremely difficult to make because the technology of energy extraction, especially by means of breeder reactors, is changing so fast. However, the Ford Foundation [4] estimates that in the United States alone recoverable resources of uranium are about 0.6 Q without the breeder and as much as 47 Q with the breeder. If one includes thorium, the recoverable resources amount to 64.5 Q with the use of the breeder reactor. Even the energy listed under "reserves" alone is impressive—about 22 Q—if we assume the development of a successful breeder.

In 1971 the National Petroleum Council in its report to the Secretary of the Interior estimated that U.S. electric utility production of electricity would increase at an annual rate of 6.7 percent. This is roughly four to seven times the population growth estimated by the Bureau of the Census. (It should be noted, however, that in the period of 1971 through 1975 electric power consumption did not increase at an annual rate of 6.7 percent but at a rate of only 4.4 percent.) The NPC has estimated that nuclear power production will rise from 23 billion kilowatt-hours in 1970 to 2068 billion kilowatt-hours in 1985, or about 48 percent of our electricity supply. Nuclear power supplied about 4 percent of the *total* U.S. energy needs in 1975 and is projected to supply 17 percent of total needs in 1985.

Nuclear power has two disadvantages that are yet to be overcome. The first is the problem of the safe disposal of the radioactive wastes that nuclear power plants produce. The second is that at present nuclear power is mostly confined to central power stations, and a convenient and safe means of making appreciable quantities of it portable to any extent is lacking. This eliminates consideration of nuclear power for the powering of most types of transportation.

1.2.3 Hydropower. The major source of energy income utilized today is water power. It has no major research and development problems to be solved. Its growth is expected to be regular and orderly.

Water power contributes about 1 percent of the energy input of the world and 4 percent of the energy input of the United States. Besides providing an inexpensive source of electricity it often aids in flood control and in helping to make rivers navigable. The total world hydroelectric power potential is estimated to be about ten times the present installed capacity. Even if this were fully exploited, the percentage contribution to the total world energy demand would remain small due to the rapid increase of this demand. While its contribution to the world's utilization of energy will never be great, it will always be important in those geographical areas where it is available.

1.2.4 Solar energy. The sun releases energy at a rate of about a million Q every three seconds. It has been estimated that about thirty-two hundred Q reach the earth every year. If we could harness but a small amount of this energy, man's energy supply problem would certainly be solved. One of the chief problems of solar energy is that it reaches the earth at a very low potential. With the sun at its zenith at sea level, only about one-tenth of a watt per square centimeter falls on the earth. Large collectors are needed to achieve appreciable amounts of power—about fifteen square feet for one kilowatt of heat or 150 square feet for one kilowatt of work utilizing a converter of 10 percent efficiency. The energy may be made more concentrated by utilizing some type of focusing arrangement but this generally requires a cloudless day and a mechanism that allows tracking of the sun.

Photochemistry is one of the frontier areas that offers some hope for the efficient storing of solar energy so that it may be used at a later date. One of the goals of people working in this field is to find a suitable reaction that can be produced by sunlight with the absorption of energy and that can, at some later time, be reversed with the evolution of energy. One of the major problems in this area is that many endothermic photochemical reactions reverse themselves so rapidly that they convert light energy into heat without allowing any time for storage. Those reactions that have shown promise respond only to ultraviolet light.

The utilization of solar energy today in any direct form (other than for the growing of crops, etc.) is all but nonexistent. Many of the satellites in orbit do obtain their instrumentation power (at most, several hundred watts) from the sun. There has also been a considerable amount of research on the use of sun for comfort heating of dwellings and the heating of hot water in sunny climates, as well as work in the development of small solar concentrators for use as domestic cookers in newly developing countries that are deficient in other primary energy sources.

1.2.5   Other primary sources. It is too early to state with certainty how much of a contribution the other primary sources—such as geothermal power, wind power, farm wastes, and the temperature difference in tropical waters—will be able to contribute toward meeting our energy needs in the next 20 years.

Some of these sources, however, present some rather interesting engineering problems and, where available, produce inexpensive power. The steam wells of Larderello, Italy, are an example of this point. The wells are drilled to depths of 1000 to 2000 ft and deliver superheated steam at pressures from 71 to 390 lb per sq in. gauge at temperatures of 290° to 400°F. A rate in excess of 4,400,000 lb of steam per hr is obtained from 140 wells; the steam also brings with it such chemicals as boric acid, borax, and ammonia. Over 500 megawatts (electrical) of installed geothermal power is now in commercial service in northern California.

Another example of naturally occurring energy sources are the "heat fields" ten miles from Reykjavik, Iceland, that deliver water at 188°F at a rate of 4200 gal per min that supplies the comfort heat of a large part of the city.

The utilization of the energy of the tides has appealed to man for many centuries. While many different schemes have been proposed, only one has been brought to fruition. The French government has constructed a power plant on the Rance River called *Maremotrice* or sea motor, which will take advantage of the unusually large tide in the river's estuary. Breton farmers had used these tides for centuries to mill grain but this new plant causes the inrushing and outgoing water to deliver as much as 240,000 kilowatts to the French electric grid. The plant is capable of delivering electricity with a difference in water level elevations as small as ten feet across the dam.

Passamaquoddy Bay which separates Maine from New Brunswick has frequently been considered a good location for a tidal power station. The long history of this project has been expensive and turbulent; none of the many studies made to date have offered conclusive evidence that significant amounts of power could be generated at rates competitive with power from more readily available energy sources. At any rate, the number of natural bays and estuaries suitable for power plants of this type is so limited that the quantity of power generated by this method will never be significant.

1.2.6 Controlled fusion. Fusion energy is encountered widely in nature because it is the basic energy of the sun and the stars. Its release on earth has been achieved only in an uncontrolled manner in the form of the hydrogen bomb, but controlled-fusion research has been going on since 1951. In theory, it should be possible to release tremendous amounts of energy by fusing the nuclei of the lightest elements to form heavier nuclei. In practice, the conditions required for success in this endeavor are extraordinary: a gas must be brought to a temperature of the order of 100 million degrees (hotter than the interior of the sun) and somehow contained for periods of the order of one second while maintaining a minimum particle density under rigorous requirements of purity.

The problem of achieving net power from a fusion reactor is fundamentally different from that of achieving power from a fission chain reaction. In a fusion reactor, there would be some level of nuclear-power production whenever any hot fuel plasma is present in the confining chamber. However, a *self-sustaining* reaction (and net power) can be achieved only when the total power released exceeds the sum of power losses from the entire system. In this way a fusion reactor does not at all resemble a fission reactor, but is more nearly analogous to a gas turbine whose operation succeeds only if its efficiencies are such that its net turbine output exceeds the power required by the compressor.

The confinement of the incredibly hot plasmas produced in fusion reactors has for a number of years seemed to fusion researchers to be an all but impossible task. However, in 1969 Soviet scientists working with a machine known as Tokamak 3 succeeded in containing a high density plasma (several trillion particles per cubic centimeter) at temperatures of about five million degrees for 25 to 50 thousandths of a second. As short as this time seems, to fusion researchers it was a major step, since heretofore such dense, superhot plasmas were breaking out of their containers in a matter of only one or two thousandths of a second.

A second generation Tokamak, the ATC (adiabatic toroidal compressor), was the next machine to be brought into operation at Princeton University. This machine demonstrated high temperatures and high-density Tokamak plasmas, showing the efficacy of two methods of heating: compression, which was the reason for its shape, and neutral beam injection. If the next generation of machines is equally successful, it is anticipated that commercial power could be generated around the turn of the century [5].

The importance of achieving a controlled fusion reaction that can be used in power generation is generally attributed to two factors:

(1) A virtually unlimited source of fuel. It has been estimated that there is enough deuterium in the oceans to provide 20 billion years' energy at current levels of consumption. Deuterium, the fuel used in certain fusion reactions, has a cost that is a small fraction of conventional fuels, even when extracted by present methods.

(2) An inherently safe energy source. There can be no explosion or runaway chain reaction, as in the case of fission power plants. The fusion process is analogous to chemical burning, rather than to fission, and the energy content of the fuel in the reaction zone at any instant is relatively small. Furthermore, the reaction products and most of the radioactivity induced in the surrounding vessel are short-lived.

The achievement of a controlled fusion reaction capable of delivering power, when achieved, will free man once and for all of the worry that he might outlive his energy sources.

1.2.7 Possible energy scenarios. Traditionally, energy policy analysis has been handled by looking to the past, but we have to live with the decisions in the future. Most energy studies base their estimate of what will happen by simply extrapolating from trends that have prevailed in the recent past. The Ford Foundation [4] has provided a more sophisticated approach in trying to divine what will happen. They have based their analysis on the premise that the future is to a certain extent within our control. They constructed three plausible but very different energy futures for the period through the year 2000. The discussion in this section is based on their analysis.

The alternatives are based on different assumptions concerning the energy growth patterns our society might adopt for the years ahead. There are, of course, many futures possible and it is most unlikely that the real energy future of the United States will conform identically to any of the three scenarios they have chosen to describe. They caution in their report that these are not predictions, but tools for rigorous thinking.

The time-dependent energy use per year is shown in Fig. 1-6. The *historical growth* scenario assumes that the use of energy will continue to

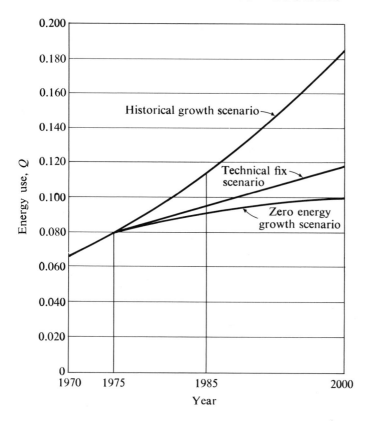

FIG. 1-6. Three possible energy scenarios according to the Ford Foundation. After Ref. [4].

grow such as it has in the past. It assumes that the nation will not deliberately impose any policies that might affect our traditional habits of energy use, but will make a strong effort to develop supplies at a rapid pace to match rising demand. The average annual energy growth comes out to the average experienced in the period 1950–72, or 3.4 percent.

The *technical fix* scenario shares with the historical growth scenario a similar level and mix of goods and services. But it reflects a determined national effort to reduce energy demand through the application of energy-saving technologies. In this scenario, energy growth is projected at about one-half the historical growth future, or about 1.7 percent annually. Only one of the major domestic energy sources—Rocky Mountain coal or shale, or nuclear power, or oil and gas—would have to be pushed hard to meet the energy growth rates of this scenario.

The *zero energy growth* scenario has the nation reaching an annual energy use of 0.1 Q per year in the year 2000, which involves an annual energy growth of about 0.9 percent. It is not an austerity program since everyone in the United States would enjoy more energy benefits in the year 2000 than he enjoys today. It does not preclude some economic growth and even allows, according to the Ford Foundation, the less privileged to catch up to the comforts enjoyed by the rest of the population today. The zero energy growth scenario would emphasize durability, not disposability, of goods. It would substitute for the idea that "more is better," the ethic that "enough is best." Supplying the energy to meet a zero energy growth scenario has far fewer problems than supplying the other scenarios. In addition to reducing demands on the traditional resources, this scenario places emphasis on renewable resources such as solar power, wind energy, and the conversion of agricultural and other wastes to energy.

The Ford Foundation stresses in its report that the nation does have energy choices. Each of the many paths that lie before us has its own advantages and pitfalls. As energy-conscious citizens, we must inform ourselves of what lies ahead before we choose our course of action.

1.3 LIMITATIONS ON ENERGY UTILIZATION

Man spends a tremendous amount of his energy resources every year. Does he get full value for what he spends? The answer is *no*. Conservative estimates place the quantity of energy wasted at about 70 percent. As the zero energy growth scenario implies, one solution to the problem of our dwindling energy reserves then appears to lie simply in reducing this waste, which would cause our supplies to last considerably longer. In this section we will consider what can and cannot be done along these lines.

Certainly one of the major factors that limits how energy will be used is the cost of that energy. In Table 1-3 we list the approximate number of dollars that must be spent to obtain a kilowatt-hour of energy (not necessarily electrical) from a particular source. This table is presented for scaling purposes only, since the cost of energy varies tremendously even within a given country.

The natural fuels such as fuel oil, natural gas, coal, and gasoline are seen to be the cheapest. If a source of energy is conveniently packaged, the price is affected, as witnessed by the cost of flashlight battery energy. If a source of energy is considered to be a rare and tasty treat, the price is affected, as witnessed by the cost of caviar. If the source of energy is considered dangerous or evil (or capable of inducing pleasant feelings in the user), the price is affected, as witnessed by the cost of martinis. It should

TABLE 1-3. COST OF ENERGY IN VARIOUS FORMS

Source of energy	Cents/kWh
Fuel oil	0.66
Natural gas⎱ Coal ⎰	0.35
Gasoline	1.5
Electricity (central station)	3.0
Sugar ⎫ Bread ⎬ Butter ⎭	16
Martini ($4\frac{27}{32}$ parts gin to $1\frac{5}{32}$ parts vermouth)	670
Flashlight battery	1340
Caviar	2000

also be noted that whereas natural fuels are the most economical in providing heat as such, an energy source such as electricity may be very competitive if the energy is to be used in the form of work rather than heat because of a fundamental limitation on converting heat to work.

We now consider in a little more detail how well we have been using our energy reserves. In Fig. 1-7 we present Putnam's estimate for the trends in efficiency on a worldwide basis; this illustration includes past performance as well as the predicted performance to the year 2050. The curves indicate that on the average the world efficiency has nearly tripled from an estimated 11.5 percent in 1900 to about 30 percent in 1950 (the last date for which firm data are available). Can this figure be increased substantially in the next century? There are several indications that this is not very likely.

It is reasonable to expect that sufficient advances can be made in the design of heat exchangers and attendant equipment to permit an overall rise of efficiency in the use of process heat to 50 percent by the year 2050. In the case of comfort heat the story is much the same. Very large central heating units now achieve efficiencies in the range of 80 to 85 percent; continued improvement in the development and design of heating equipment leads one to conclude that comfort heat will be used at an average efficiency for all units of 65 percent by the year 2050.

Both gas turbines and central station power plants that achieve efficiencies in excess of 40 percent have recently been constructed. With these developments in mind it is not unwarranted to expect that the overall efficiency for all types of work processes could go up from the present 20 percent to about 30 percent in the year 2050.

The reason for this relatively low work efficiency is partly due to the second law of thermodynamics. This ubiquitous law of nature states, in

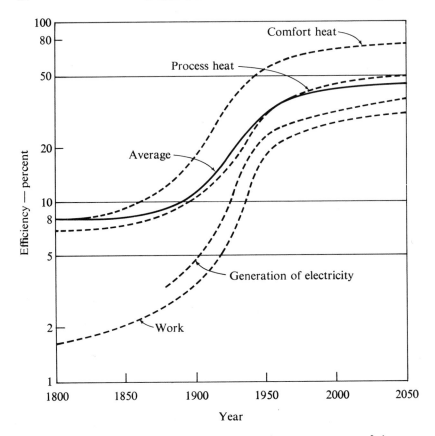

FIG. 1-7. Plausible trends in efficiency for the three components of the energy system and the generation of electricity in the United States from the year 1800 to the year 2050. The weighted average is also shown. After Putnam [2] with permission.

one of its forms, that no heat engine operating between a maximum temperature of T_1 and a minimum temperature of T_2 could be more efficient than a Carnot engine, which would have an efficiency of $(T_1 - T_2)/T_1$. Thus an engine that operates between a maximum temperature of 2000°K and a minimum temperature of 1000°K could have as its maximum efficiency 50 percent. To achieve this figure each of the processes that make up the cycle would have to be completely reversible—a state of affairs not achieved in real devices.

There are only two major forms of conversion that we will study in this book that bypass this limitation—solar energy converters and fuel cells. Both of these devices, ideally, are isothermal in their operation and do not convert the energy from their primary source to heat before generating electricity. Because they are free of the Carnot restriction, workers in direct conversion have held out great hope for them. So far the silicon photovoltaic cell has achieved conversion efficiencies in excess of 16 percent. Unfortunately, solid state physics places a maximum theoretical efficiency of 22 percent on cells made of this material—one of the best solar cell materials found to date. Some fuel cells have achieved efficiencies in the neighborhood of 50 percent; an ideal hydrogen-oxygen fuel cell operating near room temperature should enjoy an efficiency around 94 percent.

There is another reason of some consequence that helps to explain the low work efficiencies, and this is that the work totals include all forms of transportation. Nearly all of our important forms of transportation derive their power from heat engines that immediately bring them under the confines of the Carnot restriction. Moreover, the overall efficiency of most land vehicles is in the neighborhood of 5 percent. High-speed jet airplanes at their design altitude do considerably better, but lose much of their advantage during takeoff and landing.

Before we leave the subject of efficiencies we make one more comment on their usefulness. As one studies direct conversion devices, one finds that for nearly every type of device considered there is more than one efficiency number used in evaluating its performance. This point is explained by the fact that no *single* efficiency or performance number can be the sole index to how well a device will perform in every application. Performance as measured in kilowatts per pound might be the only meaningful figure of merit in the design of a power supply for a satellite. However, when a power plant for an automobile is designed, a useful figure of merit might consist of a number that combines (1) the net energy delivered to the wheels divided by the energy contained in a unit mass of fuel, and (2) the energy delivered per unit volume of power plant. The optimization of a system with respect to one parameter for one purpose could lead to an all-but-useless design if that system were used for another purpose. The importance of this point cannot be overemphasized. It is for this reason that we introduce so many indexes of performance in our study of direct conversion devices.

1.4 WHY DIRECT CONVERSION?

Now that we have reviewed the early history of direct energy conversion, the energy sources with which we are constrained to work, and the limitations under which we must work, we turn our attention to the question, Why study direct energy conversion at all? The answers are manifold, but we will try to point out the implications of some of them both now and in the future.

We have already seen that our world society is an energy society and that each year it requires a greater expenditure of energy than in the previous year. In fact, it has been said that the greatest distinction between our society and the ones that have preceded ours is that we are a society that substitutes mechanical energy for man's energy. But as was pointed out in the previous section, we are not utilizing our energy resources at great efficiency. This leads us to the first reason for studying direct energy conversion. In general, when a process can occur directly rather than by passing through several intermediate steps, it seems reasonable to assume that it may take place more efficiently. By "more efficiently" we mean with less expenditure of a primary energy reserve and with less capital investment. Furthermore, man generally derives considerable aesthetic satisfaction from carrying out a task both directly and efficiently. Certain modes of direct conversion (namely, fuel cells) have already demonstrated a capability for producing small quantities of electrical energy with considerable efficiency. Most of the other forms of direct conversion that we will study are not yet notable for their efficiency. However, many of the devices are still very much in the laboratory research stage, where refinements are continually being made.

The other reason for studying direct conversion is that we require energy in a specific form at a specific location and at a specific time. The ability to convert primary energy directly into the required form at its point of use would be a major achievement. Some of the modes of direct energy conversion now in use and under study are able to do this, and we will cite a few examples. To date the most important area for direct conversion has been the field of space exploration. We will treat in some detail the role that direct energy conversion plays and will play in this field.

Because direct conversion devices come in so many shapes, sizes, and power levels, the areas of application are practically unlimited. We will first mention a few that have already been found, and then give some uses that might be expected to occur in the not-too-distant future.

1.4.1   Terrestrial applications of direct conversion. The United States Weather Bureau has found that it can enhance the accuracy of its long-range predictions if it has timely weather information from some rather remote locations—for example, stations north of the Arctic Circle and in Antarctica. The stationing of personnel in these locations for extended periods of time could be both unpleasant and expensive. Thus, the Bureau has had constructed remote weather-sensing stations that transmit data such as temperature, wind velocity, and precipitation on a 6-hour schedule; transmissions can be made more frequent by radio command. These units draw their power from 40,000 curies of strontium 90, whose decay heat is converted directly into electricity by a thermoelectric generator that trickle charges a 32-volt sealed nickel-cadmium battery. The radioactive source and generator are buried in the ground in containers designed to prevent accidental contamination of men or animals; the only portions of the system that protrude above ground are the actual sensing elements and the transmitter aerial. These units are designed so that they need not be visited by maintenance personnel more often than about once every 10 years. Similar units fueled with bottled propane have been designed to power vhf-fm radio relay transmitters located in relatively inaccessible terrain. These areas would be radio dead spots without the relay stations.

The United States Navy has long needed a vehicle capable of locating disabled submarines. This need is being met by deep submergence search vehicles (DSSV). Such vehicles carry sophisticated electronic equipment and a crew of four, and require a highly reliable environmental control unit. These exacting conditions are met by a 4270-watt hybrid thermoelectric environmental control unit. The thermoelectric unit design was accepted after a systematic and rigorous comparison with vapor compression and absorption refrigeration systems.

Another interesting application concerns small, self-contained irrigation pumping units designed to raise the standard of living in underdeveloped areas of the world. These 50-watt units are powered by the sun, whose energy is gathered by means of a collector; the solar energy is focused onto a set of thermoelectric cells whose electrical energy is used to drive a small pump. The water is used either for irrigation or household needs. A larger unit with a 200-watt output uses an 8-ft parabolic mirror to focus the sun's rays onto the converter module, which is about 8 in. square and 2 in. deep. The power from this unit can pump to a height of 20 ft enough water to irrigate 4 acres at a rate that corresponds to 24 in. of natural rainfall per year; this is about the same precipitation that Minneapolis receives each year. This unit can also supply the personal needs of 1200 people, based on a per capita consumption of 5 gal of water per day. These calculations were made assuming only 250 days of sunshine per year with 10 hr of sunshine per day. This allows a margin of safety of about one-third for cloudy days.

Considerable developmental work has already been carried out on the construction and operating characteristics of a combustion chamber that would accept almost any type of solid fuel (coal, green wood, charcoal, etc.). The purpose of this unit is to provide a burner that could operate almost anywhere in the world on an indigenous fuel and supply enough energy to power a thermoelectric energy converter yielding an output of 150 watts. This study was initiated by the United States Army to provide a versatile power source for communication equipment.

One of the first uses to which a direct conversion device was put was the powering of a prototype telephone remote terminal in regular commercial service by means of silicon solar cells. The first tests were conducted with a panel that held 432 cells and delivered 0.5 amp into a 20-volt storage battery.

The results of this experimental field trial were completely satisfactory.

As we look to the future several more fascinating possibilities present themselves. Some of the most interesting could come in the area of medical engineering. When organs of the body are replaced or helped by auxiliary equipment, the need for reliable power sources becomes acute. For example, devices (called *pacesetters*) that are used to trigger heart action in persons who have trouble sustaining a regular heartbeat are now being designed to be powered by thermoelectric generators. These generators obtain their energy from low-level radioisotope sources. Artificial hearts are now being built and will ultimately require implantable power sources as well. Several direct conversion devices have been under active consideration for this application.

Another scheme under investigation plans to take advantage of the high operating temperatures of magnetohydrodynamic generators—in the range of 3000°K—by utilizing a portion of their waste heat to create nitrogen compounds. At these high temperatures, nitrogen combines chemically with oxygen, and the oxides can be captured in solution to make nitric acid, or nitrogen may be reacted with a mineral, such as calcium carbide (which is obtained from limestone), to form calcium cyanamide; the latter reacts readily with water to form ammonia, which is easily turned into fertilizers. The waste heat from these high temperature plants has also been considered for distillation of seawater by flash evaporation.

1.4.2 Direct conversion in space. Without a doubt, space vehicles have been the most eager users of direct conversion devices to date. It appears that this area will continue to be one of the major stimulants to, and consumers of, direct conversion generators. Fortunately, the need for electrical power in space vehicles varies from a few watts up to a megawatt; this wide range of power requirements has caused nearly every type of direct energy conversion to be subject to intensive research and development. In this section we will take a brief look at present space requirements and some estimated future needs.

The United States space program has evolved considerably since its first satellite was placed into orbit. As booster rockets increased the size of payloads that could be put into orbit, so has the demand for on-board electrical power; early systems that produced a few watts are now producing a few kilowatts.

A clue to how demand for power will grow can be obtained by examining what has happened in the aircraft industry in terms of on-board power; in 1939 a DC-3 required about 3 kW of on-board power while today's commercial jets require on the order of 300 kW. It is therefore not unreasonable to suppose that a similar, or perhaps an even more explosive growth will occur in space power needs. Table 1-4 lists the characteristics of

TABLE 1-4. CHARACTERISTIC OF SEVERAL LONG-LIFE/HIGH-POWER AUTOMATED PAYLOADS PLANNED FOR 1979-1990.†

Spacecraft	Average power, W	Desired time in orbit, yr	On-orbit maintenance, yr	Retrieve/refurbish, yr	Spacecraft weight, kg	Earth orbit altitude, km	Initial launch date
Earth-orbiting							
Large Space Telescope	1800	3–5	2.5	2.5–5	10,401	611	1980
Large X-Ray Telescope Facility	1300	5	2	5	11,350	463	1986
Extended X-Ray Survey	1310	4	1	4	7,592	371	1982
Large High-Energy Observatory A	900	4	2	4	9,518	371	1986
Large High-Energy Observatory B	844	1–3	2	1–3	5,429	371	1980
Cosmic Ray Laboratory	1000	5	2	5	18,600	371	1987
Intelsat	4400	10			1,774	35,786	1979
DOMSAT A	305	7			261	35,786	1979
DOMSAT B	4400	10			1,775	35,786	1984
Disaster Warning Satellite	5000	5			583		
Traffic Management Satellite	1100	5				35,786	1979
Foreign Communication Satellite	500	7			315	35,786	1981
DOMSAT C	400	7			311	35,786	1983
Large High-Energy Observatory D	1300	4	2	4	7,604	463	1983
Large Solar Observatory	1840	6	1	6	10,000	350	1985
Global Earth and Ocean Monitor System	1190	2	1	2	2,035	371	1986
Planetary (Deep Space)							
Pioneer Venus Multiprobe		Total Life: 8 Months to 3 yrs.	None	None	684	N/A	1980
Mercury Orbiter					3,496		1987
Pioneer Saturn/Uranus Flyby					508		1981
Mariner Jupiter	140 to 600				2,670		1981
Saturn Orbiter					11,615		1985
Ganymede Orbiter/Lander					9,745		1990
Encke Rendezvous					2,154		1981
Venus Radar Mapper					3,958		1983

† After Ref. [6]. with permission.

29

several long-life, high-power automated payloads planned by NASA for the time period between 1979 and 1990 [6]. These are the power requirements that will be deployed by the Shuttle Orbiter or Space Tug. Keep in mind that the power levels shown are average and apply only to that portion of the spacecraft that is automated; much higher power levels might be demanded for short periods of time during the mission and to provide life support.

Power needs for space can be broken into three main areas of interest: communications, manned space exploration and electric propulsion. Predictions on future power needs can be made for each of these areas.

Because spacecraft have been able to carry only limited amounts of power their transmitters have necessarily been small. This necessitated the construction of immense ground-based receiving systems. The demand for more and higher quality information will cause the number of receiving stations, as well as the power required for transmissions, to increase. Now under consideration is a system which would permit spacecraft to transmit directly to small local television stations and home receivers. Reception by small, inexpensive receiving systems would be advantageous not only within the United States but also for information dissemination to other areas of the world such as remote regions not presently accessible by conventional means. Only about 60 kW would be needed to power a system capable of being received at 210 MHz (Channel 13) over the entire United States. One-third of the earth's surface could be covered with only 300 kW at the same frequency [7].

Manned space efforts require large amounts of power for a wide range of activities not needed on unmanned vehicles. Power is needed for space-station illumination, waste management, water and food preparation, atmospheric and thermal control. Mercury spacecrafts required about 500 W/man for orbital flight. Gemini and Apollo capsules provided approximately 1.3 kW/man. As the length and complexity of a mission increases so does the on-board power.

Mars may well be the next objective of manned space exploration. Power required to support manned Mars exploration should be very similar to that required for lunar exploration. Studies which have been conducted for 6-, 8-, and 18-man bases indicate that a 6-man base will need about 40 kW whereas an 18-man base would require about 200 kW.

Electrical propulsion systems will require large amounts of power. A Mars mission using electrical propulsion might require as much as 40 MW of power. However, there are a number of missions which require much less power and could be adequately performed by electrical propulsion systems. A Jupiter flyby of a 3700 kg payload, for instance, could be made by an electrical rocket having an 11,000 kg initial Earth-orbit mass and a plant with a power density of 0.1 kW/kg generating 300 to 500 kW. During flyby its electric engines could be shut down, thus freeing considerable power for electronic exploration of Jupiter and for transmission of acquired data to Earth.

It is interesting to place in perspective just where present-day energy conversion systems are in comparison with the more conventional means of power generation. We have taken some of Giacoletto's data [8] and added to them some currently operational direct conversion systems as shown in Fig. 1-8. It is easy to see that current direct conversion efforts are a long way from the one kilowatt per kilogram of aircraft power systems.

Solar cells are relatively advanced and will continue to dominate the low power level scene because of their inherent simplicity, high state of development, and reliability. Their power-to-mass ratio is relatively low, but because they are designed to generate not very large amounts of power their total weight is generally small. The larger power level (above 25 kW) systems appear to be designed around nuclear reactors; the Brayton and Rankine cycle systems are not, of course, direct conversion systems but are nuclear-powered turbogenerators using rubidium or potassium as their working fluids. It is believed that such systems can be designed to yield power densities on the order of 0.2 kW/kg. Thermionic convertors located in a reactor core might be capable of power densities on the order of 0.3 kW/kg.

Power density is not the whole story, of course. For a given power level a space power system must be designed to yield that power for a certain period of time. Figure 1-9 is an estimated power-time continuum which indicates those regions where each system appears to have an advantage (including minimum weight) compared to all others. This drawing is rather conjectural since, as we mentioned previously, many of the systems shown are not very far along in their development. Some of them might prove to be unfeasible power sources as work continues on them. Each of the major types of systems—chemical, solar, and nuclear—shows specific advantages in certain regions of power. Chemical systems such as fuel cells are clearly suited for low power level missions of short duration, whereas photovoltaic converters retain their advantage for long missions requiring relatively little power. Nuclear systems, on the other hand, appear capable of supplying great quantities of power for long periods of time.

While weight is an important parameter in deciding the suitability of a power source for a particular mission, it is by no means the only criterion of importance. Other factors, such as cost, reliability, and integration of power source into the vehicle, can be just as important. Radioisotope-powered systems are a case in point. Though they are heavier than photovoltaic systems at power levels less than 1 kW, they offer distinct advantages in compactness and are certainly less susceptible to environmental degradation; they may even be less costly. Another example may be found in solar systems whose usefulness is a direct function of the amount of darkness

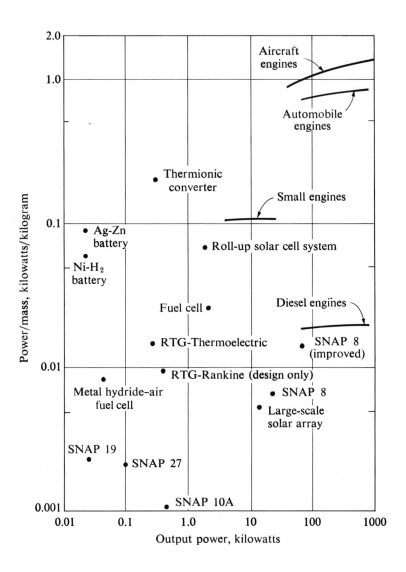

FIG. 1-8. Power per unit mass as a function of output power. The acronym SNAP stands for Systems Nuclear Auxiliary Power. SNAP 8 is a reactor-powered Rankine cycle that uses mercury as a working fluid. SNAP 10A is a reactor-powered thermoelectric unit that orbited the Earth for 43 days in 1965. SNAP 19 is a radioisotope-powered thermoelectric unit to be used on the Viking Mars Lander. SNAP 27 is a radioisotope thermoelectric unit. RTG-Rankine is a radioisotope-powered Rankine cycle unit.

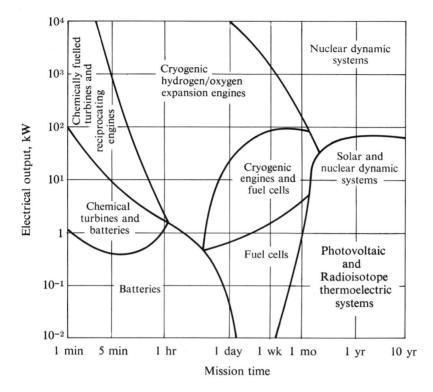

FIG. 1-9. Various types of systems in a power-time continuum showing those regions where each system appears to have an advantage (in both weight and other factors) compared to all others.

encountered in a mission; therefore, solar power might be entirely unsuitable for missions that encounter long lunar nights unless some provision for power storage in the system is made.

1.5 UNITS

Before we begin our study of direct conversion devices, let us consider briefly the problem of the units that we shall use in describing these devices. All quantities used in the physical sciences can be expressed in terms of the following fundamental ones: *mass, length, time, charge,* and *temperature.* These five quantities are considered so fundamental as to be undefinable; the problem is avoided by assigning names that serve as definitions, and these descriptive names are called *dimensions*. A dimension is said to be a name given to a measurable quality or characteristic of an entity. To reduce the number of dimensions, certain descriptions can be expressed in terms of others. That is, length, area, and volume are all dimensions describing certain size characteristics of an object. But since area is defined and measured as a length squared and volume as a length cubed, we express all three descriptions in terms of the fundamental dimension, length. Thus, area and volume are considered *derived* or *secondary* dimensions obtainable from the fundamental dimension of length. It is possible to derive secondary dimensions from the laws of nature. Newton's second law of motion requires that force be equal to mass times acceleration ($F = ma = [Ml/t^2]$). This definition assumes three primary dimensions: mass, length, and time. It is also possible to use a system of units that considers *force* as a primary dimension.

While a dimension is a descriptive word picture, a *unit* is a definite standard or measure of a dimension. A unit is an arbitrary amount of the quantity to be measured with an assigned numerical value of unity. As an example we might consider that the inch, foot, centimeter, mile, and yard are all different units but with the common dimension of length.

In much of our work we shall use the meter-kilogram-second (mks) unit system because it has found wide acceptance in many phases of the literature concerning direct energy conversion. However, there are two notable exceptions. In some of the literature on semiconductors and photocells, and in nearly all of the literature on fuel cells, the centimeter-gram-second (cgs) unit system is used. We have, as far as possible, tried to follow the practice of the literature so that the student will be able to move easily from this book to the literature and vice versa. In a few cases where it is felt that English engineering units would be more meaningful to the student than metric units, they are used in place of the metric units. Table 1-5 gives some important derived quantities and the mks units associated with them.

TABLE 1-5. SOME FAMILIAR DEFINITIONS OF DERIVED QUANTITIES

Derived quantity	Definition	Units
Speed or velocity†	$u = dl/dt$	m/sec
Acceleration	$a = du/dt = d^2l/dt^2$	m/sec²
Momentum	$p = mu$	kg-m/sec
Force	$F = dp/dt$	newtons (nt)
Work	$W = \int F \cdot dl$	joules
Power	$P_o = dW/dt$	watts

† Vectors are denoted by boldface italic type throughout the text.

We define *energy* (ε) as the ability, either latent or apparent, of a body to do work. The magnitude of a body's energy is measured by its *properties* or *state functions*, that is, macroscopic characteristics of the physical or chemical structure of the matter contained in the body, such as its pressure, density, or temperature. *Work*, on the other hand, is energy transferred, without transfer of mass, across the boundary of a system because of an *intensive property* (a property that is independent of the mass of the system) difference, other than temperature, that exists between the system and the surroundings.

We define *heat* as energy transferred, without transfer of mass, across the boundary of a system because of a temperature difference between the system and the surroundings.

The *joule* is defined as the energy that must be expended to move a unit force (a *newton*) through a unit distance (a *meter*). The unit of power, or energy per unit time, is the *watt*, defined as 1 joule per sec. In Appendix B we give a list of conversion factors that will be useful in understanding the text material and in solving problems.

The basic unit of charge is that carried by the electron. A much larger unit of charge, and the one we use to define the electronic charge, is called the *coulomb*. The coulomb is equal to 6.24273×10^{18} unit charges; or more frequently, the electronic charge is defined as 1.60209×10^{-19} coulombs. (In Appendix A are listed the values for all the physical constants we will need in our study.) A still larger unit of charge is called the *faraday*, $\mathfrak{F}$, which is equal to 96,493 coulombs. The unit of electric current is called the *ampere* and is defined as 1 coulomb per sec.

Because of the attractions or repulsion between charges, a force field is set up which for stationary charges is called an *electric field*. In general, energy is required to move charge from one position to another in an electric field. A value of potential energy can be assigned to each position in the electric field that would correspond to the energy required to bring a unit charge from infinity to the point in question. The potential energy per unit charge at a point in the electric field is called the *potential*, V. If a potential difference exists, positive charge (by convention) can flow through a conducting path from a region of high potential (energy) to a region of low potential (energy). The unit of potential is the *volt*, defined as 1 joule (energy) per coulomb (charge). Since a coulomb is a quantity of charge equivalent to 6.24273×10^{18} electrons, we have

$$1 \text{ volt} = 1.60209 \times 10^{-19} \frac{\text{joule}}{\text{electron}}.$$

Thus we have a new energy term called the *electron volt* (eV), defined as

$$1 \text{ eV} = 1.60209 \times 10^{-19} \text{ joule.}$$

In concluding this discussion of units, the student is urged to carry along the units in equations when he is working problems; in addition to preventing obvious and avoidable mistakes, this practice also tends to preserve the physical sense of the problem and to preclude its becoming just a collection of numbers.

Because we are treating such a wide variety of subjects it has been impractical to assign a single symbol to a specific physical quantity—there are simply not enough common symbols to go around. To help alleviate this problem we list the notation used in each chapter (except for the first chapter) immediately after the text of that chapter. It might be helpful to the student if before reading a chapter he were to glance over the notation at the back of that chapter.

REFERENCES

1. F. G. Zarb, "The Seven Truths of Energy," *Wall Street Journal*, September 10, 1975.

2. P. C. Putnam, *Energy in the Future* (New York: D. Van Nostrand Company, Inc., 1953).

3. A. Gerber and B. C. Netschert, "The Energy Outlook for the United States," *IEEE Spectrum*, 6 (1969), 38–45.

4. *Exploring Energy Choices* (Washington, D.C.: Ford Foundation Energy Policy Project, 1974).

5. R. G. Mills, "Problems and Promises of Controlled Fusion Power," *Mechanical Engineering*, 97 (1975), No. 9, 20–25.

6. M. S. Imamura, N. R. Sheppard, and T. D. Patterson, "Digital Techniques in Future Spacecraft Automated Power Systems," *9th* Intersociety Energy Conversion Engineering Conference, 1974 (New York: American Society of Mechanical Engineers, 1974).

7. R. I. Vachon, L. H. Wood, and R. N. Seitz, "Space Electrical Power—Quo Vadis?" *Astronautics and Aeronautics*, 5 (1967), 58–63.

8. L. J. Giacoletto, "Energy Storage and Conversion," *IEEE Spectrum*, 2 (1965), 95-102.

2 *Energy Storage*

Before coming to grips with the various forms of direct energy conversion it is both interesting and useful to consider a number of means of energy storage since, no doubt, many direct-conversion devices will be teamed with storage devices in practice. Energy storage is not a new branch of technology—indeed, its roots reach back to antiquity. The flywheel, one of the devices to be considered in some detail here, plays an essential role in the potter's wheel, which is mentioned in the Old Testament. It is clear that several methods of mechanical energy storage were well understood long before Newton formalized that subject in his treatise on the laws of motion.

Energy storage will probably play an important role in two key areas of technology: central-station power plants and medium- to light-weight vehicles.

2.1 THE USES OF ENERGY STORAGE

Storing energy for use at a later time makes sense from several viewpoints —economics, resource utilization, pollution control, and efficiency. The necessity of energy storage arises because the demand for energy is not constant over time. Sometimes we demand more energy than is available; other times available energy is not needed. The central-station power plant typifies this situation.

2.1.1 Energy storage in central-station power plants. Most electric utilities experience a marked daily, weekly, and seasonal demand for their product

—electric power. A typical daily load curve is shown in Fig. 2-1, while a weekly load curve is shown in Fig. 2-2. Utilities are required by their charters to find economical ways to generate power over large variations of electric load. At the same time they must have sufficient generating capacity to satisfy maximum demand and they must also have, for reliability, a sizeable system reserve.

In order to satisfy these conflicting demands, electric utilities use different kinds of generating equipment. So-called "base-load plants" are used to service that part of the system load that continues 24 hours a day, every day of the year. Therefore base-load plants are designed to operate with the highest efficiency on the least expensive fuel available. These two requirements generally lead to high plant capital- or first-costs, but the low fuel costs and high load factor more than compensate for the high initial cost and produce the lowest cost power in the system. Base-load plants today are primarily coal- or nuclear-powered. (Of course, if a utility had it available, hydropower would supply as much of its base load as water-level conditions would permit. Hydropower has essentially zero fuel cost.)

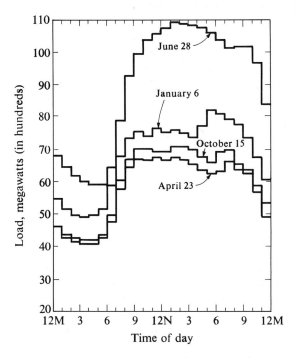

FIG. 2-1. The daily load profile of a large metropolitan utility showing the hourly swings in load. The daily peaks will differ from utility to utility, season to season, and day to day. After Ref. [15].

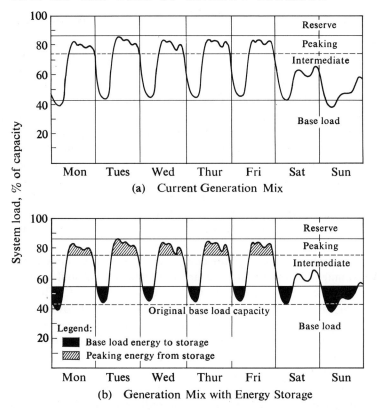

FIG. 2-2. (a) A typical weekly load curve for an electric utility. (b) How the generation mix might change if a system could employ energy storage, showing when energy might be stored and when it might be removed from storage. After Ref. [1].

The intermediate load, which represents most of the daily variation, is served by several different types of equipment. This equipment, which is generally shut down at night, is typically made up of older, less efficient fossil fuel plants and, more recently, gas turbines. The peak load, which may persist for only a few hours, is usually met by the oldest fossil fuel equipment and gas turbine units. Those utilities located in favorable geographic regions handle peak loads and sometimes intermediate loads with pumped-storage units if available.

Historically this generation mix has worked quite well for electric utilities, but as fossil fuel costs have steadily increased, the utilization of the old mix has become more costly. These sharply escalating costs have provided a big incentive to use low fuel cost base-load plants to provide the electric energy now generated by peaking and intermediate equipment.

The most cost-effective way to do this is to store the off-peak power generated by this base-load equipment.

At present, utilities must have considerable capacity that is used only a few hours a day to provide peaking- and intermediate-load power. However, if large-scale energy storage were available, relatively efficient and economical base-load power generation could be employed at higher load factors with the excess over off-peak demand being used to charge the energy storage system. During periods of peak demand the storage system would supply power, thereby reducing the need for fuel-burning peaking equipment and at the same time reducing fuel consumption. Furthermore, the increased base-load capacity would replace a part of the intermediate generation, producing additional cost and fossil fuel savings, especially if the added base-load plants were to use nonfossil primary fuels.

Using energy from a storage system is termed "peak shaving" when used to generate peaking power, and "load leveling" when used to eliminate conventional intermediate-load cycling equipment. It should be understood that the advantages of energy storage are not obtained without cost—a loss of 25 percent was estimated to size the capacities in Fig. 2-1. (The cost arises from the fact that it is impossible to get back every kilowatt-hour that is stored in the storage devices.) Thus the real significance of energy storage is not a net saving in energy but a shifting of demand from inefficient units using costly fuels to more efficient primary units using, hopefully, less expensive fuels.

If storage technologies can be developed to meet the criteria for technical and economic feasibility that electric utilities demand, then widespread energy storage will certainly be used in utility systems. Technical feasibility means that such systems must meet utility-type standards for operating life, reliability, safety, and compatibility with existing equipment. Economic feasibility implies that the total annual cost of electric energy delivered from energy storage systems must be equal to or less than the cost of energy from nonstorage equipment used for peaking and intermediate generation.

The capital cost of an energy storage system is expressed to a first approximation as

$$C_t = C_p + T \times C_s \tag{2-1}$$

where C_t is the total capital cost in dollars per kilowatt, C_p is that portion of the capital cost proportional to the power rating, C_s is that portion of the capital cost proportional to the system's energy storage capacity in dollars per kilowatt-hour, and T is the number of hours per day during which energy is delivered from storage.

Several preliminary analyses have been carried out with the goal of establishing probable ranges for technical and economic feasibility criteria. Table 2-1 gives the results of one such study [1]. In this analysis, distributed

**TABLE 2-1. FEASIBILITY CRITERIA FOR
UTILITY ENERGY STORAGE[†]**

Energy storage application	Efficiency (%)	Life (years)	Capital cost for central storage		Capital cost for distributed storage	
			C_p ($/kW)	C_s ($/kWh)	C_p ($/kW)	C_s ($/kWh)
Peak shaving	≥ 60	≥ 20	40– 90	7–20	60–150	7–25
Load leveling	≥ 70	≥ 30	50–110	5–15	50–170	5–18

† After Ref. [1].

energy storage costs are assumed to include a credit of $60 per kilowatt to reflect the fact that transmission costs will be considerably less for distributed storage systems than for central storage systems.

Kalhammer and Zygielbaum [1] come to the following conclusions about energy storage systems:

(1) Energy storage systems with what appear to be attainable technical and economic characteristics, and charged with power from modern base-load plants, promise to be more economical than gas turbines and coal gas–fired combined-cycle machines for the generation of peak and intermediate power up to approximately 2500 hours of annual operation.

(2) For operating periods between about 3000 and 5000 hours per year, coal gas–fired combined-cycle power plants promise to have more favorable economics than energy storage systems.

(3) Those energy storage devices that are economical in relatively small sizes (such as batteries or flywheels) have particularly favorable economics for peak-power generation (less than 1000 hours of annual operation) because (a) credits can be claimed for transmission and distribution capital cost savings as a result of siting close to the load and (b) capital costs are largely proportional to energy storage capacity and, thus, are low for short periods of daily operation.

(4) Depending on annual operating time and local conditions, combinations of different energy storage methods might be used to achieve the lowest-cost peak- and intermediate-power generation in future electric utility systems.

Figure 2-3 (after Ref. [1]) summarizes these results. Specific methods of storing energy and their usefulness to electric utilities will be cited in subsequent sections.

2.1.2 Energy storage in vehicles. The economic and social advantages of powering vehicles from energy storage devices are considerable because the vehicles could operate at high efficiencies and be nonpolluting. The internal combustion engine in an automobile typically converts 10 to 15

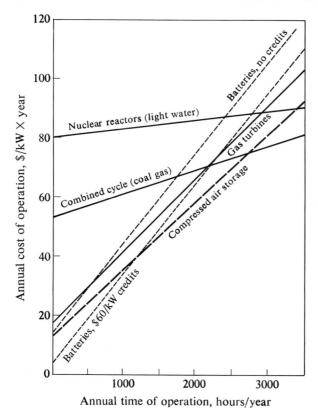

FIG. 2-3. The economics of peak- and intermediate-cycling power generation as a function of annual hours of operation. The lower dashed line for batteries gives a $60/kW credit because of savings in transmission and distribution costs. After Ref. [1].

percent of the energy in gasoline to motive power; modern central-station electric power plants burning fossil fuel have efficiencies of around 40 percent. Moreover, at the present time combustion can be better controlled in a central-station plant. Therefore automobiles using high efficiency storage systems, such as a battery array or a flywheel that obtained energy from electric power plants at off-peak times, would result in greatly improved efficiency in terms of fossil fuel consumed per vehicle mile. One barrel of crude oil fueling an electric power plant would be the equivalent of up to five barrels sent to a refinery to produce gasoline. Any new demands for electric power arising from the use of storage-powered automobiles could be met readily within the present resources of fossil fuels.

There are two important variables which must be considered in seeking an energy storage system for a vehicle: specific power, which determines to a large extent acceleration and speed capabilities, and specific energy, which determines vehicle range. Figure 2-4 summarizes requirements for a 2000-pound vehicle with a 500-pound energy storage system. This power–energy map also has some common and some uncommon energy sources marked on it. Some of these sources will be considered in greater detail in subsequent sections. It should be clear that the further to the right and the higher up a source lies, the more useful it will be as an energy source for a vehicle.

Table 2-2 summarizes the energy storage requirements for two types of vehicles—the urban car and the family car. The "urban car" in this comparison is a 2000-lb (909-kg) gross weight vehicle, while the family car is assumed to have a gross weight of 4000 lb (1818 kg).

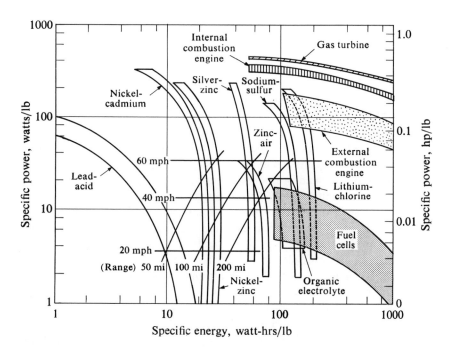

FIG. 2-4. The power and energy requirements for a 2000-lb vehicle utilizing a 500-lb motive power source for steady driving. Power and energy are assumed to be at the output of the device. After Ref. [8].

TABLE 2-2. POWER AND ENERGY DENSITY
FOR TWO TYPES OF VEHICLES

| Type of vehicle | Range (miles) [km] | Constant speed cruise | | | Acceleration |
		Velocity (mph) [kmph]	Energy density (Wh/lb) [Wh/kg]	Power density (W/lb) [W/kg]	Power density (W/lb) [W/kg]
Urban car—2000 lb	50	40	25	20	65
[909 kg]	[80]	[64]	[55]	[44]	[143]
Family car—4000 lb	200	70	122	43	73–110
[1818 kg]	[322]	[113]	[268]	[95]	[161–242]

2.2 ENERGY STORAGE IN BATTERIES

Energy storage in batteries is not a new technology for either central-station power plants or vehicles. Although it now appears to be of historical interest only, battery storage has actually been used in d-c central-station power systems. And, of course, battery-powered vehicles were quite common in the 1920's. After many years there is now renewed interest in the possible use of rechargeable batteries for bulk energy storage in utility systems and in vehicles. This new interest has two bases: (1) the specific advantages for batteries (which include distributed storage of energy for central-station plants with its significant economic and siting benefits, as well as the rapid installation and demand-responsive capacity for growth of essentially modular storage units); and (2) the emergence of new battery concepts for both central station and transportation applications that appear to offer promise of meeting the stringent cost and life requirements of these applications of energy storage.

In Ch. 8 the principles of electrochemistry governing all batteries is reviewed. It might be helpful to your understanding of this section to review those principles before reading further.

The major challenge in developing battery systems for either central-station power or transportation is to achieve a battery that has a significant cycle life and that is capable of being mass produced at low cost. Several different approaches are being pursued in current programs. One is to develop batteries of modest or low energy density around relatively in-expensive aqueous electrochemical systems. To meet cost targets, low-cost containment materials, cell designs, and production techniques must be used or developed. Reviews of various battery systems may be found in

Ref. [1], [2], and [3]. Five categories of batteries will be discussed here: aqueous electrolyte, metal-air, high-temperature, solid-state, and organic electrolyte.

2.2.1 Aqueous electrolyte batteries. Most aqueous electrolyte batteries are well developed and some have been used in the operation of commercial and research vehicles. An experimental electric vehicle operated with lead-acid batteries has obtained 145 miles range at steady speed and 65 miles range in stop-and-go traffic [2]. Acceleration was unacceptably low, however.

Lead-acid batteries have an open-circuit potential of approximately 2.05 volts, a theoretical energy density of 76 watt-hours/pound, and an achieved energy density of 10 to 24 watt-hours/pound. This is clearly the main battery source for medium- to high-power applications. Characteristics that permit this domination are high current capability, operation over a wide temperature range, good charge retention, high efficiency, long life, and, in particular, low cost for materials and manufacturing. The attainable energy density of lead-acid batteries is dependent on the discharge rate, as illustrated in Fig. 2-5. This rate dependency is caused primarily by mass transport and ionic diffusion limitations.

Cycle life of lead-acid batteries is relatively low for high-energy density designs at deep depths-of-discharge. For example, some electric vehicles made in England are equipped with batteries guaranteed to provide 200 cycles at 90 percent depth-of-discharge, good for about 12,000 miles [2]. Kalhammer [1] suggests that technically and economically feasible lead-acid batteries for utility applications could conceivably become commercial by the early 1980's.

The nickel-zinc system has an open-circuit potential of 1.706 volts, a theoretical energy density of 146 watt-hours/pound, and an achieved energy density of over 30 watt-hours/pound. Over 300 cycles at 65 percent depth of discharge and up to 1500 cycles at 50 percent depth of discharge have been attained in the laboratory. This system is of great interest for electric vehicles of the future, for the theoretical and practical energy density is nearly twice that of lead-acid batteries. Furthermore, it has good high-rate capability and can be sealed, and the cost of materials is relatively low. Cycle life of the nickel-zinc system is limited by the zinc electrode; due to volatility of zinc oxide, zinc dendrites develop during charging, causing shorts. If cycle life can be increased by a factor of three to six, then the nickel-zinc system could prove useful for electric vehicles [2].

The zinc-bromine battery has an open-circuit potential of 1.8 volts and a theoretical energy density of 196 watt-hours/pound. An energy density of 22 watt-hours/pound has been achieved on small batteries. Over 200 cycles have been reached, but the possible lifetime could be much greater. Unlike the nickel-zinc system, this battery does not suffer from zinc dendrites. The

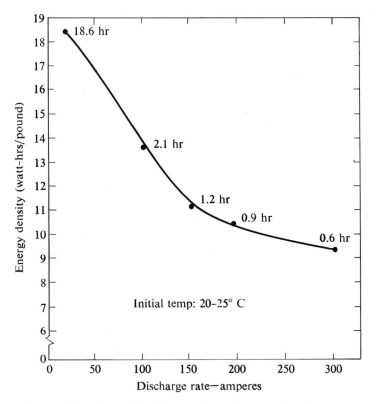

FIG. 2-5. The effect of discharge rate and time of discharge on energy density. After Ref. [2].

major drawback of the zinc-bromine system is its high self-discharge rate, losing nearly 50 percent charge in two days. A continuous trickle charge will counter this self-discharge. The high-energy density, high-rate capability, and low cost of materials might cause this system to have commercial importance [2].

The nickel-iron system has an open-circuit potential of 1.370 volts and a theoretical energy density of 121 watt-hours/pound. This is an extremely old system that is both low in cost and very long-lived. The battery marketed today is essentially the same design developed by Thomas Edison decades ago. Nickel-iron cells are the most rugged in service today, with actual lives in excess of 20 years. They are virtually foolproof electrically and are practically immune to damage caused by deep discharge, short circuits, or overcharge. An advanced nickel-iron cell has been developed that uses a metal-fiber substrate.

The nickel-cadmium battery permits a very high power drain, has outstanding cycle life, and can achieve better energy densities than the lead-acid system. The system has a theoretical energy density of 100 watt-hours/pound and an open-circuit potential of approximately 1.35 volts, depending on state-of-charge. The main drawback to widespread use of nickel-cadmium batteries is the limited world supply of cadmium and its consequent high cost. This limitation will undoubtedly hold back any extensive adoption of nickel-cadmium systems in central-station power plants or for vehicular applications.

The nickel-hydrogen cell is a relatively recent development in the area of alkaline storage batteries. This system is potentially very interesting, as it combines the best electrode from the nickel-cadmium system with the best electrode from the hydrogen-oxygen fuel cell system. The system has an open-circuit potential of 1.358 volts and a theoretical energy density of 177 watt-hours/pound. An energy density of 25 watt-hours/pound has been achieved on prototype cells and design studies reveal that 40 watt-hours/pound should be attainable. Power densities of 40 watts/pound have been realized and it is believed that the power density might be raised to 200 watts/pound in an optimized design. A nickel-hydrogen battery consists of a series stack of nickel and hydrogen electrodes installed inside of a pressure vessel filled with hydrogen gas, as shown in Fig. 2-6 (from Ref. [3]). The electrodes are separated by gas-diffusion screens, but the hydrogen gas need not be isolated from the nickel electrodes since they will not react chemically. Except for the pressure vessel, no costly material is used. Indeed the major disadvantage of the nickel-hydrogen system is the need for a pressure vessel to contain the hydrogen. A possible improvement to the nickel-hydrogen battery would be the development of a means to store hydrogen as a solid—perhaps as a metal hydride.

The zinc-chlorine battery is potentially an important system. The couple has an open-circuit potential of 2.12 volts and a theoretical energy density of more than 200 watt-hours/pound. One method of bringing this battery into practice now being investigated includes the storage of chlorine as a solid chlorine hydrate outside the battery cells proper and the use of a slightly acid electrolyte such that the zinc chloride discharge product remains in solution at all times. Potential low cost and long cycle life are attractive features of the zinc-chlorine battery, but these advantages have yet to be realized on a practical scale.

2.2.2 Metal-air batteries. In this system a metal is used to form the negative electrode, and a gas electrode using oxygen from the air forms the positive electrode. Such systems are potentially very flexible, but practical problems, such as the development of improved high-rate air electrodes

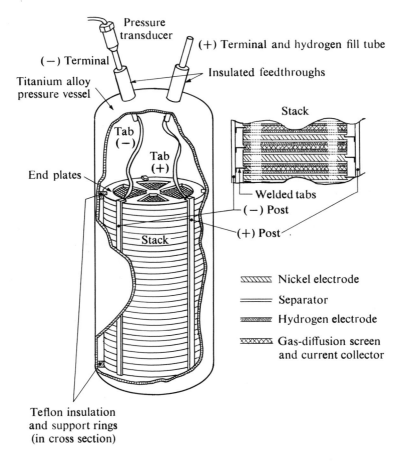

FIG. 2-6. A lightweight nickel-hydrogen multielectrode cell. After Ref. [3].

with non-noble metal catalysts, remain to be solved. High-energy density
metal-air batteries have severe thermal problems as well: they can overheat,
and, for high-temperature design, the problem of initial heating arises [2].

Though zinc has had most attention devoted to it, other metals appear
at least potentially attractive. Table 2-3 (from Ref. [2]) lists, in order of
decreasing theoretical energy density, the more promising candidate metals,
with the exotic metals eliminated from consideration. The cost per unit of
theoretical energy has been calculated based on 1972 prices for the metals in
relatively pure states. The theoretical energy density includes no penalty for
oxygen taken from the air and ranges from 8142 watt-hours/pound for
beryllium to 110 watt-hours/pound for lead. Examining the candidate
metals one finds that of the 13 metals listed, nine are superior in theoretical

TABLE 2-3. CANDIDATE METAL-OXYGEN SYSTEMS FOR BATTERIES†

Metal	Energy density (watt-hours/pound)	Energy cost (dollars/watt-hour)	Comment
Beryllium	8142	$6.63	Toxic, difficult
Lithium	6045	1.35	Studied
Aluminum	3718	0.12	Studied
Magnesium	3090	0.12	Primary system developed
Titanium	2162	0.22	Difficult
Calcium	2075	0.16	Studied
Sodium	1644	0.27	Studied
Chromium	1192	0.40	Difficult
Manganese	668	0.40	Difficult
Zinc	614	0.56	Primary system developed
Iron	556	0.45	Secondary system developed
Cadmium	262	5.72	Secondary system developed, expensive
Lead	110	1.27	Studied

† After Ref. [2], with permission.

energy density and eight are lower in metal cost per unit of theoretical energy density when compared to zinc.

The zinc-air system has received the most attention of the metal-air batteries. It has a theoretical energy density of 614 watt-hours/pound and an open-circuit potential of 1.65 volts. Primary batteries have demonstrated energy densities of 150 watt-hours/pound. Some investigators believe that the problems are so basic that they will not likely yield to additional development [2]. One such problem is the difficulty of producing, during charge, a compact enough zinc deposit to avoid interelectrode shorting. Other problems include achieving a good air electrode capable of high current densities at low gas pressure, and loss of water in the air exhausted from the air electrodes.

The aluminum-air battery appears to be an attractive battery from both a weight and cost standpoint. It has been used successfully as a primary battery but shows little promise as a secondary (rechargeable) material in aqueous electrolyte. Aluminum apparently can be cycled in nonaqueous electrolytes, but with reduced energy density. One aluminum-air battery under development is a two-kilowatt system that is mechanically recharged by replacing the aluminum and alkaline electrolyte. The air cathode uses platinum catalyst, though it is believed that non-noble metals could be substituted in commercial applications.

Considerable developmental work has been carried out in Sweden on iron-air batteries. An experimental 30 kilowatt-hour battery has been built and used to power a small truck, achieving 30 watt-hours/pound with an energy density of 45 watt-hours/pound expected in production models. The air cathode is made from pressed nickel powder with a silver catalyst. A pumped potassium hydroxide electrolyte is used to provide temperature control and the make-up water that is needed periodically. Forced air provides the oxygen needed and pressure control over the air cathodes. The auxiliary systems comprise about 10 percent of the total system weight. It is estimated that these batteries will have a lifetime of about 500 cycles, limited by the cathode.

2.2.3 High temperature batteries. These batteries are potentially attractive for both traction applications and central-station work. High power capability is achieved by use of low-resistance electrolyte materials such as fused salts and by operation at elevated temperatures which increase the charge current density. The benefits of high-temperature operation are not achieved without cost—especially troublesome are material and seal problems. The large increase in solute (up to 25 percent) when electrolyte salts melt poses a design problem, as does developing a means to heat the battery prior to use. On the other hand, high-temperature cells use electrode materials in a liquid state, thus avoiding morphological changes that occur with solid electrodes and offering at least the promise of long life.

The sodium-sulfur cell has received the most publicity of all the high-temperature battery systems. It has a theoretical energy density of 312 watt-hours/pound and an open-circuit potential of about 2.0 volts, depending on state-of-charge. The operating temperature of this cell is at approximately 300°C with all reactants and products in the liquid state. Standby temperature cannot be lower than 230°C. This system uses a solid electrolyte —most commonly called beta-alumina ($Na_2O \cdot 11Al_2O_3$), which has a very high conductivity attributable to highly mobile sodium ions in cleavage planes. This system suffers from several problems, including the accumulation of metallic sodium in the grain boundaries of the beta-alumina, causing shorts and also weakening the separator material. There is also a tendency of the beta-alumina to lose sodium after long periods at high temperature [2]. A study of the use of sodium-sulfur cells for bulk energy storage in central-station power plants, along with test results on a series of tubular cells, is presented by Mitoff and Bush in Ref. [4].

The lithium-sulfur system has a theoretical energy density of 700 watt-hours/pound when discharging to Li_2S_2. Open-circuit potential is 2.25 volts with an operating temperature of 375 to 425°C. The electrolyte is generally a eutectic salt such as LiCl-KCl. The physical arrangement of the components in the cell is typically like that shown in Fig. 2-7 (after Ref. [5]).

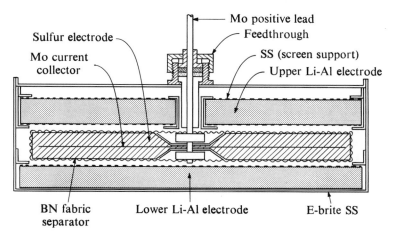

FIG. 2-7. Schematic of a lithium-sulfur cell proposed for use in load-leveling devices for electric utilities. The sulfur electrode in this cell was prepared in air and encased in a 0.15-cm thick boron nitride fabric separator. After Ref. [5].

These batteries have very high energy and power densities which exist at the expense of severe engineering problems. Some of the major problems which must be solved include materials corrosion at high temperature, retention of electrode materials during repeated cycling, attainment of a large number of cycle lifetimes, and the achievement of significant cost reductions in cell manufacture. References [5] and [6] give some goals that must be achieved by lithium-sulfur cells if they are to be used as peaking units or as power sources for vehicles. These goals are presented in Table 2-4. In some respects the peaking requirements would appear to be easier to meet than those for automobiles.

Lithium has been studied as one of the reactants in a number of battery systems. One such lithium battery system has achieved the elusive goal of cycle life in excess of 2000 cycles with neither the formation of lithium dendrites nor other problems [2]. The system which has demonstrated this remarkable goal is the lithium–tellurium tetrachloride battery which has an open-circuit potential of 3.1 volts and a theoretical energy density of 510 watt-hours/pound. The electrolyte is a molten eutectic of lithium chloride and potassium chloride operating at about 400°C. The active lithium negative materials, rather than being liquid, are alloyed with aluminum to form a solid and then encapsulated in a screen. The system has attained an energy density of 38 watt-hours/pound and a projected level of 60 watt-hours/pound. Tellurium is a by-product of the lead and copper industries and has a current production of only 100 to 200 tons/year. If demand increased, this number probably could be increased substantially.

TABLE 2-4. PERFORMANCE GOALS FOR LITHIUM-SULFUR BATTERIES

	Load leveling†	Subcompact auto‡	Compact auto‡
Peak power, kW	10,000	32	60
Specific power, W/kg			
Peak (15-sec burst)	—	237	260
Sustained discharge (≥ 2 hr)	30–40	74	76
Capacity, kWh	40,000–60,000	20	35
Specific energy, Wh/kg	120–150	148	152
Cost of capacity, dollars/kWh	15–25	30	23
Discharge period, h	4–14	2–5	2–5
Recharging time, h	4–8	5	5
Watt-hour efficiency, %	70	70	70
Cycle life	1300	1000	1000

† After Ref. [5].

‡ After Ref. [6]. A subcompact auto is assumed to be one with a loaded weight of 800 kg, range of 100 miles, and an energy consumption of 0.2 kWh/ mile. The same numbers for a compact are taken to be 1250 kg, 100 miles, and 0.35 kWh/mile.

Another high-temperature battery that potentially might find application in central-station plants and for motive uses is the aluminum-chlorine battery, which has a theoretical energy density of 650 watt-hours/pound and an open-circuit potential of 2.1 volts. The electrolyte in this system is molten $AlCl_3$-KCl-NaCl, with the latter two constituents being a binary eutectic with the amount of $AlCl_3$ varying with cell state of charge. It has been found that the electrolyte can melt as low as 70°C, but a realistic operating temperature is 150 to 250°C. At 150°C there is formation of aluminum dendrites and excessive blockage of the aluminum by $AlCl_3$, a discharge product. It is believed that operations above 200°C and the use of ceramic separators would help solve both of these problems. Overall electrical efficiencies of 87 percent have been observed with these cells, which means that they should appear especially attractive as storage units in central-station power systems.

2.2.4 Organic electrolyte batteries. Much effort has been expended on cells that use lithium as a high-energy negative electrode in an organic electrolyte. Such systems typically suffer from low discharge and charge rates; nevertheless they do appear to hold some promise because, unlike high-temperature batteries, they possess wide operating-temperature ranges.

One cell that has received some attention is the lithium-sulfur dioxide battery having a theoretical energy density of 495 watt-hours/pound and an open-circuit potential of 2.95 volts. A small primary cell has delivered 120 watt-hours/pound and appears to be capable of operating at high discharge rates. The unique characteristic of this system is that the lithium and sulfur react on the lithium electrode, forming a protective film that is porous to anodic ions and thus functions as a semipermeable membrane. This film protects the lithium from corrosion, permitting 5 to 10 years storage life with low self-discharge. At present this system is used in a primary battery but it is capable of being produced as a secondary battery.

The lithium-lamellar dichalcogenide battery is a new, rechargeable lithium system utilizing lamellar transition metal dichalcogenides, such as niobium diselenide, as host structures for cathodic nonmetals, such as iodine and sulfur. Open-circuit potentials of 3 volts have been achieved. Batteries have operated for more than 1100 cycles at low current densities at ambient temperature. Propylene carbonate was the electrolyte [2].

Another cell utilizing propylene carbonate as the electrolyte is the lithium-bromine battery, which has an open-circuit potential of 4.05 volts and a theoretical energy density of 504 watt-hours/pound. An experimental cell was cycled 1785 times, though current densities were only 30 percent of the initial value at the end of cycling. It appears that the long life of this system is due in part to a bromine shuttle mechanism which limits self-discharge [7]. This system, with further development, might find application where high energy density is required.

2.2.5 Evaluation of selected candidate secondary batteries. The required characteristics for central-station work or for motive power are in some ways different. However, each must be manufactured at low cost. The raw materials must be inexpensive and the manufacturing technique amenable to automation. A technically superb battery that is costly will not be acceptable. Likewise, long battery life is important, but there is surely a limit to the increase in acceptable first cost.

For electric vehicle use several other requirements appear to be important. These include high energy density for range and high rate capability for acceleration and hill climbing. Battery systems that lack these capabilities may need to be supplemented by auxiliary energy sources. The ability to retain charge with a self-discharge rate of less than one percent per day is believed to be an acceptable upper limit. Safety is also of paramount importance—batteries using molten or dangerous materials must be capable of being made safe during accidents or charge control failure.

Based on these requirements, Gross [2] has evaluated candidate systems. The more promising candidates are listed in Table 2-5 with an evaluation of

TABLE 2-5. EVALUATION OF SELECTED SECONDARY BATTERIES†

Battery	Major factors affecting possible use	Near-term prospects (0-5 years)	Long-term prospects (5-15 years)
Lead-acid	Low cost; better energy and power density needed; longer life needed	Excellent	Good
Nickel-iron	Uncertain cost	Good	Good
Nickel-hydrogen	Uncertain cost; weight penalty for auto use	Good	Good
Nickel-zinc	Limited cycle life	Fair	Good
Iron-air	Complexity; cost and life uncertain	Fair	Good
Sodium-sulfur	Life; cost; separator development	Fair	Good
Zinc-bromine	Need separator for long activated stand	Poor	Fair
Zinc-chlorine hydrate	Cost and reliability; weight penalty for auto use	Poor	Fair
Aluminum-air	Need rechargeable aluminum electrode	Poor	Fair
Lithium-sulfur	Improved sulfur electrode and longer life	Poor	Good
Lithium-tellurium-tetrachloride	Improved energy density	Poor	Good
Aluminum-chlorine	Improved aluminum electrode	Poor	Good
Lithium-bromine	Extensive R & D required	Poor	Good

† After Ref. [2] with permission.

their near- and long-term prospects. Of course, unforeseen technological breakthroughs could cause presently obscure systems to become attractive. Conversely, very promising systems may encounter insurmountable technical obstacles or go wanting for lack of research funds. For near-term prospects, the three best bets are the lead-acid system, the nickel-iron system, and the nickel-hydrogen system. Other promising near-term prospects are the nickel-zinc system, the iron-air system, and the sodium-sulfur system.

2.2.6 Chemical storage in hydrogen. Batteries can be considered to be a special case of chemical energy storage where conversion of electrical to chemical energy, storage, and reconversion to electrical energy are combined in a single device. One potentially important example of chemical energy storage with a *separate* device for reconversion to electrical energy is the use of hydrogen as a storage medium.

Storage of energy in hydrogen in central-station or transportation applications might be done by electrolyzing water into its constituents—hydrogen and oxygen. Another possibility is the thermochemical splitting of water using sources of high-temperature process heat—possibly nuclear reactors. At present, water electrolysis is a well-established technology but is handicapped by modest efficiency and high capital cost. Some observers [1] believe that, with the development of advanced technology, conversion efficiency might approach 100 percent with capital costs of $40 to $70 per kilowatt.

Unlike electrolysis systems, which are available essentially as off-the-shelf items, the development of thermal processes for water splitting is still in the conceptual stage. The incentives to develop such processes derive from the potential for process efficiencies and economics that might be superior to those offered by electrolysis, particularly if sources of fairly high temperature heat—such as high-temperature, gas-cooled reactors—were available. It should be recognized that the establishment of technically and economically feasible processes for thermal splitting of water will undoubtedly require very extensive development efforts for at least ten years.

After effecting separation of the hydrogen and water, the storage of hydrogen must be considered. (The storage of oxygen is a well-developed technology and should present no problems to system designers.) Storage of compressed hydrogen is technically feasible now but the economics have not been fully established because of uncertainties regarding suitable containment materials. Storage in more concentrated form—as a cryogenic liquid or chemically bound in metal hydrides—are likewise technically feasible today. However, significant energy losses are associated with liquefaction or hydride formation and decomposition. The capital cost of either of these types of storage systems are likely to be substantial.

Hydrogen reconversion to electric energy is possible in fuel cells or in gas turbines. The fuel cell approach (Ch. 8) offers potential for high efficiency with a realistic target of 60 percent for cells using hydrogen and oxygen. Advanced combustion technology could lead to efficiencies of 50 percent for combined gas turbine-steam cycles. Fuel cells will have two advantages over gas turbines: they have better load-following characteristics and fewer siting restrictions.

2.3   THERMAL ENERGY STORAGE

Energy can be stored thermally by heating, melting, or vaporizing a material; such energy then becomes available when the storage process is reversed. When energy is stored by causing a material's temperature to rise it is called sensible-heat storage. Its effectiveness depends on its specific heat and, if the volume of material is important, on the density of the storage material as well.

Another method takes advantage of phase change—that is, the transition from solid to liquid or liquid to vapor. This method is called latent-heat storage—no temperature change is involved. (On some occasions, of course, both sensible- and latent-heat storage may occur in the same material. This happens, for example, when a solid is heated, then melted, then raised further in temperature.) Considerable energy can be stored in a material undergoing a phase change. Tables 2-6 and 2-7 summarize information on a number of materials which could be used for sensible- or latent-heat storage.

Hottel and Howard [8] suggest the following generalizations concerning the storage of thermal energy:

(1) For sensible-heat storage to temperatures below 200°F, water is outstanding. One-hundred-fifty-seven cubic feet of water rising 100°F will store the energy released by burning 10 gallons of fuel oil at 70 percent efficiency. That is approximately one day's winter fuel consumption of a modest domestic dwelling.

(2) For sensible-heat storage with air as the energy transport mechanism, gravel or crushed stone in a bin has the advantage of providing a large, cheap heat-transfer surface. The bin volume will, however, be two and one-half times the volume of a tank of water that is heated over the same temperature interval.

(3) No good material utilizing latent-heat storage in the vicinity of room temperature has been found. Glauber's salt ($Na_2SO_4 \cdot 10H_2O$) has been

suggested, but its phase change at 97°F is not a complete melting but a
separation into three phases of different density and composition. If melting
is to occur near the desired space temperature (say, between 90 and 120°F)
there are limitations on materials. Most organic materials generally have
such weak crystal lattices that their heat of fusion is too low to be useful,
while inorganic salts generally melt at higher temperatures unless they are

TABLE 2-6. PROPERTIES OF HEAT STORAGE MATERIALS USING SENSIBLE HEAT†

| | Specific heat Btu/lb-°F | True density lb/ft³ | Heat capacity, Btu/ft³-°F | |
			No voids	30% Voids
Water	1.0	62	62	—
Scrap iron	0.12‡	490	59	41
Magnetite (Fe₃O₄)	0.18‡	320	57	40
Scrap aluminum	0.23‡	170	39	27
Concrete	0.27	140±	38	26
Stone	0.21	170±	36	25
Brick	0.20	140	28	20
Sodium (to 208°F)	0.23	59	14	—

† After Ref. [8] with permission.
‡ Over an interval from 77°F to 600°F.

TABLE 2-7. PROPERTIES OF HEAT STORAGE MATERIALS USING LATENT HEAT†

| | Melting point °F | Density lb/ft³ | Heat of fusion | |
			Btu/lb	Btu/ft³
Calcium chloride hexahydrate	84–102	102	75	7,900
Sodium carbonate decahydrate	90–97	90	115	10,400
Glauber's salt	90	92	105	9,700
Sodium metal	208	59	42	2,500
Ferric chloride	580	181	114	20,600
Sodium hydroxide	612	133	90	12,000
Lithium nitrate	482	149	158	23,500
Hypophosphoric acid	131	94	92	8,700
Lithium hydride	1260	51	1800	92,000
P116 wax (Sunoco)	116	49	90	4,400
$Na_2S_2O_3 \cdot 5H_2O$ (STP)	119	103	90	9,300
$FeCl_3 \cdot 6H_2O$	97	101	96	9,700
$Ca(NO_3) \cdot 4H_2O$	117	116	66	7,650

† After Refs. [8] and [11] with permission.

hydrates. The latter then commonly separate into an anhydrous solid residue and a dilute solution rather than undergo a true melting. Hottel and Howard [8] point out that a cheap inorganic hydrate with a congruent melting point is needed—the water content of the melted and unmelted parts is the same. Melting or solidification at the interface between phases is not dependent on molecular diffusion, which is slow, and rapid melting or solidification can occur as heat is added or removed.

(4) If a large temperature range is available, iron ore (magnetite) has the unusual property of exhibiting a volumetric heat capacity about the same as water at low temperature. Even if the capacity is reduced to 70 percent because of voids between the ore lumps, the capacity is still impressively high. If ore is raised in temperature to 700°F, a bin of only 37 cubic feet could store the energy in the example of item (1).

(5) Concrete can also be used to store energy over a large temperature range, though it is not as efficient, volumetrically, as magnetite. Concrete blocks have been used in England to iron out electric home-heating load.

(6) High-temperature latent-heat storage has some striking possibilities. For example, ferric chloride melts at 580°F with a heat of fusion of 20,600 Btu/ft³, lithium nitrate melts at 482°F with a heat of fusion of 23,500 Btu/ft³, and hypophosphoric acid melts at 131°F with a heat of fusion of 8,700 Btu/ft³. Heats of fusion and melting points of eutectic mixtures of various fluorides are presented by Schröder [9]. Libowitz [10] reviews the properties of various metal hydrides as thermal energy storage media.

Lorsch [11] reviews the qualities of a good thermal storage medium and presents data on various salts and hydrates of interest. He also estimates what it would cost to store various amounts of energy and what volume of material would be required to effect the storage. Figure 2-8 gives an estimate of container volume versus storage capacity for latent-heat and sensible-heat storage. The two latent-heat materials shown on this chart are a wax made by the Sun Oil Company called P116 and sodium thiosulfate pentohydrate (STP). Kalhammer and Zygielbaum [1] discuss briefly the possibility of storing energy in high-pressure steam.

2.4 MECHANICAL STORAGE OF ENERGY

The oldest energy storage systems we know about are those that have utilized some form of mechanical storage, such as hydropower. Nature took care of when to store the energy and when to release it. In winter snow in the mountains stored potential energy there; in spring and summer the snows melted, filling the streams and rivers. The energy stored in that water

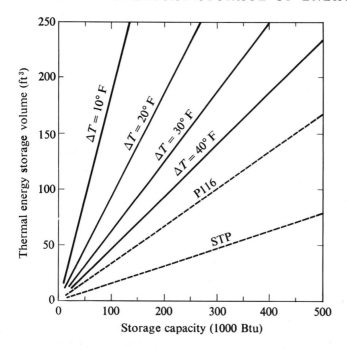

FIG. 2-8. Required container volume to achieve various amounts of energy storage as a function of temperature variations. Also shown are two materials which use latent-heat storage—a wax (P116) and sodium thiosulfate pentohydrate (STP). After Ref. [11].

was partly utilized by man—in early days by water wheels and today by hydroelectric plants. In this chapter, however, we are interested in energy storage that we can control and will not be subject to nature's capricious ways.

2.4.1 Pumped-storage hydroelectric plants. The conversion into electricity of the potential energy stored in water by virtue of its elevation can be done with an efficiency in excess of 90 percent. In recent years a technique has been developed that allows the construction of hydroelectric plants that have some of the characteristics of storage batteries. They are called pumped-storage plants. At present they are the only practical method for large-scale storage of electrical energy.

Pumped-storage plants generally operate as follows: large amounts of water from a river or lake are pumped to a reservoir at a higher elevation with reversible pump-turbines. The motors that drive the pumps are also reversible and act as electrical generators when the water falls from the upper reservoir and drives the turbines.

During off-peak load hours when other base-load plants in the system normally have excess capacity, the motor-pump units raise water from the lower reservoir to the upper reservoir by utilizing power from the slack base-load plants. Then during hours of peak demand this water is allowed to fall back down to the lower reservoir, thus adding to the system's peak capacity. The power used during off-peak hours is relatively cheap and can generally be assumed to cost only whatever the additional fuel required to generate it costs, since the base-load plants must be kept turning anyway. All efficiencies considered, it takes about three cheap kilowatt-hours to produce two kilowatt-hours to be sold at peak demand. Thus the system has an overall efficiency of about 67 percent. (As peak-demand pricing spreads throughout the utility industry, this type of energy storage will look even more attractive—the two kilowatt hours sold during a time of high demand will be able to command premium prices.)

Pumped-storage units also have the ability to respond to rapid changes in load. A spinning turbine can be fully loaded in one minute; and the newer installations can be converted from pumping to generating in 5 to 10 minutes. Pumped-storage units can be combined with conventional hydroelectric plants or can function alone. The need for this kind of system is clear from the growth now projected for them: in 1970 there was 3600 MW of pumped storage, by 1980 there will be 27,000 MW and by 1990 70,000 MW. The demand reflects the fact that peak loads are believed to be expanding much faster than base loads.

2.4.2 Compressed-gas energy storage. There are relatively few geographical locations that have a topography suitable for pumped-storage plants. However, energy can be stored in air as well as in water. Air can be stored at relatively high pressure in existing underground cavities such as those left after mining has ceased.

An air-storage power plant employs a conventional gas turbine modified so that the compressor and turbine sections may be uncoupled and operated separately, as shown in Fig. 2-9. During low-load periods the turbine clutch is disengaged and the compressor is driven by the electrical generator, which then functions as a motor, taking power from other plants in the system. The compressed air is stored for use during peak-load periods. For use, it is mixed with fuel in the combustion chamber, where it is burned and then expanded through the turbine. During these periods the entire output of the turbine is used to drive the generator.

Storing air for this purpose in fabricated containers would probably be too expensive for large storage volumes. The least expensive storage would utilize dissolved-out salt caverns, porous ground reservoirs, depleted gas and oil fields, and abandoned mines. Nuclear explosives could produce

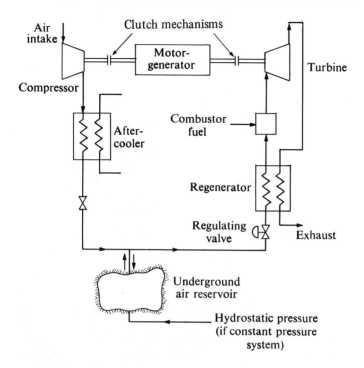

FIG. 2-9. A compressed-air energy storage system. During charging, the motor drives a compressor which stores air under relatively high pressure in an underground reservoir. During discharge, the air is used to burn a fossil fuel which drives a gas turbine connected by means of a clutch to the generator.

storage reservoirs in massive rock formations of granite, shale, or limestone. Olsson [12] suggests that the air in abandoned mine storage regions could be kept under more or less constant pressure by means of hydrostatic pressure, using water from a nearby lake or reservoir. Fortunately, wide variations in stored gas pressure can be tolerated with some penalty on performance.

The cavern volume required for a certain mass flow of compressed air is inversely proportional to the air pressure and proportional to the required number of hours of peak-load operation per day. Technical data for a 220-MW air-storage plant is given in Table 2-8. Olsson [12] asserts that such a plant could be built for $50 per kilowatt (1970 prices) excluding the cost of land, roads, and taxes. Though no such plant is presently in operation, the technology for constructing such a plant is clearly available.

TABLE 2-8. TECHNICAL DATA FOR A 220-MW
AIR-STORAGE POWER PLANT†

Station rating	220 MW
Air flow to storage at 5°C (41°F)	351 kg/sec (775 lb/sec)
Maximum storage pressure	43.5 atm (640 psia)
Air temperature in cavern	15°C (59°F)
Cavern depth	435 m (1425 ft)
Compressor power at 5°C/41°F	161 MW
Turbine inlet temperature	800°C (1470°F)
Continuous power at 5°C/41°F	73 MW
Efficiency/heat rate	
at peak load	71.5%/4770 Btu/kWh
continuous	27%/12,650 Btu/kWh
Power ratio: off-peak kWh/peak kWh	0.76
Cavern volume per hour/day peak-load operation	27,400 m³ (970,000 ft³)

† After Ref. [12].

2.4.3 Energy storage in flywheels. Flywheels, used as energy storage devices
for centuries, today find wide use in internal combustion engines to carry
the rotation of the engine between pulses of energy delivered by the pistons.
Until recently it was thought that employing flywheels in wider applications
was out of the question because of cost and because not enough energy
could be stored per unit of wheel weight. This picture has been changed by
recent advances in materials technology, largely as a result of research and
development in the aerospace industry.

Energy storage in flywheels depends on the mass of the rim and on
angular velocity; stored energy varies as the square of the rotation speed.
The limit to the stored energy is set ultimately by the tensile strength of the
material from which the rim is made. The rim must be able to withstand the
so-called "hoop stress" resulting from centrifugal forces. As with the stored
energy, these forces are proportional to the mass of the rim and increase as
the square of the rotation speed. Thus, two properties of the material
determine the amount of energy that can be stored in a flywheel: mass
density, which provides kinetic energy, and tensile strength, which resists
centrifugal forces.

Contrary to what intuition might suggest, one wants the lightest
(lowest density) available material that is strong enough. Consider a simple
thin-rim flywheel. Suppose one were to make two flywheels, identical in
dimensions and design but fabricated of different materials, having equal
tensile strength but unequal density. When these two flywheels are energized,
the heavy flywheel will of course store more energy than the light one. Note,
however, that the tensile stresses from centrifugal forces will be greater in the
heavier rim than in the lighter one, again in direct proportion to the relative

mass. As one continues to accelerate both wheels, the heavy one will be the first to approach its maximum speed as limited by its tensile strength. In other words, it will be the first to approach the limit of its energy storage. The lighter flywheel, experiencing much smaller centrifugal forces, can sustain a higher angular velocity. When the light flywheel reaches its limit, it will be storing the same total energy as did the heavier one at a lower speed. If the light material is, say, 10 times lighter per unit volume than the heavy material and both have the same tensile strength, a flywheel made of the light material will require only 10 percent as much mass to store the same amount of energy as the heavy flywheel. High strength at low density is thus the proper criterion for choosing materials for energy-storing flywheels.

Though high-strength steels might seem to be the best materials for making flywheels, it turns out that they are too heavy, too expensive, and too difficult to fabricate for the applications now being considered. The fiber composites developed initially for aerospace applications have exactly the properties required. They are lower in density than steel—by a factor of four to six—and some are far stronger. Figure 2-10 compares certain fibers

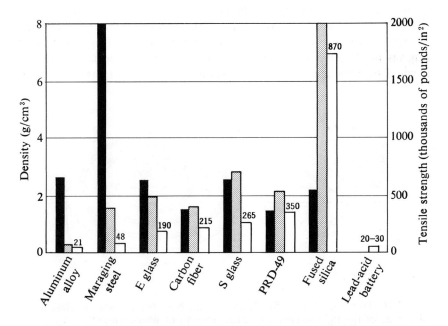

FIG. 2-10. Properties of materials for flywheels are compared. All except the first two are high-strength fibers for use in fiber composites. For each material the first bar gives the density, the second the tensile strength, and the third the maximum energy stored per unit weight of material when incorporated in a flywheel. The numbers on the top of the bar are the storage density in watt-hours per kilogram. A lead-acid battery is shown for comparison. After Ref. [13].

[13] with high-strength metals in terms of properties important to flywheels. The fiber materials do remarkably well in this comparison. A commercial fiber called E glass can store four times as much energy per unit weight as high-strength maraging steel, yet the price of the fiber is only about 15 percent of that of steel alloy. PRD-49, one of the "aromatic polyamides" and a descendent of the nylon family, can store seven times as much energy per unit weight as alloy steel. Fused silica may turn out to be the best of all for inertial storage of energy. This fiber might be able to store 10 to 15 times more energy per unit weight than flywheels made of the best alloy steels.

In order to take advantage of the capabilities of these new materials, it is necessary to reconsider the shape of the flywheel. A group at Johns Hopkin's Applied Physics Laboratory proposed a radically new design called the "superflywheel," which consists of a rimless wheel with many spokes, as illustrated in Fig. 2-11. Each spoke is a bar or rod fabricated of a fiber-composite material with the direction of the fibers being parallel to the length of the rod. Such a design converts centrifugal forces into pure tension forces. The design suffers from several drawbacks, including stress concentrations at the hub and low volume efficiency since the rods occupy only a small portion of the volume swept out by their ends.

A design which overcomes some of the disadvantages of the whirling pincushion design is made up of several concentric rings (Fig. 2-11). Each ring fits inside the next one with a small gap between them. To hold the flywheel together and to allow for relative expansions of the rings under

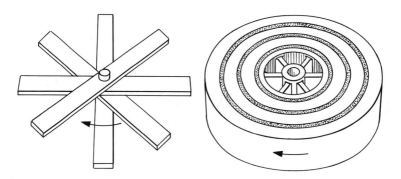

FIG. 2-11. Two new designs for flywheels that have been made to take advantage of the light weight and great strength of fiber-composite materials. At left is the rimless multispoke "superflywheel." The wheel at the right has concentric rings of fiber composite separated by small gaps filled with bonded resilient material. The design minimizes radial stresses that would cause delamination and makes efficient use of the wheel's volume. After Ref. [13].

centrifugal force, resilient elements such as bonded bands of rubberlike material fill the gaps. This design minimizes internal radial stresses and also exhibits good volume efficiency. Several improvements on this basic design have been suggested to further improve its energy storage capability [13].

Flywheels are now being considered as energy storage devices for utilities and vehicles. Small units storing 10 MW-hours of energy with a power rating of 3 MW would require an area of less than 400 ft². Compare this with two to four acres of land required for pumped-storage systems of the same capacity. Moreover, some observers believe that capital cost of flywheel storage units will be substantially less than pumped-storage units.

One proposed automobile flywheel system stores 30 kW-hours of energy in a flywheel containing 130 pounds of fused-silica fibers or 280 pounds of PRD-49. The flywheel would drive a reversible generator/motor which would then supply electric power to small motors on each wheel. The flywheel could be brought back up to speed by a reversible motor/generator unit and external power. A flywheel system, unlike a battery system, can accept a full 30-kW-hour charge in five minutes or less. A small automobile should be able to go 200 miles at 55 miles per hour on the energy stored in the flywheel.

By sealing the flywheel system in a partial vacuum, the loss of power from friction effects could be minimized. Rundown time for a rotor in a vacuum chamber is estimated at from six to twelve months. The development of high-efficiency flywheels could do much to curb our demand for more and bigger power plants to meet peak loads and our ever-increasing demand for fossil fuels to power vehicles.

2.5 SUMMARY

The energy storage systems considered here are at varying levels of development. Accordingly, some of the economic evaluations projected for these systems represent hardly more than speculation. However, it is not unreasonable to state that even these preliminary economic and technical projections indicate that several energy storage methods have reasonable potential for central-station power and selected transportation systems. Because each of these methods has specific advantages and limitations, several different energy storage methods may well be developed.

It should be ovbious from the material presented that the development of practical energy storage systems requires advances in a broad range of technical areas; solution of the problems now limiting these devices will require multidisciplinary approaches and development teams.

PROBLEMS

2-1. One problem with using solar energy to supply electricity is its intermittent nature. It has been proposed that solar energy be used to generate electricity in a solar-thermal plant during the day and this power then be used to decompose water into hydrogen and oxygen. The hydrogen is then burned with the oxygen over the 24-hour period to provide heat to run a conventional power plant.

The electrolysis process will require electrical energy of around 70 kcal/gram-mole. The solar energy plant will convert about 30 percent of the collected solar energy into electrical energy for the electrolysis process. The combustion of hydrogen will yield about 52,000 Btu/lbm and the main power plant will convert about 35 percent of this energy into electrical energy for consumer use. About 100 Btu will be collected on each square foot of solar collector surface each hour during the 10 daylight hours of each day. Calculate the following quantities of interest for a system that delivers 1000 MW on a continuous basis:

    (a) Daily solar energy collection requirements, Btu.
    (b) Solar collector area, m^2.
    (c) Daily mass of water electrolyzed, kg.
    (d) Daily hydrogen consumption rate, lbm.

What social, political, and broad economic questions do you see arising with this plant?

2-2. Suppose the hydrogen-burning conventional power plant described in Problem 2-1 is replaced with a fuel cell power plant with an efficiency of 60 percent. Each mole of hydrogen will produce 34.7 kcal of electricity. Find out how that change affects each of the answers you found in Problem 2-1.

2-3. A utility is considering building a pumped-storage plant to increase its overall system load factor and delay the construction of an additional base-load plant. Suppose the utility has options on a suitable geographical location on which an upper reservoir could be placed 500 ft above a river. The utility would like to get 100 MW of peaking power from the plant, which is assumed to have a generating efficiency of 85 percent. The pumped-storage plant is expected to deliver its power for 4 hours each day. Assume that the pumping efficiency is 65 percent—that is, 65 percent of the electrical energy input to the pump goes into actually raising the water uphill. Assume that the recreational uses of the upper reservoir require that the water level not change by more than 2 ft over the day. Find the following:

    (a) The energy that must be supplied by the rest of the system in order to get the 100 MW for 4 hours per day during the peak load time.
    (b) The acreage that must be allotted to the upper reservoir.

2-4. Consider a structure in Columbia, Missouri that is assumed to have a winter heat load of 46,780 Btu/hr (13,700 watts) based on an inside temperature of 70°F (21.1°C) and a mean outside temperature of 6°F (−14.4°C). Consider how much energy will have to be stored to supply this structure with the energy it will need for 24 hours and find the volume of storage medium required if:

    (a) Water is used as the storage medium experiencing an 80°F swing in temperature.
    (b) Concrete is used as the storage medium and the temperature swing is the same as in part (a).
    (c) Hydrophosphoric acid is used as the storage medium and it suffers no temperature change.

(d) P116 wax (Sunoco) is used as the storage medium and it undergoes no temperature change.

2-5. Consider the system load factor presented in Problem 2-3. Suppose that the utility decides to try to solve this problem by means of storage batteries instead of pumped-storage. Assume the following cost data:

	C_p ($/kW)	C_s ($/kWh)
Lead-acid	40	7
Nickel-iron	60	12
Nickel-hydrogen	80	20

Where is the break-even point for each of these systems in comparison with the pumped-storage system? Estimate the volume and weight for each of these systems. Compute the cost per kilowatt-hour delivered during the peak period assuming that the power required to charge each system is constant at 2 cents per kilowatt-hour.

2-6. Estimate the weight of batteries required for both an urban and family car for the three systems you consider to be the most attractive in the near term.

2-7. Hoffman in Ref. [14] gives design equations for electric automobiles. For the range, R, in miles he found the appropriate expression to be:

$$R = \frac{d}{4.42 \times 10^{-2} + 2.21 \times 10^{-4}v + (3.95 \times 10^{-2}/W + 1.86 \times 10^{-5})v^2}$$

The travel time between recharges, T, is

$$T = 8.6 \times 10^{-2}d \text{ (hours)}$$

The energy expended between recharges is

$$E = 5.22 \ WT \text{ watt-hours}$$

where
$\quad d$ = the energy density in watt-hours/pound
$\quad v$ = the speed in miles per hour
$\quad W$ = the vehicle weight in pounds

Make a parametric study of how the weight and energy density of a given battery system influences the range, travel time between recharges, and energy expended between recharges for a wide range of proposed battery systems for electric autos.

2-8. As another alternative to the peak-shaving unit required by the electric system in Problem 2-3, the utility is considering installing a system of super-strength flywheels made of fibers. Using the data presented in Figs. 2-10 and 2-11, make preliminary designs for a system of flywheels that will handle the peaking power situation described in Problem 2-3.

REFERENCES

1. F. R. Kalhammer and P. S. Zygielbaum, "Potential for Large-Scale Energy Storage in Electric Utility Systems," ASME Paper No. 74-WA/Ener-9.

2. S. Gross, "Review of Candidate Batteries for Electric Vehicles," *Proceedings of Battery Council International Golden Anniversary Symposium*, London, May, 1974.

3. J. F. Stockel, G. Van Ommering, L. Swette, and L. Gains, "A Nickel-Hydrogen Secondary Cell for Synchronous Orbit Application," *7th Intersociety Energy Conversion Engineering Conference, 1972* (Washington, D.C.: American Chemical Society, 1972).

4. S. P. Mitoff and J. B. Bush, Jr., "Characteristics of a Sodium-Sulfur Cell for Bulk Energy Storage," *9th Intersociety Energy Conversion Engineering Conference, 1974* (New York: American Society of Mechanical Engineers, 1974).

5. W. J. Walsh, J. W. Allen, J. D. Arntzen, L. G. Bartholme, H. Shimotake, H. C. Tsai, and U. P. Yao, "Development of Prototype Lithium/Sulfur Cells for Application to Load-Leveling Devices in Electric Utilities," *9th Intersociety Energy Conversion Engineering Conference, 1974* (New York: American Society of Mechanical Engineers, 1974).

6. E. G. Gay, W. W. Schertz, F. J. Martino, and K. E. Anderson, "The Development of Lithium/Sulfur Cells for Application to Electric Automobiles," *9th Intersociety Energy Conversion Engineering Conference, 1974* (New York: American Society of Mechanical Engineers, 1974).

7. J. L. Weininger and F. W. Secer, "Nonaqueous Lithium-Bromine Secondary Galvanic Cell," *Journal of the Electrochemical Society*, Volume 121, No. 3, March, 1974.

8. H. C. Hottel and J. B. Howard, *New Energy Technology—Some Facts and Assessments* (Cambridge, Mass.: M.I.T. Press, 1971).

9. J. Schroeder, "Thermal Energy Storage and Control," ASME Paper No. 74-WA/OcT-1.

10. G. G. Libowitz, "Metal Hydrides for Thermal Energy Storage," *9th Intersociety Energy Conversion Engineering Conference, 1974* (New York: American Society of Mechanical Engineers, 1974).

11. H. G. Lorsch, "Thermal Energy Storage Devices Suitable for Solar Heating," *9th Intersociety Energy Conversion Engineering Conference, 1974* (New York: American Society of Mechanical Engineers, 1974).

12. E. K. A. Olsson, "Air Storage Power Plant," *Mechanical Engineering*, November, 1970.

13. R. F. Post and S. F. Post, "Flywheels," *Scientific American*, December, 1973.

14. G. A. Hoffman, "Energy Requirements for Electric Automobiles," *4th Intersociety Energy Conversion Engineering Conference, 1969* (New York: American Institute of Chemical Engineers, 1969).

15. J. T. Brown and J. H. Cronin, "Battery Systems for Peaking Power Generation," *9th Intersociety Energy Conversion Engineering Conference, 1974* (New York: American Society of Mechanical Engineers, 1974).

3 Introduction to Semiconductors

In the study of the direct conversion of heat or light to electricity the role played by semiconductors is a major one. For that reason we set out early in our studies to explore their distinguishing characteristics and to decide which of these characteristics make them important for direct energy conversion purposes. The material presented in this chapter is not comprehensive, but it will provide a review of those elements of solid state theory that are germane to direct energy conversion devices. More complete discussions of solid state theory can be found in the standard references [1]–[4]. The last of these, Azaroff [4], presents the most elementary treatment.

3.1 EARLY WORK IN SEMICONDUCTORS

Research on materials we now call semiconductors has been taking place for over a hundred years. The first event that alerted early workers to the possibility of the existence of substances with interesting electrical and thermal characteristics quite different from those of metals and insulators was the discovery of materials with a negative temperature coefficient of resistance. This means that the material's resistance to the flow of an electric current decreases as the temperature is raised—completely opposite to the characteristics of a metal. (Faraday observed this phenomenon while conducting experiments on silver sulfide.) This property alone, however, is not a sufficient basis for classifying a material as a semiconductor.

Progress made in the 40 years after Faraday's discovery was not great, though several workers noted that materials belonging to the class of poor conductors had unusually high Seebeck coefficients. In 1874, Ferdinand Braun observed in lead sulfide another of the distinguishing characteristics we now attribute to semiconductors, the phenomenon of rectification. In 1873, Willoughby Smith observed that in certain materials the electrical conductivity was sensitive to light. He found this effect chiefly in metallic sulfides and oxides and the element silicon. A more complete historical review is offered by Lark-Horovitz [5], together with an extensive bibliography.

It might be well to note here that semiconductors generally have room temperature resistivities in the range 10^{-3} to 10^6 ohm-cm. A good metallic conductor has a resistivity around 10^{-6} ohm-cm whereas in a good insulator the electrical resistivity would be in the neighborhood of 10^{12} ohm-cm. Other properties that are sometimes observed in materials called semiconductors include a negative temperature coefficient of resistance and a sensitivity to light that produces a photovoltage or a change in electrical resistance.

3.2 THE BASIC IDEAS OF QUANTUM PHYSICS

In general, the men who followed Newton in developing the laws of classical mechanics and electromagnetism were concerned with matter on a macroscopic scale—that is, they dealt with problems where distances were measured in centimeters and mass in grams. The fundamentals of solid state physics, however, are determined in a region where distances are measured in angstrom units [1 angstrom unit (A) equals 10^{-8} cm] and mass is measured in micromicromicromicromilligrams (10^{-27} gm). When dealing with matter at this level, it is necessary to think in peculiar ways because the laws of physics that we apply to larger units of matter simply do not work at the submicroscopic level. This different way of looking at nature is contained in the study of *quantum mechanics.*†

Before we introduce some details of those parts of quantum mechanics pertinent to the understanding of semiconductors, we will state in a general way the principles underlying this new way of thinking. The four fundamental blocks on which the details of quantum mechanics rest are:

(1) The electron must be thought of as a dual entity—not only must it be treated as a particle, but its wave nature must be considered as well. The electron wave may be viewed as an undulation of energy. The wavelength depends upon the electron's energy—the greater the energy, the shorter the wavelength. Louis de Broglie was the first to suggest the dual nature of the electron and to deduce the exact relationship between its wavelength and its momentum.

---

† A good introduction to modern physics in general, and quantum mechanics in particular, is given by Eisberg [6].

(2) The *exclusion principle*, as enunciated by Wolfgang Pauli, states that in any atom no more than 2 electrons can occupy the same energy level. The principle says that if there are 2 electrons in the same energy level, they must have different values for their intrinsic angular momentum; an explanation based on classical or Newtonian physics would state that the 2 electrons spin in opposite directions. The energy levels referred to in Pauli's principle correspond roughly to orbits around the nucleus.

(3) The precise motion and exact position of any very small particle cannot be known at a given instant. Werner Heisenberg stated in his *uncertainty principle* that if the position of an electron were measured accurately, then there must be doubt as to its velocity, and vice versa.

(4) The mathematics of probability as applied to electrons is based on the assumption that electrons are indistinguishable.

In addition to these four fundamental ideas, the universal fact of nature's economy—applicable to phenomena on both the large and small scale—must be taken into account. Matter at ordinary temperatures left to itself tends to assume the condition that involves the least possible potential energy, whether it be water in a bucket or electrons orbiting a nucleus. We use potential energy in its broadest sense, not confining the term to gravitational potential. This type of potential energy is sometimes called *free energy*, a subject we will discuss in more detail when we take up the study of fuel cells. The state of minimum energy must be satisfied in many solid state calculations.

Before we begin our discussion of semiconductors, we will discuss briefly some of the experiments and hypotheses that have given us an understanding of the physics of semiconductors.

The photoelectric emission of electrons was one of the first experiments that quantum theory explained. If light of a certain frequency is allowed to fall on an emitter plate, as shown in Fig. 3-1, some electrons will receive enough energy to be liberated from the emitter. The positive bias supplied by the battery in the circuit causes these free electrons to be attracted to the collector and a current is caused to flow as indicated by the ammeter. The current can be caused to go to zero by making the voltage of the collector plate negative. The voltage that reduced the current to zero is called V_q, the *stopping potential*. The stopping potential repels all the electrons that are released from the emitter. Experiments of this kind demonstrated that with light of a single frequency (monochromatic) the photocurrent increased as the intensity of the light increased. It was also observed that the stopping potential was independent of the light intensity.

When light of different frequencies (wavelengths) is used, the stopping potential must be made more negative as the frequency is increased. That is, the higher the frequency (the shorter the wavelength), the greater the

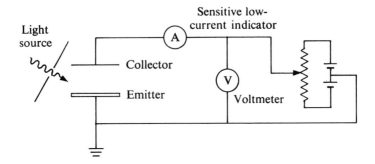

FIG. 3-1. An experimental apparatus for studying photoelectric emission. This circuit permits development of a uniformly varying voltage, changeable smoothly from positive to negative.

negative bias that must be placed on the collector to reduce the current to zero. A linear relation is seen to hold between the incident light frequency and the stopping potential, which corresponds to the maximum kinetic energy of the liberated photoelectrons. The minimum frequency of light that will cause electrons to be liberated for a given material is called the *threshold frequency* of that material. When light of a frequency less than the threshold frequency is applied to the material, regardless of its intensity, no electrons are liberated. In changing to a different emitter material, the characteristics of the curves do not change, as can be seen in Fig. 3-2. The

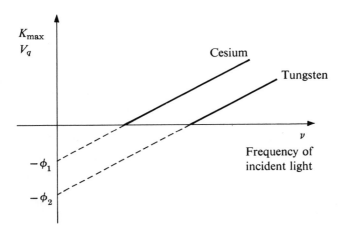

FIG. 3-2. Dependence of maximum energy (stopping potential) of photoelectrons on frequency of incident light. Note that the work functions are different but the slopes are all equal.

only thing that changes is the threshold frequency below which there is no current. The curves all have the same slope. The linear relationship between stopping potential (maximum electron kinetic energy) and frequency v can be expressed as

$$eV_q = K_{max} = a'v + b', \tag{3-1}$$

where a' is the slope and b' is a constant that depends on the metal used. It is observed in Fig. 3-2 that a' is independent of the material but b' is not.

The wave theory of light agrees well with the observed fact that an increase in intensity produces an increase in photoelectric current. However, it does not help explain the relationship between light frequency and the maximum kinetic energy of the electrons released from the surface. In 1905 Einstein explained these results by using ideas of Planck called the *quantum theory* which state that:

(1) Energy is not indefinitely indivisible. The smallest amount of energy that can be transferred in a physical process is called a *quantum*. Light is a form of energy and a quantum of light is called a *photon*.

(2) Either an electron absorbs a quantum of energy or it does not. The energy ε of a photon is proportional to the frequency v of the light, or

$$\varepsilon = hv. \tag{3-2}$$

(3) If an electron is given an amount of energy hv, then in order to escape from the metal it must use up an amount $e\phi$ of this energy, where ϕ in volts is called the *work function* of the metal; e is the electronic charge. More specifically, the work function is defined as the work required to move an electron from the Fermi level of a substance to infinity. (We will discuss the meaning of the Fermi level more fully in a later section.)

Therefore, the maximum energy an electron can have left after it gets out of the surface is

$$K_{max} = hv - e\phi. \tag{3-3}$$

This is the exact form of the empirical equation that was obtained from our experimental results. The slope a' measured from the graph agrees with the values of Planck's constant obtained in other ways and is found to be

$$h = 6.62 \times 10^{-27} \text{ erg-sec.}$$

It was particularly significant in the early days of quantum theory that the value of h determined from photoelectric data was in agreement with the value calculated from Planck's theory of radiation. In the years 1900 to 1912, the theories of Planck and Einstein were substantiated by a mass of experimental data that clearly showed that energy is not continuous but comes in discrete packets, hv. Thus, we must now consider light not only in terms of waves but also as a stream of "particles," each of which carries a discrete quantity of energy.

In 1923 A. H. Compton did an experiment that helped somewhat to rectify the long-standing conflict that existed between the wave and particle theories of light. Classical electromagnetic theory indicates that when radiation passes through matter, the resulting scattered radiation should have the same frequency as the incident radiation. Compton directed a beam of monochromatic X rays at a specimen and examined the scattered radiation with an X-ray spectrometer. In addition to finding X rays at the incident wavelength, he also found a scattered wavelength that was greater than that of the incident beam. Classical theory offers no way of introducing changes in wavelength into the scattering process; this scattering at increased wavelength (decreased frequency) is known as the *Compton effect*. The photon hypothesis provides a rather direct explanation of this phenomenon. If one assumes that the incident beam of photons has energy $h\nu$ and a corresponding amount of momentum, and then treats the scattering process as an elastic collision between a free electron at rest and a photon, one can predict the correct wavelength shift. The conservation of momentum and energy requires that the electron recoil. Thus the scattered photon must have a lower energy, and hence a lower frequency, than the incident photon. The energy of the photon is reduced by just the amount of energy that the electron gains. In interpreting the Compton effect, the photon of energy $h\nu$ is assumed to have a momentum

$$p' = h\nu/c, \qquad (3\text{-}4)$$

where c is the velocity of light. Since $c = \lambda\nu$, the wavelength associated with a photon is

$$\lambda = h/p'. \qquad (3\text{-}5)$$

The energy of an electromagnetic wave of wavelength λ is carried by massless particles (photons) of momentum h/λ.

In 1924 Louis de Broglie suggested on theoretical grounds alone that electrons might also have wave properties. By analogy to the hypothesis used in explaining the Compton effect, he proposed that the associated wavelength be inversely proportional to the particle's momentum to obtain

$$\lambda = h/p' = h/(mu) \qquad (3\text{-}6)$$

for the "wavelength" of a "particle" with mass m and velocity u. De Broglie's theory and the resulting equations were regarded as pure speculation by researchers at the time. However, in 1927 Davisson and Germer found that low energy (54 eV) electrons striking the face of a nickel crystal are actually reflected in a pattern that can be most easily interpreted as the diffraction of plane waves by the regularly spaced atoms of the crystal, thus verifying that electrons do have wave properties.

Classical mechanics recognizes no fundamental limitations on measurements of any kind. In 1927 Werner Heisenberg recognized that this assumption of measurement to any degree of accuracy was contrary to the quantum theory. His indeterminacy or uncertainty principle states that the degree of accuracy with which a set of measurements can be made is limited by the measurement process itself. The uncertainty arises because the measuring process is subject to the same quantum laws as the system being measured. Thus if one attempts to use a photon of light energy to observe the position of an electron, as the photon strikes the electron some of the photon's energy will go into the electron, causing it to recoil. Unless the photon strikes the electron, we will have no evidence in our observing instrument of the position of the object; and if the photon is scattered by the electron, then the electron's position and its momentum will change. Heisenberg summarized the limits on position and momentum as

$$(\Delta x)(\Delta p'_x) \geq h/(4\pi). \tag{3-7a}$$

Note that we make no statement on the limits of accuracy with which Δx or $\Delta p'_x$ can be measured by themselves, only on their product. The photon will not locate the particle more closely than its own wavelength λ because of diffraction effects. Therefore, to get an accurate measure of position one must use light of very short wavelength. But a photon of short wavelength is one of high momentum, as we stated in our discussion of the Compton effect $(p' = h/\lambda)$, and hence in bouncing off the particle being observed it may impart to it a high momentum.

The uncertainty relation of Eq. 3-7a can also be expressed in terms of energy and time as

$$(\Delta \mathcal{E})(\Delta t) \geq h/(4\pi). \tag{3-7b}$$

So far we have described certain interactions between electrons and electromagnetic waves. We have seen how certain experiments have led to relations such as $\mathcal{E} = h\nu$ and $\lambda = h/(mu)$, but up to this point we have had no grand unifying idea. We have had particular difficulty when we have tried to reconcile differing macroscopic observations of electron behavior; in some instances electrons exhibit wave characteristics whereas in others they act like particles.

In 1926 Erwin Schrödinger supplied the unifying key that tied all of the previous ideas of the new physics into a whole. In just one line of mathematical symbols Schrödinger encompassed virtually all the principles of quantum mechanics. The *Schrödinger equation* or *wave equation* replaces the familiar $F = ma$ of classical mechanics. Before actually stating the equation, it would be well for us to consider briefly its nature and some of its ramifications. It must be a wave equation like the equations used to describe vibrations in continuous media or acoustic phenomena. If this were not true, the wave solutions for electron diffraction experiments could not be obtained. Traditionally, wave equations are second-order partial differential equations with independent variables of space and time.

We now must consider the question of the dependent variable in the wave equation. In the case of acoustic phenomena this variable is pressure and in vibration problems it is displacement. Before we suggest a dependent variable for the Schrödinger equation we state again that we must not expect to understand atomic phenomena in the familiar classical terms. We may use crude physical models in the form of rings and shells to aid our limited imaginations, but ultimately we must come to the conclusion that particle behavior within the atom is completely alien to our macroscopic (Newtonian) experience. Therefore, we must be prepared to accept a dependent variable which at first sight seems to be more abstract than quantities such as displacement or pressure.

The variable we select is called simply the *wave function* and it is traditionally denoted by the Greek letter ψ (psi). It is important to note that it corresponds to no physical thing or occurrence. It may be given physical significance in the following way: $|\psi|^2 \, d\Omega$ is proportional to the probability that an electron will be found in the volume $d\Omega$. Admittedly, the wave function does not answer the question: Where, precisely, is the electron? In the light of electron diffraction experiments, the Compton effect, and the uncertainty principle, we must face the fact that the question really has no meaning. The most we can expect to accomplish with our wave equation is to give the probability of finding an electron in a certain region of space; we conclude then that ψ is an acceptable dependent variable.

The selection of ψ as the dependent variable leads to the possibility of a reconciliation between the observed particle and wave characteristics of the electron. If the location of a single electron is defined in terms of a wave function, then the distribution density of large numbers of electrons will exhibit wave characteristics. Concentrations of electrons will occur in those regions where $|\psi|^2$ is high. Generally large numbers of electrons are involved in the usual physical measurements and thus correspondence with theoretical probability distributions is excellent.

The Schrödinger wave equation for a single particle is

$$\frac{h^2}{8\pi^2 m}\left[\frac{\partial^2 \psi}{\partial x^2} + \frac{\partial^2 \psi}{\partial y^2} + \frac{\partial^2 \psi}{\partial z^2}\right] - P\psi = \frac{h}{2\pi i}\frac{\partial \psi}{\partial t}, \qquad \textbf{(3-8)}$$

where h is Planck's constant, P the potential energy of the particle, and $i = \sqrt{-1}$. Most physical problems require that the three-dimensional form of the wave equation be solved, but for purposes of understanding the nature of atomic phenomena, we shall work with the one-dimensional equation

$$\frac{h^2}{8\pi^2 m}\left[\frac{\partial^2 \psi}{\partial x^2}\right] - P\psi = \frac{h}{2\pi i}\frac{\partial \psi}{\partial t}. \qquad \textbf{(3-9)}$$

We also assume that potential energy P depends solely on position and not on time. This assumption is usually valid in most problems we encounter in solid state physics.

We now solve Eq. 3-9 by separating variables x and t, a procedure that is used quite often with equations of this nature. Assume there exists some function X which is only a function of x and some function T which is only a function of t and that our solution is a product of the functions, so

$$\psi(x, t) = X(x)T(t). \tag{3-10}$$

We now try this tentative solution in the Schrödinger equation (Eq. 3-9),

$$\frac{h^2}{8\pi^2 m} T \frac{\partial^2 X}{\partial x^2} - PXT = \frac{hX}{2\pi i} \frac{\partial T}{\partial t} \tag{3-11}$$

and divide Eq. 3-11 by XT to obtain

$$\frac{h^2}{8\pi^2 m} \frac{1}{X} \frac{\partial^2 X}{\partial x^2} - P = \frac{h}{2\pi i} \frac{1}{T} \frac{\partial T}{\partial t}. \tag{3-12}$$

We have achieved separation of variables, as the terms on the left are functions of x only and those on the right are functions of t alone. Each side of Eq. 3-12 involves a different independent variable and yet the two sides are equal. Therefore, we set them equal to the same quantity $-\mathcal{E}$, a symbol selection that turns out to be most propitious. The partial differential equation Eq. 3-12 now reduces to two ordinary differential equations with the attendant simplification

$$\frac{h^2}{8\pi^2 m} \frac{d^2 X}{dx^2} + (\mathcal{E} - P)X = 0 \tag{3-13}$$

$$\frac{dT}{dt} = -\frac{2\pi i}{h} \mathcal{E}T. \tag{3-14}$$

Separating the variables in Eq. 3-14 yields

$$\frac{dT}{T} = -\frac{2\pi i}{h} \mathcal{E}\, dt, \tag{3-15}$$

which is integrated to

$$T = \exp\left(-2\pi i \mathcal{E}t/h\right). \tag{3-16}$$

The function $T(t)$ is seen to be a complex oscillatory function of time whose frequency ν is given by $2\pi\nu = 2\pi\mathcal{E}/h$. Thus $\nu = \mathcal{E}/h$. But we have already stated earlier (in Eq. 3-2) that $\mathcal{E} = h\nu$ where $\mathcal{E}$ is the total energy of the particle. So our selection of $-\mathcal{E}$ as the separation constant was indeed appropriate. The arbitrary constant of integration has been omitted because the product solution of Eq. 3-10 is understood to include a constant. The solution involving time is only part of the complete solution. We now consider the solution to the part involving the variable X. The solutions to Eq. 3-13, $X(x)$, are called *eigenfunctions*. The reader is advised to keep clearly in mind the difference between the eigenfunctions $X(x)$ and the wave functions $\psi(x, t)$; the former are solutions to the time-independent Schrödinger equation while the latter are solutions to the Schrödinger equation itself.

There are three conditions that must be applied to the wave function. First, ψ must be continuous and single valued, which merely means that the probability of finding an electron should vary smoothly from point to point in the space region of interest, assuming that no electrons are created or destroyed. The single-valued condition assures us that there will be no ambiguity in the predictions of the probability. Second, the integral $\int_{-\infty}^{+\infty} |\psi|^2 \, dx$ must be finite. The normalized probability condition is specified as

$$\mathcal{P} = \frac{|\psi|^2 \, \Delta x}{\int_{-\infty}^{+\infty} |\psi|^2 \, dx}, \tag{3-17}$$

which gives† the probability $\mathcal{P}$ of finding an electron in the space between x and $x + \Delta x$. This equation states that if in the interval Δx, $|\psi|^2 \, \Delta x = 0$, the electron is certainly not in Δx, and if $|\psi|^2 \, \Delta x = 1$, and if the denominator has the conventional normalized value of one, the electron certainly is in the space Δx. If the integral $\int_{-\infty}^{+\infty} |\psi|^2 \, dx$ were not finite, the probability of finding an electron in any finite interval Δx would be zero, which is an unrealistic condition for a physical problem. Third, in the case of all finite potential energy functions $\partial \psi / \partial x$ must be continuous.

In general, solutions to the Schrödinger equation are tedious and can only be obtained for rather special cases. We will, however, consider the problem of a series of potential energy wells that we might assume constitutes an idealized crystal. Each well is of length L and everywhere within the well the potential energy is zero. At the two ends of the well the electron is forbidden from leaving the crystal by a very high potential barrier represented by P_o. A typical well on which we will concentrate our analysis is shown in Fig. 3-3. Under these assumptions the time-independent part of Eq. 3-13 becomes

$$\frac{d^2 X}{dx^2} + \left[\frac{8\pi^2 m \mathcal{E}}{h^2} \right] X = 0 \tag{3-18}$$

for the region within the well $(0 \leq x \leq L)$. This equation is identical in form to the equation of the simple harmonic oscillator or the time-independent wave equation that describes the standing waves set up in a vibrating string clamped at both ends. By standing waves we mean that the nodes of the string are stationary in space and the maximum displacement at any point does not vary with time. We will now concentrate on solving the string problem, primarily because the boundary conditions and the solutions have

† The fact that we use only $|\psi|^2$ in our probability calculations has some interesting consequences. It means that the eigenfunctions that are solutions to the time-independent Schrödinger equation can be either real or imaginary. Another way to look at this situation is to note that since Eq. 3-13 is linear in $X(x)$ we can always take a solution that is the sum of a real solution plus i times a second real solution, provided the two solutions correspond to the same value of $\mathcal{E}$.

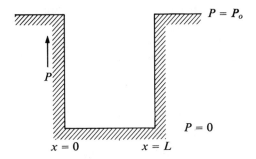

FIG. 3-3. Schematic of a crystal of length L in which the potential energy is everywhere zero within the crystal but has barriers of magnitude P_o at its two ends.

more physical significance to one unfamiliar with the ideas of quantum mechanics. We will then interpret the solutions as to what they mean for the quantum mechanics problem described by Eq. 3-18.

The equation that describes the displacement U of the string of mass per unit length γ with an applied tension T_l, analogous to Eq. 3-18, is

$$\frac{d^2U}{dx^2} + \omega^2 \frac{\gamma}{T_l} U = 0, \tag{3-19}$$

where $\omega = 2\pi\nu$ is the angular frequency of vibration. The solution to this equation has a general form

$$U = C_1 \cos \omega\sqrt{\gamma/T_l}\, x + C_2 \sin \omega\sqrt{\gamma/T_l}\, x. \tag{3-20}$$

You may verify that this is a solution to Eq. 3-19 by direct substitution. The quantity $\sqrt{\gamma/T_l}$ has the dimensions of seconds per centimeter which is the reciprocal of velocity u. We may thus relate the wavelength of a standing wave λ to its frequency and velocity in exactly the same way we did earlier for the electron, that is, $u = \lambda\nu$ so that

$$\omega\sqrt{\frac{\gamma}{T_l}} = \frac{2\pi\nu}{u} = \frac{2\pi}{\lambda}, \tag{3-21}$$

which upon substitution into Eq. 3-19 yields

$$\frac{d^2U}{dx^2} + \frac{4\pi^2}{\lambda^2} U = 0. \tag{3-22}$$

Equation 3-22 is another way of representing the time-independent part of the one-dimensional wave equation, which has a general solution

$$U = C_1 \cos (2\pi/\lambda)x + C_2 \sin (2\pi/\lambda)x. \tag{3-23}$$

The classical wave equation appears repeatedly in many branches of

physics, including acoustics, optics, mechanics, and others that are concerned with wave propagation. Consider Fig. 3-4, which shows how the
length of the string L is divided by the nodes of vibration into integral parts.
Since the distance between nodes is one-half of a wavelength, we may write

$$\frac{\lambda}{2} = \frac{L}{n} \qquad \text{where} \qquad n = 1, 2, 3 \cdots. \qquad \textbf{(3-24)}$$

Upon substituting Eq. 3-24 into Eq. 3-23, we obtain the eigenfunctions

$$U = \mathcal{C}_1 \cos \pi(n/L)x + \mathcal{C}_2 \sin \pi(n/L)x. \qquad \textbf{(3-25)}$$

We may determine the particular solution to this problem by considering
the boundary conditions that U, the displacement, must be zero at the two
ends of the string ($x = 0, L$). Thus at

$$x = 0: \qquad U = 0 = \mathcal{C}_1 \cos (0) + \mathcal{C}_2 \sin (0) = \mathcal{C}_1; \qquad \textbf{(3-26a)}$$

$$x = L: \qquad U = 0 = \mathcal{C}_1 \cos \pi n + \mathcal{C}_2 \sin \pi n = \mathcal{C}_2 \sin \pi n. \qquad \textbf{(3-26b)}$$

Equation 3-26a requires $\mathcal{C}_1$ to be zero and, excluding the trivial solution
that U is identically zero for all $x(\mathcal{C}_2 = 0)$, we require that sin πn be equal
to zero. That is indeed the case when n takes on integer values. Figure 3-4
illustrates the situation for the case of $n = 1, 2,$ and 3. We also note that $\mathcal{C}_2$
is an arbitrary constant that is a function of the amplitude but is independent
of the boundary conditions.

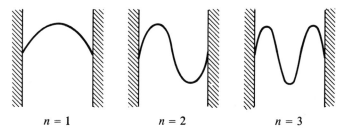

$n = 1$ $n = 2$ $n = 3$

FIG. 3-4. Several of the solutions to the vibrating string problem, showing
some of the possible standing waves that the string can assume. The integer
that is associated with each solution is shown under each sketch. We have
exaggerated the shape of the string greatly in order that the wave form
be clearly illustrated.

The most important point to remember concerning this problem is
that the solutions to boundary value wave equations such as Eq. 3-20 are
quantized; they are different from zero only for a discrete set of values of n.
In nearly everything that follows we will, again and again, encounter many
ideas in which conditions of discreteness will replace the classical conditions
of continuity.

We now return to the problem of the potential well in the crystal, which was described mathematically by Eq. 3-13. Our work is somewhat simplified if we assume the potential barrier to be infinite rather than just very large. The mathematical consequences of this assumption reduce the boundary conditions of the quantum mechanics problem to the boundary conditions of the vibrating string problem that we just considered, namely, X must be identically zero at $x = 0$ and $x = L$. For these assumptions, we conclude that if the solution is to be nontrivial, the following relationship must hold:

$$(2\pi/h)\sqrt{2m\mathcal{E}}\, L = n\pi \qquad n = 1, 2, 3 \cdots.$$

It follows, therefore, that the energy can have only the discrete values that we call the *eigenvalues*[†]

$$\mathcal{E}_n = \frac{h^2 n^2}{8mL^2}. \tag{3-27}$$

The quantity n in this equation is called a *quantum number*. If we assume, for example, a potential well the same size as the crystal, say about 1 cm, then the energy levels differ by 10^{-19} electron volts (eV).[‡]

In addition to satisfying the boundary conditions given above, quantum mechanics also requires, because of the finite probability of finding an electron anywhere in space, continuity of the solution everywhere.

Once again, we briefly review how the discreteness condition of Eq. 3-27 arose. Continuity of the solution forced $X = 0$ at $x = 0, L$. The consequence of these requirements was to make X consist of an integral number of half cycles of oscillation in the region 0 to L. Since the length of the half cycle depended on $\mathcal{E}$, this caused us to allow *only certain values of* $\mathcal{E}$. If we were to accept a value of $\mathcal{E}$ not included in the set of equations given by Eq. 3-27, then X and ψ would approach infinity outside the potential well and, consequently, when ψ was normalized inside the well, it would be zero. That is, we arrive at the unrealistic result that the probability of finding an electron inside the well with any energy would be zero. We should also keep in mind that the complete solution of Schrödinger's equation for this case would be the product of the time-dependent solution (Eq. 3-16) with the space-dependent parts for the appropriate regions.

Before leaving this problem we might note that in a real crystal the height of the potential barrier is determined in a complex way by the crystal's surface energies. If the potential barrier is high but not infinite, we then obtain nonzero values for ψ outside of the well—a result that is not expected on the basis of classical theory. In these regions the kinetic energy is negative; furthermore, quantum mechanics predicts a finite probability of pene-

---

[†] Corresponding to each *eigenvalue* is an *eigenfunction*, which is a solution to the differential equation under study.

[‡] An *electron volt* may be defined as the energy acquired or lost by 1 electron moving through a potential difference of 1 volt.

trating some distance into this "classically forbidden" region of negative kinetic energy. The ability of an electron to penetrate a potential barrier is called "tunneling." In the 1940's Enrico Fermi, at the University of Chicago, demonstrated the phenomenon of tunneling with the following problem: Given a 1-ton automobile coasting very slowly toward a hill 100 ft long and 1 ft high, what is the probability that the car will tunnel under the hill? The answer came out $10^{-10^{38}}$. The odds on tunneling on the atomic scale in semiconductors are much better, for a tunnel diode actually works; it has the unusual property of a negative resistance region. This characteristic allows the construction of a simple oscillator consisting only of a tunnel diode, capacitor, inductance, and battery. Such circuits can oscillate at very high frequencies since the tunneling is nearly instantaneous.

A more meaningful example of the wave equation occurs upon considering the hydrogen atom; the deductions based on the Schrödinger equation in this case can be verified by experiment. The system we will consider consists of a proton of charge e and an electron of charge $-e$ and mass m. If we regard the position of the proton fixed at the origin and the position of the electron at a point whose spherical coordinates are r, θ, and ϕ, the Schrödinger equation in spherical coordinates is

$$\frac{1}{r^2}\frac{\partial}{\partial r}\left(r^2\frac{\partial\psi}{\partial r}\right) + \frac{1}{r^2\sin^2\theta}\frac{\partial^2\psi}{\partial\phi^2} + \frac{1}{r^2\sin\theta}\frac{\partial}{\partial\theta}\left(\sin\theta\frac{\partial\psi}{\partial\theta}\right) + \frac{8\pi^2 m}{h}\left[\varepsilon - P(r)\right] = 0.$$

$$(3\text{-}28)$$

The solution to this equation is found to be significant only if the three constants that arise take on certain integer values. These integers are called *quantum numbers*. One of these is designated by n and can take on any integer from one to infinity. It is the *principal quantum number*. The other two constants must be integers also and their magnitudes are related to the principal quantum number n. The *azimuthal quantum number*, l, can have all integer values from $l = 0$ to $l = n - 1$ and it determines the electron's orbital angular momentum. An electron moving in an orbit has a magnetic field associated with it, since it is a moving electric charge. In the presence of an external magnetic field the orbital can orient itself in $2l + 1$ different ways. The specific orientation of the angular momentum vector assumed by the orbitals is determined by the *magnetic quantum number, m_l*, which can take on all integers, including zero, from $m = -l$ to $m = +l$. This totals to $2l + 1$ numbers. The quantum numbers are said to specify a possible *state* of the electron.

In addition to the three quantum numbers used to specify the quantum state of an electron, one more piece of information is generally given. It has been assumed that the charge of an electron is not stationary but rotates around an axis through the electron. In classical language, the electron can spin either clockwise or counterclockwise. Thus, a so-called *quantum spin number*, m_s, is usually assigned, which may take on the value $+\frac{1}{2}$ or $-\frac{1}{2}$, depending on whether or not the spin vector is parallel to the orbital momentum.

In the case of the hydrogen atom, the electron energy is completely specified by the principal quantum number n as $\varepsilon = -13.6/n^2$ electron volts. However, when we consider atoms that contain more than 1 electron, the problem becomes considerably more complicated. The complications are caused by the dependence of the energy upon n, l, m_l, and m_s instead of just upon n as with the hydrogen atom. Space will not allow us to discuss the way an electron's energy depends on its quantum numbers; the interested reader is referred to any good modern physics textbook such as Ref. [6].

In 1925 Wolfgang Pauli proposed the principle that no 2 electrons in an atom can have exactly the same set of four quantum numbers. This is known as the *Pauli exclusion principle*, and it states that there can be 2 electrons for each combination of n, l, and m_l, provided that each has a different value for m_s.

3.3 THE FERMI LEVEL

The Maxwell-Boltzmann distribution law is used in elementary kinetic theory to describe the state of molecules in a gas under ordinary conditions. Electrons are much lighter than molecules and the concentration of valence electrons (the ones that take part in chemical binding) is about ten thousand times higher than the concentration of molecules in a gas at standard temperature and pressure. Under these conditions, classical statistics are no longer valid. The classical Maxwell distribution of energies of free particles predicts an average kinetic energy of $\frac{3}{2}kT$. If all the conduction band electrons in a metal were crowded into the energy states lying within about $\frac{3}{2}kT$ of the bottom of the band, there would be nearly 1000 electrons per quantum state. This condition is at variance with the restrictions of the Pauli exclusion principle, which allows only 1 electron per state; thus it follows, when we are dealing with large numbers of electrons, that even in the lowest state of the total system, many high quantum number states of the individual electrons will be occupied. In the lowest state of a system described by classical statistics, all particles can have zero energy and momentum.

In 1928 Sommerfeld modified the free electron theory of electrical conduction in metals by applying quantum mechanics to the electron motion. The Sommerfeld modification replaced the classical statistics of Boltzmann with the quantum statistics of Fermi and Dirac. This modification caused most of the failings of the free electron theory to be removed. The quantum statistics on which the Sommerfeld theory was based depend upon the statistics developed by Enrico Fermi, which show that the probability that a particular state is occupied is given by the Fermi function

$$f(\varepsilon) = \frac{1}{\exp\left[(\varepsilon - \varepsilon_f)/(kT)\right] + 1}. \tag{3-29}$$

In this equation, ε is the energy of an allowed state as given by Eq. 3-28, ε_f is the Fermi energy, k is Boltzmann's constant, and T is temperature. Let us consider the Fermi function at absolute zero. If $\varepsilon < \varepsilon_f$, then the exponential term is zero ($e^{-\infty} = 0$) and $f(\varepsilon) = 1$. If $\varepsilon > \varepsilon_f$, then the exponential term is infinite and $f(\varepsilon) = 0$. These results are plotted in Fig. 3-5. The meaning of

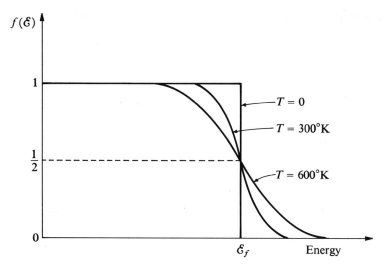

FIG. 3-5. The Fermi function and its dependence on temperature, shown somewhat exaggerated.

$f(\varepsilon) = 1$ for any $\varepsilon < \varepsilon_f$ is that all quantum states are occupied at absolute zero while all quantum states at energies greater than ε_f are unoccupied. An increase in temperature permits electrons occupying states near the Fermi level ε_f to gain sufficient thermal energy to move into the higher unoccupied states. This movement to higher states by the electrons near ε_f causes unoccupied quantum states with $\varepsilon < \varepsilon_f$ to appear. That is, it is no longer an absolute certainty that an electron will be found at states below the Fermi level. This is reflected by the curves (which have been exaggerated) drawn for temperatures of 300°K and 600°K in Fig. 3-5. *The Fermi level is by definition the energy at which the probability of a state being filled is exactly one-half.* The Fermi level also corresponds to the thermodynamic free energy (per electron) and, therefore, is *always continuous across the contact between two conductors in equilibrium.* We will discuss this point in more detail a little later.

3.4 ENERGY BANDS

In our discussion of solutions to the Schrödinger equation we observed how energy levels were quantized—that is, restricted to certain definite values in a single potential force field. We now consider briefly and qualitatively what happens when the potential energy is periodic, as in the lattice of a crystal. We use the word crystal to mean a collection of atoms arranged in a regular array.

In order to understand how electron energy levels are grouped into bands, we return once again to the concept of quantum numbers. The electronic configuration of the first thirty-six elements is given in Table 3-1. The atomic number and chemical symbol are given in the first two columns. The ionization energy in volts is given in the fourth column. The ionization energy is the energy required to remove the least tightly bound electron from the atom. The letter designation of the electron state is given in the third row; the number to the left of the letter is the principal quantum number. The letters *s*, *p*, *d*, and *f* are from the spectroscopic nomenclature and designate the azimuthal quantum number *l* that determines the electron's orbital angular momentum. That is, *s* (for *sharp*) means $l = 0$; *p* (for *principal*) means $l = 1$; *d* (for *diffuse*) means $l = 2$; *f* (for *fundamental*) means $l = 3$.

The numbers under each column heading indicate the number of electrons that have those two quantum numbers. We have not indicated the last two quantum numbers for each electron for reasons of clarity. But remember that, according to the Pauli exclusion principle, no 2 electrons can share the same four quantum numbers. A compact way of designating the electronic configuration of an atom is simply to write its quantum state notation using the number of electrons as superscripts, thus:

Carbon: $1s^2 2s^2 2p^2$;
Germanium: $1s^2 2s^2 2p^6 3s^2 3p^6 3d^{10} 4s^2 4p^2$.

It might be noted that the 6 electrons sharing the quantum state $3p$ in germanium would have either 0 or ± 1 for their magnetic quantum number m_l, and a spin quantum number of $+\frac{1}{2}$ or $-\frac{1}{2}$. That is, we can write out the quantum numbers of these electrons as

TABLE 3-1.† ELECTRONIC STRUCTURE OF ATOMS

Principal quantum number n				1	2		3			4	
Azimuthal quantum number l				0	0	1	0	1	2	0	1
Letter designation of state				$1s$	$2s$	$2p$	$3s$	$3p$	$3d$	$4s$	$4p$
Z	Symbol	Element	V_i volts								
1	H	Hydrogen	13.60	1							
2	He	Helium	24.58	2							
3	Li	Lithium	5.39	Helium core	1						
4	Be	Beryllium	9.32	Helium core	2						
5	B	Boron	8.30	Helium core	2	1					
6	C	Carbon	11.26	Helium core	2	2					
7	N	Nitrogen	14.54	Helium core	2	3					
8	O	Oxygen	13.61	Helium core	2	4					
9	F	Fluorine	17.42	Helium core	2	5					
10	Ne	Neon	21.56	Helium core	2	6					
11	Na	Sodium	5.14	Neon core			1				
12	Mg	Magnesium	7.64	Neon core			2				
13	Al	Aluminum	5.98	Neon core			2	1			
14	Si	Silicon	8.15	Neon core			2	2			
15	P	Phosphorus	10.55	Neon core			2	3			
16	S	Sulfur	10.36	Neon core			2	4			
17	Cl	Chlorine	13.01	Neon core			2	5			
18	A	Argon	15.76	Neon core			2	6			
19	K	Potassium	4.34	Argon core						1	
20	Ca	Calcium	6.11	Argon core						2	
21	Sc	Scandium	6.56	Argon core					1	2	
22	Ti	Titanium	6.83	Argon core					2	2	
23	V	Vanadium	6.74	Argon core					3	2	
24	Cr	Chromium	6.76	Argon core					5	1	
25	Mn	Manganese	7.43	Argon core					5	2	
26	Fe	Iron	7.90	Argon core					6	2	
27	Co	Cobalt	7.86	Argon core					7	2	
28	Ni	Nickel	7.63	Argon core					8	2	
29	Cu	Copper	7.72	Argon core					10	1	
30	Zn	Zinc	9.39	Argon core					10	2	
31	Ga	Gallium	6.00	Argon core					10	2	1
32	Ge	Germanium	7.88	Argon core					10	2	2
33	As	Arsenic	9.81	Argon core					10	2	3
34	Se	Selenium	9.75	Argon core					10	2	4
35	Br	Bromine	11.84	Argon core					10	2	5
36	Kr	Krypton	14.00	Argon core					10	2	6

† From Charlotte E. Moore, *Atomic Energy Levels*, Vol. II (Washington, D.C.: National Bureau of Standards Circular 467, 1952).

n	l	m_l	m_s
3	1	0	$+\frac{1}{2}$
3	1	0	$-\frac{1}{2}$
3	1	$+1$	$+\frac{1}{2}$
3	1	$+1$	$-\frac{1}{2}$
3	1	-1	$+\frac{1}{2}$
3	1	-1	$-\frac{1}{2}$

where we have demonstrated that no 2 electrons share the same four quantum numbers.

At this point it is important that we clarify the distinction between the two terms, *state* and *level*, that appear often in discussions of the properties of semiconductors. As we noted earlier, the state of an electron is fixed by four quantum numbers, n, l, m_l, and m_s. These numbers specify both the wave function and the energy. Consider the two sets of quantum numbers $(3, 1, 1, \frac{1}{2})$ and $(3, 1, -1, \frac{1}{2})$. These numbers will determine two different wave functions if we use them in the solution to the wave equation. However, they will yield the same value for the electron energy, since the energy is dependent upon the sum of squares of the first three quantum numbers. Thus, we observe that in this situation the energy levels are the same but the states are different. A situation in which energy levels are made up of more than one quantum state is called *degenerate;* the degeneracy is equal to the number of quantum states.

We are now ready to consider what happens when we bring a large number of atoms together to form a crystal. First we discuss how we will represent pictorially the electrons in a material. In Fig. 3-6 we plot the energy of an electron as a function of its distance from the nucleus of a hydrogen atom. By convention the electron's energy is taken to be zero at an infinite distance from the nucleus. As the electron moves toward the nucleus, the system comprised of the electron and the nucleus *do* work because they are of opposite sign and are attracted to each other; since the system has done work, it is at a lower energy. We recognize this fact by plotting the increasing negative energy of an electron downward as shown in Fig. 3-6. The total energy of the electron is the algebraic sum of its potential energy and its kinetic energy and locates the *energy level*, which we have discussed before. In order to ionize an atom, it is necessary to take an electron out of this orbit and move it an infinite distance away from the nucleus. The energy required to do this is given by the magnitude of the total energy.

We now consider a somewhat more complicated atom. The nucleus of a sodium atom contains 11 positive charges and consequently 11 electrons will locate themselves around this nucleus. If we add the electrons one by one, the first 2, having opposite spin, will come to rest in the $1s$ electron shell and have the largest amount of negative energy; that is, these are the electrons

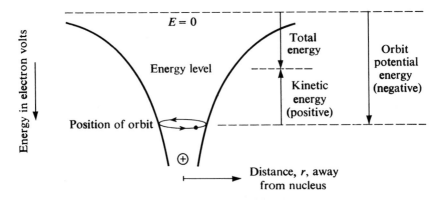

FIG. 3-6. The energy of an electron near the hydrogen nucleus. The electron's total energy which determines its energy level is the algebraic sum of its potential and kinetic energies.

that it would be most difficult to tear away from the nucleus. The Pauli exclusion principle forbids any more electrons in the first shell and dictates that the next 2 electrons will come to rest in the $2s$ shell, while the next 6 electrons occupy the $2p$ shell with magnetic quantum numbers 0, ± 1 and spin quantum numbers of $\pm\frac{1}{2}$. Because the energy levels specified by the magnetic and spin quantum numbers are very close together, we show it as one energy level with 6 electrons. The next electron that is added goes into the $3s$ or valence orbit of the atom. We have illustrated this situation in Fig. 3-7. The energy levels and potential curve have been drawn to represent the state of affairs just after the eleventh electron has been added to make the atom neutral. It should also be noted that the scale in Fig. 3-7 has been distorted to make the presentation clearer.

Now we bring together several atoms of sodium, creating a crystal of sodium. Once we have formed a crystal of the material we can no longer consider the electrons as being associated with a particular atom; rather, they must be considered as belonging to the crystal at large. The crystal is now considered as the system, and having more than 2 electrons at a single energy level would be a violation of the exclusion principle. In these circumstances the energy levels of the individual atoms are smeared into bands consisting of as many extremely closely spaced energy levels per band as there are atoms in the crystal; there are as many such bands in the crystal as there are energy levels in an isolated atom of the same substance. The exclusion principle under these conditions offers no problem because the valence electrons can now occupy slightly different energy levels within the

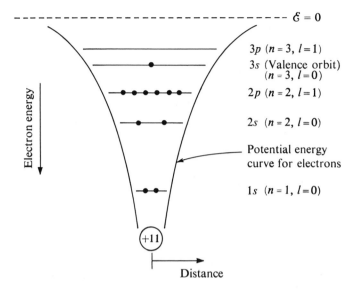

FIG. 3-7. The energy level scheme for a sodium atom which can accommodate 11 electrons. Shown along the right-hand side of the drawing are the quantum states for the electrons in the lowest energy state of the atom. After Shive [3] with permission.

3s band. We have illustrated this situation in Fig. 3-8. In sodium the bottom of the 3p band overlaps the top of the 3s band as we have shown it.

The width of an energy band from its topmost level to the lowest level is characteristic of the form of the crystal and the material of which it is constituted. The valence electron bands of most solids are a few electron volts wide. It should be made clear that the width of an energy band is independent of the size of the crystal or the total number of atoms contained in it. In two crystals, one twice as large as the other, the larger has twice as many energy levels as the smaller and these levels are packed twice as close together in the bands and accommodate twice as many electrons; the top and bottom edges, however, are at the same energy positions in both crystals.

With this background in band theory, it is now possible to indicate the nature of the distinctions between conductors, semiconductors, and insulators. If the highest energy band that contains any electrons is well separated from adjacent allowed energy bands—that is, it does not overlap any other bands and is completely full, then we have an insulator. In a full band, since all the energy levels are occupied, the electrons in this band are not permitted by the exclusion principle to take on small amounts of energy from the electric field and change their own energy to some new neighboring value. That is, they cannot acquire kinetic energy and set up a current by their

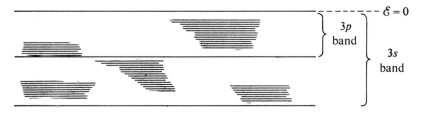

$\mathcal{E} = 0$

$3p$ band

$3s$ band

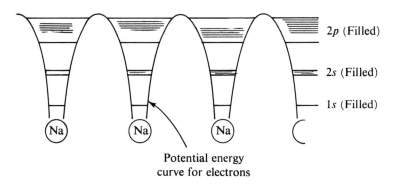

2p (Filled)

2s (Filled)

1s (Filled)

Na   Na   Na

Potential energy
curve for electrons

FIG. 3-8. In a sodium crystal that contains many atoms, the bands split into energy levels which, in general, are very close together. There are as many levels in each band as there are atoms in the crystal, and there are as many such bands in the crystal as there are energy levels in an isolated atom of the material. Each level can hold, at most, 2 electrons according to the Pauli exclusion principle.

motion. The highest occupied band corresponds to the ground state of the outermost or *valence* electrons in the atom. For this reason the upper occupied band is called the *valence band*. In an insulator the valence band is full. In addition, the width of the forbidden energy gap between the top of the valence band and the next allowed band, called the *conduction band*, is so large (much greater than kT) that under ordinary circumstances a valence electron can accept no energy at all from an applied field, because there are no empty allowed states accessible to it. For example, diamond at room temperature has an energy gap of 6 eV while the semiconductor lead telluride has an energy gap of only 0.3 eV.

In a conductor the uppermost occupied levels are very close to some unoccupied energy levels in the conduction band; that is, the conduction band is partly filled. That means an applied voltage can deliver energy to a conduction band electron, causing it to move to an unoccupied vacant state at a slightly higher energy level within the same band. In short, a partly filled conduction band means that there are mobile electrons able to accept energy from the external field and, therefore, to conduct electric current.

Semiconductors in some respects are like insulators, except that in semiconductors the forbidden gap is much narrower. At room temperature, though the valence band is full, some electrons have enough thermal energy or may receive enough energy from light so that they may jump the narrow forbidden energy gap into the empty conduction band. The raising of electrons into the conduction band in this way is called *thermal* or *optical excitation*. The higher the temperature or the higher the frequency (the shorter the wavelength) of the light source, the larger the number of electrons that will be pushed up. The electrons that are so raised are then free to accept electrical energy from an applied field and to move through the crystal. In addition the sites or "holes" left vacant in the valence band become charge carriers themselves. An electron near a hole can jump in and fill it, leaving a new hole in the place it had occupied. This in turn can be filled by a neighbor at a slightly lower energy level, and so on. Current is actually carried by electrons moving in relays but it can equally well be pictured as a flow of positive holes moving in the opposite direction. When the conduction of current is due only to those electrons excited up from the valence band to the conduction band, we say that the material is *intrinsic;* very pure germanium or tellurium at high temperature conduct this way.

By adding small amounts of impurities called *dopants* to a semiconductor material, it is possible to choose the dominant type of conduction of the material. When conduction is due to impurities, we say the material is *extrinsic.* Impurities can either supply extra electrons, in which case we call the material *n* type, or can be deficient in valence electrons, in which case we call it *p* type. If both types of impurities have been added we obtain a mixed type of extrinsic conductor. These points are illustrated in Fig. 3-9 where we have eliminated the potential curve and show only the tops and bottoms of the energy bands.

3.5 INTRINSIC SEMICONDUCTORS

Materials in which the conduction band is separated from the valence band by not too great an energy gap, so that some of the electrons occupying the upper energy levels of the valence band can be excited either optically or thermally to the lower levels of the conduction band, are given the name semiconductors. Because the temperature at which conductivity becomes appreciable depends on the width of the forbidden band, which in turn depends on the structure of the crystal, such crystals are called, appropriately enough, *intrinsic.* The energy gap between the top of the valence band and

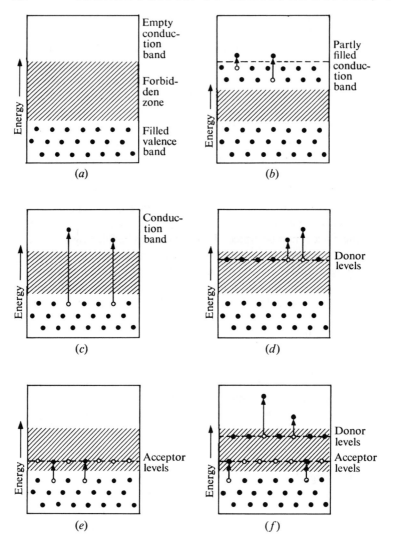

FIG. 3-9. Band theory of solids describes electrical conduction in terms of allowed and forbidden "bands" (or groups) of energy levels. Represented here are the band schemata of an insulator (*a*), metal (*b*), and four types of semiconductor: intrinsic (*c*), *n*-type (*d*), *p*-type (*e*), and mixed (*f*). Black dots are electrons. An insulator has a wider forbidden zone than a metal or semiconductor. Donor and acceptor levels are energy levels of electrons of donor and acceptor impurities in the semiconductors. After S. W. Angrist, "Galvanomagnetic and Thermomagnetic Effects," *Scientific American*, 205, No. 6 (1961), with permission.

the bottom of the conduction band we denote as $\mathcal{E}_g$. Though it makes no difference, we choose the zero energy level at the top of the valence band. This arbitrariness is allowable because only energy differences appear in the Fermi function. The density of electron energy levels $N_n(\mathcal{E})$, which is energy dependent, is measured up from the bottom of the conduction band; the density of hole energy levels $N_p(\mathcal{E})$ is measured down from the top of the valence band. We illustrate the situation graphically in Fig. 3-10. The right-

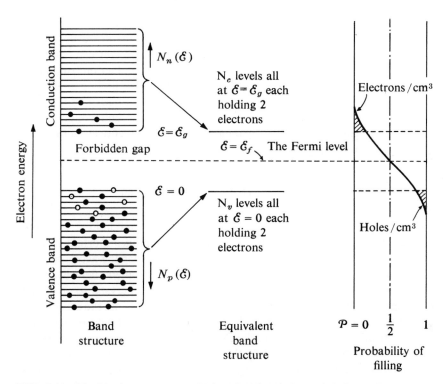

FIG. 3-10. The band structure, equivalent band structure, and the probability that a given level will be filled in an intrinsic semiconductor. After Shive [3] with permission.

hand side of Fig. 3-10 indicates the Fermi probability $f(\mathcal{E})$ that a given available energy level will be occupied. We may summarize what we know following the method of J. N. Shive [7] from Fig. 3-10 as follows:

(1) At all temperatures above absolute zero, there will be a few electrons in the conduction band and a few holes in the valence band.

(2) These numbers will increase with temperature. Their dependence on temperature we will try to determine.

(3) Because there are no donors or acceptors, the number of electrons per unit volume in the conduction band must equal the number of holes per unit volume in the valence band. This follows from the reasoning that the only way an electron can get into the conduction band is to be excited up from the valence band, thus leaving a hole there. In addition, a net charge neutrality must be maintained over dimensions larger than interatomic spacings. If this condition were not maintained the space charge would set up a field that would restore the neutrality.

(4) The Fermi level, which is that energy level whose probability of containing an electron is exactly one-half, must lie somewhere in the forbidden energy gap. This is a consequence of the fact that there are only a few electrons in the conduction band and a few holes in the valence band.

The number of electrons per unit volume in the conduction band in any range of energies $d\varepsilon$ is the product of the probability of finding an electron in this range times the density of electron levels in this range times the width of the range $d\varepsilon$. The total number n of electrons per unit volume in the conduction band can be found by integrating this product over all ranges $d\varepsilon$ from the bottom of the conduction band to the top thus

$$n = 2 \int_{\varepsilon_g}^{\substack{\text{top of conduction} \\ \text{band}}} N_n(\varepsilon) f(\varepsilon) \, d\varepsilon \text{ per unit volume.} \qquad (3\text{-}30)$$

The factor 2 accounts for the fact that each level can hold 2 electrons.

Normally, we evaluate this integral by making an important assumption. Before presenting this assumption, let us consider the acceleration of holes and electrons in solids. An electric field or magnetic field is applied to a crystal and subjects the electrons and holes in that crystal to an electric or magnetic force. At first it may seem appropriate to equate the acceleration times the mass of an electron to the force of the applied field to determine the electron's motion. After all, the electrons are only moving in response to an applied force. But to use only the laws of Newtonian mechanics would, upon reflection, be rather naive because the electron is responding not only to the applied electric or magnetic force but also to electrical forces from various atomic cores and other electrons in the periodic crystal array. Since the size scale for computing atomic or electronic forces is so small, quantum mechanics is essential to the determination of the motion produced by them. Simply utilizing classical mechanics as embodied in Newton's laws will not accurately describe an electron's motion.

A "quasi-classical" approach can be used, however, if the applied forces are much weaker than those associated with the spatially periodic electric field produced by the lattice atomic cores. In other words, the potential of the applied forces must not vary much over a few interatomic distances of the crystal structure. Under these circumstances it does turn out to be possible to represent the effect of all the periodic crystal forces in a parameter known as the *effective mass*, denoted by the symbol m^*.

This approximation, borrowed from statistical mechanics, has greatly facilitated quantitative studies of semiconductors. It permits us to apply Newtonian formulations to situations that are inherently not classical. *This classical picture of charge carriers is possible only because the major quantum features of electronic motions in solids can be buried in the "effective mass" parameter m^*.*

The quantum nature of the problem shows through in the curious fact that effective masses of conduction electrons and holes may lie in a range from less than $\frac{1}{100}$ to greater than 1 times the normal mass of an isolated electron. Values larger than the rest mass of an electron are easy to imagine because they could arise for electrons that are relatively tightly bound to an atomic core. The frequent occurrence of small effective masses cannot be visualized in classical terms at all and indicates the essential quantum nature of the problem. In fact, sometimes a different value of the effective mass must be used for each of the three space directions, so the effective mass is not just a single number but is really a tensor. Fortunately, in our work we will always be able to use a single value for the effective mass. One of the chief advantages of this approximation is that it allows, for purposes of calculation, all the distributed energy levels to be replaced by an equivalent number of energy levels all coinciding at the energy $\mathcal{E} = \mathcal{E}_g$. This equivalent number is

$$N_c = (2\pi m^* kT/h^2)^{3/2} \text{ per unit volume,} \qquad (3\text{-}31)$$

where k is Boltzmann's constant, h is Planck's constant, and m^* the effective mass. The subscript c refers to the conduction band. The distributed energy levels of the conduction band have been reduced to an equivalent number N_c all having energy $\mathcal{E}_g$ each of which may hold 2 electrons. A similar equation can be written for the number of levels in the valence band all concentrated at $\mathcal{E} = 0$. The only difference in the two equations is that m^* in this case represents the effective mass of the holes. To simplify our presentation further we assume that $m^* = m$, the rest mass of a free electron. This is not rigorously correct but the errors we will make because of this assumption will be small compared with the order of magnitude differences in electrical properties that occur with small changes in temperature, impurity content, and so forth. Thus we may write

$$N_c = N_v = (2\pi mkT/h^2)^{3/2} \text{ per unit volume.} \qquad (3\text{-}32)$$

We may compute the temperature-independent part of this function to have the numerical value $\alpha = 2.35 \times 10^{15} \text{ cm}^{-3} \, °K^{-3/2}$. Thus

$$N_c = N_v = \alpha T^{3/2} (\text{cm})^{-3}. \qquad (3\text{-}33)$$

The number of electrons in the conduction band will be given by the product of the equivalent levels N_c and the probability of filling each level times the number of electrons each can accommodate, thus

$$n = \frac{2N_c}{\exp\left[(\mathcal{E}_g - \mathcal{E}_f)/(kT)\right] + 1} \text{ cm}^{-3}. \tag{3-34}$$

The number of holes in the valence band per unit volume is given by the number of electrons per unit volume that the band could hold if it were completely full, minus the number of electrons that are actually there:

$$p = 2N_v\left[1 - \frac{1}{\exp\left[-\mathcal{E}_f/(kT)\right] + 1}\right] \text{ cm}^{-3}. \tag{3-35}$$

We have already stated that the number of electrons must equal the number of holes; thus we may equate the right-hand sides of Eqs. 3-34 and 3-35

$$n = p = 2N_c\left[\frac{1}{\exp\left[(\mathcal{E}_g - \mathcal{E}_f)/(kT)\right] + 1}\right]$$

$$= 2N_v\left[1 - \frac{1}{\exp\left[-\mathcal{E}_f/(kT)\right] + 1}\right]. \tag{3-36}$$

Noting that $N_v = N_c$, we obtain the following results

$$\mathcal{E}_f = \mathcal{E}_g/2 \tag{3-37}$$

and substituting Eq. 3-37 into Eq. 3-36 we obtain

$$n = p = \frac{2\alpha T^{3/2}}{\exp\left[\mathcal{E}_g/(2kT)\right] + 1}. \tag{3-38}$$

In any practical semiconductor, $\mathcal{E}_g$ must be at least a few kT wide or it will not be a semiconductor at all. If we assume $\mathcal{E}_g$ to be wider than $5kT$ or $6kT$, then the exponential term in the denominator will be the only one of significance and we may approximate Eq. 3-38 by

$$n = p = n_i \approx 2\alpha T^{3/2} \exp\left[-\mathcal{E}_g/(2kT)\right], \tag{3-39}$$

where n_i represents the concentration of carriers of either type in an intrinsic semiconductor. Our simplified derivation has shown that the Fermi level lies in the middle of the forbidden energy gap and remains there for all temperatures.

3.6 EXTRINSIC SEMICONDUCTORS

Up to this point we have been discussing materials that were assumed to have no impurities. Let us consider a two-dimensional representation of a silicon atom that is assumed to be intrinsic; this arrangement is shown in Fig. 3-11(a). Silicon is tetravalent and in the silicon crystal each silicon nucleus is surrounded by its 4 valence electrons. These electrons are shared with its 4 nearest neighbors, receiving from them in return a shared interest in 1 valence electron from each neighbor. Every silicon atom is, therefore, surrounded by 8 valence electrons, 4 of its own and 4 of its neighbors. This interaction of sharing valence electrons between nearest neighbors provides the forces that hold the crystal together. These electrons are in the $3s$ and $3p$ bands.

Now we consider what happens when we substitute an arsenic atom for a silicon atom. Arsenic, whose electronic configuration is $1s^2 2s^2 2p^6 3s^2 3p^6 3d^{10} 4s^2 4p^3$, has 5 electrons total in its $4s$ and $4p$ bands. Because these bands overlap, all five are considered to be valence electrons. As arsenic enters the silicon lattice as a substitute, 4 of its valence electrons assume positions similar to those assumed by the 4 valence electrons it replaces. The fifth electron of the arsenic atom is not a part of the valence band structure. It is attracted to the arsenic atom only by the electrostatic force exerted by the positive charge on the arsenic nucleus. As a consequence of this, the energy required to excite this electron into the conduction band is much less than that required to break a valence bond. This situation is illustrated in Fig. 3-11(*b*) and is shown schematically by locating an energy level in the forbidden band very close to the conduction band; the distance between the bottom of the conduction band and the energy level of the extra electron associated with the arsenic is the energy required to free the electron and is known as the *donor activation energy*. Because conduction occurs by means of electrons that have a negative charge, silicon containing this type of impurity is called *n* type. It should be noted that donors provide conduction electrons without the simultaneous creation of a hole in the valence band. The reason for this fact is that the positive ion left behind has exactly the same number of electrons around it as does any of the original semiconductor atoms. There is no vacancy in the bond structure into which other bound electrons can slide. The positive ion is therefore a *fixed* charge, which cannot help to carry current; in short it is *not* a hole.

On the other hand, if a gallium atom (with an electronic configuration of $1s^2 2s^2 2p^6 3s^2 3p^6 3d^{10} 4s^2 4p^1$) is substituted for a silicon atom, the 3 valence electrons in the $4s$ and $4p$ bands attach themselves in a manner similar to that taken by the silicon valence electrons. In the fourth bond, there is a hole left, since there is no electron from the gallium atom available to fill it. An electron from a neighboring bond may move into this hole with a very slight energy expenditure (called the *acceptor activation energy*). The hole then moves in a direction opposite to that of the electron. The energy required to excite an electron into the hole is about the same as that required to excite an arsenic atom. The energy level of these vacancies is very close to the top of the valence band. Elements substituted for parent materials that are deficient in electrons are called *acceptor elements*. The resulting material is called p type because conduction is by holes. These acceptors then create holes in the valence band without creating electrons in the conduction band. This type of material is illustrated in Fig. 3-11(c).

Let us now apply the methods of Section 3.5 to the extrinsic semiconductor. For brevity we will treat only the p-type semiconductor; the analysis of the n type follows that which we will do quite closely. A p-type

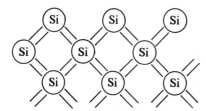

FIG. 3-11(a). Intrinsic silicon, showing the four valence electrons that each atom has. The interaction of sharing valence electrons between the atoms provides the forces that hold the crystal together.

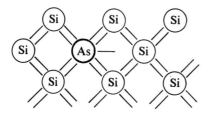

FIG. 3-11(b). Substitution of an arsenic atom for a silicon atom in the lattice of n-type silicon. An arsenic atom has 5 valence electrons; the fifth electron requires little energy to excite it into the conduction band.

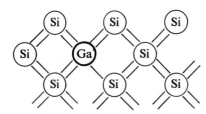

FIG. 3-11(c). Substitution of a gallium atom for a silicon atom in the lattice of p-type silicon. A gallium atom has 3 valence electrons; because the energy levels of the gallium electrons are not very much above the top of the valence band, very little energy is required to excite an electron up from the valence band, thus creating a hole there.

semiconductor, it will be recalled, is one that has a nominally filled lower band and a nominally empty conduction band with a set of acceptor states located slightly above the top of the valence band in the energy gap. These acceptor states, being shy of valence electrons, can create holes in the valence band by accepting electrons that are excited out of the valence band. It should be noted that foreign atoms occupy certain atomic sites in the structure; accordingly, their quantum states in the energy band model are spatially localized. For this reason the acceptor and donor states of extrinsic materials are sometimes called *localized states*.

For our analysis we will use the model illustrated in Fig. 3-12 and follow

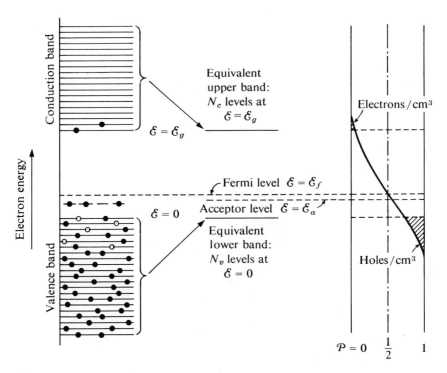

FIG. 3-12. The band structure, equivalent band structure, and the probability that a given level will be filled in a *p*-type semiconductor. After Shive [3] with permission.

Shive's [7] method. Again we define the top of the valence band as $\varepsilon = 0$, the bottom of the conduction band as ε_g, and the acceptor level as ε_a. We assume that there are N_a acceptors per unit volume but that N_a is much less than N_v so that the concentration of N_a to N_v is always less than 0.001. We wish to determine the location of the Fermi level, its dependence on temperature, and the number of holes created in the valence band at various temperatures because of the presence of the acceptor level. We again compress the energy levels of the valence band and conduction bands into the equivalent sets of N_v and N_c at $\varepsilon = 0$ and $\varepsilon = \varepsilon_g$ respectively, as we have shown in the center portion of Fig. 3-12. The right-hand portion of the diagram shows the Fermi function $f(\varepsilon)$ giving the probability that a given state will be occupied.

Our reasoning may proceed as follows. Electrons will be activated into the acceptor levels from the valence band at temperatures much lower than the temperatures it would take to activate a comparable number into the conduction band. Thus at ordinary temperatures below the intrinsic range there will be more holes in the valence band than there are electrons in the conduction band. Thus the Fermi level must be somewhere in the bottom half of the forbidden zone.

For the net charge neutrality condition to be maintained, the number of holes per unit volume must equal the number of electrons per unit volume in the acceptor level plus the number of electrons per unit volume in the conduction band. Thus

$$p = 2N_v \left[1 - \frac{1}{\exp\left[-\varepsilon_f/(kT)\right] + 1} \right]$$

Holes/cm³
in valence band

$$= \frac{N_a}{\exp\left[(\varepsilon_a - \varepsilon_f)/(kT)\right] + 1} + \frac{2N_c}{\exp\left[(\varepsilon_g - \varepsilon_f)/(kT)\right] + 1}. \quad \textbf{(3-40)}$$

Electrons/cm³   Electrons/cm³
in acceptor levels   in conduction band

The conduction and valence bands can each hold 2 electrons per level, while each acceptor level can hold but 1 electron as indicated in Eq. 3-40. We will not attempt a general solution of Eq. 3-40 but will look at a special case. (The student will be asked to consider several different cases as exercises at the end of the chapter.)

We consider the case of where the temperature is below the intrinsic range so that the number of electrons in the conduction band is negligible compared with the number of holes in the valence band. In this case the assumptions allow us to ignore the last term in Eq. 3-40, and we may solve it for ε_f to obtain

$$\varepsilon_f \approx kT \ln \left\{ \frac{N_v}{N_a} - \frac{1}{2} + \frac{1}{2} \left\{ (1 - 2N_v/N_a)^2 + (8N_v/N_a) \exp\left[\varepsilon_a/(kT)\right] \right\}^{1/2} \right\}.$$

$$\textbf{(3-41)}$$

We may further simplify this equation by placing more restrictions on it.

For example, suppose that the temperature is high enough so that the exponential factor becomes very close to unity, but not high enough for the material to become intrinsic. In this case the Fermi level reduces to

$$\mathcal{E}_f \approx kT \ln (2\alpha T^{3/2}/N_a), \qquad (3\text{-}42)$$

where we have substituted $\alpha T^{3/2}$ for N_v in Eq. 3-41. By combining Eq. 3-42 and Eq. 3-40, the hole concentration becomes approximately

$$p \approx \frac{2\alpha T^{3/2} N_a}{2\alpha T^{3/2} + N_a \exp [\mathcal{E}_a/(kT)]}. \qquad (3\text{-}43)$$

It is apparent that as the temperature is increased the hole concentration p must approach N_a, showing that more and more acceptor states become occupied. It may be shown that when the Fermi level has risen to $4kT$ higher than $\mathcal{E}_a$ the acceptors are 98 percent filled. Further increases in temperature will have little or no effect on hole concentration. The acceptors are very nearly saturated and the electrical conductivity is said to be entering the transition range between extrinsic and intrinsic conduction.

We may summarize the results of temperature on a p-type semiconductor as follows: as the temperature moves from near absolute zero, the Fermi level energy moves from halfway between the top of the valence band and the acceptor states level to the midpoint of the energy gap as the temperature approaches the intrinsic range.

Example problem.   Given a certain p-type semiconductor with 10^{14} acceptors per cubic centimeter, having their energy level 0.04 eV above the top of the valence band at a temperature of 300°K. Find the position of the Fermi level, and the concentration of conducting holes and electrons.

Solution.   To get started, we make the assumption that the number of electrons in the conduction band is negligibly small compared to the number of holes in the valence band. Thus we use Eq. 3-41,

$$\mathcal{E}_f \approx kT \ln \left\{ \frac{N_v}{N_a} - \frac{1}{2} + \frac{1}{2} \{(1 - 2N_v/N_a)^2 + (8N_v/N_a) \exp [\mathcal{E}_a/(kT)]\}^{1/2} \right\} \quad (3\text{-}41)$$

and N_v may be calculated from Eq. 3-33

$$N_v = \alpha T^{3/2} = (2.35 \times 10^{15} \text{ cm}^{-3}\,°\text{K}^{-3/2})(300)^{3/2} = 1.20 \times 10^{19}$$

and thus

$$N_v/N_a = 1.20 \times 10^{19}/10^{14} = 1.20 \times 10^5 \text{ cm}^{-3}$$

and

$$\exp [\mathcal{E}_a/(kT)] = \exp [0.04/(8.617 \times 10^{-5} \times 300)] = 4.7.$$

We may now substitute these values into Eq. 3-41:

$$\mathcal{E}_f = 2.58 \times 10^{-2} \ln \{1.20 \times 10^5 - \tfrac{1}{2} + \tfrac{1}{2}[(1 - 2 \times 1.20 \times 10^5)^2 \\ + 8 \times 1.20 \times 10^5(4.7)]^{1/2}\}.$$

We may eliminate the second term in the braces in comparison with the first and examine this equation in its expanded form:

$$\mathcal{E}_f = 2.58 \times 10^{-2} \ln \{1.20 \times 10^5 + \tfrac{1}{2}[1 - 4.80 \times 10^5 + 5.76 \times 10^{10} \\ + 4.51 \times 10^6]^{1/2}\}.$$

The first, second, and fourth terms in the brackets are negligible in comparison with the third; this means we could have started with Eq. 3-42. The Fermi level is then

$$\mathcal{E}_f = 2.58 \times 10^{-2} \ln [2 \times 1.20 \times 10^5] = 0.32 \text{ eV}.$$

The hole concentration can now be calculated from Eq. 3-43

$$p = \frac{2 \alpha T^{3/2} N_a}{2 \alpha T^{3/2} + N_a \exp [\mathcal{E}_a/(kT)]} = \frac{2 \times 1.20 \times 10^{19} \times 10^{14}}{2 \times 1.20 \times 10^{19} + 10^{14} \times 4.7} \approx 10^{14} \text{ cm}^{-3}.$$

We thus observe that the semiconductor is entering the transition region where the acceptors are said to be saturated. The reader may verify from Eq. 3-40 that the electron concentration in the conduction band is negligible.

The analysis of n-type semiconductors follows by analogy from the p-type semiconductor case. The situation for semiconductors containing both p- and n-type impurities may be conducted in exactly the same way, starting from an equation that merely restates the principle that the total net negative charge must equal the total net positive charge. We will not give the details here. In Fig. 3-13 we illustrate how the Fermi level moves toward the center of the forbidden energy zone for both n- and p-type materials; the more heavily doped materials approach the intrinsic condition much more slowly.

Our previous discussion indicated that at any temperature above absolute zero there will be some electrons in the conduction band and some holes in the valence band. If we dope a semiconductor with impurity atoms of the donor type, for example, we will increase the number of electrons in the conduction band without increasing the number of holes in the valence band. In fact, in any semiconductor that we assume to have an energy gap at least 5- or $6kT$ wide, the increasing of the majority carrier concentration is always accompanied by a decrease in the minority carrier concentration in the same proportion. This statement can be proved simply by multiplying together the electron density as given by Eq. 3-34 and the hole density as given by Eq. 3-35. Before performing this operation we make the usual assumption about the forbidden zone being 5- or $6kT$ wide and simplify the Fermi probability expressions in each equation accordingly. The result of this work is an expression that shows the constancy of the so-called pn product for a particular semiconductor at a given temperature. The product may also be recognized as the intrinsic carrier concentration squared, since in the intrinsic case $p = n$, thus

$$pn = n_i^2 \approx (2 \alpha T^{3/2})^2 \exp [-\mathcal{E}_g/(kT)]. \tag{3-44}$$

For example, consider pure germanium, which has an intrinsic electron or hole density at room temperature of about $2.5 \times 10^{13} \text{ cm}^{-3}$. Germanium of this purity is now grown routinely in semiconductor laboratories. The number of atoms of germanium in a unit volume is $4.5 \times 10^{22} \text{ cm}^{-3}$. If we were to dope the germanium with impurity atoms capable of supplying electrons in the concentration of 1 part per million, then the electron density would be $n = 4.5 \times 10^{22}/(1 \times 10^6) = 4.5 \times 10^{16} \text{ cm}^{-3}$. Because of the constancy of the pn product, $p = n_i^2/n = 1.4 \times 10^{10}$ cm^{-3}, and it is seen that $n \gg p$; and we are talking about an n-type material at

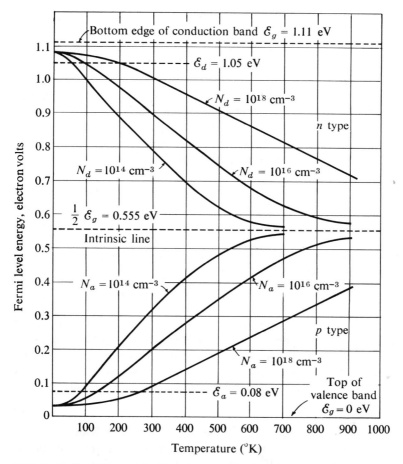

FIG. 3-13. Variation of the Fermi level with temperature for silicon with impurity concentration as a parameter. Note the symmetry of the curves as the Fermi level moves toward the intrinsic line at higher temperatures.

room temperature. If the temperature were raised to 300°C, then $n_i = 1.5 \times 10^{17}$ cm^{-3} and the intrinsic carriers predominate.

3.7 TRANSPORT PHENOMENA

We have studied in this chapter the conditions that are necessary for a material to be considered a semiconductor. In Ch. 2 we considered from a phenomenological point of view laws, such as those of Fourier and Ohm, that connect experimentally observed fluxes with the forces that produced those fluxes. We did not, however, treat the microscopic mechanisms that attempt to explain the observed effects. *Transport theory* has as its object the study of such mechanisms and the calculation of such quantities as the electrical conductivity. Mathematically, transport theory is based on a continuity equation called the *Boltzmann transport equation*. The solution to this equation, except for a few special cases, is a formidable mathematical problem. For the most part we will not attempt its solution, but we will discuss transport phenomena from a more elementary point of view. From time to time we will give results that are based on a solution of the transport equation.

First, we review those elements that are necessary to define some of the terms of interest. The *current density, $J = I/A$,* is the total current divided by the cross-sectional area perpendicular to the direction of the current. The *electric field intensity, $E = F/q$,* is defined as the force per unit charge and is related to the electrostatic potential difference (the voltage) V, through the definition of work; that is,

$$V = -\int (F/q)\,dx = -\int_l^0 E\,dx = El, \qquad (3\text{-}45)$$

where the limits on the integral are from l to 0, since in this direction work would be done on the charge. As we saw in Ch. 2, we may describe effects phenomenologically in terms of forces and fluxes. Following this procedure we take the definition of *electrical conductivity*† in an isotropic medium as the ratio of the current density (a flux) to the electric field intensity (a force)

$$\sigma = J/E \qquad \text{or} \qquad J = \sigma E. \qquad (3\text{-}46)$$

We may eliminate from Eq. 3-46 the current density in favor of the current and the area, and we may eliminate the electric field in favor of the voltage by means of Eq. 3-45 to obtain

$$I/A = \sigma(V/l) \qquad \text{or} \qquad V = Il/(\sigma A). \qquad (3\text{-}47)$$

The reciprocal of the conductivity is called the *resistivity, $\rho = 1/\sigma$,* which may be used in Eq. 3-47 to define the electrical resistance as

$$R = \rho l/A. \qquad (3\text{-}48)$$

We may now write Eq. 3-47 in the more familiar form

$$V = IR, \qquad (3\text{-}49)$$

generally called *Ohm's law.*

The current density may also be expressed in terms of the number of charge carriers in a unit cube times the speed at which they are traveling times the charge that each carries, thus

† Which corresponds to one of the L_{oo} coefficients of Ch. 2.

$$J = neu. \tag{3-50}$$

We recall that the electron velocity is in a direction opposite to that of the conventional current, J. One of the quantities that has been found useful in discussing properties of semiconductors is the *mobility* of the charge carriers. The mobility μ is an index to how rapidly a charge carrier will move on application of an electric field—that is, the average drift velocity per unit electric field

$$\mu = u/E. \tag{3-51}$$

Combining Eq. 3-51 with Eqs. 3-50 and 3-46 yields

$$\sigma = ne\mu. \tag{3-52}$$

For example, let us consider bismuth telluride, a semiconductor that has found wide application in thermoelectric devices; Bi_2Te_3 has a room temperature mobility of about 540 cm^2 per volt-sec and approximately 5×10^{18} charge carriers per cubic centimeter. Substituting these values into Eq. 3-52 yields

$$\sigma = (5 \times 10^{18} \text{ cm}^{-3})(1.6 \times 10^{-19} \text{ coulombs})(540 \text{ cm}^2/\text{volt-sec})$$
$$= 4.32 \times 10^2 \text{ (ohm-cm)}^{-1}$$

or $\rho = 1/\sigma = 2.32 \times 10^{-3}$ ohm-cm.

By comparison we might note that the resistivity of most practical insulators is extremely high—on the order of 10^{15} ohm-cm. On the other hand, typical metals such as aluminum and copper exhibit resistivities in the neighborhood of 10^{-6} ohm-cm. This low value for metals may be explained in terms of the number of free electrons available, which in a metal is on the order of the number of atoms per cubic centimeter (around 10^{22}), which is about ten thousand times larger than the number of conduction electrons in bismuth telluride.

As the electrons move in the semiconductor, they are scattered by irregularities in the crystal, so that their motion can no longer be represented by a straight line but will be some sort of a zigzag path. The average drift velocity is different for the two types of carriers that we consider, electrons and holes, because their mechanisms of motion are different. Figure 3-14 shows in an oversimplified manner the motion of a free electron in an electric field. The electron moves in a random manner through the lattice in a direction opposite to that of the field, while the hole appears to move in discrete jumps (since it merely represents the position where an electron *was*). The scattering of electrons will be discussed in more detail presently.

Because of the irregular path that the electron follows in traversing the crystal we speak of it as drifting in the electric field and call μ the *drift mobility*. The average time τ between collisions for the electron is denoted by several names, such as *collision time* or *relaxation time*. We shall generally

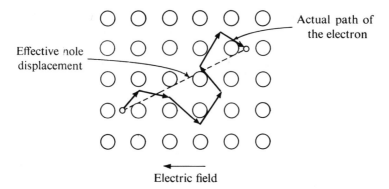

Actual path of
the electron

Effective hole
displacement

Electric field

FIG. 3-14. The schematic migration of an electron and a hole under the influence of an applied electric field. The hole travels in the direction of the field in an apparent jump.

use the latter. The acceleration of the electron a, is approximately given by Newton's law

$$a = F/m^* = eE/m^* = u/\tau, \qquad (3\text{-}53)$$

where once again we have used the effective mass concept to calculate the acceleration. The mobility as defined in Eq. 3-51 may be combined with Eq. 3-53 to yield

$$\mu = u/E = e\tau/m^* \qquad (3\text{-}54)$$

and thus the conductivity becomes

$$\sigma = ne\mu = ne^2\tau/m^*. \qquad (3\text{-}55)$$

So far we have tacitly assumed that all the collision times are the same. Let us consider the case with n_1 electrons with collision times τ_1, n_2 electrons with collision time τ_2, and so on. Then we express the conductivity as

$$\sigma = \sum_j \sigma_j = (e^2/m^*) \sum_j n_j\tau_j. \qquad (3\text{-}56)$$

We now multiply numerator and denominator by n to yield

$$\sigma = ne^2/m^* \sum_j n_j\tau_j/n. \qquad (3\text{-}57)$$

The quantity $\sum n_j\tau_j/n$ is the definition of the arithmetical average and is called the *average relaxation time* $\langle\tau\rangle$. Thus Eq. 3-57 becomes

$$\sigma = ne^2\langle\tau\rangle/m^* \qquad (3\text{-}58)$$

and the corresponding mobility becomes

$$\mu = e\langle\tau\rangle/m^*. \qquad (3\text{-}59)$$

If we consider the previous example of bismuth telluride where the mobility is 540 cm² per volt-sec, and we assume the effective mass to be 0.32 of the free electron mass of 9.1×10^{-31} kg, we obtain from Eq. 3-59 an average relaxation time of

$$\langle \tau \rangle = \frac{540 \text{ cm}^2}{\text{volt-sec}} \times \frac{m^2}{10^4 \text{ cm}^2} \times \frac{0.32 \times 9.1 \times 10^{-31} \text{ kg}}{1.6 \times 10^{-19} \text{ coulombs}}$$

$$= 9.8 \times 10^{-14} \text{ sec.}$$

The student would be well advised to convince himself of the correctness of the units used in the above calculation.

Our calculation for the relaxation time indicates that the time between collisions is very short. What causes such frequent starts and stops for the electron? To answer this question we must look further into the motion of the electron as it drifts through the crystal under the applied field.

Let us consider a perfect crystal with a perfectly periodic electrostatic force field at the absolute zero of temperature. In such a crystal electrons and holes would move as if they were in a vacuum and we would account, for the presence of the periodic force field by substituting an effective mass m^* for the free electron mass m. The application of a potential difference V to such a crystal would accelerate the carriers, giving them a kinetic energy of

$$\tfrac{1}{2}m^*u^2 = eV = eEL, \tag{3-60}$$

where L is the distance between the field applying electrodes on the crystal. The mobility in this case would simply be the velocity as calculated from Eq. 3-60 divided by the electric field E,

$$\mu = u/E = (2eL/m^*E)^{1/2} \quad \text{(INCORRECT).} \tag{3-61}$$

Unfortunately, this equation does not represent correctly the mobility of electrons in a crystal, as the mobility is not dependent on either the dimensions of the crystal or the electric field. The incorrectness of Eq. 3-61 derives from the fact that the electron is not accelerated uniformly in the field but is continually disturbed by deviations from the perfect periodicity condition assumed at the outset of our discussion. The imperfections that cause these disturbances are due to thermal motion of the crystal lattice, foreign atoms or ions, vacant lattice sites, and dislocations. These imperfections act as scattering centers for the electrons. In a sense the crystal lattice behaves much like a transmission line, and a transmission line that has local variations in its propagation characteristics will reflect its input wave to a greater or lesser extent depending on the number and severity of its variations. When the electron wave that is associated with each electron is reflected or scattered by such a scattering center, the electron is scattered with it. We term these *scattering collisions,* and we call the time between collisions, as we indicated earlier, the *relaxation time,* and the distance traveled, the *mean free path.* For specimens that have a high concentration of impurities the scattering is frequent, the mean free paths are short, and the mobilities are low. Crystals that are heavily doped almost invariable have low mobilities in the extrinsic temperature range.

A large amount of experimental evidence has been gathered that indicates that the mobility in a real crystal is very much temperature dependent. This dependence usually changes as the material changes from extrinsic to intrinsic, and so forth. This unusual phenomenon can only be explained if we are willing to accept the idea that the mean free path itself depends on temperature. We may gain a qualitative understanding of why this is so by considering two specific examples.

Consider the situation where the scattering of charge carriers by impurities is the dominating mechanism in limiting the mean free path. At low temperatures the charge carriers reside in the lower energy levels of their respective bands and have relatively small thermal velocities (that is, kT is not large). At these low velocities when a conducting particle moves near a scattering center, it remains long enough to undergo considerable deflection. On the other hand, at the higher velocities it whizzes by the scattering center at such a speed that it is hardly deflected at all. Thus an encounter at a low temperature may be a complete miss at a higher temperature. We describe this by saying that the effective cross section of the scattering center that the electron sees decreases with increasing temperature. In fact, analytical and experimental work on extrinsic semiconductors in the temperature range where impurities play the major role in the scattering process has shown that the mean free path is proportional to the temperature squared.

The second major scattering mechanism that we will consider is *lattice scattering*, which is comparatively unimportant at low temperatures, but generally is the dominant mode of scattering when impurity scattering becomes insignificant. This mechanism is the scattering of electron waves by the thermal agitation of the crystal lattice itself. When an electron or hole (or the wave associated with it) collides with the vibrating atoms in the lattice, a transfer of energy takes place.

According to the principles of quantum mechanics, the amplitude of the mechanical vibrations of the lattice at any of its natural frequencies v may change only by *discrete* amounts, such that the corresponding energy is a whole multiple of hv. Mechanical vibrations with energy equal to hv are called *phonons*, and relate to sound waves in the same way that photons relate to light waves. For this reason lattice or thermal scattering is sometimes referred to as *electron-phonon* collisions. It is generally assumed that the energy an electron loses per collision with the lattice is small compared with the total energy of the electron and thus the interaction with the lattice is restricted to the lowest energy modes of vibration, which are the longitudinal or acoustic modes. These modes are associated with the propagation of sound through the crystal and hence this type of scattering is sometimes called *acoustical scattering*. The crystal atoms are displaced from their normal lattice positions by thermal vibrations, thus the electron encounters the atoms in the lattice in a random manner and not as an ordered periodic force field. In this case when scattering does occur, it will be more severe as the temperature gets higher with a progressively decreasing mean free path. In fact, in the intrinsic region the mean free path is found to be inversely proportional to the temperature.

In general we recognize the dependence of the mean free path and the mobility on the mode of scattering by assuming that the relaxation time is energy dependent of the form

$$\tau(\mathcal{E}) = \Phi(T)\mathcal{E}^{-s} \tag{3-62}$$

where s is a scattering constant that depends on the mode of scattering and takes on values between -2 and $+2$.

Heikes and Ure [8] have given the results of calculations for the relaxation time and mobility as a function of the effective mass and the temperature. Their work, summarized in Table 3-2, also includes the case of polar, optical mode scattering in which adjacent atoms vibrate out of phase with each other, producing electromagnetic oscillations.

The scattering constant s may be determined from relatively simple mobility measurements that will evolve in later discussions.

3.7.1 Electrical conductivity. We will now begin to apply the elements of mobility and scattering theory discussed in the previous section to those properties of semiconductors that are important to many energy conversion devices.

TABLE 3-2. TEMPERATURE AND EFFECTIVE MASS DEPENDENCE OF ELECTRON RELAXATION TIME AND MOBILITY†

Scattering mechanism	s‡	τ varies as	μ varies as
Acoustic mode, lattice	$1/2$	$(m^*)^{3/2}T^{-1}$	$(m^*)^{-5/2}T^{-3/2}$
Polar, optical mode (high temperature)	$-1/2$	$(m^*)^{1/2}T^{-1}$	$(m^*)^{-3/2}T^{-1/2}$
Ionized impurity (low carrier concentration)	$-3/2$	$(m^*)^{1/2}$	$(m^*)^{-1/2}T^{3/2}$

† After Heikes and Ure [8].
‡ Exponent in Eq. 3-62: $\tau(\mathcal{E}) = \Phi(T)\mathcal{E}^{-s}$.

We will present those aspects of semiconductors pertinent to thermoelectric and photovoltaic devices in Chs. 4 and 5, which are devoted exclusively to those topics. We initiate our studies here with the electrical conductivity.

Equation 3-52 gave the electrical conductivity for all metals and for semiconductors where the product of carrier concentration and mobility for one type of charge carrier is dominant. The expression resulting when both types of carriers contribute to the electrical conductivity is

$$\sigma = e(n\mu_n + p\mu_p), \tag{3-63}$$

where n represents the number of electrons per unit volume in the conduction band and μ_n is the mobility associated with them; p represents the hole concentration in the valence band and μ_p their mobility. The number of electrons that can be thermally or optically excited into the conduction band is relatively small compared to the total number of electrons in the valence band. Because this number is small it is possible to apply classical statistics to the excitation of carriers across the forbidden energy gap. That is, we treat the excitation as a dissociation process. Thus under intrinsic conditions where the number of holes just equals the number of electrons, we use Eq. 3-39 in Eq. 3-63 to obtain

$$\sigma = 2e(2\pi kT/h^2)^{3/2}(m_n^* m_p^*)^{3/4}(\mu_n + \mu_p) \exp\left[-\mathcal{E}_g/(2kT)\right],$$

where we have used the individual effective masses of the electrons and holes in the equations for the electron and hole concentration. We can gain insight into the meaning of these equations by following the method of Shive [9] upon considering a hypothetical semiconductor which is p type at low temperatures. In Fig. 3-15 we plot for our typical semiconductor, $1/T$ in absolute temperature versus the logarithms of σ, n, μ_n, p, and μ_p. We note that as the temperature is raised ($1/T$ gets smaller) the mobility increases as the mean free path becomes longer in the range where scattering is dominated by impurities. Increasing the temperature also increases the number of holes available for conduction until the acceptor states are all filled and conduction is said to enter the *exhaustion* or *transition* range. Further increases in temperature cause the mobility to fall off as the number of carriers starts to increase rapidly, as electrons are now being excited across the forbidden energy gap from the valence band into the conduction band. In this range the number of electrons equals the number of holes, and we are clearly in the intrinsic conduction range. These changes, which occur in most semiconductors, explain the characteristic shape of the conductivity curve shown as the top curve in Fig. 3-15. Thus a curve like Fig. 3-15 used with expressions similar to Eq. 3-64 can be used to determine the energy gap, the activation energy for impurities, and the mobility and temperature dependence of charge carriers.

The electrical resistivity can be measured in a number of ways; one of the simplest is to pass a small but accurately known alternating current through a sample whose dimensions have also been accurately determined. The alternating current nulls out any Seebeck effect contribution to the volt-

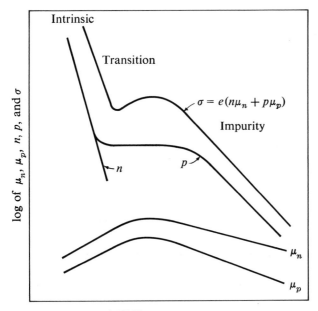

FIG. 3-15. The log σ versus $1/T$ curve deduced from a plot of log μ and log of the carrier concentration. Note that the carrier concentration in the intrinsic range plots as a straight line. The hypothetical material in this plot is p type at low temperatures. After Shive [3] with permission.

age, which is measured by two voltage probes a known distance apart on the sample. The electrical resistivity can then be determined from the measured current, voltage, and sample dimensions from Eq. 3-47.

3.7.2 Thermal conductivity. Thermal conductivity is an index of how well a solid will conduct thermal energy. If we consider a one-dimensional heat flow per unit area, per unit time q, across a slab of thickness dx, with a temperature difference of dT across the slab, then the fundamental law of heat conduction serves to define the thermal conductivity† λ_t, as

$$\lambda_t = \frac{-q}{dT/dx}, \tag{3-65}$$

where the minus sign is introduced in order that the positive direction of heat flow should coincide with the positive direction of x.

Thermal conduction on a microscopic scale is essentially a diffusion

† Which may be shown to be related in a particularly simple way to one of the conductance coefficients, such as C_1 of Appendix D.

process. Some of the entities capable of absorbing and releasing thermal energy and consequently of enabling heat to diffuse through a solid are: (1) free electrons and/or holes; (2) phonons (quantized lattice vibrations); (3) electron-hole pairs; (4) excitons†; (5) photons (radiant energy).

The diffusion property implies that these entities do not travel unlimited distances through solids, but are scattered by various processes. If there were no scattering, their wavelength would be infinite and the thermal conductivity of the material would be infinite. In general, if several heat conduction entities are present, the contributions to the thermal conductivity are additive,

$$\lambda_t = \sum_j \lambda_j. \tag{3-66}$$

Equation 3-66 is not intended to imply that the λ_j's are independent of each other. The addition of a new conducting entity may introduce a new scattering process for the other entities. In semiconductors that are used in energy conversion devices, thermal conductivity, by and large, is mostly due to free electron and phonon conduction.

In solid metals, the transport of heat is usually dominated by the motion of free electrons. Since in both electrical and thermal conductivity of metals the same type of carriers (free electrons) are involved, there should exist a relationship between these two properties. Thus the ratio of thermal to electrical conductivity should be the same for all metals and should be proportional to the absolute temperature. This is known as the Wiedemann-Franz-Lorenz law and is expressed symbolically as

$$\lambda_t/(\sigma T) = L_w = 2.45 \times 10^{-8} \text{ watt-ohm}/°K^2.$$

This law holds over a fairly wide range of temperatures for a variety of metals.

The thermal vibrations of the lattice may be quantized as phonons with a mean free path, Λ. As was first shown by Debye [1], the thermal conductivity of a dielectric crystal may be expressed as

$$\lambda_{ph} = (1/3)C_v u_{ac}\Lambda, \tag{3-67}$$

where C_v is the constant volume specific heat and u_{ac} is the velocity of sound in the material. Debye theory indicates that the dependence of C_v on temperature is determined by a single parameter, Θ, the Debye temperature, which

---

† Shive [10] explains that an exciton may be formed by the absorption of a photon that does not have enough energy to produce a free electron-hole pair. It is composed of an electron and the positive hole it has just left where the two particles are not completely separated but are held trapped in each other's electrostatic field. Thus it is electrically neutral and its motion through the crystal is random. Unless something else happens, in a short time it will deliver its energy to one of the modes of thermal lattice vibration and disappear from the scene by self-recombination. It is sometimes thought of as the excited state of an atom being transmitted to neighboring atoms by quantum mechanical resonance.

is a characteristic of the material. Θ is approximately determined by $k\Theta = h\nu_{max}/2\pi$ where the right-hand side of the equation is the vibrational mode of the highest energy; thus ν_{max} is simply the circular frequency which produces that vibration. In the Debye equation, k is Boltzmann's constant and h is Planck's constant. The Debye temperature of several typical semiconductors are: silicon, 660°K; germanium, 360°K; indium antimonide, 200°K; lead telluride, 130°K. At temperatures near the Debye temperature and above (the region of primary interest in this work), the phonons are predominantly scattered by collisions with other phonons. If the forces between atoms were purely harmonic, there would be no mechanism for collisions between different phonons and the mean free path would be limited solely by collisions of a phonon with the crystal boundary and by lattice imperfections. When anharmonic lattice interactions are present, the coupling between different phonons limits the value of the mean free path. The intensity of the vibrations is proportional to the temperature so the phonon free path, and thus, the thermal conductivity of the lattice, are related inversely to the temperature.

In certain cases scattering by impurities or lattice defects may be appreciable, giving rise to changes in the mean free path that increase the thermal conductivity even further; in other cases energy transport by excitons and radiation within the lattice can contribute substantially to the thermal conductivity.

The thermal conductivity can be measured by locating a standard with an accurately known thermal conductivity adjacent to the sample with the same width and length dimensions as the sample whose thermal conductivity is desired. By measuring the temperature drop across the standard with its known properties, the heat flow to the sample may be calculated; then, from the temperature drop and heat transfer across the sample its thermal conductivity may be calculated. The whole arrangement may be located in an evacuated chamber enclosed by a radiation shield with a temperature gradient imposed on it that matches the gradient through the sample and standard.

A somewhat more inclusive method has been described by Harman et al. [12]; it uses the Peltier heat to determine the thermal conductivity, Seebeck coefficient, and electrical resistivity of a material.

3.7.3 Hall effect.

We introduce the Hall effect at this point in our discussion because it is a phenomenon capable of telling us a great deal about transport phenomena in semiconductors. It is an effect observed easily under experimental conditions and does not require an inordinate amount of laboratory equipment. Consider a rectangular slab of material experiencing an electric current flowing in the x direction and subject to a magnetic field of flux density B in the outward z direction. If we assume for the moment that the electric current is due only to the motion of electrons in the positive x direction, then the Lorentz force, which is the fundamental interaction between an electric charge and a magnetic field, will urge the electrons to the top of the slab, as shown in Fig. 3-16. The magnitude of this force is given by the vector equation

$$F = eu \times B, \tag{3-68}$$

where the force is in newtons, e, the electronic charge in coulombs, u, the electron velocity in meters per second, and the magnetic flux density B, in webers per square meter. (Note that 1 weber per square meter is equal to 10,000 gauss.)

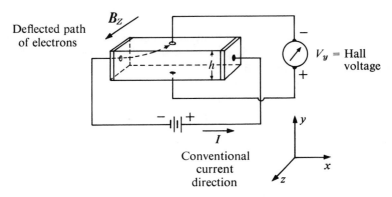

FIG. 3-16. The Hall voltage as it appears in a specimen in which charge is transported by electrons. If the charge were carried by holes, they would be deflected to the top of the specimen, thus reversing the sign of the Hall voltage.

The Hall field, which is the potential difference per unit distance set up in the y direction, is observed to be proportional to the magnetic field and the current density; that is,

$$E_y = R'BJ, \tag{3-69}$$

where R', the proportionality constant, is called the Hall coefficient. After a short period of time a field force in the y direction is established in the element due to the charge accumulation along one edge which just balances the Lorentz force; thus when equilibrium is obtained we have

$$B_z e u_x = e E_y. \tag{3-70}$$

Combining Eqs. 3-46, 3-50, and 3-52 yields

$$J_x = \sigma E_x = n e \mu E_x = n e u_x. \tag{3-71}$$

Equation 3-69 becomes, upon substitution of Eqs. 3-71 and 3-70,

$$R' = \frac{E_y}{BJ} = \frac{B_z u_x}{B_z n e u_x} = \frac{1}{ne}, \tag{3-72}$$

with units usually expressed in cubic centimeter per coulomb. A very simple expression for the carrier concentration n may be obtained by rearranging Eq. 3-72 in terms of the measurable quantities B, J, and the Hall field E_y

$$n = BJ/(E_y e). \tag{3-73}$$

Consider a specimen which is n type for which we assume that the number of donors (each contributing 1 electron) is much greater than the number of acceptors, and that no conduction electrons come from the valence band. We insure this last condition by chilling the specimen to liquid nitrogen temperature, thus reducing the probability of intrinsic conduction to almost zero. Under these conditions the Hall effect by way of Eq. 3-73 provides a particularly simple electrical means of determining the impurity concentration to great accuracy.

It should be noted, however, that the impurity concentration determined by this method is actually the difference between the acceptor and donor concentrations, $N_a - N_d$, since it is usual for a semiconductor to contain at least some of both types of impurities. Donor electrons will fill up any possible acceptor levels since the crystal must attain the lowest possible energy state consistent with its temperature. Thus, it is the difference between acceptor and donor concentrations that determines whether the crystal is n type or p type. Crystals in which either donor or acceptor concentrations dominate are said to be *partially compensated*. If we fabricate a crystal with $N_a \approx N_d$, then the crystal is said to be a *compensated intrinsic* material.

In a semiconductor in which the current is assumed to be carried entirely by holes (which move in the direction opposite to electrons), the Hall voltage is of opposite polarity as would be expected from an application of the left-hand rule for determining the direction of the force on a charge carrier moving through a magnetic field. Thus, the Hall effect is one of the easiest methods for determining whether a specimen is n or p type.

Our analysis of the Hall effect has been based on the assumption that all of the electrons travel with the same velocity and experience the same collision time as they move through the conductor. It is not difficult to demonstrate, by statistical means, that the expression for the Hall coefficient given by Eq. 3-72 must be modified by a factor that takes into account that not all of the electrons move with the same velocity. This factor is the ratio of average relaxation time squared to the square of the average relaxation time, $\langle \tau^2 \rangle / \langle \tau \rangle^2$. It is shown in more advanced books on semiconductors that if the energy surfaces of the crystal are described by a spherical wave vector and the scattering of the electrons is due to acoustic mode lattice scattering that the factor $\langle\tau^2\rangle/\langle\tau\rangle^2$ has the value $3\pi/8$ and the Hall coefficient is given by

$$R' = \frac{3\pi}{8}\frac{1}{ne}. \tag{3-74}$$

In the case where electron scatter is due chiefly to ionized impurities we find that the multiplying factor that corrects for the different velocities of the electrons is $315\pi/519$.

In a specimen in which conduction is due to the presence of both electrons and holes the derivation of the Hall coefficient becomes more complicated. Using b to represent the *mobility ratio* μ_n/μ_p, the Hall coefficient in low magnetic fields for acoustic mode lattice scattering is

$$R' = \frac{3\pi}{8}\frac{(p - nb^2)}{e(p + nb)^2}. \tag{3-75}$$

It is now possible to use the properties of the Hall coefficient and the electrical conductivity to determine a property called the *Hall mobility*, which may be obtained by combining Eqs. 3-55 and 3-72 to yield

$$\mu_H = |R'|\sigma. \tag{3-76}$$

The general solution of the Boltzmann equation for the conductivity mobility as defined by Eq. 3-52 and the Hall mobility as defined by Eq. 3-76 shows that the ratio of the Hall mobility to the conductivity mobility is given by the factor $\langle\tau^2\rangle/\langle\tau\rangle^2$.

Let us consider the example of bismuth telluride, for which we calculated the conductivity earlier. We assumed a room temperature (conductivity) mobility of 540 cm² per volt-sec and a charge carrier concentration of 5×10^{18} per cm³. Thus Eq. 3-74 yields

$$|R'| = \frac{3\pi}{8}\frac{1}{ne} = \frac{3\pi}{8}\frac{10^{-8}}{(5)(1.6 \times 10^{-19})} = 1.47 \text{ cm}^3/\text{coulomb}$$

and the conductivity may be calculated if we convert the conductivity mobility to the Hall mobility

$$\mu_H = \frac{3\pi}{8}\mu = \frac{3\pi}{8}(540) = 637 \text{ cm}^2/\text{volt-sec}$$

Now Eq. 3-76 yields for the conductivity

$$\sigma = \mu_H/R' = 637\frac{\text{cm}^2}{\text{volt-sec}}\frac{\text{coulomb}}{1.47 \text{ cm}^3} = 432 \,(\text{ohm-cm})^{-1},$$

which is the value we calculated earlier.

We may now calculate from Eq. 3-72 the Hall field we would measure on such a specimen. Assume that our specimen is 0.1 cm high and 0.1 cm deep and we pass a current of 10 ma through it while it experiences a magnetic flux density of 5000 gauss, thus

$$E_y = R'BJ = \frac{(1.47)(5 \times 10^3)(10^{-2})(10^{-8})}{(0.1)(0.1)} = 73.5 \times 10^{-6} \text{ volts/cm,}$$

or the measured Hall voltage would be

$$V_y = E_y h = (73.5 \times 10^{-6})(0.1) = 7.35 \times 10^{-6} \text{ volts,}$$

a value that can be measured with good laboratory equipment. Note that in our equation for calculating the Hall field we multiplied the magnetic flux density B, in gauss by 10^{-8} to convert it to practical units consistent with the equation. If we wish to express the results in mks units of volts/m then we must multiply the flux density in gauss by 10^{-4} to convert it to units of weber/m^2. In this case the current density must, of course, be in amp/m^2 and the Hall coefficient in units of m^3/coulomb.

3.8 SOME TECHNIQUES USED IN PRODUCING SEMICONDUCTORS

The reader will have gathered by now that one of the characteristics that distinguishes semiconductors from metals is the paucity of charge carriers that are available to take part in transport processes. Virtually a whole new technology was brought into being to control the type and concentration of charge carriers in various materials. This new technology found ways to control impurity content in substantial quantities of materials to a degree heretofore unheard of in ordinary chemical purification processes. As the demand for semiconductors increases, the literature of these techniques expands at an even faster rate. Because our treatment will be brief, we list several of the more complete references [14], [15]. A particularly good book for starting a study of crystals and crystal growing is the little book by Holden and Singer [16]; it is complete with instructions on how to make paper models of thirty-two crystal classes and on how to grow crystals at home. In this section we will touch briefly on the concepts of phase diagram and several methods for producing high purity crystals.

3.8.1 Phase diagrams. The phase diagram is a convenient way of graphically representing the state of a mixture of two or more substances as a function of temperature.† Phase diagrams, a fascinating subject in themselves, are unfortunately a topic to which we cannot devote much space. The abscissa of the phase diagram is the composition of the system which we

---

† We have eliminated a "degree of freedom" from our system by assuming that everything we will do is at constant pressure. If this were not the case we would have to describe the mixture on a phase surface. The number of degrees of freedom a given mixture will have is determined by an application of the Gibbs phase rule [4].

assume for illustrative purposes to be composed of an element that we are interested in purifying and one impurity that we are interested in eliminating. We call the element Γ and the impurity x. Any real substance would have more than one impurity, but we simplify our discussion by considering only one. The ordinate of the phase diagram is temperature. We represent our mixture of Γ and x on a phase diagram that has been exaggerated at the ends in Fig. 3-17.

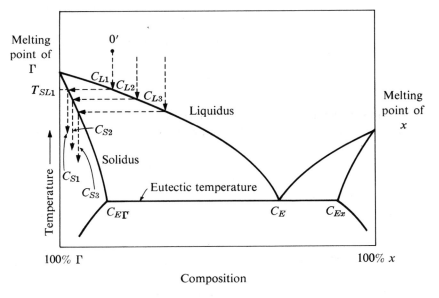

FIG. 3-17. Phase diagram of a mixture of solvent Γ and impurity x. The impurity has the effect of lowering the freezing point of Γ. The freezing point is always lowered by an impurity if the solid phase which is in equilibrium with the liquid phase is pure.

We can observe how the purification takes place by considering the effect of melting and recrystallization on a specimen of Γ that contains a small amount of the impurity x. We assume that the mixture is at a high enough temperature so that it is completely molten and that its composition is C_{L1}. This fixes its state at point $0'$ on the diagram. As we lower the temperature point, $0'$ moves down until it intersects the liquidus curve. At this temperature, T_{SL1}, the mixture begins to freeze but the portion that freezes first does not have the composition C_{L1} but has the composition C_{S1} which corresponds to the intersection of the freezing temperature T_{SL1} with the solidus curve. Thus the frozen portion is purer than the liquid portion from which it crystallizes. However, the liquid that remains after the initial freezing at T_{SL1} is more impure than that with which we started. The remaining liquid passes through successive compositions C_{L2}, C_{L3}, etc., while the succeeding freezing portions become progressively more impure with compositions C_{S2}, C_{S3}, etc., but at a slower rate. After solidification has progressed to the temperature that we call the *eutectic temperature*, the remaining liquid freezes without further change in composition—that is, C_E, until the melt is completely frozen. The solid portion that results from the freezing of the liquid of eutectic composition is called the *eutectic mixture*. In our example this consists of a physical mixture of crystals of Γ with impurity in solid solution corresponding to a composition $C_{E\Gamma}$ and crystals of impurity with Γ in solid solution to correspond to a composition C_{Ex}.

When producing high purity semiconductors only the extreme left end of the diagram is of interest; for this reason we have exaggerated it for clarity. In this region the liquidus and solidus curves are practically straight lines, and we may define a quantity called the *segregation constant*, K', as C_S/C_L. This constant is capable of indicating quantitatively the purification that can be achieved in one cycle of melting and recrystallizing. Pfann [17] has derived an expression for the purity of a solid that one can expect from a liquid of initial impurity C_{L0}

$$C_S = C_{L0}K'(1 - g)^{K'-1}, \tag{3-77}$$

where g is the fraction of the melt that has already frozen. This equation is based on the assumption that freezing takes place under conditions that insure complete homogeneity of the impurity remaining in the liquid. It is apparent that purification is greater over a larger fraction of the recrystallized ingot for impurities having the smaller K' values. The physics behind the K' values is quite complex, involving in part the relative sizes of the atoms involved (both parent and impurity atoms) and in part the directional arrangements of their valence orbits.

3.8.2 Methods of producing desirable crystals. There are many different techniques used in producing high purity semiconductors. Two of the most common are *fractional crystallization* and *zone melting*. Both methods require that one start with materials that are already quite pure—usually greater than 99.999 percent; both methods depend on the idea that impurities prefer to remain in the liquid phase. In the fractional crystallization arrangement, a charge of material is melted in a long crucible or container that is inert with respect to the charge. The boat is arranged in a furnace such that freezing commences at one end of the boat and proceeds slowly along the charge toward the other end. Thus according to our discussion of phase diagrams the solid portion will be purer than the remaining liquid and a greater than average concentration of impurities will appear in the last-to-freeze portion of the charge. We fix the speed of freezing so that it takes place slowly enough (3.6 in. per hr or slower) so that the impurities that pile up ahead of the solid-liquid interface can diffuse away into the bulk of the remaining liquid. The end portion of the recrystallized ingot now contains most of the impurities and may be cut off and discarded. The remaining portion of the crystal may now be subjected to the process again with a subsequent decrease in impurity level. After a dozen or so cycles of this process, a practical limit will be reached, since the ingot thereafter will gain as many impurities from the boat and atmosphere in which the process is carried out as are eliminated by the melting-freezing process.

In the zone melting process part of a charge, rather than all of it, is melted at one time. This slight change in procedure has produced remarkable increases in efficiency in the crystallization process as a means of separation. When we utilize the zone melting process to purify a charge, it is called *zone refining*. In this process a series of molten zones pass through the charge in one direction, causing impurities to travel with or opposite to the motion of the zones, depending on whether they lower or raise the melting point of the charge. Just as in the case of fractional crystallization, the impurities become concentrated in one end of the charge, producing a subsequent purification of the balance. As the number of passes (the number of single zones that pass through the charge) increases, the degree of separation increases, finally approaching a limit. Zone refining can also be used to concentrate desired impurities as well as to eliminate undesirable ones. A schematic of a zone refining set up is shown in Fig. 3-18. The elimination of the step of discarding the impure fraction from the pure after a single freezing is probably the chief advantage of multi-pass zone refining. In addition, time is generally saved if the molten zones are close together, because the succeeding crystallizations can begin before the first pass is completed.

Another method used frequently in preparing crystals is the *Czochralski*

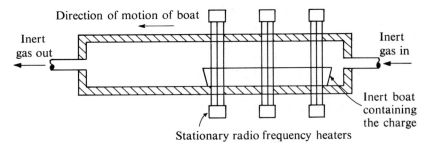

Direction of motion of boat

Inert gas out

Inert gas in

Inert boat containing the charge

Stationary radio frequency heaters

FIG. 3-18. The main items needed for a multi-pass zone refining setup. The boat is slowly drawn through a series of zone-melting coils which heat the charge by means of radio frequency heaters.

or *crystal pulling* technique. This method is illustrated in Fig. 3-19. Essentially, it involves dipping a small single crystal seed into the surface of the melt and withdrawing it at the desired freezing rate. Since the apparatus is designed so that the seed is cooler than the melt, material solidifies on the seed as it is withdrawn. The crystal pulling, or growing, as it is called, is usually done in an inert atmosphere. The greatest limitation to this method is the stability of the melt, as elements with high vapor pressure tend to condense out on the cold parts of the system. Proper design can diminish this limitation. Typical pull rates vary from 4 to 0.04 in. per hr, with the slower rates producing more perfect crystals. This system is also sensitive to thermal and mechanical fluctuations during the growing process. Crystals such as germanium, silicon, indium antimonide, and bismuth telluride have been prepared by this method.

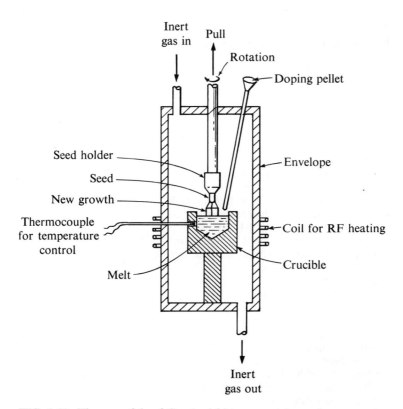

FIG. 3-19. The essentials of Czochralski-type crystal-growing apparatus. This drawing illustrates a method that provides for the controlled addition of impurities.

Figure 3-19 shows a device for adding a doping pellet. When it is desired to produce a p–n junction at some point during the growth process, a small pellet of donor material is dropped into the melt (assuming we want to change a p-type crystal to an n type). The pellet will be of such a magnitude as to overpower the initial p character of the melt and give it the desired donor concentration. Doping pellets are generally quite small—about the size of a small pinhead. Their thermal mass compared to the melt is insignificant and their introduction produces no noticeable temperature transients or growth peculiarities. In order to insure that no pile-up of impurities occurs at the liquid-solid interface, we artificially agitate the seed by means of the geometrical arrangement of crucible, heating coil, and thermal sinks, and in addition, we rotate the crystal about its vertical axis. Figure 3-20 is a photograph of some crystals that have been grown by the Czochralski method.

Another method of junction production is the *diffusion method*, which consists of heating a specimen in a gaseous atmosphere of donors or acceptors at high temperatures so that the impurities from the atmosphere diffuse into the specimen. This method is used in producing silicon junctions for solar battery use. It will be discussed in more detail in Ch. 5.

NOTATION

a	= acceleration, cm/sec^2
a'	= slope constant in Eq. 3-1, erg-sec
A	= area, cm^2
$\mathcal{C}$	= constant in Eq. 3-33, 2.35×10^{15} cm^{-3} ($^\circ$K)$^{-3/2}$
b	= mobility ratio, μ_n/μ_p, dimensionless
b'	= intercept constant in Eq. 3-1, ergs
B	= magnetic flux density, gauss or webers/m^2
$\mathbf{B}$	= magnetic flux density vector, gauss or webers/m^2
c	= velocity of light, cm/sec
C	= denotes composition
C_v	= specific heat, erg/($^\circ$K-cm^3)
$\mathcal{C}$	= constants of integration in differential equation
e	= electronic charge, coulombs
E	= electric field, volts/cm
$\mathcal{E}$	= energy, electron volts, ergs, or joules
$\mathcal{E}_f$	= Fermi energy, electron volts
$\mathcal{E}_g$	= energy gap width, electron volts
$(\mathcal{E})$	= Fermi factor or probability, dimensionless
F	= force, dynes or newtons
$\mathbf{F}$	= force vector, dynes or newtons
g	= fraction of melt frozen, dimensionless
h	= Planck's constant, erg-sec

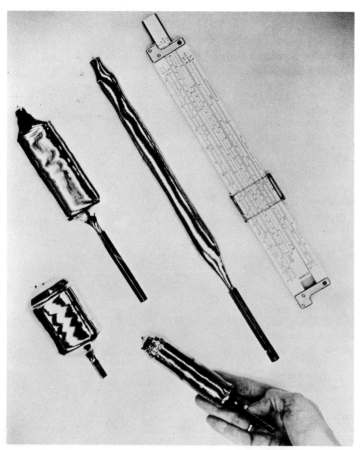

FIG. 3-20. A semiautomatic crystal-growing furnace can produce ingots of many sizes and shapes, depending on the requirement. Silicon ingots such as shown here may weigh from 300 to 500 gm, measure from 1 to $2\frac{1}{2}$ in. in diameter and from 3 to 11 in. in length. Photo courtesy of the Hoffman Electronics Corporation.

i	$= \sqrt{-1}$
I	$=$ electric current, amp
J	$=$ current density, amp/cm^2
k	$=$ Boltzmann's constant, $\text{erg}/\text{°K}$
K	$=$ kinetic energy, ergs
K'	$=$ segregation constant, dimensionless
l	$=$ quantum number
l	$=$ length, cm
L	$=$ length, cm

L_w = Wiedemann-Franz-Lorenz constant, 2.45×10^8 watt-ohm/°K^2
m = mass of electron, gm
m^* = effective mass, gm
m_l = magnetic quantum number
m_s = spin quantum number
n = indexing integer
n = quantum number
n = electron density, cm^{-3}
N_a = density of acceptor levels, cm^{-3}
N_c = equivalent number of energy levels in the conduction band, cm^{-3}
N_d = density of donor levels, cm^{-3}
N_v = equivalent number of energy levels in the valence band, cm^{-3}
$N_n(\mathcal{E})$ = density of electron energy levels, per unit energy and volume
$N_p(\mathcal{E})$ = density of hole energy levels, per unit energy and volume
p = hole density, cm^{-3}
p' = momentum, erg-sec/cm
P = potential energy, ergs
P_o = particular potential energy, ergs
$\mathcal{P}$ = probability of finding an electron, dimensionless
q = electric charge, coulombs
q = heat rate, watts/cm^2
r = radial coordinate, cm
R = electrical resistance, ohms
R' = Hall coefficient, cm^3/coulomb
s = scattering constant, dimensionless
t = time, sec
T = temperature, °K
T = a function of time alone
T_l = applied tension, dynes
u = velocity, cm/sec or m/sec
u = velocity vector, cm/sec or m/sec
$\langle u \rangle$ = mean drift velocity, cm/sec or m/sec
U = displacement, cm
V = electrical potential, volts
V_q = stopping potential, volts
x = denotes an impurity
x, y, z = coordinate directions, cm
X = a function of x alone
γ = mass per unit length, gm/cm
Γ = denotes a solvent
θ = spherical coordinate, radians
Θ = Debye temperature, °K
λ = wavelength, cm
λ_j = component of thermal conductivity, watt/(cm-°K)
λ_t = thermal conductivity, watt/(cm-°K)
Λ = phonon mean free path, cm
μ = mobility, cm^2/(volt-sec)
ν = frequency, (sec)$^{-1}$
π = 3.141 $\cdots$
ρ = electrical resistivity, ohm-cm
σ = electrical conductivity, (ohm-cm)$^{-1}$

τ = collision time or relaxation time, sec
$\langle\tau\rangle$ = average relaxation time, sec
ϕ = spherical coordinate, radians
ϕ = work function, electron volts
$\Phi(T)$ = function of temperature in Eq. 3-62
ψ = wave function, dimensionless
Ω = volume, cm^3
ω = angular frequency, radians/sec

Subscripts

a = acceptor level
ac = acoustic
c = conduction
d = donor
E = eutectic
f = Fermi level
g = energy gap
H = Hall
i = intrinsic
j = indexing integer
L = liquid state
n = indexing integer
n = electron
p = hole
ph = phonon
S = solid state
SL = freezing point
x = impurity
x, y, z = directions
Γ = solvent

PROBLEMS

3-1. Platinum has a work function of 6.2 eV. What is the lowest frequency incident radiation that can cause electrons to be ejected from the surface?

3-2. Verify that Eq. 3-16 is a solution of Eq. 3-14.

3-3. Verify that Eq. 3-20 is a solution of Eq. 3-19.

3-4. With T measured in degrees Kelvin and k the Boltzmann constant, the translational kinetic energy of a gas molecule is $\frac{3}{2}kT$. What is the corresponding de Broglie wavelength of a hydrogen atom at 0°C?

3-5. Check the accuracy of the assumption that $f(\mathcal{E}) \approx \exp\left[-(\mathcal{E} - \mathcal{E}_f)/(kT)\right]$ for $(\mathcal{E} - \mathcal{E}_f) \geq 2kT$.

3-6. What is the uncertainty in the position of the center of mass of a satellite having a mass of 1 ton when its velocity is known with an uncertainty no greater than 0.1 meter per sec?

3-7. Prepare a table showing the distribution of electrons in the allowed-energy states for the first eighteen atoms in the periodic table.

3-8. The number of charge carriers at 400°K in an intrinsic specimen of indium antimonide (InSb) is found to be 10^{17} cm^{-3}. The mobility of the electrons is 40,000 cm^2 per volt-sec while the holes have a mobility of 400 cm^2 per volt-sec. Find (a) the forbidden energy gap; (b) the Fermi level energy, assuming $m_n = m_p$. (c) If the effective mass of the holes is ten times the effective mass of the electrons, what is the Fermi level under these conditions? [Assume that the energy gap remains at the same value you found in part (a).]

3-9. Consider a p-type semiconductor experiencing a temperature low enough so that the exponential term of Eq. 3-41 dominates all the other terms in the bracket. Find the Fermi level and corresponding hole concentration.

Answer: $\mathcal{E}_f \approx (kT/2)[\ln(2N_v/N_a)] + \mathcal{E}_a/2$.

3-10. Consider a p-type semiconductor in which the Fermi level coincides with the acceptor level, that is, $\mathcal{E}_a = \mathcal{E}_f$. At this temperature, the acceptors are half occupied, so that $p = N_a/2$. Can you find the temperature at which this happens? Assume that the number of electrons in the conduction band is negligible.

3-11. Consider an n-type semiconductor in which the Fermi level coincides with donor level. Can you find the temperature at which this happens in terms of $\mathcal{E}_g$, $\mathcal{E}_d$, N_d, and the appropriate constants? Assume that the number of holes in the valence band is negligible.

3-12. A certain semiconductor has 1.5×10^{18} acceptors per cm^3. The energy level of the acceptors is 0.3 eV above the valence band. Assume that the number of electrons in the conduction band is negligible. Calculate the Fermi level and hole concentration at the temperature of liquid nitrogen, 77°K.

3-13. An n-type semiconductor has a donor concentration of 5×10^{16} cm^{-3} at an energy level of 1.4 eV. When the Fermi level is $4kT$ below the donor energy level, find the number of conduction electrons.

Answer: 4.91×10^{16} cm^{-3}.

3-14. The effective mass of electrons in extrinsic indium arsenide (InAs) is about 1/30 of the free electron mass. Assuming a room temperature mobility of 25,000 cm^2 per volt-sec, calculate the average relaxation time.

3-15. Find the electrical resistivity for the material described in Problem 3-8(b).

Answer: 3.1×10^{-3} ohm-cm.

3-16. Find the electrical conductivity for the material given in Problem 3-12 if it has a hole mobility of 80 cm^2 per volt-sec.

3-17. Calculate the Hall coefficient and Hall mobilities for the InSb of Problem 3-8. What Hall voltage will be measured in a specimen that carries an exciting current density of 1 amp per cm^2 in a field of 7.5 kilogauss? (The specimen is 0.15 cm thick.)

3-18. If a sample of gallium antimonide (GaSb) has an electron mobility of 4000 cm^2 per volt-sec and a hole mobility of 700 cm^2 per volt-sec and shows no Hall voltage, what fraction of the current is carried by the holes?

Answer: 0.85.

3-19. The segregation constant for antimony in germanium being grown at 7×10^{-3} cm per sec with the seed rotated at 144 rpm is 10^{-2}. A specimen of impure germanium containing 0.02 percent antimony is melted and slowly solidified. The last 10 percent is cut off and discarded and the rest is melted, stirred to homogeneity, and again solidified. The last 5 percent to freeze is again cut off and discarded. What is the average concentration of antimony in the resulting specimen?

3-20. Given a semiconductor where the value of the term $(2\alpha T^{3/2})^2$ in Eq. 3-44 is 10^{40} at 300°K and the material has an energy gap 1.0 eV wide. The donor concentration, N_d, is equal to 10^{15} cm^{-3}. Calculate the location of the Fermi level in electron volts for $T = 300$°K and 600°K.

3-21. In Problem 3-20 determine the fraction of the N_d levels filled at 300°K and 600°K. In this case the donor energy level is 0.98 eV above the top of the valence band.

3-22. If 5×10^{15} acceptors/cm^3 are added to the material in Problem 3-20 at an energy level of 0.02 eV above the top of the valence band, find the position of the Fermi level at 200°K.

3-23. Consider an *n*-type semiconductor at a high enough temperature so that the Fermi level has moved to an energy $4kT$ below the donor energy level. Find an expression for the Fermi level in terms of the energy gap the temperature, and the concentration of donors, N_d.

Answer: $\mathcal{E}_f = \mathcal{E}_a - kT \ln \left[(2\alpha T^{3/2})/N_d \right]$.

REFERENCES

1. C. Kittel, *Introduction to Solid State Physics.* 3rd ed. (New York: John Wiley & Sons, Inc., 1966).

2. R. B. Adler, A. C. Smith, and R. L. Longini, *Introduction to Semiconductor Physics* (New York: John Wiley & Sons, Inc., 1964).

3. J. N. Shive, *The Properties, Physics and Design of Semiconductor Devices* (Princeton, New Jersey: D. Van Nostrand Company, Inc., 1959).

4. L. V. Azaroff, *Introduction to Solids* (New York: McGraw-Hill Book Company, Inc., 1960).

5. K. Lark-Horovitz and V. A. Johnson, "The Physics of Semiconductors" in *The Science of Engineering Materials*, ed. J. E. Goldman (New York: John Wiley & Sons, Inc., 1957).

6. R. M. Eisberg, *Fundamentals of Modern Physics* (New York: John Wiley & Sons, Inc., 1961).

7. Shive, *Semiconductor Devices*, pp. 308–320.

8. R. W. Ure, Jr. and R. R. Heikes, "Theory of Thermoelectric Materials" in *Thermoelectricity: Science and Engineering*, eds. R. R. Heikes and R. W. Ure, Jr. (New York: Interscience Publishers, 1961), p. 342.

9. Shive, *Semiconductor Devices*, p. 301.

10. Shive, *Semiconductor Devices*, p. 406.

11. Kittel, *Solid State Physics*, p. 139.

12. T. C. Harman, J. H. Cahn, and M. J. Logan, "Measurement of Thermoelectric

Properties by Using Peltier Heat" in *Thermoelectricity*, ed. P. H. Egli (New York: John Wiley & Sons, Inc., 1960), p. 235.

13. Azaroff, *Solids*, pp. 333–336.

14. *Transistor Technology*, 3 vols. (Princeton, New Jersey: D. Van Nostrand Company, Inc., 1958).

15. W. G. Pfann, *Zone Melting.* 2nd ed. (New York: John Wiley & Sons, Inc., 1966).

16. A. Holden and P. Singer, *Crystal and Crystal Growing* (Garden City, New York: Doubleday and Company, Inc., 1960).

17. W. G. Pfann, "Principles of Zone Melting," *Journal of Metals* (1952), p. 747.

4 Thermoelectric Generators

The quest for a reliable, silent, energy converter with no moving parts that transforms heat to electrical power has led engineers to reconsider a set of phenomena called the thermoelectric effects. These effects, known for over a hundred years, have permitted the development of small, self-contained electrical power sources. In this chapter we will describe, once again, the thermoelectric effects, this time basing our description on observed phenomena rather than on the principles of irreversible thermodynamics. We will then conduct analyses of thermoelectric power generators and refrigerators. Using the principles and definitions of Ch. 3 concerning semiconductors, we will examine the characteristics of those materials that have properties suitable for use in thermoelectric devices. We will then consider briefly some of the problems of construction and the performance of some actual generators.

4.1 HISTORICAL INTRODUCTION

It is unfortunate, in some respects, that the first notice of the thermoelectric effects took place in 1821, just a year after Hans Christian Oersted reported that a magnetic needle is deflected by the flow of an electric current in a conductor placed near the needle. It is unfortunate because, when Thomas Johann Seebeck reported his observation that a magnetic needle is deflected when held near a circuit made of two different conductors, he attributed the deflection to the temperature difference and not to the current that was flowing in the circuit. Furthermore, he attempted to explain terrestrial magnetism as being caused by the temperature difference between the poles and the equator.

Some of Seebeck's contemporaries did recognize that a current was induced in the circuit by the temperature difference and Seebeck spent a good many years trying to convince them that they were wrong. In pursuing this elusive goal he investigated an enormous number of metals and metal oxides. Among these substances were materials that we now classify as semiconductors. Some of these materials could have been used in thermoelectric generators that would have converted heat to electricity with an efficiency of about 3 percent, a value that compared favorably with the efficiency of steam engines of that day. At the time of Seebeck's work, the only devices available for producing electric current were extremely weak electrostatic generators. Fifty years passed before steam engines drove electromagnetic generators. It was, undoubtedly, electromagnetism that caused succeeding generations of physicists and engineers to lose interest in the curious effects of thermoelectricity. The only widespread use of the effect was in the measurement of temperatures by means of thermocouples. It is difficult to say how the history of electrical engineering and electronics would have developed had Seebeck's discovery been widely employed.

Thirteen years after Seebeck reported his discovery a French watchmaker, Jean Charles Athanase Peltier, discovered that the passage of a current through a junction formed of two different conductors caused absorption or liberation of heat. Like Seebeck, Peltier failed to understand his discovery and saw it as showing only that Ohm's law may not be followed by weak currents. The nature of Peltier's discovery was made clear in 1838 by Emil Lenz, a member of the St. Petersburg Academy. He demonstrated that water could be frozen when placed on a bismuth-antimony junction by the passage of an electric current; he found that on reversing the current the ice could be melted.

Lord Kelvin (William Thomson) realized that a relation between the Seebeck and Peltier effects should exist, and proceeded to derive this relation from thermodynamic arguments. The reasoning that he used led him to conclude that there must be a third thermoelectric effect (now called the *Thomson effect*); this is a lateral heating or cooling effect that takes place in a homogeneous conductor when an electric current passes in the direction of a temperature gradient.

The basic theory of thermoelectric generators and refrigerators was derived satisfactorily in 1909 and 1911 by Altenkirch. His work indicated that for both applications materials were needed with high Seebeck coefficients, high electrical conductivities to minimize Joule heating, and low thermal conductivities to reduce heat transfer through the devices. Though Altenkirch enumerated the desirable properties for materials to be used in thermoelectric devices, 50 years passed before those materials became known and widely available. Shortly after semiconductors initiated the technologi-cal revolution of the 1950's, thermoelectricity was, in a sense, rediscovered in the old physics texts and put to use in a number of interesting ways.

4.2 THE THERMOELECTRIC EFFECTS

In Appendix D one may find defined two of the thermoelectric effects as they arose in the analysis of an even class, coupled type energy converter. We now consider these effects from a classical thermodynamics point of view. This approach is the more traditional one, one that does not depend on formalism as much as does the irreversible thermodynamics technique of Appendix D.

We begin our discussion of the thermoelectric effects by considering a thermocouple circuit connected to a potentiometer as shown in Fig. 4-1. We

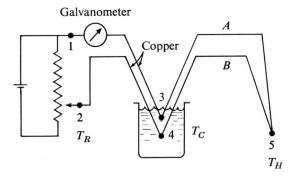

FIG. 4-1. A thermocouple circuit.

would like to use the potentiometer to measure the Seebeck voltage. Our circuit consists of two metals A and B which have their ends fastened together at point 5. Leads of a third metal, usually copper, are connected to A and B at junctions 3 and 4. Both of these junctions are maintained at some lower temperature T_C. In practice, this is generally done by means of an ice bath. The copper leads are connected to the potentiometer at points 1 and 2, both of which are at the temperature T_R, which may be room temperature. When the potentiometer is balanced as indicated by zero current in the galvanometer, the potential difference measured between 1 and 2 is the Seebeck voltage, $V_{A,B}$.

Figure 4-2 has been drawn to have the same corresponding states as Fig. 4-1 but shows only the essential features of the thermocouple. At the

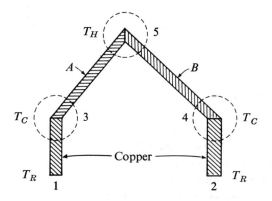

FIG. 4-2. The thermocouple of Fig. 4-1 reduced to its essentials.

steady state, temperature differences exist along the wire but there is no electric current flowing in the circuit. Equations 2-56 and 2-51 defined the Seebeck voltage as

$$(\Delta V)_{\substack{I=0 \\ \Delta T \to 0}} = \alpha \, \Delta T. \tag{4-1}$$

We may now apply this equation to each segment of the circuit in Fig. 4-2. We replace ΔV and ΔT by dV and dT and integrate around the circuit

$$V_3 - V_1 = \int_{T_R}^{T_C} \alpha_{Cu} \, dT,$$

$$V_5 - V_3 = \int_{T_C}^{T_H} \alpha_A \, dT,$$

$$V_4 - V_5 = \int_{T_H}^{T_C} \alpha_B \, dT,$$

$$V_2 - V_4 = \int_{T_C}^{T_R} \alpha_{Cu} \, dT.$$

Upon adding these equations, the left side reduces to $V_2 - V_1 = V_{A,B}$. The first and last terms on the right side add out to yield

$$V_{A,B} = \int_{T_C}^{T_H} (\alpha_A - \alpha_B) \, dT. \tag{4-2}$$

The Seebeck voltage is thus seen to be independent of the room temperature and the Seebeck coefficient of the lead wires α_{Cu}.

If we wish to use the arrangement in Fig. 4-1 to measure the temperature T_H, then we are more interested in the rate of change of the Seebeck voltage than in the value of the voltage itself. Thus, upon differentiating Eq. 4-2, we obtain

$$\frac{dV_{A,B}}{dT} = \alpha_A - \alpha_B, \tag{4-3}$$

which is called the Seebeck coefficient† (or sometimes, quite inappropriately, the thermoelectric power) of the couple.

We show in Fig. 4-3 a junction in which an electric current I is flowing

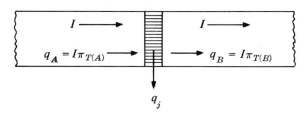

FIG. 4-3. A junction of two dissimilar materials experiencing an electric current. Heat is absorbed or liberated at the junction, depending on the materials and the direction of the current.

from conductor A to conductor B. The junction is maintained at the uniform temperature T. The electric current causes an exchange of heat with the environment; however, if this exchange is measured, it will be found to be greater or less than the I^2R Joule heating that is experienced by any ordinary conductor. The difference between what is evolved in our example and what would be expected in a homogeneous conductor due simply to Joule heating depends on the magnitude and direction of the current, on the temperature, and on the materials A and B. The phenomenon we have just described is known as the *Peltier effect*.

We now compute the rate at which heat must be removed from the junction in order to maintain the temperature constant. Let V_A and V_B be the potentials of conductors A and B on opposite sides of the junction. The rate at which electrical work is done on the junction is simply the current times the potential drop across the junction $IV_{A,B} = I^2R_j$, where R_j is the resistance of the junction. In the next section we will describe how, in a semiconductor/metal junction, energy is absorbed or liberated as electrons or holes are forced to change their energy levels because of the continuity of the Fermi level. The same ideas govern the junction of any two dissimilar materials and the index to how much energy will be absorbed or released is given by the Peltier coefficient π_T (watts per amp). Thus, at the left face of the junction, the current transports in $q_A = I\pi_{T(A)}$ and at the right face of the junction the current transports out $q_B = I\pi_{T(B)}$. If we let q_j represent the rate at which energy must be removed from the junction to maintain its temperature constant, we have, from the first law of thermodynamics

$$q_j = I^2R_j + I(\pi_{T(A)} - \pi_{T(B)}) \qquad \text{[watts]}, \qquad (4\text{-}4)$$

† We might note that this quantity corresponds to the interaction coefficient $\alpha_1' = L_{oi}/L_{oo}$ derived by means of irreversible thermodynamics in Appendix D, specifically in Eq. D-35.

or by using the second Kelvin relation

$$q_j = I^2 R_j + IT(\alpha_A - \alpha_B) \qquad [\text{watts}]. \qquad (4\text{-}5)$$

It should be recognized that q_j can be a term that represents heat absorbed or heat liberated depending on the relative magnitude of the two terms. Since the Peltier heat is reversible, the second term can be made to add or subtract from the first at will, simply by reversing the direction of the current.

We next consider a rod (illustrated in Fig. 4-4) at the steady state in

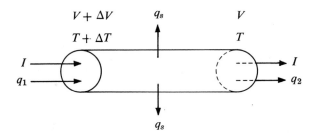

FIG. 4-4. A heat current and an electric current flowing in a homogeneous rod in which there is a temperature gradient.

which a heat current is flowing due to an applied temperature difference ΔT. We also send an electric current through the element, but we find that the heat developed is greater or less than $I^2 R$, the difference depending upon the magnitude and direction of the current, the temperature, and the material. This is known as the Thomson effect.

We will now compute the rate at which heat must flow out the sides of the rod in order for the temperature at every point in the rod to be maintained constant. The conduction heat flow through the left face of the rod is exactly the same as that flowing out the right face. We let q_s denote the heat flow out the side walls of the rod. The rate at which electrical work is done on the element is $I \Delta V$. At the left face the electrical current transports $q_1 = I \pi_{T(1)}$ and at the right face $q_2 = I \pi_{T(2)}$. Because we are at the steady state, the first law yields for the heat transfer through the side of the rod†

$$\begin{aligned} q_s &= I \Delta V + I\pi_{T(1)} - I\pi_{T(2)} \\ &= I[\Delta V + (T + \Delta T)\alpha_1 - T\alpha_2], \end{aligned} \qquad (4\text{-}6)$$

but we can always write to first-order terms

$$\alpha_1 = \alpha_2 + \frac{d\alpha}{dT}\Delta T$$

† We have ignored the conduction terms since they are the same at both faces.

and thus

$$q_s = I\left(\Delta V + T\frac{d\alpha}{dT}\Delta T + \alpha\,\Delta T\right), \qquad (4\text{-}7)$$

where we have neglected the second-order term ΔT^2 and dropped the subscripts from α. We may eliminate the voltage from Eq. 4-7 simply by recalling from Section D.2.3 that the voltage drop across the rod is the usual IR drop minus that contributed by the Seebeck effect; thus $\Delta V = IR - \alpha\,\Delta T$ and we express the heat transfer through the sides of the rod as

$$q_s = I^2 R + I\left(T\frac{d\alpha}{dT}\Delta T\right). \qquad (4\text{-}8)$$

The last term is the heat that must be transferred away from the element over and above the Joule heat $I^2 R$; it is called the *Thomson heat*. From purely thermodynamic reasoning Sir William Thomson, who later became Lord Kelvin, predicted in 1855 that a conductor carrying an electric current along a temperature gradient should experience a heating or cooling in addition to, and independent of, the irreversible Joule heating, depending on the direction of the current. Thomson's deduction was verified for a number of substances long before the solid state physics of the phenomenon were understood.

The product $T(d\alpha/dT)$ is called the *Thomson coefficient* and is usually defined positive if heat must be added to keep the temperature the same. Thus we write

$$\tau' = -T\frac{d\alpha}{dT} \qquad (4\text{-}9)$$

and Eq. 4-8 becomes

$$q_s = I^2 R - I\tau'\,\Delta T. \qquad (4\text{-}10)$$

By combining Eqs. 4-2 and 4-9 we obtain *Kelvin's first relation*

$$\tau'_A - \tau'_B = -T\frac{d^2 V_{(A,B)}}{dT^2} = -T\frac{d}{dT}\left[\frac{\pi_{T(A,B)}}{T}\right]. \qquad (4\text{-}11)$$

Kelvin's second relation, which was found (in Appendix D) by means of irreversible thermodynamics, is repeated here:

$$\pi_{T(A,B)} = T\frac{dV_{A,B}}{dT} = T\alpha_{(A,B)}. \qquad (4\text{-}12)$$

It should be noted that Kelvin found both of these equations by ignoring the irreversible processes of heat conduction and Joule heating and setting the net change of entropy in the reversible processes associated with the Peltier and Thomson effects equal to zero.

Both the Seebeck and Peltier coefficients are defined for junctions between two conductors, but the Thomson coefficient is a property of a single conductor. Equation 4-9 suggests a way of defining the absolute

Seebeck coefficient for a single material. The third law of thermodynamics establishes that the Seebeck coefficient is zero for all junctions at absolute zero. Thus Eq. 4-9 can be integrated to yield

$$\alpha = -\int_0^T \frac{\tau'}{T} dT. \qquad \text{(4-12)}$$

The absolute Seebeck coefficient of a material at very low temperatures may be determined by forming a junction between the material and a super-conductor, the latter possessing a Seebeck coefficient of zero. A procedure like this has been carried out for pure lead up to 18°K and the Thomson coefficient for lead has been measured between 20°K and room temperature. The value of the Thomson coefficient between 18°K and 20°K can be accurately extrapolated. Thus by means of Eq. 4-12, the absolute Seebeck coefficient of lead has been established. The absolute Seebeck coefficient of any other conductor may now be determined simply by joining it to lead.

4.3 A SOLID STATE DESCRIPTION OF THE THERMOELECTRIC EFFECTS

In Appendix D the thermoelectric effects were introduced to analyze a thermoelectric generator from an irreversible thermodynamics point of view. In the previous section we considered these same effects from a classical thermodynamics point of view. We now consider, from an electron energy aspect, the definition of these coefficients in terms of solid state parameters. Figure 4-5 illustrates a p-type semiconductor connected between two metal contacts. We assume that the contacts are ohmic (that is, the current across the contact is linearly proportional to the applied voltage) and that a battery has been placed in the circuit to supply a potential across the sample.

The Peltier coefficient†, π_T, gives the magnitude of the heating or cooling that occurs at a junction of two different materials over and above the ordinary Joule heating that is taking place at the contact. Since the Peltier coefficient is the ratio of energy liberated or absorbed at the contact per coulomb of charge crossing the contact it has the dimensions of voltage.

We now interpret the Peltier heating or cooling as being due to the change in the average kinetic energy of a current carrier when it crosses a contact. We may obtain a physical understanding of the phenomenon by considering Fig. 4-5 again. The Fermi level in the metal is continuous with the Fermi level in the semiconductor because we have assumed that equilibrium exists across the interface; the position of the Fermi level in the metal

---

† Which is recognized as the interaction coefficient, $\alpha_1 = L_{oi}/L_{oo}$, of Appendix D.

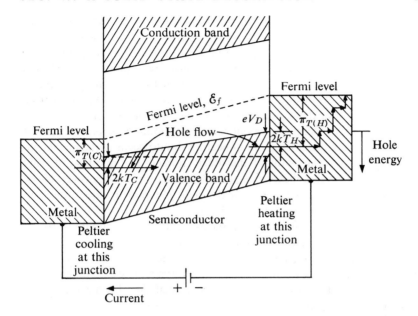

FIG. 4-5. Energy diagram for a circuit containing a *p*-type semiconductor and two metal contacts. The energy of the carriers in the metal is the Fermi energy, whereas in the semiconductor they are at the Fermi energy plus $2kT$.

by definition is coincident with that position which causes it to lie in the center of the electron energy distribution in the partly filled band. Assume that a hole current is flowing from left to right across the junction; as long as the hole travels in the metal, it carries on the average only the Fermi energy of that metal; but in order for it to cross the left-hand junction, it must have at least the Fermi energy of the semiconductor, $\mathcal{E}_f$ (measured positively downward), more than its average energy in the metal. Thus, only a fraction of the total number of holes in the metal have enough energy to cross the contact. Using the methods of transport theory, one may show that *of the holes that are able to cross* the contact, each one will carry an average energy of $2kT$ more than the Fermi energy.

The metal is thus forced into the position of continuously supplying energy to each hole that crosses the interface. The magnitude of the *energy per coulomb* that each hole takes out of the metal into the semiconductor is the Peltier coefficient and is the sum of the Fermi energy and the additional energy required to permit hole travel in the semiconductor. That is

$$\pi_{T(p)} = \frac{1}{e}(\mathcal{E}_f + 2kT). \tag{4-13}$$

The additional energy required by the semiconductor is supplied by the metal lattice, thus causing a selective passing on to the semiconductor of high energy holes. It is interesting to note that this energy is *not* delivered to the semiconductor by the holes, since these holes are in thermal equilibrium with the holes that are already in the semiconductor. The energy required by the holes to gain entrance to the semiconductor simply disappears from the neighborhood of the contact, thus cooling it in the process.

By applying the same process in reverse, it should be apparent that for the same current, an equal amount of heating should occur in the metal contact within a few mean paths of the other contact. The question of what happens to the heat that disappears at the left junction is now answerable by merely noting that it must appear at the right junction to satisfy the conservation of energy for the complete circuit.

The derivation presented here for the Peltier coefficient should be recognized as being approximate. One of the reasons that it is approximate is that we have not taken into account the scattering mechanism that the charge carriers encounter as they wander through the crystal. If we do take scattering into account, the equation for the Peltier coefficient for a *p*-type semiconductor with a relaxation time of the form $\tau = \Phi(T)\varepsilon^{-s}$ is

$$\pi_{T(p)} = \frac{1}{e}\,[\varepsilon_f + (5/2 - s)kT] \qquad (4\text{-}14)$$

and for acoustic scattering by the lattice, where $s = \frac{1}{2}$, we obtain the previously derived Eq. 4-13. For an *n*-type semiconductor the equivalent expression for the Peltier coefficient is

$$\pi_{T(n)} = -\frac{1}{e}\,[(\varepsilon_g - \varepsilon_f) + (5/2 - s)kT]. \qquad (4\text{-}15)$$

The Seebeck coefficient for a *p*-type material may be found simply by applying Kelvin's second relation derived in Ch. 2:

$$\alpha_p = \pi_{T(p)}/T. \qquad (4\text{-}16)$$

Thus

$$\alpha_p = \frac{k}{e}\,[\varepsilon_f/(kT) + (5/2 - s)] \qquad (4\text{-}17)$$

and for an *n*-type material

$$\alpha_n = -\frac{k}{e}\,[(\varepsilon_g - \varepsilon_f)/(kT) + (5/2 - s)]. \qquad (4\text{-}18)$$

At high enough temperatures the Fermi level lies relatively close to the center of the forbidden energy gap, so that we may write Eq. 3-39 in terms of the Fermi level (where we have made the usual approximation that the energy gap is at least 5- or $6kT$ wide):

$$p = 2aT^{3/2}\exp\,[-\varepsilon_f/(kT)]. \qquad (4\text{-}19)$$

Equation 4-17 gives an independent method for determining the Fermi level; hence it may be used in conjunction with Eq. 4-19 to predict the hole concentration from the easily measured Seebeck voltage.

It is seen that the sign of the Peltier or Seebeck coefficient gives a simple direct test for determining whether a conductor is n or p type, assuming that the scattering constant is less than $5/2$. Since the Fermi level is generally a few kT above the top of the valence band, Eqs. 4-17 and 4-18 predict a Seebeck coefficient in a semiconductor on the order of a few hundred microvolts per degree where $k/e = 86$ microvolts per degree.

In an intrinsic semiconductor, both the electrons and holes diffuse in the temperature gradient, so that they cancel each other's contribution if both types of charge carriers have the same mobility; if their mobilities are different, however, the net Seebeck coefficient can be found from a weighted average such as

$$(\mu_n + \mu_p)\alpha_i = \mu_n\alpha_n + \mu_p\alpha_p. \tag{4-20}$$

We may simplify this expression by assuming that the Fermi level lies in the center of the forbidden energy gap so that $(\mathcal{E}_g - \mathcal{E}_f) = (\mathcal{E}_f - 0) = \mathcal{E}_g/2$, a reasonable assumption for most purposes. Then when Eqs. 4-17 and 4-18 are combined with Eq. 4-20 we find

$$\alpha_i = \left[\frac{1-b}{1+b}\right]\frac{k}{e}[\mathcal{E}_g/(2kT) + (5/2 - s)], \tag{4-21}$$

where $b = \mu_n/\mu_p$.

The most complicated case is when $n \neq p$ and the mobilities are not equal; for this situation of mixed conduction, we have

$$\alpha = \frac{k}{e}\left\{\frac{p\mu_p[\mathcal{E}_f/(kT) + (5/2 - s)] - n\mu_n[(\mathcal{E}_g - \mathcal{E}_f)/(kT) + (5/2 - s)]}{p\mu_p + n\mu_n}\right\}. \tag{4-22}$$

We now briefly consider the third of the thermoelectric phenomena— the Thomson effect. As a hole flows from left to right in the uniformly doped specimen shown in Fig. 4-5, it loses potential energy of eV_D due to the fact that it resides at a lower energy level (measured positively downward) in the valence band at the right-hand end. At the same time, however, it gains thermal kinetic energy as it moves up the temperature gradient established by the Peltier effect at the ends of the bar; this gain in thermal energy is about $2k\,\Delta T$. The sum of the two quantities represents the net gain in energy per charge carrier. This quantity may be either positive or negative, depending on the relative magnitude of the two terms. Thus energy is either delivered to or given up by the lattice of the crystal with the consequent heating or cooling of the specimen. The magnitude of this energy exchange is given by the Thomson coefficient, which is defined as positive if a positive current flowing in the direction of the positive temperature gradient increases the average total energy of the carrier, thereby cooling the specimen.

The Thomson coefficient for a p-type semiconductor with acoustic scattering by the lattice in volts per degree is

$$\tau'_p = -V_D/\Delta T + 2k/e. \qquad (4\text{-}23)$$

4.4 ANALYSIS OF A THERMOELECTRIC GENERATOR

In this section we will utilize the definitions developed in the previous section to analyze a power-producing thermoelectric generator. In addition, we will briefly treat a Peltier effect refrigerator. Our analysis will not be exact because the complexities of such analyses have a tendency to obscure physical insight into the way devices operate. Studies [1] have shown that the results obtained from an exact analysis differ very little from those obtained from an approximate one. (We will discuss those differences briefly in a later section.)

4.4.1 Basic assumptions. To obtain an analysis that highlights the phenomena taking place in a thermoelectric generator it is necessary to make certain simplifying assumptions. Our analysis will be based on the model illustrated in Fig. 4-6. It consists of two semiconductor elements, one of which is a p-type material and the other an n-type material. We make the following simplifying assumptions:

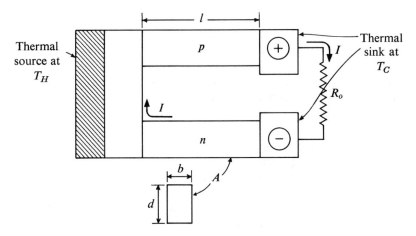

FIG. 4-6. The model of the thermoelectric generator that is used in the analysis in this section.

(1) The generator works between the two temperatures T_H and T_C which are the actual temperatures at the junctions between the active semiconducting materials and the straps or reservoirs to which they are connected.

(2) There is no heat transfer between the reservoirs at T_H and T_C except through the thermoelectric elements with no lateral heat transfer from the arms of the device.

(3) The junction electrical contact resistance is negligible compared with the bulk resistance of the arms.

(4) The arms are of constant cross-sectional area.

(5) The electrical resistivity ρ, the thermal conductivity λ, and the Seebeck coefficient α of the material are independent of temperature.

(6) Thermal contact resistance between the source and connecting bus bar between the p- and n-type elements can be made small while providing good electrical insulation. A similar assumption holds for the sink.

Assumption number (5) is probably the weakest one in the list. While convenient for making calculations, it can sometimes lead to significant errors in predicting results. Section 4.4.7 gives several techniques that can be used when this condition is relaxed.

4.4.2 Temperature distribution and thermal energy transfer for the generator.
Consider a section of length dx of one leg of a thermoelectric generator as shown in Fig. 4-7. The bar is assumed to be experiencing a temperature gradient and carrying an electric current in the x direction as shown. The bar has unit cross-sectional area. From Fourier's law of heat conduction for a one-dimensional element, the heat entering the infinitesimal section through the left face is

$$-\lambda \frac{dT}{dx}. \qquad \text{(4-24)}$$

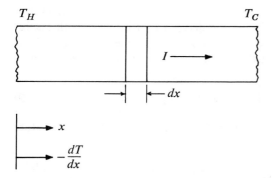

FIG. 4-7. A portion of a bar carrying an electric current in a temperature gradient.

The heat leaving the section through the right face is the thermal conductivity times the temperature gradient at the right face:

$$-\lambda \left[\frac{dT}{dx} + \frac{d}{dx}\left(\frac{dT}{dx}\right) dx \right]. \tag{4-25}$$

The Joule heat generated in the volume of the element is the current density ($J = I/A$) squared times the electrical resistivity ρ and the length of the element dx:

$$J^2\rho \, dx. \tag{4-26}$$

Since we have assumed temperature independent properties, that is, $d\alpha/dT = 0$, the Thomson coefficient must be zero. Under steady-state conditions the heat out of the element must equal the heat in, plus any heat generated internal to the element, thus

$$\lambda \left(\frac{d^2T}{dx^2}\right) + J^2\rho = 0. \tag{4-27}$$

The solution to Eq. 4-27 may be found by utilizing the following boundary conditions:

$$T = T_H \quad \text{at} \quad x = 0$$
$$T = T_C \quad \text{at} \quad x = l$$

and is found to be

$$T = [T_H - (x/l)\,\Delta T] + [J^2\rho/(2\lambda)]x(l - x), \tag{4-28}$$

where $\Delta T = T_H - T_C$. Note that this equation has two independent terms, one of which gives the normal linear relationship in the absence of a current; the second term is of a parabolic nature reflecting the Joule heating. The effect of these two terms is shown in Fig. 4-8.

The heat that enters or leaves a junction of a thermoelectric device under our stated assumptions may be divided into two parts: (1) that due to the presence of a temperature gradient at the junction; (2) that associated with the absorption or liberation of energy due to the Peltier effect. The magnitude of the first part may be found by application of Fourier's law of heat conduction. This is done by taking the derivative of Eq. 4-28 with respect to x and multiplying by the cross-sectional area of the elements and the thermal conductivity. Thus at the hot junction $x = 0$, the Fourier term is found to be

$$-A\lambda \frac{dT}{dx}\bigg|_{x=0} = \gamma\lambda\,\Delta T - \tfrac{1}{2}I^2\rho/\gamma, \tag{4-29}$$

where $\gamma = A/l$. At the cold junction the heat out due to a temperature gradient is evaluated as

$$-A\lambda \frac{dT}{dx}\bigg|_{x=l} = \gamma\lambda\,\Delta T + \tfrac{1}{2}I^2\rho/\gamma. \tag{4-30}$$

It is seen that at the hot end of the bar the heat transfer to the element is reduced by one-half of the Joule heat flowing into the source. At the cold end the usual conduction term is enhanced by one-half of the Joule heat flowing into the sink. This division of the Joule heat is a consequence of the temperature distribution as given by Eq. 4-28 and does not involve heat flowing up a temperature gradient. This fact becomes somewhat easier to understand if we assume that the Joule heat flows along its own temperature gradient as indicated in Fig. 4-8.

We now calculate the energy transfer due to the Peltier effect at each junction. We do this by application of the definitions set forth in Section 4.2. Since there will be heat absorbed between each reservoir and each leg of the generator, the total Peltier heat is defined to be

$$-(\pi_{T(pr)} + \pi_{T(rn)})I_{pn} = -\pi_{T(pn)}I_{pn}, \tag{4-31}$$

where I_{pn} is the current flowing from the p-type arm to n-type arm at the junction in question. By application of Kelvin's second relation (Eq. 2-57) we may write Eq. 4-31 as

$$-\pi_{T(pn)}I_{pn} = -\alpha T I_{pn}, \tag{4-32}$$

where α is simply the combined Seebeck coefficient for the junction

$$\alpha = |\alpha_n| + |\alpha_p|.$$

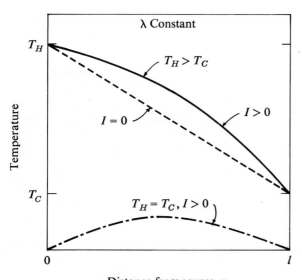

FIG. 4-8. Temperature distribution in a bar under various conditions of temperature difference and electrical current.

Seebeck coefficients of n-type and p-type materials add because they act like seats of electromotive force in series. This can be observed from Fig. 4-6. For present-day materials this allows, for all practical purposes, the doubling of the open circuit voltage of the generator.

4.4.3   Maximum thermal efficiency of a generator. We now may calculate the efficiency of a thermoelectric generator by application of the laws of thermodynamics. The *thermal efficiency* is defined as the ratio of the electrical power output P_o to the thermal power input q_H to the hot junction

$$\eta_t = P_o/q_H. \tag{4-33}$$

Note that this definition is different from the one given in Appendix D, which was a comparison of a device's efficiency with its Carnot efficiency $\Delta T/T_H$,

$$\eta = \eta_t/\eta_{ca} = \eta_t T_H/\Delta T. \tag{4-34}$$

The thermal input to the hot junction is given by Eq. 4-29 plus the Peltier effect term as defined by Eq. 4-32, thus

$$q_H = K\,\Delta T + \alpha T_H I - \tfrac{1}{2}I^2 R, \tag{4-35}$$

where the thermal conductance K and electrical resistance R are defined as they were in Appendix D:

$$K = \lambda_n A_n/l_n + \lambda_p A_p/l_p = \lambda_n \gamma_n + \lambda_p \gamma_p \tag{4-36}$$

and

$$R = \rho_n/\gamma_n + \rho_p/\gamma_p. \tag{4-37}$$

Since the current flowing at the hot junction is from the n-type material to the p-type material, opposite to the definition we set forth in Eq. 4-31 with the minus sign, the Peltier term in Eq. 4-35 must carry a plus sign. That is, the Peltier effect causes the absorption of additional heat at the source while half the Joule heat is returned to the source.

   The output power is simply the current squared times the load resistance R_o,

$$P_o = I^2 R_o. \tag{4-38}$$

The open circuit voltage is $\alpha\,\Delta T$, so the electric current drawn from the generator is

$$I = \frac{\alpha\,\Delta T}{R + R_o}. \tag{4-39}$$

The thermal efficiency may be computed from Eq. 4-33 to be

$$\eta_t = \frac{I^2 R_o}{K\,\Delta T + \alpha T_H I - \tfrac{1}{2}I^2 R}. \tag{4-40}$$

If possible, we would like to maximize the thermal efficiency. The feasibility of doing this becomes clearer if we introduce a new variable, m', which represents the ratio of the load resistance to the internal resistance of the device

$$m' = R_o/R. \tag{4-41}$$

Thus Eq. 4-40 in terms of m' is

$$\eta_t = \frac{m'(\Delta T/T_H)}{\dfrac{(1+m')^2}{T_H} \cdot \dfrac{RK}{\alpha^2} + (1+m') - \dfrac{1}{2}\dfrac{\Delta T}{T_H}}. \tag{4-42}$$

We note the appearance of the product RK in the denominator of Eq. 4-42. All other things being equal, the smaller RK is, the higher the efficiency. Let us form this product from the definitions given by Eqs. 4-36 and 4-37

$$RK = \lambda_n\rho_n + \lambda_n\rho_p(\gamma_n/\gamma_p) + \lambda_p\rho_n(\gamma_p/\gamma_n) + \lambda_p\rho_p. \tag{4-43}$$

We minimize this product by taking the derivative of Eq. 4-43 with respect to γ_n/γ_p and setting the result equal to zero, to obtain

$$\gamma_n/\gamma_p = (\rho_n\lambda_p/\rho_p\lambda_n)^{1/2} \tag{4-44}$$

and the value of RK when γ_n/γ_p has this magnitude is

$$(RK)_{\min} = [(\rho_n\lambda_n)^{1/2} + (\rho_p\lambda_p)^{1/2}]^2. \tag{4-45}$$

Here again, we briefly consider the grouping of properties, called the *figure of merit*, that was introduced in Appendix D. This grouping, it will be recalled, related those properties that are important in the design of a thermoelectric generator:

$$Z = \alpha^2/RK.$$

Utilizing the minimum value of the RK product given in Eq. 4-45 in the above definition, we find the maximum value of the figure of merit (denoted by an asterisk) for any combination of n- and p-type materials to be

$$Z^* = \frac{(|\alpha_n| + |\alpha_p|)^2}{[(\rho_n\lambda_n)^{1/2} + (\rho_p\lambda_p)^{1/2}]^2}. \tag{4-46}$$

We may now express the thermal efficiency of a thermoelectric generator which has had its geometry optimized by means of Eq. 4-44 as

$$\eta_t = \frac{m'(\Delta T/T_H)}{\dfrac{(1+m')^2}{Z^*T_H} + (1+m') - \dfrac{1}{2}\dfrac{\Delta T}{T_H}}. \tag{4-47}$$

The value of the resistance ratio m' that maximizes the thermal efficiency is found by taking the derivative of Eq. 4-47 with respect to m' and setting the result equal to zero to obtain

$$m'_{\mathrm{opt}} = (1 + Z^*T_{\mathrm{av}})^{1/2}, \tag{4-48}$$

where $T_{\mathrm{av}} = \frac{1}{2}(T_C + T_H)$. The thermal efficiency with both geometry and load resistance optimized is found by substituting Eq. 4-48 into Eq. 4-47, which yields

$$\eta_{t(\text{max})} = \frac{(m'_{\text{opt}} - 1)(\Delta T/T_H)}{m'_{\text{opt}} + T_C/T_H}. \tag{4-49}$$

The thermal efficiency under these conditions is a function of Z^*T_{av} and T_C/T_H. Figure 4-9 shows how the thermal efficiency depends upon the figure of merit and the temperature ratio.

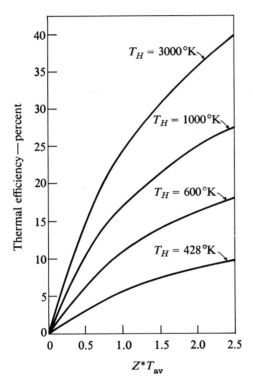

FIG. 4-9. Thermal efficiency of a thermoelectric generator as a function of the source temperature and the figure of merit. The sink temperature is assumed to be 300°K.

Equation 4-49 should be compared with the expression (Eq. D-81) derived in Appendix D for the effectiveness of a thermoelectric generator; it is repeated here† for clarity:

† We have multiplied it by the Carnot efficiency to convert it from an effectiveness to an efficiency expression.

$$\eta_{t(max)} = \frac{[(1 + Z_1 T)^{1/2} - 1][\Delta T/T_H]}{(1 + Z_1 T)^{1/2} + 1}. \tag{D-81}$$

It is observed from this comparison that for small temperature differences Eq. 4-49 approaches Eq. D-81.

4.4.4 Maximum power output of a generator. Instead of maximizing the efficiency, it is sometimes desirable to maximize the power output of a generator. If we express the power output in terms of the resistance ratio m' and the current as given by Eq. 4-39 we obtain

$$P_o = \frac{(\alpha \, \Delta T)^2 m'}{(1 + m')^2 R}, \tag{4-50}$$

which may be maximized by the usual procedure. This operation yields the well-known result that for maximum power, the resistance ratio m' is identically equal to unity—that is, $R_o = R$. Thus, the efficiency of a generator operating at maximum power is given by Eq. 4-47 with m' set equal to one:

$$\eta_{t(mp)} = \frac{\Delta T/T_H}{4/(Z^*T_H) + 2 - \frac{1}{2}(\Delta T/T_H)}. \tag{4-51}$$

In designing a generator for maximum power output one tries to attain the given power with minimum volume, minimum weight, or minimum thermoelectric material. To obtain these objectives it is necessary to maximize the power output per unit of total cross-sectional area, P_o/A_{tot}. In addition, the length of the element should be kept as short as is practicable. A lower limit on this factor is imposed, because with extremely short elements the contact resistance is no longer negligible in comparison with the resistance of the elements. The power output per unit of cross-sectional area may be found by setting m' equal to one in Eq. 4-50 and dividing by the area of the elements A_n and A_p, thus

$$\frac{P_o}{A_{tot}} = \frac{(\alpha \, \Delta T)^2}{4l[(\rho_n/A_n) + (\rho_p/A_p)][A_n + A_p]}, \tag{4-52}$$

where $A_{tot} = A_n + A_p$ and where we have assumed that the lengths of the n- and p-type elements are the same. This quantity will be a maximum when the denominator is a minimum. Taking the derivative of the denominator with respect to (A_n/A_p) we obtain the area ratio which maximizes Eq. 4-52

$$\frac{A_n}{A_p} = \left[\frac{\rho_n}{\rho_p}\right]^{1/2}. \tag{4-53}$$

Note the similarity between this quantity and the one that maximizes the efficiency; the significant difference is that for the maximum power case Eq. 4-53 does not involve the thermal conductivity. It is possible to derive expressions for the internal resistance, thermal conductance, and maximum power output in terms of this area ratio. This will be left as an exercise at the end of the chapter.

4.4.5   Multistage generators. Single-stage power generation by a thermo-electric device has inherent output voltage and load limitations. Staging of generators by any method rarely results in outstanding gains in efficiency or power density, but substantial changes in optimum load resistances and output voltages are possible. There are many different modes of staging; we will discuss two or three of the most widely exploited methods.

One of the simplest methods of staging is a series couple as illustrated in Fig. 4-10. It is analogous to a number of batteries placed in series. The output voltage for N couples is simply N times the voltage of a single couple, whereas the current is the same as for a single couple. The optimal load resistance is N times the optimal load resistance of a single-stage device whereas the electrical power output and thermal input increase linearly with N. Thus, the thermal efficiency is independent of the number of couples.

Nearly all thermoelectric materials are very much temperature depend-ent. For a given temperature difference, one type of material will have the highest figure of merit, but in another temperature range another type of material may have a higher figure of merit, as is clearly illustrated in the property charts in Appendix C. Thus, to obtain maximum performance over a large temperature range, one would like to use a number of materials, each being used over the particular temperature interval where it has better

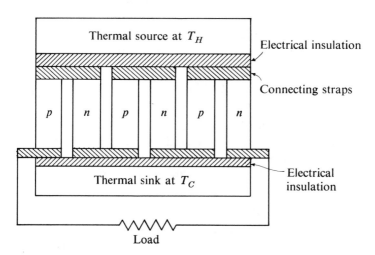

FIG. 4-10. Single-stage thermoelectric devices that have been arranged to be thermally in parallel and electrically in series.

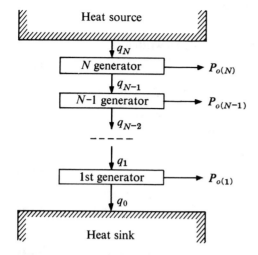

FIG. 4-11. A cascaded generator consisting of N units thermally in series.

properties than other materials. One method of achieving this is to place a number of generators thermally in series as is shown in Fig. 4-11. This is called a *cascaded generator;* the upper bound on its efficiency is found by considering an infinite-stage device, as we will do in the latter part of this section.

The efficiency of the cascaded generator illustrated in Fig. 4-11 may be derived by applying the first law of thermodynamics to the generator, and is no different than the analysis of any cascaded heat engine. Applying the first law to the Nth stage gives

$$q_N - q_{N-1} = P_{o(N)} \tag{4-54}$$

and by definition the thermal efficiency of the Nth generator is

$$\eta_{t(N)} = \frac{P_{o(N)}}{q_N}. \tag{4-55}$$

Eliminating $P_{o(N)}$ from Eq. 4-54 by use of Eq. 4-55 gives

$$q_N(1 - \eta_{t(N)}) = q_{N-1}. \tag{4-56}$$

Applying the first law to the $N - 1$ generator yields

$$q_{N-1} - q_{N-2} = P_{o(N-1)}, \tag{4-57}$$

but by definition the thermal efficiency of this stage is

$$\eta_{t(N-1)} = \frac{P_{o(N-1)}}{q_{N-1}}, \tag{4-58}$$

which allows Eq. 4-57 to be written as

$$q_{N-1}(1 - \eta_{t(N-1)}) = q_{N-2}. \tag{4-59}$$

For the entire cascade the first law may be written as

$$q_N - q_0 = P_{o(1)} + P_{o(2)} + \cdots + P_{o(N)}, \tag{4-60}$$

but again, by definition, the system has an overall thermal efficiency of

$$\eta_t = \frac{P_{o(1)} + P_{o(2)} + \cdots + P_{o(N)}}{q_N} \tag{4-61}$$

so that Eq. 4-60 may be written as

$$q_0 = q_N(1 - \eta_t). \tag{4-62}$$

Combining Eqs. 4-56 and 4-59 yields

$$q_{N-2} = q_N(1 - \eta_{t(N)})(1 - \eta_{t(N-1)}), \tag{4-63}$$

which may be generalized to

$$q_0 = q_N(1 - \eta_{t(N)})(1 - \eta_{t(N-1)}) \cdots (1 - \eta_{t(1)}). \tag{4-64}$$

Substituting Eq. 4-64 into Eq. 4-62 gives

$$q_N(1 - \eta_{t(N)})(1 - \eta_{t(N-1)}) \cdots (1 - \eta_{t(1)}) = q_N(1 - \eta_t),$$

which upon simplification is simply

$$\eta_t = \eta_{t(1)} + \eta_{t(2)} + \cdots + \eta_{t(N)} - \eta_{t(1)}\eta_{t(2)} \cdots \eta_{t(N)}, \tag{4-65}$$

or, more compactly

$$\eta_t = 1 - \prod_{i=1}^{i=N} (1 - \eta_{t(i)}), \tag{4-66}$$

where $\prod$ signifies the product of terms.

Obviously, as a first approximation, the efficiencies of multistage cascaded generators add. However, the temperature drop across each stage will be smaller, giving lower stage efficiencies.

We now turn our attention to designing a multistage generator for maximim efficiency. In order to do this we must add one more assumption to those made in Section 4.4.1. We require that each stage be electrically insulated along its mating surface from the adjacent stage. The electrical insulation will be assumed to offer no resistance to heat transfer from one stage to the next; hence, there will be no finite temperature drop across the insulation. This assumption is almost impossible to achieve in practice. Temperature drops of 5° to 6°K across hot side junctions, simply due to the thermal contact resistance of two materials electrically insulated from each other, are quite common in real generators. This consideration will place another limitation on staging; the addition of more than two stages, in most cases, would cause such an increase in power input as to prohibit further staging from efficiency considerations alone.

We follow the procedure Harman [2] used in analyzing multistage thermoelectric generators. An equivalent circuit diagram for the arrangement of Fig. 4-11 is shown in Fig. 4-12. By Kirchhoff's law, the electrical circuits will be independent if the branch currents $I_1, I_2 \cdots I_N$ are equal. We may now find the current that maximizes the efficiency or power output by using the relations of Section 4.4.3 or 4.4.4.

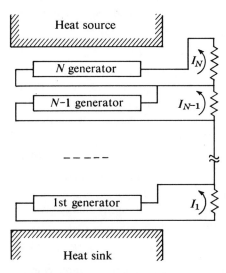

FIG. 4-12. An equivalent circuit for an N-stage generator in which the branch circuits are independent.

The branch current for the kth stage is

$$I_k = \frac{V_k}{R_k + R_{o(k)}},\qquad(4\text{-}67)$$

where V_k is the thermoelectric voltage produced in the kth stage while R_k and $R_{o(k)}$ are the internal and load resistance of the kth stage, respectively. The kth stage will operate at maximum efficiency if the resistance ratio $m'_{\text{opt}(k)}$ is chosen consistent with the following criterion

$$m'_{\text{opt}(k)} = (1 + Z_k T_{\text{av}(k)})^{1/2}.\qquad(4\text{-}68)$$

The optimum current under these conditions is then

$$I_{\text{opt}(k)} = \frac{\alpha_k \, \Delta T_k}{R_k(1 + m'_{\text{opt}(k)})}.\qquad(4\text{-}69)$$

It is now easy to generalize that the efficiency of the kth stage is simply

$$\eta_{t(k)} = \frac{\Delta T_k}{T_k} \cdot \frac{m'_{\text{opt}(k)} - 1}{m'_{\text{opt}(k)} + T_{k-1}/T_k}. \tag{4-70}$$

To satisfy the requirement that the branch circuits be independent as mentioned earlier it is necessary to have

$$(I)_{\text{opt}(1)} = (I)_{\text{opt}(2)} = \cdots = (I)_{\text{opt}(N)}. \tag{4-71}$$

So far we have developed the procedure for maximizing the efficiency of each stage. We now consider the problem of satisfying the first law of thermodynamics as it is applied to the kth stage. The energy per unit time *rejected* by the kth stage at temperature T_{k-1} is

$$q_{c(k)} = K_k \, \Delta T_k + \pi_{T(k)} I + \tfrac{1}{2} I^2 R_k, \tag{4-72}$$

where $\Delta T_k = T_k - T_{k-1}$ and K_k, R_k are the thermal conductance and electrical resistance of the kth stage respectively. The quantity $\pi_{T(k)}$ is the Peltier energy rejected per unit of electric current per unit time, at the temperature T_{k-1} which may also be expressed as $\alpha_k T_{k-1}$. The energy absorbed per unit time by the next stage—the $k - 1$ stage—is

$$q_{H(k-1)} = K_{k-1} \, \Delta T_{k-1} + \pi_{k-1} I - \tfrac{1}{2} I^2 R_{k-1}, \tag{4-73}$$

where $\Delta T_{k-1} = T_{k-1} - T_{k-2}$ and K_{k-1} and R_{k-1} are the thermal conductance and electrical resistance of the $k - 1$ stage. The Peltier term π_{k-1} in this case may be written as $\alpha_{k-1} T_{k-1}$. At the steady state condition the energy given off must equal the energy absorbed between junctions, so

$$K_k \, \Delta T_k + \pi_{T(k)} I + \tfrac{1}{2} I^2 R_k = K_{k-1} \, \Delta T_{k-1} + \pi_{T(k-1)} I - \tfrac{1}{2} I^2 R_{k-1}. \tag{4-74}$$

We may make this equation more useful by making some simplifying approximations. Since, in general, the Peltier coefficients will be very close in magnitude and they are both multiplied by the common value of I, then the two terms may be added out as an approximation. The electrical resistances of the two stages will also be very close in value and so the two Joule heating terms may be combined into one. The results of these approximations are

$$K_k \, \Delta T_k \approx K_{k-1} \, \Delta T_{k-1} - I^2 R_{k-1}. \tag{4-75}$$

We may summarize our work as follows: the entire generator will operate at maximum efficiency if the external load is adjusted for each stage so that the current drawn is the optimum as predicted by Eq. 4-69; the temperature drop required across each stage is that predicted by Eq. 4-75; the efficiency of the entire generator is given by Eq. 4-66, where the maximum efficiency is found for each stage from Eq. 4-70.

A similar analysis can be carried out for a maximum power generator in which the load resistance is set equal to the internal resistance of the generator as was indicated in Section 4.4.4.

We next consider a device consisting of an infinite number of stages, each having an infinitesimal temperature difference across it. Each stage will be assumed to have had its resistance ratio adjusted to maximize its efficiency. It is useful to consider such a device since (1) the result places an upper limit on the efficiency obtainable with a given material over a given temperature range; and (2) the result can be shown to be exact, even for an arbitrary temperature dependence of the material parameters [1]. However, in our development we will make the usual assumption of temperature independent properties.

We consider an infinite-stage generator similar to that illustrated in Fig. 4-11. In Appendix D we developed an expression for the efficiency of a thermoelectric generator with an infinitesimal temperature difference of dT across it as

$$\eta_t = \frac{dT}{T} \frac{(1 + ZT)^{1/2} - 1}{(1 + ZT)^{1/2} + 1}. \qquad (4\text{-}76)$$

We recall our use of the term "effectiveness" or "reduced efficiency" in Appendix D as

$$\eta = \frac{(1 + ZT)^{1/2} - 1}{(1 + ZT)^{1/2} + 1}. \qquad (4\text{-}77)$$

We may then state the thermal efficiency for the kth stage, by combining Eqs. 4-76 and 4-77:

$$\frac{dq_k}{q_k} = \eta(T) \frac{dT_k}{T_k}. \qquad (4\text{-}78)$$

Integrating Eq. 4-78 from the first stage to the last stage yields

$$\ln (q_0/q_N) = -\int_{T_C}^{T_H} \eta(T) \frac{dT}{T}. \qquad (4\text{-}79)$$

The overall thermal efficiency is, of course, by definition

$$\eta_t = 1 - q_0/q_N. \qquad (4\text{-}80)$$

Thus, combining Eqs. 4-79 and 4-80 gives

$$\eta_t = 1 - \exp\left[-\int_{T_C}^{T_H} \eta(T) \frac{dT}{T} \right]. \qquad (4\text{-}81)$$

The integration of this equation may be carried out graphically or numerically. Ure and Heikes [1] have reported that even theoretically, infinite staging causes very little increase in thermal efficiency. They showed that using an average parameter analysis on a single-stage device gives a good approximation (within 7 percent) to an infinite-stage device operating over the same temperature difference. Any real thermoelectric device will always have an efficiency less than that predicted by Eq. 4-81.

4.4.6 Segmented arm generators. There is another approach besides staging that allows the use of several different materials to span a given tem-

perature range. This approach consists of fabricating segmented couples
such that each of the materials is operating over a temperature range where
its figure of merit is highest. Figure 4-13 illustrates a segmented generator
in which the *p*-type arm is made up of *j'* different materials and the *n*-type
arm is made up of *j* different materials.

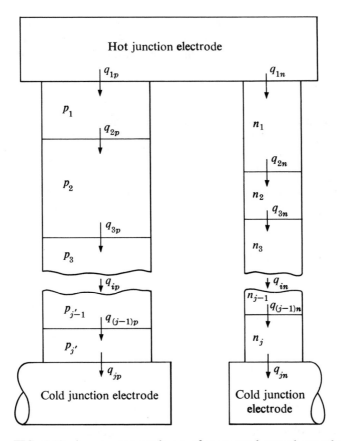

FIG. 4-13. A generator made up of segmented arm thermoelectric elements.

Ure and Heikes [1] have demonstrated why the theoretical efficiency
of a generator having segmented arms is always less than or equal to the
theoretical efficiency of the corresponding multistage generator which uses
the same materials over the same temperature ranges. They note that the
difference in efficiency may be small if the materials in each arm have similar
properties, but the segmented generator will have a significantly lower theo-

retical efficiency than the cascaded generator if the various materials in each arm have widely different properties.

The calculation of the efficiency of a segmented device is not so simple as for the multistage device which was done in Section 4.4.5. No such simple analytical solution exists in this case because the relative lengths of the segments are a function of the current and hence of the load resistance. The lengths of the segments are determined by specifying the desired interface temperature and the condition that the total heat flowing into any interface must be zero. For the interface between the ith and ith $+ 1$ segments in the p-type material in the generator illustrated in Fig. 4-13 the boundary condition can be expressed as

$$\lambda_{p,i}(\Delta T_{p,i}/l_{p,i}) + \tfrac{1}{2}\rho_{p,i}J_p^2 l_{p,i} - \lambda_{p,i+1}(\Delta T_{p,i+1}/l_{p,i+1})$$
$$+ \tfrac{1}{2}\rho_{p,i+1}J_p^2 l_{p,i+1} - (\alpha_{p,i+1} - \alpha_{p,i})T_{p,i}J_p = 0, \quad (4\text{-}82)$$

where $J_p = I/A_p$ is the current density in the p-type arm and $\Delta T_{p,i} = T_{p,i} - T_{p,i+1}$. The first four terms represent the heat added to the interface by the thermal conduction process, while the last term is a Peltier heat due to the junction of dissimilar materials.

An expression for the efficiency of a device like that in Fig. 4-13 can be written as

$$\eta_t = \frac{I^2 R_o}{\lambda_{n1}\gamma_{n1}\,\Delta T_{n1} + \lambda_{p1}\gamma_{p1}\,\Delta T_{p1} - \tfrac{1}{2}I^2[\rho_{n1}/\gamma_{n1} + \rho_{p1}/\gamma_{p1}] + \pi_{p1,n1}I}, \quad (4\text{-}83)$$

where

$$I = \frac{\sum\limits_i (\alpha_{p,i}\,\Delta T_{p,i} - \alpha_{n,i}\,\Delta T_{n,i})}{R_o + \sum\limits_i [(\rho_{n,i}/\gamma_{n,i}) + (\rho_{p,i}/\gamma_{p,i})]}. \quad (4\text{-}84)$$

At each interface a boundary condition similar to Eq. 4-82 must be satisfied. In general, it is not possible to determine analytically the optimum values of R_o and the γ's as can be done in the case of single element arms. It is usually necessary to resort to various approximation techniques or to use a high-speed computer. In fact, Swanson, Somers and Heikes [3] have shown that this problem may be solved to any degree of accuracy desired. However they also show that there is a simpler procedure that is accurate enough for most applications. Their procedure consists of simply determining the required length of each segment by treating the heat flow at zero current. Using these lengths it is then possible to calculate average values of ρ, λ, and α for the entire segmented arms. Using these values of ρ, λ, and α along with the hot and cold junction temperatures, one may calculate R_o, A_n/A_p, and η by the use of the equations developed for the single-stage generator.

Bates and Weinstein [4] constructed a segmented generator of PbTe and Si-Ge which compliment each other over the temperature interval from

50°C to 1000°C. Their experimental results agreed to within 5 percent of their theoretical calculations. Their generator achieved an efficiency of 8.7 percent with a hot shoe temperature of 800°C. They felt that if a hot junction temperature of 1000°C were used, efficiencies greater than 10 percent could be achieved.

4.4.7   Temperature dependent material properties. Even a cursory examination of the material properties given in Appendix C reveals that thermoelectric properties are far from temperature independent. While the derivation of the differential equations that describe the performance of such materials in generators and refrigerators is relatively straightforward, obtaining exact solutions from them is not. Because the exact procedure [5] is lengthy and requires computer methods in most cases, approximate methods have usually been used to incorporate temperature dependence of properties. These methods are based on determining suitable averages of α, ρ, and λ. Once these averages have been determined, they are then treated as temperature independent quantities. The methods described here are from Ref. [1].

The simplest approach is to use the notion of a simple average,

$$\bar{x} \equiv (1/\Delta T) \int_{T_C}^{T_H} x(T)\, dT. \qquad (4\text{-}85)$$

Ure and Heikes [1] suggest a slight modification of this approach; calculate $\bar{\alpha}$ and $\bar{\lambda}$ by Eq. 4-85 and ρ_{av} as follows:

$$\rho_{av} = (1/\bar{\lambda}\,\Delta T) \int_{T_C}^{T_H} \rho(T)\lambda(T)\, dT. \qquad (4\text{-}86)$$

The reason for using this technique is that for $I = 0$ they give the correct internal resistance R, thermal conductance K, and voltage V when used in the constant property equations [1].

It may also be shown that for $I \neq 0$ when $\bar{\alpha}$, $\bar{\rho}$, and $\bar{\lambda}$ are defined by Eq. 4-85 they will yield the correct values for K, R, and V if the temperature is a linear function of x.

Except in those cases where the temperature differences are extremely large or errors greater than 10 percent are not tolerable, more elaborate techniques do not appear to be justified [1]. It should also be noted that dependence on properties other than temperature may also influence device performance. Ybarrondo and Sunderland [6] have analyzed the effect of spatially dependent properties on the performance of thermoelectric heat pumps.

4.4.8   Design of a thermoelectric generator. We now consider in some detail the design of a thermoelectric generator using the properties of real materials. We will calculate all the relevant quantities that a designer would

be interested in knowing in order to accomplish a specific task. The properties of the materials are from Appendix C.

Problem. Design a thermoelectric generator to operate between 27°C and 327°C. Consider both a maximum efficiency and maximum power design. In addition to finding the power output and thermal efficiency of the device, find its voltage, current, and the required heat input.

Solution. From Appendix C we find that at the mean temperature of the generator, 177°C (450°K), the n- and p-type materials with the highest figures of merit are:

n-type	p-type
75% Bi$_2$Te$_3$, 25% Bi$_2$Se$_3$	25% Bi$_2$Te$_3$, 75% Sb$_2$Te$_3$ (1.75% excess Se)
$\alpha = -195 \times 10^{-6}$ volts/°C $\rho = 1.35 \times 10^{-3}$ ohm-cm $Z = 2.05 \times 10^{-3}$ (°K)$^{-1}$	$\alpha = +230 \times 10^{-6}$ volt/°C $\rho = 1.75 \times 10^{-3}$ ohm-cm $Z = 2.50 \times 10^{-3}$ (°K)$^{-1}$

Equation 4-46 expresses the figure of merit for a combination of materials that make up a couple. The figure of merit for a single material is generally defined as

$$Z = \frac{\alpha^2}{\rho\lambda}. \tag{4-87}$$

We may now use this definition to obtain the thermal conductivity† for the two materials;

$$\lambda_n = \frac{\alpha_n^2}{\rho_n Z_n} = \frac{(-195 \times 10^{-6})^2}{(1.35 \times 10^{-3})(2.05 \times 10^{-3})} = 0.014 \frac{\text{watt}}{\text{cm°C}};$$

$$\lambda_p = \frac{\alpha_p^2}{\rho_p Z_p} = \frac{(230 \times 10^{-6})^2}{(1.75 \times 10^{-3})(2.5 \times 10^{-3})} = 0.012 \frac{\text{watt}}{\text{cm°C}}.$$

The optimal figure of merit with respect to geometry adjustments for the combination of materials‡ is found from Eq. 4-46:

$$Z^* = \frac{\alpha^2}{[(\rho_n\lambda_n)^{1/2} + (\rho_p\lambda_p)^{1/2}]^2}$$

$$= \frac{[(195 + 230) \times 10^{-6}]^2}{[(1.35 \times 10^{-3} \times 14 \times 10^{-3})^{1/2} + (1.75 \times 10^{-3} \times 12 \times 10^{-3})^{1/2}]^2}$$

$$= 2.26 \times 10^{-3} \text{ (°K)}^{-1}.$$

† Researchers have found it considerably easier to measure the Seebeck coefficient, electrical resistivity, and figure of merit than to measure the thermal conductivity and calculate the figure of merit of a material. Methods of obtaining these values may be found in the standard references on thermoelectricity [7], [8].

‡ It should be noted that, in general, the figure of merit for the combination of materials is not the simple average of the two separate figures of merit. In this example, however, it is very close to that value.

The ratio of areas to lengths which minimizes the RK product is found from Eq. 4-44 to be

$$\gamma_n/\gamma_p = [\rho_n\lambda_p/(\rho_p\lambda_n)]^{1/2} = [1.35 \times 1.2/(1.75 \times 1.4)]^{1/2} = 0.81.$$

We now make one further assumption: that the ratio of the area of the n-type element to its length is 1 cm and that the length of each element is 1 cm,

$$\gamma_n = \frac{A_n}{l_n} = 1 \text{ cm}$$

and thus

$$\gamma_p = 1/0.81 = 1.24 \text{ cm}.$$

The thermal conductance from Eq. 4-36 is

$$K = \lambda_n\gamma_n + \lambda_p\gamma_p = (14 \times 10^{-3})(1) + (12 \times 10^{-3})(1.24) = 28.8 \times 10^{-3} \text{ watts/}^\circ\text{C}$$

and the internal electrical resistance may be calculated from Eq. 4-37 as

$$R = \rho_n/\gamma_n + \rho_p/\gamma_p = 1.35 \times 10^{-3}/1 + 1.75 \times 10^{-3}/1.24 = 2.76 \times 10^{-3} \text{ ohm}.$$

The optimum resistance ratio is found from Eq. 4-48:

$$m'_{\text{opt}} = (1 + Z^*T_{\text{av}})^{1/2} = (1 + 2.26 \times 10^{-3} \times 450)^{1/2} = 1.42$$

and thus the external resistance is

$$m'_{\text{opt}} = 1.42 = R_o/2.76 \times 10^{-3}$$
$$R_o = 3.92 \times 10^{-3} \text{ ohms}.$$

The open circuit voltage is simply the Seebeck coefficient for both legs combined times the temperature difference across the legs,

$$V_{oc} = \alpha \Delta T = [(|-195| + |+230|) \times 10^{-6}][300] = 0.128 \text{ volt}$$

and the optimum current may be found from Eq. 4-39:

$$I_{\text{opt}} = \frac{\alpha \Delta T}{R(m'_{\text{opt}} + 1)} = \frac{0.128}{2.76 \times 10^{-3}(1.42 + 1)} = 19.2 \text{ amp}.$$

The power output is the current squared times the load resistance,

$$P_o = I^2R_o = (19.2)^2(3.92 \times 10^{-3}) = 1.44 \text{ watts}.$$

We now find the power density by computing the total cross-sectional area of the semiconducting material. We assumed earlier that $\gamma_n = 1$ cm and that the length of both elements is 1 cm. Thus

$$A_n = 1 \text{ cm}^2$$

and from the calculated value for the p-type element of $\gamma_p = 1.24$ cm then

$$A_p = 1.24 \text{ cm}^2.$$

Thus the total cross-sectional area of both legs is

$$A_{\text{tot}} = 2.24 \text{ cm}^2$$

and the power density is

$$P_o/A_{\text{tot}} = \frac{1.44}{2.24} = 0.642 \text{ watt/cm}^2.$$

The power input to the device is found from Eq. 4-35

$$q_H = K\,\Delta T + \alpha T_H I - \tfrac{1}{2}I^2 R$$
$$= (28.8 \times 10^{-3})(300) + (425 \times 10^{-6})(600)(19.2) - \tfrac{1}{2}(19.2)^2(2.76 \times 10^{-3})$$
$$= 8.65 + 4.90 - 0.51$$
$$= 13.04 \text{ watts.}$$

It is observed that most of the heat supplied is due to simple thermal conduction; the Peltier effect, however, accounts for almost 40 percent of the total. The thermal efficiency may be computed from Eq. 4-40 as

$$\eta_t = \frac{P_o}{q_H} = \frac{1.44}{13.04} = 11.03 \text{ percent.}$$

We may check the accuracy of these calculations by means of Eq. 4-49,

$$\eta_{t(\text{max})} = \frac{(m'_{\text{opt}} - 1)(\Delta T/T_H)}{m'_{\text{opt}} + T_C/T_H} = \frac{(1.42 - 1)(300/600)}{1.42 + 300/600} = 10.95 \text{ percent,}$$

which checks within slide rule accuracy.

We consider next the problem of operating this same generator at maximum power. Under this condition the load resistance has the same value as the internal resistance, thus the current is

$$I_{mp} = \frac{\alpha\,\Delta T}{2R} = \frac{0.128}{2(2.76 \times 10^{-3})} = 23.2 \text{ amp};$$

the power delivered is

$$P_o = I^2 R_o = (23.2)^2(2.76 \times 10^{-3}) = 1.48 \text{ watts};$$

and the power density is

$$P/A_{\text{tot}} = 1.48/2.24 = 0.662 \text{ watt/cm}^2.$$

The generator's thermal efficiency is calculated from Eq. 4-51 to be

$$\eta_{t(mp)} = \frac{\Delta T/T_H}{4/(Z^*T_H) + 2 - \tfrac{1}{2}(\Delta T/T_H)}$$
$$= \frac{300/600}{4/(2.26 \times 10^{-3} \times 600) + 2 - \tfrac{1}{2}(300/600)} = \frac{0.5}{2.93 + 2 - 0.25}$$
$$= 10.70 \text{ percent.}$$

In this case we have increased the power output at the expense of the thermal efficiency.

We next consider the possibility of designing the generator to yield the maximum power density. Equation 4-53 gives the area ratio which maximizes the power per total cross-sectional area:

$$\frac{A_n}{A_p} = \left[\frac{\rho_n}{\rho_p}\right]^{1/2} = \left[\frac{1.35}{1.75}\right]^{1/2} = 0.88.$$

If $\gamma_n = 1$ cm (with $A_n = 1$ cm^2 and $l_n = 1$ cm), then $\gamma_p = (1/0.88) = 1.14$.

From Eq. 4-37 we find the electrical resistance is

$$R = \rho_n/\gamma_n + \rho_p/\gamma_p = 1.35 \times 10^{-3}/1 + 1.75 \times 10^{-3}/1.14$$
$$= 2.88 \times 10^{-3} \text{ ohms,}$$

which for maximum power is also the external load resistance R_o. Thus the current is

$$I_{mpd} = \frac{\alpha \, \Delta T}{2R} = \frac{0.128}{2(2.88 \times 10^{-3})} = 22.20 \, \text{amp.}$$

The power output is

$$P_{o(mpd)} = I^2 R_o = (22.2)^2 (2.88 \times 10^{-3}) = 1.42 \, \text{watts.}$$

The total cross-sectional area of the elements is

$$A_{\text{tot}} = A_n + A_p = 1 + 1.14 = 2.14 \, \text{cm}^2$$

and thus the power density is

$$\frac{P_{o(mpd)}}{A_{\text{tot}}} = \frac{1.42}{2.14} = 0.665 \, \text{watt/cm}^2,$$

a very slight increase in power density over the simple maximum power case. On a large generator even this small difference could be important. The efficiency of the maximum power density case is the same as that found for the maximum power case. This is easily observed from Eq. 4-51.

4.5 ANALYSIS OF A THERMOELECTRIC COOLER

We will now briefly consider the performance of a direct energy conversion device that does not have the goal of converting heat to electrical power; a thermoelectric cooler transports heat from a low temperature reservoir to a high temperature one by the passage of an electric current through a junction of dissimilar materials. Once again we consider a unit made of n-type and p-type semiconductors as is illustrated in Fig. 4-14. The positive direction for the current is from n to p at the cold junction as in the figure.

The three quantities of interest in evaluating the performance of a thermoelectric cooler are: the coefficient of performance, the heat pumping rate, and the maximum temperature difference that the device will produce. All three quantities are very much dependent on the temperature at which the device operates. All the assumptions made in carrying out the analysis on the thermoelectric generator are assumed to hold for the thermoelectric cooler.

4.5.1 Coefficient of performance. The coefficient of performance β_t is defined as the rate of heat removed from the cold reservoir q_C divided by the electrical power input P,

$$\beta_t = q_C / P. \tag{4-88}$$

The rate at which heat is removed from the cold reservoir depends on

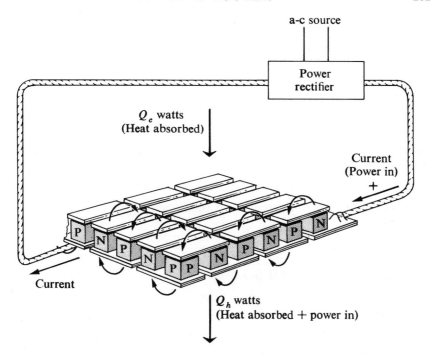

FIG. 4-14. A thermoelectric cooler.

the same three terms that appeared in calculating the heat supplied to the power generator in Section 4.4. The heat removed is that due to the Peltier effect, minus one-half of the Joule heat that flows back to the cold junction, minus the conduction heat due to the temperature difference of the two junctions. Thus

$$q_C = \alpha T_C I - \tfrac{1}{2}I^2 R - K\,\Delta T. \tag{4-89}$$

The voltage that must be applied to the couple is the sum of two terms: (1) the IR rise across the couple, and (2) the voltage that must be overcome because of the Seebeck effect,

$$V = \alpha\,\Delta T + IR. \tag{4-90}$$

The power input is

$$P = VI = \alpha I\,\Delta T + I^2 R. \tag{4-91}$$

The coefficient of performance of the couple is now obtained by substituting Eqs. 4-89 and 4-91 into Eq. 4-88:

$$\beta_t = \frac{\alpha T_C I - \tfrac{1}{2}I^2 R - K\,\Delta T}{\alpha I\,\Delta T + I^2 R}. \tag{4-92}$$

The problem of maximizing the coefficient of performance may be most easily handled by defining a new grouping of terms,

$$f = IR/\alpha, \tag{4-93}$$

which allows Eq. 4-92 to be written as

$$\beta_t = \frac{fT_C - \frac{1}{2}f^2 - RK\,\Delta T/\alpha^2}{f\,\Delta T + f^2}. \tag{4-94}$$

Maximization of Eq. 4-94 is dependent on minimizing the RK product and selecting an optimum value for f. The minimum value of RK was found to be given by Eq. 4-45 as

$$(RK)_{\min} = [(\rho_n\lambda_n)^{1/2} + (\rho_p\lambda_p)^{1/2}]^2. \tag{4-45}$$

The coefficient of performance of the couple with optimum geometry as given by Eq. 4-45 is

$$\beta_t = \frac{fT_C - \frac{1}{2}f^2 - \Delta T/Z^*}{f\,\Delta T + f^2}, \tag{4-95}$$

where Z^* is defined by Eq. 4-46 as

$$Z^* = \frac{\alpha^2}{[(\rho_n\lambda_n)^{1/2} + (\rho_p\lambda_p)^{1/2}]^2}. \tag{4-46}$$

We may now find the value of f that maximizes β_t by taking the derivative of β_t with respect to f and setting it equal to zero. The results of this operation are

$$f_{\text{opt}} = \frac{\Delta T}{(1 + Z^*T_{\text{av}})^{1/2} - 1} \tag{4-96}$$

and the optimum current is

$$I^* = \frac{\alpha\,\Delta T}{R[(1 + Z^*T_{\text{av}})^{1/2} - 1]}. \tag{4-97}$$

The maximum coefficient of performance may be found by substituting Eq. 4-96 into Eq. 4-95 to obtain

$$\beta_{t(\max)} = \frac{T_C}{\Delta T}\left[\frac{(1 + Z^*T_{\text{av}})^{1/2} - T_H/T_C}{(1 + Z^*T_{\text{av}})^{1/2} + 1}\right]. \tag{4-98}$$

In Fig. 4-15 the maximum coefficient of performance is plotted as a function of the cold junction temperature and the figure of merit. The applied voltage for optimum operation may be found by combining Eqs. 4-97 and 4-90 to yield

$$V = \frac{\alpha\,\Delta T(1 + Z^*T_{\text{av}})^{1/2}}{(1 + Z^*T_{\text{av}})^{1/2} - 1} \tag{4-99}$$

and the power input for maximum β_t is obtained from Eq. 4-91

$$P = \frac{(1 + Z^*T_{\text{av}})^{1/2}}{R}\left[\frac{\alpha\,\Delta T}{(1 + Z^*T_{\text{av}})^{1/2} - 1}\right]^2. \tag{4-100}$$

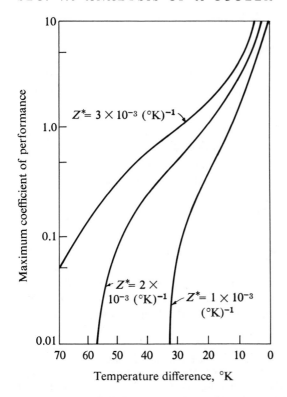

FIG. 4-15. The maximum coefficient of performance that can be achieved with a given temperature difference and a specified figure of merit for the couple. The hot shoe temperature is assumed to be 300°K.

4.5.2 Maximum heat-pumping rate.

The maximum rate of heat pumping may be found by taking the derivative of Eq. 4-89 with respect to the current I and setting the result equal to zero to obtain

$$I^* = \alpha T_C/R \qquad \text{(4-101)}$$

and the applied voltage under these conditions is found from Eq. 4-90 to be

$$V = \alpha T_H. \qquad \text{(4-102)}$$

The heat-pumping rate at the optimum current is simply

$$q_C = (\alpha^2 T_C^2/2R) - K \, \Delta T. \qquad \text{(4-103)}$$

Further optimizations with respect to the amount of thermoelectric material needed may also be carried out.

4.5.3 Maximum temperature difference. If we set the heat removed from the cold reservoir equal to zero, the temperature difference that the thermoelectric cooler will produce becomes a maximum. Thus from Eq. 4-103

$$\Delta T = \alpha^2 T_C^2 / (2RK). \tag{4-104}$$

This can be further increased by using the minimum value of the RK product as given by Eq. 4-45. Thus Eq. 4-104 becomes

$$\Delta T_{\max} = \frac{T_C^2 \alpha^2}{[(\rho_n \lambda_n)^{1/2} + (\rho_p \lambda_p)^{1/2}]^2} = \tfrac{1}{2} T_C^2 Z^*. \tag{4-105}$$

It should be noted that an estimate for the figure of merit of a given couple can be found by simply measuring the maximum temperature difference that the couple will produce and the cold junction temperature.

The minimum value of the cold junction temperature for a given hot junction temperature is obtained by solving Eq. 4-105 for T_C:

$$T_C = [(1 + 2Z^* T_H)^{1/2} - 1]/Z^*. \tag{4-106}$$

4.5.4 Design of a thermoelectric cooler. We now consider a set of numerical calculations for the design of a thermoelectric cooler. The material we will use will be the same material that was used in the design of the thermoelectric generator.

Problem. Design a thermoelectric cooler that will maintain one face of a piece of electronic equipment at 273°K (0°C). Heat will be dissipated from the hot junction at 327°K (54°C) to the surroundings at 300°K (27°C). The hot junction must be at a higher temperature than the surroundings in order to provide a driving force for the heat dissipation. Three watts must be continuously removed from the electronic equipment. We desire to minimize the power input to the cooler.

Solution. The temperature difference that the cooler must maintain is $T_H - T_C = 327 - 273 = 54\text{K}°$. The material properties at the average temperature of 300°K are:

n type	p type
75% Bi₂Te₃ 25% Bi₂Se₃	25% Bi₂Te₃ 75% Sb₂Te₃ (1.75% excess Se)
$\alpha = -165 \times 10^{-6}$ volts/°C $\rho = 1.05 \times 10^{-3}$ ohm-cm $Z = 2.00 \times 10^{-3}$ (°K)⁻¹	$\alpha = +210 \times 10^{-6}$ volts/°C $\rho = 0.98 \times 10^{-3}$ ohm-cm $Z = 3.50 \times 10^{-3}$ (°K)⁻¹

The thermal conductivity for each of the materials may be calculated from Eq. 4-87

$$\lambda_n = \frac{\alpha^2}{\rho Z} = \frac{(-165 \times 10^{-6})^2}{(1.05 \times 10^{-3})(2.00 \times 10^{-3})} = 0.013 \frac{\text{watt}}{\text{cm}^\circ\text{C}}$$

$$\lambda_p = \frac{\alpha^2}{\rho Z} = \frac{(210 \times 10^{-6})^2}{(0.98 \times 10^{-3})(3.50 \times 10^{-3})} = 0.012 \frac{\text{watt}}{\text{cm}^\circ\text{C}}.$$

The ratio of γ_n/γ_p that maximizes the coefficient of performance is the same as that given by Eq. 4-44

$$\gamma_n/\gamma_p = (\rho_n\lambda_p/\rho_p\lambda_n)^{1/2} = \left(\frac{1.05 \times 1.2}{0.98 \times 1.3}\right)^{1/2} = 0.995 \approx 1.00.$$

The maximum figure of merit for this combination of materials at room temperature is

$$Z^* = \frac{[(165 + 210) \times 10^{-6}]^2}{[(1.05 \times 10^{-3} \times 13 \times 10^{-3})^{1/2} + (0.98 \times 10^{-3} \times 12 \times 10^{-3})^{1/2}]^2}$$

$$= 2.76 \times 10^{-3} \, (^\circ\text{K})^{-1}.$$

We now make the same assumption that was made for the thermoelectric generator, that is, the ratio of the area of the n-type element to its length is 1 cm

$$\gamma_n = \frac{A_n}{l_n} = 1 \text{ cm}.$$

The thermal conductance is simply

$$K = \lambda_n\gamma_n + \lambda_p\gamma_p = (13 \times 10^{-3})(1) + (12 \times 10^{-3})(1) = 25 \times 10^{-3} \text{ watt/}^\circ\text{C}$$

and the internal electrical resistance is

$$R = \rho_n/\gamma_n + \rho_p/\gamma_p = 1.05 \times 10^{-3} + 0.98 \times 10^{-3} = 2.03 \times 10^{-3} \text{ ohm}.$$

The materials-temperature quantity that is used in calculating the optimum current is

$$(1 + Z^*T_{\text{av}})^{1/2} = (1 + 2.76 \times 10^{-3} \times 300)^{1/2} = 1.35,$$

where the mean temperature of the device is 286°K. From Eq. 4-97 the current that maximizes the coefficient of performance is

$$I^* = \frac{\alpha \, \Delta T}{R[(1 + Z^*T_{\text{av}})^{1/2} - 1]} = \frac{(375 \times 10^{-6})(54)}{2.03 \times 10^{-3}[1.35 - 1]} = 28.7 \text{ amp}.$$

Each couple will pump heat away from the cold junction at a rate given by Eq. 4-89

$$\begin{aligned} q_C &= \alpha T_C I - \tfrac{1}{2}I^2R - K\,\Delta T \\ &= (375 \times 10^{-6})(273)(28.7) - \tfrac{1}{2}(28.7)^2(2.03 \times 10^{-3}) - (25 \times 10^{-3})(54) \\ &= 2.93 - 0.83 - 1.35 = 0.74 \text{ watt}. \end{aligned}$$

Since we must remove 3 watts from the equipment, this means we require four coolers.

The coefficient of performance for a device operating at the optimum current is given by Eq. 4-98 as

$$\beta_{t(max)} = \frac{T_C}{\Delta T}\left[\frac{(1 + Z^*T_{av})^{1/2} - T_H/T_C}{(1 + Z^*T_{av})^{1/2} + 1}\right]$$

$$= \frac{273}{54}\left[\frac{1.35 - 327/273}{1.35 + 1}\right]$$

$$= 0.32$$

and thus the power input to each cooler is

$$P = q_c/\beta_t = \frac{0.75}{0.32} = 2.35 \text{ watts}$$

and for all four units the required power is 9.35 watts.

4.6 THE FIGURE OF MERIT

In our analysis of both the thermoelectric generator and cooler the importance of the materials parameter called the *figure of merit* has been amply demonstrated. The equations of performance and the plotted results show that even small increases in the figure of merit can produce significant changes in the thermal efficiency and coefficient of performance. In this section we will set forth some guide lines on materials selection, but we must recognize that the development of new thermoelectric materials to a certain extent is still more of an art than a science. Ure and Heikes [1] give the following warning:

It cannot be emphasized too strongly that the present state of solid-state theory is inadequate to handle this problem. Only vague guidelines can be given and it is necessary to use a considerable amount of empiricism in the selection and improvement of materials.

4.6.1 Why semiconductors? In Ch. 3 we defined the Wiedemann-Franz-Lorenz law as

$$\lambda\rho/T = (\pi^2/3)(k/e)^2 = L_w = 2.45 \times 10^{-8} \text{ watt-ohm/}^{\circ}\text{K}^2 \quad \textbf{(4-107)}$$

which holds over a fairly large range of temperatures for a variety of metals. Thus, an examination of the definition of the figure of merit for a single material, that is,

$$Z = \frac{\alpha^2}{\lambda\rho}, \quad \textbf{(4-108)}$$

reveals that for many metals the larger the Seebeck coefficient, the larger the figure of merit, since $\lambda\rho$ is a constant for a given metal. So far, no metallic thermocouple has realized a differential Seebeck coefficient of more than about 100 microvolts per degree Kelvin.

Certain semiconductors have absolute Seebeck coefficients of around 1000 microvolts per degree Kelvin. However, these compounds generally have a larger $\lambda\rho$ product than that predicted by the Wiedemann-Franz-Lorenz law. Thus one does not immediately arrive at the conclusion that semiconductors are better materials than metals for thermoelectric devices. However, it has been found that higher values of the figure of merit may be obtained in *certain semiconductors* than for any metal. Therefore, it is proper that we devote all of Ch. 3 and this section to a study of semiconductors.

The problem essentially boils down to finding materials with large figures of merit in the temperature ranges of interest. This involves the simultaneous control of three macroscopic parameters: the Seebeck coefficient, the electrical resistivity, and the thermal conductivity. Each of the three quantities is a function of the density of charge carriers. The Seebeck coefficient decreases as the charge carrier concentration increases; the electrical resistivity decreases as the charge carrier concentration increases, whereas the total thermal conductivity increases as the charge carrier concentration increases. The interrelationship among these parameters is illustrated in Fig. 4-16. The Seebeck coefficient is a complicated function of the density of charge carriers, n; the electrical resistivity, however, as will be recalled from Ch. 3, is

$$1/\rho = \sigma = ne\mu, \tag{4-109}$$

where e is the electronic charge and μ is the mobility of the charge carrier. The thermal conductivity for semiconductors is generally assumed to be made up of at least two parts, an electronic portion that may be calculated from the Wiedemann-Franz-Lorenz law and a lattice or phonon portion; thus

$$\lambda = \lambda_{el} + \lambda_l. \tag{4-110}$$

Since the phonon portion is generally regarded as independent of the carrier concentration, while the electronic portion is directly dependent on the carrier concentration, the total thermal conductivity increases as the carrier concentration increases.

Figure 4-16 has been divided rather arbitrarily into three sections. In the insulator portion the electrical resistivity is too large to produce thermoelectric materials of any value. At the other end of the scale, the metals have very low Seebeck coefficients and large thermal conductivities, which preclude them from having any value as thermoelectric materials. However, highly doped semiconductors or semimetals with carrier concentrations near 10^{19} (cm)$^{-3}$ have substantial Seebeck coefficients, low electrical resistivities, and fairly low thermal conductivities. This is shown by the peaking of the Z versus n curve near the right-hand end of the section classed as semiconductors.

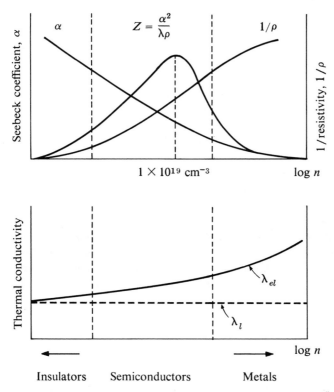

FIG. 4-16. A schematic representation of how the Seebeck coefficient, resistivity, and thermal conductivity depend on the concentration of extrinsic charge carriers.

4.6.2 Transport considerations of importance in the figure of merit.

We will now apply the transport theory outlined in Ch. 3 to define the solid state parameters of importance in calculating the figure of merit. To keep our discussion as simple as possible we make the following assumptions:

(1) The material is extrinsic and n type at the temperature in question. The extension to p-type material is easily carried out.

(2) The energy surfaces in the valence and conduction band are spheres in which the carrier energy is a parabolic function of the wave vector k. In this case the effective mass m is a constant. This assumption is sometimes called the *simple band approximation*.

(3) The material is assumed nondegenerate.†

† We now explain the meaning of the term nondegenerate in a manner slightly different from the approach used in Ch. 3. The term nondegenerate implies that the number of charge carriers is much less than the maximum number that could be packed into a given volume, considering an electron as having the dimension of a wave packet. One half of

By the addition of dopants to the material it is possible to adjust the carrier concentration so that the figure of merit is maximized. In Ch. 3 we found that the number of energy levels in the upper band in a given volume is given by

$$N_c = (2\pi m^* kT/h^2)^{3/2} \text{ per cm}^{-3}. \tag{4-111}$$

Furthermore, if the Fermi level expressed in units of kT is sufficiently below the bottom of the conduction band, that is,

$$\mathcal{E}_g/(kT) - \mathcal{E}_f/(kT) = \xi_g - \xi_f = \xi_{gf} > 1.25, \tag{4-112}$$

then the number of conduction electrons may be approximated as follows:

$$n = \frac{2N_c}{1 + \exp(\xi_{gf})} \approx 2N_c \exp(-\xi_{gf}), \tag{4-113}$$

where ξ_{gf} is a positive quantity. This rather simple expression is similar to the expression for the number of holes per unit volume obtained for a p-type material given in Ch. 3 as Eq. 3-43. As the carrier concentration is increased by increasing the concentration of donors, the Fermi level increases and the Fermi level moves from below the conduction band ($\xi_{gf} > 0$) up into the conduction band ($\xi_{gf} < 0$).

We will assume the electrical conductivity to be given by Eq. 3-52, that is,

$$\sigma = ne\mu. \tag{4-109}$$

The mobility μ is determined by the rate at which electrons are scattered by various defects in a rigid lattice. Following the notation of Ch. 3 we describe the scattering by a relaxation time τ that may be defined as the reciprocal of the rate at which a non-equilibrium distribution returns to equilibrium. We assume a relaxation time of the form

$$\tau(\mathcal{E}) = \Phi(T)\mathcal{E}^{-s}, \tag{4-114}$$

where s is the scattering constant corresponding to the mode of scattering that the electrons encounter. For acoustical scattering, s has the value $\frac{1}{2}$. Table 3-2 tabulates s for the most important scattering processes. From Eq. 4-18 we define the Seebeck coefficient for an n-type material as

$$\alpha_n = -k/e[(5/2 - s) + \mathcal{E}_g/kT - \mathcal{E}_f/kT] \tag{4-18}$$

and if we let

$$\delta = 5/2 - s \tag{4-115}$$

we may write Eq. 4-18 as

$$\alpha_n = -k/e(\delta + \xi_{gf}). \tag{4-116}$$

---

the maximum number that can be packed into a unit volume is given by Eq. 4-111. In the nondegenerate case the charge carriers may be treated as a classical electron or hole gas, each charge carrier having the kinetic energy kT. Under these conditions the familiar Boltzmann statistics of kinetic theory may be applied.

The thermal conductivity is assumed to consist of a lattice portion† and an electronic portion. The electronic portion is expressed in terms of the electrical conductivity by means of the Wiedemann-Franz-Lorenz law and a multiplying factor δ', which replaces the constant $(\pi^2/3)$ that appeared in Eq. 4-107 with a number that depends on the mode of scattering. Thus

$$\lambda = \lambda_l + \lambda_{el} = \lambda_l + \delta'(k/e)^2 T\sigma. \tag{4-117}$$

For the nondegenerate case δ and δ' are equal, both being defined by Eq. 4-115. Substituting Eqs. 4-109, 4-116, and 4-117 into Eq. 4-108 we obtain

$$Z = \frac{(k/e)^2 2 N_c e\mu(\delta + \xi_{gf})^2 \exp{(-\xi_{gf})}}{\lambda_l + \delta'(k/e)^2 2 N_c e\mu T \exp{(-\xi_{gf})}}. \tag{4-118}$$

If we multiply both sides by T to form a dimensionless figure of merit and divide the numerator and denominator by λ_l this expression becomes

$$ZT = \frac{A'(\delta + \xi_{gf})^2 \exp{(-\xi_{gf})}}{1 + \delta A' \exp{(-\xi_{gf})}}, \tag{4-119}$$

where

$$A' = (k^2/e)N_s T(m^*/m)^{3/2}(\mu/\lambda_l) \tag{4-120}$$

and

$$N_s = 2(2\pi mkT/h^2)^{3/2}, \tag{4-121}$$

which is similar to N_c, except that we have replaced the effective mass with the free electron mass. If we express μ in square centimeters per volt-second, T in degrees Kelvin, and λ_l in watts per centimeter-degree centigrade, the parameter A' is

$$A' = 0.8955(T/300)^{5/2}(m^*/m)^{3/2}(10^{-3}\mu/10^2\lambda_l). \tag{4-122}$$

We may now take the derivative of Eq. 4-119 with respect to ξ_{gf} and set it equal to zero to obtain the value of this quantity which maximizes the figure of merit, that is,

$$(\delta - 2 + \xi_{gf}) \exp{(\xi_{gf})} = 2\delta A'. \tag{4-123}$$

The values of ξ_{gf} that satisfy this expression are shown in Fig. 4-17 for the case of acoustic mode scattering ($s = \frac{1}{2}$, $\delta = \delta' = 2$). The dimensionless figure of merit to which this corresponds is also shown in the figure. This theory was first developed by Goldsmid and Douglas [9] and the development presented here follows Ure and Heikes [1].

Figure 4-17 indicates that values of ξ_{gf} that maximize the figure of merit lie in the range $0 < \xi_{gf} < 1.5$ for materials in which the scattering constant $s = \frac{1}{2}$. For $s = -1/2$ or $-3/2$, ξ_{gf} lies in the range $-5 < \xi_{gf} < 1$. The nondegenerate theory set forth here is not valid in this range, although the maximum figure of merit is reasonably close to that found by exact calcu-

---

† The lattice portion of the thermal conductivity is assumed to include all other forms of conductivity that might occur, such as excitons, radiation, and so forth.

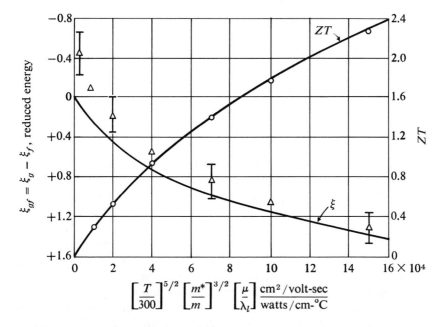

FIG. 4-17. The value of the reduced Fermi energy measured from the bottom of the conduction band which maximizes the figure of merit of an *n*-type semiconductor with acoustic lattice scattering. The maximum figure of merit is also shown. The figure of merit is within 0.5 percent of its maximum when ξ is within the limits shown. After Ure and Heikes [1].

lation. The exact calculation is given in Ref. [1]. The maximum figure of merit is determined by the values of s and A'. The larger A' is, the larger the figure of merit will be. Furthermore, if ξ_{fg} is fixed within the limits shown in Fig. 4-17, the figure of merit will be near its maximum, under the assumptions that were made at the beginning of this section.

It has been found in materials that have been doped to a maximum figure of merit, that the Seebeck coefficient is between 200 and 300 microvolts per degree centigrade. The carrier concentration that maximizes the figure of merit is found to lie in the range from 10^{18} to 10^{21} cm^{-3}. These carrier concentrations are much higher than those desired in many semiconductor devices, such as transistors and rectifiers. Thus, materials to be used in thermoelectric elements often do not have to be as pure as material used in other devices. In some materials it has been difficult to find dopants that are soluble enough to allow the carrier concentration to be raised to its optimum value.

Today, many researchers in the area of thermoelectric materials feel that an order of magnitude increase in the figure of merit of an n-type and p-type material would make thermoelectric power generation (and cooling) competitive with most of the contemporary modes of power generation and cooling. At present a materials breakthrough does not seem imminent, despite tremendous research efforts in this area.

4.7 DEVICE CONFIGURATIONS

The actual configuration that a thermoelectric device will assume in practice generally depends on two things:

(1) The location and primary function of the power generator: Is the generator to power the transmitter in a communications satellite, or is it to operate the light and horn on a harbor buoy?

(2) The primary source of energy to be used in the generator: Will the generator in the communication satellite be powered by a nuclear source, or will it use a mirror to concentrate sunlight on the hot junction?

In this section we will outline some of the major problems that must be solved preliminary to a configuration design, some of the actual configurations used in various generators, and the heat sources and sinks associated with these designs.

4.7.1 Major design problems. Utilizing the expanding technology associated with the transistor industry, researchers working on thermoelectric materials developed intermetallic compounds with good thermoelectric properties. At that time the thermoelectric device designer faced two problems almost as difficult to solve as the materials problem. They were:

(1) The fitting of thermoelectric elements with electrodes that would provide semiconductor-to-metal interfaces through which heat and electric current could easily flow.

(2) The development of a thermocouple structure that would accommodate the mechanical properties of thermoelectric materials. During thermal cycling a generator is subjected to thermal expansion and contraction due to temperature differences. Moreover, since the generator is a high heat flux device, good efficiency requires that the various interfaces be placed in compressive engagement, thereby mechanically stressing the semiconductor components as well.

With regard to the first problem, it has been necessary in almost every case to find a different solution for each alloy that has been used to construct generators. At low temperatures where Bi_2Te_3 and $BiSbTe_3$ can be used, a soft solder is permissible but direct soldering to the semiconductor is generally not possible. The usual procedure is to plate a thin layer of nickel onto the ends of the semiconductor and then solder to the nickel.

Care must be taken to avoid the presence of copper during this operation, since copper diffuses rapidly into Bi_2Te_3 at low temperatures.

For higher temperatures, with Bi_2SeTe_2, GeTe or PbTe contacts are usually made using nickel, iron or stainless steel. The semiconductor may be heated until just molten at the surface and then brought into contact with the metal. There is still more art than science in this method of bonding. Alternatively, a junction may be made by tin soldering, in which case tin is first diffused into the iron or steel and into the semiconductor. Iron electrodes simply held in place by compression have also been successfully used with PbTe elements. Very low contact resistances have been reported with this type of element-electrode junction.

Silicon germanium alloys are particularly well-suited to generators operating at relatively high temperatures. The material can be successfully metallurgically bonded to tungsten, whose thermal expansion coefficient matches that of the alloy quite closely. Tungsten has not been used as a hot junction electrode for air because it oxidizes quite rapidly at elevated temperatures. However, silicon-germanium itself or some other alloy of silicon has been used to form hot junction electrodes. The hot shoes serve both as heat reception plates and electrical connectors. The cold ends are connected to the heat rejection plate by means of an insulating disc as shown in Fig. 4-18. This configuration is known as an "Air-Vac" type thermo-

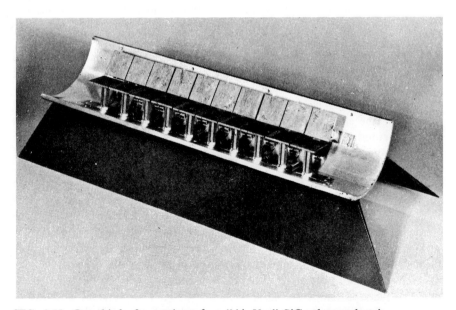

FIG. 4-18. One-third of a section of an "Air-Vac" SiGe thermoelectric module of the type used with radioisotope and fossil fuel heat sources. Photograph courtesy of RCA Corp.

couple [10]. Except for the metal cold junction contacts, the "Air-Vac" thermocouple is constructed from low vapor pressure, oxidation-resistant silicon alloys and so, as the name suggests, is suitable for operation in both high temperature air and vacuum environments. Because of the low weight of the silicon alloys from which the "Air-Vac" thermocouple is fabricated, this configuration has a low moment of inertia and has excellent resistance to dynamic shock. Thermocouples of this design have operated in air at temperatures to 950°C for prolonged periods with no degradation.

Another technique that has been used with silicon germanium alloys is ion plating. When hot shoe temperatures of approximately 1035°C are utilized with shoes made of silicon alloys with 15 weight percent molybdenum added, the silicon germanium legs undergo several reactions, including: (1) evaporation of silicon from the hot shoe, which is then free to react with SiO_2 or Al_2O_3 and generate the volatile SiO; (2) the residual O_2 and H_2O in the generator, especially at start-up, are free to react with the Si or Ge to form SiO and GeO respectively; and (3) the formation of GeO which can also lead to the generation of liquid Ge. With all three of the above reactions, the SiO and possibly the GeO condense on a cooler part of the thermoelectric legs. This condensate can cause increased thermal conductance by thermal shorting of the insulation and electrical shorting between the SiGe couple and the molybdenum foils in the insulation. By applying a thin coating of Si_3N_4 to the whole couple by means of ion plating, silicon vaporization is suppressed while insulating the couple. Reference [11] describes techniques for achieving this goal.

Because most semiconductors are relatively weak mechanically, device design could not proceed unless some safe means of mechanically holding the elements between the hot and cold junctions could be found. Compressive loading was finally decided upon as a relatively simple method of holding the elements between the thermal reservoirs; Fig. 4-19 illustrates this method of loading.

Some interesting observations were made on the mechanical behavior of n-type lead telluride ingots compressively mounted in a temperature gradient. It was found that very large single crystals bent readily without breaking, and that such elements when loaded compressively were subject to columnar buckling. The presence of grain boundaries was found to be desirable, as it rendered the ingot more resistant to creep or plastic flow.

Polycrystalline ingots of intermetallic compounds, while relatively brittle at room temperature, nevertheless do plasticly deform at elevated temperatures. Intimate mating of a hot junction electrode with the thermoelement takes place at temperatures near 1000°F under compression. The rate of creep of materials such as lead telluride alloys fortunately decreases with time at constant stress, so that a compressively loaded element gradually approaches an equilibrium length in service.

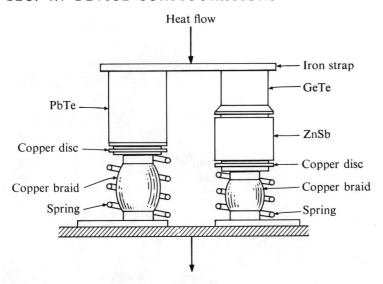

FIG. 4-19. A schematic of a spring-loaded thermoelectric element made of several different materials. This arrangement allows a material to be used in a temperature range where its properties are optimum.

   The solution of these two major problems on single couple devices allowed the design and construction of reliable generator structures composed of couple alloys that could produce sizable quantities of power over years of service.

4.7.2 Radioisotope-powered generators. The possibility of utilizing nuclear-powered thermoelectric generators in space vehicles is especially inviting because of their reliability and simplicity. Furthermore, radioisotopes suitable for fueling such units will become more plentiful in the future as by-products of nuclear reactors. We will outline some of the principles that must be kept in mind when designing a unit that is to be powered by a nuclear source. Complete details on the design of this type of unit may be found in Ref. [14].

   Radioisotopes present sources of energy with relatively high power densities whose natural decay rates determine, to a great extent, the lifetime of the power plant. This type of energy source lends itself to the following kinds of missions:

   (1) Earth orbit missions that require low power for long periods of time;

   (2) Lunar landings for which power is required during long lunar nights;

   (3) Probes into the dense atmosphere of Venus;

FIG. 4-20. Photograph of a simple, economical, thermoelectric generator that operates from the heat of combustion of an ordinary kerosene lamp yielding 0.2 watt at 9 volts. The unit stands 13 inches high and weighs $3\frac{1}{2}$ pounds when filled with kerosene. This system, which also provides light and heat, will run continuously for 24 hours on one tank of fuel. In the top view the hermetically sealed thermocouples, power leads, and the fins used to dissipate the waste heat can be seen in relation to the flame. Design details for conventionally fired units can be found in Refs. [12], [13]. Photograph courtesy of 3M Company.

(4) In general, missions that preclude the use of solar cells, or missions for which other energy sources are, for one reason or another, unsuitable.

This type of energy source loses some of its attractiveness for terrestrial converters because of the need for shielding to protect humans from the radiation. Nevertheless, these units are now beginning to find some application in supplying power for automatic weather information transmitters located above the Arctic Circle. In this type of installation the radio-active source is buried to a depth that makes remote the possibility of a man or animal receiving a harmful radiation dose. Two more disadvantages must be considered when utilizing nuclear sources: the availability of pres-ent-day isotopes is small and, based on today's energy conversion efficiency, the power-producing capability is on the order of several hundred watts. It should be noted that large quantities of isotopes are available, but the facilities to separate, purify, and process active materials into forms useful for power application are limited.

We will describe briefly the mechanism by which an atom or nucleus decays. A more detailed description can be found in a modern physics text such as Ref. [15]. If the outer electronic structure of an atom is given some extra energy so that the atom exists in an excited state with an energy higher than the ground state, then the atom will almost always get rid of this extra energy very quickly. Either the atom will emit one or more photons, thus causing it to go to the ground state, or if there is enough extra energy, an electron might be thrown off. In any event the atom, except under rare circumstances, will dispose of the extra energy and drop back to the ground state in about 10^{-8} sec. Many nuclei, on the other hand, have the ability to exist, for as long as billions of years in some cases, in a state that is unstable—that is, in a state in which the nucleus can, and eventually will, decay to a stable state. A nucleus may make a transition to a state of lower energy by emitting an alpha particle (alpha decay), an electron or positron† (beta radioactivity), or a photon (gamma radioactivity).

Alpha-emitting isotopes of practical interest are produced by reactor irradiation of heavy elements such as bismuth. The energy range of alphas from isotopes of emitters with useful half-lives is from 6 to 7 million electron volts (MeV), while the beta and gamma emissions are less than 3 MeV. For this reason alpha sources permit higher thermal power densities than do other isotopes. Because nearly all the energy of the alpha is absorbed in the source, the biological shielding requirements are greatly reduced.

Nearly all the radioactive fission products formed from reactor fuels are beta emitters. The attentuation of beta particles in the fuel and encapsulating material will often result in the generation of heat with a simultaneous re-lease of gamma or X rays. When large quantities of these fission products are concentrated in a capsule, the isotopic decay results in the release of thermal energy.

There are several hundred radioisotopes in existence today, but only a few of these can meet the criteria that would make them useful in the design of a generator. The most important criteria are:

---

† A positron, it will be recalled, is a particle with the mass of an electron but carrying a positive charge instead of a negative one.

(1) High specific power (watts per gram);

(2) Sufficient half-life to accomplish the mission;

(3) Benign effect of radiation from the source on encapsulation material and animal life in instances of release in air or water. (This includes the problem of supplying shielding necessary for adequate protection of personnel.)

(4) Reasonable cost of purifying and processing to a suitable form.

(5) Sufficient availability of isotope to make its use as an energy source practical.

In Table 4-1 we present some of the properties of isotopes which might be used to power generators. The data were compiled from Refs. [16] and [17] and, of course, are subject to revision.

The design of a thermoelectric generator energized by a nuclear source is identical to that carried out in Section 4.4.8. The design of the shell, however, and the structural problems that must be solved in arranging the thermocouple units around the nuclear source and providing adequate shielding for the source are considerable and are beyond the scope of this book. Some of the problems that must be considered in utilizing this type of generator in a space vehicle are: shielding for ground personnel before launch, shielding to provide adequate protection in case of abort during the launch period, the ablative qualities of the source enclosure, and the source during reentry. These problems and many more are described in detail in Ref. [14]. Once the required electrical energy output is stated, the design can be carried back to find the amount of source material necessary to yield the required output. The geometrical configuration of the source material and relevant structure can then be adjusted to give the maximum temperature the thermoelectric elements can stand.

An illustration of a low-cost, high-performance, 500-watt, radioisotope-powered thermoelectric generator is shown in Fig. 4-21.

In order to gain a feel for radioisotope-powered generators, we will examine a design that has been completed for the Viking mission to Mars. The Viking missions are to take place in the late 1970's and will conduct scientific investigations from orbit, during entry, and on the surface of Mars. Each Viking spacecraft will consist of an orbiter and lander. This mission will be man's first opportunity to obtain direct measurements within the Mars atmosphere and on the Mars surface.

The proposed power supplies follow the basic design of the units used on the Nimbus satellite (see Fig. 4-22). The Viking units incorporate a lead telluride/silver antimony telluride alloy thermoelectric material) segmented at the hot side with tin telluride. The 90 thermoelectric units are connected in a series-parallel array to provide current path redundancy. The Pu-238 heat source delivers 675 thermal watts to the thermoelectric units which in turn delivers 40 watts electrical at 4.4 volts for an overall efficiency of nearly

TABLE 4-1. PROPERTIES OF SEVERAL RADIOISOTOPES THAT MIGHT BE USED IN NUCLEAR-FUELED GENERATORS†

Isotope	Fuel form	Decay mode	Compound power density W/cm³	Compound power density W/gm	Half-life, years	Shielding required	Maximum operating temp, °C	Availability kW/yr (thermal)	Cost dollars/watt
Polonium 210	GdPo	α	820	82	0.38	minor	1600	70	150
Plutonium 238	PuO₂	α	3.7	0.41	86.4	minor	1000	11	750
Curium 242	Cm₂O₃	α	1050	98	0.45	neutron	1600	1.5	
Curium 244	Cm₂O₃	α	28.6	2.6	18.0	neutron	1600	8	3650
Promethium 147	Pm₂O₃	β	2.1	0.28	2.6	minor	1000	2	1000
Strontium 90	SrO SrF₂	β	1.2	0.24	28	heavy	1000	31	90

† Refs. [16] and [17].

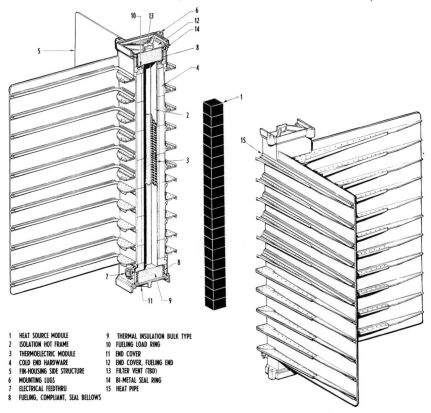

1	HEAT SOURCE MODULE	9	THERMAL INSULATION BULK TYPE
2	ISOLATION HOT FRAME	10	FUELING LOAD RING
3	THERMOELECTRIC MODULE	11	END COVER
4	COLD END HARDWARE	12	END COVER, FUELING END
5	FIN-HOUSING SIDE STRUCTURE	13	FILTER VENT (TBD)
6	MOUNTING LUGS	14	BI-METAL SEAL RING
7	ELECTRICAL FEEDTHRU	15	HEAT PIPE
8	FUELING, COMPLIANT, SEAL BELLOWS		

FIG. 4-21. A schematic of a low-cost, high-performance, 500-watt, radioisotope-powered thermoelectric generator. This design incorporates
an isothermal fin design that is made possible by water-filled heat pipes
extending out to the tips of the fins. Drawing courtesy of Teledyne Isotopes Energy Systems Division.

6 percent. The long half-life (86.4 years) ensures that there will be no appreciable decrease in power output during the life of the mission.

The unit has a hot junction temperature of 840°K and a cold junction
temperature of 470°K. Each of the two units to be mounted on the spacecraft (see Fig. 4-22) weighs less than 35 pounds and is about 16 inches high
and 24 inches across the fin tips. The unit has a specific power of 1.2 watts/
pound (2.6×10^{-3} kW/kg) [18].

Teledyne Corporation has been active in developing advanced RTG
units, including a generator for which they claim an initial efficiency in
excess of 10 percent [19]. Their design is in modular form for a 400-watt(e)
end-of-mission power output which is fueled by curium 244 and has a begin-
ning-of-life specific power of 5 watts/pound (1.1×10^{-2} kW/kg). The

1. RESERVOIR
2. THERMAL INSULATION
3. HEAT REJECTION FIN (6)
4. HEAT SHIELD END PLUG (2)
5. GETTER (2)
6. RADIOISOTOPE FUEL
7. CAPSULE SUPPORT RING (2)   12. RTG POWER OUTPUT RECEPTACLE
8. RADIOISOTOPE CAPSULE   13. THERMOELECTRIC COUPLE (90)
9. HEAT SHIELD
10. THERMOELECTRIC MODULE COLD SINK ASSEMBLY (6)
11. MODULE THERMAL INSULATION

FIG. 4-22. The SNAP-19 power supply for the Viking Lander vehicle. The unit uses plutonium 238 as a power source to supply an initial thermal power input of 682 watts. It delivers 35 watts(e) at 4.4 vdc. The unit has an overall mass of 16 kg (35.3 lb). The ninety thermocouples operate between a source temperature of 845°K (1060°F) and a fin root temperature of 440°K (330°F). The container is 39.6 cm high (15.6 in.) and has an overall diameter of 58.4 cm (23 in.). Drawing courtesy of Teledyne Isotopes Energy Systems Division.

modular design allows convenient selection of unit power levels from 80 watts to 800 watts in 80-watt increments with only minor changes to the housing length and configuration. Some of the details of this design are given in Table 4-2.

TABLE 4-2. 400-WATT HIGH-PERFORMANCE-DESIGN RTG GENERATOR†

	Beginning of life	End of life
Hot junction temperature, °C	800	708
Cold junction temperature, °C	183	161
Fuel (Cu_2O_3), outer surface temp., °C	962	—
Output power, watts(e)	519	400
Input power, watts(t)	4663	3778
Overall efficiency, percent	11.1	10.6
Load voltage, volts	30	30
Generator total weight, kg	45.4	
Specific power, watts/kg	11.4	8.8
Number of T/E couples	660	—
Total thermoelectric area, cm^2	486	—
n-leg material	gadolinium selenide	
p-leg material	copper selenide	

† After Ref. [19].

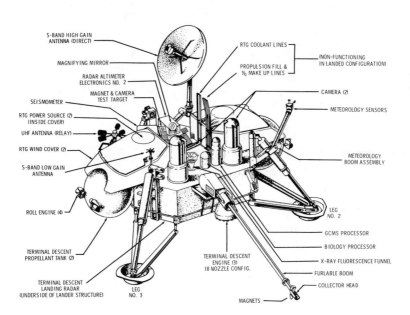

FIG. 4-23. Artist's concept of the Viking Spacecraft in the landed configuration. The completely outfitted Lander measures approximately 3 m (10 ft) across and is about 2 m (7 ft) tall. It has a mass of approximately 576 kg (1270 lb) without fuel. Drawing courtesy of Teledyne Isotopes Energy Systems Division.

4.7.3   Thermoelectric environmental control unit. Large amounts of electronic equipment can now be found in almost every location—from the bottom of Mariana Trench in the Pacific Ocean to the television equipment truck parked outside the local sports stadium. Since all electronic equipment generates heat and since its performance is frequently dependent on its environmental temperature, the need for effective compact cooling units has steadily grown. Purcupile, *et al.* [20] have presented a convincing argument and design for a thermoelectric environmental control unit to be used to cool the inside of U.S. Army electronic equipment vans. They argue that their design is one of high reliability, presenting a unit that eases the problem of maintenance because of its solid state nature.

The unit they designed and which is illustrated in Fig. 4-24 can provide

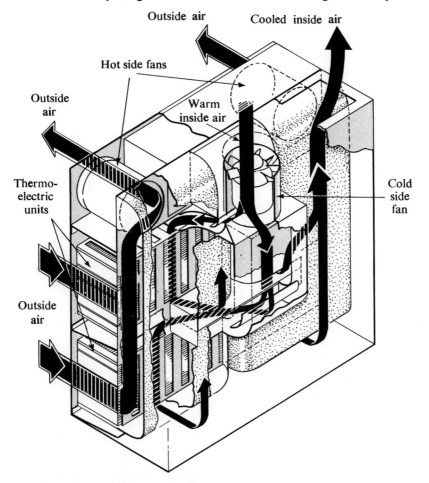

FIG. 4-24. Thermoelectric environmental control unit for an electronics van. After Ref. [20] with permission.

24,000 Btu/hr (2 tons or 7 kW) of cooling. The unit has overall dimensions of 40 in. by 40 in. by 20 in. and an overall weight of 338 lbs, including 142 lbs of thermoelectric material. The unit has a coefficient of performance of 1.0, requiring a nominal power input of 7 kW. The unit's design was based on an outside air temperature of 120°F and assumes that the return air that the unit draws in to be cooled is also at 120°F. In order to cool the hot side of the junctions the unit uses 1800 ft³/min of outside air drawn in by means of two ducted fans. At the same time 940 ft³/min of inside air is drawn downward by a single fan where it is then split into two paths. 100 ft³/min of the incoming air is directed over the power supply leaving a net flow of 840 ft³/min to pass over the cold side of thermoelectric modules. The cooled air is then returned to the van through one or both of the discharge openings at the top of the unit. Since the thermoelectric units require direct current and the power most likely to be available in the field is 50/60 or 400 Hz a-c, a power supply must be included in the unit.

Cooling is done by two thermoelectric cores, one located on top of the other. Each of the cores contains 12 modules with 108 thermocouples in each of the 12 modules. The p-type material is made from a pressed and sintered compound of bismuth-tellurium-antimony. The n-type material is a bismuth-tellurium-selenium compound made by the Bridgman method. The average figure of merit of each of the materials is about 3×10^{-3} (°K)$^{-1}$.

The design presented in Ref. [20] makes a strong argument for the use of thermoelectric cooling units to handle even difficult cooling jobs.

NOTATION

A	= area, cm²
A'	= function defined by Eq. 4-120, dimensionless
$\mathfrak{a}$	= constant in Eq. 3-33, 2.35×10^{15} cm^{-3} (°K)$^{-3/2}$
b	= mobility ratio, μ_n/μ_p, dimensionless
b	= dimension, cm
e	= electronic charge, coulombs
$\mathcal{E}$	= energy, electron volts, ergs, or joules
f	= IR/α, °K
h	= Planck's constant, erg-sec
I	= electric current, amp
J	= current density, amp/cm²
k	= Boltzmann's constant, erg/°K
k	= wave vector
K	= thermal conductance, watt/°K
l	= dimension, cm
L_w	= Wiedemann-Franz-Lorenz constant, 2.45×10^{-8} watt-ohm/°K²
m	= electron mass, gm

m^*	=	effective electron mass, gm
m'	=	R_o/R, dimensionless
n	=	electron density, cm^{-3}
N	=	number of couples or stages
N_c	=	equivalent number of energy levels in the conduction band, cm^{-3}
N_s	=	function defined by Eq. 4-121, cm^{-3}
p	=	hole density, cm^{-3}
P	=	electrical power, watts
P_o	=	electrical power output, watts
q	=	heat rate, watts
R	=	electrical resistance, ohms
R_o	=	load resistance, ohms
s	=	scattering constant, dimensionless
T	=	temperature, °K
V	=	electrical potential, volts
x	=	coordinate direction, cm
x	=	generalized material property
Z	=	figure of merit, (°K)$^{-1}$
α	=	Seebeck coefficient, volt/°K
β_t	=	coefficient of performance, dimensionless
γ	=	A/l, cm
δ	=	function defined by Eq. 4-115, dimensionless
δ'	=	multiplying constant in Eq. 4-117, dimensionless
η	=	efficiency, dimensionless
η_t	=	thermal efficiency, dimensionless
λ	=	thermal conductivity, watt/(cm-°K)
μ	=	mobility, cm²/(volt-sec)
ξ	=	$\mathcal{E}/(kT)$, dimensionless
π	=	$3.141\cdots$
π_T	=	Peltier coefficient, watt/amp
Π	=	product of terms
ρ	=	electrical resistivity, ohm-cm
σ	=	electrical conductivity, (ohm-cm)$^{-1}$
τ	=	relaxation time, seconds
τ'	=	Thomson coefficient, volt/°K
$\Phi(T)$	=	function of temperature in Eq. 4-114

Subscripts

A, B	=	signifies two different materials
av	=	average
C	=	cold
ca	=	Carnot
Cu	=	copper
el	=	electronic
f	=	Fermi level
g	=	energy gap
gf	=	defined by Eq. 4-112
H	=	hot
i	=	intrinsic, or indexing integer
j	=	junction
k	=	kth stage

l	= lattice
max	= maximum
min	= minimum
mp	= maximum power
mpd	= maximum power density
n	= electron
N	= nth item or stage
oc	= open circuit
opt	= optimum
p	= holes
R	= room
s	= side
tot	= total
0	= sink

Superscripts

*	= maximum or optimum value
overbar	= average

PROBLEMS

4-1. Find the current that will make the junction heat transfer be zero for a thermocouple with a Seebeck coefficient of 200 microvolts per °K; the temperature of the junction is 600°K with a junction resistance of 0.01 ohm.

Answer: 12 amp.

4-2. Derive Eq. 4-42 starting with Eq. 4-40.

4-3. Verify Eqs. 4-44 and 4-45.

4-4. Prove the correctness of Eqs. 4-48 and 4-49.

4-5. Derive Eq. 4-53.

4-6. For the case of maximum power per unit of cross-sectional area, derive an expression for the internal resistance, thermal conductance, and maximum power.

4-7. Find the thermal efficiency and power density for the example problem in Section 4.4.8 under the assumption that γ_n/γ_p is equal to one and that γ_n remains equal to 1 cm. Compare your results with those calculated in Section 4.4.8.

4-8. It is desired to design an electrical generator to produce 10 watts and to operate between room temperature and 100°C. Utilizing the same materials used in Section 4.4.8, complete the design. How many couples are required to produce the desired output? What is the heat input under the assumption of maximum efficiency, under the assumption of maximum power output? If the fuel used in the generator (CH_4, with a heat of combustion of 194 kcal per mole) is burned and transfers heat to the thermoelectric elements with an overall efficiency of 50 percent, find the rate of fuel consumption per hour.

4-9. Carry out the design of the generator described in Problem 4-8 utilizing as an n-type material a compound of 75 percent lead telluride (PbTe) and 25 percent tin telluride (SnTe) and a p-type material silver antimony telluride ($AgSbTe_2$). Assume that heat is supplied at 400°C and rejected at 327°C.

4-10. Find the maximum temperature difference that the material used in the generator of Problem 4-8 could produce if it were operated as a refrigerator.

4-11. Develop an expression for the heat delivered to the hot junction for a thermoelectric heating device similar to that given by Eq. 4-89 for heat removed from the cold junction. What is the coefficient of performance for this type of device? Derive an expression for the maximum coefficient of performance.

4-12. A thermoelectic heat pump is designed to extract heat from the atmosphere at 0°C and deliver it to a home to be maintained at 30°C. Choose the best of the materials from those listed in the Appendix C and find the maximum percentage savings in electric power consumed compared to direct I^2R heating.

4-13. Find the number of thermoelectric units required to maintain a special 25-watt amplifier at 100°C below room temperture (27°C) using the best material listed in Appendix C. Design the unit on the basis of operating it at the maximum heat pumping rate. Find the power input to the system. Assume that the entire 25-watt output must be removed from the amplifier.

4-14. Preliminary data from a competing manufacturer of thermoelectric materials indicate that a new thermocouple that they have developed will produce a maximum temperature drop of 100°C at a cold shoe temperature of 200°K. What is the figure of merit they are claiming for their material?

4-15. Derive Eq. 4-123.

4-16. If short elements are used in thermoelectric generators or coolers, contact resistance must be taken into account. If the contact resistance is given by r_n/A_n and r_p/A_p and they are the same at both ends of the elements, develop an expression for the apparent resistivity ρ' that may be used in all the equations derived in the chapter.

Answer: $\rho' = \rho + 2(r/l)$.

4-17. Find the maximum figure of merit at 300°K of an *n*-type extrinsic material with acoustic lattice scattering and a value of $A' = 1.4$. What must be the distance in electron volts between the bottom of the conduction band and the Fermi level for this to be a maximum?

4-18. If the material described in Problem 4-17 has the effective mass of its electrons equal to the rest mass of the electron and has a mobility of 1000 cm² per volt-sec, what is its lattice thermal conductivity?

4-19. Compute the volume and weight of strontium 90 required to fuel the generator designed in Section 4.4.8. Assume that the material will contain 25 percent impurities with a density of 4 gm per cm³. We desire the power output of the generator to be no less than that computed in Section 4.4.8 at the end of the first half-life.

4-20. If we elect to use curium 244 in the generator described in Problem 4-19 but still require that at the end of 285 days it have the power output of the example problem of Section 4.4.8, will we increase or decrease the weight of the generator? Assume that the impurity content and density of impurities remains the same.

4-21. Consider the same requirements as put forth in Problem 4-19, assuming this time that the fuel is polonium 210. Does the generator weight increase or decrease?

4-22. A specimen of a certain *p*-type material is found to produce a voltage of 2.4 mV when it has a temperature difference of 10°K imposed on it. The mean temperature of the specimen is 320°K. If scattering is by the acoustic lattice modes, what is the concentration of holes in the valence band?

Answer: 8.3×10^{18} cm⁻³.

4-23. For an extrinsic p-type semiconductor whose Fermi level is $4kT$ above the top of the valence band and whose charge carriers are scattered by ionized impurities, what is the Seebeck coefficient? If scattering is by the acoustic modes, what is the Seebeck coefficient?

4-24. Using the value of the Fermi level you found in Problem 3-8, calculate the material's Seebeck coefficient. Assume scattering by the optical modes.

4-25. You have been asked to design a power supply for a small solid state portable television set. It will be powered by an exothermic chemical reaction activated by dropping a catalyst into a container on the back of the set. The television set requires 15 watts at 9 volts. The generator will have a hot shoe temperature of 800°C and will dump heat to the environment from a radiator at a cold shoe temperature of 70°C. The unit will be designed so that each thermoelectric element is 1.2 cm long. Basing your design on maximum efficiency considerations and choosing your materials from those listed in Appendix C find: (a) the minimum number of thermoelectric couples required to meet the design requirements, (b) the size of the radiator required to dump the waste heat assuming an emissivity of 0.9, no convection, and surroundings that are at 20°C.

4-26. A certain p-type material has a Seebeck coefficient given by the expression

$$\alpha_p = (10^2 + 10T - 0.1T^2)\mu V/°C,$$

where T is in degrees centigrade. Find the following:
- (a) The average value of the Seebeck coefficient over the temperature range of interest.
- (b) The location of the Fermi level, in units of kT, assuming acoustic scattering by the lattice.
- (c) The hole concentration.

4-27. The material described in Problem 4-26 is to be used in a thermoelectric cooler. The n-type material always has a Seebeck coefficient of $\alpha_n = -\alpha_p$. The cooler is to maintain a diode at $-5°C$ while the hot junction is at 40°C. Find the amount of energy absorbed at the cold junction due to the Peltier effect if the junction is passing a current of 20 amp.

4-28. Using the materials and current given in Problem 4-27 and assuming that the following average properties also hold:

	p-type	n-type
resistivity, ohm-cm	1.0×10^{-3}	1.1×10^{-3}
thermal conductivity, watt/cm-°K	13.0×10^{-3}	15×10^{-3}

Find the net heat removed from the diode per unit time and the unit's coefficient of performance.

4-29. You have been asked to design a solar-powered thermoelectric generator for a satellite to be placed in orbit about Mercury. The temperature of the hot and cold junctions have been estimated to be 730°K and 560°K respectively.

The n-type material is a new one and you have only been supplied with some of its solid-state parameters: lattice-type scattering of electrons, width of energy gap 6.8 kT, Fermi level location 5.6 kT above top of valence band, conduction electron density equal to 10^{18} cm^{-3}, electron mobility 2×10^3 cm^2/volt-sec, thermal conductivity $\lambda = 11.0 \times 10^{-3}$ watt/cm-°C.

The p-type material should be chosen from those materials available in Appendix C.

The equipment that this unit will power requires 60 watts and is found to have an overall equivalent resistance of 6.67 ohms.

Pick some appropriate design criteria and determine the following:
(a) The load voltage.
(b) The least number of couples required to deliver the power.
(c) The least collector area required assuming that the collector is perfect and that the incident radiation in the neighborhood of Mercury is 0.89 watt/cm².

4-30. A design is desired for a thermoelectric power supply for an ice-formation warning device to be used on bridges in remote locations. A sensitive detector determines when ice has formed on the bridge surface and the warning device then transmits a signal to switch on caution lights ahead of the bridge and warning lights in the nearby highway patrol office.

The generator will be kerosene-fired, having a hot shoe temperature of 600°C. The generator will dump its heat to the environment from a plate radiator which has a temperature of 90°C.

You may select a *p*-type material from Appendix C.

The solid-state engineers are still working on the *n*-type material but they have given you the following information (at the mean temperature of the generator) based on their preliminary work:

lattice thermal conductivity = 6.65×10^{-3} watt/cm-°C
electrical resistivity = 2×10^{-3} ohm-cm

and the bottom of the conduction band is $1.2\,kT$ above the Fermi level. Scattering in this material is by acoustic modes and the engineers believe they can achieve the maximum figure of merit potential (according to the theory of Ure and Heikes) for this material.

The warning device operates at 28 volts and has an effective internal resistance of 14 ohms. Each thermoelectric element in the power supply is 1.2 cm long.

Pick some appropriate design criteria and determine the following:
(a) The properties of the *p*- and *n*-type material.
(b) The least number of couples required to deliver the power.
(c) The thermal efficiency of the generator.
(d) The power input to the generator.

4-31. The following pieces of information are known about a fully optimized thermoelectric cooler: the maximum heat-pumping rate is 10 watts with a cold shoe temperature of 5°C and a hot shoe temperature of 50°C; the zero load maximum ΔT is 85°C; the geometry parameter, γ, is 1.0 for both *n* and *p* elements; the supply voltage is 2.0 volts with a supply current of 16.65 amperes. Determine whether or not this unit will perform as expected. If it cannot perform as expected, how much cooling will it do?

REFERENCES

1. R. W. Ure, Jr. and R. R. Heikes, "Theoretical Calculation of Device Performance," in *Thermoelectricity: Science and Engineering*, eds. R. R. Heikes and R. W. Ure, Jr. (New York: Interscience Publishers, Inc., 1961), Chapter 15.

2. T. C. Harman, "Multiple Stage Thermoelectric Generation of Power," *Journal of Applied Physics*, 29 (1958), 1471.

3. B. W. Swanson, E. V. Somers, and R. R. Heikes, "Optimization of a Sandwiched Thermoelectric Device," *Journal of Heat Transfer*, 83 (1961), 77–82.

4. H. E. Bates and M. Weinstein, "On the Efficiency of Segmented SiGe-PbTe Thermocouples," *Intersociety Energy Conversion Engineering Conference, 1968*

Record, I.E.E.E. Publication 68 C 21 Energy (New York: Institute of Electrical and Electronic Engineers, Inc., 1968).

5. B. Sherman, R. Heikes, and R. Ure, "Calculation of Efficiency of Thermoelectric Devices," *Journal of Applied Physics*, 31 (1960), 1–16.

6. L. J. Ybarrondo and J. E. Sunderland, "Influence of Spatially Dependent Properties on the Performance of a Thermoelectric Heat Pump," *Advanced Energy Conversion*, 5 (1965), 383–405.

7. Paul H. Egli, ed., *Thermoelectricity* (New York: John Wiley & Sons, Inc., 1960), Chapters 14–22.

8. J. E. Bauerle, P. H. Sutter, and R. W. Ure, Jr., "Measurements of Properties of Thermoelectric Materials," in *Thermoelectricity: Science and Engineering*, eds. R. R. Heikes and R. W. Ure, Jr. (New York: Interscience Publishers, Inc., 1961), Chapter 10.

9. H. J. Goldsmid and R. W. Douglas, "The Use of Semiconductors in Thermoelectric Refrigeration," *British Journal of Applied Physics*, 5 (1954), 386.

10. R. L. Klem and A. G. F. Dingwall, "Silicon-Germanium Thermoelectric Power-Generating Devices," *Engineering Developments in Energy Conversion* (New York: American Society of Mechanical Engineers, 1965).

11. N. B. Elsner, "Ion Plating of SiGe Thermoelectric Couples with Si_3N_4 for Vaporization Suppression and Electrical Suppression," *9th Intersociety Energy Conversion Engineering Conference*, 1974 Proceedings (New York: American Society of Mechanical Engineers, 1974).

12. B. W. Swanson and E. V. Somers, "Optimization of a Conventional-Fuel–Fired Thermoelectric Generator," *Journal of Heat Transfer*, 81 (1959), 245–248.

13. A. Bayne Neild, Jr., "Portable Thermoelectric Generators," Paper No. 645A, Transactions of the SAE (1963).

14. W. H. Corliss and D. L. Harvey, *Radioisotope Power Generation* (Englewood Cliffs, New Jersey: Prentice-Hall, Inc., 1964).

15. C. H. Blanchard, C. R. Burnett, R. G. Stoner, and R. L. Weber, *Introduction to Modern Physics*. 2nd ed. (Englewood Cliffs, New Jersey: Prentice-Hall, Inc., 1969).

16. E. T. Mahefkey, Jr. and D. F. Berganini, "Radioisotope Power Subsystems for Space Application," Society of Automotive Engineers Paper No. 650791.

17. W. G. Ruehle, "The Kernel-Heater Concept for Multikilowatt-Radioisotope Power," *Intersociety Energy Conversion Engineering Conference, 1968 Record*, I.E.E.E. Publication 68 C 21 Energy (New York: Institute of Electrical and Electronic Engineers, Inc., 1968).

18. W. M. Brittain and S. T. Christenberry, "SNAP 19 Viking RTG Flight Configuration and Integration Testing," *9th Intersociety Energy Conversion Engineering Conference*, 1974 Proceedings (New York: American Society of Mechanical Engineers, 1974).

19. A. R. Lieberman and W. E. Osmeyer, "A 10% Efficient Economic RTG Design," *9th Intersociety Energy Conversion Engineering Conference*, 1974 Proceedings (New York: American Society of Mechanical Engineers, 1974).

20. J. C. Purcupile, R. E. Stillwagon, and R. E. Franseen, "Development of a Two-Ton Thermoelectric Environmental Control Unit for the U.S. Army," *Transactions of the American Society of Heating, Refrigeration, and Air Conditioning Engineers*, 74 (1968), Part II.

5   Photovoltaic Generators

Much of this book is concerned with the conversion of heat to electrical energy by various means. In this chapter we consider a method that does not involve heat but converts electromagnetic radiation directly to electrical power. By eliminating the intermediate step of conversion to heat we bypass the Carnot limitation on efficiency of heat engines. For this reason photovoltaic conversion has held out great promise to those who have worked in direct energy conversion. Unfortunately, for various reasons which we shall discuss, this promise has not yet been completely fulfilled.

In this chapter we shall discuss producing electrical power by exposing p–n junctions to electromagnetic radiation. The two chief sources of energy that have been considered for powering this type of converter are: (1) short wavelength† radiation such as that produced by radioactivity with wavelengths in the neighborhood of 0.01 A; and (2) sunlight, whose wavelength is in the range of 5000 A. We will concentrate our attention on the latter in this chapter; in Ch. 9 we will discuss briefly the possibility of utilizing the former in this type of energy converter. Because those converters that use light as their energy source have proved more practical, we will often refer to p–n junction energy converters as photovoltaic devices even though many of the principles we will discuss apply equally well to radioactively powered devices.

5.1   HISTORICAL PERSPECTIVE

Like most of the principles on which energy conversion devices are based, the photovoltaic effect is not a new discovery. Edmond Becquerel in 1839

† Where we give wavelengths in angstrom units, A; 1 angstrom = 10^{-8} cm.

noted that a voltage was developed when light was directed onto one of the electrodes in an electrolyte solution. The effect was first observed in a solid in 1877 by W. G. Adams and R. E. Day, who conducted experiments with selenium. Other early workers with solids included Schottky, Lange, and Grondahl, who did pioneering work in producing photovoltaic cells with selenium and cuprous oxide. This work led to the development of photo-electric exposure meters. In 1954 researchers turned to the problem of utiliz-ing the photovoltaic effect as a source of power. In that year several groups, including workers at the RCA and Bell Telephone Laboratories, achieved conversion efficiencies of about 6 percent by means of junctions of p-type and n-type semiconductors. These early junctions, commonly called p–n junctions, were made of cadmium sulfide and silicon. Later workers in the area have achieved efficiencies near 15 percent by using improved silicon p–n junctions. A review of developments in this field has been given by Bube [1].

5.2 A REVIEW OF RADIATION PRINCIPLES

We introduced in Ch. 3 the idea that energy is not indefinitely indivisible. We stated that the smallest piece of energy that could be transferred in a process was called a *quantum;* that light is a form of energy and a quantum of light we termed a *photon.* Planck suggested that the energy of a photon is proportional to the frequency of the radiation associated with it,

$$\varepsilon = h\nu, \tag{5-1}$$

where ε is the energy of the photon, h is Planck's constant [$= 6.62 \times 10^{-27}$ erg-sec], and ν is the frequency in cycles per second. Because we have asso-ciated a frequency with the radiation, giving it a wave characteristic, and at the same time have stated that energy is transferred in discrete amounts, giving it a corpuscular characteristic, we say that light has a dual nature—not explainable solely in terms of either waves or particles.

We note that Eq. 5-1 states that at any given frequency—which implies any given wavelength, since they are related by $c = \lambda\nu$ where c is the speed of propagation—radiation energy is always in whole multiples of $h\nu$, which represents a minimum energy. It can never be a fraction of this value because a photon of a given wavelength could not have less. We therefore consider radiation from the sun or any other source of radiation as a stream of energy chunks called photons, each one carrying an energy exactly equal to its frequency times Planck's constant.

Consider a beam of red light with a wavelength $\lambda = 6000$ A. We may find its energy in electron volts (using 3×10^{10} cm per sec for the speed of light) by a direct application of Eq. 5-1:

$$\varepsilon = h\nu = hc/\lambda = 6.62 \times 10^{-27} \text{ erg-sec}$$

$$\times \frac{3 \times 10^{10} \text{ cm/sec}}{6000 \times 10^{-8} \text{ cm}} = 3.31 \times 10^{-12} \text{ erg},$$

but by definition

$$1 \text{ electron volt (eV)} = 1.60 \times 10^{-19} \text{ joule} = 1.60 \times 10^{-12} \text{ erg}$$

so

$$\varepsilon = \frac{3.31 \times 10^{-12} \text{ erg}}{1.60 \times 10^{-12} \text{ erg/(eV)}} = 2.08 \text{ eV}.$$

It follows that the energy of a photon with a wavelength of 3000 A would have an energy of a little more than 4 eV.

Now we may consider the energy source with which we must work in utilizing photovoltaic devices. The spectral distribution of sunlight depends on many factors, including the three sources of atmospheric absorption, namely (a) atmospheric gases (O_2, N_2, and so on); (b) water vapor; and (c) dust. Each of these absorption mechanisms tends to deplete the ultraviolet in a preferential manner. The effect of these sources of absorption can be described by means of an optical path length m through which the light passes, and by means of the number of centimeters of precipitable water vapor w in the atmosphere. We define m by the relation $m = 1/\cos z$ where z is the angle between the line drawn through the observer and the zenith and the line through the observer and the sun. In the course of a day z varies from 90 deg to a minimum, $z_{\min}$, that occurs at noon; $z_{\min}$ also is a function of the season of the year between the limits $z_{\min} = \text{latitude} \pm 23.50$ deg. The simplest case is, of course, when $z_{\min} = 0$ and then $m = 1$.

The *photon flux* is a quantity useful in solar cell calculations; it is defined as the number of photons crossing a unit area perpendicular to the light beam per second. If we let Φ denote the intensity of the light in watts per square centimeter, then the number of photons carrying that energy N_{ph} may be computed quite simply if we make an assumption concerning the average energy of each photon. That is

$$\Phi = N_{ph}\varepsilon = N_{ph}h\nu_{av} = N_{ph}hc/\lambda_{av}. \tag{5-2}$$

If we assume that outside the atmosphere the solar spectrum has an intensity of 0.135 watt per cm² and that each photon carries on the average 1.48 eV, then we may calculate the photon flux as

$$N_{ph} = 0.135 \frac{\text{watts}}{\text{cm}^2} \times \frac{1}{1.48 \text{ eV}} \times \frac{\text{eV}}{1.60 \times 10^{-19} \text{ joule}} \times \frac{\text{joule}}{\text{watt-sec}}$$

$$= 5.8 \times 10^{17} (\text{cm}^2\text{-sec})^{-1}.$$

Table 5-1 gives some indication of the variation in solar intensity and the photon density for various values of m and w. The total number of solar photons N_{ph} as given by Table 5-1 is computed by summing the number of photons in the energy range from zero up to the maximum energy (about 4 eV) found in the solar spectrum.

TABLE 5-1. PARAMETERS OF THE SOLAR SPECTRUM AS A FUNCTION OF ABSORPTION CONDITIONS [2]

m	w	Comments	Φ (W/cm²)	$\mathcal{E}_{av}$ (eV)	N_{ph} (No./sec-cm²)
0	0	Outside atmosphere	0.135	1.48	5.8×10^{17}
1	0	Sea level, sun at zenith	0.106	1.32	5.0×10^{17}
2	0	Sea level, sun at 60 deg from zenith	0.088	1.28	4.3×10^{17}
3	0	Sea level, sun at 70.5 deg from zenith	0.075	1.21	3.9×10^{17}
1	2	About 50% relative humidity	0.103	1.25	4.8×10^{17}
3	5	Extreme condition	0.059	1.18	3.2×10^{17}
1	0	Cloudy day (7000°K Black Body)	0.012	1.44	5.2×10^{16}

In Fig. 5-1 we plot in arbitrary units an actual spectral distribution as a function of energy for several of the cases listed in Table 5-1. In Fig. 5-2 we show how these same conditions will affect the photon density as a function of the cutoff energy. That is, we plot the number of photons in the solar distribution per unit area per unit time whose energy exceeds the energy gap of the material.

5.3 OPTICAL EFFECTS IN SEMICONDUCTORS AND $p-n$ JUNCTIONS

To set the stage for considering the physical process of turning light into electricity in a $p-n$ junction it will be helpful to consider several other optical phenomena in semiconductors. It is interesting to note that many semiconductors that exhibit unusual properties under electrical and thermal excitation also exhibit interesting properties when irradiated with electro-magnetic waves of various frequencies. For example, silicon, a material that has found wide application in transistors, appears to have the typical metallic luster when viewed with ordinary light. When viewed under longer wavelength infrared radiation, however, silicon becomes transparent. If we

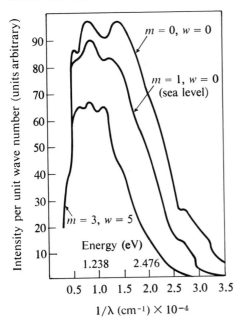

FIG. 5-1. The solar spectrum intensity per unit wave number as a function of the reciprocal of the wavelength (the energy) for various conditions. After Loferski [2] with permission.

view a specimen of silicon with very long-wave infrared radiation and slowly reduce the wavelength of the radiation, we note that the transparency of the specimen increases. Further reduction in wavelength brings us to a point where the specimen's opaqueness increases abruptly. The shorter wavelength radiation is of higher energy (recall Eq. 5-1: $\varepsilon = h\nu = hc/\lambda$) and thus when the radiation has a wavelength of 1.108 microns (10^{-6} meter $=$ 1 micron) it corresponds to an energy of 1.12 eV, which is the forbidden band width of silicon. Therefore, photons of this energy or greater are capable of exciting electrons from near the top of the valence band into energy levels near the bottom of the conduction band. This transition is accomplished at the expense of the photon's energy, which is absorbed during the process and makes the crystal opaque to this frequency of radiation. From this introduction we see that radiation experiments are capable of telling us quite a lot about the band structure of semiconductors. We will now explore briefly several more semiconductor properties which are useful in understanding photoconversion devices.

Photoconductivity is generally defined as the increase in electrical conductivity of a semiconductor element when radiation of the proper frequency

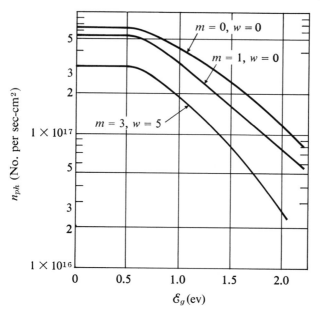

FIG. 5-2. The potential number of absorbed photons as a function of the cutoff energy (the width of the forbidden energy band). After Loferski [2] with permission.

is directed onto the semiconductor. The property has been widely exploited in devices designed to detect radiation. Photoconductivity occurs appreciably whenever radiation having an energy greater than the forbidden energy gap of the specimen is used to irradiate the semiconductor. We describe the phenomena of photoconductivity following the method of Azaroff [3].

When radiation is allowed to fall on a semiconductor and produces f electron-hole pairs per cm³-sec, we denote the increase in the density of electrons and holes by the following two equations:

$$\Delta n = f\tau_n^* \qquad \Delta p = f\tau_p^*, \qquad (5\text{-}3)$$

where the symbol τ^* denotes the effective lifetime of the carriers and the subscripts denote whether or not we are describing electrons or holes. We should note that this τ^* is not the same quantity as the mean relaxation time. We may now use an equation such as Eq. 3-63 to describe the change in electrical conductivity:

$$\Delta\sigma = e(\Delta n\mu_n + \Delta p\mu_p)$$
$$= ef(\tau_n^*\mu_n + \tau_p^*\mu_p). \qquad (5\text{-}4)$$

The contribution of electrons and holes to the increase in conductivity may be a function of their relative lifetimes or their mobilities or both. To measure $\Delta\sigma$ with accuracy it is necessary that it be of the same order of magnitude as the conductivity of the semiconductor without radiation. Thus crystals that are fairly good insulators (having relatively low dark conductivities), in general, make good photoconductors. For example, pure or compensated crystals of cadmium sulfide (CdS) are essentially insulators in the dark, having conductivities of about 10^{-12} (ohm-cm)$^{-1}$. When illuminated with light of a frequency that corresponds to an energy that is the width of the crystal's forbidden band, the conductivity may increase many-fold. Cadmium sulfide and cadmium telluride have similar characteristics in this respect.

The photocurrent I_s that is produced by illumination of a semiconductor that is an insulator in the dark may be expressed as a function of the following variables: F', the total number of electrons and holes produced each second by the absorbed photons; the effective lifetime; and the transit time

$$I_s = eF'\tau^*/T_r,\tag{5-5}$$

where T_r is the *transit time*—the time spent by an electron in moving between the two electrodes connected to the semiconductor. It may be determined from the interelectrode spacing and the mean drift velocity of the electrons to be

$$T_r = \frac{L}{\langle u \rangle} = \frac{L}{\mu E},\tag{5-6}$$

where μ is the drift mobility and E is the applied electric field. By expressing the electric field as the applied voltage divided by the interelectrode spacing, we write Eq. 5-6 as

$$T_r = \frac{L^2}{\mu V}.\tag{5-7}$$

The larger the effective lifetime τ^*, the greater will be the photocurrent I_s. If we imagine that the lifetime of an electron is greater than the lifetime of a hole, this means that holes are trapped quickly in recombination centers† while the free electron exists long enough to be swept out of the crystal

† The term *recombination center* or *trapping center* is another name for a spatially *localized energy state* such as those created by donor and acceptor impurities, dislocations, interstitial atoms, and so forth. As an example of the role these states play, consider a localized energy state lying far above the top of the valence band in an n-type semiconductor. These states are normally empty but there exists a finite probability that a free electron may transfer from a state in the conduction band to one of these lower-lying states. Because these states are at a lower energy, the transition by the electron is accompanied by an energy release either in the form of a photon or a phonon. The crystal imperfection is thus a "trap" for electrons. Similarly, a p-type specimen can contain *hole traps*. The term recombination center is generally reserved for an imperfection that has a high probability for capturing an electron from the conduction band and then losing the electron to the valence band, thus "capturing a hole"; recombination centers are generally located near the center of the forbidden band.

by the applied field. Since charge neutrality must be preserved, the negative electrode injects another electron until the free electron can recombine with a hole. Thus a photon may appear to cause more than one electron to be made available for conduction. This apparent gain is denoted by a gain factor

$$G = \frac{\tau^*}{T_r},$$ (5-8)

which is a direct index to the efficiency of a photoconductor, as can be seen by substituting G into Eq. 5-5. The gain factor can be increased by decreasing the transit time through the interelectrode spacing. It may also be increased by increasing the effective lifetime, which is inversely related to the drift velocity, the number of sites available for trapping, and the effectiveness of trapping centers.

The photoconversion device that has attained the highest efficiency is the p–n junction. A p–n junction can be made during the growing of a crystal, for example, by suddenly adding an excess of donor impurities to the melt from which the solidified crystal is being drawn (see Section 3.8.2 on the growth of semiconductor crystals).

Since the density of electrons is larger in the n-type region than in the p-type region, electrons on the n side of the junction diffuse down the concentration gradient to the p-type region where they recombine with free holes. Positive holes will flow at the same time toward the n-type region in the valence band. In a very short time (on the order of a millimicrosecond) the charging up process is completed, with the p-type region possessing an excess of negative charge and the n-type region taking on an excess of positive charge. A contact potential difference having an energy $\Delta \varepsilon$ develops across the junction of such a magnitude to just oppose the further flow of electrons and holes due to the concentration gradient. The region adjacent to the junction is said to contain a *space charge* and is sometimes referred to as a *transition region*. The extent of this region around the junction is 10^{-4} to 10^{-6} cm wide. The energy-level diagram corresponding to this final equilibrium condition is illustrated in Fig. 5-3. This contact potential causes the energy levels of the n-type region to be displaced downward and p-type region to be shifted upward so that the Fermi levels of the two regions remain horizontal and continuous at the junction. We generalize this observation further by restating a condition that had been previously assumed: *in a system in thermal equilibrium the Fermi level energy is constant throughout the entire system.* This is analogous to two containers filled with a liquid connected by a pipe in which the liquid seeks the same level in both containers so long as nothing disturbs the system. It should also be noted that this contact potential cannot be used to deliver power to an external load. As soon as we introduce connecting leads to the p–n junction, we introduce

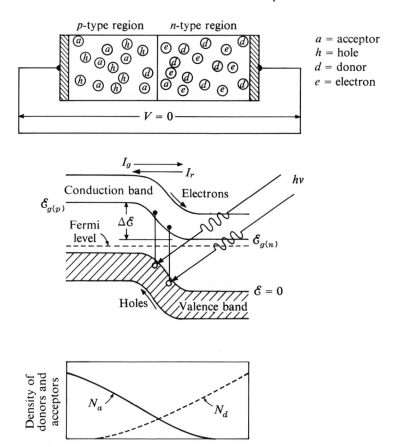

FIG. 5-3. A *p-n* junction schematic showing the junction, the energy band scheme, and the density of donors and acceptors as a function of position in the junction.

new contact potentials; this brings the total circuit voltage to zero as long as all parts of the system are kept at the same temperature. Thermodynamically speaking, we say that a contact potential is totally unavailable in a system in thermal equilibrium.

The small number of thermally excited electrons that take up residence in the conduction band of the *p*-type region can easily flow "down" into the *n*-type region. This gives rise to a thermally generated current I_g which is directly proportional to the number of thermally excited electrons in the *p*-type region

$$n_p \approx A_1 \exp\left[-(\mathcal{E}_{g(p)} - \mathcal{E}_f)/(kT)\right],\tag{5-9}$$

where the *p* subscript denotes values in the *p*-type region. In the *n*-type region, the number of thermally excited electrons in the conduction band is given by

$$n_n \approx A_1 \exp\left[-(\mathcal{E}_{g(n)} - \mathcal{E}_f)/(kT)\right].$$

If these electrons can cross the potential barrier $\Delta\mathcal{E} = \mathcal{E}_{g(p)} - \mathcal{E}_{g(n)}$, they can enter the p-type region to recombine with the holes. This produces a recombination current I_r flowing to the left that is proportional to

$$A_1 \exp\left[-(\Delta\mathcal{E} + \mathcal{E}_{g(n)} - \mathcal{E}_f)/(kT)\right]$$
$$= A_1 \exp\left[-(\mathcal{E}_{g(p)} - \mathcal{E}_{g(n)} + \mathcal{E}_{g(n)} - \mathcal{E}_f)/(kT)\right]$$
$$= A_1 \exp\left[-(\mathcal{E}_{g(p)} - \mathcal{E}_f)/(kT)\right]. \qquad \textbf{(5-10)}$$

We note that the right-hand side of Eq. 5-10 is exactly the same as Eq. 5-9. That is, the potential barrier adjusts itself to such a value that at equilibrium the current flowing to the right is the same as the current flowing to the left, or $I_r = I_g$.

We continue our exploration of the p–n junction by performing some simple experiments. If we bias the p-type region, so that it is more negative with respect to the n-type region, by applying a so-called *reverse bias* of

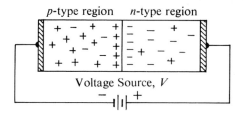

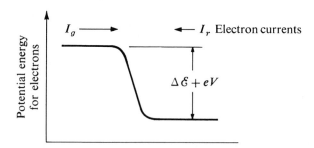

FIG. 5-4(a). The dependence of the electron generation and recombination currents across a *p-n* junction with a reverse bias. The reverse saturation current is due to the flow of particles that are minority carriers in the regions from which they come. This reverse current is due entirely to diffusion resulting from the minority particle concentration gradients at and near the junction and thus is not dependent on the applied voltage. In this case the saturation current is due to electrons in the *p*-type region and holes in the *n*-type region.

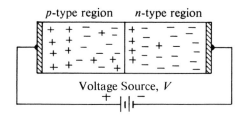

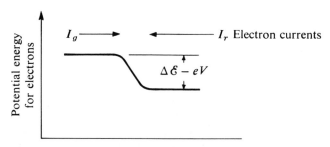

FIG. 5-4(b). The dependence of the electron generation and recombination currents across a *p-n* junction with a forward bias. The forward current across a junction is due to the majority carriers in the regions from which they come. They cross the junction because of the concentration gradient from one side of the barrier to the other. The electric field influences these gradients so as to favor a diffusion current in the forward direction. The forward current in this case is due to electrons in the *n*-type region and holes in the *p*-type region.

magnitude† V, the energy barrier that electrons in the *n*-type region will see is now $\Delta\mathcal{E} + eV$, and it is virtually impossible for any electrons from the *n*-type region to surmount this barrier and enter the *p*-type region. This is shown in Fig. 5-4(*a*). Thus the recombination current for electrons I_r is very small. This biasing does not affect the generation current for electrons I_g to any extent, because the number of thermally excited electrons in the *p*-type region is not changed. The reverse bias also limits the number of holes in the valence band that can go from the *p* side to the *n* side. Recall that holes, unlike electrons, prefer to go "uphill." We thus have about the same I_g and a reduced I_r for holes.

If we *forward bias* our *p–n* junction, we get the situation illustrated in Fig. 5-4(*b*). Once again we have done nothing to change the number of thermally excited electrons in the *p*-type region and thus the current I_g is not affected. However, the applied voltage in this situation reduces the energy

† By convention we normally assume the voltage V to be less than zero when the *p*-side is negative, and we assume V to be greater than zero when the *p*-side is positive. Thus when we apply a reverse bias, the potential barrier that electrons on the *n* side see is $\Delta\mathcal{E} - (-eV) = \Delta\mathcal{E} + eV$.

barrier the electrons in the n-type region of the conduction band see and thus increases I_r for electrons according to the Boltzmann distribution law by a factor exp $[eV/(kT)]$. Because I_g does not change and I_r equals I_g at equilibrium we may write

$$I_r = I_g \exp [eV/(kT)]. \tag{5-11}$$

The net electron current that will flow in the circuit is the difference between the two currents I_r and I_g; thus from Eq. 5-11 we obtain

$$I_r - I_g = I_g \exp [eV/(kT)] - I_g$$
$$= I_g \{\exp [eV/(kT)] - 1\}. \tag{5-12}$$

This current is zero when $V = 0$ and increases to large values for positive eV, and decreases when eV is negative toward a negative saturation value $-I_g$.

The hole current flowing across the junction behaves similarly. The applied voltage that lowers the height of the barrier for electrons also lowers it for holes, so that large numbers of holes flow from the p region to the n region under the same voltage conditions that produce large electron currents in the opposite direction. We note that electron and hole currents going in different directions add; the total current, including the effects of both holes and electrons, is given by

$$I_j = I_o \{\exp [eV/(kT)] - 1\}, \tag{5-13}$$

where I_o is called the *saturation* or *dark current*. Equation 5-13 is sometimes called the *rectifier equation*.

The equivalent circuit of a photovoltaic cell can be drawn as shown in Fig. 5-5. The elaborate realistic model of Fig. 5-5(a) is generally replaced

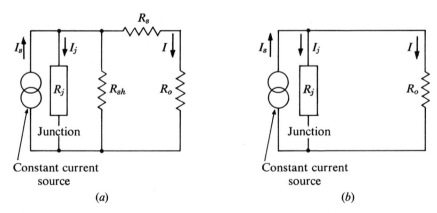

FIG. 5-5. (a) Equivalent circuit of an illuminated p-n junction photovoltaic cell showing the internal series and shunt resistance. (b) The simplified equivalent circuit that is used in this chapter.

with the simplified circuit shown in Fig. 5-5(b). For our purposes the simplified circuit is perfectly adequate and yields essentially the same result as the more realistic model. Because the operation of a photovoltaic converter involves the microscopic action previously detailed, we describe its operation in terms of a macroscopic device that yields an equivalent result. The equivalent circuit consists of a constant-current generator delivering a current I_s into a network of impedances, which include the nonlinear impedance of the junction R_j, an intrinsic series resistance R_s, an intrinsic shunt resistance R_{sh}, and the load resistance R_o.

Application of Kirchhoff's law to the simplified circuit will yield several interesting relationships. When a p–n junction is illuminated, the light causes a current I to flow in the load; the magnitude of this current is the difference between the current that would flow if the junction were short circuited I_s and the current that flows across the junction I_j, which we found in Eq. 5-13. Thus we have

$$I = I_s - I_j \tag{5-14}$$

or

$$I = I_s - I_o\{\exp\,[eV/(kT)] - 1\}, \tag{5-15}$$

where I_j is the total current due to both electron and hole flow across the junction, I_o is the *dark* or *saturation* current, and V is the voltage across the junction.

We will now make an analysis of this device as an energy converter. In so doing we will try to find those characteristics that lead to high efficiency devices. Since it is more common to analyze photovoltaic converters in terms of current densities, rather than in terms of currents, we now switch to that notation. The current densities are based on the area of exposed junctions. The current density that flows through the load, J, is the difference between the current that would flow if the junction were short circuited, J_s, and the current that flows across the junction, J_j, which was defined by Eq. 5-13. Thus, we have

$$J = J_s - J_j \tag{5-16}$$

or

$$J = J_s - J_o\{\exp\,[eV/(kT)] - 1\}. \tag{5-17}$$

The maximum voltage that we could measure on the cell would occur under open circuit conditions, $J = 0$, which is

$$V_{oc} = (kT/e) \ln (J_s/J_o + 1) \tag{5-18}$$

To find the voltage that will produce maximum power density we compute the power output of the device

$$P = JV = (J_s - J_o\{\exp\,[eV/(kT)] - 1\})V. \tag{5-19}$$

Taking the derivative of this equation with respect to V and setting the result equal to zero yields an implicit equation for the voltage that maximizes the power

$$\exp\left[eV_{mp}/(kT)\right]\left[1 + eV_{mp}/(kT)\right] = 1 + J_s/J_o = \exp\left[eV_{oc}/(kT)\right]. \quad \textbf{(5-20)}$$

The current density that maximizes the power may be found by combining the expression for the maximum power voltage as given by Eq. 5-20 with the expression for the current as given by Eq. 5-17:

$$J_{mp} = \frac{[eV_{mp}/(kT)]J_s}{1 + eV_{mp}/(kT)}\left[1 + \frac{J_o}{J_s}\right]. \quad \textbf{(5-21)}$$

The maximum power density is then simply

$$P_{max} = J_{mp}V_{mp} \quad \textbf{(5-22)}$$

or

$$P_{max} = \frac{[eV_{mp}/(kT)]V_{mp}J_s}{1 + eV_{mp}/(kT)}\left[1 + \frac{J_o}{J_s}\right]. \quad \textbf{(5-23)}$$

The power density input to the junction is simply the total number of photons in the solar spectrum, N_{ph}, times the average energy of each of those photons, $\mathcal{E}_{av}$. Since the dark current density J_o is usually five or more orders of magnitude smaller than the short circuit current density J_s, we may approximate the maximum efficiency of the converter as

$$\eta_{max} \approx \frac{[eV_{mp}/(kT)]V_{mp}J_s}{[1 + eV_{mp}/(kT)]N_{ph}\mathcal{E}_{av}}. \quad \textbf{(5-24)}$$

We should note that the number of photons with energy greater than $\mathcal{E}_g$ decreases as $\mathcal{E}_g$ increases, while the ratio J_s/J_o and consequently, V_{mp}, increases with $\mathcal{E}_g$; it is evident that η_{max} will pass through a maximum as a function of $\mathcal{E}_g$.

In our analysis we have assumed that the internal shunt resistance R_{sh} is much greater than the load resistance R_o, and the internal series resistance R_s is much less than R_o. Whereas the first condition, which causes most of the junction current to be delivered to the load, is easy to achieve, creating a small series resistance is a more difficult task. The larger R_s is, the greater is the power that is dissipated in the junction and the smaller the voltage across the load.

We now examine in Fig. 5-6 a typical voltage-current plot for an actual solar cell; we show the effect that load resistance has on the power yield of the cell. The nonlinear characteristic of the junction is clearly evident in this plot.

5.4 PROPERTIES DESIRED IN SEMICONDUCTORS FOR CELL USE

In the previous section we considered the mechanism by which a *p–n* junction converts radiation energy into electrical energy. We also derived an

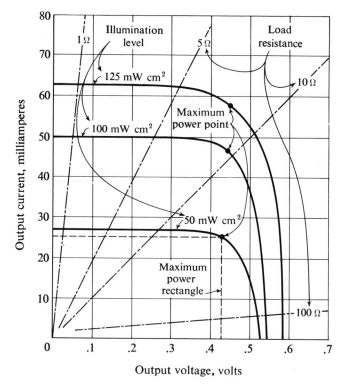

FIG. 5-6. Typical voltage-current characteristics for a silicon *p*-on-*n* cell. The open circuit voltage depends logarithmically on the illumination, while the short circuit current is a linear function of the illumination. The actual voltage to the load is independent of cell area and is a function only of load resistance and illumination level; however the output current depends on the illumination level, load resistance, and cell area.

expression for the efficiency of a photovoltiac device in terms of such macroscopic parameters as dark current density, short circuit current density, and voltage at the maximum power point. These expressions, while useful for some tasks in cell design, tell us nothing about the microscopic properties that would be desirable in the semiconductor of which the cell is made. In this section we will indicate what those properties are and which materials have proved successful in photovoltaic cell use.

We begin by considering some of the ramifications of the series resistance introduced in the circuit analysis of the last section. To achieve a high conversion efficiency it is desirable to produce electron-hole pairs within a very short distance of the *p-n* junction. Electrons and holes produced far from the junction simply recombine without contributing to the cell's output.

The average distance a carrier diffuses before recombination is called the *diffusion length* and we now consider what it means and how it is calculated.

If we generate excess carriers in a small region of a semiconductor, they tend to diffuse away from their point of generation because of the concentration gradient; they diffuse down the concentration gradient away from the high concentration at the point of generation. These excess carriers have a finite lifetime, τ^*, so that they will ultimately disappear by recombination. The average distance a carrier diffuses before recombination is called the diffusion length L, and is related to the diffusion constant D and the lifetime by

$$L = (D\tau^*)^{1/2}. \tag{5-25}$$

We may interpret the diffusion constant, physically, by considering a semiconductor that has a concentration gradient of carriers as is shown in Fig. 5-7. The carriers' motion in response to the gradient is analogous to the

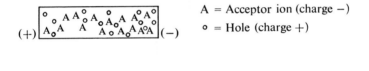

A = Acceptor ion (charge $-$)

o = Hole (charge $+$)

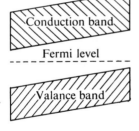

FIG. 5-7. By doping a specimen so that it has a concentration gradient of acceptors, an electrostatic field can be set up along the specimen. The electrostatic field is set up because the higher hole concentration at the right hand causes more holes to drift from right to left than from left to right.

mixing† of two different gases or liquids. The electric current density that a concentration gradient will produce in the x direction is simply

$$J_D = -eD \frac{dn}{dx}, \tag{5-26}$$

† If two different gases or liquids are allowed to remain in contact, there will be a gradual mixing of the two, even in the absence of convection currents. These processes of mixing are described by Fick's laws; the first one has a form identical to Eq. 5-26.

where the minus sign occurs because diffusion occurs toward the region of decreasing concentration. If this diffusion produces an electric field E, steady state conditions are reached when the conduction current, $J_{cd} = \sigma E$, is equal to the diffusion current J_D,

$$J_{cd} = J_D$$

$$ne\mu E = -eD\frac{dn}{dx}. \qquad (5\text{-}27)$$

The presence of the field E will cause a potential energy difference of magnitude eEx to exist over a distance x. Thus, if the carrier concentration is low enough so that we may use Boltzmann statistics to describe the energy distribution of the carriers, then the concentration gradient as a function of x is

$$n = C\exp\left[-eEx/(kT)\right], \qquad (5\text{-}28)$$

where C is a constant. Upon combining Eqs. 5-27 and 5-28 we find a relation between the diffusion constant and the mobility

$$D = \frac{kT}{e}\,\mu, \qquad (5\text{-}29)$$

which is known as the *Einstein relation*. This equation is quite useful in determining D because μ can be easily determined from Hall effect experiments.

How does the diffusion length relate to the series resistance with which this discussion began? As we stated earlier, only those carriers produced near the junction (10^{-6} cm $< L < 10^{-2}$ cm) contribute to the output of the cell. For this reason cells are generally fabricated with the junction located very near the surface so that the junction intercepts the maximum amount of incident light. In the case of an n-type on p-type cell as shown in Fig. 5-8, the n-type layer is about 10^{-4} cm thick. This very thin layer, through which the load current must flow, is the origin of the series resistance R_s that we mentioned earlier. The thickness of the n-type layer therefore must be a compromise between the value of R_s and the collection efficiency of the junction for photoexcited electrons and holes.

Equation 5-24 reveals that the efficiency of a photovoltaic energy converter is linearly dependent on the short circuit current density J_s. The short circuit current density is proportional to the efficiency with which the carriers generated in the bulk are collected and delivered to the external circuit, the fraction of the incoming photons absorbed in the effective volume, the fraction of the radiation not transmitted completely through the junction, and the number of photons per second per unit area of p-n junction whose energy is great enough to generate electron-hole pairs in the semiconductor. We express this symbolically as

$$J_s = \eta_{co}(1 - r)[1 - \exp(-\alpha l)]en_{ph}, \qquad (5\text{-}30)$$

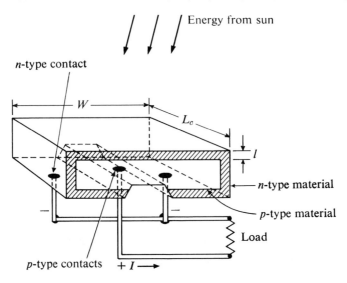

FIG. 5-8. A cross section of an *n*- on *p*-type material photovoltaic junction.

where η_{co} is the collection efficiency, r is the reflection coefficient, $\exp(-\alpha l)$ is the fraction of the radiation transmitted, α is the absorption coefficient, l is the thickness of the absorbing semiconductor, and n_{ph} is the number of photons per second per unit area whose energy is great enough to generate electron-hole pairs.

The mathematical description of the absorption of light by a solid is very similar to the description of the attenuation of gamma rays, X rays, or molecular beams, topics that are discussed in any well-written modern physics book such as Blanchard *et al.* [4]. Photons are removed from the incident beam by collisions that produce excited states or free electrons and holes. If Φ_1 is the original light intensity of a beam and Φ is the intensity after traversing a thickness x of the solid, then

$$\Phi = \Phi_1 \exp(-\alpha x), \qquad (5\text{-}31)$$

where α is the absorption coefficient. It may be demonstrated that the absorption coefficient is inversely related to the mean free path. Since $\exp(-\alpha l)$ is the fraction transmitted through the junction, then $[1 - \exp(-\alpha l)]$ is the fraction of the original beam that has been absorbed at the distance l.

We note that not all the minority carriers that are generated in the solid by the radiation contribute to the power developed in the load, because some of them recombine with majority carriers either inside the bulk of the semiconductor or at the surface. We have recognized this by defining the collection efficiency η_{co}, as the ratio of the carriers passing through the circuit (the short circuit current density, J_s) to the total number of carriers generated in the solid per unit time. Rearrangement of Eq. 5-30 serves as the definition of the collection efficiency:

$$\eta_{co} = \frac{J_s}{(1 - r)[1 - \exp{(-\alpha l)}]en_{ph}}. \tag{5-32}$$

η_{co} has been computed [5] for the simple geometry case of an infinite plane $p\text{-}n$ junction at $x = l$; it was found to be a function of the absorption constant for the radiation α, the minority carrier lifetime τ^* (the lifetime of a hole in an n-type region or the lifetime of an electron in a p-type region), and the surface recombination velocity s. The surface recombination velocity is the effective velocity at which all minority carriers appear to be swept into the surface where they disappear in surface trap energy levels. Surface recombination is evaluated by measurement of the total recombination rate as a function of surface-to-volume ratio. The surface recombination velocity is very sensitive to surface treatment; high surface recombination velocities are found for ground or sandblasted surfaces whereas low surface velocities occur in surfaces polished by chemical etching. In Table 5-2 we tabulate the

TABLE 5-2. THE COLLECTION EFFICIENCY† η_{co} AS A FUNCTION‡ OF s, L, AND α

s (cm/sec)	L (cm)	α (cm^{-1})	η_{co}
0	10^{-2}	10^3	0.61
0	10^{-3}	10^3	0.47
0	10^{-3}	10^6	0.65
100	10^{-3}	10^3	0.61
∞	10^{-2}	10^3	0.25
∞	10^{-3}	10^3	0.23
∞	10^{-3}	10^6	0.001
∞	10^{-6}	10^3	6×10^{-5}

† From Ref. [2].
‡ With l assumed equal to 10^{-3} cm.

collection efficiency as a function of the surface recombination velocity, the diffusion length L, and the absorption coefficient α.

Examination of Table 5-2 reveals that the most favorable condition for a high collection efficiency is that for which $l/L \ll 1$ and for which the surface recombination velocity is low. These calculations indicate the advisability of chemically etching the surface of photovoltaic cells. For efficient absorption it is necessary that the thickness of the top surface of the cell be approximately equal to the reciprocal of the absorption constant, $l \approx \alpha^{-1}$, thus $10^{-6} < l < 10^{-4}$ cm. The lifetime of the minority carriers can be determined if we assume that the thickness of the top surface l is equal to 0.1 of the diffusion length, $L = (D\tau^*)^{1/2}$. Then if $D = 10$ cm² per sec, the lifetime of the minority carriers should lie in the range 10^{-5} sec $> \tau^* >$ 10^{-13} sec. It can be shown [5] that s will not reduce the collection efficiency if $s/D \ll 1/L$ and $s/D \ll \alpha$. With $l = 0.1L = \alpha^{-1}$ for α in the range given in Table 5-2, both of these conditions are satisfied if s is less than 10^5 cm per sec. These modest requirements on τ^* and s predict that many materials should be capable of yielding high values of η_{co}, and the collection efficiency should not affect the choice of the best materials for solar conversion.

The magnitude of reflection losses can be estimated by using the relation between the index of refraction γ and the reflection coefficient r, namely,

$$r = (\gamma - 1)^2/(\gamma + 1)^2. \tag{5-33}$$

Because γ has not been measured for many materials that are of interest in photovoltaic devices, an empirical relation due to Moss [6] is used to estimate the index of refraction

$$\mathcal{E}_g(\gamma)^4 = 173 \tag{5-34}$$

that has been found to be approximately true for materials of the zinc blend or diamond lattice structure. If $\mathcal{E}_g = 1$ eV, then $\gamma = 3.6$ and $r = 0.31$. If $\mathcal{E}_g = 2$ eV, then $\gamma = 3.05$ and $r = 0.26$. We conclude that materials that have energy gaps that make them of interest for use in photovoltaic energy converters will all have about the same reflection loss.

We are now in a position to further simplify the efficiency expression given by Eq. 5-24 and to find an upper bound for the efficiency at which a cell can operate. This may be done by writing the short circuit current as $J_s = Kn_{ph}$ where K is a constant that includes all the losses we have just discussed, namely, reflection, transmission, and collection. If we assume that $K \approx 1$ and that eV_{mp}/kT is much greater than unity, then Eq. 5-24 can be written as

$$\eta_{max} \approx \frac{n_{ph}V_{mp}}{N_{ph}\mathcal{E}_{av}}. \tag{5-35}$$

We can interpret this equation for a silicon cell by noting that n_{ph} is about $\frac{2}{3}N_{ph}$ and the voltage at maximum power is about one-third the energy of the average impinging photons. The results of these approximations yield an upper limit on the efficiency of a silicon cell of about 22 percent.

The last parameter that we will consider involving the microscopic properties of semiconductors is the saturation current density J_o. Shockley [7] has presented a detailed analysis of this problem; we will give a simpler picture of the events in the neighborhood of the junction.

We first assume that the junction region is thin in comparison with the diffusion length and so recombination within the junction proper may be neglected. We consider a heavily doped p region in contact with a moderately doped n region which is a favorable condition for achieving a low value of J_o. Thus, we assume that the current is carried solely by the holes generated in the n region that diffuse over to the p region. The current carried by these holes is equal approximately to the absolute value of the electronic charge, $|e|$, times the equilibrium hole density, p_n, in the n region, times the mean diffusion velocity u_p, which we assume to be the diffusion length $L_p = (D_p \tau_p^*)^{1/2}$ divided by the hole lifetime τ_p^*, thus yielding

$$u_p = \frac{(D_p \tau_p^*)^{1/2}}{\tau_p^*} = \frac{D_p}{L_p}. \tag{5-36}$$

In germanium at room temperature values of 200 cm per sec for holes having a lifetime of 10^{-3} sec are typical. In silicon, holes having a lifetime of 10^{-7} sec yield a mean diffusion velocity of 10^4 cm per sec. The hole generation current density is then approximately

$$J_{o(p)} = p_n e D_p / L_p = p_n \mu_p kT / L_p, \tag{5-37}$$

where we have used the Einstein relation $D = \mu kT/e$. We recall from Eq. 3-44 that the product of the hole and electron densities in a given region must be a constant

$$p_n = \frac{n_i^2}{n_n} = \frac{2.23 \times 10^{31} T^3 \exp\left[-\mathcal{E}_g/(kT)\right]}{n_n}, \tag{5-38}$$

where n_i = equilibrium density of electrons in the intrinsic semiconductor and n_n is the equilibrium density of electrons in the n region. The latter quantity may be expressed in terms of the electrical resistivity (as was done in Ch. 3) as

$$n_n = (\rho_n e \mu_n)^{-1}. \tag{5-39}$$

Combining Eqs. 5-37, 5-38, and 5-39 yields

$$J_{o(p)} = 2.23 \times 10^{31} T^3 \rho_n \mu_n \mu_p kTeL_p^{-1} \exp\left[-\mathcal{E}_g/(kT)\right], \tag{5-40}$$

where the results are in amperes per square centimeter. Multiplication by the area of the junction converts the answer to I_o. Other methods of calculating J_o are outlined by Loferski [2]. The strong temperature dependence of J_o is apparent from Eq. 5-40. Keeping in mind that the lower J_o is, the greater is the efficiency, it is apparent why the lower the temperature at which the solar converter is maintained, the better its performance will be.

The only other quantities needed to evaluate the efficiency and the saturation current are the density of photons that have energy exceeding the energy gap of the material, the total photon density, and the average energy of those photons; these quantities were given in Section 5.2.

5.4.1 Choice of materials. Based on the principles set down in Section 5.4, we may now make some statements on the selection of materials for use in photovoltaic converters.

Two effects take place in semiconducting materials used in solar converters. First, the number of photons absorbed with energy greater than the
band gap, n_{ph}, decreases as the band gap increases. (This point was illustrated
in Fig. 5-2 where we plotted the number of photons absorbed against the
semiconductor energy gap.) As the band gap increases, the saturation current density J_o decreases, thus causing an increase in the output voltage. This
point becomes clearer when Eqs. 5-40 and 5-18 are combined. The results of
this operation are messy, but qualitatively we observe that a reduction in J_o,
which occurs on increasing the energy gap, increases the open circuit voltage
as the log of the ratio J_s/J_o. The effect of these two forces on the maximum
conversion efficiency of a photovoltaic converter is illustrated in Fig. 5-9. This
curve was obtained by Loferski [8] using a set of equations similar to those
derived in the preceding section. In computing J_o a material with silicon's
properties was assumed; reflection, recombination, and transmission losses
were ignored in computing J_s since it was demonstrated earlier that these
quantities do not vary appreciably among different materials. This curve
gives the maximum *theoretical* efficiency which could be expected under the
assumptions set down in deriving the governing equations. A small cross on

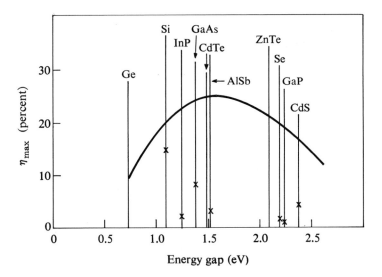

FIG. 5-9. The maximum solar energy conversion efficiency as a function
of the energy gap of the semiconductor. The maximum measured efficiency
for various materials is denoted by a cross at the energy gap of the material.
The curve has been calculated for an ideal junction outside the atmosphere.
After Refs. [8] and [9].

the energy gap value line of each material indicates the *actual* conversion efficiency which has been achieved in real converters.

We note that the curve passes through a broad maximum due to the operation of the previously described opposing forces. The curve, however, predicts values of η_{max} higher than that of silicon for semiconductors with energy gaps between 1.1 and 2.3 eV.

Materials having energy gaps in this range include indium phosphide, InP (1.27 eV); gallium arsenide, GaAs (1.35 eV); aluminum antimonide, AlSb (1.49 eV); cadmium telluride, CdTe (1.5 eV); zinc telluride, ZnTe (2.1 eV); aluminum arsenide, AlAs (2.16 eV); and gallium phosphide, GaP (2.24 eV). This range of energy gaps would also include mixed semiconductors formed by combining materials from the III-V and II-VI semiconductors in different proportions. An example of this type material would be $GaAs_x P_{1-x}$, which would have an energy gap between 1.35 eV (GaAs) and 2.24 eV (GaP). Other materials that have energy gaps that would make them of interest for converter use are junctions composed of two semiconductors, so-called heterojunctions such as that between selenium (Se) and cadmium selenide (CdSe) and cadmium sulfide (CdS) and cupric sulfide (CuS).

To indicate the order of magnitude of some of the quantities that are involved in computing efficiencies of solar converters, we have taken results and data from Ref. [9] in formulating Table 5-3 on the performance of solar energy converters.

It is interesting to note that the theoretical efficiency actually increases in some materials as the optical path length m and the number of centimeters of precipitable water vapor w increase† as shown in Fig. 5-10. The increased absorption of the atmosphere resulting from atmospheric gases, humidity, and dust tend to deplete the ultraviolet wavelengths (see Figs. 5-1 and 5-2) thus favoring converters with small band gaps; the performance of large band gap materials is severely penalized because an insufficient number of photons with energies necessary to create electron-hole pairs reaches the converter. We note finally that the difference between silicon and the optimum material is greatest for conversion of solar energy outside the atmosphere. Under these conditions η_{max} for silicon is 19.4 percent, whereas η_{max} for a material with an energy gap of 1.6 eV is 24.6 percent. Thus, none of the materials discussed here appears to offer improvements of as much as a factor of two.

The maximum power output under various conditions of atmospheric absorption are shown in Fig. 5-11. These curves may be obtained by multiplying the energy densities given in Table 5-1 for various atmospheric conditions times the efficiencies presented in Fig. 5-10. Even though efficiencies for

† The case of $w = 2$ corresponds to a relative humidity of about 50 percent.

TABLE 5-3.   PERFORMANCE† OF SOLAR ENERGY CONVERTERS‡

Material	$\mathcal{E}_g$ (eV)	μ_n cm²/V-sec	μ_p cm²/V-sec	τ_p^* (sec)	Cost‖ (Dollars/watt)		J_o (amp/cm²)	J_s mA/cm²	V_{oc} (V)	η_{max} (percent)
Si	1.12	1200	250	10^{-5}	15 to 60	Theory	5.9×10^{-12}	44.5	0.58	22
						Exp'tl	10^{-8}	35	0.61	15
CdS§	1.2	1200	250	10^{-5}	45	Theory	10^{-14}	51	0.73	23
						Exp'tl	7×10^{-11}	34	0.50	8.3
CdTe	1.45	300	30	10^{-8}		Theory	10^{-19}	39	0.95	21
						Exp'tl	2.2×10^{-12}	24	0.58	6.5
GaAs	1.35	3000	600	10^{-8}	800	Theory	10^{-16}	41	0.84	21
						Exp'tl	4.7×10^{-11}	21	0.50	4.2

† Illumination taken to be 140 mW/cm².
‡ From Ref. [9].
§ Band gap is controlled by width of energy gap in Cu_2S. All other properties are those of Si [9].
‖ Bare cell.

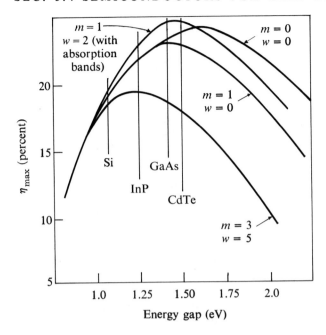

FIG. 5-10. Maximum conversion efficiency of a solar cell as a function of energy gap for various atmospheric conditions. After Loferski [2] with permission.

small band gap materials might be higher with atmospheric absorption, power densities suffer losses of as much as 50 percent under these conditions.

The load impedance at maximum power can be found by combining Eqs. 5-20, 5-21, and 5-22 derived in Section 5.3. The result of these operations is simply

$$R_{mp} = \frac{\exp\left[-eV_{mp}/(kT)\right]}{I_o e/(kT)}, \tag{5-41}$$

where I_o and V_{mp} are computed by the methods indicated in the earlier section. The load impedance for maximum power is seen to be dependent on the energy gap through the quantities I_o and V_{mp}. As the energy gap increases, the load impedance rises rapidly.

5.4.2 Limitations on photovoltaic energy converters. We will briefly describe some of the factors, as detailed in Refs. [9] and [10], that prohibit real photovoltaic converters from achieving the efficiencies predicted in Table 5-3. Some of these factors were previously encountered when we initiated our discussion of semiconductor properties. The major factors are:

   (1) Reflection losses on the surface;

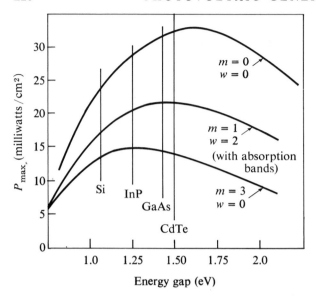

FIG. 5-11. Maximum power from an ideal photovoltaic converter as a function of energy gap for different absorption conditions. After Loferski [2] with permission.

(2) Incomplete absorption;

(3) Utilization of only part of the photon energy for creation of electron-hole pairs;

(4) Incomplete collection of electron-hole pairs;

(5) A voltage factor;

(6) A curve factor related to the operating point at maximum power;

(7) Additional degradation of the curve due to internal series resistance.

These factors can be divided into several groups as follows: Factors 1, 2, and 4 can be combined and called the overall collection efficiency, as was done earlier; all three of these factors are related to the absorption characteristics of the material. Factors 1 through 4 determine the short circuit current. Factors 5 and 6 are related to voltage-amperage characteristics of the device. Factors 1, 4, and 7 are mainly determined by techniques, and improvements in these areas may all but eliminate these factors from consideration. Factors 2, 3, 5, and 6, however, have absolute physical limitations beyond which improvement is not possible. It should be noted that these basic limitations are also technique-influenced to a certain extent. We will briefly discuss each of the seven factors.

(1) Reflection losses have been reduced to almost zero, by means of transparent coatings with appropriate thickness and index of refraction.

Losses as low as 3 percent for silicon cells have been reported in the literature [9]. We conclude that these losses are no longer of major consequence in making improvement in cell performance.

(2) Figure 5-12 shows the energy spectrum of sunlight at sea level on a bright, clear day. The figure also indicates the maximum amount of energy utilized in the generation of electron-hole pairs in semiconductors with

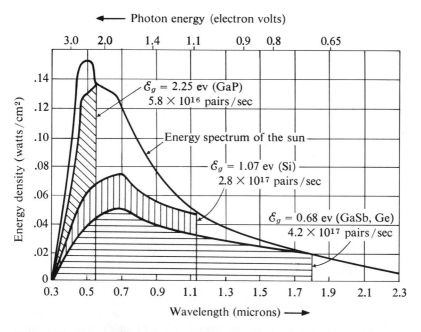

FIG. 5-12. The energy spectrum of the sun at sea level on a bright, clear day, and the parts of this spectrum utilizable in the generation of electron-hole pairs in semiconductors with energy gaps of 2.25, 1.07, and 0.68 eV, respectively. Listed for each of these cases is the number of electron-hole pairs generated under the assumption of the existence of an abrupt absorption edge with complete absorption and zero reflection on its high-energy side. After Wolfe [10] with permission.

different energy gaps. For every value of the energy gap a cutoff line is obtained beyond which the photons possess insufficient energy to create an electron-hole pair. It is also observed that the smaller the energy gap, the larger the portion of the sun's spectrum that can be utilized by the cell.

The problem of incomplete absorption can be alleviated somewhat by turning to materials that have absorption coefficients that increase very rapidly with photon energy. Figure 5-13 shows the absorption characteristics

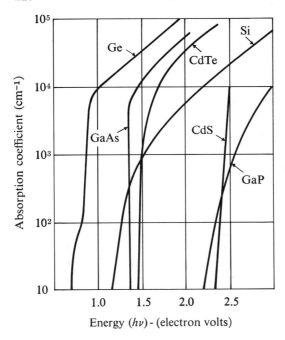

FIG. 5-13. The optical absorption coefficient as a function of photon energy ($h\nu$) in electron volts. After Loferski [9] with permission.

of some semiconductors of interest for cell use. A rapidly rising absorption coefficient, such as that of GaAs, means that a larger fraction of the carriers generated by the absorption of solar photons will be within a short distance of the surface of incidence. The importance of this fact can be more fully appreciated if we recall our earlier interpretation of the absorption coefficient as the reciprocal of the mean free path of the photon in a solid. Consequently, the "active region" of the cell—that is, the sum of the diffusion lengths ($L_n + L_p$) on the two sides of the junction—can be smaller. This means that shorter lifetimes can be tolerated, thus opening the possibility of creating a cell approaching its theoretical maximum. Materials with shorter minority carrier lifetimes are generally easier and cheaper to make than materials that have previously been considered for cell use. Furthermore, less material will be needed in any given solar cell since it will require a thinner film to insure effective absorption of the incident radiation.

(3) Figure 5-12 reveals that a large number of the photons that will be absorbed will have more energy than is needed to create an electron-hole pair. Any energy that an impinging photon has in excess of the energy gap of the material will contribute to the lattice vibrations of the material and will eventually be dissipated as heat. Thus, those photons whose energy is

less than the energy gap of the material do not contribute at all to electron-hole pair generation and those photons whose energy exceeds the energy gap of the material while creating an electron-hole pair have their excess energy dissipated as heat. Wolf presents a curve that shows that 46 percent of the impinging solar energy can be utilized in electron-hole pair generation in a semiconductor with an energy gap of 0.9 eV, assuming that all photons with sufficient energy to create pairs are actually absorbed. This limit and the number of electron-hole pairs generated by sunlight per square centimeter of exposed area per second as a function of energy gap (as given in Fig. 5-2) represent basic limitations and are completely independent of technique factors.

(4) A significant number of the electron-hole pairs generated by photon absorption will not be created within the space charge region of the p–n junction; only those pairs created within a diffusion length of the junction can be collected and separated by the built-in field. The majority of those created at greater distances from the junction will recombine, causing the collection efficiency to fall below 100 percent. In Section 5.4 we listed the major factors of which the collection efficiency is a function. Wolf [10], in a more elaborate analysis, solves a diffusion differential equation for the steady-state condition to obtain an expression for the overall collection efficiency.

(5) The largest recoverable voltage in a photovoltaic cell is the open circuit voltage given by Eq. 5-18. The energy required to generate an electron-hole pair is equal to the energy gap of the material which, on a per electron basis, can be expressed as a voltage. The open circuit voltage is always observed to be less than the energy gap voltage for the material of which the cell is made. There are two reasons for this:

(a) The barrier height is equal to the maximum forward voltage across the junction; this is determined by the difference in Fermi levels in the n- and p-type material on both sides of the junction. The Fermi levels, as discussed in Ch. 3, are a function of impurity concentration and temperature, and are normally located within the forbidden gap, thus causing the barrier height to be less than the energy gap.

(b) A voltage equal to the barrier height would be obtained only if an extremely large number of electron-hole pairs were generated; this number can never be reached by photon absorption from direct sunlight.

The so-called voltage factor (V.F.), a measure of how much of the cell potential is being realized, can be formed by dividing the open circuit voltage, as calculated by Eq. 5-18, by the energy gap of the material (in volts) to yield

$$\text{V.F.} = V_{oc}/\mathcal{E}_g = [kT/(e\mathcal{E}_g)] \ln [J_s/J_o + 1]. \qquad (5\text{-}42)$$

The calculations of the quantities appearing in this equation have already been given in Section 5.4.

(6) In Section 5.3 we indicated that the maximum power that can be obtained from a converter is obtained at the operating point which encloses the largest area in the voltage-current characteristic curve of Fig. 5-6. This point is defined by the maximum power voltage and current, V_{mp} and J_{mp}. Forming the ratio of the products $V_{mp}J_{mp}$ to $V_{oc}J_s$, we obtain what Wolf [10] calls the curve factor (C.F.):

$$\text{C.F.} = \frac{V_{mp}J_{mp}}{V_{oc}J_s} = \frac{J_o(eV_{mp}/kT)^2 \exp(eV_{mp}/kT)}{J_s \ln(J_s/J_o + 1)}. \qquad (5\text{-}43)$$

Both the curve factor and the voltage factor depend on the saturation current J_o. As we outlined earlier, the saturation current is dependent upon the material properties. In Fig. 5-14 we plot both the voltage factor and the

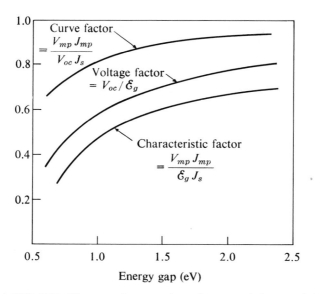

FIG. 5-14. The curve factor, voltage factor, and characteristic factor for a solar energy converter as a function of semiconductor energy gap width. After Wolf [10] with permission.

curve factor and their product, which we call the *characteristic factor*. All three factors are slightly dependent on energy gap and increase as the energy gap increases. The characteristic factor is pretty much independent of technique, being sensitive only to the nature of the material used in the converter.

(7) It has been found in actual converters that the series resistance of the cell can cause deviation from the ideal voltage-current characteristics. This deviation causes the curve to flatten, resulting in a reduction in the net power output. In earlier discussions we noted that if the layer of mate-

rial on top of the junction was reduced in thickness, the collection efficiency was improved because of the larger photon absorption. This solution, however, conflicts with resistance requirements, because as the layer is reduced in thickness, its resistance goes up. The ohmic contacts applied to the cell also cause its resistance to go up, but improvements in the techniques of applying contacts have caused this resistance to become all but negligible.

The voltage drops around the circuit are

$$V = IR_s + V_{load} \tag{5-44}$$

and the current flowing in the circuit is given by Eq. 5-17, which we have converted from a current density equation to a current equation.

$$I = I_s - I_o\{\exp[eV/(kT)] - 1\}. \tag{5-45}$$

Combining Eqs. 5-44 and 5-45 we find that the voltage across the load when we include the internal voltage drop of the cell is

$$V_{load} = (kT/e)\ln[1 + (I_s - I)/I_o] - IR_s. \tag{5-46}$$

The output power would obviously be reduced by the presence of the I^2R_s dissipation in the generator. Possibilities for reducing series resistance through the development of improved techniques appear good.

5.5 THE DESIGN OF A CONVERTER

Now we will consider the methods used in the design of a photovoltaic converter. This design will be based on properties of existing materials in order that the calculations be as realistic as possible.

Problem. We wish to design a solar power plant to operate a small radio used as a community listening center in an underdeveloped section of the world. The power required is 5 watts; this power is stored in a battery system where it is used for 2 or 3 hours in the late afternoon or evening period to energize a transistor radio. Daytime charging by the solar cell system would be expected to store 20 to 30 Whr. Our design will include finding the performance parameters for the energy converter. We assume that the unit is energized by the sun under conditions given by $m = 1$, $w = 2$ which correspond to the sun at the zenith with a 50 percent relative humidity. The energy of the photons and their density are given in Table 5-1.

Solution. We will assume that the converter units are p–n junctions made from silicon with the following properties:

$\mathcal{E}_g = 1.11$ eV	$T = 300°K$
$\mu_p = 400$ cm^2/volt-sec	$\mu_n = 10^3$ cm^2/volt-sec
$\tau_p^* = 10^{-5}$ sec	$\tau_n^* = 10^{-7}$ sec
$N_a = 10^{19}$ cm^{-3} acceptors in the p-layer	$N_d = 10^{17}$ cm^{-3} donors in the n-layer

We begin our work by calculating the reverse saturation current density $J_{o(p)}$ of the holes, utilizing Eq. 5-37:

$$J_{o(p)} = \frac{p_n e D_p}{L_p}. \tag{5-37}$$

The density of holes in the n-type region may be found by calculating the pn product using Eq. 5-38. The pn product is

$$\begin{aligned} pn = n_i^2 &= 2.23 \times 10^{31} T^3 \exp\left(-\mathcal{E}_g/kT\right) \text{ cm}^{-6} \\ &= 2.23 \times 10^{31} \, (300)^3 \exp\left(-1.11/.026\right) \\ &= 1.56 \times 10^{20} \text{ cm}^{-6}, \end{aligned}$$

where we have used $kT = 0.026$ eV.

Now we assume that the temperature of the device is not high enough to ionize all the donor electrons but is just high enough to cause the Fermi level to be at the donor energy level. Let us examine this assumption by considering the expression for the concentration of electrons in the conduction band. This number must be equal to the number of vacant donor levels plus the number of holes in the valence band:

$$n = \frac{2N_c}{1 + \exp\left[(\mathcal{E}_g - \mathcal{E}_f)/(kT)\right]} = N_d \left[1 - \frac{1}{1 + \exp\left[(\mathcal{E}_d - \mathcal{E}_f)/(kT)\right]}\right]$$

$$+ 2N_v \left[1 - \frac{1}{1 + \exp\left[-\mathcal{E}_f/(kT)\right]}\right].$$

We may simplify this expression by noting that $\exp\left[-\mathcal{E}_f/(kT)\right]$ is a very small number (about 10^{-18}) and hence the last term may be neglected. Since we have assumed $\mathcal{E}_f \approx \mathcal{E}_d$ we find that concentration of electrons in the n-type region is

$$n_n = \tfrac{1}{2}N_d = \tfrac{1}{2} \times 10^{17} \text{ cm}^{-3}.$$

Thus

$$p_n n_n = 1.56 \times 10^{20} = p_n(\tfrac{1}{2} \times 10^{17})$$
$$p_n = 3.12 \times 10^3 \text{ cm}^{-3}.$$

We repeat again that, since the number of holes in the p-type region (10^{19} cm^{-3}) is greater than the number of excess electrons in the n-type region (10^{17} cm^{-3}), the current flow is nearly all carried by holes, because the p-type region is injecting a large number of holes into the n-type region. For this reason we calculate only the hole contribution to the saturation current. We now use Eq. 5-25 to calculate the diffusion length for the holes in the n-type region, first calculating the hole diffusion constant by means of the Einstein equation

$$D_p = \frac{\mu_p kT}{e} = \frac{400 \text{ cm}^2}{\text{volt-sec}} \times \frac{\text{volt}}{11{,}600^\circ\text{K}} \times 300^\circ\text{K} = 10.4 \text{ cm}^2/\text{sec}$$

and the hole diffusion length is

$$L_p = (D_p \tau_p^*)^{1/2} = [(10.4 \text{ cm}^2/\text{sec})(10^{-5} \text{ sec})]^{1/2} = 1.02 \times 10^{-2} \text{ cm}.$$

The saturation current density from Eq. 5-37 is

$$J_{o(p)} = \frac{p_n e D_p}{L_p} = \frac{(3.12 \times 10^3 \text{ cm}^{-3})(1.60 \times 10^{-19} \text{ coulomb})(10.4 \text{ cm}^2 \text{ sec}^{-1})}{1.02 \times 10^{-2} \text{ cm}}$$

$$= 5.06 \times 10^{-13} \text{ amp/cm}^2.$$

We now calculate the short circuit current, which requires that we estimate the collection efficiency. To do this we use the data in Table 5-2. Using an absorption coefficient of about 10^3 and assuming an etched surface for our cell, which gives us a low surface recombination velocity, we find a collection efficiency of 0.61. Since our answer is not too dependent on this number, we do not carry out the elaborate calculations required to obtain a better estimate. The reflection coefficient is obtained by using the empirical Eq. 5-23 for the index of refraction

$$\mathcal{E}_g(\gamma)^4 = 173$$
$$1.11(\gamma)^4 = 173 \tag{5-34}$$
$$\gamma = 3.54$$

and Eq. 5-33 for the reflection coefficient

$$r = \frac{(\gamma - 1)^2}{(\gamma + 1)^2} = \frac{(3.54 - 1)^2}{(3.54 + 1)^2} = 0.31.$$

Our earlier discussion of collection efficiency pointed out a condition that would produce a high collection efficiency, namely $l/L \ll 1$. Using the previously recommended condition of $l = 0.1L = \alpha^{-1}$, we find that the thickness of the n-type layer should be $l = \alpha^{-1} = 0.1L = 0.001$ cm. Thus the fraction of the impinging radiation that is transmitted is

$$\exp(-\alpha l) = \exp(-10^3 \times 10^{-3}) = 0.368.$$

The number of photons under conditions $m = 1$, $w = 2$ with energy in excess of the energy gap of silicon is, from Fig. 5-2, 3×10^{17} cm^{-2} sec^{-1}. Thus the short circuit current density is, from Eq. 5-30,

$$\begin{aligned} J_s &= \eta_{co}(1 - r)[1 - \exp(-\alpha l)]en_{ph} \\ &= 0.61(1 - 0.31)(1 - 0.37)(1.60 \times 10^{-19} \text{ coulomb})(3 \times 10^{17} \text{ sec}^{-1} \text{ cm}^{-2}) \\ &= 12.7 \times 10^{-3} \text{ amp/cm}^2. \end{aligned} \tag{5-30}$$

We may now calculate the open circuit voltage from Eq. 5-18:

$$V_{oc} = (kT/e) \ln(J_s/J_o + 1). \tag{5-18}$$

The factor kT/e is simply 0.026 volt, so

$$V_{oc} = 0.026 \ln(12.7 \times 10^{-3}/5.06 \times 10^{-13} + 1),$$

where we may drop the one in the parentheses in comparison with the current ratio term. Thus

$$V_{oc} = 0.026 \ln(2.51 \times 10^{10}) = 0.62 \text{ volt.}$$

Since we are interested in operating the converter under maximum power conditions we must now determine the voltage that permits this operation. This requires a trial and error solution to Eq. 5-20:

$$\exp[eV_{mp}/(kT)][1 + eV_{mp}/(kT)] = 1 + J_s/J_o$$
$$\exp(V_{mp}/0.026)(1 + V_{mp}/0.026) = 2.51 \times 10^{10}. \tag{5-20}$$

The correct answer lies between 0.54 and 0.55 volt. We will take 0.54 volt as the maximum power voltage. The maximum power current density can now be found from Eq. 5-21:

$$J_{mp} = \frac{[eV_{mp}/(kT)]J_s}{1 + eV_{mp}/(kT)}[1 + (J_o/J_s)]$$

$$J_{mp} = \frac{(0.54)/(0.026)(12.7 \times 10^{-3})}{1 + (0.54)/(0.026)} \left[1 + \frac{5.06 \times 10^{-13}}{12.7 \times 10^{-3}} \right]$$

$$= 12.1 \times 10^{-3} \, \text{amp/cm}^2. \tag{5-21}$$

The maximum power density is simply the product of the maximum power current density and maximum power voltage:

$$P_{mp} = J_{mp}V_{mp} = (12.1 \times 10^{-3})(0.54) = 6.54 \times 10^{-3} \, \text{watts/cm}^2.$$

The photon density arriving at the cell surface is found from Table 5-1 to be 4.8×10^{17} cm^{-2} sec^{-1} each one carrying on the average 1.25 eV. Thus the incident energy density is

$$N_{ph}\mathcal{E}_{av} = 4.8 \times 10^{17} \, \text{cm}^{-2} \, \text{sec}^{-1} \times 1.25 \, \text{eV} \times 1.60 \times 10^{-19} \, \text{joule (eV)}^{-1}$$
$$\times 1 \, \text{watt-sec (joule)}^{-1} = 9.6 \times 10^{-2} \, \text{watts/cm}^2.$$

The maximum efficiency of our cell may now be computed by dividing the output power density by the input power density:

$$\eta_{\text{max}} = \frac{P_{mp}}{N_{ph}\mathcal{E}_{av}} = \frac{6.54 \times 10^{-3}}{96 \times 10^{-3}} = 6.81 \, \text{percent.}$$

Equation 5-35 gives a means of estimating the theoretical maximum efficiency of a photovoltaic converter; we may use this equation to see how close our converter is coming to the theoretical maximum:

$$\eta_{\text{max}} \approx \frac{n_{ph}V_{mp}}{N_{ph}\mathcal{E}_{av}} = \frac{3 \times 10^{17}}{4.8 \times 10^{17}} \times \frac{0.54}{1.25} = 27 \, \text{percent.}$$

So we see that our converter is operating a long way from its theoretical limit.

We now consider the assembly of this array into a unit that will supply the needed power. Considerable work has been devoted to finding a cell geometry that maximizes the power output of the cell by minimizing the power dissipated in the cell itself. Photovoltaic converters made of silicon generally have a thin n-type layer superimposed on a base of p-type silicon. The n-type layer is made by diffusing phosphorus into the surface of p-type silicon. The problem of securing large single crystals of silicon for cell use has been, to a certain extent, alleviated by the use of current collector grids on the surface of the cell. These grids (illustrated in Fig. 5-15) offer a means of increasing cell efficiency by dividing cell structure into sections about $\frac{1}{2}$ cm wide by 2 cm long instead of the usual 1 by 2 cm size. Wolf [10] reports that this causes increases of as much as 20 percent in cell efficiencies. The reason for this improvement is that the smaller width of the cell represents in effect a shorter mean path for the hole current and a lower current density in the n-type layer. This allows a reduction in n-type layer thickness while simultaneously obtaining a decrease in series resistance.

The grid structure as illustrated in Fig. 5-15 consists of fine metal strips in contact with the n-type layer separated by a suitable distance. It is necessary, again, to satisfy two conflicting requirements: wide grid lines have low resistance but decrease the active area of the cell, while narrow grid lines expose most of the surface to the impinging radiation, but have high resistance. Wolf optimizes grid line width and spacing for this type of cell.

For the sake of completeness let us calculate the resistance of the thin n-type surface layer of the cell.

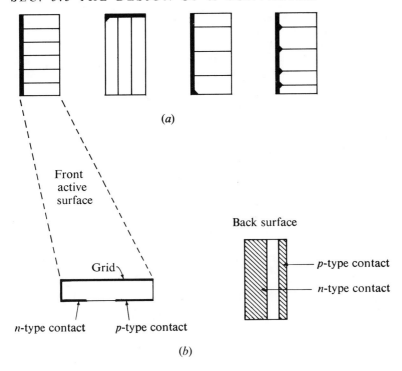

FIG. 5-15. (*a*) Standard (far left) and nonstandard gridded configurations of solar cells. (*b*) One way of providing large area contacts to the *p-n* junction.

Chapin [12] has estimated the resistance across the width of a cell L_c units long, W units wide, and having either a *p*- or *n*-type material layer *l* units thick (as illustrated in Fig. 5-8) to be

$$R_{su} = \frac{W\rho_n}{4L_c l}. \tag{5-47}$$

We may find out what this value is for our cell by calculating the resistivity of the *n*-type layer:

$$\rho_n = (n_n e \mu_n)^{-1} = [(\tfrac{1}{2} \times 10^{17} \text{ cm}^{-3}) \times (1.60 \times 10^{-19} \text{ coulomb})(10^3 \text{ cm}^2/\text{volt-sec})]^{-1}$$
$$= 0.125 \text{ ohm-cm},$$

where we have again assumed half the donor states to be filled. We also assume that the *n*-type layer is $\frac{1}{2}$ cm wide and 2 cm long and has a depth of 0.001 cm, which is the reciprocal of the absorption coefficient. Thus

$$R_{su} = \frac{0.5 \times 0.125}{4 \times 2 \times 0.001} = 7.8 \text{ ohms}.$$

Thus each cell of $\frac{1}{2}$ by 2 cm has a surface resistance of 7.8 ohms. For comparison purposes we might note that the load impedance at maximum power may be found from Eq. 5-41 to be about 52 ohms per sq cm of cell surface.

We are now ready to complete the design with respect to cell area. We found in our power calculations that the available power density was 6.54×10^{-3} watts per cm² and the transistor radio system requires an input of about 5 watts to keep the radio battery system at an adequate level of charge. The area required then is

$$(A \text{ cm}^2)(6.54 \times 10^{-3} \text{ watts/cm}^2) = 5 \text{ watts}$$
$$A = 765 \text{ cm}^2.$$

Since we do not plan on incorporating a sun-tracking mechanism into the system for reasons of cost and simplicity, we decide to use an area of 900 cm² to take into account that the incident radiation falls off considerably (see Table 5-1) as the sun moves away from the zenith.

Before we conclude our discussion of this problem we must take into account one more factor concerning the solar power supply—the sun and the power available from it. The sun in a very real sense constitutes an integral part of any photovoltaic system and we would be remiss in not taking it into account in our calculations. We have already decided, for reasons of cost and simplicity, not to include a tracking mechanism in our system, but we still need to know what the sun delivers under various conditions and how this affects storage capacity.

Chapin [12] has reported on the charging capacity for a solar cell system mounted at an angle to the horizontal of 40 deg (corresponding to the lati-

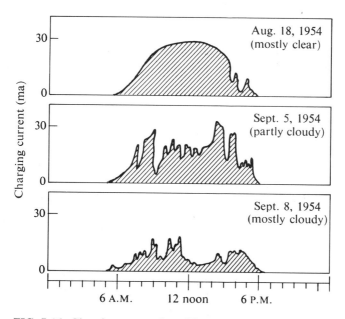

FIG. 5-16. Charging current in milliamperes to a load of about 1.35 volts as function of the time of day under various weather conditions. After Chapin [12] with permission.

tude at Murray Hill, New Jersey) with the intention of getting a compromise between the summer and winter sun angles. The load was a nickel-cadmium storage cell presenting an approximate constant voltage load to the generator. Continuous readings of voltage and current were recorded and these results are presented in Fig. 5-16 for three typical days. The top curve is for a clear day showing the expected increase in charging toward the forenoon and the decrease in late afternoon. The middle curve is for a partly cloudy day with some clear spots and with large clouds occurring occasionally. Just before and after a bright cloud obscures the sun, the charging rate becomes greater than that for a clear day because of the reflections off the clouds. The bottom curve is for a dark day with periods of rain; even on this day there was some charging.

Using the data collected at Murray Hill, it is possible to estimate the energy available throughout the year. This estimate will vary from place to place, but Fig. 5-17 illustrates the monthly trend. Curves similar to those shown in Fig. 5-16 were averaged over 24 hr for each day and then for each month to show the equivalent number of hours of full sunlight (0.1 watt per cm²) that could be expected at any time of year. In December we note that we expect only 2.4 hr of full sun each day compared with June's 4.8 hr. The upper line shows the computed number of hours of full sun that would be

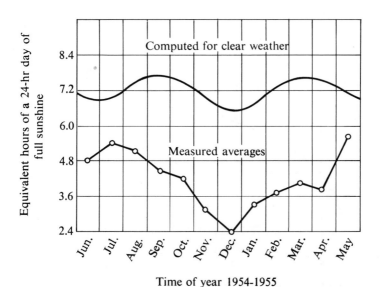

Time of year 1954-1955

FIG. 5-17. The equivalent number of hours of full sunshine as a function of the time of the year computed for clear weather and actually measured. The angle of mounting was 40 deg to the horizontal. Computations were for 41 deg north latitude. After Chapin [12] with permission.

obtained for this mounting and latitude, assuming full sun all of each day and taking into account the changing angle of the sun for the different seasons. The difference between the two curves can be called a weather factor.

The radiation available in December can be improved by increasing the mounting angle; we must bear in mind, however, that an increase in mounting angle will cause a decrease in the June performance. Work carried out at Murray Hill indicates that increasing the mounting angle to 65 deg will improve the December performance by 10 percent without causing June to be the new low point.

Average power, however, is not the full story. We must take into account storage that will allow continuous operation of equipment during the light and dark periods. In Fig. 5-18 we plot the number of days of storage capacity at full load current required to yield a *continuous* percentage of the maximum solar cell output for that time. For example, if we wish to operate the system continuously (24 hr per day) at 10 percent of the cell's maximum power output—that is, if we wish to operate our 5-watt unit at 0.5-watt output—we will need 8 days of storage capacity (at full load current). If we wish to operate at 17 percent of the rated capacity of the cell system then we must provide 30 days of storage. Considering the cost of solar cells it might

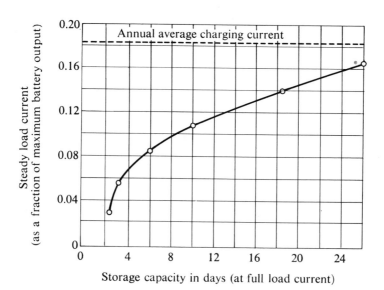

FIG. 5-18. The fraction of the maximum continuous current that can be drawn as a function of the storage capacity in terms of full load current. After Chapin [12] with permission.

be more economical to increase storage capacity at the expense of solar cell system size.

Since we only intend to operate our listening center for about 3 hr per day we decide that large storage capacity is not required; this is especially true if we consider the use of our community listening center in areas of Africa, South America, and Asia where the solar insolation in duration and intensity exceeds that of the northeastern United States (the area for which these charts were computed) by a considerable margin. If the radio consumed 20 Whr of energy operating at 12 volts, then for a 3-hr period a storage capacity of only 10 amp-hr would provide 6 days of listening capacity without benefit of solar recharging.

We may summarize the results of our design as follows: Radio consumes 20 Whr in each 3-hr period of listening. Energy supplied by a 900-cm² solar collector consisting of nine hundred 1-cm² grids, each delivering about 6.5×10^{-3} watts with the sun at the zenith. The maximum power density voltage of each grid is 0.54 volt. The maximum power density current of each grid is 12.1×10^{-3} amp. The conversion efficiency of the unit is 6.8 percent. The energy is stored in a battery that will deliver 10 amp-hr of current at 12 volts.

5.6 FABRICATION OF CELLS

Before we discuss any of the associated problems of collection, reliability, radiation damage, and so forth, we would like to outline the steps involved in making two different types of cells.

5.6.1 Silicon cells. We will first consider the manufacture of silicon solar cells since they are the ones that are most widely used. Next to oxygen, silicon is the most abundant element on earth; the pure silicon used in cell manufacture is extracted from sand, which is mostly silicon dioxide (SiO_2). The silicon required for solar cell use, because of its high purity, is expensive. The prevailing price for very pure silicon suitable for processing into solar cells is between 50 and 100 dollars per pound. How much this price can be reduced by technological improvements remains to be seen.

The pure silicon is placed in an induction furnace as described in Section 3.8, where boron is added to the melt. This turns the crystal resulting from the melt into p-type material. A small seed of single crystal silicon is dipped into the melt and withdrawn at a rate slower than 4 in. per hr; the resulting ingot looks like a medium-sized carrot. Ingots from which solar cells may be sliced are shown in Fig. 3-20.

The rate of growth and other conditions are adjusted so that the crystal that is pulled is a single crystal. It is not necessary to use single-crystal silicon in solar cells but performance of polycrystalline material is generally about one-tenth of that found in the single-crystal cells.

Wafers are then sliced from the grown crystal by use of a diamond cutting wheel. The slices are then lapped, generally by hand, to remove the saw marks and strained regions. After a fine lap the slabs are etched in hydrofluoric acid (HF) or nitric acid (HNO_3) to complete the first phase of preparation of the cells. We now have thin slices of p-type silicon with a carefully finished surface.

The wafers are then sealed in a quartz tube partly filled with phosphorous pentoxide (P_2O_5) and the arrangement is placed in a diffusion furnace where temperature is carefully controlled; this process causes the phosphorous to diffuse into the p-type silicon to a depth of about 10^{-4} to 10^{-5} cm. The cells are then etched in a concentrated acid to remove unwanted coatings that formed during manufacture. Wax or Teflon masking tape is used to protect the surfaces not to be etched. Generally an anti-reflection coating of silicon monoxide about 800 A thick is evaporated onto the surface of the cell.

Historically, the solar cell size of 1×2 cm predominated until 1965. The 2×2 cm and 2×6 cm are now more widely used. The number of electrical contacts that must be made to build a unit of a given power output goes down as the square of areas of the individual cells used goes up.

Even larger area silicon solar cells have been successfully produced by means of webbed dendrite silicon. This material is made by seeding two coplanar dendrites from a single seed. A silicon web freezes between the two coplanar dendrites as they are pulled from the melt. The thickness of the web is controlled by the pull rate. When the web is first seeded, the edge dendrites are about 1/4 inch apart. They then separate, thus widening the silicon sheet, at a rate which is generally not constant but averages about 0.1 inch per foot of web pulled. Both p on n cells and n on p cells have been made with the areas ranging in size from 1×15 cm up to 1×30 cm. Average efficiencies greater than 10 percent have been routinely achieved in these cells. They do, however, break rather easily as they are only on the order of 0.01 to 0.015 inch thick.

Contacts have always been a problem. A number of approaches have been tried. In one of them a stencil or mask is fabricated the size of the desired grid lines, then a thin layer (a few hundred A) of either chromium or titanium is evaporated onto the silicon surface wherever the mask permits. This is followed by a much thicker layer (10^{-4} cm) of silver. The surface is then sintered slightly above 600°C to improve contact strength and provide low resistance. The other approach is to deposit an extremely thin layer of gold by chemical deposition and then deposit a nickel layer over the gold to which electrical connections can be made.

5.6.2 The violet cell. One of the most significant advances in the 1970's in photovoltaics was the development of the so-called violet cell [13, 14]. This cell represented a major advance in solar cell technology, combining the use of a very shallow diffused junction about 10^{-5} cm below the top surface, a new grid pattern for collecting the current from this shallow region, a new Ta_2O_5 antireflective coating and other innovations [14]. For covered cells under air-mass zero conditions, 14 percent efficiencies were observed. Of particular significance was the fact that the performance gain occurred in the blue response region of the cell and should therefore be radiation resistant.

The use of Ta_2O_5 antireflective coatings on these cells resulted in actual performance gains when they were covered. This is contrary to the usual losses experienced when cells with SiO_x coatings are covered. Routine production of 14-percent-efficiency cells represents a 25 percent improvement over the 11-percent cells that had become the standard in solar cell work.

5.6.3 Thin film solar cells. When power generation by solar cells became a practical reality in the late 1950's, it became immediately apparent that cells made in the form of thin films would have the following potential advantages:

(1) Low material cost.

(2) Low manufacturing cost, possibly avoiding the need for single crystal growth.

(3) High power-to-weight ratios.

(4) Low array costs, because the number of connections needed will be greatly reduced.

Many research groups have attempted to gain these advantages, which could be achieved by a thin film solar cell. But because the potential reward is so great, the fabrication of such cells has not come easily. The limited success that has been achieved has been done with thin film cadmium sulfide (CdS) cells.

CdS cells having areas of 50 cm² have been made by evaporating the semiconductor onto a flexible substrate such as Kapton, a metallized plastic substrate. A barrier layer of copper sulfide is then deposited on top of the CdS. A cross-section of such a cell is shown in Fig. 5-19. Power to weight ratios of 100 watts/pound are claimed for such cells. The resulting cell is generally about 0.004 inch thick. So far there has been no significant commercial production of such cells.

The two main problems holding back thin film cells have been their low efficiency and their instability. Cells delivered to NASA have achieved beginning of life average efficiencies of about 4 percent. A recent report of environmental tests on a number of CdS cells shows that the power output

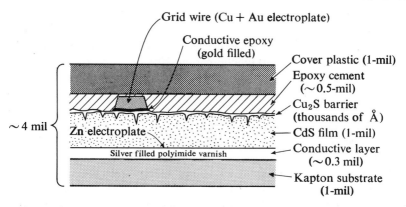

FIG. 5-19. CdS thin film solar cell. After Ref. [15].

of these cells as presently constructed will degrade as much as 50 percent when freely suspended in a space environment, due to thermal cycling between 60°C and −190°C. The degradation was attributed to the severe mismatch in the thermal expansion coefficients between the cadmium sulfide layer and the other layers making up the cell [15]. It has been found that CdS cells will also degrade from moisture in the air.

It has been pointed out that such devices, if fabricated into large arrays (1000 m²), could supply power in the kilowatt range and compete strongly on a cost, weight and availability basis with nuclear power systems now being designed for use in space. The thin film area is certainly one in which research will be continued [9].

5.7 SOLAR CELLS IN SPACE

Photovoltaic cells have provided the electric power for almost every space-craft the United States and the Soviet Union have launched in the first decade of the Space Age. For missions which will be completed in a few weeks or less primary batteries and fuel cells may be used in space vehicles, but for missions longer than that their weight and volume penalties simply become too great. Photovoltaic power provided the electricity for instruments on board the spacecraft that flew past Venus, powered the television cameras for photographic studies of the Moon, and have taken exciting television photos of Mars and Jupiter. The original Early Bird communication satellites produced only 75 W of power, while INTELSAT 4 has a 600-W power capability. Skylab manned space stations had nearly 20 kW available from 312,000 cells mounted on six structural wings with a total area of about 3000 ft². Units of up to 50 kW are planned for space stations beyond Skylab. These units have been designed as a four-wing array, providing 10,000 ft² of solar cells, or slightly more than 2 million equivalent 2 cm × 2 cm cells. The units are designed to permit rotation of the station to provide artificial gravity.

Estimates by NASA, DOD, and COMSAT indicate a likely requirement for over 10 million solar cells during the 1970's. It is likely that over $150 million will be expended through 1979 to design, develop, and procure assembled solar cell arrays (if the efficiency remains at the current 10 to 11 percent). Another $70 million would be required to launch such arrays, assuming 35,000 ft² of array area at 0.5 lbm/ft² and $4000 per pound launch cost.

The components of a typical solar cell power system are illustrated in Fig. 5-20 [15]. For power levels of several hundred watts or greater, the solar cells are usually mounted on structures continuously turned broadside to the sun in order to intercept the maximum amount of solar energy. Sun sensors, drive logic, and a drive motor function to rotate the solar panel assembly about an axis of the spacecraft. For satellites stabilized with respect to the earth, rotation about one axis is usually adequate.

A rotary transformer or slip rings may be used to transfer power from the rotating solar panel to the spacecraft. The day power so generated is split into two parts. Part of this power is supplied to the power conditioning circuits to be regulated and converted to the required voltage and frequency for immediate use by the spacecraft loads; the other part is supplied to the battery charge controller to recharge the batteries which supply night power.

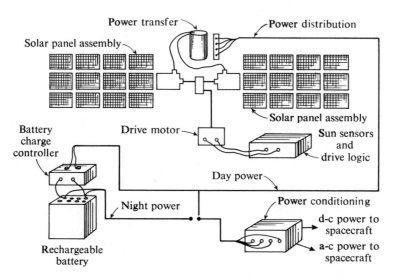

FIG. 5-20. The components that make up a solar cell power system.

Considerable progress has been made in developing lightweight body-mounted arrays for space use. Somberg [16] has. reported the successful construction and testing of three arrays fabricated with extremely high power-to-weight ratios. Two of the substrates were of magnesium, while the third was of conventional aluminum honeycomb. All of the arrays used 2 cm $\times$ 2 cm n/p cells, 200×10^{-6} m (8×10^{-3} in.) thick with a base resistivity of 2 ohm-cm. The contacts were titanium-palladium-silver and had a vacuum deposited antireflection coating of titanium oxide, which enhances cell output approximately 4 percent after the application of the cover slide. The cells were welded with silver-plated molybdenum interconnections. The cells on the two magnesium substrates were protected with thin microsheet cover slides, while those on the conventional aluminum honeycomb used a ceria-doped microsheet.

The two arrays mounted on magnesium substrates had power-to-weight ratios of 7×10^{-2} kW/kg (32 W/lbm) and 8.1×10^{-2} kW/kg (36 W/lbm). The conventional array delivered 4.5×10^{-2} kW/kg (20.6 W/lbm). In 1966 the Nimbus 2 meteorological satellite was placed in orbit with an array that delivered 1.3×10^{-2} kW/kg. Thus the magnesium-mounted arrays exhibit about a five-fold improvement over the 1966 state of the art. Figure 5-21 illustrates a 520-watt power system body-mounted on a defense communications satellite.

5.7.1　Reliability of a solar cell system. Because of their low individual outputs, solar cells are generally not used singly but are connected into panels or arrays that produce substantial voltages and currents. An individual cell failure could cause a total outage for the system. The mechanism for failure of solar cells on a power panel can generally be classified as follows:

(1) an open circuit due to a poor interconnection;

(2) an increased series resistance due to deterioration of a contact on the solar cell or terminal post;

(3) melting of a solder contact, causing the shorting of the p–n junction. In the case of a cell system used in space, the following are also relevant:

(4) a short due to micrometeorite damage;

(5) radiation-induced damage.

Failure in a space system is the most serious condition because of the impossibility of being able to make a repair. The probability of each of these failure mechanisms occurring cannot be reliably established. It would seem, however, that the most likely occurrence is for failure by an open circuit. This would be caused by excessive shock and vibration or by overheating of the solder contacts. Failure of an entire panel by such a defect is prevented by using a series-parallel matrix arrangement as illustrated in Fig. 5-22. Thus, should an open circuit occur, current normally flowing through one panel will be diverted to parallel cells.

FIG. 5-21. The Defense Satellite Communications System Phase II is designed to provide a secure worldwide telecommunications system. Power is supplied by eight solar panels using silicon cells located on the surface of the satellite. The panels will provide 520 watts at the beginning of the satellite's life, declining to 390 watts at the end of five years. Three 12-ampere-hour, nickel-cadmium batteries support full satellite operation through all eclipses for five years. The two steerable, narrow-coverage dish antennas and the two earth-average antennas are visible on the top of the satellite. Photograph courtesy of the Systems Group of TRW Inc.

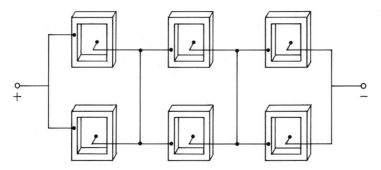

FIG. 5-22. A series-parallel matrix, which prevents complete failure of a solar cell system in the event of the failure of a single cell or connection to a cell.

5.7.2   Radiation damage. The greatest research effort expended on solar cells to date has been concentrated on the effects of high-energy electrons and protons on their electrical characteristics. This topic became of importance after the first satellites discovered intense radiation belts surrounding the earth. It was realized then that if earth satellites were going to be powered by solar cells more would have to be known about the effect these high-energy particles would have on the output of their power supplies.

According to the best information available to date, the Van Allen radiation belt can be described in terms of an inner doughnut-shaped belt whose axis coincides with the axis of the earth and attains a maximum intensity at an altitude of about 10^4 km; the second or outer belt attains its peak intensity at an altitude of 2.7 to 3.7×10^4 km. It is believed that the latter belt may extend even farther into space. The outer belt is subject to extreme temporal variation, but one measurement indicated an omnidirectional flux of 10^4 protons per cm²-sec with a proton energy in excess of 30 MeV. The radiation of the inner belt, which has been measured more thoroughly, is estimated to have an electron flux of about 10^7 particles per cm²-sec; their energy spectrum extends past 1 MeV, though a large part of them have energies less than this. The protons found in the inner belt have a range in energy of 0.5 MeV to 1 MeV; the number in this energy range is about 3×10^8 protons per cm²-sec.

On the basis of laboratory studies and this information it has been concluded [8] that an unshielded solar cell might experience an appreciable decrease in its power output after about 3 months of exposure to the electron flux and after about 30 hours of exposure to the proton flux of the inner radiation belt.

It has been found that the ability to resist radiation damage varies from material to material. The semiconductor parameter that has been found most sensitive to radiation is the minority carrier lifetime τ. The rate of change of this lifetime is found to be inversely proportional to the probability $\mathcal{P}$ of producing a defect by bombardment with particles of energy $\mathcal{E}_B$ and the minority carrier capture cross section Q_{CB} of these defects,

$$1/\tau \sim Q_{CB}\mathcal{P}. \qquad (5\text{-}48)$$

One can expect moderate variation in the probability and rather large variation in the capture cross section among various semiconductors. The minority carrier capture cross section may be thought of as a measure of the chance of a collision between an irradiating particle (an electron or proton) and a minority carrier (a hole on the n-type side of the junction or an electron on the p-type side of the junction).

We might also note that if a material has a sharp absorption edge (as has, for example, GaAs) and is therefore able to achieve a given maximum efficiency with a smaller minority lifetime, this can lead to a higher radiation resistance even if the product of Q_{CB} and $\mathcal{P}$ has the same value as another material.

Research in this area has indicated several methods for improving the radiation resistance of silicon solar cells [9], [17] which we will summarize under the assumption that the proposed solutions or variations on them are applicable to all types of solar cells:

(1) One way to minimize the effect of carrier lifetime is to maximize carrier mobility. Since electron mobility is two to three times hole mobility, the use of very thin n-type material as the surface material on top of p-type base material has notably improved the radiation resistance of solar cells.

(2) However, research [18] has indicated the unusual self-healing properties of lithium-doped p/n solar cells. Lithium is known to be highly mobile in silicon and is introduced into the base region of p/n cells to interact with radiation induced damage centers to reduce the effect of such centers on minority carrier lifetimes. Lithium appears to impart to such cells a room temperature self-healing capability that potentially makes them the most radiation-resistant solar cells yet studied. Based on these early results, which are not yet completely understood, it has been estimated that lithium solar cells should provide a 50-fold improvement in radiation resistance over the conventional n/p silicon cells.

(3) The last method of improving cell performance under radiation conditions is perhaps the most obvious; it includes coordination of the design of the cell to include optimization of the non-radiation-sensitive portions of the design, allowance for a protective cover and mounting arrangements, and so forth. Considerable inhibition of radiation damage occurred when sapphire covers of a thickness corresponding to 0.25 gm per cm² were placed over the face of the cells. In fact, electrons up to 1 MeV caused no deterioration in cell performance with the 0.25-gm per cm² shield

in place. Protection from high energy protons is considerably more difficult to achieve, but shields to protect against these particles have found some success.

5.7.3 Large solar arrays. The development of large spacecraft for both manned and unmanned applications has encouraged the design and construction of large, lightweight, deployable solar cell arrays. One such spacecraft is Skylab, an experimental space station designed to expand knowledge about orbital operations and to accomplish carefully selected scientific, technological, and medical investigations.

Raw power for Skylab was supplied by two separate solar arrays: one unit provided power to the Apollo Telescope Mount (ATM) and one unit provided power to the Orbital Workshop System (OWS). Figure 5-23 is a sketch of Skylab in orbital configuration.

The ATM solar array was one of the largest solar cell arrays ever flown in space. It had a beginning-of-mission power capability in excess of 11,000 watts. The ATM and OWS solar arrays together were capable of supplying in excess of 20,000 watts. The ATM solar array consisted of 20 solar panels divided into four wings oriented at 45 degrees to the longitudinal axis of the Skylab vehicle. Each wing consists of four complete panels, with each panel containing 20 solar cell modules and a half-panel containing 10 modules. Four half-panels, one from each wing, are paired

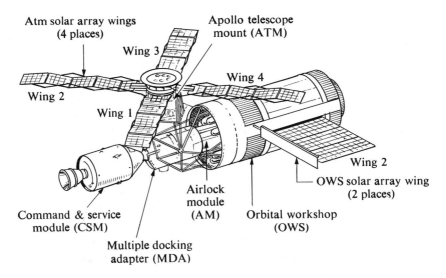

FIG. 5-23. A sketch of the Skylab in orbital configuration. After Ref. [19] with permission.

TABLE 5-4. PHYSICAL AND ELECTRICAL CHARACTERISTICS OF THE ATM SOLAR ARRAY[†]

Size of each wing	13.23 m (521 in.) long 2.65 m (104.5 in.) wide
Mass	1954 kg (4300 lbm) including deployment structure
Total solar cells	2 cm $\times$ 2 cm : 123,120 2 cm $\times$ 6 cm : 41,040
Power output	11,340 W at 55°C at BOM 10,343 W at 55°C at EOM
Overall power-to-weight ratio	1.2 $\times$ 10^{-3} kW/kg (2.6 W/lbm)

† See Refs. [19] and [20] for further details.

to form two complete panels, making a total of 18 complete panels in the array.

The ATM solar cell array is deployed by means of a pantograph system, which unfolds after Skylab reaches orbit. Details of the physical and electrical characteristics of the array are given in Table 5-4.

The *n*- or *p*-type cells had an overall conversion efficiency of 10 percent with a base resistivity of 7 to 14 ohm-cm. The cell contacts were fully covered AgTi.

A photograph of another high-performance, folding, solar wing-panel system is shown in Fig. 5-24. The frontispiece illustrates one of the biggest solar arrays ever built.

5.8 PHOTOVOLTAICALLY-PRODUCED ELECTRICAL POWER ON EARTH

The earth receives an abundant quantity of solar power each day. Table 5-5 summarizes the total number of kilowatt-hours available under various conditions for a ground power station that covers one square mile. Even though the amount of energy available is immense, the widespread use of solar cells to produce significant amounts of electrical power on earth does not appear to be at hand.

The overriding deterrent to their use is, without question, their cost. The solar arrays used on the Apollo Telescope Mount described in the preceding section cost about $2 million per kilowatt. Some work suggests that cells for terrestrial application could be made for about $15,000 per

FIG. 5-24. A rigid solar array wing made up of two curved panels, each approximately 2.5 ft (0.76 m) by 5 ft (1.52 m). The "gull wing" shape provides extra stiffness and maximum volume utilization when the wing is folded up. Power output from this unit is 240 watts. This is the only "welded" (as opposed to soldered) solar array produced in the United States. Photograph courtesy of the Lockheed Missiles and Space Company, Inc.

TABLE 5-5. INCIDENT AND AVAILABLE SOLAR
ENERGY AT 40 DEG. N. LATITUDE, SEA LEVEL†

Season and type of day	Incident solar energy	5% conversion	10% conversion	15% conversion
	[in millions of kilowatt-hours per square mile per day]			
Clear summer day	17.3	.86	1.73	2.6
Clear winter day	6.5	.32	.65	.96
Cloudy summer day	3.5	.17	.35	.51
Cloudy winter day	nil	nil	nil	nil

† After Ref. [21].

kilowatt by using existing silicon solar cell manufacturing methods, relaxing the stringent space cosmetic and performance specifications, changing the cells' shape for better utilization of single-crystal silicon, and automating many of the manufacturing processes. The use of simple concentrators (as illustrated in Figure 5-25) would require fewer cells to generate the same electrical power and could lower the cost of power to about $10,000 per kilowatt [22]. The costs for conventional fossil fuel or nuclear plants range from $500 to $1500 per installed kilowatt.

Cherry [21] believes that automated processes might produce thousands of square feet of solar array at costs near $50 per kilowatt, or about 50

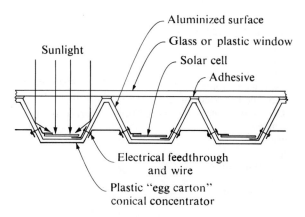

FIG. 5-25. Proposed design for a solar concentrator using the egg carton design. After Ref. [21] with permission.

cents per square foot. A square mile of array would cost about $14 million. Cherry also estimates that construction of the necessary ground support equipment might cost about $1 per square foot or about $28 million and that storage and switching gear could be installed for about $10 million. It is further assumed that the storage equipment and solar arrays are replaced after 10 years and that annual maintenance charges of $1 million are incurred. The "farm" is assumed to be installed in the southwestern part of the United States where it could easily generate 2.1×10^8 kWh/yr per square mile. If the power were sold for 3 cents per kWh, such a "farm" would have an annual before-tax rate of return of about 5 percent.

Before solar energy can be used to generate electricity on a large scale, the cost of solar arrays must be reduced three to four orders of magnitude. The present nonautomated method of producing cells must be replaced by massive automated techniques using abundant low-cost materials.

Further increases in efficiency, while desirable, are not absolutely necessary; methods of constructing large-area arrays on the ground from materials that can withstand many years of sunlight and weather must be developed. Large-scale batteries capable of long life and deep discharges must also be developed to solve the 24 hour per day requirement for power. While the batteries can be operated in ideal environments, they must have high storage density and be made of abundant and inexpensive materials, preferably materials that can be reprocessed time and again.

NOTATION

A = area, cm² or proportionality constant in Eq. 5-9
c = velocity of light, cm/sec
C = constant of integration
C.F. = curve factor as defined by Eq. 5-43
D = diffusion constant, cm²/sec
e = electronic charge, coulombs
E = electric field, volt/cm
$\mathcal{E}$ = energy, electron volts, ergs, or joules
f = number of electron-hole pairs produced, cm⁻³-sec⁻¹
F' = total number of electrons and holes produced, sec⁻¹
G = gain factor, dimensionless
h = Planck's constant, erg-sec
I = electric current, amp
I_g = thermally generated current, amp
I_j = junction current, amp
I_o = dark or saturation current, amp
I_r = recombination current, amp
I_s = short circuit current, amp
J = current density, amp/cm²

J_j = junction current density, amp/cm²
J_o = dark or saturation current density, amp/cm²
J_s = short circuit current density, amp/cm²
k = Boltzmann's constant, erg/°K
K = loss coefficient
l = thickness of absorbing semiconductor, cm
L = diffusion length or electrode spacing, cm
L_c = cell length, cm
m = optical path length, cm
n = electron density, cm⁻³
n_{ph} = photon flux with enough energy to generate an electron-hole pair, (sec-cm²)⁻¹
N_a = density of acceptor levels, cm⁻³
N_c = equivalent number of energy levels in the conduction band, cm⁻³
N_d = density of donor levels, cm⁻³
N_{ph} = photon flux, (sec-cm²)⁻¹
N_v = equivalent number of energy levels in the valence band, cm⁻³
p = hole density, cm⁻³
P = power density, watts/cm²
$\mathcal{P}$ = probability of producing a defect with particles of energy $\mathcal{E}$, dimensionless
Q_{CB} = minority carrier capture cross section, cm²
r = reflection coefficient, dimensionless
R = electrical resistance, ohms
R_j = nonlinear junction impedance, ohms
R_o = load resistance, ohms
R_s = series resistance, ohms
R_{sh} = shunt resistance, ohms
s = surface recombination velocity, cm/sec
T = temperature, °K
T_r = transit time, sec
u = velocity, cm/sec
V = electrical potential, volts
V.F. = voltage factor defined by Eq. 5-42, dimensionless
w = amount of precipitable water vapor, cm
W = cell width, cm
x = coordinate
z = angle between observer and the zenith, radians
α = absorption coefficient, cm⁻¹
γ = index of refraction, dimensionless
η = efficiency, dimensionless
λ = wavelength, angstroms or cm
μ = mobility, cm²/(volt-sec)
ν = frequency, (sec)⁻¹
ρ = electrical resistivity, ohm-cm
τ^* = minority carrier lifetime, sec
Φ = light intensity, watts/cm²

Subscripts

a = acceptor
av = average

cd	=	conduction
co	=	collection
d	=	donor
D	=	diffusion
g	=	energy gap
i	=	initially
max	=	maximum
min	=	minimum
mp	=	maximum power
n	=	in the *n*-type region
oc	=	open circuit
p	=	in the *p*-type region
s	=	short circuit
su	=	surface

PROBLEMS

5-1. What percent of the potential number of photons in the solar spectrum on a day when conditions are termed "extreme" will have energy enough to create an electron-hole pair in a material with a 2-eV forbidden energy zone? In a 1-eV forbidden energy zone material?

5-2. Assuming that the photons carry the average energy listed in Table 5-1, what will be the average energy density for the photons which can create an electron-hole pair in a 1-eV forbidden energy zone material?

5-3. What is the wavelength in angstroms for a photon of average energy outside the atmosphere? For the photon of average energy under conditions $m = 3$, $w = 0$? For a photon of average energy under conditions $m = 3$, $w = 5$?

5-4. Assume that the earth receives 0.135 watt per cm² of radiation from the sun. Suppose that this radiation did not have a spectral distribution, but was received at the sodium resonance wavelength (5890 A). (a) Calculate the number of photons arriving at the surface per square centimeter. (b) Calculate the current generated in a surface junction of 1 cm² assuming that no radiation is reflected and that each photon gives rise to one collected electron-hole pair.

Answer: (b) 12.8×10^{-2} amps.

5-5. Derive the equation for the voltage and current density that maximizes the power as given by Eqs. 5-20 and 5-21. Also derive the open circuit voltage expression as given by Eq. 5-18.

5-6. The differential equation that describes the excess hole concentration in the *n* region of a *p*–*n* junction is

$$D_p \left[\frac{d^2p}{dx^2} \right] - \frac{p}{\tau_p^*} = 0.$$

Solve this equation for *p* as a function of *x*.

Answer: $p(x) = p(0)e^{-x/L_p}$.

5-7. Derive Eq. 5-29.

5-8. Calculate the diffusion length and mobility of holes in *n*-type germanium (a) if the hole lifetime is 10^{-6} sec; (b) if the hole lifetime is 10^{-4} sec. The hole diffusion constant is 44 cm² per sec.

5-9. For material with a surface recombination velocity of 100 cm per sec, a diffusion length 10^{-3} cm, an absorption coefficient of 10^3 cm^{-1}, a depth of surface of n-type material of 10^{-3} cm, an energy gap of 1.3 eV, and which is irradiated by a photon flux (possessing energy in excess of the energy gap) of 1.5×10^{17} photons per cm^2-sec, find the short circuit current density.

Answer: 6.5×10^{-3} amps/cm^2.

5-10. For a material that has a hole lifetime of 10^{-6} sec, a hole mobility of 400 cm^2 per volt-sec, and a density of holes in the n-type region of 10^5 cm^{-3} at room temperature, find the hole saturation current density. If the equilibrium density of free electrons in the n-type region is 10^{16} cm^{-3} what is your estimate of the energy gap of the material?

5-11. A material has an intrinsic density of electrons of 10^{13} cm^{-3} and has 10^{17} cm^{-3} electrons in the n-type region at 280°K. The diffusion coefficient for holes is 60 cm^2 per sec with a hole lifetime of 10^{-4} sec. Find the saturation current density due to holes.

Answer: 1.24×10^{-11} amps/cm^2.

5-12. Consider a photocell operating at 310°K made from cadmium telluride having properties as listed in Table 5-3. Find the voltage factor, the curve factor, and the characteristic factor for the cell. Make two sets of calculations, one based on theoretical values, the other on experimental values.

5-13. Compare the voltage factor, curve factor, and characteristic factor for each of the cell materials listed in Table 5-3, using both experimental and theoretical values for each material.

5-14. In the example problem solved in Section 5.5 the operating temperature of the device was assumed to be 300°K. Assume that the temperature dependence of the hole and electron mobilities are given by the following expressions:

$$\mu_p = 400(300/T)^{-2.3} \text{ cm}^2/\text{volt-sec}$$
$$\mu_n = 1000(300/T)^{-2.6} \text{ cm}^2/\text{volt-sec}$$

and that all other properties of the cell remain the same. Calculate the maximum power density voltage, current density, and efficiency of the cell at 270°K, 330°K, and 375°K, and compare your results with those found in Section 5.5.

5-15. A photovoltaic cell made of germanium has a p-type surface layer that has 10^{19} acceptors per cm^3 and 10^{16} donors per cm^3 in the n-type layer. Assuming a gap width of 0.72 eV, a hole lifetime of 10^{-6} sec, and a diffusion constant of 44 cm^2 per sec, calculate for a cell at a temperature of 300°K: (a) the equilibrium hole density in the n-type region; (b) the saturation current density; (c) the short circuit current density, assuming that it is irradiated by light of the intensity and wavelength described in Problem 5-4; (d) the maximum power density generated by the cell under the conditions given in part (c).

Answers: (a) 1.11×10^{11} cm^{-3}; (b) 1.17×10^{-4} amp/cm^2.

5-16. It is proposed to fabricate a photovoltaic cell of GaAs having the properties listed in Table 5-3. For the case of $m = 0$, $w = 0$, calculate the open circuit voltage and the maximum power voltage. If they are necessary, make assumptions similar to those that were made in Section 5.5.

5-17. Based on the following densities, a solar intensity of 140 milliwatts per cm^2 and the efficiencies given in Table 5-3, calculate the area and weight of material to deliver 1 watt of power. The densities of the photovoltaic materials of interest are as follows: Si, 2.33 gm per cm^3, GaAs, 5.31 gm per cm^3, CdTe, 6.20 gm per cm^3;

CdS, 4.82 gm per cm^3. Assume that all of the cells have the same thickness of 0.5 mm.

5-18. Combine Eqs. 5-18 and 5-40 and determine how the output voltage of a photovoltaic cell is related to forbidden gap width of a material through the saturation current density. Make some calculations that will allow you to graph this change.

5-19. Consider a specimen of gallium arsenide used as a photoconductor. It has an electron mobility and lifetime of 3000 cm^2 per volt-sec and $\tau_n^* = 10^{-3}$ sec. Its hole mobility and lifetime are 600 cm^2 per volt-sec and 10^{-8} sec. The specimen is illuminated with light of a frequency that produces 10^{14} electron-hole pairs per sec-cm^3. Electrodes are separated by 2 cm, and 100 volts are applied across the electrodes. Calculate the increase in electrical conductivity, the transit time, and gain for the electrons.

5-20. The reverse saturation current I_o of a silicon cell at 40°C is 1.2 × 10^{-7} amp. The short circuit current when exposed to sunlight is 5 amp. From this information compute (a) the open circuit voltage; and (b) the maximum power output of the cell.

5-21. A certain thin-film CdS cell had the following properties at 55°C: short circuit current density, 13.0 ma/cm^2; maximum power current density, 10.9 ma/cm^2; open circuit voltage, 0.47 V; voltage at maximum power 0.36; efficiency, 3.3 percent. A space probe to Venus needs 1200 watts at 28 volts. Design a power system from these cells which will supply the required power. What is the area required?

5-22. Consider the power requirements presented in Problem 5-21 but now carry out the design using silicon cells with the following properties at 55°C: short circuit current density, 35 ma/cm^2; open circuit voltage, 0.58 V; efficiency, 13 percent.

5-23. Laboratory measurements on a CdTe solar cell reveal that it has a dark current density of 1.2 × 10^{-9} amp/cm^2 with a short circuit current density of 6 × 10^{-4} amp/cm^2 at 310°K. The voltage factor has been calculated and found to be 0.24. Find: (a) the maximum power voltage; (b) the maximum power current density; (c) the number of 2 cm × 6 cm size cells which would be required to supply 15 watts at 28 volts. How must the cells be arrayed?

5-24. While rummaging around in an electronic junk yard you stumble upon a photovoltaic device with an exposed area of 2 cm × 2 cm. Taped to the device was a voltage current characteristic curve that was identical to Fig. 5.6. You examine this curve and decide that weather in your area most closely matches conditions described by $m = 1$ and $w = 0$. If you operate the cell at 27°C, determine: (a) the saturation current density; (b) the cell efficiency as a function of load resistance (you may present your results either in graphical or equation form); (c) the theoretical maximum efficiency for this cell under the stated conditions.

REFERENCES

1. R. H. Bube, *Photoconductivity of Solids* (New York: John Wiley & Sons, Inc., 1960).

2. J. J. Loferski, "Theoretical Considerations Governing the Choice of the Optimum Semiconductor for Photovoltaic Solar Energy Conversion," *Journal of Applied Physics*, 27 (1956), 777–784.

3. L. V. Azaroff, *Introductions to Solids* (New York: McGraw-Hill Book Company, Inc., 1960).

4. C. H. Blanchard, C. R. Burnett, R. G. Stoner, and R. L. Weber, *Introduction to Modern Physics*. 2nd ed. (Englewood Cliffs, New Jersey: Prentice-Hall, Inc., 1969).

5. P. Rappaport, J. J. Loferski, and E. G. Lindner, "The Electron-Voltaic Effect in Germanium and Silicon *p–n* Junctions," *RCA Review*, XVII (1956), 100–128.

6. T. S. Moss, *Photoconductivity in the Elements* (New York: Academic Press, Inc., 1952), p. 244.

7. W. Shockley, "The Theory of *p–n* Junctions in Semiconductors and *p–n* Junction Transistors," *Bell System Technical Journal*, 28 (1949), 435–489.

8. J. J. Loferski, "Recent Research on Photovoltaic Solar Energy Converters," *Proceedings of the IEEE*, 51 (1963), 667–674.

9. P. A. Crossley, G. T. Noel, and M. Wolf, "Review and Evaluation of Past Solar Cell Development Efforts," RCA Astro-Electronics Division Report, AED R-3346, Contract NASW-1427, 1968.

10. M. Wolf, "Limitations and Possibilities for Improvement of Photovoltaic Solar Energy Converters. Part I: Considerations for Earth's Surface Operation," *Proceedings of the IRE*, 48 (1960), 1246–1263.

11. J. J. Loferski, "Possibilities Afforded by Materials Other Than Silicon in the Fabrication of Photovoltaic Cells," *Acta Electronica*, 5 (1961), 350–361.

12. D. M. Chapin, "The Direct Conversion of Solar Energy to Electrical Energy," in *Introduction to the Utilization of Solar Energy*, eds. A. M. Zarem and D. D. Erway (New York: McGraw-Hill Book Company, Inc., 1963), Chapter 8.

13. W. J. Billerbeck and D. J. Curtin, "Flexible Solar Array Applications in Communications Satellites," *9th Intersociety Energy Conversion Engineering Conference*, 1974 Proceedings (New York: American Society of Mechanical Engineers, 1974).

14. D. J. Curtin and R. Cool, "Qualification Testing of Laboratory Produced Violet Solar Cells," *Proceedings of the Tenth IEEE Photovoltaic Specialists Conference* (New York: Institute of Electrical and Electronic Engineers, 1973).

15. Arvin Smith, "Status of Photovoltaic Power Technology," *Journal of Engineering for Power, Transactions of the American Society of Mechanical Engineers*, Series A, 91 (1969), 1–12.

16. H. Somberg, "Development of a Lightweight Body-Mounted Solar Cell Array with a High Power-to-Weight Ratio," *8th Intersociety Energy Conversion Engineering Conference*, 1973 Proceedings, (New York: American Institute of Aeronautics and Astronautics, 1973).

17. D. J. Curtin and R. L. Statler, "Status of Silicon Solar Cell Radiation Damage," *7th Intersociety Energy Conversion Engineering Conference*, 1972 Proceedings (Washington, D.C.: American Chemical Society, 1972).

18. J. J. Wysocki, P. Rappaport, E. Davison, R. Hand, and J. J. Loferski, "Lithium-Doped Radiation-Resistant Silicon Solar Cells," *Applied Physics Letters*, 9 (44) July 1, 1966.

19. M. S. Imamura, H. S. Wassen and J. D. Stroud, "An Approach to Performance Assessment and Management of a Large Solar Array/Battery Power System," *7th Intersociety Energy Conversion Engineering Conference*, 1972 Proceedings (Washington, D.C.: American Chemical Society, 1972).

20. J. P. Thornton and L. W. Crabtree, "ATM Solar Array in Flight Performance Analysis," *9th Intersociety Energy Conversion Engineering Conference*, 1974 Proceedings (New York: American Society of Mechanical Engineers, 1974).

21. W. R. Cherry, "The Generation of Pollution-Free Electrical Power From Solar Energy," *Journal of Engineering for Power*, Vol. 94, Series A, Number 2, April, 1972.

22. E. L. Ralph, "A Plan to Utilize Solar Energy as an Electric Power Source," *Proceedings of the Eighth IEEE Photovoltaic Specialists Conference* (New York: Institute of Electrical and Electronic Engineers, 1970).

6   Thermionic Generators

A thermionic converter can be analyzed from at least three different points of view: (1) in terms of *thermodynamics* it may be viewed as a heat engine that uses an electron gas as a working substance; (2) in terms of *electronics* it may be viewed as a diode that transforms heat to electricity by the law of thermionic emission; (3) in terms of *thermoelectricity* it may be viewed as a thermocouple in which an evacuated space or a plasma has been substituted for one of the conductors. Regardless of the point of view adopted in analysis, a thermionic converter works because of the phenomenon of thermionic emission.

6.1   HISTORICAL INTRODUCTION

Over two hundred years ago Du Fay observed that the space in the vicinity of a red-hot body is a conductor of electricity. Little theoretical information about this phenomenon was available until the publication in 1853 by Edmond Becquerel of a paper devoted to the topic. One of the observations he published was that a potential of only a few volts was sufficient to drive a current measurable by a galvanometer through air heated between platinum electrodes to a temperature corresponding to red heat.

Elster and Geitel in the years 1882 to 1889 worked on a sealed device that contained two electrodes, one that could be heated and one that could be cooled. By connecting an electrometer to the cold cathode they noted that charge flowed from the hot electrode to the cold one. It was established that at relatively low temperatures the current passed more readily if the hot filament was charged positively. At moderately higher temperatures charge passed just as easily from a negatively charged filament as from a positively charged one, and at the highest temperatures the currents from a negatively charged filament predominated.

Thomas Alva Edison, in a request for a patent in 1883, indicated that he was an early observer of the phenomenon of thermionic emission in a vacuum. A portion of his patent application reads:

"I have discovered that if a conducting substance is interposed anywhere in the vacuous space within the globe of an incandescent electric lamp and said conducting substance is connected outside the lamp with one terminal, preferably the positive one of the incandescent conductor, a portion of the current will, when the lamp is in operation, pass through the shunt circuit thus formed, which shunt includes a portion of the vacuous space within the lamp. The current I have found to be proportional to the degree of incandescence of the conductor or candle power of the lamp."

Several years later, Preece and Fleming showed that this effect was due to "negative electricity" leaving the negative end of the main filament, traversing the vacuum, and then being collected by the relatively positive independent electrode. The effect is still known as the *Edison effect*, though he quickly lost interest in it, being involved at the time in the perfection of his electric light system. The nature of the carriers of the negative charge emitted by an incandescent conductor in a vacuum was not revealed until 1899 by J. J. Thomson, who found that their ratio of charge to mass agreed within the limits of experimental uncertainty with the value he found for electrons.

By 1933 Langmuir had achieved sufficient physical understanding to construct several types of thermionic converters if he had chosen to do so. However, for the most part the subject lay dormant until 1956, when Hatsopoulos [1] described two types of thermionic converters in his doctoral thesis at the Massachusetts Institute of Technology. Since that time developmental work in the field has progressed at a very rapid rate.

6.2 BASIC PHYSICAL PRINCIPLES

In its simplest form, a thermionic energy converter consists of two electrode surfaces, one of which (called the *emitter*) is maintained at a high temperature, whereas the other (called the *collector*) is maintained at a lower temperature; they are separated by either a vacuum or a plasma (see Fig. 6-1). Electrons are given sufficient thermal energy in the emitter to impart to them a random jostling type motion that encourages some of them to escape from the surface of the emitter. They then traverse the vacuum or plasma that separates the emitter from the collector, enter the collector, and

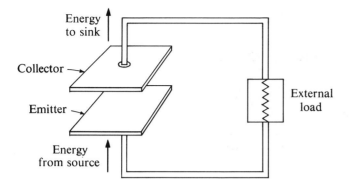

FIG. 6-1. Schematic of a thermionic converter as a heat engine.

return through an external load to the emitter, thus producing electrical power. In each of the steps described there are complications that tend to hinder the transport of electrons. Our analyses will treat these problems in some detail.

6.2.1 Work function. An electrode structure can be visualized as atoms arranged in some orderly geometrical pattern (called the *lattice*) and vibrating about their equilibrium positions. The atom is made up of a positively charged nucleus with a small number of negatively charged electrons orbiting around the nucleus. The number of electrons in each orbit and the number of orbits around each nucleus depend upon the type of atom and vary from one material to another. The attractive force between electrons and nucleus is due to the opposite charges the two masses carry. The electrons that move in the outermost orbits of the atom are held to their mother atom by a very weak force and, hence, may leave their own orbit to enter another orbit around some other nucleus. Thus the electrons in the outermost orbits do not belong to specific atoms but are generally given the name of free (or valence) electrons. When an atom loses an electron, the atom becomes positively charged (due to the deficiency of negative charge). Thus an electrode consists of positively charged atoms or ions submerged in a sea of electrons as is shown in Fig. 6-2. Different types of materials possess free electrons to a lesser or greater extent. Copper has about one free electron to every atom, while the semiconductor indium antimonide has one free electron to about every million atoms.

We now review the concept of the Fermi level introduced in Section 3.3. At absolute zero the kinetic energy of the free electrons would occupy quantum states (energy levels) from zero up to some maximum value called the Fermi level. These energy levels are separated from one another by very

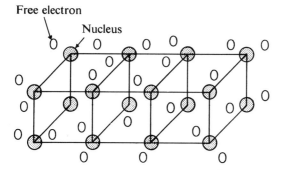

FIG. 6-2. Lattice structure of an electrode shown composed of a lattice of positive ions submerged in a sea of electrons.

small but discrete amounts of energy. Each quantum level contains a limited number of free electrons, just as each electron orbit surrounding a nucleus contains a limited number of electrons. An energy level can be filled, partly empty, or completely empty. One can imagine free electrons as stored on shelves with respect to their energy levels. The ones with low energy are on the bottom shelves while the higher energy ones are on the top shelves. At absolute zero the top shelf corresponds to the Fermi level, and its electrons have the highest energy of all the free electrons. At temperatures other than absolute zero some electrons start to have energies greater than the Fermi level. It will be recalled from our discussion in Ch. 3 on the Fermi level that at any temperature other than absolute zero the probability that a quantum state will be occupied is exactly one-half when the energy of that allowed state is equal to the Fermi level.

It is presumed that free electrons are retained in a metal by the forces of attraction between two unlike charges, since there must be as many positively charged atoms as there are free electrons. The magnitude of this force of attraction could be calculated by conventional techniques, but it would be a tedious procedure to calculate the positive charge on the surface as a function of position and then to calculate the force exerted on the electron by the total of this charge; this situation is illustrated in Fig. 6-3(a). The short cut that may be used to solve this electrostatic problem is based on the "method of images." The field to the right of $x = 0$ is identical in both Figs. 6-3(a) and 6-3(b). Thus, we may reason that the force on the electron at a distance x from the surface is the same as if the metal surface were replaced by a positive charge of magnitude e at $-x$. The force may then be calculated from the inverse square law, using a separation of $2x$, since that is the distance between the electron and its "image." The magnitude of the force on the electron is, therefore, $e^2/(16\pi\epsilon_0 x^2)$. The energy required to

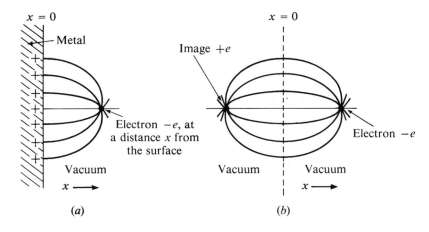

FIG. 6-3. (a) The electric field lines for an electron near the surface of a metal. (b) Electric field lines for an image charge $+e$ and an electron at equal distances on either side of $x = 0$. The field for x greater than zero is identical with the field in (a).

overcome this force is called the surface work or work function, ϕ. We note that it is normally expressed in *electron volts per electron or, more than likely, just volts.* We also note that the work that must be supplied to lift the electron to some energy level $\phi + \mathcal{E}_f$, where $\mathcal{E}_f$ is the Fermi level outside the surface, is merely ϕ, because it is presumed that any electron that escapes comes from the effective top of the Fermi distribution and, hence, already possesses the Fermi energy $\mathcal{E}_f$.

The electrodes in a thermionic energy converter have different Fermi levels; the emitter has a low Fermi level whereas the collector has a relatively high Fermi level. Thus if an electron in the emitter is to be lifted out of the emitter surface, it will require a larger amount of energy than would a corresponding electron to be lifted out of the collector. We interpret this statement to mean that free electrons in the collector Fermi level have more energy than free electrons in the emitter Fermi level. *Thus the emitter work function is greater than the collector work function.*

When sufficient heat is supplied from a high temperature source to the emitter, some of the high energy free electrons at the Fermi level will obtain enough energy to escape from the emitter surface. That is, they gain energy equal to the emitter work function with some kinetic energy left over. In the ideal case the electrons will pass the interelectrode gap between emitter and collector without expending any energy. When the electrons strike the collector, they will give up their kinetic energy plus energy equal to the collector work function, since it requires an amount of energy equal to the collector work function to cause an electron to pass through the collector surface. This energy must be rejected as heat from the low temperature collector.

Once the electron has reached the Fermi energy level of the collector, it is still at a higher energy than an electron at the Fermi energy level of the emitter. Its higher potential may now be utilized to cause it to pass through some external load.

6.2.2 Derivation of the emission formula. By making several simplifying assumptions, thermodynamical methods may be used to arrive at the electron current that a solid body will emit if supplied with sufficient energy.

Consider an electron gas in equilibrium with a hot conductor. We ignore the mutual repulsion forces that the electrons exert on one another and assume that the gas obeys the same law as an uncharged perfect gas. If we know the pressure of such a gas, from kinetic theory we will know how many electrons will strike on a unit area of hot conductor surface each second. Of these, a certain fraction will be absorbed while the remainder will be reflected. Because we hypothesized an equilibrium condition, the number of electrons that impinge on the surface must equal those that leave it. The electrons that are absorbed must be compensated for by those that are emitted. Thus the fraction of emitted electrons are $1 - r$ where r is the so-called mean reflection coefficient. One further assumption that must be made in this analysis (which is patterned after Reimann [2]) is that the electrons that are emitted leave at the same rate as if they were being emitted into a vacuum. We now seek the pressure of the external electron gas.

To obtain our goal we employ classical thermodynamics. Consider a Carnot engine, operating between two temperatures T and $T + dT$, that evaporates material from the saturated liquid state to the saturated vapor state during the heat addition process, as is shown in Fig. 6-4. The efficiency of such an engine is approximately

$$\eta_t = \frac{\text{work out}}{\text{heat supplied}} = \frac{v_{fg}dp}{h_{fg}}. \tag{6-1}$$

The efficiency of any ideal or Carnot engine is simply the temperature difference that the engine operates across divided by the temperature at which the heat is supplied. Thus for our engine we approximate its efficiency in terms of temperature as

$$\eta_t \approx \frac{dT}{T}. \tag{6-2}$$

By combining Eqs. 6-1 and 6-2 we obtain

$$h_{fg} = v_{fg}T\frac{dp}{dT}, \tag{6-3}$$

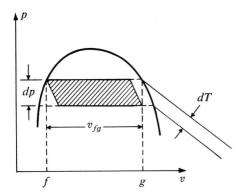

FIG. 6-4. Pressure versus specific volume plot used in the derivation of the Richardson-Dushman equation.

which is the well-known Clausius-Clapeyron equation of thermodynamics. In terms of thermionic emission we interpret h_{fg} to be the latent heat of evaporation of 1 mole of electrons and v_{fg} to be the increase in volume of the system accompanying the evaporation of this quantity of electrons.

It is also assumed that v_{fg} is the molecular volume of the external electron gas, which we may define in terms of the perfect gas law as

$$v_{fg} = \frac{\Re T}{p},$$ (6-4)

where $\Re$ is the gas constant. Thus we may combine Eq. 6-4 with Eq. 6-3 to yield

$$\frac{dp}{p} = \frac{h_{fg}}{\Re T^2} \, dT.$$ (6-5)

It is now necessary for us to define the relationship between the latent heat of evaporation and the temperature of a "subliming" solid. The thermodynamic definition of the constant pressure specific heat is

$$C_p = \left(\frac{\partial h}{\partial T}\right)_p$$ (6-6)

and if we apply this definition to a subliming solid we obtain

$$\frac{dh_{fg}}{dT} = C_{p(\text{gas})} - C_{p(\text{solid})} = C_p - C_p'.$$ (6-7)

From measurements of the Thomson effect, it is deduced that the specific heat of the internal electrons in almost all metals is negligible in comparsion with the specific heat of electrons in the gaseous phase. The general statement of the principle of equipartition of energy states that for all degrees of freedom for which the energy is a quadratic function, each degree of freedom will share equally the total energy. Using this principle, elementary classical mechanics, and thermodynamics, we can show that the total energy of N molecules is

$$N\mathcal{E}_M = \frac{f}{2} n' \mathcal{R} T, \tag{6-8}$$

where $\mathcal{E}_M$ is the mean total energy per molecule, f the number of degrees of freedom, n' the number of moles, and $\mathcal{R}$ the universal gas constant. We therefore identify Eq. 6-8 as the internal energy of a gas and call it

$$\mathcal{E}_{\text{int}} = \frac{f}{2} n' \mathcal{R} T, \tag{6-9}$$

or, on a per mole basis,

$$\mathcal{E}'_{\text{int}} = \frac{f}{2} \mathcal{R} T. \tag{6-10}$$

The molal specific heat at constant volume is defined from thermodynamics as

$$C_v = \left(\frac{\partial \mathcal{E}'_{\text{int}}}{\partial T} \right)_v \tag{6-11}$$

and thus

$$C_v = \frac{f}{2} \mathcal{R}. \tag{6-12}$$

From thermodynamic considerations of a perfect gas we know

$$C_p - C_v = \mathcal{R}. \tag{6-13}$$

Hence

$$C_p = \frac{f+2}{2} \mathcal{R}. \tag{6-14}$$

Considering a monatomic gas for which the energy is wholly kinetic energy of translation (with, of course, three degrees of freedom) we find

$$C_p = \tfrac{5}{2} R. \tag{6-15}$$

We now write Eq. 6-7 as

$$h_{fg} = \int_0^T C_p \, dT + h_0, \tag{6-16}$$

where h_0, the constant of integration, is equal to the molecular latent heat at absolute zero. Thus

$$h_{fg} = \tfrac{5}{2} \mathcal{R} T + h_0. \tag{6-17}$$

We now substitute Eq. 6-17 into Eq. 6-5 to obtain

$$\frac{dp}{p} = \frac{h_0}{\mathcal{R} T^2} \, dT + \frac{5}{2} \frac{dT}{T} \tag{6-18}$$

and integrate

$$\ln p = -h_0/(\Re T) + 5/2 \ln T + C \qquad \textbf{(6-19)}$$

or

$$p = T^{5/2} \exp\left[-h_0/(\Re T)\right] \exp(C). \qquad \textbf{(6-20)}$$

It may be found from the elements of the kinetic theory that the number of particles, $\dot{N}$, striking a unit area of wall per unit time coming in from all directions with all speeds is

$$\dot{N} = \tfrac{1}{4}nu_{av}, \qquad \textbf{(6-21)}$$

where n is the number of particles per volume and u_{av} is the arithmetic mean speed. The perfect gas law allows us to express n in terms of other properties as

$$n = \frac{p}{kT}. \qquad \textbf{(6-22)}$$

The average speed, u_{av}, can also be expressed in terms of the properties of the particle gas, providing we are willing to make an assumption about how the speeds of the particles are distributed. If we make the usual kinetic theory assumption of a Maxwellian distribution then the mean speed is

$$u_{av} = \left[\frac{8kT}{\pi m}\right]^{1/2}, \qquad \textbf{(6-23)}$$

where m is the mass of the particle. Thus the number of particles striking a unit area per unit time in terms of the properties of the particles may be found by combining Eqs. 6-21, 6-22, and 6-23 to yield

$$\dot{N} = p/(2\pi mkT)^{1/2}. \qquad \textbf{(6-24)}$$

Since an electric current is nothing more than a stream of charged particles, we can now convert our pressure equation (Eq. 6-20) into a current equation by dividing by the factor $(2\pi mkT)^{1/2}$. The fraction of emitted electrons are $(1 - r)$ of those that impinge on the emitter; thus, we write that our emission current is

$$J = (1 - r)A_0 T^2 \exp\left[-h_0/(\Re T)\right], \qquad \textbf{(6-25)}$$

or if we assume that r is independent of temperature we may write

$$J = A_1 T^2 \exp\left[-h_0/(\Re T)\right], \qquad \textbf{(6-26)}$$

where A_1 is called the *emission constant*.

We now complete the changeover from our gaseous model by redefining the work function, ϕ. By the term *work function* we mean that part of the latent heat of evaporation per electron which must be added to permit its escape at 0°K and which does not include the energy that goes into the electrons already in the vapor phase. Thus to a good approximation, we write

$$\frac{\phi}{k} = \frac{h_0}{\mathfrak{R}},\qquad\qquad\text{(6-27)}$$

where ϕ is the work function† and k is Boltzmann's constant, sometimes called the gas constant for one molecule. Thus Eq. 6-26 can be written as

$$J = A_1 T^2 \exp\left[-\phi/(kT)\right].\qquad\qquad\text{(6-28)}$$

This equation is known as the *Richardson-Dushman equation*‡ and gives the maximum electron current that an emitting surface can supply per unit area at temperature T. This current is called the *saturation current* because if we assume that an evacuated tube contains only the emitter (sometimes called the *cathode*) and a collector (sometimes called the *anode*), then if the collector is sufficiently positive it will take all the electrons that are emitted from the emitter. Under these conditions the tube is saturated. The theoretical value for the constant A_1 is usually assumed to have the value of 120 amp per $\text{cm}^2\text{-}{}^\circ K^2$.

A word of caution is in order with respect to the quantities A_1 and ϕ as they appear in Eq. 6-28. Experiments conducted to determine values of A_1 and ϕ in effect turn Eq. 6-28 into an empirical equation where A_1 and ϕ are considered constants that will fit, within the limits of experimental error, the data obtained from the measurements. The derivation of Eq. 6-28 is then merely a guide to the form of the empirical equation. The fact that A_1 may take on different values for different materials may be attributed to some of the assumptions that were made in the analysis. The reason given for allowing A_1 to exceed the theoretical value is usually attributed to changes in the chemical composition of the emitter or to the fact that the work function might decrease with increasing temperature. Later in the chapter we will tabulate some values for A_1 and ϕ for various substances.

6.3 THERMODYNAMIC ANALYSIS OF A THERMIONIC CONVERTER

In order to obtain an understanding of the parameters that govern the operation of a thermionic converter, we will conduct a thermodynamic analysis of a converter with a rather general configuration. Our approach

† If the work function is given in volts, it must be multiplied by the electronic charge, e, to make the exponential quantity dimensionless. If the work function is in electron volts, this multiplication is not required.

‡ It should also be noted that this equation can be derived in a straightforward manner by means of statistical mechanics. This technique is given in most modern physics texts and in a good electronics text such as Levine [3].

will follow rather closely that given by Houston [4]. A simple schematic of the converter is shown in Fig. 6-5.

The emitter region is maintained at temperature T_e by the heat transfer q_s and the collector region is maintained at a lower temperature T_c by heat transfer away from the collector of q_r. The emitter and collector have work functions (expressed in volts) of ϕ_e and ϕ_c respectively and are separated by a gap of width w. Because the plates are at different temperatures they will emit electrons at different rates, thus establishing a potential difference

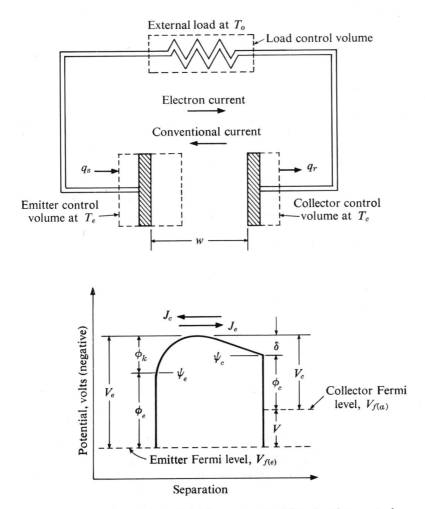

FIG. 6-5. Schematic of a thermionic energy converter showing control volumes (top) and electron potential (bottom).

between them. If they are not connected by an external load, then the cooler plate will acquire a negative potential of a magnitude that will reduce the current flow between the two plates to zero. Of course, if they are connected through an external load of resistance R_o then the potential difference between the two plates will adjust itself to a value that will be consistent with this net flow of current.

We assume that the collector and emitter reside in isothermal regions at temperatures T_c and T_e respectively. We call the Fermi level of the collector $\mathcal{E}_{f(c)}$ and the Fermi level of the emitter $\mathcal{E}_{f(e)}$ which are also assumed to be the Fermi levels of the adjacent portion of the connecting wire. We note that the Fermi level varies continuously across the converter.

In a completed circuit after electron emission becomes significant a space charge will be established in the gap and the potential distribution takes on the characteristic shape of the drawing at the bottom in Fig. 6-5. The magnitude of the space charge depends upon the emission current and the difference $\psi_c - \psi_e$. Several types of thermionic converters have been proposed and analyzed in the literature; these include the close-spaced diode, the plasma diode, and the magnetic triode among others. These devices differ only in the method by which they control the space charge. The thermodynamic analysis presented here is applicable to all of them. The details of how each of these devices controls the space charge will be taken up after the general analysis sets down the fundamentals.

The current density of electrons that the emitter will deliver to the collector may be found by utilizing Eq. 6-28. That current will be the fraction of the saturation current electrons that have sufficient initial velocities to overcome a retarding potential barrier of magnitude[†]

$$\delta + \phi_c + V - \phi_e;$$

thus

$$\begin{aligned} J_e &= A_1 T_e^2 \exp\left[-e\phi_e/(kT_e)\right] \exp\left[-e(\delta + \phi_c + V - \phi_e)/(kT_e)\right] \\ &= A_1 T_e^2 \exp\left[-eV_e/(kT_e)\right], \end{aligned} \qquad (6\text{-}29)$$

where $V_e = \phi_k + \phi_e = \delta + \phi_c + V$.

The current density that the collector will deliver to the emitter—the so-called back emission—will be that fraction of the saturation current electrons of the collector that have sufficient initial velocities to overcome the retarding potential barrier δ that the collector electrons see, that is

$$\begin{aligned} J_c &= A_1 T_c^2 \exp\left[-e\phi_c/(kT_c)\right] \exp\left[-e\delta/(kT_c)\right] \\ &= A_1 T_c^2 \exp\left[-eV_c/(kT_c)\right], \end{aligned} \qquad (6\text{-}30)$$

where $V_c = \phi_c + \delta$.

The net current density available then is the difference between J_e and J_c

[†] We note that the retarding barrier is reduced by $-\phi_e$ because the electrons already have overcome that barrier in forming the saturation current.

$$J = J_e - J_c = A_1 T_e^2 \exp\left[-eV_e/(kT_e)\right] - A_1 T_c^2 \exp\left[-eV_c/(kT_c)\right]. \quad \text{(6-31)}$$

Physically, Eqs. 6-29, 6-30, and 6-31 indicate that the net electron flux from emitter to collector, or the net current per unit area of emissive surface, is dependent upon the temperature of the emitter and collector, the space charge barrier δ, and the work function ϕ_c of the collector, provided, of course, that

$$\delta + \phi_c + V > \phi_e$$

or
$$V_e > \phi_e. \quad \text{(6-32)}$$

The output voltage V is simply

$$V = [V_e - V_c] = [(\phi_e - \phi_c) + (\phi_k - \delta)]$$

$$= \frac{1}{e}[\mathcal{E}_{f(c)} - \mathcal{E}_{f(e)}]. \quad \text{(6-33)}$$

It should be noted that ϕ_e and ϕ_c, simply being properties of the emitter and collector respectively, are independent of the current density while the space charge terms $\phi_k - \delta$ vary with the current density. We will treat the space charge term variation in the next section.

The voltage across the load will be the output voltage minus the voltage drop across the lead wire from the converter to the load. The thermoelectric voltage of the lead wire has been ignored, generally being a few millivolts or less, a small value compared to the output voltage.

$$V_{\text{load}} = V_e - V_c - IR_l, \quad \text{(6-34)}$$

where R_l is the resistance of the lead wire.

The open circuit voltage may be found by setting $J = 0$ in Eq. 6-31, redefining V_e and V_c from Eqs. 6-29 and 6-30 and solving for V to yield

$$V_{oc} = (2kT_e/e)\ln(T_e/T_c) + (\phi_c + \delta)(T_e/T_c - 1). \quad \text{(6-35)}$$

Let us consider three special cases in which $\phi_k = \delta = 0$ or complete cancellation of the space charge between the electrodes. In Fig. 6-6(a) the output voltage V is greater than the difference $(\phi_e - \phi_c)$ of the electrode work functions. Under this condition the current J that can flow from emitter to collector is

$$J_e = A_1 T_e^2 \exp\left[-(\psi_c - V_{f(e)})/(kT_e)\right] \quad \text{(6-36)}$$

or, equivalently,

$$J_e = A_1 T_e^2 \exp\left[-(\phi_c + V)/(kT_e)\right].$$

This emitter current is also the net output current of the converter, provided the temperature of the collector is sufficiently low so that no appreciable back emission occurs at the collector surface. The relation between J and V for the conditions described in Fig. 6-6(a) is given by the line XY in Fig. 6-7. This line is called the Boltzmann line and is a straight line in the semi-log plot of Fig. 6-7; it has a slope of $1/kT_e$.

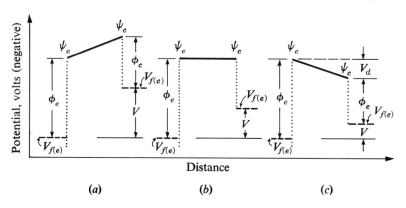

FIG. 6-6. Potential diagrams for various operating conditions.

When V, the load voltage, becomes equal to $(\phi_e - \phi_c)$ as in Fig. 6-6(b), the current density J equals the saturation current density of the emitter because ψ_c equals ψ_e and all the emitted electrons have sufficient energy to reach the collector. For voltages V less than $(\phi_e - \phi_c)$ as in Fig. 6-6(c) the current density remains at the saturated value and the relation between J and V simply becomes the horizontal line YZ of Fig. 6-7.

We now return to our thermodynamic analysis and evaluate the heat input into the isothermal region that is assumed to surround the emitter. A control volume is drawn such that it encloses the emitter and passes through the potential maximum as is shown in Fig. 6-5.

The first law of thermodynamics applied to the control volume states that in the steady state the energy leaving the control volume must equal the energy the control volume receives, that is,

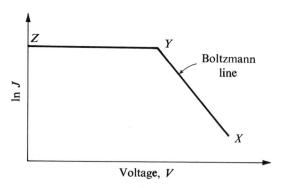

FIG. 6-7. Theoretical voltage-current density characteristics of a thermionic converter.

Energy Out = Energy In

$$q_e + q_{fg} + q_{cd} + q_{ra} = q_c + q_j + q_s, \qquad (6\text{-}37)$$

where q_e is the cooling of the emitter due to electrons carrying energy away. This term is analogous to the Peltier cooling that takes place in the thermoelectric converter. It should be noted that the average kinetic energy† (in equivalent volts) of all electrons emitted from the emitter surface is $2kT_e/e$, but only a small fraction have sufficient kinetic energy to overcome the retarding potential that the emitter electrons see of magnitude $\phi_c + \delta + V - \phi_e$. Thus the energy electrons take with them is

$$q_e = J_e(\phi_c + \delta + V - \phi_e + 2kT_e/e). \qquad (6\text{-}38)$$

q_{fg} corresponds to the heat leaving the emitter due to the so-called latent heat of evaporation of the electrons. That is, the energy used to overcome the work function of the emitter

$$q_{fg} = J_e\phi_e. \qquad (6\text{-}39)$$

q_{cd} is the heat leaving due to conduction and in the most general case consists of that portion which is conducted down the lead wire and that portion which would be conducted away by a plasma (if we were considering a plasma-type generator); thus

$$q_{cd} = \Delta T\,[\lambda_l A_l/(A_e l) + \lambda_w A_w/(A_e w)], \qquad (6\text{-}40)$$

where $\Delta T = T_e - T_c$ and the subscript l refers to the lead wires and w to the interelectrode gap.

The net loss of energy by radiation from the emitter to the collector is q_{ra}. If we consider two parallel surfaces whose distance apart is small compared with their size, so that nearly all the radiation emitted by one surface will fall upon the second, we will obtain a radiation shape factor of unity for either surface. If we further restrict our analysis to gray surfaces, that is, surfaces whose absorptivities and thus emissivities are the same for all wavelengths, we may use the Stefan-Boltzmann law [5] of radiation as given by

$$q_{ra} = 5.67 \times 10^{-12}(T_e^4 - T_c^4)(\epsilon_e^{-1} + \epsilon_c^{-1} - 1)^{-1}. \qquad (6\text{-}41)$$

We now modify this result by evaluating the emitter emissivity ϵ_e at T_e and the collector emissivity ϵ_c at the geometric mean temperature $\sqrt{T_e T_c}$ to reflect the fact that the collector and emitter are not true gray bodies. The Stefan-Boltzmann constant used in Eq. 6-41 is given so that the results are in watts per square centimeter.

Now we consider those terms that make up the input to the emitter: q_c is the energy the collector supplies to the control volume by back emission, that is, the back emitted electrons must climb exactly the same hill as those

† A discussion of the motion of electrons in solids is given in Section 4.3.

from the emitter except that their kinetic energy due to temperature is just $2kT_c/e$; thus

$$q_c = J_c(\phi_c + \delta + V + 2kT_c/e). \tag{6-42}$$

q_j is the Joule heating that takes place in the lead wires and in the plasma if one exists, half of which is assumed to go to the emitter and half to the collector, thus

$$q_j = \tfrac{1}{2}(J_e - J_c)^2(R_l + R_w). \tag{6-43}$$

We may now calculate the heat supplied q_s from Eq. 6-37 and Eqs. 6-38 through 6-43 as

$$q_s = J_e(V_e + 2kT_e/e) - J_c(V_e + 2kT_c/e) + \sigma\omega(T_e^4 - T_c^4)$$
$$+ \Delta T \left[\lambda_l A_l/(l A_e) + \lambda_w A_w/(w A_e)\right] - \tfrac{1}{2}(J_e - J_c)^2(R_l + R_w). \tag{6-44}$$

The thermal efficiency may now be calculated by dividing the output power $V(J_e - J_c)$ by the heat supplied to yield

$$\eta_t = V(J_e - J_c)/q_s. \tag{6-45}$$

We note that all heat fluxes in the preceding equations have been calculated on the basis of watts per square centimeter, and in Eqs. 6-44 and 6-45 we used the relationship $V_e = \phi_c + V + \delta$.

There are several particularly simple cases, which we consider first for their usefulness in telling us about the thermodynamics of thermionic converters.

The first case is one that ignores all energy losses from the emitter except electron emission cooling. We are interested in this case because it tells us how the back emission from the collector sets a lower limit on the value of V_c. Each electron traveling from the emitter to the collector will carry away an energy (in volts) of $V_e + 2kT_e/e$, while those electrons that form the back emission from the collector to the emitter will give up on striking the emitter energy (in volts) equal to $V_e + 2kT_c/e$. Under these assumptions Eq. 6-45 becomes

$$\eta_t = \frac{(V_e - V_c)(J_e - J_c)}{J_e(V_e + 2kT_e/e) - J_c(V_e + 2kT_c/e)}. \tag{6-46}$$

We now define three dimensionless quantities:

$$\beta_e = eV_e/(kT_e); \qquad \beta_c = eV_c/(kT_c); \qquad \theta = T_c/T_e;$$

introducing them and Eqs. 6-29 and 6-30 into Eq. 6-46 to obtain

$$\eta_t = \frac{[\beta_e - \theta\beta_c][1 - \theta^2 \exp(\beta_e - \beta_c)]}{(\beta_e + 2) - \theta^2(\beta_e + 2\theta)\exp(\beta_e - \beta_c)}. \tag{6-47}$$

Only if $\beta_c > \beta_e - 2\ln(\theta)^{-1}$ is Eq. 6-47 meaningful. That is, we require $J_e > J_c$ or else the device does not give up power to an external load. It is interesting to note that β_e does not vary greatly over the range of emitter temperatures and currents typically found in strongly emitting thermionic emitters. If we let J_e range from 1 to 10 amp per cm² while T_e varies from 1000° to 2000°K, we find that β_e will range only from 16.3 to 20.0. In Fig. 6-8 we plot Eq. 6-47, that is, η_t versus β_c, for a value of $\beta_e = 18$ as a function of θ. This plot tells us that the efficiency is very near a maximum value where

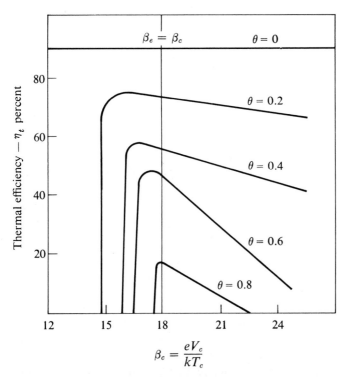

FIG. 6-8. Thermal efficiency versus a collector parameter as a function of temperature ratio. After J. M. Houston [4] with permission.

$\beta_c = \beta_e$ that is for $\beta_c = 18$. Thus for maximum efficiency under our stated assumptions we conclude

$$\beta_e \approx \beta_c$$

or
$$V_c = V_e T_c / T_e. \tag{6-48}$$

The meaning of this equation becomes clear if we consider a thermionic converter in which we hold V_e, T_c, and T_e constant and vary the collector work function ϕ_c, which is simply V_c minus the potential barrier δ. At $V_c = V_e$ the efficiency of the device is zero simply because there is no output potential. As V_c is lowered the efficiency increases until at some particular point the collector starts to back emit significantly. The efficiency then goes through a maximum at the point given by Eq. 6-48 and if V_c is reduced more, the efficiency quickly falls to zero as J_c approaches J_e. At the optimum value of V_c the magnitude of the back emission current is given by $J_c = \theta^2 J_e$, which may be easily obtained from Eqs. 6-29, 6-30, and 6-48.

At the optimum value of V_c as given by Eq. 6-48 the maximum efficiency as obtained from Eq. 6-47 is

$$\eta_t = \frac{\beta_e(1 - \theta)}{\beta_e + 2}\left[\frac{1 - \theta^2}{1 - \theta^2(\beta_e + 2\theta)/(\beta_e + 2)}\right]. \qquad \textbf{(6-49)}$$

The bracketed term is always near unity. The Carnot efficiency is simply $1 - \theta$, so that if β_e is approximately equal to 18, the efficiency in this case is about 90 percent of the Carnot efficiency.

If we assume that the electrons drift over the barrier with no kinetic energy $\phi_k = 0$, thus making $2kT = 0$, then Eq. 6-46 becomes simply $(V_e - V_c)/V_e$. At the optimum value of V_c as given by Eq. 6-48 the device has an efficiency exactly equal to the Carnot efficiency.

The quantity V_c may be solved for explicitly by eliminating V_e in favor of β_e in Eq. 6-48, thus

$$V_c = T_c\beta_e k/e = T_c\beta_e/11{,}606. \qquad \textbf{(6-50)}$$

If we assume that $\beta_e = 18$ and $T_c = 300°K$ we find that $V_c = 0.47$ volt, which is unattainably low. However, if we assume $\beta_e = 18$ and $T_c = 1200°K$ then $V_c = 1.88$ volts—a value not difficult to attain in practice. [The constant 11,606 comes from dividing Boltzmann's constant (1.38×10^{-23} joule per °K) by the electronic charge (1.60×10^{-19} coulomb). By substituting units into the given equation we can always tell when we need to include the charge constant.] The use of a material with a value of V_c less than this would lower the efficiency because of increased back emission. Thus we conclude that if we are working with room temperature collectors we assume the back emission to be negligibly small and merely strive for as low a value of V_c as can be achieved.

It is also possible to fix the value of V_c and find the maximum permissible collector temperature that does not reduce efficiency because of back emission. Equation 6-50 does this when solved for T_c.

6.4 SPACE CHARGE CONTROL

Because electrons are charged particles that constitute the working fluid of a thermionic converter, they produce a space charge in the region between the emitter and collector. Unless steps are taken to limit this buildup of charge it will act to severely limit the efficiency of a thermionic converter.

While a number of different methods have been tried to limit the effect of the space charge retarding force, in recent years all methods but one have been discarded. The method that has produced the best results so far is the one that provides for introduction of positive ions in the interelectrode space. For this reason we will devote most of our attention to it. Other methods of space charge control will be considered briefly in subsequent sections, merely for the sake of completeness.

The introduction of an ionized gas into the interelectrode space gives rise to a variety of potential distributions. Factors complicating this phenomenon are surface ionization, electron scattering and surface adsorbed layers. Let us consider the most common electron cloud neutralization medium, cesium. As the cesium pressure in a thermionic generator is increased while the emitter temperature is held fixed, the emitted ion current will increase proportionally at first [6]. When cesium adsorption on the surface begins, however, the corresponding reduction of the surface work function will slow down the rate of increase of ion emission; in fact, as the pressure continues to go up a point will be reached where further increases in cesium pressure may result in a decrease in ion emission. On the other hand, electron emission will, in general, increase with increasing cesium pressure. As will be shown in Section 6.4.7, there is a value of the cesium pressure that produces just enough ions to neutralize the space charge. The surface work function ϕ_{nn} corresponding to that pressure is called the neutralization work function. It follows that if an emitter is operated at a pressure greater than p_{nn} or, equivalently, if it has a work function less than ϕ_{nn}, surface ionization is not adequate for complete space charge neutralization. Ions will be in excess however, if $\phi > \phi_{nn}$.

The value of ϕ_{nn} for a given metal is a weak function of the surface temperature and since the practical range of emitter temperatures actually employed in thermionic converters is rather narrow (1200°C to 1800°C) for practical purposes one single value of ϕ_{nn} for each metal is adequate. The approximate values of ϕ_{nn} for some commonly used emitter materials are listed in Table 6-1.

TABLE 6-1. APPROXIMATE NEUTRALIZATION WORK FUNCTION OF VARIOUS EMITTER SURFACES*

Material	Neutralization Work Function ϕ_{nn}, volts
Polycrystalline Tungsten	2.65
Polycrystalline Rhenium	2.80
Polycrystalline Niobium	2.55

* After Ref. [6].

Because of the nature of the state of the ionized gas between the electrodes, Hernquist [7] suggested three principal modes of operation of cesium vapor thermionic converters:

(1) The plasma mode. This mode is characterized by low cesium pressures and high emitter temperatures. The low cesium pressure results in a cesium-free emitter.

(2) The high pressure mode. In this mode of operation, the cesium pressure may be in the range of a few torrs (1 torr = 1 mm of Hg). The high cesium pressure causes the emitter to be cesium covered and requires a small interelectrode spacing to limit the loss due to electron collisions.

(3) The arc or ball-of-fire mode. This mode of operation occurs at lower temperatures than mode 2. Impact ionization is the main mode of ion generation.

We will discuss each of these three modes of operation in turn.

6.4.1   The low-pressure diode. The first method of space charge control that is explored is one that utilizes the principle of resonance ionization. When positive ions are created within the generator, the negative space charge cloud between the collector and emitter can be neutralized. A gas whose ionization potential is less than the work function of the emitter is introduced into the generator. As an atom of this gas strikes the hot emitter surface, the outermost electron of the gas becomes more strongly bound to the emitter and hence the atom leaves the emitter without its outermost electron; that is, the gas atom leaves as a positive ion. If the gas pressure in the generator is kept at such a value that electrons making the transit from emitter to collector encounter few or no collisions, the generator is said to be a low-pressure one. A low-pressure converter is said to be one with cesium pressure of about 10^{-4} mm of mercury. A cross-sectional schematic of a low-pressure converter is shown in Fig. 6-9. The various processes taking place in such a converter are illustrated in Fig. 6-10.

The gas most often used in this type of generator is cesium, which has an ionization potential of 3.89 volts. For a tungsten emitter whose work function is 4.52 volts the resonance ionization condition is satisfied; that is, the ionization potential of the gas is less than the work function of the emitter. In addition to neutralizing the space charge, the cesium can serve another purpose: it will condense on the collector if the latter is kept cool enough, imparting to the collector a work function approximately equal to that of cesium. In some cases a monatomic layer of cesium on a metal oxide can produce a polarized atomic layer with a work function lower than that obtained by just the condensation of the ionizing gas.

Nottingham [8] has analyzed the work of Taylor and Langmuir [9] to determine the minimum temperature that will produce complete ionization of every cesium atom as it arrives at the hot emitter. He found that if less

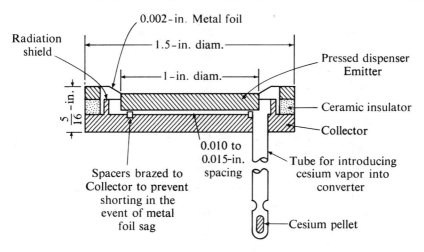

FIG. 6-9. Cross section through a cesium vapor converter.

than 10^{13} atoms per sec arrive from a pool of liquid cesium at 0°C, then an emitter at 970°K will have a negligible coating of cesium atoms and every atom that arrives will leave the emitter as a cesium ion. As the arrival rate increases, the minimum emitter temperature for complete ionization goes up correspondingly. Nottingham found the following empirical formula between minimum emitter temperature for complete ionization of cesium and temperature of the liquid cesium source by utilizing Taylor's and Langmuir's graphical data on atom arrival rate, temperature, and the ideal gas law:

$$T_{\min} = 3.6T_{cs}. \tag{6-51}$$

Nottingham suggests that the linear relationship between these two quantities is perhaps more than an accident of numbers because the physical phenomena of the evaporation of an atom from a liquid surface and the evaporation from a tungsten surface may involve attractive forces not too different from each other. If the temperature of the emitter is slightly below the minimum as given by Eq. 6-51, the production of ions at any given arrival rate is discontinuously reduced by approximately a factor of ten.

For complete neutralization of the space charge the density of ions must equal the density of electrons, which for plane parallel geometry can be represented as

$$J_p/u_{av(p)} = J_{sat}/u_{av(n)}, \tag{6-52}$$

where the subscript p denotes ions; sat, the saturation condition; and n, electrons.

If, however, the electrons and ions are in thermal equilibrium, the mean

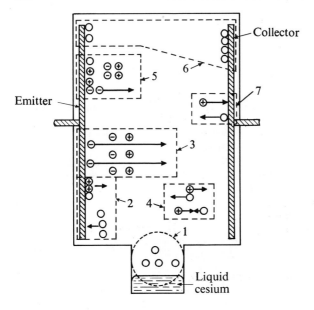

Emitter

Collector

O Neutral cesium atom
⊕ Positive cesium ion
⊖ Electron

Liquid cesium

FIG. 6-10. Schematic representation of the various processes in a gas-filled converter. (1) Evaporation of liquid cesium; (2) Cesium atoms arrive at emitter and depart as ions; (3) Space charge neutralization; (4) Energy sharing of ions with atoms; (5) Formation of an ion space charge sheath; (6) Reduction of work function due to cesium deposition; (7) Cesium ion recombination at the collector surface.

velocities of the electrons and ions will not be the same, as can be shown from kinetic theory and Eq. 6-23:

$$u_{\text{av}(p)} = \left[\frac{8kT}{\pi m_p}\right]^{1/2} \qquad u_{\text{av}(n)} = \left[\frac{8kT}{\pi m_n}\right]^{1/2}, \tag{6-53}$$

where m_p and m_n represent the mass of the ion and of the electron respectively. Thus Eq. 6-52 may be rewritten as

$$J_p = J_{\text{sat}}(m_n/m_p)^{1/2}. \tag{6-54}$$

The number of atoms striking the emitter surface per unit time per unit of emitter area is given by Eq. 6-21 as

$$\tfrac{1}{4}nu_{\text{av}}. \tag{6-21}$$

If it is assumed that each cesium atom that strikes the emitter is ionized, the ion current density becomes

$$J_p = \tfrac{1}{4}nu_{av(p)}. \qquad (6\text{-}55)$$

Combining Eqs. 6-52 and 6-55 yields

$$n = 4J_{sat}/u_{av(n)}$$

and by utilizing the definition of the mean velocity given in Eq. 6-23 and the perfect gas law as given by Eq. 6-22, we find that the required cesium pressure is

$$p = 4.12 \times 10^{-6}(T_{av})^{1/2}J_{sat} \text{ mm of Hg}, \qquad (6\text{-}56)$$

where T_{av} is the mean of the emitter and collector temperatures.

If we have adjusted the cesium pressure so that the space charge is completely neutralized, then the output voltage becomes, from Eq. 6-33, simply

$$V = \phi_e - \phi_c. \qquad (6\text{-}57)$$

The number of electrons that succeed in reaching the collector is simply the number yielded under saturation conditions minus those that combined with ions, thus

$$J_e = J_{sat} - J_p. \qquad (6\text{-}58)$$

The ratio of electrons reaching the collector to the saturation value is then

$$\frac{J_e}{J_{sat}} = 1 - \left[\frac{m_n}{m_p}\right]^{1/2}. \qquad (6\text{-}59)$$

The power density output becomes

$$P = J_{sat}[1 - (m_n/m_p)^{1/2}][\phi_e - \phi_c]. \qquad (6\text{-}60)$$

Thus the power lost in ion generation is simply

$$J_{sat}(\phi_e - \phi_c)(m_n/m_p)^{1/2},$$

which may be of the order of a few hundredths of a watt per ampere. We may now use Eq. 6-29 to calculate the saturation current density, and then use Eq. 6-59 to calculate the actual current. The efficiency may be calculated by using Eq. 6-60 in the numerator of an equation such as Eq. 6-45, thus

$$\eta_t = J_{sat}[1 - (m_n/m_p)^{1/2}][\phi_e - \phi_c]/q_s \qquad (6\text{-}61)$$

where q_s is given in Eq. 6-44.

Any time a plasma comes in contact with a material body, a sheath or contact potential region is formed between the plasma and the body. A voltage drop occurs across the sheath region which in many ways is similar to the contact potential appearing at a semiconductor-metal junction or at a p–n semiconductor junction. The reason that a sheath forms can be explained by considering the physical situation. If we assume that the electrons and ions are in thermal equilibrium in a plasma, then the speed of the electrons must be many times the speed of the ions as can be reasoned from Eq. 6-53, since the mass of the ion is many times the mass of the electron.

Now in each case Eq. 6-21 will predict the random particle current density for each of the species; for electrons when the electron speed is used and for the ions when the ion speed is used. This means that if the particle density, n, *in the plasma* is the same for each species, the current density of electrons leaving the plasma (and entering the sheath) will exceed by many times the current density of the ions.

Imagine that an isolated electrode is brought into contact with the plasma (though the argument can be shown to hold for conductors as well [10]); at first the electron current to the electrode will be much greater than the ion current. The isolated body will be charged negatively, therefore, until its potential is reduced enough to make the net charge arriving at the body zero; that is, since no current can flow through the isolated body, an equal number of positive and negative charges must arrive at the body per unit time for equilibrium to exist. This gives rise to a potential difference between the plasma and the body that we call the sheath; it is this sheath that repels some of the negative charges trying to leave the plasma. The positive ions which enter the sheath will be rapidly swept to the electrode by the sheath's electric field; thus the positive and negative charge densities *within the sheath region* will be unequal.

Now we return to the situation that prevails in a low-pressure diode. When there are a sufficient number of positive ions to exactly neutralize the space charge, the motive diagram looks like Fig. 6-11(a). This zero field condition is in general not stable. A slight excess of ions will cause electrons to be injected with increased velocity into the space between the emitter and collector. If the ion production is increased to a greater value, an ion space charge sheath will form as is shown in Fig. 6-11(b). The width of this sheath is generally less than a mean free path and therefore electrons that have energy enough to leave the emitter can generally enter the emitter-collector space. Details on experimental operation of low-pressure converters may be found in an article by Hernquist, Kanefsky, and Norman [11].

6.4.2 The high-pressure cesium converter. Increasing the pressure in the converter until it reaches values in the neighborhood of 1 mm of mercury or higher causes some notable changes in the characteristics of a converter. Under the high-pressure situation conditions are much more like those in ordinary discharge plasmas, with the motion of the ions and electrons more or less randomized by collisions between electrons and ions as they traverse the interelectrode space. In this case the collision mean free path is much smaller than the electrode spacing. Under these conditions the current to or from electrodes is largely determined by thin space charge sheaths [see Fig. 6-11(b)] that are a few Debye lengths in thickness. Again, ion generation is mainly due to resonance ionization at the emitter. The recommended emitter temperature is between 1500 to 1800°C.

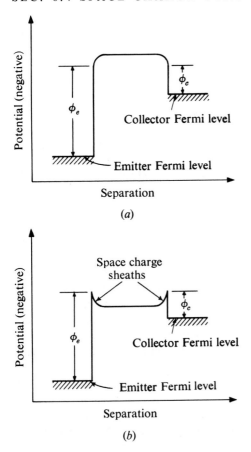

FIG. 6-11. Potential diagram for electrons in a thermionic converter where the space charge has been (a) partially neutralized by positive ions; (b) completely neutralized by positive ions.

A detailed treatment of the high-pressure or plasma converter has been presented by Lewis and Reitz [12]–[14]. To obtain a complete set of working equations it is necessary to solve the heat conduction problem in the plasma. We consider the reason for this in a qualitative way.

Electrons that traverse the interelectrode space in this type of converter experience several phenomena not generally found in the previously discussed converters. Because of the electron-ion collisions previously mentioned, the interelectrode space offers considerable resistance to the passage of the electric current. For cesium this resistance may be approximated by

$$\rho \approx 0.16(3000/T)^{3/2} \text{ ohm-cm.} \qquad \textbf{(6-62)}$$

If a large current density J is fed into this plasma, the plasma must find a way of disposing of this energy. For example, a generator delivering a current density of 40 amp per cm^2 utilizing a plasma offering an electrical resistivity of, say, 0.25 ohm-cm, will be faced with the problem of dissipating 400 watts per cm^3. Lewis and Reitz [14] estimate that the plasma is totally incapable of disposing of this much energy. This heat has no choice but to go into heating the electrons that are in the interelectrode space. Thus it is possible for the electrons at the collector to be hotter than the emitter temperature, producing an increase in the collector barrier and output voltage. Thus the Joule heat need not be completely wasted.

The thin space charge sheaths at the emitter and collector also affect the electron gas. At the emitter the electrons fall down a potential barrier. The potential energy is converted into heat, thus raising the temperature of the electron gas to a value greater than the emitter temperature. The potential barrier at the collector has the property of draining from the electron cloud near it only those electrons that have enough energy to surmount the barrier. These energetic electrons are replaced by means of collisions with slower electrons. Because it drains energetic electrons away from the plasma, the collector barrier has a cooling effect on the electron cloud. By considering the Joule heating in the plasma and the cooling and heating at the collector and emitter, the heat conduction problem in the interelectrode space can be solved. The output voltage equation in final form is the difference between the work functions of the emitter and collector plus a term involving the emitter and collector temperatures and the temperature of the electron gas just outside the emitter.

The thermal efficiency is calculated in the usual way, taking into account conduction in the plasma and the lead wires and the other terms that are given in Eq. 6-44.

The high-pressure plasma diode offers the advantage of almost complete space charge neutralization. The disadvantage is the large internal voltage drop due to the relatively high impedance of the plasma.

6.4.3 The ignited mode converter. At even lower temperatures (from 1200 to 1500°C) more efficient conversion is obtained in the ignited or arc mode of operation. In fact, the majority of all thermionic converters in operation today operate in this ignited mode, characterized by volume ionization of the cesium vapor. The ignited cesium vapor has the nature of an externally heated hot cathode discharge. The so-called ball-of-fire mode refers to an external power source, whereas the arc, or ignited, mode refers to internal heating by the emission current. This method of operation is characterized by two distinct regions containing "bright" and "dark" plasmas. In the dark region the electrons do not have sufficient energy to ionize and excite significant numbers of cesium atoms. Neutralization occurs in this region via ion flow from the bright region. Electrons accelerated into this bright region over the emitter sheath have picked up sufficient energy to ionize and excite cesium atoms through inelastic collisions and so produce the bright discharge. See Fig. 6-12. Ions produced in this manner are sufficient not only to neutralize any existing negative space charge, but also to produce a strong positive space charge. Figure 6-13 presents the potential diagrams

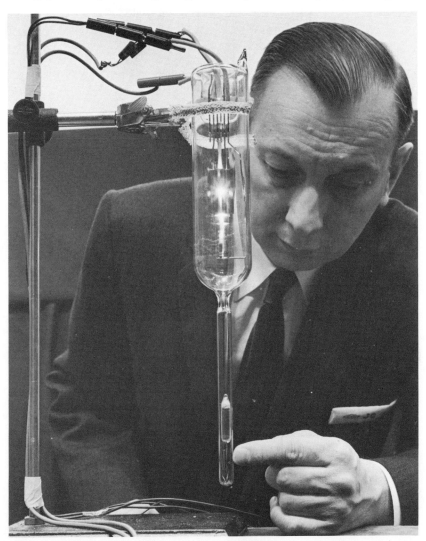

FIG. 6-12. Photograph of a thermionic converter which uses an ionized cesium gas to reduce the space charge in the converter. Photograph courtesy of the Westinghouse Electric Corporation.

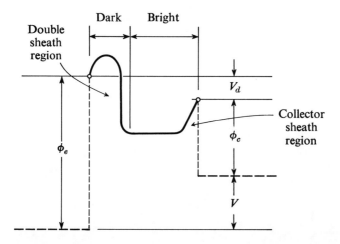

FIG. 6-13. Potential distribution in a cesium converter operating in the ignited mode.

corresponding to the ignited mode. An internal voltage drop, V_d, is needed to maintain the volume ionization of the cesium. To provide V_d the output voltage is, of course, reduced by an equivalent amount. The ignited mode current-voltage characteristic is shown in Fig. 6-14. At low voltages the current approaches the saturation current of the emitter.

For given electrode temperatures, given work functions and a given output voltage, a thermionic converter reaches the highest attainable output

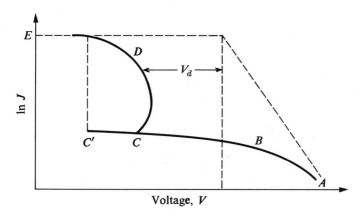

FIG. 6-14. Typical voltage-current density characteristic of a thermionic converter at relatively low temperatures.

power and efficiency if the effects of space charge and collision are completely eliminated. The first effect is eliminated if a sufficient number of positive ions are present in the interelectrode space and the second is reduced if the product of the pressure of the cesium vapor times the electrode spacing, $p_{cs}w$, is made sufficiently small. When these two conditions are satisfied, the voltage-current curve is that described in Fig. 6-7 and the diode is said to be operating with ideal performance.

A real converter, though, has the ionization loss V_d and has a current-voltage curve as shown in Fig. 6-14. This curve can be divided conveniently into two regions. The region ABCC′ may be qualitatively described as being current deficient in comparison to the ideal voltage-current curve, and a region CDE that may be qualitatively described as being voltage deficient in comparison to the ideal curve. The first region is called the passive region of operation. The current deficiency observed in this region is due either to lack of sufficient ion emission from the emitter for space-charge neutralization, if $\phi_e < \phi_{nn}$, or to elastic collisions, or both.

The second region, CDE, is called the ignited mode region of operation of a cesium diode. The voltage deficiency observed in this region is due to both elastic and inelastic collisions between electrons and cesium atoms. It is believed that in this mode of operation the electrons that enter the interelectrode space are accelerated and acquire additional kinetic energy which is proportional to the internal voltage drop V_d. This excess kinetic energy is randomized by means of elastic collisions. The randomized kinetic energy of the electrons is sufficient to ionize the cesium atoms in the interelectrode space. The ions produced in this manner are sufficient not only to neutralize any existing negative space charge but, in addition, produce a strong positive space charge which gives rise to the concave upward potential diagram shown in Fig. 6-13. It has been found experimentally and justified theoretically that the voltage deficiency V_d in the ignited mode of operation depends primarily on the product $p_{cs}w$ [15]. The V_d versus $p_{cs}w$ curve possesses a minimum of about 0.5 V at a $p_{cs}w$ value of about 20 mil-torr. Figure 6-15 depicts this minimum. A generalized correlation of ignited mode current-voltage characteristics has been developed [16] and is shown in Fig. 6-16. The characteristics are plotted in the form of normalized current against the output voltage less the difference in work functions for the emitter and collector. The pressure-spacing product is plotted as a parameter. The use of these curves will be illustrated by means of an example in the next section. Because of the complex nature of the transport phenomena in the interelectrode space it is extremely difficult to predict with accuracy the performance of real devices. This problem is discussed in more detail in Refs. [6], [15], [16].

An enormous amount of experimental data on converter performance has been obtained in the past few years. These data assist the designers of

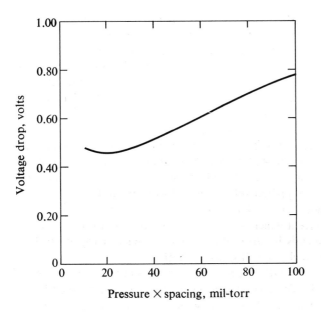

thermionic systems to select design parameters best suited for each application. Figure 6-17 of Ref. [6] gives the maximum power density as a function of output voltage for a number of different converter combinations. The best performance attained in 1962 was by a polycrystalline tungsten emitter (WS-Mo) and is represented by the lowest line in Fig. 6-17. Subsequent testing of rhenium emitters (ReB-Mo) improved performance considerably. This improvement is attributed to the fact that polycrystalline rhenium requires a lower cesium pressure to attain a given work function than does polycrystalline tungsten. Further improvements were attained by etching the emitter surface to expose preferred orientations that adsorb cesium better. But the most spectacular improvement was attained by introducing vapor additives in the interelectrode space (WBPH-Mo with additive). These results were first attributed to cesium fluoride in the additive but were subsequently found to be caused by oxygen that was present in the cesium fluoride.

It now appears that the use of additives in cesium diodes is probably the most promising technique for achieving further improvements in converter performance [6]. Such additives may either be electronegative, such as

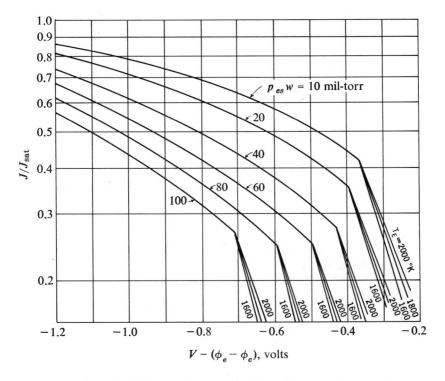

FIG. 6-16. The ratio of the actual current density to the saturation current density as a function of a corrected voltage (the load voltage less the difference in electrode work functions). The interelectrode pressure times spacing product is the parameter. After Ref. [16] with permission.

oxygen, or electropositive, such as barium. The electronegative additives increase the work function of the refractory metal emitters in the absence of cesium. When cesium is introduced in the converter, it adsorbs better on the emitter surface and results in a lower work function for a given cesium pressure than that achieved in the absence of the electronegative additive. On the other hand, electropositive additives directly reduce the work function of the refractory metal emitter. The net result for both types of additives is the same: namely, lower cesium pressures are required to produce a given work function on the emitter.

Other improvements in the performance of converters that have been made in recent years include reduction in interelectrode spacing, reduction of collector work functions by means of additives, and reduction of the internal voltage drop of diodes operating in the ignited region by means of inert gas additives.

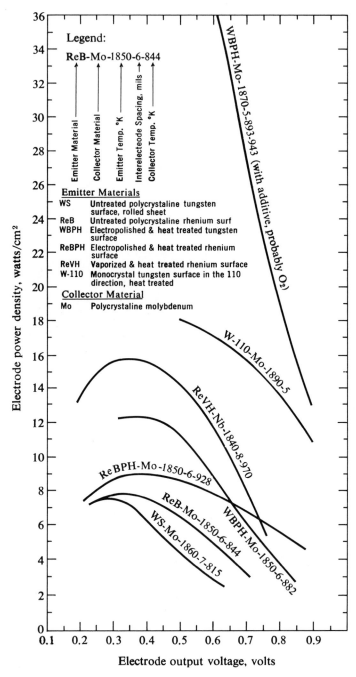

FIG. 6-17. The power density as a function of output voltage in converters with optimized cesium pressures for various emitter-collector surface pairs. After Ref. [6] with permission.

6.4.4 A numerical example of the analysis of a cesium diode. In this section we will try to bring together the work of our previous sections in solving a numerical example of a cesium-filled diode. In doing this we will make certain assumptions consistent with obtaining reasonably accurate engineering answers without undue labor. The numerical work will be treated as if this were a preliminary design; therefore, answers in general will not be carried beyond two decimal places.

Problem. It is proposed to design a solar-powered cesium-filled thermionic diode operating in the ignited mode to supply power for a satellite. The device is to operate with an emitter temperature of 1850°K and is to be made of polycrystalline rhenium. The cesium pressure is to be 4 torr and is sufficient to provide a neutralization work function on the emitter of 2.80 volts. The collector is molybdenum and is assumed to have a work function of 1.70 volts. Find the output voltage, maximum power, maximum current density and thermal efficiency.

Solution. Is back emission important? is our first question. Since we are assuming no space charge loss, then $V_e = \phi_e$ and $V_c = \phi_c$ and Eq. 6-48 yields

$$T_c = (\phi_c/\phi_e)T_e = (1.7/2.80)(1850) = 1125°K.$$

Let us assume that the radiator for this unit will keep the collector at 1000°K and since this temperature is below the temperature calculated by Eq. 6-48, we may ignore back emission in the rest of our calculations.

We now proceed to calculate the output voltage. The pressure in the converter was given as 4 torr. Since we wish to maximize power we propose to use a pressure-spacing product of 20 mil-torr. This fixes the spacing at 5 mils (0.005 in.). From Fig. 6-15 we read an internal voltage drop of $V_d = 0.45$ volt. Then from Fig. 6-13 we can compute the load voltage as follows:

$$V = \phi_e - \phi_c - V_d = 2.80 - 1.70 - 0.45 = 0.65 \text{ volt.}$$

This load voltage can now be used to find what fraction of the saturation current is being drawn. The abscissa on Fig. 6-16 is the load voltage less $(\phi_e - \phi_c)$ or

$$0.65 - (2.80 - 1.70) = -0.45 \text{ volt.}$$

From Fig. 6-16 we now use this number to read $J/J_{sat} = 0.40$ on the 20 mil-torr line. Although Ref. [16] reports a somewhat more complicated method of calculation, we choose to calculate the saturation current by means of Eq. 6-30,

$$J_{sat} = 120 \, T_e^2 \exp\left(-11{,}606 \, \phi_e/T_e\right),$$

where once again we have included the electronic charge in our calculations because ϕ_e is in volts. Thus the saturation current density is

$$J_{sat} = 120 \, (1850)^2 \exp\left[-11{,}606 \, (2.80)/1850\right]$$
$$= 8.4 \text{ amps/cm}^2.$$

But the actual current is only 0.4 of the saturation current density or

$$J = 0.4 \times 8.4 = 3.35 \text{ amps/cm}^2.$$

The power density output can now be computed as

$$P = VJ = (0.65)(3.35) = 2.18 \text{ watts/cm}^2.$$

We are now in a position to calculate the magnitude of the external load that will yield maximum power. To simplify our work we assume that our device has an emitter area of 4 cm², thus yielding a current of 13.4 amps and a power output of 8.72 watts. The load resistance is calculated from the familiar equation for the dissipation of electrical energy $P = I^2R_o$ and thus $R_o = P/I^2 = 8.72/(13.4)^2 = 0.048$ ohm.

Before moving on to the efficiency calculations we should note that the cost of ionizing the cesium used up about 40 percent $[0.45/(2.80 - 1.70)]$ of the voltage available between the emitter and collector work functions. The saturation current from collector to emitter may be calculated and found to be only 3 percent of that from emitter to collector. Therefore neglecting it will have no appreciable effect on the results of this example.

Kitrilakis and Meeker [17] report a thermal conductivity for cesium vapor of about 1.24×10^{-4} W/cm-°K. Using this figure and the temperature difference between the emitter and collector we may calculate the energy loss by conduction from the emitter to collector:

$$q_{cd} = \lambda_w \Delta T/w = 1.24 \times 10^{-4} \times (1850 - 1000)/1.27 \times 10^{-2}$$
$$= 8.30 \text{ watts/cm}^2.$$

To find the energy leaving the emitter by radiation Eq. 6-41 is used. From emissivity data reported by Wilson [18] we use $\epsilon_e = 0.3$ and $\epsilon_c = 0.1$ and thus

$$q_{ra} = 5.672 \times 10^{-12}[(1850)^4 - (1000)^4][(0.3)^{-1} + (0.1)^{-1} - 1]^{-1}$$
$$= 5.0 \text{ watts/cm}^2.$$

Next we calculate the cooling of the emitter due to electrons carrying energy away from it. This quantity is composed of all electrons with kinetic energy $2kT_e$ that can surmount the potential barrier ψ_e. Thus by combining Eqs. 6-39 and 6-38 we obtain

$$q_e = J_e (V_e + 2kT_e)$$
$$= 3.35 (2.80 + 2 \times 8.62 \times 10^{-5} \times 1.850 \times 10^3)$$
$$= 3.35 (2.80 + 0.32)$$
$$= 10.4 \text{ W/cm}^2.$$

Houston [4], in an analysis conducted on the terms that make up the heat supplied to the emitter of a thermionic converter, found an interesting relationship between the Joule heat generated in the lead wire q_jA_e, the heat conducted from the emitter along the lead $q'_{cd}A_e$ (where the prime denotes the fact that we are including the Joule heating terms in our expression), the voltage drop in the lead V_l, and the thermal efficiency of the device, η_t.

The Joule heat developed in the lead by the current J_eA_e is the familiar I^2R term and is given by

$$q_jA_e = (J_eA_e)^2\rho_l l/A_l. \tag{6-63}$$

The heat conducted away from the emitter is simply that which is calculated from the Fourier conduction equation minus one-half the Joule heat that is assumed to be returned to the emitter,

$$q'_{cd}A_e = \lambda_l A_l(T_e - T_o)/l - \tfrac{1}{2}q_jA_e, \tag{6-64}$$

where T_o is the temperature of the load which is assumed to be room temperature. The product of Eqs. 6-63 and 6-64 is

$$q_j(q'_{cd} + \tfrac{1}{2}q_j) = J_e^2\lambda_l(T_e - T_o)\rho_l. \tag{6-65}$$

The Wiedemann-Franz-Lorenz relation, as we have seen earlier, is defined as the ratio of the thermal conductivity to the electrical conductivity times the absolute temperature, and is a constant that holds fairly well for most metals over a fairly wide range of temperatures;

$$L_w = \lambda_l/(\sigma_l T_{av}) = 2.45 \times 10^{-8} \text{ watt-ohm/}°K^2. \tag{6-66}$$

Using Eq. 6-66 in Eq. 6-65 we obtain

$$q_i(q'_{cd} + \tfrac{1}{2}q_i) = J_e^2 L_w T_{av}(T_e - T_o). \tag{6-67}$$

The term $q_i(q'_{cd} + \tfrac{1}{2}q_i)$ is practically independent of the dimensions of the lead wire and the material. By making the lead wire diameter large the Joule heat terms can be made small while the conduction term will be made large due to large cross-sectional area A_l, or vice versa. By lengthy but straightforward calculations one may find the following four relationships when efficiency is maximized with respect to lead geometry,

$$q_i = \eta_t q'_{cd}/(1 - \eta_t), \tag{6-68}$$

$$V_l = \left[\frac{L_w T_{av}(T_e - T_o)\eta_t}{1 - \tfrac{1}{2}\eta_t}\right]^{1/2}, \tag{6-69}$$

$$q'_{cd} = J_e V_l(1 - \eta_t)/\eta_t \tag{6-70}$$

and

$$l/A_l = V_l/(J_e A_e \rho_l). \tag{6-71}$$

We may now apply these equations to our example problem by making the following assumptions: $T_e - T_o = 1550°K$; $T_{av} = 1075°K$; $\eta_t = 0.08$. (We assume a value for the efficiency here, and if our estimate is very far off in our later calculation for thermal efficiency, we can come back and correct this assumed value and the resulting calculations.)

Thus the voltage drop in the lead is, from Eq. 6-69,

$$V_l = \left[\frac{2.45 \times 10^{-8} \times 1.075 \times 10^3 \times 1.550 \times 10^3 \times 8 \times 10^{-2}}{1 - 4 \times 10^{-2}}\right]^{1/2}$$

$$= 5.85 \times 10^{-2} \text{ volts,}$$

which is less than 9 percent of the load voltage.

We have previously calculated a value for the emitter current of $J = 3.35$ amp/cm² which we will now use in Eq. 6-70

$$q'_{cd} = 3.35 \times 5.85 \times 10^{-2} \times (1 - 0.08)/0.08$$
$$= 2.25 \text{ watts/cm}^2.$$

The optimum value of lead length to lead area may now be obtained by assuming an electrical resistivity of 5×10^{-5} ohm-cm (tantalum at 1425°K) and an emitter area of 4 cm². Using these values in Eq. 6-71 we obtain

$$l/A_l = 5.85 \times 10^{-2}/(3.35 \times 4 \times 5 \times 10^{-5}) = 87.3 \text{ cm}^{-1}.$$

Thus if we choose #14 wire (16.3×10^{-2} cm diameter) we find that the optimum length of lead to the emitter is 1.82 cm.

We may now calculate the heat supplied as follows:

$$q_s = q_{cd} + q_{ra} + q_e + q'_{cd}$$
$$= 8.30 + 5.00 + 10.40 + 2.25 = 25.95 \text{ watts/cm}^2,$$

where the term q'_{cd} includes the Joule heat contribution as given by Eq. 6-63. The thermal efficiency is then

$$\eta_t = P/q_s = 2.18/25.95$$
$$= 8.4 \text{ percent,}$$

which is approximately one-fifth of the Carnot efficiency. This value compares rather well with the value of efficiency we assumed to make the final series of calculations. Therefore for preliminary design purposes it will not be necessary to recalculate the last set of calculations.

6.5 THERMIONIC CONVERTER MATERIALS

The problem of developing materials suitable for use in thermionic converters ranks next to the space charge control problem in the development of efficient thermionic generators. We will briefly describe the properties we desire in materials suitable for converters.

First we consider the emitter. The most important properties required in a good emitter material are:

(1) A high electron emission capability coupled with a low rate of deterioration;

(2) Low emissivity, to reduce heat transfer by radiation from the emitter.

(3) The material must be such that in the event some of it vaporizes and subsequently condenses on the collector it will not poison the collector (that is, change the collector properties, thereby making it less effective).

The relative importance of these properties is dependent upon the type of converter being designed. It should be noted that efficiency is a much slower rising function of electron emission capability if space charge is present than if there is no space charge. It was also noted in the section on low-pressure diodes that for reasonable ionization, at least a portion of the emitter must have a work function in excess of the ionization potential of the neutralizing gas. In the case of cesium this means 4 volts or more. Converters utilizing other means of space charge control can use emitters that have a lower work function.

The work function may be reduced considerably by an absorbed single layer of foreign atoms. This comes about by the establishment of a dipole layer at the surface. The layer can be formed by atoms or molecules. This is essentially what happens in a cesium converter, which is designed so that cesium condenses on the emitter or collector. Table 6-1 presented earlier gives some approximate values for work functions for some commonly used emitter materials.

The main criteria for choosing a collector material is that it have as low a work function as possible. Because the collector temperature is held below any temperature that will cause significant electron emission, its actual emission characteristics are of no consequence. The lower the collector work function, however, the less energy the electron will have to give up as it enters the collector surface. In practice the lowest value of ϕ_c that can be maintained stably is about 1.5 eV. For applications in which it is desirable to maintain the collector at elevated temperatures (greater than 900°K), such as space applications, an optimum value of ϕ_c may be determined. For example, Ref. [6] reports that for a collector temperature of 1273°K, $\phi_{c(opt)}$ is about 1.6 eV, a value rather easy to achieve in practice. Molybdenum has been used widely as a collector; it is frequently assumed to have a work function of 1.7 eV.

Morris in Ref. [19] gives a rather complete review of the literature for the better metallic electrodes used in thermionic cesium converters. Power densities as high as 36 watts/cm² are reported for some of the earlier converters.

Most investigators agree that high operating temperatures make the realization of practical thermionic converters an extremely difficult technological feat. This problem is being skirted by the development of converters that operate at lower temperatures. Henne and Weber [20] have built converters that utilize pressed and sintered cermets of uranium oxide and molybdenum for emitters; cesium is still used to provide ions for charge neutralization. The UO_2 is responsible for a low work function while the molybdenum provides mechanical strength and good thermal and electrical conductivity.

Experiments carried out with this material show encouraging results. The collector was polycrystalline molybdenum. Figure 6-18 summarizes the operating results for this diode, giving the power output density as a function of interelectrode spacing and emitter temperature. As the emitter temperature increases, the power density also increases but so does the optimum cesium pressure, and therefore there is increased dependence on interelectrode spacing. An output power density of 2.5 watts/cm² at an emitter temperature of 1250°C was achieved. Five watts per square centimeter was achieved with an emitter temperature of 1350°C. A thermal efficiency of 15 percent was reached on some runs. Operating lifetimes of several hundred hours have been demonstrated with these converters. Producing a converter with a lifetime of several thousand hours is the next goal.

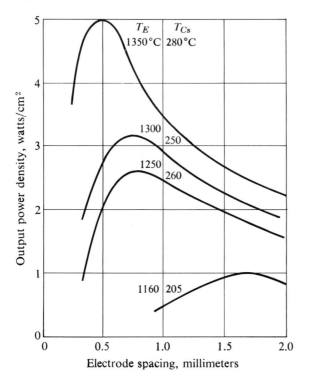

FIG. 6-18. The dependence of power output density on electrode spacing in a low-pressure cesium diode utilizing pressed and sintered cermets of uranium oxide and molybdenum emitters. After Ref. [20].

6.6 HEAT PIPES

As the previous sections indicate, thermionic converters require a great deal of thermal energy to be supplied to the emitter over a small area and since their efficiency is not high, a great deal of thermal energy must be carried away from the collector. This apparently simple problem has caused the designers of thermionic (and thermoelectric) systems to give a great deal of thought to the problem of thermal energy transport. One of the solutions that has been proposed is as simple as it is elegant. Technically, it has been called [21] a "structure of very high conductance"; in practice it is called a *heat pipe*.

Heat pipes are devices capable of transferring large thermal energy densities at efficiencies greater than 90 percent by utilizing the evaporation, condensation, and surface tension properties of a working fluid. They are capable of transferring up to 500 times as much heat per unit weight as can a solid thermal conductor of the same cross section. Other than a working fluid the heat pipe normally has some kind of closed outer shell and a porous capillary wick (see Fig. 6-19). Heating one region of the heat pipe evaporates working fluid and drives the vapor to other regions where it condenses, giving up its latent heat. In the wick, surface tension forces return the condensate back to the evaporator region through capillary channels. In actual practice heat flux densities of up to 400 watts/cm² have been obtained using liquid silver as the working medium at 2300°K. Theoretical calculations indicate that with development much higher heat fluxes can be attained.

The heat pipe is appealing as an auxiliary to energy conversion devices because it can be used as a thermal transformer to couple heat sources and sinks of different heat flux densities. Heat flux density transformation ratios as large as 10 to 1 have been achieved. Such ratios arise, for example, in thermionic converters where the boiler end receives heat at a very high flux density and rejects it by radiation from a larger condenser area of the heat pipe at a low flux density.

The operating temperature of a heat pipe is determined by the choice of the working fluid and the operating pressure. In theory the heat pipe operates almost at a single temperature—the boiling-condensing temperature at the working pressure which is constant along the pipe. In practice a small temperature gradient exists, because a small vapor pressure gradient is generated between the boiler and condenser sections. Thus a heat pipe can be designed to operate with a temperature gradient of only a few degrees. In practice nearly 5 kW have been driven down a 2 ft long molybdenum heat pipe at 1700°K with a temperature drop of less than 6K°.

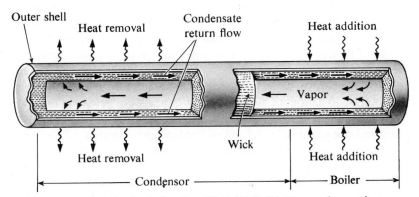

FIG. 6-19. Schematic of a heat pipe. Heat applied to one end vaporizes the working fluid and causes it to travel to the other end where it condenses, giving up its latent heat of vaporization. The working fluid then returns to the evaporation section by capillary action along a wick.

The heat pipe concept has been attributed to G. M. Grover and associates of the Los Alamos Scientific Laboratory [21]. An out-of-core version of a six-cell, heat-pipe–heated, thermionic converter array has been described by Kroeger, Ward, and Breitwieser [22]. Their major extension of technology is in the area of heat pipes for cooling a reactor and carrying thermal energy from the reactor to the converters. The performance characteristics of an out-of-core thermionic system at power levels between 40 and 70 kW(e) are summarized. The use of the heat pipe in a relatively inexpensive line-focussing solar concentrator is described by Swet [23]. This unit provides near-isothermal heat transport at otherwise unachievable rates. The heat pipe is located at the focus of a parabolic collector and tracks the sun by means of a bimetallic thermal heliotrope. Russo [24] describes a radioisotope-powered thermoelectric generator that uses 48 copper/water heat pipes to pump energy out of the thermoelectric units.

6.7 THERMIONIC SYSTEM CONSIDERATIONS

In this section we shall briefly consider some systems that utilize thermionic generators as their power sources. These designs point out some of the types of engineering problems that must be solved before thermionic power can become practical.

6.7.1 Thermionic reactor power systems for space. Three thermionic nuclear-reactor–powered systems have been designed for a variety of space applications [25]. Studies have included both manned and unmanned applications for auxiliary power and electrical propulsion. Specific systems reported on are for auxiliary power units providing 5 to 10 kW(e) for unmanned satellites, 40 kW(e) for manned space laboratories, and 120 kW(e) for electric propulsion. All of these systems employ the same basic thermionic fuel element.

The power system that has been proposed for the manned orbital laboratory typifies work that has been done on space thermionic systems. It was designed to produce 40 kW(e) for five years of operation. Two different configurations have been examined: one boom-mounted on the laboratory and one mounted at the end of a tether approximately 3.2 km long. The tethered version reduces the amount of shielding that must be carried aloft to protect laboratory personnel. Table 6-2 summarizes the two systems.

The thermal power produced in the reactor that is not converted to electricity is removed by the heat-rejection system. In the boom-mounted configuration, circulating liquid metal (NaK) passing through the reactor becomes radioactive and would be a radiation hazard to personnel in the spacecraft if it flowed directly to the radiator. The heat is transferred to

TABLE 6-2. SPACE THERMIONIC POWER SYSTEM SUMMARY

	Boom-mounted	Tethered
Net conditioned power (kW(e))	40	40
Beginning-of-life capability (kW(e))	55	65
Overall length (m)	10	12
Maximum diameter (m)	3.66	3.06
Radiator area (m²)	75	
Power system mass (kg)	5,360	5,180
Station shield mass (kg)	6,770	
Support boom mass (kg)	1,800	
Cable tether mass (kg)		1,090
Total power subsystem mass (kg)	13,950	6,220

five radiator loops in a heat exchanger, which surrounds the reactor but is shielded from both the reactor and the spacecraft. The radiator loops carry the heat to the radiator panels, each of which consists of 1150 heat pipes making up an isothermal radiating surface. In the tethered configuration, a single circulating NaK loop is used with no intermediate heat exchanger.

The power-conditioning system takes the electrical power from the reactor at 9 volts d-c and converts it to a higher regulated voltage. To meet the requirement of providing 40 kW(e) net after five years of operation, a redundant power capability of 35 percent is built in to compensate for thermionic fuel element degradation or failures during life.

6.7.2   Thermionic power for fossil fuel central-station plants. Thermionic units have also been proposed for use in fossil fuel central-station plants. Present power plant practice limits the usable source temperature to approximately 800°K (1000°F). This restriction is primarily the result of the pressure-temperature characteristic of the steam along with the allowable stress values for economically feasible materials. Fossil fuels are capable of delivering much higher temperatures than 800°K. Thus it is obvious that the efficiency of central-station power plants can be raised by using more of the temperature potential of fossil fuels. Thermionic topping is one means of using this high temperature potential; the heat rejected from the thermionic converters can then be supplied to a conventional steam plant. Engdahl, Cassano, and Dowdell [26] describe a plan for adding a thermionic topper to the existing T.V.A. Bull Run Station. Figure 6-20 presents a schematic of their design.

A forced draft fan delivers inlet air to the air preheater and final air heater and thence into the main combustion chamber where pulverized coal

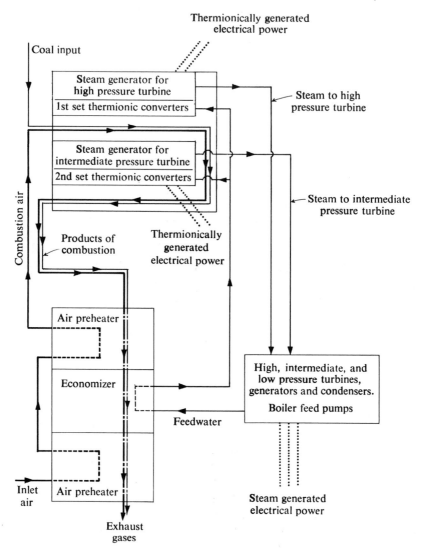

FIG. 6-20. Block diagram of a thermionic topping unit for a coal-fired power plant. The addition of topping is designed to increase the efficiency and output of the plant without substantially increasing the cost.

is introduced and fired. The hot combustion gases pass over the first group of thermionic modules and then they go to the other side of the furnace where they pass over another group of thermionic modules. From this point they flow through the final air heater, economizer and air preheater, before entering ducting which leads to the precipitators and exhaust stack.

Heat rejected from the first set of modules is used to produce superheated steam. Heat rejected from the second group of modules is used to produce reheat steam for the intermediate pressure turbine. The thermionic converters are assumed to have an efficiency of 15 percent; therefore they deliver 85 percent of the energy supplied to them to the steam generator sections. The thermionic modules use a silicon carbide envelope as protection against the corrosive effects of the high temperature fossil fuel combustion gases. The emitter is assumed to be at 1785°K. Superheated steam at 239 atm and 800°K is generated by the heat rejected from the first thermionic unit's collectors and the reheat steam is produced at 37 atm and 800°K by the heat rejected from the second bank of units.

The low voltage, high current output of the thermionic units is fed to an acyclic motor which is coupled directly to an 1800 rpm a-c generator. The cost of such a motor in the power range of interest (225 d-c megawatts) was about $6/kW in 1968 and is estimated to have an efficiency of 98 percent. The integration of the thermionic topping unit into the conventional a-c output of the plant is achieved in this one piece of equipment, the acyclic motor.

The study cited claims that the plant's total output power and efficiency increases because of thermionic topping from 914 megawatts at 41.3 percent to 1139 megawatts at 50.6 percent while the fuel flow increases only 2 percent. Primarily because of reductions in boilerhouse volume, Engdahl, et al. [31] claim an 8 percent reduction in direct plant costs as well as a $3 million per year saving in fuel cost. They claim that their studies indicate that thermionic energy conversion does have a place in the field of large central station power plants. As an additional bonus to those already mentioned, they expect such plants to produce significant reductions in thermal pollution (because of reductions in the amount of energy ultimately rejected by the plant) and atmospheric pollution (because of the significantly higher temperatures in the combustion chambers) that supply energy to the thermionic converters.

6.7.3 Miniature thermionic converters.
Thermionic converters have also been considered to supply miniscule amounts of power. On the low end of the scale, they have been designed to supply 100 microwatts for medical telemetry units and up to 100 milliwatts for special purpose space and terrestrial units.

Gasper and DeSteese [27] have described the design and operation of several miniature radioisotope-fueled thermionic converters. Such a converter is illustrated in Fig. 6-21. The units are generally constructed around a right circular cylinder fuel pellet. The emitter forms the first case around the fuel element; the collector is maintained in place by small sapphire or ruby balls located between the emitter and collector. A cesium reservoir appendage is added for those devices using cesium as a space charge inhibitor.

FIG. 6-21. A low-powered thermionic unit designed to produce about 20 milliwatts. Photograph courtesy of Donald W. Douglas Laboratories.

Because these devices operate at inherently lower temperatures than the converters described previously, electrode materials other than rhenium, tungsten, and niobium have been found suitable for these units. Oxides of barium and strontium on tungsten and nickel were two of the materials which proved suitable for the small units described in Ref. [27]. Emitter temperatures were between 573°K and 865°K, while collector temperatures were around 500°K. These low temperatures and the low current densities (less than 100 ma/cm^2) give rise to very long-lived units, with a high degree of reliability and a wide choice of construction materials.

Promethium-147 in the promethia fuel form (Pm_2O_3) is the low energy beta emitter which was used in the first units built. It was found that acceptable radiation dose rates could be obtained from low power units (0.01 to 5 milliwatts) with as little as one centimeter of shielding.

One of the units tested delivered 19 milliwatts at 0.14 V with an overall efficiency of 0.55 percent. It has been suggested that the volume (7.9 cm^3), weight (87 gm), and efficiency of these prototype units can be significantly improved with continued development.

NOTATION

A = area, cm^2

A_0 = constant in Eq. 6-25, amp/cm^2-°K

A_1 = emission constant in Richardson-Dushman equation, amp/cm^2-°K

C = constant of integration in Eq. 6-19

C_p = molal constant pressure specific heat for a gas, kcal/(mole-°K)

C'_p = molal constant pressure specific heat for a solid, kcal/(mole-°K)

C_v = molal constant volume specific heat, kcal/(mole-°K)

e = electronic charge, coulombs

$\mathcal{E}$ = energy, electron volts or ergs

$\mathcal{E}_M$ = energy per molecule, electron volts or ergs

$\mathcal{E}_{\text{Int}}$ = internal energy, electron volts or ergs

$\mathcal{E}'_{\text{Int}}$ = internal energy per mole, electron volts or ergs/mole

f = number of degrees of freedom

h_{f_g} = latent heat of vaporization per mole of electrons, ergs/mole

h_0 = molecular latent heat at absolute zero, ergs/mole

I = electric current, amp

J = electric current density, amp/cm^2

k = Boltzmann's constant, ergs/°K

l = lead wire length, cm

L_w = Wiedemann-Franz-Lorenz constant, 2.45×10^{-8} watt-ohm/°K^2

m = mass, gm

n = number of particles per unit volume, cm^{-3}

n' = number of moles

N = number of molecules

$\dot{N}$ = number of particles striking a unit area per unit time

p = pressure, dynes, mm of mercury, or torrs

P = power density, watts/cm^2

q = heat rate density, watts/cm^2

q'_{cd} = conduction heat density including Joule heat, watts/cm^2

r = mean reflection coefficient, dimensionless

R = electrical resistance, ohms

R_o = external load resistance, ohms

$\mathcal{R}$ = universal gas constant, ergs/(mole-°K)

T = temperature, °K

u = speed, cm/sec

v_{f_g} = change in specific volume in the evaporation of 1 mole of electrons, cm^3/mole

V = electrical potential, volts

V_d = volume ionization potential, volts

w = gap width, cm

β = $eV/(kT)$, dimensionless

δ = retarding potential barrier, volts

ϵ = emissivity, dimensionless

ϵ_0 = permittivity of free space, farad/meter

η_t = thermal efficiency, dimensionless

θ = T_c/T_e, dimensionless

λ = thermal conductivity, watt/(cm-°K)

π $= 3.141\cdots$
ρ $=$ electrical resistivity, ohm-cm
σ $=$ Stefan-Boltzmann constant, watts/(cm^2-$^\circ$K^4)
ϕ $=$ work function or potential function, electron volts or volts
ψ $=$ electrical potential as denoted in Fig. 6-5, volts
ω $=$ emissivity factor as defined in Eq. 6-44, dimensionless

Subscripts

av $=$ average
c $=$ collector
cd $=$ conduction between emitter and collector
cd' $=$ conduction along leads
cs $=$ cesium
e $=$ emitter
f $=$ Fermi level
fg $=$ evaporation
int $=$ internal
j $=$ Joule
k $=$ kinetic energy
l $=$ lead wires
min $=$ minimum
n $=$ electrons
nn $=$ neutralization
M $=$ per molecule
o $=$ room
oc $=$ open circuit
p $=$ positive ions
r $=$ rejected
ra $=$ radiation
s $=$ supplied
sat $=$ saturation
w $=$ interelectrode gap

PROBLEMS

6-1. Could a thermionic converter with identical work functions for both emitter and collector yield a useful power output? Explain your answer briefly.

6-2. A thermionic converter has an emitter with a work function ϕ_1 and a collector with a work function ϕ_2. The emitter and collector are maintained at the same temperature. Can such a converter yield a useful power output? What is the open circuit voltage of such a device?

6-3. Derive Eq. 6-35.

6-4. Derive Eq. 6-47.

6-5. Calculate the saturation current density from an ideal thermionic converter with a tungsten emitter at 2500°K. Tungsten has a work function of 4.52 volts.

6-6. Consider a close-spaced high vacuum converter with an emitter and collector each having an area of 6 cm². The emitter is made of thorium carbide ($\phi_e = 3.2$ volts, $A_1 = 100$ amp/cm² − K²) and the collector is made of barium oxide on tungsten ($\phi_c = 1.2$ volts, $A_1 = 0.9$ amp/cm² − °K²). The space charge has the following properties: $\phi_k = 0.20$ volt and $\delta = 0.13$ volt. The emitter is kept at a temperature of 1900°K. Find the diode's output voltage, current and thermal efficiency.

6-7. Compute a quantity analogous to the Seebeck coefficient for a thermionic converter.

6-8. Manufacturing difficulties prevented the construction of the converter analyzed in Section 6.4.4. It was decided to double the interelectrode spacing to 10 mils. What effect does this have on the significant performance parameters of that converter if all other conditions are maintained the same as in the example problem?

6-9. A small thermionic converter is designed to be implanted in the body to power a heart pacemaker. The unit will use plutonium-238 as a fuel and must deliver 160 micro-watts. The emitter with an area of 4 cm² will be made of lanthanum boride on tungsten ($\phi_e = 2.66$ volts, $A_1 = 29$ amp/cm²-°K²) while the collector is made of strontium oxide on tungsten ($\phi_c = 1.3$ volts, $A_1 = 0.3$ amp/cm²-°K²). In this high vacuum converter $\phi_k = \delta = 0.1$ volt. The collector will reject heat to the body and will be kept at 43°C (the upper limit tolerable for blood and tissue). Find the output voltage and the required emitter temperature.

6-10. A low-pressure cesium converter operates at an emitter temperature of 2300°K and a collector temperature of 1100°K. The monolayer of cesium on tungsten produces an emitter work function of 1.5 volts and a value of $A_1 = 3$ amp/cm²-°K². Find the cesium pressure for complete neutralization of the space charge. Also find the ion current density in the converter.

Answer: $p = 1.45$ mm Hg.

6-11. A certain thermionic converter has an open circuit voltage of 2.5 volts but while under load at the same temperature it has an output potential of 0.7 volt and delivers a current of 3.0 amp. The emitter has an area of 2 cm² and is maintained at 1600°K while the collector is kept at 600°K, which causes back emission to be negligible. The retarding potential barrier, δ, is found to be equal to 0.09 volt. Find the energy leaving the emitter due to the so-called electron cooling and the unit's thermal efficiency considering electron cooling as the only mode of energy loss.

6.12. You recently found an old thermionic converter in the rubbish bin of your electronics shop. The nameplate had the following data on it: "Emitter: $\phi_e = 2.6$ volts, $A_{1e} = 33$ amp/cm²-°K², Area = 5 cm²; the interelectrode spacing is 20 mil and the interelectrode pressure is 5 torr. Back emission for converter is negligible." You take this unit over to the lab and measure the following values: $V_{\text{load}} = 0.7$ volts with $I = 5$ amps; $V_{oc} = 1.7$ volts. You discover that you have no way to measure temperatures in the lab and so you must make do with these numbers. Assuming that the retarding potential barrier, δ, is negligible find: (a) the emitter temperature; (b) the recommended collector temperature; (c) the cooling of the emitter due to electron emission, in watts/cm².

REFERENCES

General

1. G. N. Hatsopoulos, "The Thermoelectron Engine" (Sc.D. dissertation, M.I.T., 1956).

2. A. L. Reimann, *Thermionic Emission* (New York: John Wiley & Sons, Inc., 1934).

3. S. N. Levine, *Quantum Physics of Electronics* (New York: The Macmillan Company, 1965).

4. J. M. Houston, "Theoretical Efficiency of the Thermionic Energy Converter," *Journal of Applied Physics*, 30 (1959), 481–487.

5. F. Kreith, *Principles of Heat Transfer*. 3rd ed. (Scranton: International Textbook Company, 1974).

6. G. N. Hatsopoulos, "Thermionic Energy Conversion," *Intersociety Energy Conversion Engineering Conference, 1966 Record* (New York: American Institute of Aeronautics and Astronautics, 1966).

7. K. G. Hernquist, "Analysis of the Arc Mode Operation of the Cesium Vapor Thermionic Energy Converter," *Proceedings of the IEEE*, 51 (1963), 748–754.

Low-Pressure Diode

8. W. B. Nottingham, "Cesium Plasma Diode as a Heat-to-Electrical-Power Transducer," in *Direct Conversion of Heat to Electricity*, eds. J. Kaye and J. A. Welsh (New York: John Wiley & Sons, Inc., 1960), Chapter 8.

9. J. B. Taylor and I. Langmuir, "The Evaporation of Atoms, Ions and Electrons from Cesium Films on Tungsten," *Physical Review*, 44, Section 2 (1933), 423–458.

10. M. A. Uman, *Introduction to Plasma Physics* (New York: McGraw-Hill Book Company, 1964).

11. K. G. Hernquist, M. Kanefsky, and F. H. Norman, "Thermionic Energy Converter," *RCA Review*, XIX, No. 2 (1958), 244.

High-Pressure Converter

12. H. W. Lewis and J. R. Reitz, "Thermoelectric Properties of the Plasma Diode," *Journal of Applied Physics*, 30 (1959), 1439–1445.

13. H. W. Lewis and J. R. Reitz, "Open Circuit Voltages in the Plasma Thermocouple," *Journal of Applied Physics*, 30 (1959), 1838.

14. H. W. Lewis and J. R. Reitz, "Efficiency of the Plasma Thermocouple," *Journal of Applied Physics*, 31 (1960), 723.

Ignited Mode Converter

15. S. S. Kitrilakis, A. Shavit, and N. S. Rasor, "The Departure of the Observed Performance from the Idealized Case in Cesium Thermionic Converters," *Proceedings of the Twenty-Fourth Annual Conference on Physical Electronics*, M.I.T., March, 1964,. p. 171.

16. S. S. Kitrilakis and F. Rufeh, "Experimental Correlation of Converter Variables in the Ignited Mode," *Proceedings of the International Conference on Thermionic Electrical Power Generation*, 1965, London, England.

17. S. S. Kitrilakis and M. Meeker, "Experimental Determination of the Heat Conduction of Cesium Gas," *Advanced Energy Conversion*, 3 (1963), 59.

18. V. C. Wilson, "Thermionic Power Generation," *IEEE Spectrum* (1964), pp. 75–83.

Thermionic Materials

19. J. F. Morris, "Performances of the Better Metallic Electrodes in Cesium Thermionic Converters," *7th Intersociety Energy Conversion Engineering Conference*, 1972 Proceedings (Washington, D.C.: American Chemical Society, 1972).

20. R. Henne and W. Weber, "Experiments with Low Pressure Cs Diodes with Cermet Emitters, Operating at Emitter Temperatures of 1250°C," *9th Intersociety Energy Conversion Engineering Conference*, 1974 Record (New York: American Society of Mechanical Engineers, 1974).

Heat Pipes

21. G. M. Grover, T. P. Cotter, and G. F. Erickson, "Structures of Very High Conductance," *Journal of Applied Physics*, 35 (1964), 1990–1991.

22. E. W. Kroeger, J. J. Ward, and R. Breitwieser, "An Out-of-Core Version of a Six-Cell Heat-Pipe Heated Thermionic Converter Array," *7th Intersociety Energy Conversion Engineering Conference*, 1972 Proceedings (Washington, D.C.: American Chemical Society, 1972).

23. C. J. Swet, "Heliotropic Thermal Generators," *8th Intersociety Energy Conversion Engineering Conference*, 1973 Proceedings (New York: American Institute of Aeronautics and Astronautics, 1973).

24. F. A. Russo, "Operational Testing of the High Performance Thermoelectric Generator (HPG-02)," *9th Intersociety Energy Conversion Engineering Conference*, 1974 Proceedings (New York: American Society of Mechanical Engineers, 1974).

Systems

25. A. J. Gietzen and W. G. Hohmeyer, "Thermionic Reactor Power Systems," *7th Intersociety Energy Conversion Engineering Conference*, 1972 Proceedings (Washington, D.C.: American Chemical Society, 1972).

26. R. E. Engdahl, A. J. Cassano, and R. B. Dowdell, "Thermionic Energy Conversion for Central Power Stations," *3rd Intersociety Energy Conversion Engineering Conference*, 1968 Record, I.E.E.E. Publication 68C 21 Energy (New York: Institute of Electrical and Electronic Engineers, Inc., 1968).

27. K. A. Gasper and J. G. DeSteese, "Miniature Isotope Thermionic Electrical Power Supply," *3rd Intersociety Energy Conversion Engineering Conference*, 1968 Record, I.E.E.E. Publication 68C 21 Energy (New York: Institute of Electrical and Electronic Engineers, Inc., 1968).

7 Magnetohydrodynamic Power Generators

In this chapter we will analyze a mode of power generation that utilizes a conducting fluid moving through a magnetic field. This subject is a broad one and a detailed study is beyond the scope of this text.

Because this field is rapidly changing, there has been no agreement even on the name by which the subject should go. The plasma aspects of the field have been called cosmical electrodynamics by astrophysicists, plasma physics or plasma dynamics by electrical engineers and physicists, magneto-aerodynamics by aerodynamicists. The more general term of magnetofluid-mechanics was proposed by von Karman and probably is the least restrictive of all the names that have been suggested. Traditionally, most of the work that has been done in power generation has gone under the name of *magneto-hydrodynamics* (MHD) and that is the practice we will follow here.

In brief, in an MHD generator a stream of hot ionized gas replaces the whirling copper armature of the conventional turbogenerator as is shown in Fig. 7-1. In either case a rather good electrical conductor is forced to move through a magnetic field, thereby inducing an electric field in the conductor; power can now be withdrawn from the induced electric field by a number of methods. Because the kinetic energy of the gas stream is converted directly to electric energy, the MHD generator is a much simpler device than its conventional counterpart. Moreover, because it has no hot, highly stressed moving parts, the MHD generator duct can be built to handle gas conditions that would quickly destroy a conventional turbine. As a consequence, MHD power plants are potentially much more efficient than steam power stations.

After a brief historical introduction, we will discuss the modes of creating plasmas and their properties; we will then conduct a thermodynamic

Turbogenerator   MHD generator

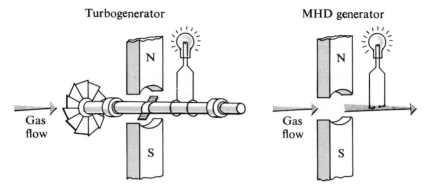

FIG. 7-1. Comparison between the conventional turbogenerator and the MHD generator.

analysis of an MHD generator, and will conclude with a discussion of the major problems to be solved in the field.

7.1 HISTORICAL INTRODUCTION

The idea of using a fluid conductor instead of a solid conductor to pass through the poles of a magnet to generate power is not new. Michael Faraday in 1831 experimented with mercury flowing in a glass tube in a magnetic field; he also suggested that the tidal currents flowing in the earth's magnetic field might be used for power generation.

Most of the present-day devices for power generation are concerned with the conversion of the thermal energy of a gas to electrical energy. The reason for this is that a gaseous conductor has certain advantages as a working substance. However, it should be noted that other materials, such as liquid metals, can also be used as working fluids. Sir William Crookes in 1879 considered the special properties of matter in discharge tubes, tentatively advancing the idea that such gases should be considered as a "fourth state of matter" that follows the solid, liquid, and gaseous states. In the 1930's, Langmuir, whose work we mentioned in Ch. 6, began using the designation "plasma" to describe ionized gases. Depending on the degree of ionization, such gases exhibit properties similar to those of metals, semiconductors, strong electrolytes, and ordinary gases.

The patent literature of the 1920's and 1930's [1–3] contains numerous references to generators that utilized ionized gases as their conducting media.

Karlovitz [3], in particular, carried out extensive experiments with a gaseous MHD generator in the period between 1938 and 1944. Because of the particular field arrangement chosen and the low conductivity of the gases, this generator did not produce appreciable power.

Early work concentrated on the utilization of an electric arc to heat the gas whereas more recent studies favor the utilization of combustion gas, since it appears more practical from an economic point of view. One of the chief reasons this type of generator is of interest is because it bypasses development of nuclear reactors or other elaborate schemes to produce the high temperature gas.

7.2 GASEOUS CONDUCTORS

Before we begin our analysis of an MHD generator we turn our attention to the gaseous conductor, which has proved to be the most feasible working substance. These gaseous conductors are called *plasmas* and while there are many definitions of plasma we will use the following: A plasma is an ionized gas in which the presence of charged particles has considerable influence on its properties—particularly its electrical properties. A plasma is electrically neutral except in microscopic regions.

7.2.1 Ionization of a gas. Now that we have defined a plasma in terms of an ionized gas we consider in some detail a phenomenological description of the ionization process. This description necessarily takes some liberties with what actually transpires during the process. Our description of the ionization process and the different modes of producing ions follows that of Cambel [4].

Ionization is an endothermic process whereby one or more electrons are removed from an atom. Ionization mechanisms may be broadly categorized into three classifications: thermal ionization processes, which are due to the collision of agitated particles constituting the gas; ionization brought about by irradiation of the gas with high-energy particles; and cumulative ionization, which is sometimes called ionization by stages. Most of the ionization processes in which engineers are interested are not self-sustaining; hence they must have energy fed continually to them.

We now describe the steps that might occur in the thermal ionization of a diatomic gas. We begin by considering this gas at some temperature near absolute zero. We represent a molecule of this gas as a "dumbbell" or rigid rotator as shown in Fig. 7-2. Depending on how close we are to absolute zero, the molecule will be able to engage in translational motion

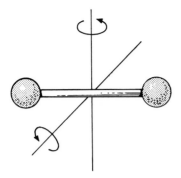

FIG. 7-2. Rigid rotator having translational and rotational degrees of freedom.

in any direction, and as the temperature is increased slightly the dumbbell will begin rotation as well, thus exhibiting three more degrees of freedom. The vibrational degree of freedom does not start until the temperature is increased to nearly 1000°K. This is shown in Fig. 7-3. As the temperature is increased, the molecular impacts contain sufficient energy so that the bond between the two atoms is broken, thus causing dissociation as shown in Fig. 7-4. At atmospheric pressure oxygen starts to dissociate at about 3000°K, while nitrogen starts to dissociate at about 4500°K. The dissociation reaction of oxygen may be written as

$$O_2 + \varepsilon_D \rightarrow 2O. \tag{7-1}$$

The dissociation energy ε_D is most often given in electron volts per molecule. In Table 7-1 we list dissocation energies of some common gases.

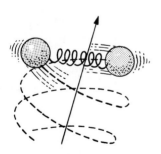

FIG. 7-3. Diatomic molecule having translational, rotational, and vibrational degrees of motion.

FIG. 7-4. Dissociation of molecule to neutral atoms.

If we continue to increase the temperature, the electrons in orbit around the atomic nucleus become excited to quantum states above the ground state. This kind of excitation contributes to the total energy, but is generally assumed to be negligible up to about 5000°K. If the temperature

TABLE 7-1. TYPICAL DISSOCIATION ENERGIES †

Molecule	$\mathcal{E}_D$ (ev)
H_2	4.48
N_2	9.76
O_2	5.08
CO	11.11
NO	6.48
OH	4.37
CO_2	16.56

† From Cambel [4].

of the gas is raised yet further beyond the dissociation state, the gas becomes ionized as is seen in Fig. 7-5. That is, the electron leaves the atom, causing it to become a positively charged ion. For the single ionization of oxygen we have

$$O + \mathcal{E}_i \rightarrow O^+ + e, \qquad (7\text{-}2)$$

●   Electron

   Positive ion

FIG. 7-5. Ionization of atom.

where ε_i is the ionization energy of the atom in electron volts per atom. The fraction of air molecules that are thermally ionized at 1 atm pressure is given in Fig. 7-6. We define the *ionization energy* or the *ionization potential* as the energy expended in removing a given electron from its atomic orbit and placing it at rest at an infinite distance from the nucleus of the atom. Usually, the ionization energy is given in electron volts, while the ionization

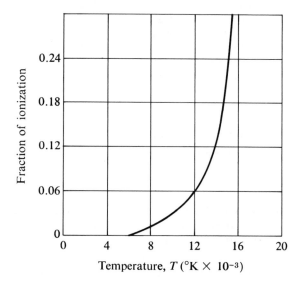

FIG. 7-6. The fraction of molecules thermally ionized in air at 1 atm. After Ref. [4] with permission.

potential is given in volts. For any particular case the ionization energy and the ionization potential are numerically equal. The ionization energies for some representative elements are given in Table 7-2. The number of electrons stripped from the atom is an index to its stage of ionization.

Reduction of the pressure on a gas can cause a significant reduction in the temperature at which a gas will ionize. If the pressure on oxygen or nitrogen is reduced to one-millionth of an atmosphere, then significant ionization takes place at 6000°K rather than 10,000°K. Some of the major dissociation and ionization reactions in air are shown in Fig. 7-7 from the work of Hansen [6].

7.2.2 Methods of ionizing a gas. There are a number of processes that may be used to ionize a gas. Of the three broad classes of ionization mentioned in Section 7.2.1 the one most important in the design of MHD

**TABLE 7-2. REPRESENTATIVE IONIZATION
ENERGIES IN ELECTRON VOLTS†**

Element	Stage of ionization		
	I	II	III
Aluminum	5.96	18.74	28.31
Argon	15.68	27.76	40.75
Calcium	6.09	11.82	50.96
Cesium	3.87	23.4	
Helium	24.46	54.14	
Hydrogen	13.527		
Magnesium	7.61	14.96	79.72
Nitrogen	14.48	29.47	47.40
Oxygen	13.55	34.93	54.87
Potassium	4.318	31.66	46.5
Sodium	5.12	47.06	70.72
Strontium	5.667	10.98	

† From Ref. [5].

generators involves collisions between the constituents of the hot gas. For the sake of completeness, at the end of our discussion of collisional ionization we will mention some of the other processes that can be used to ionize a gas.

In *electron collisional ionization* the energy delivered as an electron collides with an atom of gas strips off another electron from that atom. The idea of a cross section plays a fundamental role in the study of ionization. The *ionization cross section* is a measure of the probability that electrons of a given energy will ionize a given atom. In general the cross section is a function of the energy of the incident electron and the energy state of the atom to be ionized. If a single collision is to ionize an atom, the energy of the incident electron must at least equal the ionization energy of the atom. This value is the minimum or *threshold energy* for ionization. The number S of ion pairs produced by an electron in traveling 1 cm through a gas at a pressure of 1 mm of mercury is a function of the initial energy of the electron. It has been found that for single ionizations S reaches a maximum for initial electron energies from five to ten times the ionization energy of the atom and continues to decrease for higher electron energies. S is called by various names, including *differential ionization coefficient, ionization efficiency,* and *ionizing ability*. It should be noted that electrons can lose energy in nonionizing collisions before they ionize an atom. If the electron that collides with the atom has energy in excess of the minimum required to

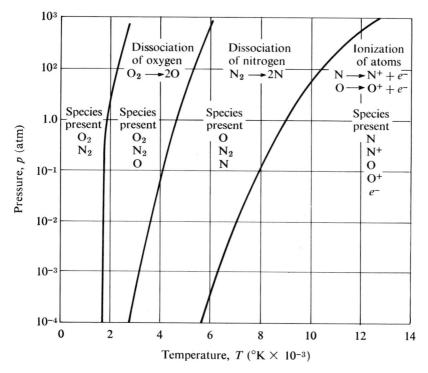

FIG. 7-7. The regions of pressure and temperature for major chemical reactions in air. After Ref. [6].

ionize the atom, the excess energy may be retained by the electron, transferred to an electron liberated in the ionizing process, or used to excite or further ionize the atom. There is also the possibility that a combination of these things may occur. Another form of collisional ionization is called thermal ionization.

Thermal ionization occurs when the average kinetic energy of the molecules is high enough so that the energy transferred in a collision between two neutral molecules is sufficient to ionize one of them. This can occur only at very high temperatures. The name is somewhat misleading since the process is essentially one of collision. The process has been encountered in electric arcs, high temperature flames and, more recently, behind strong shock waves in hypersonic flow fields and in thermonuclear energy research. This type of ionization usually does not occur alone; as the number of electrons increases appreciably in the gas they begin to act as ionizing agents themselves, and since they are much more efficient than neutral atoms or ions, electron collision ionization soon dominates the ionization process.

We will now discuss some of the other methods of ionization used for special purposes in energy conversion studies. A *high frequency electric field* can be applied to a gas which can cause an electron to acquire sufficient energy to excite and ionize the gas. This method is convenient for producing plasmas in a laboratory for study. *Surface ionization*, a method of ionization discussed in Ch. 6, offers a rather simple way to produce ions. When a neutral atom hits a hot surface, it may lose its least strongly held electron to the surface and leave the surface as an ion. A *photon* may also be used to ionize a gas if its energy as computed by Planck's law, $\varepsilon = h\nu$, is greater than the ionization energy of the atom. It can be shown that air cannot be ionized by light in the visible range; in fact, even an atom of cesium with an ionization energy of 3.88 eV cannot be ionized by visible light. Ultraviolet or X ray radiation is required.

Ionization by collisions of the second kind occurs when an excited atom strikes another atom and ionizes it. The probability of this occurring is at a maximum when the available energy of the excited atom is just equal to the ionization energy of the neutral atom with which it collides. The most important source of excited atoms are atoms in so-called metastable states. Atoms in metastable states have electrons in energy levels from which they cannot drop to a lower level by radiating energy. These transitions are not actually "forbidden" but are highly improbable.

Cumulative ionization refers to a process in which ionization occurs in two or more stages. Thus an atom that was raised to an excited state by one method may have its ionization completed by one or more of the other processes. *Electron attachment* occurs when an electron attaches itself to a neutral gas atom or molecule, thus forming a negative ion. Electron attachment increases as the electron energy decreases, because the electron remains within the sphere of influence of the atom for a longer time.

Before we close our discussion of the ionization process it might be well to mention the recombination processes by which an ion becomes electrically neutral again. Recombination processes are important because they liberate energy, and the engineer is sometimes faced with problems of disposing of this energy. Experiments have shown that neutralization rates can greatly exceed collision rates between neutral gas particles. This difference in rates is due to the attractive forces between particles of opposite charge that urge them together. There are more modes of recombination than there are modes of ionization; however, the details of the recombination processes are beyond the scope of this book. Because there are so many different ways for recombination to take place, there are no simple approaches to this problem. Cambel [4] gives a brief discussion and outline of the recombination processes as well as a good list of references for these and ionization processes.

7.2.3 Electrical conductivity. The successful generation of power by use of the principles of magnetohydrodynamics requires the attainment of large electrical conductivities in gases at relatively low temperatures. The electrical conductivity of a plasma does not conform to the simple characteristics of a metal. Under certain conditions the plasma will display nonlinear effects; the conductivity will depend on the magnitude of the applied field strength or voltage gradient. Some plasmas even show a negative voltage dependence; that is, an increase in voltage causes a decrease in resistance.

One of the most important parameters governing the electrical conductivity of a gas is the degree of ionization of the gas. The reason for this is that the conductivity depends on how many electrons and ions there are available to do charge carrying. One of the most successful analyses of ionization was made by Saha [7] on the basis of equilibrium thermodynamic reasoning. His analysis assumed that the process of ionization is a completely reversible reaction as defined by an equation such as Eq. 7-2. The analysis does not take into account the time required to establish internal equilibrium or the ionization mechanism but depends solely on the physical properties of the gas. The concentration of neutral atoms n_{ng}, of singly ionized atoms n_i, and of electrons n_n are assumed to be in complete thermal equilibrium; that is, they all have the energy of agitation corresponding to the temperature T. These concentrations of neutral particles, positive ions, and electrons act as the constituent particles of a gas mixture and produce partial pressures that contribute to the total gas pressure p,

$$p = p_{ng} + p_i + p_n. \tag{7-3}$$

If n is the original concentration of atoms in the gas, $n = n_{ng} + n_i$, then the fraction of ionized atoms is $X = n_i/n = n_n/n$ and the relation developed by Saha is

$$\frac{X^2}{1 - X^2} p = 3.16 \times 10^{-7} T^{5/2} \exp\left[-\mathcal{E}_i/(kT)\right], \tag{7-4}$$

where p is the total pressure in atmospheres, T is the temperature of the gas in degrees Kelvin, and $\mathcal{E}_i$ is the ionization energy.

Researchers in the field of plasma physics have developed expressions for the conductivity of gases in various degrees of ionization. Reference [4] gives an expression for the conductivity of a slightly ionized gas, which is arbitrarily defined as one with $X < 10^{-4}$, as

$$\sigma = 3.34 \times 10^{-12} \frac{X}{QT^{1/2}} \text{ (ohm-cm)}^{-1}, \tag{7-5}$$

where Q is the *collision cross section* in cm². The collision cross section Q is defined as an area about the center of a particle such that a collision occurs as soon as another particle comes within the area Q. This area is defined to be perpendicular to the relative motion of the two particles. Owing to the attractive forces between electrons and positive ions, the likelihood of a collision between them is much higher than between an electron and a neutral particle. Some representative electron-atom collision cross sections for engineering materials are given in Fig. 7-8. These data are found in Ref. [8].

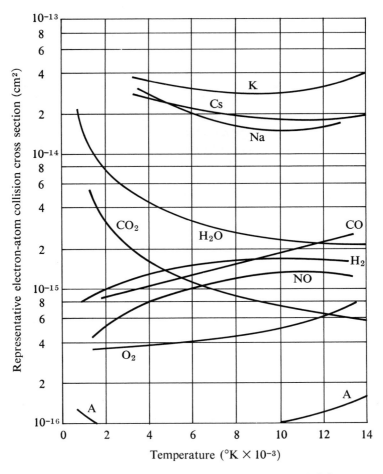

FIG. 7-8. Electron-atom collision cross sections. From Ref. [8].

We may now calculate, for example, the conductivity of argon gas at 7000°K and 1 atm. From Eq. 7-4 we find the degree of ionization as follows:

$$\frac{X^2}{1-X^2}(1) = 3.16 \times 10^{-7}(7 \times 10^3)^{5/2} \exp\left[-\varepsilon_i/(kT)\right]$$

$$\exp\left[-\mathcal{E}_i/(kT)\right] = \exp\left[(-15.68\,\text{eV} \times 1.60 \times 10^{-19}\,\text{joule/eV})/(1.38 \times 10^{-23} \right.$$
$$\left. \text{joule}/{}^\circ\text{K} \times 7 \times 10^3\,{}^\circ\text{K})\right]$$
$$= 5.09 \times 10^{-12}$$

and if we assume X is small we may approximate $X^2/(1 - X^2)$ by X^2 to find

$$X = 8.08 \times 10^{-5}.$$

We conclude that ionization is slight. Extrapolating from Fig. 7-8 we assume that Q is 5×10^{-17} and from Eq. 7-5 we find

$$\sigma = 3.34 \times 10^{-12}\,\frac{8.08 \times 10^{-5}}{5 \times 10^{-17}(7000)^{1/2}} = 6.72\ (\text{ohm-cm})^{-1}.$$

Present materials technology limits generators to operating temperatures less than 3000°K. Therefore another method of increasing the conductivity of gases used in MHD generators has been developed: this method is called *seeding*. (It should be kept in mind that while seeding is the most frequently proposed method of achieving non-thermal ionization of the gases to be used in MHD generators, it is by no means the only method, as was indicated in Section 7.2.2.) Seeding materials are substances which are added to the working fluid of an MHD generator. They generally have low ionization energies; this means that substantial conductivities can be achieved at relatively low temperatures. Examination of Table 7-2 reveals that the alkali metals and alkaline earths have relatively low ionization potentials. The injection of seed material into a high velocity gas stream involves some practical complexities; therefore, it is desirable to deal with seed materials that melt easily. Seed material must be inexpensive, especially if the generator is of an open cycle design. No matter how low the cost of the seeding material an open cycle generator would require some type of seed recovery system. Some relative cost data are given in Section 7.5.1.

The calculation of the conductivity of a seeded gas is no simple task. Lin, Resler, and Kantrowitz [9] have conducted some work in this area. The results of these calculations depend on the concentration of neutral seed material, ions, and neutral gas. Figure 7-9 gives the electrical conductivity of propane-air flames seeded with various concentrations of alkali compounds. Figure 7-10 gives the calculated conductivity of the gaseous reaction products at 1 atm from the burning of C_2H_4 with stoichiometric oxygen while being seeded with potassium. The conductivity is, approximately, inversely related to the square root of the pressure.

7.3 ANALYSIS OF AN MHD GENERATOR

In this section we will consider the analysis of a constant velocity MHD generator. Our work, in some respects, will follow that of Refs. [10] and

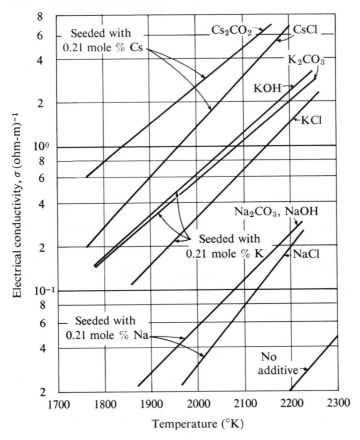

FIG. 7-9. The effect of seeding on the electrical conductivity of propane-air flames. From Ref. [4].

[11]. As is the case with a turbine, MHD generators will probably be designed with a constant flow velocity, the primary effect being a drop in pressure as the gas forces itself through the successive turbine stages of the former, or the magnetic field of the latter. This assumption of strictly constant velocity is useful in that it greatly simplifies the equations of motion and makes clear the processes occurring in the generator. In practice one might design for constant Mach number; however, the difference for present purposes is not great. One might also design for constant temperature, constant pressure, or constant area. The paths that would be followed on a TS diagram in these generators are shown schematically in Fig. 7-11.

A schematic of the generator we intend to analyze is shown in Fig. 7-12. At the entrance the generator duct has a width d and height b.

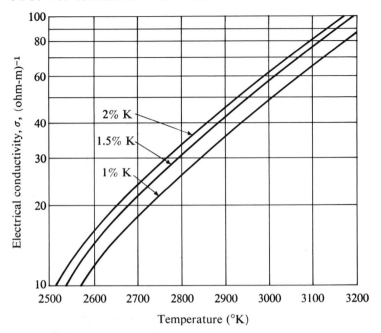

FIG. 7-10. Some representative curves showing the electrical conductivity characteristics of the products of combustion of C_2H_4 burned in stoichiometric oxygen while being seeded with potassium.

With the axial velocity held constant, electrical energy is extracted from only the thermal energy of the gas. We may consider this as a two-stage process—the Faraday induction removes electrical energy only from the kinetic energy of the flow as the conductive gas cuts the magnetic lines of force; however, the gas is then accelerated to restore the velocity, but in this process of acceleration the static temperature decreases.

7.3.1 Assumptions. We make the following assumptions concerning the analysis:

(1) The gas is assumed to enter at a constant rate into the generator at station 1 in the positive x direction with a uniform velocity u_1, pressure p_1, and temperature T_1.

(2) A uniform magnetic flux density B is assumed to exist in the $+z$ direction. The walls at $z = \pm b/2$ are insulators and the walls at $y = \pm d/2$ are conductors that serve as electrodes to collect the current and deliver it to the external load R_o.

(3) The state properties and flow speed of the gas are uniform over any section.

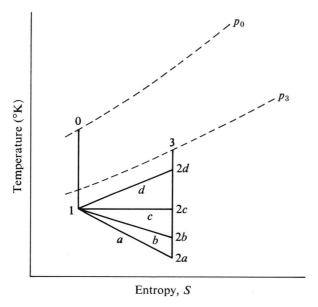

FIG. 7-11. The paths that are followed on a *TS* diagram for MHD generator systems designed for (*a*) constant velocity, (*b*) constant Mach number, (*c*) constant temperature, (*d*) constant pressure. State 0 represents the stagnation conditions upstream of the nozzle; state 1 is the exit of the nozzle and the entrance to the generator; state 2 is the exit to the generator and the entrance to the diffuser; state 3 is the exit of the diffuser.

(4) The fluid is assumed to be a frictionless, compressible, perfect gas.

(5) The perturbation of the applied magnetic field by the current is neglected.

(6) Leakage currents at the ends of the electrode are neglected.

(7) The electrical conductivity is a scalar quantity with a value determined by the mean temperature and pressure in the generator duct.

(8) Heat transfer from the duct is neglected.

(9) The coordinate system we will use to describe the phenomena taking place in the generator is shown in Fig. 7-13. We have previously assumed an electrically conducting fluid with a velocity u in the positive x direction and a magnetic field B at right angles to this in the positive z direction. The interaction of the velocity field with the magnetic field induces an electric field E_{ind} at right angles to both u and B. The magnitude of this field is given by the cross product

$$E_{\text{ind}} = u \times B. \tag{7-6}$$

Since we have assumed that the conductivity is a scalar quantity, we may relate the induced current density to the induced field

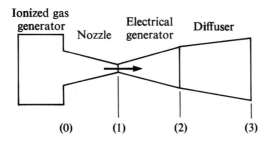

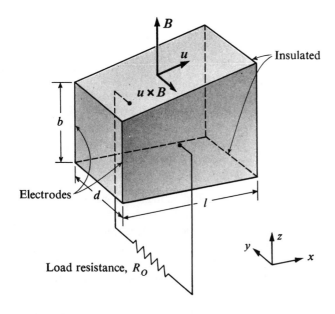

FIG. 7-12(a). Schematic of the gas generator, nozzle, electric generator, and diffuser arrangement.

FIG. 7-12(b). The electrical generator and coordinate system in detail.

$$J_{ind} = \sigma E_{ind}. \tag{7-7}$$

At the same time the induced current interacts with the magnetic field to induce a Lorentz force given by the vector cross product

$$F_{ind} = J_{ind} \times B. \tag{7-8}$$

This is the same force that occurs in an electric generator as the induced current in the armature cuts the lines of the generator's field. The induced

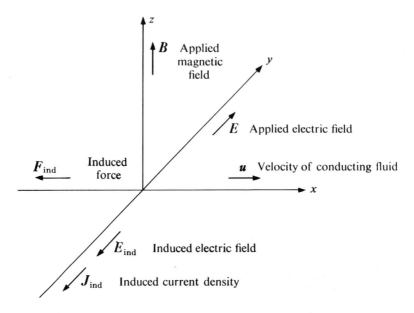

FIG. 7-13. The coordinate system we will use in analyzing the flow of a conducting fluid through a magnetic field and an electric field.

force is perpendicular to both J_{ind} and B thus making it parallel but in an opposite direction (by the left-hand rule) to the velocity vector u.

To generalize we now apply an electric field E at right angles to both the magnetic field B and the velocity u but in an opposite sense to the induced current density J_{ind}. The net current density J through the conducting fluid and the one that we would measure with a suitably placed ammeter is then

$$J = \sigma(E + u \times B) = \sigma(E + E_{ind}) = \sigma E'. \qquad (7\text{-}9)$$

The effective Lorentz force due to both currents is then

$$F = J \times B = \sigma(E + u \times B) \times B. \qquad (7\text{-}10)$$

We note that if the applied electric field E is greater than the induced electric field $u \times B$ we have an accelerator that may be used as a thrust-producing device. If the polarity of the imposed voltage is reversed, the Lorentz force will retard the flow.

7.3.2   Governing equations. We will now give the basic equations that we will use in analyzing the MHD generator. First we will present the basic fluid mechanics equations, then the electrical equations for three important cases and lastly we will combine both the electrical and fluid mechanics equations.

Consider a small element of space of length dx and cross-sectional area A at the left and $A + dA$ at the right face as is shown in Fig. 7-14. Since we have previously assumed steady flow with no sources or sinks in the generator, the mass rate of flow is a constant,

$$m = \rho_1 A_1 u_1 = \rho b \, du = \rho A u. \tag{7-11}$$

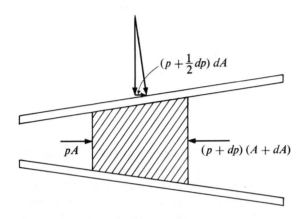

FIG. 7-14. The forces on the control volume used to derive the momentum equation.

We next consider the momentum equation. The rate of flow of momentum into the control volume is the mass rate of flow across the left-hand boundary, $\rho A u$, times the velocity u. Hence

$$\rho A u^2.$$

The rate of momentum flow out of the control volume is

$$\rho A u^2 + d(\rho A u^2)$$

and the net rate of flow of momentum is

$$+[\rho A u^2 + d(\rho A u^2)] - \rho A u^2 = +d(\rho A u^2) = \frac{d}{dx}(\rho A u^2)\, dx. \tag{7-12}$$

The force on the left face is pA and that on the right face is

$$(p + dp)(A + dA) = pA + p\, dA + A\, dp,$$

where we have neglected the small term $dA\, dp$. The average pressure on the side walls is $p + \frac{1}{2} dp$ and the component of this force to the right due to this pressure is

$$(p + \tfrac{1}{2} dp)\, dA = p\, dA.$$

The resultant force including the body force due to $\mathbf{J} \times \mathbf{B}$ over the volume bounded by the planes x and $x + dx$ is to a good approximation

$$= (pA + p \, dA) - (pA + p \, dA + A \, dp) - JBA \, dx$$

$$= -A \frac{dp}{dx} dx - JBA \, dx. \tag{7-13}$$

Newton's second law states that the rate of change of momentum must equal the resultant force

$$+\frac{d}{dx} (\rho A u^2) \, dx = -A \frac{dp}{dx} dx - JBA \, dx$$

and upon dividing through by A one obtains

$$+\frac{m}{A} \frac{du}{dx} + \frac{dp}{dx} = -JB \tag{7-14}$$

or upon dividing through by A
For constant velocity Eq. 7-14 simplifies to

$$\frac{dp}{dx} = -JB. \tag{7-15}$$

Next we consider the conservation of energy equation for the steady state situation. The rate of flow of energy into the control volume across the left face equals the product of the mass rate of flow, $\rho A u$, and the energy per unit mass $\mathcal{E}$. The energy per unit mass we assume to be made up of three parts: the internal energy, the flow energy, and the kinetic energy. The first of these two we group together following the usual thermodynamic practice, calling the result the enthalpy h. The kinetic energy per unit mass is simply $\frac{1}{2}u^2$. Thus the energy of the entering stream per unit mass is

$$\mathcal{E} = \mathcal{E}_{\text{int}} + p/\rho + \tfrac{1}{2}u^2 = h + \tfrac{1}{2}u^2 \tag{7-16}$$

and the rate of flow of energy into the element across its left face is

$$\rho A u \times \mathcal{E} = \rho A u (h + \tfrac{1}{2}u^2).$$

The net rate of flow of energy into the control volume is

$$+d[\rho A u (h + \tfrac{1}{2}u^2)] = +\frac{d}{dx} [\rho A u (h + \tfrac{1}{2}u^2)] \, dx.$$

This net rate of energy flow in an adiabatic, steady state system must be equal to the power delivered or supplied per unit volume by or to the system

$$+\frac{d}{dx} [\rho u (h + \tfrac{1}{2}u^2)] = -JE,$$

which in a constant velocity system is simply

$$-\rho u \frac{dh}{dx} = JE, \tag{7-17}$$

where we have ignored changes in density.

We have assumed a perfect gas whose equation of state is

$$p = \rho \mathcal{R} T, \tag{7-18}$$

where $\mathcal{R}$ is the gas constant.† Since the enthalpy of a perfect gas is a function of temperature alone, we may relate the enthalpy to the various other state variables by

$$h = c_p T = \frac{\gamma}{\gamma - 1} \frac{p}{\rho} \tag{7-19}$$

where γ denotes the ratio of specific heats c_p/c_v.

Sound waves propagated through the fluid travel at a characteristic velocity, called the *sonic velocity*, which for a perfect gas is given by

$$a = \sqrt{\gamma p/\rho} = \sqrt{\gamma \mathcal{R} T}. \tag{7-20}$$

The ratio of the velocity at any point to the sonic velocity is called the *Mach number*

$$M = u/a.$$

We will now discuss one more concept found useful in analyzing compressible flow problems. If we could devise a thermometer that could travel at the stream velocity, the temperature it would measure as it moved with the stream would be the static temperature. However, if we insert a stationary thermometer into a stream of compressible fluid, the fluid immediately adjacent to the thermometer will be brought to rest—the fluid will stagnate at that point. The temperature measured by such a thermometer is called the stagnation temperature. Assuming an adiabatic work-free process between the undisturbed flow and the stagnation point, the first law of thermodynamics as given by Eq. 7-16 yields

$$\frac{u^2}{2} = h_0 - h = c_p(T_0 - T), \tag{7-21}$$

where we have denoted the stagnation or total state by the zero subscript. The ratio of the total temperature to the static temperature is

$$\frac{T_0}{T} = 1 + \frac{u^2}{2c_p T} = 1 + \frac{(\gamma - 1)u^2}{2\gamma \mathcal{R} T},$$

which in terms of the Mach number definition and Eq. 7-20 is

$$\frac{T_0}{T} = 1 + \frac{\gamma - 1}{2} M^2. \tag{7-22}$$

By definition, the stagnation pressure and temperature are related to the static pressure and temperature by an isentropic process, thus

$$\frac{p_0}{p} = \left[\frac{T_0}{T}\right]^{\frac{\gamma}{\gamma - 1}} = \left[1 + \frac{\gamma - 1}{2} M^2\right]^{\frac{\gamma}{\gamma - 1}}. \tag{7-23}$$

† We show the equation with the universal gas constant $\mathcal{R}$. If the density is in units of mass per unit volume, then $\mathcal{R}$ must be divided by the molecular weight to make the relationship dimensionally homogeneous.

7.3.3 Details of the analysis. We are now ready to apply the equations of the previous section to the analysis of the constant velocity generator. But first we must reexamine Ohm's law to see what effect the magnetic field has on the electric fields produced. In Section 3.7.3 the Hall effect was described for solids; however, it should be recognized that the Hall effect can manifest itself in any situation where charged particles move through a magnetic field. Because of the Hall effect several different types of generators can be constructed. The three most important are the continuous electrode generator, the segmented electrode generator and the Hall generator, each of which will be discussed in turn.

The electric field referred to the gas moving with velocity u in magnetic field B is

$$E' = E + u \times B. \tag{7-24}$$

When the electron current flows the electrons drift through the gas at some average drift velocity u_n relative to the gas. The electrons therefore will also respond to a transverse induced field, $u_n \times B$ as well as to E' and therefore u_n is not directed just opposite to E' as might be expected, but is skewed somewhat because of the additional field as shown in Fig. 7-15. In this

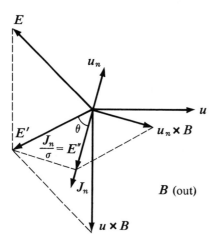

FIG. 7-15. Vector diagram for fields and currents in a moving ionized gas.

drawing the B field is out of the paper. E' is the vector sum of the electric field E due to external charges and the induced field $u \times B$. The field E'' is the vector sum resulting from E' and $u_n \times B$. An observer moving at the electron drift velocity would observe the E'' electric field.

The electrons behave as though they were moving in a medium of conductivity σ in a field of E'' and thus the electron current becomes

$$J_n = \sigma E'' \tag{7-25}$$

or

$$J_n = \sigma E' + \sigma(u_n \times B). \tag{7-26}$$

The electron current is related to u_n by

$$J_n = -u_n n_n e, \tag{7-27}$$

where as usual n_n is the electron density and e is the electronic charge. From Section 3.7.1 it will be recalled that the conductivity can also be expressed as

$$\sigma = n_n \mu_n e \tag{7-28}$$

where μ_n is the electron mobility in the gas. Equations 7-27 and 7-28 can be combined to yield

$$\frac{J_n}{\sigma} = \frac{u_n}{\mu_n} \tag{7-29}$$

or in scalar form

$$\frac{J_n}{\sigma} = \frac{u_n}{\mu_n}. \tag{7-30}$$

Equation 7-26 becomes by substitution

$$J_n = \sigma E' - \mu_n J_n \times B. \tag{7-31}$$

From Eq. 7-25 it should be noted that E'' is simply J_n/σ and thus from Fig. 7-15 we may write

$$\tan \theta = \frac{u_n B \sigma}{J_n} \tag{7-32}$$

$$\tan \theta = \mu_n B.$$

The angle θ is called the *Hall angle*.

The simple Ohm's law expression has now been modified by the presence of the term $\mu_n J_n \times B$. This expression does not take into account ionic current in the gas nor does it account for electron inertia effects. Because the mobility of electrons is so much higher than the mobility of ions, we will ignore the presence of ions in the rest of the analysis.

The components of the vector J_n in the x, y and z directions are:

$$\begin{aligned} J_{nx} &= \sigma E'_x - \mu_n J_{ny} B \\ J_{ny} &= \sigma E'_y - \mu_n J_{nx} B \\ J_{nz} &= \sigma E'_z = 0 \end{aligned} \tag{7-33}$$

where we will assume $E_z = 0$ and therefore $E'_z = 0$. We designate $\mu_n B$ by β_n and call it the *Hall parameter*. Equations 7-33 can be solved for J_{nx} and J_{ny} to yield

$$J_{nx} = \frac{\sigma(E'_x - \beta_n E'_y)}{1 + \beta_n^2} \tag{7-34a}$$

$$J_{ny} = \frac{\sigma(E'_y + \beta_n E'_x)}{1 + \beta_n^2}. \tag{7-34b}$$

In Table 7-3 we now set down the components of the various vectors that arise in analyzing MHD generators.

In Section 3.7 it was shown that the mobility of an electron is related to its relaxation time in a particularly simple way: $\mu = e\tau/m^*$. It can also be shown that an electron's angular frequency in orbit perpendicular to a

TABLE 7-3.   VECTOR COMPONENTS IN AN MHD GENERATOR

Vector	x component	y component	z component
u	u	0	0
B	0	0	B
J_n	J_{nx}	J_{ny}	0
E'	E_x	$E_y - uB$	0
$u \times B$	0	$-uB$	0
$F = J_n \times B$	$J_{ny}B$	$-J_{nx}B$	0

magnetic field is a particularly simple function of the magnetic field and mass of the electron, namely: $\omega = eB/m^*$. Combining these two simple relations one finds that

$$\omega\tau = \mu_n B = \beta_n. \tag{7-35}$$

Consider a generator with continuous electrodes such as is shown schematically in Fig. 7-12(b). In this case $E_x = 0$ because the electrodes are of uniform potential axially. The local current components are from Eqs. 7-34 and Table 7-3:

$$J_{nx} = \frac{\sigma\beta_n(E_y - uB)}{1 + \beta_n^2} \tag{7-36a}$$

$$J_{ny} = \frac{\sigma(E_y - uB)}{1 + \beta_n^2}. \tag{7-36b}$$

If $J_{ny} = 0$ (open circuit condition) we have $E_y = uB$. It is convenient to define the ratio of the electric field in the y-direction to uB product, namely $K = E_y/(uB)$, as the *loading factor*. In two of the three types of generators discussed here the loading factor is equal to the electrical conversion efficiency, η_e.

The power generated in length δx is δP_o

$$\delta P_o = -J_{ny}E_y bd\,\delta x = \frac{\sigma u^2 B^2 bd\,K(1 - K)\,\delta x}{1 + \beta_n^2}. \tag{7-37}$$

The mechanical power input is the product of the force in the y-direction times the velocity times the volume:

$$\delta P_M = -J_{ny}B\,u\,bd\,\delta x. \tag{7-38}$$

Dividing Eq. 7-37 by Eq. 7-38 yields the loading factor or conversion efficiency K. We note that the power density is reduced by the factor $1 + \beta_n^2$ because of the Hall effect. Equation 7-36a tells us that a current is flowing axially in the duct. If this axial current could be reduced or eliminated, then the power density could be raised.

As a second case, suppose we have a generator with many electrode segments, as in Fig. 7-16. All load circuits are mutually insulated, and insu-

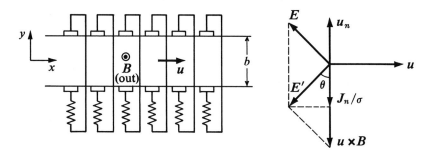

FIG. 7-16. Segmented electrode MHD generator and vector diagrams of fields and currents.

lated from ground. In this generator $J_{nx} = 0$. Then from Eq. 7-34a we have $E_x' = \beta_n E_y'$ or

$$E_x = \beta_n(E_y - uB). \tag{7-39}$$

The current components from Eqs. 7-33 and Table 7-3 are:

$$J_{nx} = 0$$
$$J_{ny} = \sigma(E_y - uB). \tag{7-40}$$

Again, under open circuit conditions $J_{ny} = 0$ and we have the relation $E_y = uB$ and thus retain the definition of the loading factor K.

The power generated in length δx is

$$\delta P_o = \sigma u^2\, B^2 bd\, K(1 - K)\, \delta x. \tag{7-41}$$

The mechanical input power remains the same as given by Eq. 7-38. The use of segmented electrodes prohibits current from flowing in the axial direction and thus removes the penalty imposed by the Hall effect which occurs in the case of the continuous electrode generator. Note that the coefficient $(1 + \beta_n^2)$ has now disappeared from the denominator of the expression for the electrical power delivered.

A third possibility is to short circuit the transverse current and collect power by connecting the load between upstream and downstream electrodes; this results in the so-called Hall generator configuration. Figure 7-17 illustrates such a device.

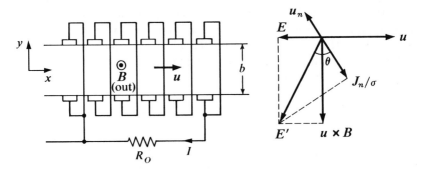

FIG. 7-17. Hall-type MHD generator and associated field and current diagram.

This device is characterized by a zero transverse electric field, $E_y = 0$ and from Table 7-3 we note

$$E_x' = E_x \quad \text{and} \quad E_y' = -uB. \tag{7-42}$$

The current equations are from Eqs. 7-34:

$$J_{nx} = \frac{\sigma(E_x + \beta_n uB)}{1 + \beta_n^2}$$

$$J_{ny} = \frac{\sigma(-uB + \beta_n E_x)}{1 + \beta_n^2}. \tag{7-43}$$

The open circuit condition is realized when $J_{nx} = 0$, resulting in the open circuit electric field and transverse current

$$E_{x(oc)} = -\beta_n uB$$

$$J_{ny(oc)} = -\sigma uB. \tag{7-44}$$

The *Hall generator loading factor* in this case is defined as

$$K_H = \frac{E_x}{E_{x(oc)}} = -\frac{E_x}{\beta_n uB}. \tag{7-45}$$

The power generated in length δx is

$$\delta P_o = \frac{\sigma u^2 B^2}{1 + \beta_n^2} \beta_n^2 K_H (1 - K_H) bd \, \delta x. \tag{7-46}$$

The input power is

$$\delta P_M = -J_{ny} B \, bd \, u \, \delta x = \frac{\sigma u^2 B^2 (1 + \beta_n^2 K_H)}{1 + \beta_n^2} bd \, \delta x, \tag{7-47}$$

so that the conversion efficiency, η_c, which is found by dividing Eq. 7-46 by Eq. 7-47, equals

$$\eta_e = \frac{\beta_n^2 K_H (1 - K_H)}{1 + \beta_n^2 K_H}. \tag{7-48}$$

Solving Eq. 7-48 for K_H yields

$$K_H = \frac{(1 - \eta_e) \pm \sqrt{(1 - \eta_e)^2 - 4\eta_e/\beta_n^2}}{2}. \tag{7-49}$$

For any η_e there are two K_H values and two corresponding power levels. There is a maximum η_e which cannot be exceeded. The optimum value of K_H for a particular value of β_n can be obtained by taking the derivative of Eq. 7-48, with respect to K_H, and setting the result equal to zero to obtain

$$K_{H(\text{opt})} = \frac{1}{\beta_n} \sqrt{1 + \frac{1}{\beta_n^2}} - \frac{1}{\beta_n^2} \tag{7-50}$$

and similarly the maximum value of η_e can be obtained from Eq. 7-49, yielding

$$\eta_{e(\text{max})} = 1 + \frac{2}{\beta_n^2} - \frac{2}{\beta_n} \sqrt{1 + \frac{1}{\beta_n^2}}. \tag{7-51}$$

Equation 7-51 indicates that in order to obtain a high conversion efficiency a large value of β_n is required. For example, in order to obtain an efficiency of 75 percent, β_n must equal 7. The corresponding load factor is 0.124. This means that the Hall generator must operate close to the short circuit condition rather than the open circuit condition to obtain reasonably high efficiencies.

The electrical power density for each type of generator can be normalized by dividing each unit's output by $\sigma u^2 B^2 \, bd \, \delta x$. The results of this normalization are presented in Fig. 7-18. For the Hall effect generator the power density at maximum efficiency for large β_n is approximately half the power density at the $\beta_n = \infty$ value. In designing such a generator one would normally run at something less than $\eta_{e(\text{max})}$ to obtain a more favorable power density. In most cases it now appears that the segmented electrode generator would be most advantageous. However, if β_n is less than about 0.7 it would probably pay to use continuous electrodes. There are ways to connect the load circuits of the segmented generator in a manner that results in a single load circuit of high voltage and low current.

Now we return to the gas flow part of our analysis for a constant velocity generator by relating the loading factor to the temperature and pressure in the generator. The loading factor may also be interpreted as the fraction of the electric power generated that is actually delivered to the external load, the difference being dissipated in the internal resistance of the generator itself. This dissipated energy shows up either as an increased pressure drop or as a departure from reversibility. We may demonstrate

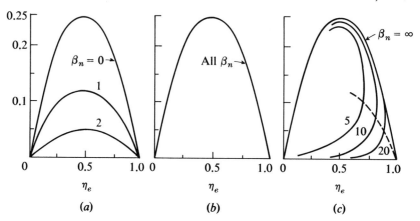

FIG. 7-18. Normalized power density for the three basic MHD generator configurations: (*a*) continuous electrode; (*b*) segmented electrode; and (*c*) Hall-type generator.

this by writing the loading factor in terms of the constant pressure specific heat and the temperature

$$K = \rho c_p \frac{dT}{dp},$$ (7-52)

which upon substitution of the perfect gas law $\rho = p/\Re T$ and the ratio of the specific heats γ yields

$$\frac{K(\gamma - 1)}{\gamma} \frac{dp}{p} = \frac{dT}{T},$$ (7-53)

which may be integrated between the inlet and any other point to obtain

$$\frac{T}{T_1} = \left[\frac{p}{p_1} \right]^{K(\gamma - 1)/\gamma}.$$ (7-54)

Equation 7-54 then indicates that the actual temperature drop is always less than the isentropic temperature drop. This is analogous to the "turbine reheat" effect that occurs when a gas flows through the stages of a turbine, entering each stage at a temperature slightly higher than it would have had if it experienced an isentropic temperature drop in the preceding stage. The reheat in the case of a turbine is due to the frictional heating of the fluid rather than to Joule heating.

We consider next the area variation required to produce constant velocity. The continuity equation (Eq. 7-11) may be written in terms of the perfect gas law as

$$\frac{A}{A_1} = \frac{p_1}{\rho} = \frac{p_1}{p} \frac{T}{T_1} = \left[\frac{p}{p_1}\right]^{\frac{K(\gamma-1)}{\gamma} - 1} \tag{7-55}$$

Thus the area with respect to the inlet area may be found if the pressure ratio and loading factor for the point in question are known.

Earlier we considered an electrical efficiency that was the ratio of the voltage across the load to the maximum possible voltage—the open circuit condition. Because an MHD generator is a fluid-dependent device, we might well consider a measure of how efficiently energy is being removed from the fluid as it traverses the generator. An overall generator adiabatic efficiency does precisely this by comparing the enthalpy drop from the entrance of the generator nozzle to the exit of the generator with the same enthalpy drop across an adiabatic reversible device:

$$\eta_{ad} = \frac{h_0 - h_3}{h_0 - h_3'}, \tag{7-56}$$

where the prime denotes the isentropic state. We have used the static enthalpy at exit because in the model we are analyzing we do not plan to use the exhaust velocity any further. Since we have previously assumed constant specific heats, Eq. 7-56 may be written as

$$\eta_{ad} = \frac{T_0 - T_3}{T_0 - T_3'} = \frac{1 - T_3/T_0}{1 - T_3'/T_0}. \tag{7-57}$$

The process 0 to 1 occurs in the nozzle and in a well-designed nozzle is nearly isentropic. The process 2 to 3 occurs in the diffuser; even well-designed diffusers experience entropy increases. In order that our presentation be kept simple, we will assume an isentropic diffuser. We may now calculate the temperature ratio T_3/T_0 as follows:

$$\frac{T_3}{T_0} = \frac{T_3}{T_2} \frac{T_2}{T_1} \frac{T_1}{T_0}. \tag{7-58}$$

But we have assumed that the inlet and exit states of the nozzle and diffuser are related isentropically, so

$$\frac{T_1}{T_0} = \left[\frac{p_1}{p_0}\right]^{(\gamma-1)/\gamma} \quad \text{and} \quad \frac{T_3}{T_2} = \left[\frac{p_3}{p_2}\right]^{(\gamma-1)/\gamma} \tag{7-59}$$

and if we assume the loading factor K to be constant for the entire generator, Eq. 7-54 will describe the process across the generator

$$\frac{T_2}{T_1} = \left[\frac{p_2}{p_1}\right]^{K(\gamma-1)/\gamma}. \tag{7-60}$$

Substituting Eqs. 7-59 and 7-60 into Eq. 7-58 yields

$$\frac{T_3}{T_0} = \left[\left(\frac{p_1}{p_2} \right)^{1-K} \frac{p_3}{p_0} \right]^{(\gamma - 1)/\gamma}. \tag{7-61}$$

The static pressure ratio across the generator p_2/p_1, in terms of the desired stagnation pressure ratio p_3/p_0, can be found from

$$\frac{p_3}{p_0} = \frac{p_3}{p_2} \frac{p_2}{p_1} \frac{p_1}{p_0}. \tag{7-62}$$

From Eq. 7-23 the pressure ratios across the nozzle and diffuser can be found to be

$$\frac{p_1}{p_0} = \frac{1}{[1 + \frac{1}{2}(\gamma - 1)M_1^2]^{\gamma/(\gamma - 1)}}$$

$$\frac{p_3}{p_2} = [1 + \frac{1}{2}(\gamma - 1)M_2^2]^{\gamma/(\gamma - 1)}, \tag{7-63}$$

since the total pressure across an adiabatic, isentropic device is constant. The Mach number at the exit of the generator is related to the Mach number at the entrance by

$$M_2^2 = \frac{u^2}{\gamma \mathcal{R} T_2} = \frac{u^2}{\gamma \mathcal{R} T_1} \frac{T_1}{T_2} = M_1^2 \left(\frac{p_1}{p_2} \right)^{K(\gamma - 1)/\gamma}. \tag{7-64}$$

The ratio in Eq. 7-62 may be evaluated now by combining Eqs. 7-63 and 7-64 to yield

$$\frac{p_3}{p_0} = \left(\frac{p_2}{p_1} \right) \left[\frac{1 + \frac{1}{2}(\gamma - 1)M_1^2 \left(\frac{p_1}{p_2} \right)^{K(\gamma - 1)/\gamma}}{1 + \frac{1}{2}(\gamma - 1)M_1^2} \right]^{\gamma/(\gamma - 1)}, \tag{7-65}$$

which unfortunately is an implicit relation for p_2/p_1 in terms of p_3/p_0.

The isentropic temperature drop across the system is simply

$$\frac{T_3'}{T_0} = \left(\frac{p_3}{p_0} \right)^{(\gamma - 1)/\gamma}. \tag{7-66}$$

Thus we may evaluate the overall adiabatic efficiency by substituting Eqs. 7-61 and 7-66 into Eq. 7-57 to obtain

$$\eta_{ad} = \frac{1 - \left[\left(\frac{p_1}{p_2} \right)^{1-K} \left(\frac{p_3}{p_0} \right) \right]^{\gamma - 1/\gamma}}{1 - \left(\frac{p_3}{p_0} \right)^{\gamma - 1/\gamma}}, \tag{7-67}$$

where p_1/p_2 is found from Eq. 7-65. As K approaches unity (the open circuit condition), the overall adiabatic efficiency approaches one, as expected. With K less than unity the adiabatic efficiency may still become large if the pressure ratio p_3/p_0 is sufficiently large. This is analogous to the familiar internal reheat of turbomachines, except in this case the Joule heating is passed downstream and is available for conversion into electrical power.

Now we will consider the formulation of an overall thermodynamic efficiency for a simple open cycle MHD generator. In the simple open cycle a fuel and oxidizer without preheating are burned and then seed material is added to make the gas sufficiently conducting. Even with seeding most combustion gases are not sufficiently conducting below about 2300°K at 1 atm, so the flame temperature must exceed 2300°K to extract any electrical power. Because air as an oxidizer will not yield such temperatures, it is necessary to use some pure oxygen with the air or a chemical oxidizer.

The simplest way to define an overall thermal efficiency for such a system is the ratio of the net power available to the energy released in the combustion chamber. If some of the energy left in the exhaust gases were used to provide comfort or process heat, a more sophisticated definition would be required.

The net power output is found by subtracting from a power equation such as Eq. 7-37 the power to the auxiliaries, which would include the power that must be supplied to the magnet. The energy supplied in the combustion chamber is simply the change in enthalpy for the combustion reaction, which may be calculated from the heats of formation for the reactants and the products. (This method is explained in detail in Ch. 8.) Thus the thermal efficiency for the simple open cycle is

$$\eta_t = \frac{IV - P_{\text{aux}}}{\Delta H}. \tag{7-68}$$

A further disadvantage of the simple open cycle is that seed material must be continually supplied, which adds to the cost of power generation. The cost of seeding is discussed in Section 7.5.1. In Section 7.6 we will consider more complex power systems that bypass some of the limitations of the simple open cycle systems.

7.4 SOLUTION OF AN MHD GENERATOR PROBLEM

We will now consider the solution to a simple MHD continuous electrode generator problem, using the assumptions and equations of the previous sections. The data that are given require no technical breakthroughs to be achieved and might be considered reasonable for an open cycle power plant. Following is the given information where the state numbers refer to the points on Fig. 7-12.

The source of high temperature gas is assumed to be the products of combustion of ethylene C_2H_4 in stoichiometric air. These products are assumed to be seeded with 2 percent potassium; the conductivity is given in Fig. 7-10.

Combustion temperature	$T_0 = 3000°K$
Combustion pressure	$p_0 = 5$ atm
Exhaust pressure	$p_3 = 1$ atm
Magnetic flux density	$B = 30$ kilogauss $= 3$ tesla
Hall parameter	$\omega\tau = 1.25$
Entrance geometry	$b = 0.5$ meter
	$d = 2.0$ meters
Mach number at entrance to generator	$M_1 = 0.80$
Loading factor	$K = \frac{1}{2}$
Ratio of specific heats	$\gamma = 1.2$

Solution. The molecular weight of the gases passing through the generator may be found simply by writing the combustion equation for the stoichiometric reaction

$$C_2H_4 + 3O_2 + 3 \times 3.76N_2 \rightarrow 2CO_2 + 2H_2O + 11.29N_2$$

and thus the average molecular weight of the products of combustion is:

$$\text{Mol. Wt.} = \frac{2 \times 44}{15.29} + \frac{2 \times 18}{15.29} + \frac{11.29 \times 28}{15.29} = 28.73 \approx 29,$$

where 15.29 is the total number of moles of reaction products. The heat of combustion for this reaction is 1.32×10^9 joules per kg-mole of fuel.

The static temperature at the inlet to the generator may be found by use of Eq. 7-22:

$$\frac{T_0}{T_1} = 1 + \frac{\gamma - 1}{2} M_1^2 = 1 + \frac{1.2 - 1}{2}(0.8)^2 = 1.064.$$

$$T_1 = 3000/1.064 = 2820°K.$$

The static pressure is found from Eq. 7-23:

$$\frac{p_{01}}{p_1} = \left[1 + \frac{\gamma - 1}{2} M_1^2\right]^{\gamma/(\gamma-1)} = (1.064)^6 = 1.45$$

$$p_1 = 5/1.45 = 3.45 \text{ atm.}$$

The pressure ratio across the generator itself may be found by trial and error from Eq. 7-65:

$$\frac{p_3}{p_0} = \frac{p_2}{p_1}\left[\frac{1 + \frac{1}{2}(\gamma - 1)M_1^2(p_1/p_2)^{K(\gamma-1)/\gamma}}{1 + \frac{1}{2}(\gamma - 1)M_1^2}\right]^{\gamma/(\gamma-1)}$$

$$0.2 = \frac{p_2}{p_1}\left[\frac{1 + 0.064(p_2/p_1)^{0.083}}{1.064}\right]^6.$$

A value of $p_2/p_1 = 0.19$ satisfies this equation thus:

$$p_2 = 0.19(3.45) = 0.66 \text{ atm.}$$

The average pressure in the generator is simply

$$p_{av} = (3.45 + 0.66)/2 = 2.05 \text{ atm.}$$

The average temperature may be found by first computing the temperature at the discharge of the generator section by utilizing Eq. 7-60:

$$\frac{T_2}{T_1} = \left[\frac{p_2}{p_1}\right]^{K(\gamma-1)/\gamma} = (0.19)^{0.083} = 0.873$$

$$T_2 = (2820)(0.873) = 2460°\text{K.}$$

The average temperature is then $T_{av} = (2460 + 2820)/2 = 2640°\text{K.}$

Now that we have the average properties in the generator we may find the average conductivity. From Fig. 7-10 the conductivity at 2640°K and 1 atm pressure is found to be 17(ohm-m)$^{-1}$. The average pressure in our generator is 2.05 atm. The conductivity is approximately inversely related to the square root of the pressure [12] so that the conductivity at 2.05 atm is

$$\frac{\sigma_1}{\sigma_{av}} = \sqrt{\frac{p_{av}}{p_1}} = \frac{17}{\sigma_{av}} = \sqrt{\frac{2.05}{1}}$$

$$\sigma_{av} = 11.8 \text{ (ohm-m)}^{-1}.$$

The velocity at entrance to the generator may be calculated from the definition of Mach number given in Eqs. 7-19 and 7-20, thus:

$$u_1 = M_1\sqrt{\gamma \Re T_1}$$

$$= 0.8 \left[\frac{1.2 \times 8.31 \times 10^3 \text{ joules} \times 2820°\text{K kg-mole}}{\text{kg-mole-°K}} \times \frac{\text{nt-m}}{29 \text{ kg}} \times \frac{\text{kg-m}}{1 \text{ joule } 1 \text{ nt-sec}^2}\right]^{1/2}$$

$$u_1 = 790 \text{ m/sec.}$$

We may now compute the length of the generator required to attain the desired pressure ratio. This is done by substituting the current density J_{ny} from Eq. 7-36b into Eq. 7-15 and integrating to obtain

$$l_2 - l_1 = -\frac{(1 + \beta_n^2)(p_2 - p_1)}{\sigma u B^2 (K - 1)}$$

$$l_2 - l_1 = -\frac{[1 + (1.25)^2] \times (0.66 - 3.45) \text{ atm} \times 1.01 \times 10^5 \text{ nt/(m}^2 - \text{atm)}}{11.8 \text{ (ohm-m)}^{-1} \times 790 \text{ m/sec} \times (3)^2 \text{ tesla}^2 \times (1/2 - 1)}$$

$$= -17.2 \text{ meters,}$$

where the minus sign arises because in our coordinate system the induced current carries a negative sign. The student would be well advised to verify the correctness of the units in the last calculation.

The current density may be calculated from Eq. 7-36b:

$$J_{ny} = \frac{\sigma u B (K - 1)}{1 + \beta_n^2}$$

$$= \frac{11.8 \text{ (ohm-m)}^{-1} \times 790 \text{ m/sec} \times 3 \text{ tesla} \times 1 \text{ volt-sec/m}^2 - \text{tesla} \times (1/2 - 1)}{2.56}$$

$$= 5470 \text{ amp/m}^2.$$

The area over which this density exists may be approximated by a trapezoid, once we know the required exit area. The area variation required to produce constant velocity may be found from Eq. 7-55 as follows:

$$\frac{A_2}{A_1} = \left[\frac{p_2}{p_1}\right]^{[K(\gamma-1)/\gamma]-1} = (0.19)^{-0.917} = 4.6$$

$$A_2 = 4.6 \, A_1 = 4.6 \text{ m}^2.$$

Thus if we keep the distance between electrodes constant, then the dimension b must increase from 0.5 meter at the entrance to 2.3 meters at the exit. An illustration of the duct cross section and the electrode area is shown in Fig. 7-19. The area of one electrode is equal to

$$\text{Electrode area} = \frac{1}{2}(b_1 + b_2)l = \left(\frac{0.5 + 2.3}{2}\right)(17.2) = 24.1 \text{ m}^2.$$

The total current available is the electrode area times the current density:

$$I = J \times A = \left(5470 \, \frac{\text{amp}}{\text{m}^2}\right)(24.1 \text{ m}^2) = 1.32 \times 10^5 \text{ amp.}$$

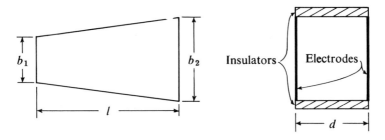

FIG. 7-19. A side and end view of the electrodes in the MHD generator.

The voltage available to the load is found from the definition of the loading factor $(K = E_y/uB)$ and the electric field $(E_y = V/d)$ to yield

$$V = KuBd = \frac{1}{2} \times 790 \, \frac{\text{m}}{\text{sec}} \times 3 \text{ tesla} \times \frac{1 \text{ volt-sec}}{\text{m}^2\text{-tesla}} \times 2 \text{ m} = 2370 \text{ volts}$$

The power density is simply the electric field times the current density:

$$P_o/\Omega = \frac{2370 \text{ volts}}{2m} \times \frac{5470 \text{ amps}}{\text{m}^2} = 6.48 \times 10^6 \, \frac{\text{watts}}{\text{m}^3}$$

and the total power is

$$P_o = (P_o/\Omega)\Omega = (6.48 \times 10^6 \text{ watts/m}^3) \times (24.1 \text{ m}^2 \times 2m)$$
$$= 312 \text{ megawatts.}$$

The resistance of the fluid, excluding the electrodes, is simply the distance between the electrodes divided by the conductivity and the area over which the current flows:

$$R = \frac{d}{\sigma A} = \frac{2m}{11.8 \text{ (ohm-m)}^{-1} \times 24.1 \text{ m}^2} = 7.0 \times 10^{-3} \text{ ohms.}$$

Thus, for matched impedance conditions the external load must be very small, because of the large electrode areas. The matched load resistance could be raised markedly by utilizing a segmented electrode generator in which the area of each segment would be quite small.

We can now calculate the so-called adiabatic conversion efficiency for the device as defined by Eq. 7-57. The actual temperature at the discharge of the diffuser is given by Eq. 7-61.

$$\frac{T_3}{T_0} = \left[\left(\frac{p_1}{p_2} \right)^{1-K} \frac{p_3}{p_0} \right]^{(\gamma-1)/\gamma} = [(5.25)^{1/2}(0.2)]^{0.166}$$

$$T_3 = 2640°K.$$

The isentropic temperature drop is, however,

$$\frac{T_3'}{T_0} = \left[\frac{p_3}{p_0} \right]^{(\gamma-1)/\gamma} = (0.2)^{0.166}$$

$$T_3' = 2300°K.$$

Thus the adiabatic conversion efficiency in comparison with an isentropic device is

$$\eta_{ad} = \frac{T_0 - T_3}{T_0 - T_3'} = \frac{3000 - 2640}{3000 - 2300} = 51.5 \text{ percent.}$$

The overall thermal efficiency can be found if we know the energy being delivered to the generator. The energy released in the combustion process is found from tables of combustion data to be $\Delta h_{comb} = 1.56 \times 10^9$ joules per kg. The mass rate of flow is simply $uA\rho$. The density at the inlet to the generator is

$$\rho_1 = \frac{p_1}{\mathcal{R}T_1} = \frac{3.45 \text{ atm kg-mole-}°K}{8.31 \times 10^3 \text{ joules} \times 2820°K} \times \frac{1.01 \times 10^5 \text{ nt}}{\text{m}^2\text{-atm}}$$

$$= 1.465 \times 10^{-2} \text{ kg-mole.}$$

Thus the mass rate of flow at 1 is

$$m = 1.465 \times 10^{-2} \text{ kg-mole} \times 1 \text{ m}^2 \times 790 \frac{m}{\text{sec}} = 11.58 \text{ kg-mole/sec.}$$

The rate of energy input into the generator is

$$\mathcal{E}_1 = m \times \Delta h_{comb} = 11.58 \frac{\text{kg-mole}}{\text{sec}} \times \frac{1 \text{ kg-mole of fuel}}{15.29 \text{ kg-mole}} \times \frac{1.32 \times 10^9 \text{ joules}}{\text{kg-mole of fuel}}$$

$$= 10.0 \times 10^8 \text{ watts.}$$

The thermal efficiency without allowing any energy for auxiliaries, such as magnets etc., then is

$$\eta_t = \frac{P_o}{\mathcal{E}_1} = \frac{3.12 \times 10^8 \text{ watts}}{10.0 \times 10^8 \text{ watts}} = 31.2 \text{ percent.}$$

It should be kept in mind that we are exhausting gases at a temperature of 2640°K, a temperature that is high enough to utilize as a source of energy in a conventional power plant; in Section 7.6 we will discuss ways in which this can be done.

The power required to supply the magnetic field in large installations is not great; this subject is discussed in Section 7.5.4.

7.5 PROBLEMS ASSOCIATED WITH MHD POWER GENERATION

We will now consider in some detail several of the problems that must have at least partial solution before economically competitive MHD power generation can be attained.

7.5.1 Increasing electrical conductivity by means of seeding. In Section 7.2.2 we discussed several methods of ionizing gases in order that they may be made electrically conducting to an extent that would permit their use in an MHD generator. The method that has appeared most promising to date is the use of an easily ionized substance such as an alkali metal to provide the necessary conductivity in a closed cycle power plant where seed recovery can be achieved.

The electrical conductivity is approximately proportional to the square root of the seeding concentration, whereas the cost of the seed is proportional to the quantity of seed lost in any subsequent recovery equipment, the cost of installing the seeding plant, and the cost of operation of the seed recovery plant. Optimum seed concentration is then determined by evaluating the relative importance of a large power density associated with a high conductivity versus the seed and seed equipment costs. The cost of seeding with different potassium compounds as reported by Wright *et al.* [13] is given in Table 7-4.

One of the factors that must be considered in the use of seeding material is the possible deleterious effect the alkali metals can have on the components of the generator that come in contact with them. It is highly probable that this material will cause increased corrosion of the generator components.

The study described in Ref. [13] indicates that if only 90 percent seed recovery can be achieved it is more economical to inject a quantity of seed that yields a concentration of only 0.1 percent of the combustion gases. However, if 99 percent recovery can be achieved, then 1 percent seeding concentration becomes economically feasible because of the increased power density that results from the increased electrical conductivity.

TABLE 7-4. COST† OF SEEDING WITH DIFFERENT POTASSIUM COMPOUNDS‡

Ratio of N_2/O_2 →	3.727	2.0	1.0	0.5	0
Seed ↓	(Air)				(Pure oxygen)
K_2CO_3	0.0129	0.0082	0.0058	0.0046	0.0033
KNO_3	0.0140	0.0095	0.0067	0.0053	0.0039
KOH (flakes)	0.0129	0.0084	0.0060	0.0047	0.0034
KOH (50% solution)	0.0090	0.0060	0.0042	0.0033	0.0023

† In cents per kilowatt-hour (c/kWh) of the plant output.
‡ From Wright *et al.* [13].

7.5.2 High temperature materials. One of the chief problems in the design of long-life MHD generators is the finding of materials that can survive the high operating temperatures of such generators. This problem is formidable when one considers that both an insulator and a conductor are required that can sustain temperatures of 2000 to 3200°K for long periods of time in an atmosphere that might include alkali metal vapors used for raising the conductivity of the gas. It is necessary to include the possibility of two types of generators—those that use inert gases such as helium or argon which have been heated by a nuclear reactor, and the open cycle type generator in which a fossil fuel has been burned to give the high temperatures and in which the duct gases will be a mixture of carbon monoxide (CO), carbon dioxide (CO_2), water vapor (H_2O), nitrogen (N_2), and the thermal decomposition products of these molecules.

Tungsten and tantalum appear to be the most promising materials for use as electrodes with inert gas generators, assuming they do not react with alkali metals and are compatible with the electrical insulation used in the duct.

In the early stages of electrode development it was believed that water-cooled metallic electrodes could be used in MHD generators. However, this leads to a cool electrode boundary layer (large electrode voltage drops with arc spots) and is generally conducive to poor electrical performance. The use of calcia- or yttria-stabilized zirconia has led to promising results. Other tests have indicated that the zirconia electrode material can be replenished continually by introduction of a very small amount of the electrode material into the combustion products, thus "flame spraying" the electrode surfaces. Another approach that has met with some success is to use metallic electrodes bathed in an atmosphere of CO to prevent oxidation. The Soviets have reported some success with ceramic (silicon carbide) electrodes.

For providing electrical insulation, many ceramic materials must be omitted from consideration because of low melting point, low decomposition temperature, or high electrical conductivity. Experience has shown that stabilized zirconia is attractive both as an insulating wall material and an electrode material if certain precautions are observed in its use; it is a material with good refractory properties and a low vapor pressure. To prevent electrical leakage in the zirconia insulating walls, as well as in the boundary layer, a transpiration flux of hot air may be used, the air entering between and around the ZrO_2 blocks. Reference [14] gives a rather complete list of papers on MHD power generation, including work on electrode and insulating wall construction.

7.5.3   Heat transfer problems. The materials problems discussed in the preceding section can be ameliorated to a certain extent by cooling the walls. One limitation, however, must be considered: the electrodes should not be cooled to such an extent that electrons recombine with ions in their vicinity, thereby reducing the effective conductivity of the gas. There is no limitation to the extent to which the insulated walls may be cooled. The cooling, however, must not reduce the bulk temperature more than a few percent. The extent of the cooling may be calculated in the usual ways for turbulent flow in closed channels. For open cycles in which solid particles such as carbon are present, radiation heat transfer must also be considered. In the next section we will present some estimates of the loss by heat transfer as a fraction of the thermal input.

Aerodynamic losses, including viscous drag and diffuser losses, will also occur. However, MHD power generators have the possibility of being much cleaner than turbines and thus such losses may be relatively small.

The problem of boundary layer formation on electrodes is considerably more serious, however. In addition to the growth of the usual viscous and thermal boundary layers adjacent to the electrodes, a space charge sheath and potential drop forms at the electrode surface as in the thermionic converter or the conventional arc discharge device. The true mechanism at the conducting wall is not fully understood and is the focus of considerable experimental and theoretical research effort.

7.5.4   Magnet losses. One of the characteristics of an MHD generator is that the power required for the magnetic field can be an appreciable fraction of the generated power. The calculations and assumptions that must be made to determine this fraction are extensive. One can consider the case of an air-core electromagnet, an iron-core electromagnet, or a cryogenic superconducting magnet. Reference [15] treats the first two cases.

A superconducting magnet is one whose coil is wound with a material whose electrical resistance goes to zero below a certain temperature (generally not more than 10°K). This usually requires that the coil of the magnet be submerged in a liquid helium bath which has a boiling point of 4.2°K at 1 atm. Alloys of niobium and zirconium, and alloys of niobium and tin have shown promise in the production of wire for use in superconducting magnets.

A superconducting magnet offers two principal advantages over a magnetic field produced by a copper-wound magnet. First, the current-carrying capacity of the superconductors now available is much greater than can be achieved with copper by a factor of nearly a hundred. Thus the volume of the windings can be greatly reduced. Secondly, since a superconductor has zero electrical resistivity, no Joule losses arise in the magnet and the power required to create the field decreases by several orders of magnitude.

At present, the cost of construction of a conventional magnet system and a superconducting magnet system are approximately the same. However, the cost of operating a superconducting magnet would be considerably lower, requiring only that power needed to maintain the temperature of the coils in the superconducting state. In addition, we can expect the cost of superconducting materials to drop markedly as their technology becomes further developed. An analysis of the design of a superconducting magnet system has been carried out by Wilson and Roberts [16]. A complete review of the state-of-the-art of superconducting magnets may be found in Refs. [17] and [18].

Lindley [19] has carried out an interesting study comparing the heat transfer and magnetic field power losses for plants of various sizes. He found the minimum output for a plant that utilizes a conventionally produced magnetic field using water-cooled copper coils producing a field of 3 tesla, and for a plant that utilizes a superconducting field of 10 tesla. The results of his calculations are shown in Figs. 7-20 and 7-21.

7.5.5 End current losses. A pressure loss peculiar to MHD generators is that due to circulating electrical currents that occur at each end of the generator section of the duct; these currents are sometimes called eddy currents.

Because the moving conductor in an MHD device is a three-dimensional continuum instead of a bundle of essentially one-dimensional wires, eddy currents may occur wherever there is a rapid variation in electric or magnetic field strength or fluid velocity. These currents induce a pressure loss in the flow because of the interaction of the current and the magnetic field. Under typical conditions it appears that this pressure loss will not exceed 10 percent of the entrance stagnation pressure. These variations can be avoided to a great extent in a linear configuration generator by the insertion of guide vanes in the regions near the entrance and exit of the generator region which would block the eddy current circulation. Sutton [10] has analyzed these entering and leaving losses for several different cases.

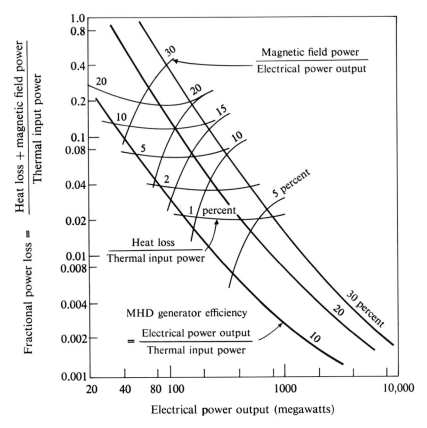

FIG. 7-20. Power losses in an MHD generator as a function of the electrical power output. The magnetic field is supplied by a copper field coil; the flux density is 3 tesla. After Ref. [19] with permission.

7.5.6 A-C power generation. The types of generators discussed so far have been d-c devices; for efficient power distribution, however, alternating current is required. Inversion equipment is fairly standard at the present time, although the development of long-term reliability at high power levels still poses somewhat of a problem.

The possibility of generating alternating current directly in an MHD channel is of some interest; the so-called electrodeless configuration devices have been investigated [10]. By a suitable arrangement of magnetic field coils supplied with properly phased power, a sinusoidal magnetic wave may be made to travel the length of the channel. If the speed of travel of this wave is made less than that of the fluid, electrical currents will be induced in the flow, which in turn will create an electric field inducing an additional voltage in the coils of the magnet. The net effect will be to retard the flow and generate

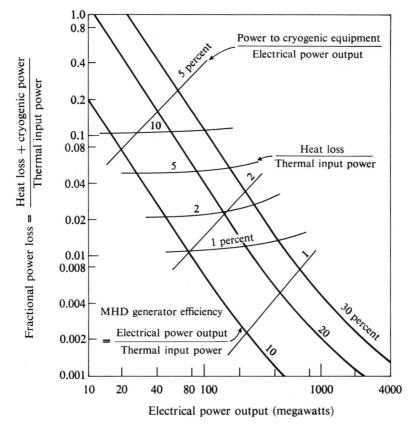

FIG. 7-21. Power losses in an MHD generator as a function of the electrical power output. The magnetic field is supplied by a superconducting field coil; flux density 10 tesla. After Ref. [19] with permission.

power in the windings. For this scheme to be effective, however, electrical conductivities considerably greater than those now available in combustion gases will be required.

7.6 POSSIBLE PLANT CONFIGURATIONS FOR LARGE SCALE MHD POWER GENERATION

The example problem worked in Section 7.4 clearly showed the practicality of utilizing the exhaust gases of an MHD generating plant after they pass through the electrodes of the generator. The temperature of the exhaust gases is so high that most of the energy released during the combustion process passes out the exhaust stack. For that reason we will consider in this section several alternative schemes for the generation of electrical power.

7.6.1   Fossil-fueled, open cycle generators. The simplest scheme calls for the addition of a compressor to raise the pressure of the combustion air, a preheater using the exhaust gases of the MHD generator to raise the temperature of the combustion air, and a conventional steam power plant to use the energy remaining in the exhaust gases to power the auxiliaries and supply additional output power. A further refinement would be to use oxygen-enriched air for combustion to raise the combustion temperature even higher.

The scheme most likely to be realized uses coal as a fuel. Because hydroxyl radicals have a tendency to participate in electron-removal reactions, the presence of hydrogen in an MHD combustion plasma is undesirable. Coal has a higher ratio of carbon atoms to hydrogen atoms than either fuel oil or methane, and thus produces a more conductive MHD combustion plasma. Furthermore, coal is the most abundant domestic fossil fuel.

The major problems associated with using coal as an MHD fuel can frequently be traced back to its mineral matter content. Some of the problems associated with the use of coal include: (1) erosion of electrodes and insulators by slag condensing in the MHD duct; (2) corrosion and erosion of heat-transfer surfaces and refractories in the steam boiler and air preheater; and (3) the necessity of recovering seed from a complex seed-slag mixture. Bergman, Plants, Demeter, and Bienstock [20] have examined the question of whether or not an MHD-steam power plant employing coal gasification can compete economically with other power plants.

Ordinarily the term "gasification of coal" is used to describe the reacting of coal with steam and either air or oxygen to produce a fuel gas that contains CO and H_2 and that can then be upgraded to methane. Because of the need to minimize the amount of H_2 in the combustion plasma, only those gasification processes which yield a low-Btu, low-H_2 producer gas provide a satisfactory cycle working fluid.

Reference [20] assesses the efficacy and economics of producing a clean, low-Btu fuel gas from coal for MHD power generation by means of four processing schemes. Each involved a different mode of coal combustion and level of gas cleanliness. Suspension gasification with slag removal prior to combustion yielded the most favorable combination of operating characteristics and power cost.

In that scheme a two-stage combustion system is utilized with a suspension gasifier as the first stage. The hot gas leaving the first stage is almost completely cleaned (99 percent by weight particulate removal is assumed); secondary air and seed are introduced in the second stage where final combustion occurs. Figure 7-22 is a power flow diagram of this proposal and Fig. 7-23 is the corresponding mass flow diagram.

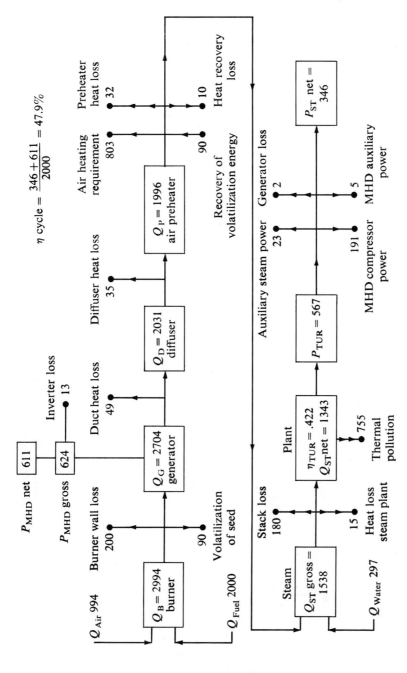

FIG. 7-22. Power flow diagram of a combined MHD–conventional power plant using suspension gasification with air. All power flows are in megawatts. After Ref. [20].

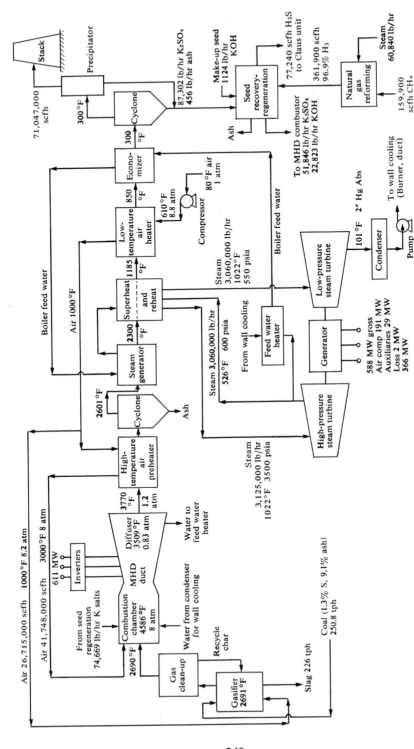

FIG. 7-23. Mass flow diagram for a combined MHD-conventional power plant using suspension gasification with air. After Ref. [20].

Raw coal is gasified with hot air, using 41.3 percent stoichiometric air at 810°K; molten slag is drained off from the bottom of the gasifier. The endothermic C-CO₂ and C-H₂O reactions occur in the dilute-gas phase where there is a relatively low concentration of fuel in suspension. The gas generated is 30.7 percent CO and 12.1 percent H_2 and contains little tar and no methane because of the high operating temperature. Unconsumed char is captured by a combination of ceramic cyclones and expanded bed filters. Carryover char is recycled back to the bottom of the gasifier. The gas produced is fed to a secondary combustor at 1750°K and 8 atm with the remaining 60 percent of the total air preheated to 1922°K to produce a flue gas temperature of 2803°K at the entrance to the MHD duct.

The prime operating constraint for this system is to avoid the coke-softening temperature range at the top of the first-stage gasifier. The formation of a viscous, tacky carryover material complicates the task of gas cleaning. For most cokes, the ash melting range lies between 1422°K and 1810°K. This analysis was based on the use of Pittsburgh-seam coals, which tend to have fairly high ash-melting temperatures, so that a gasifier-exit temperature of 1750°K was chosen. Exit-gas temperatures can be controlled by either varying the air-preheat temperature or introducing flue-gas recycle. In this study a reduced air-preheat temperature of 810°K was adopted.

The MHD generator duct in this design would be a linear, segmented Faraday generator. It would have a loading factor of 0.8 with an average duct velocity of 800 m/sec. The magnet would provide 6 tesla over the length of the duct, tapering down toward the end to maintain a Hall parameter of less than 4.

Operating and capital costs of this design were competitive with conventional power plants for coal prices starting at $4 per ton. Increasing coal prices simply made this design look more attractive. The system had a design efficiency of 47.9 percent, a capital cost of $217 per installed kW, and an operating cost of 9.6 mills per kWh with coal at $4 per ton. With coal at $24 per ton the operating costs become 14.8 mills per kWh.

Steam plant engineering is a relatively mature technology for which only minor cost and efficiency improvements can be anticipated. The same is not true of MHD energy conversion systems where, as the technology evolves, substantial cost reductions can be expected for major components such as ac-dc inverters, MHD ducts, superconducting magnets, and air preheaters. If the capital costs of constructing MHD power plants can be kept within bounds, then the advantages inherent in improved cycle efficiency, such as conservation of natural resources, reduced fuel costs, and lowered emission of pollutants, can be exploited to the fullest degree. Figure 7-24 illustrates a prototype MHD generator that has been used to study materials and other problems of power generation.

FIG. 7-24. View of the Mark VI MHD generator from the burner end. This unit has accumulated more than 150 hours of operating experience at power levels up to 550 kW under operating conditions simulating those encountered in a full-scale base-load power plant. The horizontal overhead pipe carries cooling water to the burner and vertical pipes feed cooling water to the MHD channel (covered with electrode connectors) downstream of the burner. The magnet at center right is a conventional room-temperature magnet, with iron yoke and copper magnet coils. The vertical tanks contain ceramic zirconia used to coat the electrodes continuously to prevent their erosion and coal ash to simulate the residue from burning coal. Photograph courtesy of Avco Everett Research Laboratory, Inc.

7.6.2 Nuclear-fueled, closed-cycle generators. In order for closed-cycle nuclear MHD power plants to become practical for central-station power generation, high-temperature nuclear reactors must be developed which can operate economically, reliably, and for long periods of time with an exit temperature in excess of about 2300°K. A great deal of difficulty has been encountered in developing reactors utilizing solid fuel elements which meet these requirements. Various theoretical studies done over the past few years have shown that a gaseous core reactor power plant utilizing an MHD-steam cycle has the potential of achieving very high thermal efficiency with a low fuel cycle cost and a breeding ratio greater than 1. In addition, the gaseous reactor MHD system offers the advantages in space of relatively high efficiency, high radiation temperature, and high specific power.

Williams, *et al.* [21] have explored in some detail the possibility of building an electric power plant utilizing a gaseous core reactor with MHD conversion. The reactor would operate with a central region of gaseous U-233 mixed with hydrogen, surrounded by a region of hydrogen gas contained within a spherical cavity. Unlike gaseous core rocket reactors, the power reactor would be internally moderated by hydrogen gas within the gaseous uranium core. The graphite or beryllium blanket surrounding the cavity would contain fertile thorium.

The gas mixture leaving the core is at an average temperature of 4000°K. It exits the reactor through a film-cooled subsonic exit region below the core and enters the MHD duct through a transpiration-cooled graphite nozzle. Pressure in the reactor is at several hundred atmospheres.

A simplified cycle diagram for the proposed cycle is shown in Figure 7-25. The MHD generator for this system is a high-pressure device with high power output per unit volume. The ceramic-coated hot electrodes are film-cooled by hydrogen at about 2000°K in order to provide some wall cooling and to protect the electrodes from an undesirable build-up of uranium droplets.

Because the MHD generator duct is small due to its high pressure, the magnetic field requirement is reduced below that of conventional MHD generator plants. (For example, for a 3600-MW electrical plant, the duct inlet area is 0.13 ft² with a corresponding exit area of 1.2 ft², for a pressure ratio of 10 to 1.) A magnetic field of 8 tesla has been assumed to be provided by a shielded cryogenic magnet.

After exiting the MHD duct, the uranium droplets are removed from the hydrogen gas by four cyclone-type separators. The molten uranium collected at the bottom of the separator is pumped by an electromagnetic pump back to the reactor inlet. The uranium-free hydrogen gas flows into turbine-compressor units. Hydrogen from each separator expands through a turbine, is cooled in a sodium-to-hydrogen heat exchanger, enters the first stage compressor, is cooled again by a second heat exchanger before entering the second-stage compressor, and is cooled again before final compression.

The liquid sodium, heated by the hydrogen in the heat exchangers, circulates through the steam generators. In the system under consideration, two steam generators are used with each turbine-compressor unit. The primary advantages of using multiple turbine-compressor and steam generators is that a failure of one of these units would result in only a 25% loss of plant capacity.

The thermodynamic cycle of the plant was examined based on a reactor operating pressure of 200 atm and a reactor exit temperature of 4000°K.

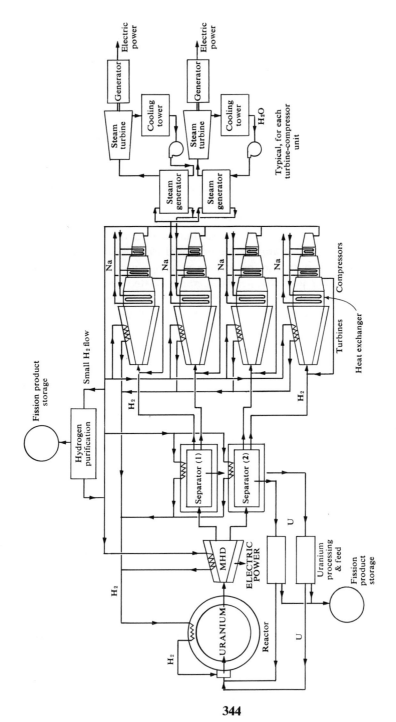

FIG. 7-25. A simplified cycle diagram of a combined nuclear-fueled, MHD, gas-turbine, steam-power plant. Such plants become economic in the thousands-of-megawatt range. After Williams, *et al.* [21].

The corresponding hydrogen flow is 34 kg/sec for a 3600-MW electrical reactor. The MHD duct inlet temperature was 3540°K. The average electrical conductivity of the gas in the duct was estimated at 43 mhos/meter. The projected MHD electrical power output is 0.23 MW(e) for each thermal megawatt. For a turbine pressure drop of 15-to-1, the turbine is estimated to provide 0.31 MW(e) for each thermal megawatt supplied. The steam plant is estimated to provide 0.19 MW(e) for each thermal megawatt, yielding an overall cycle efficiency of about 73 percent.

7.6.3 Liquid-metal MHD generators. MHD devices using liquid metals, sometimes called LMMHD, were originally conceived in the early 1960's as compact power systems for space and for other special applications. These early studies were very limited in scope. Subsequent investigations utilizing sophisticated mathematical models were broadened enough to reveal basic power cycles that appear to be attractive for central-station power generation with maximum cycle temperature in the range of 1000 to 2000°F.

A number of advanced heat sources currently under development are projected to supply heat in this range of temperatures. It appears that two-phase LMMHD energy conversion systems might provide a suitable companion to several of these heat sources. Included in this list are the liquid-metal fast breeder reactor (LMFBR), the fusion reactor, and the high-temperature gas-cooled reactor (HTGCR). Furthermore, fluidized-bed combustors are being developed to provide "clean" thermal energy from high sulfur in the appropriate temperature range for the LMMHD. Studies have also been carried out showing that the LMMHD cycle could be utilized as a bottoming cycle with a plasma MHD topping unit.

Cutting and Amend [22] have analyzed several cycles utilizing the LMMHD. One of the most attractive cycles combines an MHD generator with a gas turbine and a steam power plant. A schematic of the system is shown in Fig. 7-26. The cycle uses an inert gas as the thermodynamic working fluid and a liquid metal as the electrical conductor (electrodynamic fluid). In operation, the gas and liquid are mixed and the mixture enters the MHD generator, where the expansion of the gas drives the liquid across the magnetic field and generates electrical power. The two phases are then separated, with the liquid phase being returned to the mixer via an intermediate heat exchanger, where it once again picks up energy from the primary coolant from the reactor. The gas phase then expands further through a gas turbine, which produces power for sale or to run auxiliaries. The gas phase enters another heat exchanger, where it supplies energy to a steam loop for powering an otherwise conventional steam plant. System cycle studies indicate efficiencies in the neighborhood of 50 percent are attainable.

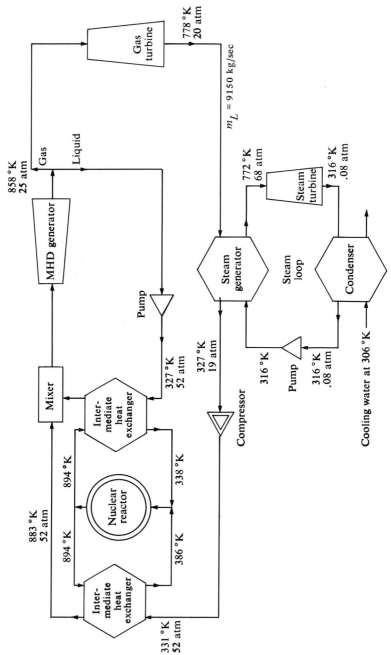

FIG. 7-26. Two-phase LMMHD and steam cycle plant interfaced with a sodium-cooled nuclear reactor. After Ref. [22].

It appears that systems such as the one illustrated in Fig. 7-26 have excellent potential for advanced energy-conversion systems in central-station power generation. The advantages of the LMMHD are: (1) an effective coupling to fossil heat sources, such as fluidized-bed combustors, or to liquid-metal–cooled heat sources, such as the breeder or fusion reactor; (2) elimination of the liquid-metal–to–water interference in liquid-metal–cooled reactors; and (3) improved cycle performance at limiting steam temperatures and the potential to operate at elevated temperatures.

NOTATION

A	=	area, m²
a	=	speed of sound, m/sec
b	=	dimension, meters
B	=	magnetic flux density, gauss
$\mathbf{B}$	=	magnetic flux density vector, tesla
c_p	=	constant pressure specific heat, joules/(°K-kg)
d	=	dimension, meters
e	=	electronic charge, coulombs
$\mathcal{E}$	=	energy, joules
$\mathcal{E}_D$	=	dissociation energy, electron volts
$\mathcal{E}_i$	=	ionization energy, electron volts
E	=	electric field, volts/meter
$\mathbf{E}$	=	electric field vector, volts/meter
$\mathbf{E}'$	=	electric field vector as defined by Eq. 7-24, volts/meter
$\mathbf{E}''$	=	electric field vector as seen by moving observer, volts/meter
F	=	force, newtons
$\mathbf{F}$	=	force vector, newtons
h	=	specific enthalpy, joules/kg
h	=	Planck's constant, joule-sec
I	=	electric current, amp
J	=	current density, amp/m²
$\mathbf{J}$	=	current density vector, amp/m²
k	=	Boltzmann's constant, joule/°K
K	=	loading factor or electrical efficiency, dimensionless
K_H	=	Hall generator loading factor, dimensionless
l	=	length, meter
L	=	interaction length defined by Eq. 7-32, meters
m	=	mass rate of flow, kg/sec
m^*	=	effective electron mass, gm or kg
M	=	Mach number, dimensionless
n	=	concentration, m⁻³
p	=	pressure, atmospheres
P_o	=	output power, watts
P_M	=	mechanical input power, watts
Q	=	collision cross section, m²

R	=	internal resistance, ohms
R_o	=	external load resistance, ohms
$\mathcal{R}$	=	universal gas constant, joules/(kg-mole °K)
S	=	number of ion pairs produced by an electron
T	=	absolute temperature, °K
u	=	velocity, m/sec
$\mathbf{u}$	=	velocity vector, m/sec
V	=	electrical potential, volts
x	=	coordinate direction, m
X	=	fraction ionized, dimensionless
y	=	coordinate direction, m
z	=	coordinate direction, m
β_n	=	Hall parameter, dimensionless
γ	=	ratio of specific heats, dimensionless
η_e	=	electrical efficiency, dimensionless
η_{ad}	=	adiabatic efficiency, dimensionless
η_t	=	thermal efficiency, dimensionless
θ	=	Hall angle, radians
μ	=	mobility, cm²/(volt-sec) or m²/(volt-sec)
ν	=	frequency, sec⁻¹
ρ	=	fluid density, kg/m³ or kg-mole/m³
σ	=	conductivity, (ohm-cm)⁻¹ or (ohm-m)⁻¹
τ	=	mean time between collisions, sec
ω	=	electron cyclotron frequency, sec⁻¹
Ω	=	volume, m³

Subscripts

ad	=	adiabatic
av	=	average
aux	=	auxiliary
comb	=	combustion
i	=	ions
ind	=	induced
int	=	internal
max	=	maximum
n	=	electrons
ng	=	neutral
oc	=	open circuit
opt	=	optimum
x	=	coordinate direction
y	=	coordinate direction
z	=	coordinate direction
0	=	stagnation state
$1, 2 \cdots$	=	stations

Superscript

	=	isentropic state

PROBLEMS

7-1. Find the wavelength of the energy that would be needed to ionize an oxygen or nitrogen atom. Is it possible for visible light to ionize air? Explain briefly.

Answer: $\lambda_N = 853$ A; $\lambda_O = 910$ A.

7-2. Find the degree of ionization of nitrogen and oxygen at 0.1 atm pressure and 8000°K. Do these substances meet our definition of a slightly ionized gas?

7-3. Using the degree of ionization you found in Problem 7-2, find the conductivity of this gas, assuming it to be slightly ionized. If the pressure is reduced by a factor of 10, what happens to the conductivity? If the temperature goes up by a factor of 50 percent, what happens to the conductivity?

7-4. Derive Eqs. 7-22 and 7-23.

7-5. Derive Eq. 7-50. Plot a curve of $K_{H(\text{opt})}$ for β_n from 0.1 to 10.

7-6. Derive Eq. 7-51. Plot a curve of $\eta_{e(\text{max})}$ for β_n from 0.1 to 10.

7-7. Derive Eq. 7-67. Justify every step of the operation.

7-8. Solve the example problem worked in Section 7.4, but in this case assume the combustion temperature is 2700°K. How does this 10-percent reduction in combustion temperature affect the power output, the adiabatic efficiency, and the overall cycle efficiency of the system?

Answer: $P_o = 297$ megawatts; length $= 90$ m.

7-9. A constant area MHD accelerator jet has the following given data:

Distance between electrodes	0.25 meter
Electrical conductivity	40 $(\text{ohm-m})^{-1}$
Mean flow velocity	2000 m/sec
Area of each electrode	0.3 m²
Applied voltage	1000 volts
Magnetic flux density	1 weber/m²

Find the rate at which mechanical energy is delivered to the gas stream. At what rate is electrical energy delivered to the accelerator? What is the efficiency of the accelerator?

Answer: Efficiency $= 50$ percent.

7-10. If the applied voltage is halved and the magnetic flux density is doubled, what effect does this have on the accelerator's effectiveness, described in Problem 7-9?

7-11. An MHD generator that uses helium seeded with 2 percent K_2CO_3 as its working fluid has an average conductivity of 50 $(\text{ohm-m})^{-1}$. At the entrance the generator and gas have the following properties:

$d = 25$ cm	T_{01}	$= 2800$°K
$b = 15$ cm	p_{01}	$= 2$ atm
$B = 1.4$ weber/m²	$u_1 = u_2$	$= 1000$ m/sec

The output voltage is maintained everywhere at 220 volts with a constant electrical efficiency. The gas at the exit of the generator section is $T_{02} = 2200°K$. Find (a) the outlet dimension b_2 assuming d stays constant; (b) the output power; and (c) the adiabatic efficiency, across the generator. Ignore the Hall effect in your calculations.

7-12. The design of the generator analyzed in Section 7.4 is changed so that the fluid leaves the generator (section 2) at a Mach number of unity. Find p_2, T_2 and u_2. How will this design change influence the operating characteristics of the generator?

Answer: $u_2 = 915$ m/sec.

7-13. A certain MHD generator uses helium seeded with cesium at $2200°K$ to give a conductivity of 10 (ohm-m)$^{-1}$. The gas travels at 750 m/sec in a magnetic field of 2.5 weber/m^2, through a duct with a cross-sectional area of 0.5 m^2. The generator operates at 75 percent of open circuit voltage. The working fluid has a mobility of 2.3 m^2/(volt-sec). Find the power per unit length of generator if it is designed to have continuous electrodes.

7-14. Consider the generator in Problem 7-13 again except now consider it to be a segmented electrode type generator. Find its power per unit length.

7-15. Assume that the generator in Problem 7-13 is a Hall generator. Find the power generated per unit length.

7-16. Compute the short circuit current densities of the three basic MHD configurations.

7-17. A gas accelerator that uses the Hall effect has been proposed to accelerate the products of combustion of C_2H_4. The gas will be initially accelerated by means of a nozzle as it moves from a holding tank where it is stored at 2.75 atmospheres and $3200°K$. After passing through the nozzle and before entering the generator, the gas is at a static pressure of 1.25 atmospheres. It is then seeded with 2 percent potassium. The exit velocity of the gas from the accelerator is twice the entrance velocity. The area of each electrode is 0.3 m^2 and the length of the MHD accelerator is 0.5 m. The magnetic flux density in the accelerator is 15 tesla and the mobility of the electrons in the ionized gas is 2.2 m^2/volt-sec.

Make a set of reasonable assumptions and find: (a) the velocity of the gas at the entrance to the accelerator; (b) the mechanical power delivered to the gas; (c) the electrical power output; (d) the efficiency of the device.

7-18. Using the data given in Section 7.6.2, estimate the power output and efficiency for the MHD portion of the reactor-fired power plant described there. Are your results comparable to the given number of 0.23 megawatts electrical power out per thermal megawatt in? What assumptions did you have to make to arrive at your numbers?

7-19. Using the data on Fig. 7-25 and in Section 7.6.3, estimate the power output and efficiency of the MHD generator, gas turbine, and steam plant of the two-phase LMMHD power plant illustrated and described there. Also estimate the overall plant efficiency if possible. State your assumptions.

REFERENCES

1. C. Petersen, "Method for Transforming the Kinetic Energy of Gases into Electrical Energy," U.S. Patent No. 1,443,091 (January 23, 1923).

2. E. Rupp, "Method of an Apparatus for Generating Electrical Energy," U.S. Patent No. 1,916,076 (June 27, 1933).

3. B. Karlovitz, "Process for the Conversion of Energy," U.S. Patent No. 2,210,-918 (August 13, 1940).

4. A. B. Cambel, *Plasma Physics and Magnetofluidmechanics* (New York: McGraw-Hill Book Company, Inc., 1963).

5. C. D. Hodgman, R. C. Weast, R. S. Shankland, and S. M. Selby, eds., *Handbook of Chemistry and Physics* (Cleveland, Ohio: The Chemical Rubber Publishing Company, 1962), p. 2586.

6. C. F. Hansen, "Approximations for the Thermodynamic and Transport Properties of High-Temperature Air," NACA TN 4150 (1958).

7. M. N. Saha, "Ionization in the Solar Chromosphere," *Philosophical Magazine*, 40 (1920), 472–488.

8. V. H. Blackman, M. J. Jones, and A. Demitriades, "MHD Power Generation Studies in Rectangular Channels," in *Proceedings 2nd Symposium Engineering Aspects of Magnetohydrodynamics*, eds. C. Mannal and N. W. Mather (New York and London: Columbia University Press, 1962), pp. 180–210.

9. S. C. Lin, E. L. Resler, and A. R. Kantrowitz, "Electrical Conductivity of Highly Ionized Argon Produced by Shock Waves," *Journal of Applied Physics*, 28 (1955), 95.

10. G. W. Sutton and A. Sherman, *Engineering Magnetohydrodynamics* (New York: McGraw-Hill Book Company, Inc., 1965).

11. L. P. Harris and J. D. Cobine, "The Significance of the Hall Effect for Three MHD Generator Configurations," *Transactions of the ASME, Journal of Engineering for Power*, 83A (1961), 392.

12. S. Way, S. M. DeCorso, R. L. Hunstad, G. A. Kemeny, W. Stewart, and W. E. Young, "Experiments with MHD Power Generation," *Transactions of the ASME, Journal of Engineering for Power*, 83A (1961), 397.

13. J. K. Wright, R. V. Harrowell, D. C. Gore, and C. V. Barnett, "Some Factors Influencing the Design of Open-Cycle Fossil-Fuel MHD Generators for the Electricity Supply Industry," in *Symposium on Magnetoplasmadynamic Electrical Power Generation*, at King's College, University of Durham (Newcastle upon Tyne: The Institution of Electrical Engineers, 1962).

14. J. B. Dicks, S. Way, T. R. Brogan, and M. S. Jones, Jr., "MHD Power Generation: Current Status," *Mechanical Engineering*, 91, No. 8 (1969), 18–25.

15. R. Wall, D. Erway, R. Spies, J. D. Burns, and D. McDowell, *Energy Conversion Systems Reference Handbook*, Vol. VII—*Other Devices* (Washington, D.C.: Office of Technical Services, U.S. Department of Commerce, 1960), p. VIII-D-20.

16. G. W. Wilson and D. C. Roberts, "Superconducting Magnet for Matnetoplasmadynamic Power Generation" in *Symposium on Magnetoplasmadynamic Electrical Power Generation, op. cit.* (Ref. [13]).

17. D. C. Freeman, Jr., "Superconducting Magnets—Part 1, The Role of Cryogenics," *Mechanical Engineering*, 89, No. 2 (1967), 46–52.

18. D. C. Freeman, Jr., "Superconducting Magnets—Part 2, Applications," *Mechanical Engineering*, 89, No. 3 (1967), 36–43.

19. B. C. Lindley, "Some Economic and Design Considerations of Large-Scale MPD Generators," in *Symposium on Magnetoplasmadynamic Electrical Power Generation, op. cit.*

20. P. D. Bergman, K. D. Plants, J. J. Demeter, and D. Bienstock, "An Economic Evaluation of MHD-Steam Powerplants Employing Coal Gasification," Bureau of Mines Report of Investigation 7796, U.S. Department of the Interior, 1973.

21. J. R. William, Y. Y. Yung, K. D. Kirby, and J. D. Clement, "Exploratory Investigation of an Electric Power Plant Utilizing a Gaseous Core Reactor with MHD Conversion," *7th Intersociety Energy Conversion Engineering Conference*, 1972 Proceedings (Washington, D.C.: American Chemical Society, 1972).

22. J. C. Cutting and W. E. Amend, "Status of the Two-Phase Liquid-Metal MHD Program at the Argonne National Laboratory," *9th Intersociety Energy Conversion Engineering Conference*, 1974 Proceedings (New York: American Society of Mechanical Engineers, 1974).

8　Fuel Cells

To a great extent the energy that the earth's population utilizes is initially derived from the energy stored within the chemical bonds of hydrocarbon fuels such as coal, gasoline, and natural gas. When this energy is converted to electrical power most of it, according to the dictates of the second law of thermodynamics, must be discarded. The conversion process transforms energy that was stored in a highly ordered manner in the chemical bonds to energy associated with great disorder after the combustion process. The maximum amount of useful power that can be obtained from this energy now is that which a Carnot engine would obtain operating between the temperature at which the energy was released and, in general, the natural temperature of the surroundings. In a real power plant the various conversion processes limit the system to an overall thermal efficiency of, at best, about 40 percent.

In this chapter we will consider a means of conversion that eliminates the high temperature combustion and subsequent processes found in nearly all energy conversion schemes designed to produce electrical power. By means of devices known as fuel cells it is possible to bypass the conversion-to-heat process and the associated mechanical-to-electrical processes; that is, a *fuel cell* is an electrochemical device in which the chemical energy of a conventional fuel is converted directly and efficiently into low voltage, direct-current electrical energy. One of the chief advantages of such a device is that because the conversion, at least in theory, can be carried out isothermally, the Carnot limitation on efficiency does not apply. A fuel cell is often described as a primary battery in which the fuel and oxidizer are stored external to the battery and are fed to it as needed. Figure 8-1 illustrates the elements of a fuel cell. It is implied in the use of the term battery, in this case, that the battery components themselves (electrodes and electrolytes) are not con-

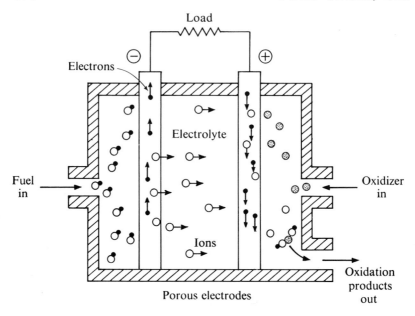

FIG. 8-1. Schematic of a fuel cell. The fuel gas diffuses through the anode and is oxidized, thus releasing electrons to the external circuit; the oxidizer diffuses through the cathode and is reduced by the electrons that have come from the anode by way of the external circuit.

sumed in the energy conversion process. The principle underlying any combustion reaction, whether it be in a fuel cell or a heat engine, is the same. The combustion reaction involves a transfer of electrons from the fuel molecules (thus oxidizing them) to the oxidizer molecules (thus reducing them). In the heat engine, fuel and oxidizer molecules are intimately mixed so that electrons pass directly from fuel molecules to oxidizer molecules. The fuel cell is a device that keeps the fuel molecules from mixing with the oxidizer molecules, permitting, however, the transfer of electrons by a metallic path that may contain a load.

8.1 HISTORICAL INTRODUCTION

In 1801, Humphrey Davy, one of the pioneers in electrochemical research, built a fuel cell that used carbon and nitric acid. However, another English investigator, William Grove, is generally acknowledged as the originator of the fuel cell. In 1839 he constructed a chemical battery in which the water-forming reaction of hydrogen and oxygen generated an electric current. While the purpose of Grove's experimental work was to help him study the decomposition of water, he noted with interest that his device, which used platinum electrodes in contact with dilute sulfuric acid, would cause "the permanent deflection" of a galvanometer connected to the cell. Grove did succeed in decomposing water by using twenty-six of his cells in series as a power source. Grove was the first worker to note the difficulty of producing high current densities in a fuel cell that uses gases. The problem he faced is still being wrestled with by present-day workers in the area. His insight into this problem is demonstrated by the following quotation:

"As the chemical or catalytic action could only be supposed to take place, with ordinary platina foil, at the line or water mark where the liquid, gas and platina met, the chief difficulty was to obtain anything like a notable surface of action."

Later in the chapter we will discuss this problem and some of the solutions to it that have been proposed. Figure 8-2 illustrates one of Grove's cells.

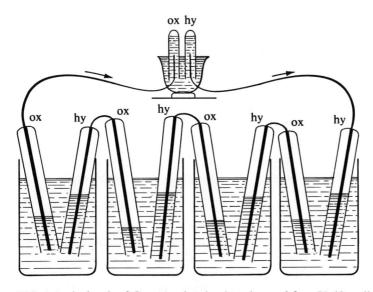

FIG. 8-2. A sketch of Grove's, showing how he used four H_2/O_2 cells to drive an electrolysis cell "to effect the decomposition of water by means of its composition."

Fifty years later in England two chemists, Ludwig Mond and Carl Langer, developed a device they actually called a fuel cell. Their cell had an output of about 6 amp per ft^2. The successful development of the dynamo at the time of Mond's and Langer's work overshadowed their effort and fuel cells quickly and quietly dropped into oblivion until the early 1940's. At that time Berl published the results of his studies on the peroxide mechanism of a carbon-oxygen electrode. Justi in Germany worked initially with carbon electrodes but realized that the surface-of-action problem was critical and hence started to work with porous metal electrodes.

Bacon in 1954 published the results of his high-pressure cell, which seemed to have good prospects. Since that time the number of workers in the area has increased at a very high rate. In the latter portion of the chapter we will briefly describe the work on those cells that have been most successful. There have been several excellent reviews of fuel cell work to which the interested reader may refer [1]–[3]. In order to analyze and determine the operating characteristics of fuel cells, we will briefly review the thermodynamic concepts pertinent to them.

8.2 THERMODYNAMIC PRINCIPLES

First we consider the role of the Gibbs free energy in finding the maximum useful work of a fuel cell. We will also determine what factors determine the theoretical open circuit voltage of a fuel cell by deriving the Nernst voltage equation. Finally, we will consider the various definitions of efficiency that may be applied to fuel cells.

8.2.1 The maximum work of a system. In order for us to formulate some efficiency definitions for fuel cells, we need some standards on which to base them. In this section we will consider what is the maximum work that one can expect to obtain from a system, regardless of its state before or after a given process.

We will use the term *reversible work* to mean the maximum work that can be done by a system during a given change of state, assuming that the system undergoes heat transfer with the surroundings. It is also evident that the only way that the work can be a maximum is for the process to be completely reversible.

We will consider a system similar to the one illustrated in Fig. 8-3. It has mass dm_i entering it, mass dm_e leaving it, heat $d\bar{Q}$ is transferred to the system, and work $d\bar{W}$ is done by the system.† Since we will be working with gaseous systems, which generally do not involve large changes in elevation

---

† Where the mass units are given in gram-moles. To avoid confusion in units we will place a bar over a symbol to denote an extensive property such as $\bar{H}$ in kilocalories. The unbarred symbol, following the chemist's notation, denotes a molar specific property such as H in kilocalories per mole. We will denote the units after some of the equations to reinforce this convention.

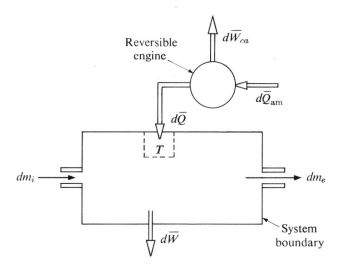

FIG. 8-3. A system in which maximum work can be done during a process.

or velocity, we will consider changes in potential and kinetic energy to be negligible. The change in stored energy for the systems will be represented by $d\mathcal{E}_{int}$. For the work to be completely reversible the process must be reversible and, therefore, any heat transfer to the surroundings must take place through a Carnot engine. We show the heat transfer on our sketch as taking place at the point where the system has a temperature T. We write the first law of thermodynamics for this system as

$$d\bar{Q} + dm_i(H_i) = d\bar{W} + dm_e(H_e) + d\mathcal{E}_{int} \quad [\text{kcal}], \quad \text{(8-1)}$$

where H is the enthalpy in units of kilocalories per mole.

Because the process is reversible, we find that the change of entropy is that due to heat transfer plus any change caused by mass transfer across the boundaries:

$$d\bar{S} = d\bar{Q}/T + dm_i\, S_i - dm_e\, S_e \quad [\text{kcal/°K}]. \quad \text{(8-2)}$$

The work of the Carnot engine can be found from an application of the first law to yield

$$d\bar{W}_{ca} = d\bar{Q}_{am} - d\bar{Q}, \quad \text{(8-3)}$$

where the subscript am denotes heat transfer with the environment. Because the Carnot engine is reversible, the change of entropy for the environment must equal the change of entropy for the system

$$\frac{d\bar{Q}_{am}}{T_{am}} = \frac{d\bar{Q}}{T}.$$

Thus the work for the Carnot engine is

$$d\overline{W}_{ca} = T_{am}(d\overline{Q}/T) - d\overline{Q}. \tag{8-4}$$

If we eliminate $d\overline{Q}/T$ from the above equation by using Eq. 8-2 we obtain

$$d\overline{W}_{ca} = T_{am}(d\overline{S} - dm_i\,S_i + dm_e\,S_e) - d\overline{Q} \quad \text{[kcal]}. \tag{8-5}$$

Since the reversible work is the maximum work, we must add to the work of the system the work of the Carnot engine:

$$d\overline{W}_{rev} = d\overline{W} + d\overline{W}_{ca}. \tag{8-6}$$

We may now substitute Eqs. 8-5 and 8-1 into Eq. 8-6 to obtain

$$d\overline{W}_{rev} = d\overline{Q} + dm_i(H_i) - dm_e(H_e) - d\mathcal{E}_{int}$$
$$+ T_{am}(d\overline{S} - dm_i\,S_i + dm_e\,S_e) - d\overline{Q}.$$

This equation simplifies to

$$d\overline{W}_{rev} = dm_i(H_i - T_{am}S_i) - dm_e(H_e - T_{am}S_e) - d(\mathcal{E}_{int} - T_{am}\overline{S}) \quad \text{[kcal]}. \tag{8-7}$$

The reversible work in this case, which involves heat transfer with the surroundings only, is a function of the initial and final states of the system and also depends on the temperature of the surroundings.

We now consider a system in which a chemical reaction might be taking place. In many cases the system will be in temperature equilibrium before and after the reaction takes place (if we wait a little while for the system to return to the environmental temperature). Let us consider a system that is closed—that is, it does not involve mass transfer and is assumed to be in temperature equilibrium with its environment; thus Eq. 8-7 becomes

$$d\overline{W}_{rev} = -d(\mathcal{E}_{int} - T\overline{S}) \tag{8-8}$$

$$_1\overline{W}_{2(rev)} = (\mathcal{E}_{int(1)} - T_1\overline{S}_1) - (\mathcal{E}_{int(2)} - T_2\overline{S}_2), \tag{8-9}$$

where $T_{am} = T_1 = T_2$ in Eq. 8-7. The quantity $\mathcal{E}_{int} - T\overline{S}$ is called the *Helmholtz function* and is denoted by the symbol $\overline{A}$. That is, when a closed system is in temperature equilibrium with the surroundings, the reversible work will be given by

$$d\overline{W}_{rev} = -d\overline{A}, \tag{8-10}$$

or, if we integrate from state 1 to state 2,

$$_1\overline{W}_{2(rev)} = \overline{A}_1 - \overline{A}_2 \quad \text{[kcal]}. \tag{8-11}$$

Let us now consider the more restricted case of a system in both pressure and temperature equilibrium with the surroundings. Since the system may undergo a volume change during the process, work may be done on the system by the surroundings if the volume of the system Ω decreases, or the system may do work on the surroundings if its volume increases. The work done on the surroundings, if we assume that the pressure of the system is the pressure of the surroundings, is given by

$$\overline{W}_{am} = P_{am}(\overline{\Omega}_2 - \overline{\Omega}_1) = P_2\overline{\Omega}_2 - P_1\overline{\Omega}_1 \qquad \text{[kcal]}. \qquad (8\text{-}12)$$

The maximum useful work is the reversible work minus the work done on the surroundings; thus we may combine Eq. 8-9 with Eq. 8-12 to obtain the maximum useful work

$$\overline{W}_{\max} = \overline{W}_{\mathrm{rev}} - \overline{W}_{am} = (\mathcal{E}_{\mathrm{int}(1)} - T_1\overline{S}_1) - (\mathcal{E}_{\mathrm{int}(2)} - T_2\overline{S}_2) - (P_2\overline{\Omega}_2 - P_1\overline{\Omega}_1)$$
$$= (\overline{H}_1 - T_1\overline{S}_1) - (\overline{H}_2 - T_2\overline{S}_2). \qquad (8\text{-}13)$$

The quantity $(\overline{H} - T\overline{S})$ is also a thermodynamic property and is called the *Gibbs function*. It is often denoted by the symbol $\overline{G}$. Thus, for a closed system in temperature and pressure equilibrium with the surroundings we have

$$\overline{W}_{\max} = \overline{G}_1 - \overline{G}_2 \qquad \text{[kcal]}. \qquad (8\text{-}14)$$

Consider a steady flow process that is in temperature equilibrium but not necessarily pressure equilibrium with the surroundings. Equation 8-7 represents this process if we assume that the storage term $d(\mathcal{E}_{\mathrm{int}} - T_{am}S)$ is identically zero and that the mass flow into the system must equal the mass flow out. Thus, Eq. 8-7 integrates to

$$\overline{W}_{\mathrm{rev}} = (\overline{H}_i - T_i\overline{S}_i) - (\overline{H}_e - T_e\overline{S}_e),$$

or

$$\overline{W}_{\mathrm{rev}} = \overline{G}_i - \overline{G}_e \qquad \text{[kcal]}. \qquad (8\text{-}15)$$

We may generalize our results by saying that for a steady flow system or closed system in both temperature and pressure equilibrium the maximum useful work is given by

$$-\overline{W}_{\max} = \Delta\overline{G} \qquad \text{[kcal]}. \qquad (8\text{-}16)$$

Thus Eq. 8-16 could apply equally well to a closed system such as a Daniell cell or a steady flow gas fuel cell.

8.2.2 Some electrochemical fundamentals. Since fuel cells operate on the well-established principles of electrochemistry, it is appropriate that we review those ideas that are germane to the understanding of the fuel cell.

We begin our study by considering a typical galvanic cell—a generic name for a device that converts chemical energy to electricity. The cell we consider is a Daniell cell (illustrated in Fig. 8-4) which consists of a container divided into two parts by a partition that permits the diffusion of ions between them. In the left-hand compartment, which contains zinc sulfate, we insert a bar of zinc; in the right-hand compartment, which contains copper sulfate, we insert a bar of copper. We complete the circuit by connecting the two electrodes by a wire that can deliver current to an external load.

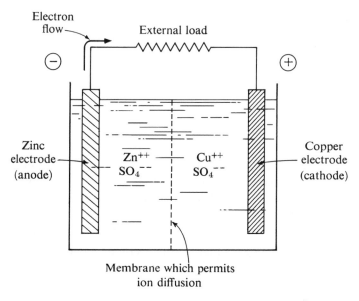

FIG. 8-4. The Daniell cell.

By considering the important properties of electrochemical cells, we hope to be able to predict the relative *ease* and relative *rate* of possible electrode reactions. Thermodynamics provides answers to questions of the relative ease of electrode reactions and, conversely, electrochemical experiments yield thermodynamic data. Rates will have to be considered separately.

Electrons go out of the cell electrode marked ⊖ and go into the cell electrode marked ⊕. We will use the notation ⊕ and ⊖ to indicate positive and negative in the electrical sense, and the uncircled symbols, + and −, to indicate positive and negative in the algebraic sense. We will always use the term *anode* to mean the electrode at which oxidation takes place. Oxidation for our purposes means the losing of electrons. That is, electrons at the anode are free to leave it and flow in the external circuit. The *cathode* is the electrode at which reduction takes place (where electrons are gained). In our example the cathode receives these electrons from the external circuit.

The electrons that go into the cathode are captured in reaction with the Cu^{++} ions and used in the reaction†

$$Cu^{++} + 2e^- \rightarrow Cu(s) \qquad \text{[cathode reaction].} \qquad \textbf{(8-17)}$$

Copper ions are removed from the solution at the cathode and zinc ions go into solution from the anode. Cations Zn^{++} and Cu^{++} in the solution

---

† The symbol (*s*) which follows Cu in Eq. 8-17 denotes the solid state. Similarly (*l*) (*g*), and (*aq*) denote the liquid, gaseous, and aqueous states respectively.

move toward the cathode (the copper bar) and anions SO_4^{--} move toward the anode.

The electrons that leave the anode are released by the reaction

$$Zn(s) \rightarrow Zn^{++} + 2e^- \qquad \text{[anode reaction]}. \qquad \textbf{(8-18)}$$

The zinc ions migrate away from the anode into the solution. To complete the process, electrons flow from the anode to the cathode through the wire and a current is obtained from an oxidation-reduction reaction. This reaction, which causes a gradual eating away of the zinc bar and plating out of Cu^{++}, will continue until one of the two quantities is exhausted.

Combining the anode and the cathode reaction yields

$$Zn(s) + Cu^{++} \rightarrow Zn^{++} + Cu(s). \qquad \textbf{(8-19)}$$

The equation representing the cell reaction must be balanced because equal numbers of electrons go to the cathode and leave the anode.

By examining Eq. 8-17 we observe that the passage of 2 moles of electrons through the cell results in the plating out of 1 mole of copper and produces 1 mole of zinc ions as shown by Eq. 8-18. One gram-mole of electrons is Avogadro's number (6.02×10^{23}) of electrons and has a total charge of 96,493 coulombs. Since the coulomb is an ampere-second, a wire that carries a current of 1 amp for 96,493 sec will pass 1 mole of electrons or a charge of 96,493 coulombs. A charge equal to Avogadro's number of electrons is called a faraday, usually denoted by the symbol $\mathfrak{F}$ in honor of the man who first carried out quantitative studies of the chemical effects of currents.

As an example we again consider the Daniell cell. How much copper will plate out on the cathode if a current of 10 amp is drawn for 1 hr?

10 amp $\times$ 3600 sec/hr = 36×10^3 coulombs/hr drawn from the cell.

Since there are approximately 96,500 coulombs per faraday, we find

$$\frac{36 \times 10^3 \text{ coulombs/hr}}{96.5 \times 10^3 \text{ coulombs/faraday}} = 0.373 \text{ faraday/hr.}$$

Since 2 faradays of electrons will produce 1 mole of copper, we conclude that 0.373 faraday per hr will produce 0.186 mole of copper in an hour or approximately 11.8 gm per hr.

If we were to connect the copper-zinc Daniell cell to an external circuit containing a source of electrical energy (that is, "charge the cell,") then electrons would flow in a direction opposite to that shown in Fig. 8-4. The corresponding electrode reactions are

$$Zn^{++} + 2e^- \rightarrow Zn(s) \qquad \text{[cathode reaction]} \qquad \textbf{(8-20)}$$

and

$$Cu(s) \rightarrow Cu^{++} + 2e^- \qquad \text{[anode reaction]}. \qquad \textbf{(8-21)}$$

Because copper is being oxidized and Zn^{++} ions are being reduced, we now call the copper electrode the anode, and the zinc electrode the cathode. The cell reaction in this case is given by

$$Cu(s) + Zn^{++} \rightarrow Cu^{++} + Zn(s). \tag{8-22}$$

In deriving Eqs. 8-14 or 8-15, which give the maximum possible work for a system, we placed no restrictions on the type of work that the system was doing or having done on it. If we assume that the only *useful* work our system can do is electrical work, then for an open or closed system in pressure and temperature equilibrium with the environment, Eq. 8-16 may be written on a per mole basis as

$$-W_{\max(el)} = \Delta G \quad [\text{kcal/mole}]. \tag{8-23}$$

The electrical work done by a cell is given by the amount of charge that flows from the cell multiplied by the driving force that causes it to flow—that is, the potential difference of the cell V. The amount of charge is given by the product of the number of moles of electrons involved in the cell reaction (sometimes called the number of equivalents) times the number of coulombs per mole of electrons. Thus

$$W_{el} = n\mathfrak{F}V \quad [\text{kcal/mole}], \tag{8-24}$$

where n represents the number of moles of electrons. Upon combining Eq. 8-24 with Eq. 8-23 we obtain

$$-W_{\max(el)} = \Delta G = -n\mathfrak{F}V \quad [\text{kcal/mole}]. \tag{8-25}$$

The potential difference represented by V must be the reversible potential of the cell, which is the potential measured under open circuit conditions. Following the usual chemical practice we will use a superscript degree sign (°) to indicate thermodynamic quantities in their standard states, usually a pressure of 1 atm. Sometimes we specify a standard-state temperature as well; this temperature will be 298°K (77°F) unless noted otherwise. We may denote a standard-state temperature for a property by writing it as a subscript on a symbol, for example, ΔG°_{298}.

To facilitate the calculation of enthalpies or free energies of reaction, a table of relative enthalpies or free energies can be constructed. The procedure is to arbitrarily set equal to zero the enthalpy or free energy of each element in its standard state. The enthalpy of a compound relative to its elements is called the *heat of formation*. The *enthalpy of reaction* can be found simply by subtracting from the enthalpy of formation of the products the enthalpy of formation of the reactants; a similar procedure may be followed to find the change in free energy for a reaction. That is,

$$\Delta H_{\text{reaction}} = \sum_{\text{products}} \Delta H_f - \sum_{\text{reactants}} \Delta H_f$$

and

$$\Delta G_{\text{reaction}} = \sum_{\text{products}} \Delta G_f - \sum_{\text{reactants}} \Delta G_f.$$

TABLE 8-1. HEATS OF FORMATION AND GIBBS FREE ENERGIES OF FORMATION IN THE STANDARD STATE†

Compound	ΔH_f° (kcal/ mole)	ΔG_f° (kcal/ mole)	Ion	ΔH_f° (kcal/ mole)	ΔG_f° (kcal/ mole)
$AgCl(g)$	22.23	16.79	$Ag^+(aq)$	25.31	18.43
$AgCl(s)$	−30.36	−26.22	$Br^-(aq)$	−28.90	−24.57
$CO(g)$	−26.42	−32.81	$Cl^-(aq)$	−40.02	−31.35
$CO_2(g)$	−94.05	−94.26	$CO_3^{--}(aq)$	−161.63	−126.22
$CO_2(aq)$	−98.69	−92.31	$Cu^{++}(aq)$	15.39	15.53
$CH_4(g)$	−17.89	−12.14	H^+	0	0
$C_8H_{18}(g)$	−49.82	4.14	$I^-(aq)$	−13.37	−12.35
$C_8H_{18}(l)$	−59.74	1.77	$K^+(aq)$	−60.04	−67.47
$H_2SO_4(aq)$	−216.9	−177.34	$Li^+(aq)$	−66.54	−70.22
$H_2O(l)$	−68.32	−56.69	$Mg^{++}(aq)$	−110.4	−109.0
$H_2O(g)$	−57.80	−54.64	$Na^+(aq)$	−57.28	−62.59
$LiH(g)$	30.7	25.2	$OH^-(aq)$	−54.96	−37.60
$NaCO_3(s)$	−270.3	−250.4	$Zn^{++}(aq)$	−36.43	−35.18

† At 298°K and 1 atm. From Ref. [4].

In Table 8-1 we list some properties of formation for compounds of interest to fuel cell workers. Consider the example of the reaction of carbon monoxide with oxygen

$$CO(g) + \tfrac{1}{2}O_2(g) \rightarrow CO_2(g).$$

From Table 8-1 we find

$$\Delta H_{f(CO)}^\circ = -26.42 \text{ kcal/mole} \qquad \Delta G_{f(CO)}^\circ = -32.81 \text{ kcal/mole}$$
$$\Delta H_{f(O_2)}^\circ = 0 \text{ (by definition)} \qquad \Delta G_{f(O_2)}^\circ = 0 \text{ (by definition)}$$
$$\Delta H_{f(CO_2)}^\circ = -94.05 \text{ kcal/mole} \qquad \Delta G_{f(CO_2)}^\circ = -94.26 \text{ kcal/mole};$$

thus

$$\Delta H^\circ = \Delta H_{f(CO_2)}^\circ - \Delta H_{f(CO)}^\circ - \tfrac{1}{2}\Delta H_{f(O_2)}^\circ = -94.05 - (-26.42) - 0$$
$$= -67.63 \text{ kcal/mole}$$

and

$$\Delta G^\circ = \Delta G_{f(CO_2)}^\circ - \Delta G_{f(CO)}^\circ - \tfrac{1}{2}\Delta G_{f(O_2)}^\circ = -94.26 - (-32.81) - 0$$
$$= -61.45 \text{ kcal/mole}.$$

It is also possible to calculate the enthalpy of formation of a compound from the enthalpy of reaction.

We now return to the problem of calculating the voltage associated with the change in free energy with all products and reactants in their standard state. We call $V°$ the *standard cell potential* (also called the *standard emf*) corresponding to the standard free energy change, $\Delta G°$, for the cell reaction. Then from Eq. 8-25

$$\Delta G° = -n\mathfrak{F}V° \quad [\text{kcal/mole}]. \tag{8-26}$$

Next we consider a means for predicting the reversible cell voltage for any electrochemical cell. To do this we must review several more principles used in electrochemistry. The specific Gibbs free energy we defined as

$$G = H - TS = \mathcal{E}_{int} + P\Omega - TS \quad [\text{kcal/mole}] \tag{8-27}$$

and upon differentiation we obtain

$$dG = d\mathcal{E}_{int} + P\,d\Omega + \Omega\,dP - T\,dS - S\,dT. \tag{8-28}$$

The familiar equation that represents a combination of the first and second laws of thermodynamics is

$$d\mathcal{E}_{int} = T\,dS - P\,d\Omega \quad [\text{kcal/mole}]. \tag{8-29}$$

Upon substituting Eq. 8-29 into Eq. 8-28 we obtain

$$dG = \Omega\,dP - S\,dT \tag{8-30}$$

and for an isothermal change of state

$$dG = \Omega\,dP$$

or

$$G - G° = \Delta G = \int_{p°}^{p} \Omega\,dP, \tag{8-31}$$

where $G°$ is the value of the Gibbs function at 1 atm, $p°$, and G is the value of the Gibbs function at any other pressure, p. Assuming a perfect gas gives us a functional relationship between Ω and P, so that we may now write Eq. 8-31 as

$$G - G° = \Delta G = \int_{p°}^{p} \mathfrak{R}T\frac{dP}{P} \quad [\text{kcal/mole}],$$

where $\mathfrak{R}$ denotes the gas constant per mole. Upon integration we obtain

$$G - G° = \mathfrak{R}T\ln p - \mathfrak{R}T\ln p° = \mathfrak{R}T\ln(p/p°)$$

and if we use the fact that $p°$ is identically equal to 1 atm, the above equation simplifies to

$$G - G° = \mathfrak{R}T\ln p, \tag{8-32}$$

where p is always expressed in atmospheres.

Let us consider a general chemical reaction such as

$$\alpha A + \beta B \rightleftarrows \gamma C + \delta D, \tag{8-33}$$

where A, B, C, and D represent various substances and α, β, γ, and δ represent corresponding stoichiometric coefficients. The double arrow indicates that when equilibrium is achieved each of the substances, assumed to be ideal gases, will be present in certain quantities existing at its partial pressure. We now write Eq. 8-32 for each of the components of Eq. 8-33 on a per mole basis:

$$G_A - G_A^\circ = \Re T \ln p_A$$
$$G_B - G_B^\circ = \Re T \ln p_B$$
$$G_C - G_C^\circ = \Re T \ln p_C$$
$$G_D - G_D^\circ = \Re T \ln p_D. \tag{8-34}$$

The change of the Gibbs function for the reaction is simply

$$\Delta G = G_{\text{products}} - G_{\text{reactants}} = \gamma G_C + \delta G_D - \alpha G_A - \beta G_B. \tag{8-35}$$

We now substitute Eq. 8-34 into Eq. 8-35:

$$\Delta G = \gamma[G_C^\circ + \Re T \ln p_C] + \delta[G_D^\circ + \Re T \ln p_D]$$
$$- \alpha[G_A^\circ + \Re T \ln p_A] - \beta[G_B^\circ + \Re T \ln p_B] \tag{8-36}$$

and we define

$$\Delta G^\circ = \gamma G_C^\circ + \delta G_D^\circ - \alpha G_A^\circ - \beta G_B^\circ. \tag{8-37}$$

ΔG° is the change in Gibbs function during the chemical reaction if the reaction goes to completion and if each constituent in the reactants is at a pressure of 1 atm and the given temperature before the reaction begins, and if each constituent in the product is also at a pressure of 1 atm and at the given temperature after the reaction has taken place. Thus, upon substituting Eq. 8-37 into Eq. 8-36, we obtain

$$\Delta G = \Delta G^\circ + \Re T \ln \left[p_C^\gamma p_D^\delta / (p_A^\alpha p_B^\beta) \right]. \tag{8-38}$$

As a general requirement for equilibrium, we suppose that two systems are in equilibrium if there is no possibility for any work to be done by an interaction between them. Figure 8-5 illustrates two systems with an engine placed between them. If for all the possible interactions between the two

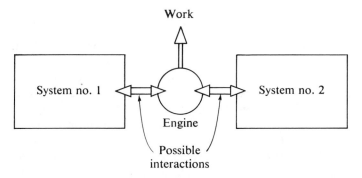

FIG. 8-5. Two systems that communicate with each other through an engine.

systems the maximum useful work is zero, we conclude that the two systems are in equilibrium. One of the systems could be the surroundings, and therefore our discussion includes interactions between a system and the surroundings. We, of course, require that the two systems be at the same temperature, for otherwise we could operate a heat engine between the two systems. We also require that the two systems be in pressure equilibrium or else we could operate a turbine between them. They must also be at the same kinetic and potential energy levels, or else an engine could be devised to utilize this difference. We could formulate other equilibrium requirements for surface, electrical, or magnetic effects.

Equation 8-23 stated the condition for maximum useful work for a system in pressure and temperature equilibrium with its surroundings and where changes in kinetic and potential energy are negligible is

$$-W_{max} = \Delta G. \tag{8-16}$$

Since we have required that for equilibrium $W_{max} = 0$, we deduce the general requirement that

$$\Delta G = 0. \tag{8-39}$$

We thus conclude that two systems or a system and its surroundings which are at the same pressure and temperature are in equilibrium when for all possible changes of state $\Delta G = 0$. This general requirement for equilibrium can be applied to our typical chemical reaction from which we derived Eq. 8-38. Thus

$$0 = \Delta G° + \Re T \ln \left[p_C^\gamma p_D^\delta / (p_A^\alpha p_B^\beta) \right]$$

or

$$\Delta G° = -\Re T \ln \left[p_C^\gamma p_D^\delta / (p_A^\alpha p_B^\beta) \right]. \tag{8-40}$$

The equilibrium constant is defined as

$$K_p = \left[p_C^\gamma p_D^\delta / (p_A^\alpha p_B^\beta) \right], \tag{8-41}$$

so we may write

$$\Delta G° = -\Re T \ln K_p. \tag{8-42}$$

We have already defined $\Delta G°$ as being based on a standard pressure of 1 atm and therefore we deduce that K_p must also be pressure independent. Likewise, we note from our previous discussion that $\Delta G°$ is dependent on temperature and thus K_p must be temperature dependent. In fact we will find values of the equilibrium constant tabulated as a function of temperature. Most references tabulate the equilibrium constant based on values of pressure in atmospheres. Our work can be extended to chemical reactions involving any number of reactants and products and is often considered to be a thermodynamic proof of the law of chemical equilibrium. Equation 8-42 relates the standard free-energy change to the equilibrium constant in the chemical reaction. From thermodynamic data we are able to calculate the equilibrium constant and thus the concentration of products from any given concentration of reactants.

For substances that do not follow the ideal gas law (such as solutions in condensed phases, heterogeneous systems, and so forth), the partial pressures of Eq. 8-40 are often eliminated in favor of a function, defined by Lewis, that is derived from a more general equation of state. The function, generally denoted by f, is called the *fugacity* and is a measure of the tendency of a component to escape from a solution [7]. It is equal to the partial pressure only when the vapor behaves like an ideal gas.

Whenever we form the ratio of the fugacity of a component, say f_A, to the fugacity of the component in some standard state f_A°, then we have defined the *activity*, a_A. Furthermore, by dividing the fugacity by the pressure of interest we define a new quantity called the *activity coefficient:* $\lambda = f/p$. This leads us to a method of defining a new equilibrium constant as follows

$$K_f = \frac{f_C^\gamma f_D^\delta}{f_A^\alpha f_B^\beta} = \frac{\lambda_C^\gamma \lambda_D^\delta}{\lambda_A^\alpha \lambda_B^\beta} \cdot \frac{p_C^\gamma p_D^\delta}{p_A^\alpha p_B^\beta} \qquad (8\text{-}43)$$

or

$$K_f = K_\lambda K_p.$$

We note that K_λ is not an equilibrium constant but simply the ratio of activity coefficients needed to convert the partial pressures in K_p into the fugacities in K_f. At the appropriate time we will discuss the roles these concepts play in fuel cell theory; at present, however, we will assume that the partial pressures of the components in a reaction regardless of the state of the substances will be sufficient to define an equilibrium constant.

We may now substitute Eq. 8-26 into Eq. 8-42 to obtain

$$-\Re T \ln K_p = -n\mathfrak{F} V^\circ, \qquad (8\text{-}44)$$

which is the relationship between the reversible cell potential and the equilibrium constant. Values and units of $\mathfrak{F}$ and $\Re$ are as follows: $\mathfrak{F} = 23,060$ cal(volt)$^{-1}$ (mole of electrons)$^{-1}$, $\Re = 1.987$ cal(deg)$^{-1}$ (gm-mole of reaction)$^{-1}$. If we choose T to be 298°K, and substitute these values for $\mathfrak{F}$ and $\Re$ in the above equation, we obtain

$$\ln K_p = 39.0 \, nV^\circ \qquad \text{or} \qquad \log_{10} K_p = 16.9 \, nV^\circ. \qquad (8\text{-}45)$$

Recalling that n is defined as the number of moles of electrons per mole of reaction and that V° is expressed in volts, readers may verify that K_p is dimensionless, as it should be.

As an example of how one might use the above equations in determining one equilibrium constant, we will consider the example of the copper-zinc Daniell cell again where the cell reaction equation was

$$Zn(s) + Cu^{++} \rightarrow Cu(s) + Zn^{++} \qquad (8\text{-}22)$$

and the electrode reactions are

$$Zn(s) \rightarrow Zn^{++} + 2e^- \quad \text{(anode)} \tag{8-20}$$

and

$$Cu^{++} + 2e^- \rightarrow Cu(s) \quad \text{(cathode).} \tag{8-21}$$

Measurements on the Daniell cell show that the reversible cell potential V° is $+1.100$ volts at 25°C. The electrode reaction equations indicate that there are 2 moles of electrons evolved for every mole of copper or zinc; thus from Eq. 8-45

$$\ln K_p = (39)(2)(1.100) = 86;$$

then

$$K_p = e^{86} \approx 10^{37}.$$

The large value of K_p indicates that zinc spontaneously reduces aqueous cupric ions to metallic copper. Recall that oxidation takes place at the anode and reduction at the cathode. Furthermore we can calculate the change in Gibbs free energy from Eq. 8-26 which is also the maximum useful work

$$\Delta G^\circ = -n\mathfrak{F}V^\circ = -2(96,500)(1.100) = -212,300 \text{ volt-coulomb,}$$

which is also

$$\Delta G = -212,300 \text{ joules} = \frac{-212,300}{4.184} = -50,780 \text{ cal/mole,}$$

since there are 4.184 joules per cal. That is, the maximum useful work we can expect from our cell is 50,780 cal per mole of copper and zinc.

Let us consider the meaning of these calculations. In deriving the expression involving the equilibrium constant we used the partial pressures of the constituents involved in the reaction; the partial pressure of the ith constituent, it will be recalled from thermodynamics, is equal to

$$p_{ith} = \frac{n_{ith}}{n_t} P_t,$$

where P_t is the total pressure of the mixture and n_{ith}/n_t is the mole fraction of the ith constitutent. In our general reaction it is given by

$$\frac{n_a}{n_t} = \frac{\alpha}{\alpha + \beta + \gamma + \delta}.$$

Thus in general the equilibrium constant represents the ratio of the concentration of products to the concentration of reactants

$$K = \frac{\text{concentration of products}}{\text{concentration of reactants}}. \tag{8-46}$$

The equilibrium constant we found was related to the change in standard free energy as was described by Eq. 8-42 by

$$\ln K = -\Delta G^\circ/(\mathfrak{R}T). \tag{8-42}$$

We now interpret this equation to mean:

(a) If the reaction is accompanied by a large decrease in free energy, it proceeds virtually to completion. This is deduced from the fact that K will be large and thus the concentration of products will be many times the concentration of reactants. We found this in our Daniell cell example.

(b) If $\Delta G°$ increases greatly during a reaction, K will be small and no discernible change will take place; the reaction will not proceed very far.

(c) If $\Delta G°$ is small or near zero the concentration of reactants and products are of the same order of magnitude.

Though the change in free energy prescribes the extent to which a reaction will take place, thermodynamics will not tell us how fast it will proceed. The answer to this vital question lies in the study of chemical kinetics. This subject is especially important for fuel cells, and we will discuss its more salient features in a later section.

We now return to Eq. 8-38, which gave the relationship between the standard change in free energy and any other change in free energy in terms of the equilibrium constant. Equation 8-38, written in slightly different form, is

$$\Delta G° = \Delta G - \mathcal{R}T \ln K_p. \tag{8-47}$$

We now write this equation with the *actual* rather than the *equilibrium* concentration or activities, denoting this new ratio by Q'

$$\Delta G° = \Delta G - \mathcal{R}T \ln Q'. \tag{8-48}$$

We may now eliminate ΔG in favor of potentials by Eq. 8-26 to obtain

$$-n\mathcal{F}V° = -n\mathcal{F}V - \mathcal{R}T \ln Q',$$

or, more simply,

$$V° = V + \frac{\mathcal{R}T}{n\mathcal{F}} (\ln Q'). \tag{8-49}$$

Equation 8-49 is called the *Nernst equation* and we will find it or variations of it useful in determining the open circuit voltage of a fuel cell.

Chemists have long found it useful to attribute part of a cell's standard potential $V°$ to each of the half-reactions that go to make up the cell reaction. Many scientists, in fact, maintain that it is impossible to measure unambiguously a *single* electrode potential. We will, therefore, follow the practice of dividing the cell's potential. We arbitrarily define the potential of the half-reaction

$$H_2(g) \rightarrow 2H^+ + 2e^- \qquad \text{to have} \qquad V° = 0, \tag{8-50}$$

which is also consistent with the free energies of formation tabulated in Table 8-1. Lewis and Latimer, two of the pioneers of electrochemistry, tabulated half-reaction potentials for half-reactions written with electrons on the right so that the half-reaction is an oxidation. For this reason half-reaction potentials are called *oxidation potentials*. Table 8-2 lists many oxida-

TABLE 8-2. SOME HALF-REACTIONS AND THEIR OXIDATION POTENTIALS.†

	Half-reaction	Potential (volts)
Li(s)	$\rightarrow Li^+ + e^-$	+3.05
Na(s)	$\rightarrow Na^+ + e^-$	+2.71
Mg(s)	$\rightarrow Mg^{++} + 2e^-$	+2.37
Al(s)	$\rightarrow Al^{+3} + 3e^-$	+1.66
Zn(s)	$\rightarrow Zn^{++} + 2e^-$	+0.763
Fe(s)	$\rightarrow Fe^{++} + 2e^-$	+0.44
$H_2(g)$	$\rightarrow 2H^+ + 2e^-$	0
Sn^{++}	$\rightarrow Sn^{+4} + 2e^-$	−0.15
Cu(s)	$\rightarrow Cu^{++} + 2e^-$	−0.337
$2I^-$	$\rightarrow I_2 + 2e^-$	−0.536
Ag(s)	$\rightarrow Ag^+ + e^-$	−0.799
Hg(l)	$\rightarrow Hg^{++} + 2e^-$	−0.85
$2Br^-$	$\rightarrow Br_2 + 2e^-$	−1.06
$H_2O(l)$	$\rightarrow \frac{1}{2}O_2(g) + 2H^+ + 2e^-$	−1.23
$2Cl^-$	$\rightarrow Cl_2(g) + 2e^-$	−1.36
$4H_2O + Mn^{++}$	$\rightarrow MnO_4^- + 8H^+ + 5e^-$	−1.51
$2F^-$	$\rightarrow F_2(g) + 2e^-$	−2.87

† After Ref. [5].

tion half-reactions and their potentials. For reversible reactions we know that if $\Delta G° = X$ for the reaction $A \rightarrow B$, then $\Delta G° = -X$ for the reaction $B \rightarrow A$. Since the free energy and standard potential are linked by Eq. 8-26, the standard potentials for half-reactions that are the reverse of those already considered can be obtained merely by changing the sign of the value listed in Table 8-2. Thus, for the half-reaction

$$Cu(s) \rightarrow Cu^{++} + 2e^- \qquad V° = -0.337 \text{ volt}$$

and so

$$Cu^{++} + 2e^- \rightarrow Cu(s) \qquad V° = +0.337 \text{ volt.}$$

In Table 8-2 we list reactions in order of decreasing oxidation potential. In other words, there is a decreasing tendency for the forward half-reaction to occur from top of the table to the bottom. Lithium has a great tendency to engage in the half-reaction

$$Li(s) \rightarrow Li^+ + e^- \qquad V° = +3.05 \text{ volt,}$$

but has very little interest in engaging in the reaction

$$e^- + Li^+ \rightarrow Li(s) \qquad V° = -3.05 \text{ volt.}$$

Fluorine, on the other hand, is reluctant to become involved in a reaction such as

$$2F^- \rightarrow F_2(g) + 2e^- \qquad V^\circ = -2.87 \text{ volt,}$$

but eagerly takes part in one that has the nature of

$$F_2(g) + 2e^- \rightarrow 2F^- \qquad V^\circ = +2.87 \text{ volt.}$$

As an example of the use of oxidation potentials, we again consider the case of the Daniell cell. Can we deduce from oxidation potentials given in Table 8-2 whether or not zinc will reduce aqueous cupric ions to metallic copper? We solve the problem by finding the equilibrium constant for the reaction

$$Zn(s) + Cu^{++} \rightarrow Cu(s) + Zn^{++},$$

with the half-reactions

$$Zn(s) \rightarrow Zn^{++} + 2e^- \qquad \text{(anode)}$$

and

$$Cu^{++} + 2e^- \rightarrow Cu(s) \qquad \text{(cathode)}.$$

The oxidation potential for the Zn to Zn^{++} reaction is listed in Table 8-2 as $+0.763$ volt. The potential for the reaction Cu^{++} to $Cu(s)$ is not listed; the oxidation potential for the half-reaction of Cu to Cu^{++}, however, is listed as -0.337 volt. The reverse V° of this half-reaction is merely $+0.337$ volt. The cell potential is the sum of these half-reaction potentials, so

$$V^\circ = 0.763 + 0.337 = 1.100 \text{ volts.}$$

As we demonstrated earlier, this potential yielded an equilibrium constant of about 10^{37}, which means that Zn can easily reduce Cu^{++} ions to metallic copper. In general, we conclude from Eq. 8-45 that positive values for V° lead to large equilibrium constants whereas negative values for V° lead to small equilibrium constants.

Some scientists (mostly in Europe) use, instead of the *half-reaction potential*, the *electrode potential*. By our convention, the Latimer sign convention, we write

$$Zn(s) \rightarrow Zn^{++} + 2e^- \qquad V^\circ = +0.763 \text{ volt}$$

and

$$Zn^{++} + 2e^- \rightarrow Zn(s) \qquad V^\circ = -0.763 \text{ volt,}$$

because we have concerned ourselves with *half-reaction potentials*. The standard *electrode potential* for zinc dipped in an aqueous solution of zinc ions is $\ominus 0.763$ volts. It is written this way to emphasize that the potential is negative in an *electrical* sense. The potential for the Zn^{++} to Zn reaction is written as -0.763 volts because it is negative in the *algebraic* sense.

Many of the details of electrochemistry have been omitted in this brief survey; the interested reader, however, may fill these in by referring to any good physical chemistry text such as Moore [6] or Sheehan [7]. An excellent elementary introduction to the subject of physical chemistry may be found in Hepler [8].

8.3 THE EFFICIENCY OF A FUEL CELL

We now consider in somewhat more detail the general descriptive statements we made about fuel cells in the introduction and how the fundamental relations of Section 8.2 can be applied to a fuel cell. One of the most interesting features of a fuel cell is that under certain conditions it is not subject to the Carnot cycle limitation with respect to its efficiency.

Let us review the way this evasion takes place in producing useful work. In ordinary combustion, as a fuel reacts with an oxidizer (usually oxygen in air), the chemical energy stored in the bonds of the fuel molecule is released as heat. Fuels can be oxidized because their valence electrons desire to go to the states of lower energy that they would occupy as products resulting from the oxidation process. By forcing the valence electrons to take a path that causes them to do useful work before they take up residence as oxidation products, their chemical energy can be converted directly to useful work without going through the process of being converted to heat and consequently without becoming subject to the Carnot bound on efficiency.

This process is achieved in a device similar to any other electrochemical cell; it consists of two electrodes, connected externally by a metallic circuit through which the valence electrons must pass from the fuel electrode, and internally by a conducting medium (the electrolyte), through which ions flow to complete the circuit.

The chemical equation that describes this reaction is simply

$$\text{Fuel} + \text{Oxidizer} = \text{Products.} \qquad \textbf{(8-51)}$$

We can be more specific than this by considering the reaction that takes place at each electrode (the half-cell reactions)

$$\text{Anode:} \quad \text{Fuel} = \text{Ions} + \text{Electrons} \qquad \textbf{(8-52)}$$

$$\text{Cathode:} \ \text{Oxidizer} + \text{Electrons} = \text{Ions.} \qquad \textbf{(8-53)}$$

As we observed earlier, the electromotive force that will drive electrons liberated at the anode through the external load is proportional to the Gibbs free energy change.

The Gibbs free energy, it will be recalled, is defined as

$$\Delta G = \Delta H - T\,\Delta S \qquad [\text{kcal/mole}], \qquad \textbf{(8-54)}$$

where ΔH is the enthalpy change for the reaction, often called the *heat of reaction* or *heat of combustion*. It is of the same magnitude as, but usually of opposite sign to, the constant pressure heating value, which is always defined as a positive number; ΔS, of course, is the entropy change for the process. If the process is reversible, the quantity $T \Delta S$ represents the isothermal heat transfer. The magnitude of the driving voltage is defined from Eq. 8-25 as

$$\Delta G = -n\mathfrak{F}V, \qquad (8\text{-}25)$$

where V, in this case, is the magnitude of the reversible electromotive force that sends electrons from anode to cathode. In general, Eq. 8-25 represents the maximum electrical work we can expect from the complete reversible oxidation of a mole of fuel. Once again, we state that thermodynamics can tell us nothing about current density because generation of an electrical current is determined by the rates of the electrode reactions, a subject we will treat briefly in a later section.

Many fuel cells that appear promising reject heat—that is, they utilize exothermic reactions. Concerning exothermic reactions we note the following: (1) The isothermal rejection of heat does not, a priori, make a fuel cell into a heat engine; (2) Heat rejected need not be wasted, especially at higher temperatures; (3) Rejection of heat causes ΔG to be numerically† smaller than ΔH.

8.3.1 Efficiency of a simple cell. There are several ways of calculating the efficiency of a simple fuel cell—that is, a cell without regeneration. The ideal efficiency for such a cell is simply the change in free energy, which is the maximum useful work we can obtain from any system, divided by the heat of reaction

$$\eta_i = \frac{\Delta G}{\Delta H} = 1 - \frac{T \Delta S}{\Delta H}, \qquad (8\text{-}55)$$

which is less than unity, even in a cell operating reversibly, so long as heat $(T \Delta S)$ is being rejected. The heat of reaction‡ is used in Eq. 8-55 in order to compare the efficiency of a fuel cell with that of a conventional power plant. The efficiency defined by Eq. 8-55 represents in one sense the thermal efficiency of the fuel cell alone and does not include losses that would be associated with the attendant accessories required in any real installation. In terms of the reversible electromotive force of the cell, the efficiency given by Eq. 8-55 is simply

$$\eta_i = -n\mathfrak{F}V/\Delta H = -ItV/\Delta H, \qquad (8\text{-}56)$$

where I is the current and t the time for which the current flows.

---

† This point is made somewhat clearer if we consider that for most chemical reactions of interest, both ΔG and ΔH are normally negative, and thus the decrease in entropy associated with a heat rejection reduces the absolute value of ΔG. We have used the sign convention that heat transfer to a system is positive, and away from a system is negative.

‡ The heat of reaction used in this calculation is usually the one that assumes liquid water in the products and hence is the one associated with the higher heating value of the fuel.

In a fuel cell under load, the actual electromotive force that drives the electrons through the external circuit will fall below V to some lower value we will call V_{ac}. The reasons for this drop are generally attributed to one or more of the following: (1) An undesirable reaction may be taking place at the electrodes or elsewhere in the cell; (2) Something may be hindering the reaction at the anode or cathode; (3) A concentration gradient may become established in the electrolyte or in the reactants; (4) Joule heating associated with the IR drop occurs in the electrolyte. We will discuss the importance of these factors in Section 8.4.

These unwanted effects lead us to define an actual efficiency as

$$\eta_{ac} = -n\mathfrak{F}V_{ac}/\Delta H. \tag{8-57}$$

By combining the definition of the actual work, the maximum useful work, and the first law of thermodynamics, it may be shown that the difference between the two work expressions must appear as rejected heat.† This quantity will be larger than the reversible isothermal heat transfer $T\,\Delta S$. Thus we obtain another measure of efficiency by dividing Eq. 8-57 by Eq. 8-56:

$$\eta_v = V_{ac}/V. \tag{8-58}$$

This ratio decreases as we increase the current density and is a convenient index to the irreversibilities of the cell.

Another efficiency used to define the fraction of the reaction which is occurring electrochemically to give current is called the *faradaic* or *current* efficiency, η_F. It should be considered for each electrode separately since the fuel consumption might not equal the oxidant consumption. In order to keep things simple, though, most of the time we will write just one faradaic efficiency expression. It is equal to

$$\eta_F = \frac{I}{n\mathfrak{F}N_{fu}}, \tag{8-59}$$

where N_{fu} is the total number of moles of fuel reacted electrochemically per second. The quantity $(1 - \eta_F)$ is that fraction of the reactants that may react directly to give heat release in the cell or may react to products other than those desired. The part of the chemical free energy that actually results in electrical energy is $\eta_v\eta_F$. There are other definitions of efficiency but the ones that have been cited here are sufficient for most purposes.

8.3.2   Efficiency calculations for a simple fuel cell

Problem. Examine how the ideal efficiency of a simple hydrogen-oxygen fuel cell changes as its operating temperature is raised from 298°K to 2000°K. Also calculate the four efficiencies given in Section 8.3.1 for a hydrogen-oxygen

---

† The rejected heat is the heat that must be removed from the cell if the reaction is to proceed isothermally.

cell operating in the standard state of 298°K and 1 atm. The actual cell voltage is 0.75 V while the cell delivers 1.5 amps. The fuel flow (hydrogen) is 0.25 cm³/sec. Independent measurements reveal that 5.5×10^{-2} cm³/sec of fuel is escaping through the electrolyte unreacted.

Solution. The cell we consider for our example is, perhaps, the most widely exploited cell; it is the cell that consumes hydrogen as fuel at the anode while reducing oxygen to hydroxide ions at the cathode and producing water. The cell is illustrated in Figs. 8-6, 8-7, and 8-8. The half-cell reactions that describe this cell are:

Anode: $H_2(g) \rightarrow 2H^+ + 2e^-$ $V° = 0$ **(8-60a)**

Cathode: $\frac{1}{2}O_2(g) + 2H^+ + 2e^- \rightarrow H_2O(l)$ $V° = 1.23$ volts,   **(8-60b)**

which for the cell yields

$$H_2(g) + \tfrac{1}{2}O_2(g) \rightarrow H_2O(l).$$ **(8-60c)**

For this reaction we may now tabulate the functions $\Delta H°$ and $\Delta G°$ and compute the ideal efficiency for cells operating at the given temperatures. In addi-

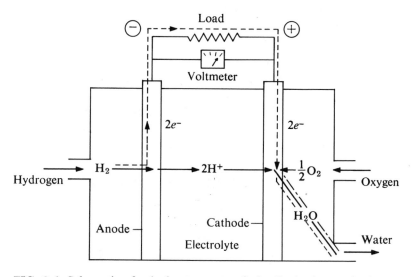

FIG. 8-6. Schematic of a hydrogen-oxygen fuel cell. At the anode-electrolyte interface hydrogen dissociates into hydrogen ions and electrons. The hydrogen ions migrate through the electrolyte to the cathode interface where they combine with the electrons that have traversed the load.

tion we may calculate the Carnot efficiency for an engine that operates between the given temperature and a sink temperature of 298°K. Table 8-3 lists the results of this calculation, assuming that steam is the product of the reaction; we make this assumption so that we see the effect of increasing temperature on the efficiency of the fuel cell, while the pressure remains constant.

EXPERIMENTAL UNIT – MODULE CELL COMPONENTS

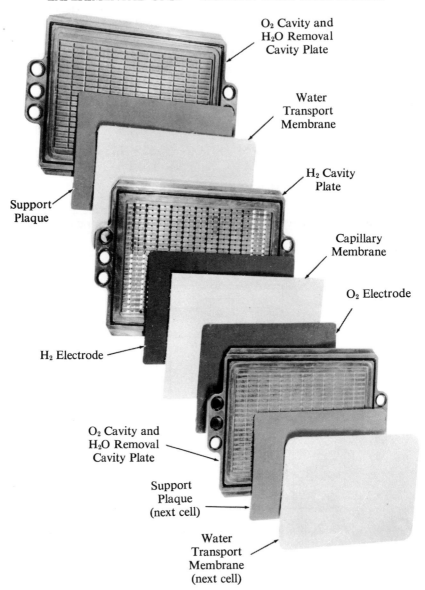

O₂ Cavity and
H₂O Removal
Cavity Plate

Water
Transport
Membrane

H₂ Cavity
Plate

Capillary
Membrane

O₂ Electrode

H₂ Electrode

Support
Plaque

O₂ Cavity and
H₂O Removal
Cavity Plate

Support
Plaque
(next cell)

Water
Transport
Membrane
(next cell)

FIG. 8-7. Exploded view of a fuel cell that uses a special asbestos matrix to immobilize the KOH electrolyte and a special H₂O removal system as described in Section 8.6.1. Photograph courtesy of Allis-Chalmers Manufacturing Company.

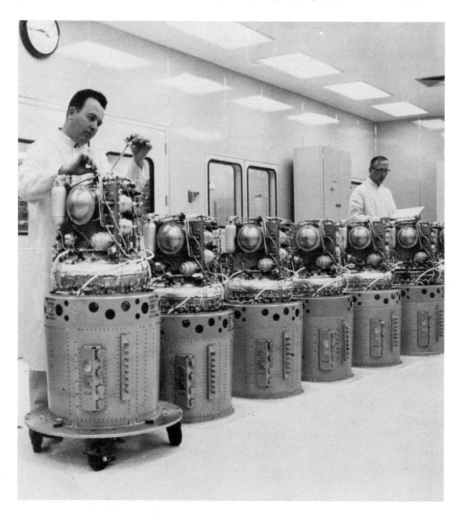

FIG. 8-8. Three of these fuel cell power plants operating on hydrogen and oxygen provided the electricity in the Apollo vehicle on all the flights to the moon. The product water formed in the cell provided the astronauts' drinking water. Photograph courtesy of United Technologies, Inc.

Table 8-3 reveals that at low temperature the ideal fuel cell enjoys a considerable advantage over the best heat engine, but this advantage disappears near 1500°K.

Now we direct our attention to the other efficiencies. Table 8-3 reveals that

TABLE 8-3. RELEVANT THERMODYNAMIC
PROPERTIES† FOR THE HYDROGEN-OXYGEN
FUEL CELL‡

T (°K)	$\Delta H°$ (kcal/mole)	$\Delta G°$ (kcal/mole)	η_i $(\Delta G°/\Delta H°)$	Carnot efficiency $(T_H - T_C/T_H)$
298	−57.80	−54.64	0.94	0
400	−58.04	−53.52	0.92	0.26
500	−58.27	−52.36	0.90	0.40
1000	−59.21	−46.03	0.78	0.70
2000	−60.26	−32.31	0.54	0.85

† The values of $\Delta G°$ and $\Delta H°$ listed here are for the reaction which produces H_2O from hydrogen and oxygen. The sign on these values must be reversed if hydrogen and oxygen are produced from H_2O.

‡ After Ref. [9].

at 298°K the ideal efficiency is 0.94. The actual efficiency can be found by computing the actual cell work which is the numerator of Eq. 8-57

$$-n\mathfrak{F}V_{ac} = -2\frac{\text{mole-elec}}{\text{mole}} \times \frac{23.060 \text{ kcal}}{\text{volt-mole-elec}} \times 0.75 \text{ volt} = -34.6 \text{ kcal},$$

which gives an actual efficiency of

$$\eta_{ac} = -\frac{n\mathfrak{F}V_{ac}}{\Delta H} = \frac{-34.6}{-57.8} = 0.598.$$

The voltage efficiency is simply the ratio of the actual cell voltage to the reversible cell voltage

$$\eta_v = \frac{V_{ac}}{V} = \frac{0.75}{1.23} = 0.61.$$

The current efficiency is based on the fuel reacted electrochemically which for the cell under consideration is $25 \times 10^{-2} - 5.5 \times 10^{-2} = 19.5 \times 10^{-2}$ cm³/sec. Since 1 mole of H_2 occupies 24,481 cm³ under the standard conditions given (which you may verify by use of the ideal gas law) the fuel flow rate in moles per second is then

$$N_{fu} = \frac{19.5 \times 10^{-2} \text{ cm}^3/\text{sec}}{24,481 \text{ cm}^3/\text{mole}} = 7.96 \times 10^{-6} \frac{\text{mole}}{\text{sec}}.$$

Now from Eq. 8-59 we find

$$\eta_F = \frac{I}{n\mathfrak{F}N_{fu}} = \frac{1.5 \text{ amp} \times 1 \text{ coul}/(\text{sec-amp})}{2\frac{\text{mole-elec}}{\text{mole}} \times 96,500 \frac{\text{coul}}{\text{mole-elec}} \times 7.96 \times 10^{-6} \frac{\text{mole}}{\text{sec}}} = 0.975.$$

The high current efficiency is characteristic of hydrogen unless a side reaction occurs at the anode.

8.4 FACTORS LIMITING FUEL CELL PERFORMANCE

In Section 8.3.1 we listed the factors that have a tendency to degrade the performance of a fuel cell below the theoretical value. Before we discuss these factors in detail, it is necessary for us to set forth two additional general requirements for all fuel cells. These are *reactivity* and *invariance*.

The first requirement, reactivity, is very closely related to the factors set down in Section 8.3.1. To satisfy the reactivity requirement it is necessary that we have proper stoichiometry. For example, carbon should always be oxidized to carbon dioxide so that the maximum amount of electrical energy is released in the reaction; when carbon is oxidized only to carbon monoxide the reaction yields only 2 faradays of electricity per mole of fuel instead of 4 faradays as is the case when carbon dioxide is the product of the reaction.

We also require high electrode activity, which results in large current densities. These two reactivity requirements are controlled to a great extent by the rates and mechanisms of electrode reactions. These areas need considerable research before high efficiency fuel cells can be realized. So far the reactivity problem has been met by using porous electrodes to increase the area at the gas-electrode-electrolyte interface, by increasing pressure, by raising temperature, or by using catalysts. In general, the limitation on current density comes about because of the failure to meet the reactivity requirements.

The second general requirement, invariance, means that a fuel cell should only be a converter of energy and should remain, unlike a conventional battery, invariant throughout its life. This requirement implies no corrosion or side reactions, no change in the electrolyte, and no change in the electrodes. The invariance requirement is fairly subtle, but extremely important. It means that fuel must not be allowed to diffuse over and mix with the oxidizer. Catalysts can become poisoned and the pores of gas electrodes can become clogged with liquid ("drowning") or gas ("blow-through") or extraneous material making the electrode inoperative. If the wrong ions carry the current, the electrolyte may lose its invariance and the cathode and anode reactions may be thrown out of balance. The invariance requirement is met by the proper choice of materials and operating conditions.

Unfortunately, the reactivity and invariance requirements are interrelated; if we increase the temperature to improve reactivity we might cause the electrodes to become involved in the cell reaction, thereby causing them to lose their invariance. However, if we operate the cell near room temperature, we might keep the cell invariant but it would deliver precious little electricity.

We may now consider in some detail the principles that are used to explain some of the losses that take place in fuel cells.

The losses that take place at the electrodes are generally attributed to some form of *polarization*—a term used to denote the difference between the theoretical voltage of a given electrode and the experimental voltage when current is drawn from the cell. We will generally classify electrode losses into three categories: (1) chemical polarization; (2) concentration polarization; (3) resistance polarization.

In addition we will consider briefly other factors that tend to reduce the output of a fuel cell, but we will avoid detailed consideration of these losses.

When a load is applied to a fuel cell and current is drawn we find that the output voltage drops below the theoretical value V to some smaller value V_{ac}. Figure 8-9 illustrates the losses that act at each electrode to reduce the value of the open circuit voltage. Thus we write the actual cell voltage as

$$V_{ac} = V - \Delta V_{conc(c)} - \Delta V_{chem(c)} - \Delta V_{conc(a)} - \Delta V_{chem(a)} - \sum IR, \quad \text{(8-61)}$$

where c denotes cathode and a denotes anode. We now consider each of these losses in turn.

8.4.1 Activation or chemical polarization. *Activation or chemical polarization*, or *overvoltage* as it is sometimes called in electrolysis work, is a surface phenomenon, the magnitude of which depends in part upon how ions are discharged at the electrodes and in part upon the rate at which they are discharged. The electrochemical oxidation of fuel involves a *chemisorption process* in which the adsorbed molecules (those collected on the surface) are held to the surface by bonds comparable to those that form in the production of chemical compounds. The fuel gas engages in chemisorption either as molecules or atoms while electrons are removed from the adsorbed atoms. This involves a breakage of the molecule bonds and formation of new bonds between the fuel atoms and those of the catalyst. Subsequently, the latter bonds are broken and somehow electrons are released and the charged fuel ion combines with the electrolyte ion to form a product. Energy is required to cause all of these things to happen, so we simply say a certain activation energy is required to permit the reaction to occur. This energy must be subtracted from that which is theoretically available.

It is customary to express the voltage drop due to chemical polarization by a *strictly empirical* equation, called the *Tafel equation* [6], [13], as

$$\Delta V_{chem} = a' + b' \ln J, \quad \text{(8-62)}$$

where J is the apparent current density at the electrode. Even though the

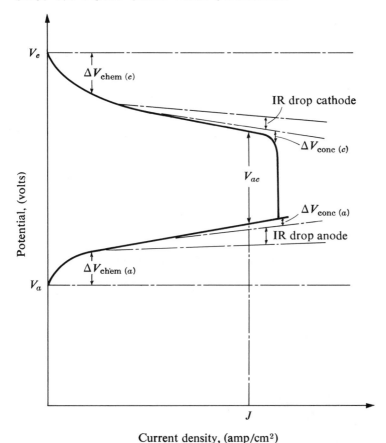

Current density, (amp/cm²)

FIG. 8-9. Potential versus current density showing the various polarizations as a function of current density.

Tafel equation is empirical, electrochemists have been able to ascribe theoretical importance to the constants a' and b'. The definitions of a' and b' most often given are

$$a' = -\Re T/(\alpha n \mathcal{F}) \ln (j_o) \qquad (8\text{-}63)$$

and

$$b' = -\Re T/(\alpha n \mathcal{F}). \qquad (8\text{-}64)$$

The quantities α and j_o are kinetic parameters, the former being a constant that represents the fraction of ΔV_{chem} that aids a reaction in proceeding, the latter being the exchange current density, intimately related to the height of the activation energy barrier. To reduce chemical polarization the gas diffusion electrode has been developed, while electrocatalysts have tried to achieve the same end chemically. The purpose of the gas diffusion electrode is simply to maximize the three-phase interface of gas-electrode-electrolyte. It is, therefore, an electronic conductor with many small pores in it ranging from 10 to 100 microns in diameter. The pores create large reactive surface areas per unit geometrical area and allow free entrance to reactants and exit to products. The removal of products such as water in a hydrogen-oxygen cell is especially important in order to prevent "drowning" of the electrode, which precludes further reaction. Figure 8-10 is a cross-sectional schematic of a typical gas diffusion electrode, exaggerated to show the gradation in pore size. The solution to the problem of achieving "a notable surface of action," as Grove termed it in 1839, is still being sought. Nearly every variation in fuel cell design is aimed at achieving this goal. Increases in pressure and temperature will also generally decrease chemical polarization.

Figure 8-11 illustrates the effect of current density and the exchange current density on the chemical polarization loss. As exchange current density increases, polarization loss decreases almost independently of the current drawn from the cell. By measuring the slope and y intercept of a plot of

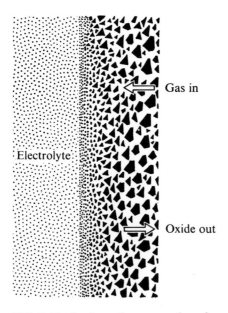

Gas in

Electrolyte

Oxide out

FIG. 8-10. A schematic cross section of a gas diffusion electrode that shows how the pore size varies. This arrangement provides a large surface area on which reactions may occur. The gas pressure is maintained at a value sufficiently high to keep the electrolyte from flooding the electrode but not high enough to cause gas bubbles in the electrolyte.

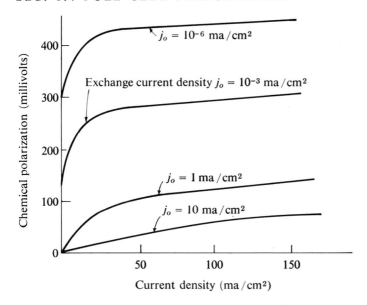

FIG. 8-11. Chemical polarization as a function of current density. After Austin [13] with permission.

ΔV_{chem} versus current density plotted on semilogarithmic paper it is possible to determine the empirical constants of Eq. 8-62.

8.4.2 Concentration polarization. After current begins to flow in an electrochemical cell, there is a loss of potential due to the inability of the surrounding material to maintain the initial concentration of the bulk fluid. For example, in the Daniell cell problem considered earlier, as Cu^{++} ions plate out on the surface of the cathode a layer of solution is formed in which the concentration of Cu^{++} is nearly depleted. This gradient is equivalent to a concentration cell—a type of electrochemical cell. This uneven concentration produces a *back electromotive force* which opposes the voltage that a fuel cell would deliver under completely reversible conditions. This type of polarization may often be reduced by vigorous stirring of the electrolyte or by increases in temperature, which tend to accelerate ionic diffusion within the cell. This type of loss has been found especially troublesome in fuel cell applications for space, because of the absence of a gravitational field which tends to encourage ion drift.

The first type of concentration polarization we consider is the reduction in potential due to a change in concentration of the electrolyte in the vicinity of an electrode during a reaction. We attack this problem by supposing that there exists an equivalent film thickness or diffusion layer of stagnant fluid of thickness δ'. Fick's first law of diffusion states that systems will change in such a way as to eliminate concentration gradients, and it may be integrated for this case to give the relation that defines the equivalent film thickness

$$N_d = \frac{D(c_b - c_{if})}{\delta'}, \tag{8-65}$$

where N_d = mass transfer rate at any point on the electrode, gram-mole per square centimeter-second; c_b = average concentration in bulk electrolyte, gram-mole per cubic centimeter; and c_{if} = concentration at the interface; D = diffusion coefficient, square centimeters per second, and δ' in centimeters. Nernst originally formulated this "diffusion layer" concept in 1904. We represent its meaning in Fig. 8-12. The mass transfer of Eq. 8-65

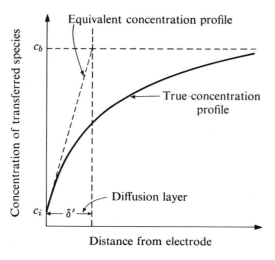

FIG. 8-12. The equivalent film thickness theory used to explain concentration polarization.

can be expressed as a function of current density J and the number of moles of electrons transferred per mole of fuel

$$\frac{J}{n\mathfrak{F}} = \frac{D(c_b - c_{if})}{\delta'}. \tag{8-66}$$

The maximum current occurs when the electrolyte near the electrode is completely depleted, $c_{if} = 0$

$$J_L = \frac{n\mathfrak{F}D}{\delta'} c_b. \tag{8-67}$$

If one assumes that the diffusion layer thickness is independent of the rate of diffusion, the concentration at the interface c_{if} can be related to the current density by combining Eqs. 8-66 and 8-67 to yield

$$\frac{c_{if}}{c_b} = 1 - \frac{\delta' J}{D\, n\mathfrak{F} c_b} = 1 - \frac{J}{J_L}. \tag{8-68}$$

The voltage loss due to this change in concentration is given by an equation similar to that used to predict the voltage of an electrochemical cell with transference.[†] Assuming that migration of the potential determining ion is negligible and that the ions in the bulk fluid and near the electrode have the same activity coefficients we write

$$\Delta V_{conc(c)} = \frac{\mathfrak{R}T}{n\mathfrak{F}} \ln\left(c_{if}/c_b\right), \tag{8-69}$$

or, in terms of the limiting current density from Eq. 8-68

$$\Delta V_{conc(c)} = \mathfrak{R}T/(n\mathfrak{F}) \ln\left[J_L/(J_L - J)\right], \tag{8-70}$$

where the logarithmic term has been rearranged to yield a positive number for the potential drop. This equation refers to a consumptive electrode process such as at the cathode in the fuel cell where ions are being removed from the electrolyte. At the anode, where ions are being discharged into the electrolyte and a concentration buildup may occur, the concentration potential is given by

$$\Delta V_{conc(a)} = \mathfrak{R}T/(n\mathfrak{F}) \ln\left[(J_L + J)/J_L\right]. \tag{8-71}$$

Note that $\Delta V_{conc(a)}$ will always be small as the logarithmic term can never exceed $\ln 2$ as J approaches J_L.

Circulation by means of a pump has been found to be one of the most effective methods of reducing concentration polarization. References [10] and [11] discuss in some detail analytical methods for predicting the effect of forced convection of the electrolyte on the limiting current that can be drawn from a cell. The solution to this problem is obtained by solving an equation analogous to the Navier-Stokes equation for velocity distribution in a fluid

$$u\frac{\partial c}{\partial x} + v\frac{\partial c}{\partial y} = D\left[\frac{\partial^2 c}{\partial x^2} + \frac{\partial^2 c}{\partial y^2}\right], \tag{8-72}$$

where the viscosity has been eliminated in favor of the diffusion coefficient D, and the inertia terms $\partial u/\partial x$ and so on have been replaced by concentration gradient terms.

We will consider only two solutions to this problem, both for parallel flat plates. If we ignore the entrance effects, the viscous boundary layer

---

† An electrochemical cell with transference is a cell that has solutions of different concentration in direct contact. Ions diffuse from one part of the solution to the other because they differ in nature, mobility, and concentration. The slight deviation from electroneutrality that results at the interface between solutions causes a measurable potential difference.

begins to grow at the lower edge of the electrodes. According to Schlichting
[12] they merge at a certain "entrance length" l_E predicted by

$$l_E = 0.04 \ w \ uw/\nu = 0.04 \ w \ \mathrm{Re}_w, \qquad (8\text{-}73)$$

where Re_w is the Reynolds' number based on the plate separation w. The
limiting current density over the entrance length region is given by an equation calculated from hydrodynamic methods for flow over a single flat plate.

$$J_{L,\mathrm{av}(el)} = 0.667 \ n\mathfrak{F}c_b D(\mathrm{Sc})^{1/3}(u/\nu l)^{1/2}, \qquad (8\text{-}74)$$

where Sc is the Schmidt number $= \nu/D$.

After the viscous boundary layers have merged as shown in Fig. 8-13,

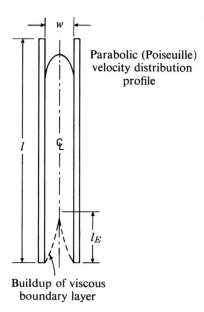

Buildup of viscous
  boundary layer

FIG. 8-13. Laminar flow of electrolyte between flat plate electrodes. The
flow remains laminar even at high electrolyte velocities because of the
narrow separation of the electrodes, w. The electrodes are d units wide
(into the plane of the paper).

the fully developed Poiseuille flow with its associated parabolic velocity
profile continues downstream. For this type of flow the limiting current
density is given by the equation

$$J_{L,\mathrm{av}(fd)} = 1.62 \ n\mathfrak{F}c_b \ u(\mathrm{Re}_w)^{-2/3}(\mathrm{Sc})^{-2/3}(w/l)^{-1/3}. \qquad (8\text{-}75)$$

For flow velocities in which the entrance length is not negligible, it is
desirable to calculate the limiting current in the entrance length region by
means of Eq. 8-74 and the limiting current density in the remaining section

by means of Eq. 8-75; the two are then combined into an arithmetically weighted average. When the entrance length is negligible (less than a tenth of the electrode length) as is the case with low flow velocities, Eq. 8-75 may be used to predict the current density for the entire length of the electrode.

For vertical electrodes in gravitational fields density gradients are established because of concentration differences or temperature differences that give rise to buoyancy forces, $g\Delta\rho$. Reference [11] gives the average limiting current density for an electrode of height l

$$J_{L,\mathrm{av}(fc)} = 0.505 \, n\mathfrak{F}D \, c_b^{5/4}(\mathrm{Sc})^{1/4}(g\alpha_b/\nu^2)^{1/4}(l)^{-1/4}, \qquad (8\text{-}76)$$

where g is the acceleration of gravity and α_b is a density coefficient defined by

$$\alpha_b = \frac{1}{\rho_b}\left[\frac{\partial\rho}{\partial c}\right] \approx \frac{\rho_b - \rho_{if}}{\rho_b(c_b - c_{if})}. \qquad (8\text{-}77)$$

Because substantially higher limiting currents can be sustained in forced convection fuel cells, it is often necessary to subtract from the net cell output the power that must be supplied to the pump. The pump power required is a function of fluid velocity, geometrical factors, entrance conditions, and the presence of external force fields. After determining the velocity required to produce the desired limiting current density, it is possible to use the techniques of fluid mechanics to estimate the pressure loss in each cell compartment, the connecting pipes, and auxiliaries. Reference [10] gives some examples of such calculations.

Once the limiting current density has been calculated from the appropriate equation (8-74, 8-75, or 8-76) and the operating current density selected, the concentration polarization may be calculated from Eqs. 8-70 and 8-71.

The next type of concentration polarization we consider is that due to changes in concentration of the reactant gas in the immediate vicinity of the reaction zone at the electrode. These concentrations are expressed in terms of the partial pressure of the gas as it diffuses through the electrode. The situation is illustrated in Fig. 8-14.

The total pressure on the gas side is designated as P_g while the pressure on the electrolyte side is denoted by P_{ey}. The gas pressure in the pores of the electrode P_r must be at a value sufficiently great to prevent the drowning of the electrode by the electrolyte (that is, it must be great enough to maintain three-phase equilibrium within the pores of the electrode). This difference in pressure between the gas supply and the pressure found at the reaction zone causes a reduction in potential similar to the concentration gradient in the electrolyte; thus we write

$$\Delta V_{\mathrm{conc}(g)} = \mathfrak{R}T/(n\mathfrak{F}) \ln (P_r/P_g), \qquad (8\text{-}78)$$

where we have written the logarithm terms so as to yield a positive number for the potential drop.

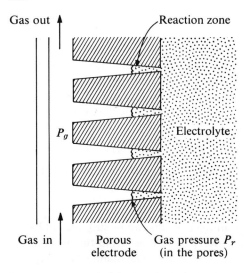

Gas out

Reaction zone

P_g

Electrolyte

Gas in

Porous electrode

Gas pressure P_r (in the pores)

FIG. 8-14. A schematic of a porous electrode that shows the pressure differences that can cause gas side concentration polarization.

In general, this loss is small and may be neglected, but if the oxidizer is air then P_g must be the partial pressure of the oxygen in the air while the electrolyte might be at the pressure of the air. In this case gas concentration potential loss may be significant. Further discussion of concentration polarization may be found in Eisenberg [10] and Tobias *et al.* [11].

8.4.3 Resistance polarization. When an electrochemical reaction occurs at an electrode there is generally a significant change in the specific conductivity of the electrolyte which involves an additional loss of potential. Eisenberg [10] quotes an equation that gives this loss as a function of the fraction of the current carried by a given ionic species in solution (the *transference number* of that ion), the limiting current density, the actual current density, and the number of faradays transported per mole of fuel.

There is ample evidence for hydrogen-oxygen fuel cells employing concentrated solutions of potassium or sodium hydroxide as electrolytes to show that resistance polarization is negligibly low even at fairly high current densities. In ion exchange membrane cells this is not always true and resistance polarization calculations must be carried out. In some cases the decrease in conductivity at one electrode may be accompanied by an increase in conductivity at the other electrode so that the net result on the cell is to eliminate any voltage drop due to resistance polarization. Furthermore, no matter what the electrodes are made of, they will have a finite resistance that must also be subtracted from the open circuit voltage in determining the cell's operating voltage.

8.4.4 Heat transfer. Often it is important to be able to calculate the heat released within a fuel cell, especially in cells with high current densities. Heat transfer comes from three distinct effects taking place in the cell:

(1) The electrochemical reaction producing the current in the cell is not adiabatic which gives rise to a reversible heat transfer whose magnitude depends on $T \Delta S$;

(2) Some of the fuel reacts chemically with the oxidizer rather than electrochemically to generate an irreversible heat transfer; and

(3) The cell operates at some voltage less than the theoretical open circuit voltage with the difference manifesting itself as I^2R and $I \Delta V$ heat in the cell, where I is the current drawn and R and ΔV represent irreversible resistances and voltage drops.

First, let us consider the electrochemical reaction which gives rise to the reversible heat transfer. (You may establish the presence of this heat transfer term simply enough by writing the first law for the cell and using the definition of the Gibbs free energy, $\Delta G = \Delta H - T \Delta S$.) The reversible heat transfer is obtained only from those moles of fuel that react electrochemically to produce an electrical current, namely $\eta_F N_{fu}$. Thus the reversible heat transfer rate is

$$\dot{Q}_{rev} = \eta_F N_{fu}(T \Delta S) = \eta_F N_{fu}(\Delta H - \Delta G) = \frac{I}{n\mathfrak{F}}(T \Delta S), \qquad \text{(8-79)}$$

where the $\eta_F N_{fu}$ has been eliminated in favor of the current by use of Eq. 8-59. Since $T \Delta S$ for most reactions of interest is negative, we infer that the reversible heat transfer in most cases will be away from the cell.

That part $(1 - \eta_F)$ of the fuel supplied that reacts chemically, but not electrochemically, with the oxidant is also turned into heat. This amounts to

$$\dot{Q}_{chem(irr)} = (1 - \eta_F)N_{fu}(\Delta H) = \frac{I}{n\mathfrak{F}}\left[\frac{1 - \eta_F}{\eta_F}\right](\Delta H). \qquad \text{(8-80)}$$

Once again since ΔH is negative for most reactions of interest, this results in heat transfer away from the cell.

Finally, we must consider the heat transfer that takes place because of the irreversible voltage drops that occur throughout the cell. At each electrode there will be activation and concentration voltage drops as discussed in the previous sections. There will also be I^2R type voltage drops occurring in each electrode and in the electrolyte. The net result of all these is to cause the cell operating voltage to be below the theoretical open circuit voltage Once again we consider only that fuel that reacts electrochemically to produce an electrical current

$$\dot{Q}_{\Delta V} = \eta_F N_{fu}(n\mathfrak{F})(V_{ac} - V) = I(V_{ac} - V), \qquad \text{(8-81)}$$

where again we have eliminated the fuel flow rate in favor of the electric current. The voltages have been arranged to automatically produce a sign consistent with heat transfer away from the cell.

The total heat transfer is then

$$\dot{Q}_t = \dot{Q}_{rev} + \dot{Q}_{chem(irr)} + \dot{Q}_{\Delta V} = \frac{I}{n\mathfrak{F}} \left[T\,\Delta S + \frac{1 - \eta_F}{\eta_F}(\Delta H) + n\mathfrak{F}(V_{ac} - V) \right].$$

(8-82)

The second term will generally be small since η_F is usually close to one.

8.5 DESIGN CALCULATIONS FOR A FUEL CELL

We will now consider in some detail an example problem that illustrates the principles we have discussed in the previous sections. We will assume physical data that are representative of the materials encountered in fuel cell work. In some cases, because of a scarcity of real data, estimates that are believed to be sufficiently accurate for use in the preliminary design of a fuel cell are employed. The example problem will be kept simple so that main ideas may be kept in the fore at all times.

   Problem.   Analyze the performance of a single cell operating on hydrogen as the fuel and using the oxygen in air as the oxidizer. The porous electrodes (of either carbon or nickel) employed are separated by a 30 percent solution of KOH. We will assume the cell operates at a temperature of 25°C and that the fuel and the air are supplied at 1 atm. The faradaic efficiency for this type of cell has been estimated to be 95 percent. Preliminary independent measurements indicate that 20 percent of the fuel supplied to the cell will escape through the electrolyte unreacted. The physical dimensions according to the notation of Fig. 8-13 are as follows:

Separation between electrodes	$w = 0.25$ cm	
Height of cell	$l = 12$ cm	
Depth of cell	$d = 6$ cm	
Average electrolyte velocity	$u = 5$ cm/sec	
	(supplied by an external pump)	

The physical properties of the electrolyte at 25°C are as follows:

Concentration	30% KOH (wt) or
	$c_b = 6.9 \times 10^{-3}$ mole/cm³
Density	$\rho = 1.294$ gm/cm³
Dynamic viscosity	$\mu = 2.43 \times 10^{-2}$ poise
Kinematic viscosity	$\nu = 1.887 \times 10^{-2}$ cm²/sec
Conductivity	$\sigma = 0.625$ (ohm-cm)$^{-1}$
Diffusion coefficient for OH⁻ ions†	$D = 1.5 \times 10^{-7}$ cm²/sec

   † This value is an estimate, since data on this type of process are not easily obtainable; the actual value might be two or three times larger. The real picture is complicated by the unknown viscosity in the boundary layer on the electrode.

Solution. We may now calculate the open circuit voltage by considering what goes on at each electrode. We assume that each electrode reaction follows the half-cell reactions that were set down as Eqs. 8-60a and 8-60b:

Anode: $H_2(g) \rightarrow 2H^+ + 2e^-$ $V° = 0$ **(8-60a)**
Cathode: $\frac{1}{2}O_2(g) + 2H^+ + 2e^- \rightarrow H_2O(l)$ $V° = 1.23$ volts   **(8-60b)**

yielding a cell reaction of

$$H_2(g) + \tfrac{1}{2}O_2(g) \rightarrow H_2O(l). \qquad \textbf{(8-60c)}$$

We may now apply the Nernst equation (Eq. 8-49) to our cell potential:

$$V = V° - \frac{\mathcal{R}T}{n\mathcal{F}} \ln \frac{a_{H_2O}}{a_{H_2}(a_{O_2})^{1/2}}. \qquad \textbf{(8-83)}$$

The activity of the H_2O to be used in this equation should be that for water in 30 percent KOH solution. This value is somewhat less than one, but we may take it as one to make our answer conservative. The hydrogen is supplied at 1 atm (and has an activity of 1 since the activity is equal to the partial pressure of an ideal gas), and the activity of the oxygen is 0.21 since that is the partial pressure of oxygen in air. Thus the open circuit voltage (which is the same as the reversible voltage) is

$$V = 1.23 - \frac{(1.99)(298)}{(2)(23,060)} \ln \frac{(1)}{(1)(0.21)^{1/2}} = 1.23 - 0.013 \ln (2.18)$$

$$= 1.22 \text{ volts.}$$

Austin, in Ref. [13], indicates that the reactions in a hydrogen-oxygen fuel cell do not follow the reaction equations given by Eqs. 8-60a and 8-60b; he indicates more complicated reactions at the electrodes due to the chemisorption process of hydrogen at the anode and the creation of peroxide ions at the cathode. This process, according to Young and Rozelle [14], causes a loss that results in an open circuit voltage of around 1.10 volts. However, for the purpose of illustration we will use the value we calculated of 1.22 volts. If we were to raise the supply pressure of the hydrogen and the air to 10 atm and allow the product to continue to exhaust at 1 atm, the open circuit voltage would be increased to about 1.26 volts. We should keep in mind that the value of the open circuit voltage as given by an equation similar to Eq. 8-83 reflects the fact that not all the reactants and products are at the standard pressure of 1 atm.

We next calculate the value of the limiting current density based on an assumed velocity for the electrolyte of 5 cm per sec. We will use the data given, checking first to determine the entrance length relevant to our problem by Eq. 8-73:

$$l_E = 0.04 \, w(\mathrm{Re}_w) = 0.04(0.25)(5 \times 0.25/1.89 \times 10^{-2})$$
$$= 0.01(66.2) = 0.66 \text{ cm.}$$

Since this value is less than one-tenth of our electrode length we ignore the laminar flow at the entrance and calculate the limiting current density based on a fully established flow as given by Eq. 8-75

$$J_{L,\mathrm{av}(fd)} = 1.62 \, n\mathcal{F}c_b u (\mathrm{Re}_w)^{-2/3} (\mathrm{Sc})^{-2/3} (w/l)^{-1/3}. \qquad \textbf{(8-75)}$$

In calculating the entrance length we found a Reynolds number of 66.2, and we may now compute the Schmidt number as

$$Sc = \frac{\nu}{D} = \frac{1.89 \times 10^{-2}}{1.5 \times 10^{-7}} = 1.26 \times 10^5$$

and a length ratio of

$$\frac{w}{l} = \frac{0.25}{12} = 0.0208.$$

Thus the limiting current density is

$$J_{L,\mathrm{av}(fd)} = 1.62 \times 2 \frac{\text{mole-elec}}{\text{mole}} \times \frac{96,500 \text{ amp-sec}}{\text{mole-elec}} \times \frac{6.9 \times 10^{-3} \text{ mole}}{\text{cm}^3} \times \frac{5 \text{ cm}}{\text{sec}}$$

$$\times (66.2)^{-2/3}(1.26 \times 10^5)^{-2/3}(0.0208)^{-1/3} = 0.956 \text{ amp/cm}^2.$$

We initially assume an operating current density for our fuel cell of 0.5 amp per cm² because larger current densities lead to chemical polarization losses that greatly exceed those predicted by Eq. 8-62. An equation typical of one that might represent the activation loss at the anode for a hydrogen-oxygen cell is

$$\Delta V_{\mathrm{chem}(a)} = 0.14 + 0.005 \ln J_{ma}$$

and for the cathode

$$\Delta V_{\mathrm{chem}(c)} = 0.20 + 0.007 \ln J_{ma},$$

where the operating current density must be expressed in milliamperes per square centimeter to retain the significance of the equation. Thus the chemical polarization loss in our example is

$$\Delta V_{\mathrm{chem}(a)} = 0.14 + 0.005 \ln (500) = 0.17 \text{ volt}$$

and

$$\Delta V_{\mathrm{chem}(c)} = 0.20 + 0.007 \ln (500) = 0.24 \text{ volt.}$$

We now calculate the polarization due to concentration gradients in the electrolyte near the electrodes. At the cathode a consumptive process is taking place as the reaction on the surface of the electrode captures H^+ ions out of the electrolyte. The magnitude of this potential loss is given by Eq. 8-70, which predicts a functional dependence on the ratio of the current density drawn to the limiting current density, thus

$$\Delta V_{\mathrm{conc}(c)} = \Re T/(n\mathfrak{F}) \ln [J_L/(J_L - J)] = \frac{(1.99)(298)}{(2)(23,060)} \ln \left[\frac{0.956}{0.956 - 0.500}\right]$$

$$= 0.013 \ln (2.1) = 0.01 \text{ volt.}$$

At the anode, where a concentration buildup is expected due to creation of H^+ ions, the concentration-polarization is given by Eq. 8-71:

$$\Delta V_{\mathrm{conc}(a)} = \Re T/(n\mathfrak{F}) \ln [(J_L + J)/J_L]$$
$$= 0.013 \ln (1.52) = 0.0055$$
$$\approx 0.01 \text{ volt.}$$

The gas side concentration polarization at the anode is ignored, since both the fuel and the products in the electrolyte are assumed to be at 1 atm. However, we will calculate the gas side polarization at the air electrode by means of Eq. 8-78. We use the partial pressure of the oxygen in the air for P_g

$$\Delta V_{\mathrm{conc}(g)} = \frac{\Re T}{n\mathfrak{F}} \ln (P_r/P_g) = 0.013 \ln (1/0.21) = 0.02 \text{ volt.}$$

We will assume that the high concentration of OH^- ions in the bulk electrolyte precludes any potential drop due to resistance polarization.

The IR drop in the cell may be calculated simply by multiplying the current density times the resistivity times the length of current flow in the electrolyte; thus

$$IR = Jw/\sigma = 0.5\,\frac{amp}{cm^2} \times 0.25\ cm \times \frac{ohm\text{-}cm}{0.625} = 0.20\ volt.$$

We now compute the actual operating voltage of the fuel cell by subtracting from the open circuit voltage, 1.22 volts, the various polarization losses and IR drop across the cell; thus

$$V_{ac} = 1.22 - 0.17 - 0.24 - 0.01 - 0.01 - 0.02 - 0.20 = 0.57\ volt.$$

It should be noted that the highest polarization is that due to chemical activation at the anode and cathode. This loss in our example represents nearly 25 percent of the potentially available voltage.

The power output of the cell is the actual potential times the current

$$P_o = V_{ac}I = V_{ac}JA = (0.57\ volt)\left(0.50\,\frac{amp}{cm^2}\right)(72\ cm^2) = 20.5\ watts.$$

If we were to scale up this cell by combining several cells either in parallel or series, we might wish to attribute part of the power output to the pump that circulates the electrolyte. The role played by pump power in an array of fuel cells that have been combined to achieve larger power outputs is a complex one; it generally represents a small part of the total power output (see Ref. [10]). We will ignore it in our calculations.

In Section 8.3.1 we set down several expressions for efficiency, which we now apply to our example fuel cell. The thermodynamic or "pseudo-thermal" efficiency as given by Eq. 8-57 (assuming the product of the reaction is liquid water) is

$$\eta_{ac} = \frac{-n\mathfrak{F}V_{ac}}{\Delta H} = \frac{-\ [2\ mole\text{-}elec/mole][23.06\ kcal/(volt\text{-}mole)][0.57\ volt]}{[-68.32\ kcal/mole]}$$

$$= 38.5\ percent.$$

The efficiency based on the ratio of the actual voltage to the open circuit voltage is, from Eq. 8-58,

$$\eta_v = \frac{V_{ac}}{V} = \frac{0.57}{1.22} = 46.7\ percent.$$

At $298°K$ we may calculate from Table 8-1 an ideal efficiency based on the ratio of the change in free energy to the heat of reaction $(\Delta G°/\Delta H°)$ for a hydrogen-oxygen cell of 83 percent. In our operating cell we achieve only about half of what was theoretically available.

Now we may estimate the fuel requirements by use of the definition of the faradaic efficiency as given by Eq. 8-59:

$$\eta_F = \frac{JA}{n\mathfrak{F}N_{fu}} = 0.95 = \frac{(0.5\ amp/cm^2)(72\ cm^2)}{\left(2\,\dfrac{mole\text{-}elec}{mole}\right)\left(96,500\,\dfrac{amp\text{-}sec}{mole\text{-}elec}\right)\left(N_{fu}\,\dfrac{mole}{sec}\right)}$$

$$N_{fu} = 1.96 \times 10^{-4}\ mole\ H_2/sec.$$

Since a mole of hydrogen at standard conditions occupies 24,481 cm³, the flow rate of the reacted fuel is 4.78 cm³/sec. But 20 percent of the fuel supplied escapes through the electrolyte unreacted; therefore, the fuel rate that must be supplied may be determined as follows:

$$0.20 \, \dot{\Omega}_{su} + \dot{\Omega}_{fu} = \dot{\Omega}_{su}$$

$$0.20 \, \dot{\Omega}_{su} + 4.78 \text{ cm}^3/\text{sec} = \dot{\Omega}_{su}$$

$$\dot{\Omega}_{su} = 5.97 \text{ cm}^3/\text{sec.}$$

We may also calculate the energy that will have to be removed from the cell as heat because of reversible and irreversible processes taking place in the cell. The formation of water from hydrogen and oxygen, even if carried out reversibly, is an exothermic reaction and will give rise to heat transfer as predicted by Eq. 8-79; using data from Table 8-3 again we find

$$\dot{Q}_{rev} = \eta_F N_{fu}(\Delta H - \Delta G)$$

$$= (0.95) \left(1.96 \times 10^{-4} \frac{\text{mole}}{\text{sec}} \right) [-68.32 - (-56.69)] \frac{\text{kcal}}{\text{mole}}$$

$$= -2.17 \times 10^{-3} \frac{\text{kcal}}{\text{sec}} \times 4.184 \times 10^3 \frac{\text{joule}}{\text{kcal}} = -9.1 \text{ watts.}$$

The fuel that is simply reacted chemically also produces heat in accordance with Eq. 8-80:

$$\dot{Q}_{chem(irr)} = (1 - \eta_F)N_{fu}(\Delta H) = (1 - 0.95) \left(1.96 \times 10^{-4} \frac{\text{mole}}{\text{sec}} \right) \left(-68.32 \frac{\text{kcal}}{\text{mole}} \right)$$

$$= -0.67 \times 10^{-3} \frac{\text{kcal}}{\text{sec}} \times 4.184 \times 10^3 \frac{\text{joule}}{\text{kcal}}$$

$$= -2.8 \text{ watts.}$$

Lastly, the irreversible voltage drops that are occurring in the cell also produce heat that must be removed as predicted by Eq. 8-81:

$$\dot{Q}_{\Delta V} = I(V_{ac} - V) = (72 \text{ cm}^2) \left(0.5 \frac{\text{amp}}{\text{cm}^2} \right) (0.57 - 1.22) \text{ volts}$$

$$= -23.4 \text{ watts.}$$

The total heat that must be removed from the cell for it to stay in steady state is 35.3 watts, a quantity roughly 50 percent larger than the net power out of the cell.

To appreciate the role that the current density plays in the operating characteristics of a fuel cell, we calculate the voltage, power output, and efficiency as a function of current density; we give the results for power output and efficiency in Fig. 8-15. We note that the power output is a maximum near current densities of 0.8 amp per cm², but the efficiency as measured by η_{ac} falls steadily as the current density is increased. High efficiency at low current density is not always a desirable goal because power-producing units then grow to very large sizes. Thus efficiencies must never be thought of without considering current densities. As the power density of a cell designed to handle a given load for a given period of time increases, more fuel and storage containers would have to be provided to yield the same energy output because of the reduced efficiency of the unit. The optimization of an

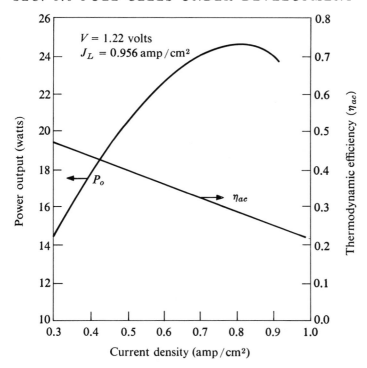

FIG. 8-15. The power output and thermodynamic efficiency of the example fuel cell as a function of the current density.

entire system then is not a simple problem but must include all the parameters that bear on the problem. In providing power for a satellite, for example, a fuel cell operating at a low current density (and a high efficiency) might be an acceptable solution, because the weight of stored gases and their containers might be less than the extra cells that would have to be carried to supply the given power if low efficiency but high current density cells were used.

8.6 FUEL CELLS UNDER DEVELOPMENT

A large number of different types of fuel cells are under development today. Some are at a rather advanced stage, others are still little more than labora- tory curiosities. We will describe examples of both types of cells. We will not attempt to list each of the nearly one hundred different types of fuel cells that have been investigated to date, but will describe some typical cell charac- teristics for several different cells representative of the several classes into which they have been divided.

8.6.1 Hydrogen-oxygen cells. The cells which have been most extensively developed are those that use hydrogen as their fuel and either oxygen or oxygen in air as the oxidant. The electrochemical process and losses occurring in such cells has been described in earlier sections of this chapter.

Allis-Chalmers has successfully developed three basic building-block fuel cell modules for space use. Their cells include a radiation-cooled 200 watt module; a gas/liquid-cooled 2000 watt module and a liquid-cooled 5000 watt module. Each of these fuel cell modules employs a capillary matrix electrode-electrolyte concept. A brief description of the capillary matrix used by Allis-Chalmers will illustrate one method of reducing a laboratory fuel cell into an operational system.

Water management and heat transfer are intimately related; often evaporation of water consumes about one-third of the heat to be rejected. The static moisture removal system developed for spacecraft is an interesting example of how this problem can be solved. In each cell the KOH electrolyte is immobilized in an asbestos matrix. The porous electrodes are held firmly against the faces of the matrix. A second matrix, also containing KOH and supported on both sides by porous nickel plaques, forms a wall between the anodes chamber and a space called the moisture-removal cavity. Water evaporates from the fuel cell electrolyte, diffuses as vapor to the second matrix, diffuses as a liquid through this matrix, and finally evaporates into the moisture-removal cavity. The driving force for this transport process is the chemical potential of water as measured by its vapor pressure, and this driving force is controlled by a temperature compensated electronic controller that vents water vapor to vacuum when the vapor pressure in the cavity exceeds the desired value. An exploded view of one section of such a module is shown in Fig. 8-7; Fig. 8-16 is a schematic of what is taking place in the cell.

The 2000-watt system is typical of fuel cell space power systems. The fuel cell stack used in this module consists of 32 series-connected cell sections with each section consisting of two parallel-connected cells. Each module contains its own electronic control assembly, control values, condenser and water pump assemblies, coolant pump and, where required, its own three-phase 400-cycle inverter supply.

The search for lightweight, portable power sources of rather modest size have turned engineers more and more towards fuel cell systems. A number of these systems incorporate their own fuel-generation devices. Most commonly this is done by use of a metal hydride, such as sodium aluminum hydride pellets or calcium hydride pellets, and water.

Baker and Onischak [16] have pointed out that the generation of 60 watts of regulated power for four hours requires either 20 pounds of secondary batteries or eight pounds of currently available primary batteries. The latter would be quite expensive. The system they have developed consists of

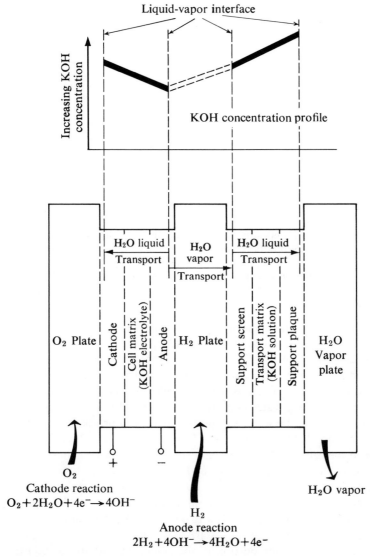

FIG. 8-16. Schematic of H_2O transport in the Allis-Chalmers fuel cell to be used in space systems. After Ref. [15].

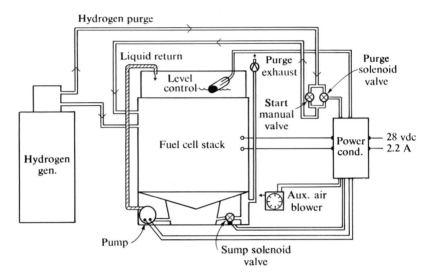

FIG. 8-17. Schematic of a 60-watt metal hydride-air fuel cell system. The Kipp hydrogen generator produces hydrogen by reacting sodium aluminum hydride pellets and water. It supplies 42 liters/hour of hydrogen fuel to the fuel cell for four hours on a single charge of 113 grams. After Ref. [16] with permission.

three subsystems, as illustrated in Fig. 8-17: (1) a Kipp hydrogen generator; (2) a 19-volt d-c fuel cell stack; and (3) a d-c/d-c power conditioner delivering 28 ± 0.2 volt d-c. The Kipp generator produces hydrogen by reacting sodium aluminum hydride pellets and water. The gas is produced on demand by the fuel cell, and when no demand exists the pressure builds in the generator forcing water away from the fuel pellet. The unit is vented to the atmosphere on the water side so that hydrogen pressure in the Kipp unit never exceeds 15 cm of water. The Kipp unit supplies 42 liters/hour of hydrogen to the cell for four hours on a single 113-gram fuel charge.

The fuel cell stack has an electrolyte reservoir above it and a sump basin below, as shown in Fig. 8-18. The power conditioner unit (PCU) converts the 19 volts d-c from the fuel cell into 28 volts regulated d-c power. A secondary function of the PCU is to provide all the logic and control circuits necessary to automatically start and regulate the overall system. Furthermore, the converter portion of the circuit, in addition to boosting the voltage level of the output fuel cell power, guarantees the regulated output in the face of fuel cell subsystem aging. For a single mission of four hours the unit is able to deliver 33 watt-hours/kilogram (15 watt-hours/pound).

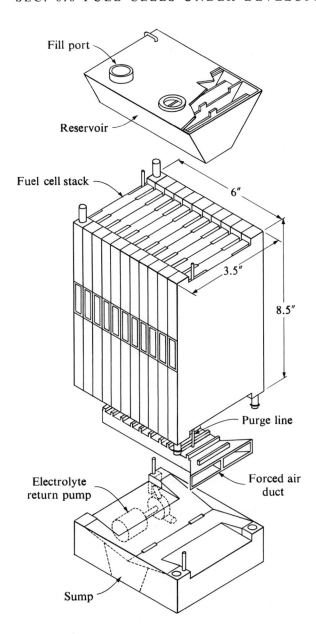

FIG. 8-18. The arrangement of the fuel cell stack and electrolyte pump in the 60-watt metal hydride-air fuel cell system. After Ref. [16] with permission.

Taschek [17] has described a system that uses calcium hydride that has even more impressive performance figures than those of the sodium aluminum hydride system described in the previous paragraphs. The system delivers an average power of only 4.5 watts but at a specific power of 264 watt-hours/kilogram (120 watt-hours/pound). The fuel cost for metal hydride fuel cell systems is approximately one-tenth that of the energy cost of a primary battery. Of course, the cost of the fuel cell itself (and any power conditioning unit) must be amortized over the useful life of the system and that quantity must be added to the fuel cost in order to obtain the total cost of system power. The fuel cell systems described here are not expensive since they operate at low power levels and low temperatures.

Camp and Baker [18] have also designed a milliwatt metal-hydride fuel cell system designed to power a remote electrical sensor and transmitter. The sensor or equipment requirements generally call for a high energy density on both a weight and volume basis, long shelf life, a steady voltage and, hopefully, low cost.

8.6.2   Electrolyte soluble fuels. Gaseous fuels demand a porous electrode so constructed that the required electrochemical reaction takes place at the gas/liquid/solid interfaces. If the fuel is soluble in the electrolyte, electrode construction is simpler; a thin conducting sheet, supporting a catalytically active material if necessary, is basically all that is required. Moreover, liquid fuels are generally easier to store and transport in comparison with gaseous fuels. For these reasons, the development of fuel cells utilizing electrolyte-soluble fuels has become the object of intense research in recent years.

A number of fuels have been considered, including ammonia, hydrazine and methanol [2], [23]. Both ammonia (NH_3) and hydrazine (N_2H_4) are convenient ways to store and transport hydrogen in liquid form for reaction at a fuel cell anode. Hydrazine is much more reactive and much more costly than ammonia and methanol. Hydrazine will probably find early application where its cost can be tolerated ($3/kWh).

The U.S. Army has had a hydrazine fuel cell under development for a number of years [19]. A recent model of this unit weighs 6.6 kg (14.5 lb) and delivers approximately 860 watt-hours per kilogram (390 watt-hours/lb) of fuel. A schematic of the system is shown in Fig. 8-19. Hydrazine fuel is injected into an electrolyte tank to provide a constant level of hydrazine concentration in the anolyte. The anolyte is circulated through the anolyte compartment of the fuel cell module and air is blown through the cathode compartment. Other components are required to maintain heat and moisture. This cell would normally be used to recharge a 24-volt nickel-cadmium battery or supply power directly to an external load.

Icenhower and Urbach [20] have described work they have done on a high power density hydrazine fuel cell. Using oxygen as the oxidizer, they

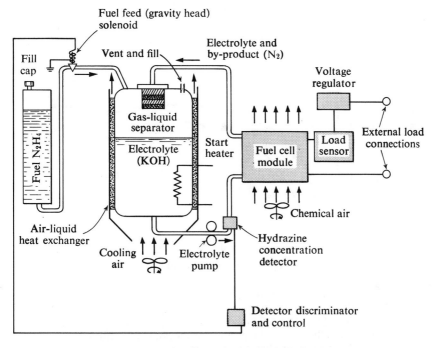

FIG. 8-19. Flow diagram for a portable hydrazine-powered fuel cell power source developed for the U.S. Army. The fuel is soluble in the electrolyte which is pumped through the cell module. After Ref. [19].

achieved power densities up to 0.65 watts/cm². At this output, a power efficiency of 32 percent was obtained at 70°C at less than one molar hydrazine concentration. Power efficiencies exceeding 48 percent were obtained over a power density range from 4.3×10^{-2} to 21×10^{-2} watts/cm² by optimal matching of the temperature (50 to 80°C) and hydrazine concentration (0.1 to 1.0 molar) to the electrical load. Figure 8-20 shows the terminal voltage, coulombic efficiency, and power efficiency as a function of concentration for a 0.43 amp/cm² load at 70°C. The power efficiency is the product of the coulombic efficiency and the voltage efficiency. The power efficiency exhibits a peak of 45 percent at an intermediate concentration of 0.6 M, where the voltage and coulombic efficiencies are moderately high. A projected cell thickness of 0.1 in. and a power density of only 21×10^{-2} watts/cm² corresponds to a calculated stack power/volume ratio of 565 kilowatts/m³.

Böhm and Maass [21] have developed a fuel cell capable of utilizing unpurified methanol as the fuel and air as the oxidizer. The cell actually uses hydrogen, which it obtains from a built-in cracking unit, as the fuel. The catalytic cracking unit cracks the methanol at 300 to 330°C without the

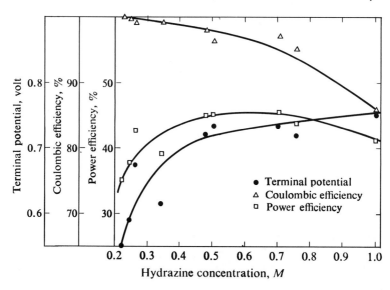

FIG. 8-20. The influence of hydrazine concentration on terminal voltage, coulombic efficiency, and power efficiency in the hydrazine fuel cell described in Ref. [20]. The cell was operated at a 0.43 amp/cm² load at 70°C. The power efficiency is the product of the coulombic efficiency and the voltage efficiency. Reproduced with permission.

addition of any other substance such as water. The produced gas consists mainly of hydrogen and carbon monoxide. The hydrogen is anodically oxidized in the cell to produce electricity, while the carbon monoxide, after passing through the fuel cell, is burned to heat the reactor. A schematic of this cell is shown in Fig. 8-21. The electrodes in the fuel cell are activated charcoal that have been sprayed with a platinum compound to act as a catalyst. The cell showed remarkable stability through 5000 hours of operation.

A number of attempts have been made to develop cells that use ammonia as a fuel. The merits of ammonia are numerous. It is a commodity readily available worldwide, costing only slightly more than fossil fuels. The impurity content of commercial-grade ammonia is 0.5 percent and the main contaminant is water, which is not detrimental to the fuel cell operation. Ammonia is hardly flammable and of relatively low toxicity, yet it can be detected in very small concentrations. The fuel is stored as a liquid and has a vapor pressure/temperature characteristic almost identical to that of propane. It can thus be fed to a fuel cell down to a temperature of −29°C.

Collins, Michalek, and Brink [22] have described their development of an ammonia fuel cell system that uses an air-cooled phosphoric acid fuel

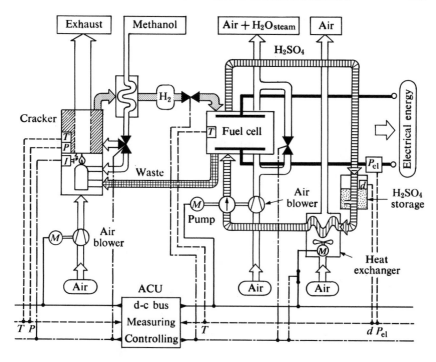

FIG. 8-21. Block diagram of the methanol-air fuel cell system described in Ref. [21]. With 200 grams of catalyst, more than one liter of methanol can be cracked, which is enough to supply a one-kilowatt fuel cell system. Temperature, pressure, electrical power, and acid density are monitored by the automatic control unit (ACU).

cell. The heat for cracking the ammonia into hydrogen and nitrogen is obtained from the fuel cell bleed gas. The cracking process takes place over a precious metal catalyst at a nominal temperature of 850°C. The reported system operated unattended for many months, delivering a net power of 300 watts at 18 volts from 26 cells. The operating temperature of the cell was 130°C. Fuel consumption was 159 grams/hour; parasitic power for the cell was 29 watts.

8.6.3   Biochemical cells. Certainly one of the most intriguing types of fuel cells that has been considered to date is a cell in which one or both electrode reactions are promoted or catalyzed by biological processes. Research impetus has stemmed from two considerations: first, the vast quantities of vegetable and animal wastes that might be used as a source of electrical energy; second, the need to eliminate organic waste material from closed environments, such as spacecraft.

Biochemical cells can be conveniently divided into two main types: (1) indirect cells in which the fuel fed to the organism is converted into a waste product which can be removed and utilized in a separate fuel cell; and (2) direct cells in which the organism provides a continuous supply of the enzymes required by the biochemical/electrochemical process, in which case the organism derives no benefit from the process and perishes. Alternatively, the organism in a direct cell may grow in the neighborhood of the electrode and the waste product of its metabolism (ammonia, ethanol, hydrogen, etc.) may be utilized directly for the production of electricity.

Since in the indirect cell a large part of the energy supply is utilized by the organism itself, such cells are not likely to prove to be efficient energy converters. The direct biocell runs into the difficulty that conditions favorable to the growth of living organisms, for example neutral or nearly neutral solutions, ambient or near ambient temperatures, are distinctly unfavorable for the efficient production of electrical energy in fuel cell devices [23].

However, the literature now shows that in at least two cases indirect biochemical fuel cells have been actually built [24]. One cell used the juice from a single coconut as its fuel and air as its oxidant, functioning intermittently over a period of 45 days for a total of 50 hours operation. During this time the cell delivered about 380 milliwatt-hours of electricity at a potential of 1.5 volts. Under ambient conditions the cells which have been built have achieved faradaic efficiencies near 100 percent. Ion exchange membranes were used in both successful cells.

A related area which has been the subject of intensive research is the development of an implantable fuel cell to power an artificial heart. These studies have been motivated by the fact that about a half million adults in the United States could be considered candidates for various modes of devices designed to assist or replace part or all of the heart muscle. A major component of any assist device is its power supply. Hospitalized patients can tolerate bulky boxes of accessory equipment to power the assist devices; however, it is believed that a permanent left ventricular assist device or a total heart replacement device should be capable of total implantability if the patient is to lead a reasonably normal life.

A number of studies have investigated the possibility of constructing a fuel cell that would extract a fuel, such as glucose, or other readily oxidizable chemicals from the blood. Reference [25] gives a good list of sources that describe the work done in this area, as well as describing a set of experiments carried out on an implantable glucose fuel cell.

All such cells must meet three requirements: (1) the anode must be able to contact with enough venous blood so that the cell's fuel requirements can be met; (2) the cathode must have adequate access to a source of oxygen; and (3) the implant must not react with surrounding body tissue and must not by virtue of its size, weight, shape, or location, seriously modify essential body functions, nor should it create any discomfort that would render its presence unacceptable to the recipient. These strenuous requirements will certainly tax the ingenuity of those working in this field, but if they are successful, they will offer new lives to thousands of people now suffering with various cardiac ailments.

8.6.4 Regenerative cells. A regenerative cell may be defined as a fuel cell in which the reactants are regenerated from the products and thence recycled. Regeneration can be arranged to take place within or externally to the fuel cell, the latter method being the more generally acceptable because the requirements of the regenerator and the fuel cell are frequently incompatible.

A number of methods of regeneration are at least theoretically available, including: (1) thermal, (2) electrical, (3) chemical, (4) radioactive, and (5) photochemical. A generalized schematic of a regenerative cell is shown in Fig. 8-22. No matter what method of regeneration is employed, the plan of operation is the same: energy in some form is supplied in the regenerator while electrical power is delivered by the fuel cell.

Cells using thermal regeneration might find application where there is an abundant supply of waste heat, as in the vicinity of nuclear power plants. Electrical regenerative cells are similar to ordinary storage batteries and might be useful in meeting power plant peak loads. The so-called "redox cell" is a chemically regenerative cell; in such cells the fuel and oxidizer are made to react with other substances outside the cell. These other substances are chemical intermediates which in turn generate current in the cell in the usual way. Radioactive regeneration might be found to be helpful in increasing the efficiency of nuclear power plants by utilizing some of the wasted radiation energy of the plants. Photochemical regenerative devices

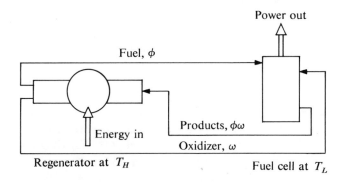

FIG. 8-22. Schematic of a generalized regenerative fuel cell system. In theory the energy supplied to the regenerator can be in almost any form.

have been proposed for satellite applications where sunlight provides a cheap and abundant form of energy. Reference [23] gives a fairly complete review of developments in the field of regenerative fuel cells.

Only two types of regenerative cells—the thermally regenerative cell and the chemically regenerative, or redox, cell—have had much significant research done on them. Reference [26] gives a general evaluation of those chemicals that might prove useful in regenerative fuel cell systems.

In a thermally regenerative cell a fuel ϕ is reacted with an oxidizer ω at T_C to form a product $\phi\omega$. This reaction produces electrical energy; the product is returned to a regenerator where it is dissociated back into the reactants at a higher temperature T_H. Under these circumstances the products may be regarded as the working fluid in a thermal cycle in which heat is changed into electrical work and thus must be subject to the Carnot limitation on efficiency. This limitation holds even though the working fluid undergoes dissociation and recombination. Although the fuel cell itself is still exempt from the Carnot limitation, the combination is not. Reference [27] presents a rather detailed thermodynamic analysis of a thermally regenerative fuel cell.

A thermally regenerative cell using the lithium-tin system has been under investigation at Argonne National Laboratories [28]. Some of the conclusions resulting from this investigation are as follows:

(1) Thermally regenerative cells are medium efficiency devices (5 to 20 percent) with proven cell lifetimes of up to 12,000 hours but with only short proven system lifetimes.

(2) In air-cooled systems, the regenerator size will depend primarily on the condenser-to-air heat transfer coefficient.

(3) It is reasonable to expect that complete thermally regenerative systems in the size range of 1 to 10 kilowatts will have specific power capabilities of about 10^{-2} kW/kg (5 W/lb), excluding heat source weight.

(4) The materials problems are not yet solved, but some promising refractory metals and alloys have been found.

Considerable attention has been devoted to the use of regenerative systems in space. Wynveen and Schubert [29] have designed an electrically regenerative system to be used aboard a modular space station. Electrical energy comes from solar panels and is fed to a set of electrolysis cells that produce hydrogen and oxygen to be used in fuel cells. A regenerative fuel cell system teamed with a solar array offers the following important advantages over the solar array/nickel-cadmium battery electrical power system: (1) lower overall cost; (2) 3 percent less solar array area; (3) 2700 kilogram lower launch mass; (4) fewer information subsystem interfaces; and (5) greater growth potential. Figure 8-23 presents a block diagram of a modular fuel cell/solar cell system and also summarizes the flow, power, and weight characteristics evolved during the previously cited study.

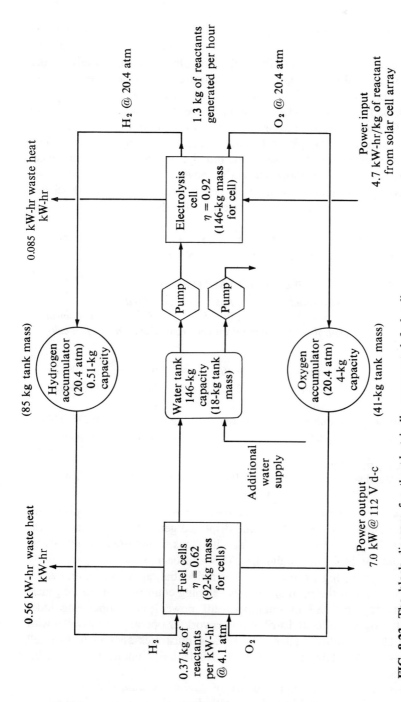

FIG. 8-23. The block diagram for the electrically regenerated fuel cell system. The cells utilized in this system can operate in either the fuel cell or electrolysis mode. After Ref. [29].

8.6.5 Central-station fuel cell plants. Fuel cells are now receiving considerable attention as potential sources of power in central-station power plants. The inherent characteristics of fuel cell power plants offer many advantages over conventional power supplies. Fuel cells are very efficient even in small ratings. Furthermore, high efficiency and effective operation are achieved over a broad range of off-design conditions. Because the power plants are essentially static, maintenance is expected only at infrequent intervals. The modular nature of the plants facilitates maintenance by permitting field replacement of component assemblies. Finally, fuel cell power plants meet demands for environmentally acceptable power. As shown in Table 8-4, measured exhaust emissions are well below federal standards. Fuel cell operation is quiet and waste heat is rejected directly to air.

TABLE 8-4. POWER SYSTEM EXHAUST EMISSION STANDARDS AND COMPARISONS†

	FEDERAL STANDARDS‡			
	Gas-fired utility central station	Oil-fired utility central station	Coal-fired utility central station	Experimental fuel cells
SO_2	no requirement	7.36	10.90	0–0.00026
NO_x	1.96	2.76	6.36	0.139–0.236
Hydrocarbons	no requirement	no requirement	no requirement	0.225–0.031
Particulates	0.98	0.92	0.91	0.00003–0

† After Ref. [30] with permission.
‡ Federal standard (effective 8-17-71) values converted to lb/1000 kWh

Because of their numerous attractive features, fuel cell power plants are being developed for both on-site and dispersed generation. On-site generation would employ relatively low-capacity (tens to hundreds of kilowatts) generators for individual buildings. This approach would be particularly effective in providing electric power for residential, agricultural, and small industrial users in the rural areas of developing countries. Dispersed generation involves the use of multimegawatt power plants operating independently to serve a local distribution network or operating in parallel with a large electric utility system. Figure 8-24 illustrates an on-site fuel cell power system available for multifamily residential, commercial, and light-industrial use.

Fuel cells provide improved use of capital because capacity can be added in small increments consistent with demand (as shown schematically

FIG. 8-24. A 40-kilowatt fuel cell power plant operating on a hydrocarbon fuel and air is capable of providing electrical energy to multifamily residential, commercial, and light-industrial buildings. Photograph courtesy of United Technologies, Inc.

in Fig. 8-25). If one assumes that an ideal power system could be expanded annually to just meet load-demand growth, then Fig. 8-26 indicates the cost penalty associated with the time between the equipment installation and its full utilization [30]. [The higher the discount rate (or, as sometimes called,

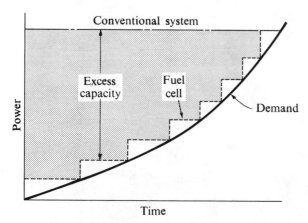

FIG. 8-25. Because fuel cells can be added in small increments, power plant capacity can be much more closely matched with demand for power. Thus capital need not be tied up in idle generating equipment. After Ref. [30] with permission.

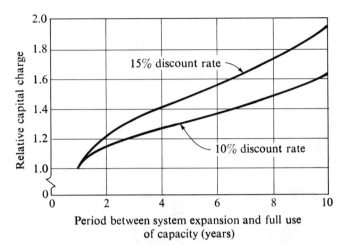

Period between system expansion and full use
of capacity (years)

*Relative capital charge component total cost over a
twenty-year period

FIG. 8-26. The penalty for underutilizing installed generating equipment
depends on the discount rate and the number of years between expansion
and full utilization. The higher the discount rate, the greater the relative
capital charge. After Ref. [30].

FIG. 8-27. Model of a 26-megawatt fuel cell power plant designed to
operate on liquid and gaseous hydrocarbon fuels. A power plant of this
size would occupy only one-half acre at a substation and provide the
electrical needs of a community of 20,000 people. Photograph courtesy of
United Technologies, Inc.

the opportunity cost of money) the higher the penalty. That statement simply reflects the fact that money tied up in equipment could be earning 12 or 15 percent or whatever the discount rate is.]

Because of their short lead time and their effectiveness at low power levels, fuel cells could be added annually while conventional systems would not be fully utilized for 5 to 10 years. Such a condition would lead to capital charges which are 30 to 50 percent lower with fuel cells. The ability to add capacity in small increments minimizes penalties resulting from inaccurate load forecasts. Figure 8-27 is a photograph of a model of a 26-megawatt fuel cell power system located at a power substation.

NOTATION

a	$= f/f^\circ$, activity, dimensionless
a'	$=$ empirical constant defined by Eq. 8-63, volts
A	$=$ area, cm^2
$\overline{A}$	$=$ Helmholtz function, kcal
b'	$=$ empirical constant defined by Eq. 8-64, volts
c	$=$ concentration, gram-mole/cm^3
C_p	$=$ molar constant pressure specific heat, kcal/(mole-°K)
D	$=$ diffusion coefficient, cm^2/sec
$\mathcal{E}$	$=$ specific energy, kcal/mole
$\overline{\mathcal{E}}$	$=$ energy, kcal
f	$=$ fugacity, dimensionless
$\mathfrak{F}$	$=$ Avogadro's number of electrons
g	$=$ acceleration of gravity, cm/sec^2
G	$=$ specific Gibbs function, kcal/mole
$\overline{G}$	$=$ Gibbs function, kcal
H	$=$ specific enthalpy, kcal/mole
$\overline{H}$	$=$ enthalpy, kcal
j_o	$=$ exchange current density, ma/cm^2
J	$=$ current density, ma/cm^2 or amp/cm^2
I	$=$ current, amp
K	$=$ equilibrium constant, dimensionless
K_f	$=$ fugacity equilibrium constant defined by Eq. 8-43, dimensionless
K_p	$=$ pressure equilibrium constant defined by Eq. 8-41, dimensionless
K_λ	$=$ conversion factor in Eq. 8-43, dimensionless
l	$=$ length, cm
l_E	$=$ entrance length, cm
m	$=$ mass, moles
n	$=$ number of moles of electrons, reactants, or products
N_d	$=$ mass transfer rate at any point on the electrode, gram-mole/cm^2-sec
N_{fu}	$=$ fuel rate reacted electrochemically, gram-mole/sec
p	$=$ partial pressure in atmospheres or with respect to 1 atm, dimensionless
P	$=$ pressure, atm
P_o	$=$ power output, watts
$\underline{Q}$	$=$ specific heat transfer, kcal/mole
$\overline{Q}$	$=$ heat transfer, kcal

$\dot{Q}$ = heat transfer rate, kcal/sec or watts
Q' = actual ratio as used in Nernst equation (Eq. 8-49), dimensionless
R = cell resistance, ohms
$\mathcal{R}$ = universal gas constant, cal/(gm-mole °K)
Re = Reynolds' number, dimensionless
S = specific entropy, kcal/(mole-°K)
$\bar{S}$ = entropy, kcal/°K
Sc = Schmidt number, dimensionless
t = time, sec
T = absolute temperature, °K
u = velocity in x direction, cm/sec
v = velocity in y direction, cm/sec
V = voltage, volts
$V°$ = standard cell potential, volts
w = separation between electrodes, cm
W = specific work, kcal/mole
$\bar{W}$ = work, kcal
x, y, z = coordinate directions, cm
$\alpha, \beta, \gamma, \delta$ = stoichiometric coefficients in Eq. 8-33, moles
α = fraction of $\Delta V_{chem.}$ that aids a reaction in proceeding, dimensionless
α_b = density coefficient defined by Eq. 8-77, cm³/mole
δ' = stagnant fluid layer thickness, cm
η_{ac} = actual efficiency defined by Eq. 8-57, dimensionless
η_{ca} = Carnot efficiency, dimensionless
η_F = faradaic efficiency defined by Eq. 8-59, dimensionless
η_i = ideal efficiency defined by Eq. 8-55, dimensionless
η_v = voltage efficiency defined by Eq. 8-58, dimensionless
λ = f/p, activity coefficient, dimensionless
μ = dynamic viscosity, poise
ν = kinematic viscosity, cm²/sec
σ = conductivity, (ohm-cm)⁻¹
ρ = density, gm/cm³
ϕ = a generic fuel
ω = a generic oxidizer
$\bar{\Omega}$ = volume, cm³
$\dot{\bar{\Omega}}$ = volume rate, cm³/sec
Ω = volume, cm³/mole

Subscripts

a = anode
ac = actual
am = surroundings or environment
av = average
A, B, C, D = products and reactants in Eq. 8-35
b = bulk
c = cathode
ca = Carnot
C = cold
chem = chemical
conc = concentration
e = leaving

el	= electrical	
ey	= electrolyte	
f	= formation	
fc	= free convection	
fd	= fully developed	
fu	= fuel	
g	= gas	
H	= hot	
i	= entering	
if	= interface	
*i*th	= typical	
int	= internal	
irr	= irreversible	
L	= limiting	
ma	= milliamperes	
max	= maximum	
r	= pores	
rev	= reversible	
su	= supplied	
t	= total	
1, 2···	= state points	
ΔV	= irreversible voltage drop	

Superscripts

°	= standard state
pr	= products
re	= reactants

PROBLEMS

8-1. Calculate the maximum work that can be theoretically obtained from the steady flow process of the burning of pure carbon monoxide in atmospheric air at 25°C. Assume heat transfer with the atmosphere only, and that air is composed of 21 percent oxygen and the balance nitrogen. (a) Assume that the air and fuel enter at 1 atm and that the products leave at 1 atm. (b) Assume that the products leave the system at the partial pressures of these products in the atmosphere. The partial pressure of CO_2 in the atmosphere is 0.0004 atm.

Answer: (a) 60.73 kcal/mole.

8-2. How much silver will 1 amp plate out in 15 min?

Answer: 1.0 gm.

8-3. A given Daniell cell initially has 95 gm of zinc and 450 ml of 0.100 M $CuSO_4$ where M denotes the molarity (moles of solute per liter of solution). What is the longest possible time that this cell can deliver a current of 2 amp?

Answer: 72.5 min.

8-4. Determine the Gibbs function for saturated liquid water and for saturated vapor at 1.7 atm. What is interesting about these two values and why?

8-5. Derive an equation for the enthalpy of reaction as a function of dV/dT. You may need the fact that $[\partial(\Delta G)/\partial T] = -\Delta S$. The result of this derivation is known as the Gibbs-Helmholtz equation.

8-6. A galvanic cell has the reaction

$$2Ag(s) + Hg_2Cl_2(s) \rightarrow 2AgCl(s) + 2Hg(l) \qquad V^\circ_{298^\circ K} = 0.0455 \text{ volt.}$$

If $dV^\circ/dT = 0.000338$ volt/$^\circ$K, calculate ΔG°, ΔS°, and ΔH°.

8-7. For the reaction

$$Ag(s) + \tfrac{1}{2}Cl_2(g) \rightarrow AgCl(s) \qquad V^\circ_{298^\circ K} = 1.1360 \text{ volts}$$

and $dV^\circ/dT = -0.000595$ volt/$^\circ$K. With these data and those of Problem 8-6, calculate V°, ΔG°, and ΔH° for the cell wherein

$$2Hg(l) + Cl_2(g) \rightarrow Hg_2Cl_2(s).$$

8-8. By means of oxidation potentials, calculate the equilibrium constant at 25°C for the reaction

$$Ag^+(aq) + \tfrac{1}{2}Cu(s) \rightarrow Ag(s) + \tfrac{1}{2}Cu^{++}(aq).$$

8-9. Calculate the heat of reaction and the change in free energy for the reaction given in Problem 8-8.

8-10. Which of the following reactions might be used as a source of electrical energy?

(a) $I_2(s) + 2Br^-(aq) \quad \rightarrow 2I^-(aq) + Br_2(l)$
(b) $2Ag(s) + Zn^{++}(aq) \rightarrow 2Ag^+(aq) + Zn(s)$
(c) $Cl_2(g) + 2Br^-(aq) \quad \rightarrow 2Cl^-(aq) + Br_2(l)$
(d) $CH_4(g) + 2O_2 \quad\quad \rightarrow CO_2(g) + 2H_2O(g).$

8-11. Find ΔG and ΔH for the reactions of Problem 8-10 at 298°K.

8-12. For each of the following reactions design a workable galvanic cell by writing the cathode and anode reactions, predicting the direction of current flow when the cell is discharging, and predicting the measured open circuit voltage of the cell when all concentrations are unity.

(a) $Mg(s) + 2Ag^+(aq) \quad\quad \rightarrow Mg^{++} + 2Ag(s)$
(b) $Cu(s) + Cl_2(g) \quad\quad\quad \rightarrow Cu^{++} + 2Cl^-$
(c) $2MnO_4^- + 5Hg(l) + 16H^+ \rightarrow 5Hg^{++} + 8H_2O + 2Mn^{++}.$

8-13. Find ΔH for reactions in parts (a) and (b) of Problem 8-12.

8-14. By using the data from Table 8-1, calculate the open circuit potential for the reactions in Problem 8-10. Check your results against those that you calculated by means of oxidation potentials.

8-15. Calculate the ideal gas equilibrium constant for the complete reaction of octane $[C_8H_{18}(g)]$ with oxygen at 77°F.

Answer: $\ln K = 2120.$

8-16. A hydrogen-oxygen fuel cell delivers one ampere at 0.72 V with a fuel flow of 10.00 cm³/min. Independent measurement shows that 2.25 cm³/min of fuel is escaping through the electrolyte unreacted. The cell operates in the standard state of 298°K and 1 atm. (a) Find the actual voltage and current efficiency. (b) Find the magnitude of the three major contributions to heat transfer from the cell.

8-17. A regenerative fuel cell that operates on AsI_3 has been proposed. The properties of this compound in kilocalories per mole as:

	298°K	700°K
$\Delta H°$	-35.9	-40.3
$\Delta G°$	-21.9	-4.5.

The cell will operate at 298°K and the products will be regenerated at 700°K. What is the maximum work one can expect from this system? What is the ideal thermal efficiency of the system? How close does the system come to Carnot efficiency? How much heat must be ideally absorbed in the regeneration process? Assume that all the reactants and products are in the liquid phase throughout the system.

8-18. The number of faradays produced by a given amount of reactants is directly related to their equivalent weights. The equivalent weight is defined as the sum of the molecular weights of the reactants divided by the number of moles of electrons transferred in the reaction. What is the equivalent weight of each of these fuel cell reactions: (a) hydrogen-oxygen to water; (b) carbon-oxygen to carbon dioxide; (c) carbon-oxygen to carbon monoxide; (d) carbon monoxide-oxygen to carbon dioxide.

8-19. For each of the fuel cell reactions given in Problem 8-18, determine the number of grams of reactants required to produce 1 kW over a period of 10 hr. Assume the cells operate at one-half of their open circuit theoretical voltage.

Answer: (a) 5.45×10^3 gms; (d) 1.24×10^4 gms.

8-20. Using the data from the example problem worked in Section 8.5, design a system to deliver 25 volts. Find the number of cells required and estimate the net power output. Consider the effect on the fuel consumed of selecting operating points away from the point of maximum power output. Assume that the pump power is 10 percent of the power output but never less than 10 watts. Find the efficiency of your systems by several meaningful methods.

8-21. A high temperature fuel cell (820°C) that has been investigated intensely in Great Britain is one that uses a solid electrolyte of a mixture of sodium and lithium carbonate. If the cell is supplied with air as an oxidizer and carbon monoxide as a fuel, the cell might follow reactions such as these:

$$\text{Anode:} \quad CO + CO_3^{--} \quad \rightarrow 2CO_2 + 2e^-$$
$$\text{Cathode:} \quad CO_2 + \tfrac{1}{2}O_2 + 2e^- \rightarrow CO_3^{--}$$

with the overall cell reaction

$$CO + \tfrac{1}{2}O_2 \rightarrow CO_2.$$

What is the calculated open circuit voltage at the operating temperature? Assume the CO and CO_2 are at atmospheric pressure. What is the equilibrium constant for this reaction? What is the ideal efficiency of this cell? If performance data for the cell indicate an actual open circuit voltage of 1.02 volts and an operating voltage of 0.84 volt at a current density of 33 ma per cm², and the electrolyte has a resistance of 4 ohm-cm and an electrode spacing of 0.3 cm, what is the total potential drop due to all polarizations other than simple IR drop?

8-22. Reference [31] reports that the National Carbon Company has a hydrogen-oxygen cell with an operating voltage characteristic of $V = 0.936 - 0.00244J$ where the current density is in milliamperes per square centimeter. Find the current density that maximizes the power output of the cell. What is the current density that maximizes the voltage efficiency? Plot efficiency and power output as a function of current density. Interpret your results for a design situation in which weight must be minimized.

8-23. It is necessary to design a fuel cell to supply power for a particular space mission. The power requirements of the mission are 15 kW for 1 week at 12 volts. The cell selected is a G.E. Ion Membrane Cell with a voltage characteristic [31] of $V = 1.00 - 0.000931J$ with J, the current density, in milliamperes per square centimeter. The weight of the cell, encapsulation, and fixed electrolyte per watt is 1.46 kg per 1000 cm² of electrode surface. Find the operating conditions for your cell system that minimize the weight that must be carried aloft.

8-24. The Kings College regenerative fuel cell is reported to operate on the reaction

$$Br_2 + Sn^{++} \rightarrow Sn^{4+} + 2Br^-.$$

Find the theoretical open circuit voltage. The cell is reported to have a voltage-current density characteristic [31] of $V = 0.70 - 0.0096J$ with J in milliamperes per square centimeter. The power allowance for the pump is assumed to be $0.2J$. From the reported data find the optimum current density.

Answer: $J_{opt} = 26$ ma/cm².

8-25. A hydrogen-oxygen fuel cell is cube-shaped and uses as an electrolyte yttria-stabilized zirconia with a resistivity of 10 ohm-cm. It produces a voltage across the load of 0.592 volt while yielding a power density 0.106 watt/cm³ of cell. The device loses heat through its walls at the rate of 0.72 watt/cm² of cell external wall surface. The reactants enter at 25°C and leave at 105°C. You may assume that the change in ΔH (not including the reaction) due to the temperature and phase change is +11.080 kcal/gm-mole of fuel. Find at what power output the fuel cell will become self-sustaining with respect to heat losses and find the size of the cell.

8-26. Your company is now considering manufacturing a fuel cell power supply for a portable television set. The set requires 19.8 watts. You have available a cell that stoichiometrically reacts gaseous methane (CH_4) with oxygen to produce the desired power. The cell has an operating characteristic described by the following equation:

$$V_{ac} = V^\circ - 0.314I$$

where V_{ac} is the actual voltage of the cell across the load, V° is the theoretical open-circuit voltage, and I is the current in amperes. (a) Find the current and voltage per cell which maximizes the power output of a cell. (b) Find the minimum number of cells needed to meet the power requirements of the load if the cells are operated at the optimum condition. (c) Find the number of grams of reactants required per hour to operate the power supply.

Answer: (a) $V_{opt} = 0.52$ volts; (c) 14.3 grams/hr.

REFERENCES

1. H. C. Howard, "Direct Generation of Electricity from Coal and Gas (Fuel Cells)," in *Chemistry of Coal Utilization*, ed. H. H. Lowry (New York: John Wiley & Sons, Inc., 1945).

2. H. A. Liebhafsky and E. J. Cairns, *Fuel Cells and Fuel Batteries* (New York: John Wiley & Sons, Inc., 1968).

3. C. Berger, ed., *Handbook of Fuel Cell Technology* (Englewood Cliffs, New Jersey: Prentice-Hall, Inc., 1968).

4. F. D. Rossini, D. D. Wagman, W. H. Evans, S. Levine, and I. Jaffe, *Selected Values of Chemical Thermodynamic Properties*, Circular of the National Bureau of Standards 500 (Washington, D.C.: 1952).

5. Wendell M. Latimer, *Oxidation States of the Elements and Their Potentials in Aqueous Solutions* 2nd ed. (Englewood Cliffs, New Jersey: Prentice-Hall, Inc., 1952).

6. W. J. Moore, *Physical Chemistry* 3rd ed. (Englewood Cliffs, New Jersey: Prentice-Hall, Inc., 1962).

7. W. F. Sheehan, *Physical Chemistry* 2nd ed. (Boston: Allyn and Bacon, Inc., 1969).

8. L. G. Hepler, *Chemical Principles* (New York: Blaisdell Publishing Company, 1964).

9. H. A. Liebhafsky, "The Fuel Cell and the Carnot Cycle," *Journal of the Electrochemical Society*, 106 (1959), 1068.

10. M. Eisenberg, "Design and Scale-Up Considerations for Electrochemical Fuel Cells," in *Advances in Electrochemistry and Electrochemical Engineering*, Vol. 2, ed. Charles W. Tobias (New York: Interscience Publishers, a Division of John Wiley & Sons, 1962).

11. C. W. Tobias, M. Eisenberg, and C. R. White, "Diffusion and Convection in Electrolysis—A Theoretical Review," *Journal of the Electrochemical Society*, 99 (1952), 359C.

12. H. Schlichting, *Boundary Layer Theory* (London: Pergamon Press, Ltd., 1955), p. 149.

13. L. G. Austin, "Electrode Kinetics of Low Temperature Hydrogen-Oxygen Fuel Cells," in *Fuel Cells*, ed. G. J. Young (New York: Reinhold Publishing Corporation, 1960).

14. G. J. Young and R. B. Rozelle, "Fuel Cells," *Journal of Chemical Education*, 36 (1959), 68.

15. J. L. Platner, "Allis-Chalmers Capillary Matrix Fuel Cell Systems—An Advanced Aerospace Power Source," *Intersociety Energy Conversion Engineering Conference 1968 Record*, Publication 68 C-21 Energy (New York: Institute of Electrical and Electronics Engineers, 1968).

16. B. S. Baker, M. Onischak, and R. Tripp, "60-Watt Hydride-Air Fuel Cell System," *9th Intersociety Energy Conversion Engineering Conference*, 1974 Proceedings (New York: American Society of Mechanical Engineers, 1974).

17. W. G. Taschek, "Metal Hydride Fuel Cell Power Source," *9th Intersociety Energy Conversion Engineering Conference*, 1974 Proceedings (New York: American Society of Mechanical Engineers, 1974).

18. R. N. Camp, B. S. Baker, and E. H. Reiss, Jr., "Milliwatt Fuel Cell System for Sensors," *9th Intersociety Energy Conversion Engineering Conference*, 1974 Proceedings (New York: American Society of Mechanical Engineers, 1974).

19. G. R. Frysinger, "The Economical Fuel Cell," *IEEE Spectrum*, 6 (1969), 83.

20. D. E. Icenhower and H. B. Urbach, "High Power Density Hydrazine Fuel Cells," *8th Intersociety Energy Conversion Engineering Conference, 1973 Proceedings* (New York: American Institute of Aeronautics and Astronautics, 1973).

21. H. Böhm and K. Maass, "Methanol/Air Acidic Fuel Cell System," *9th Intersociety Energy Conversion Engineering Conference*, 1974 Proceedings (New York: American Society of Mechanical Engineers, 1974).

22. M. F. Collins, R. Michalek, and W. Brink, "Design Parameters of a 300-Watt Ammonia-Air Fuel Cell System," *7th Intersociety Energy Conversion Engineering Conference*, 1972 Proceedings (Washington, D.C.: American Chemical Society, 1972).

23. K. R. Williams, ed., *An Introduction to Fuel Cells* (Amsterdam: Elsevier Publishing Company, 1966).

24. J. M. Brake, *Biochemcial Fuel Cells, Report No. 11*, Final Report, 1 July 1962 to 31 March 1965 (AD 619 665), (Washington, D.C.: Clearinghouse for Federal Scientific and Technical Services, U.S. Department of Commerce, 1965).

25. S. K. Wolfson, Jr. and S. J. Yao, "Implantable Fuel Cells: Effects of Added Endogenous Dialyzable Materials," *7th Intersociety Energy Conversion Engineering Conference*, 1972 Proceedings (Washington, D.C.: American Chemical Society, 1972).

26. L. G. Austin, *Fuel Cells, A Review of Government Sponsored Research*, NASA SP-120 (Washington, D.C.: National Aeronautics and Space Administration, 1967).

27. S. W. Angrist, *Direct Energy Conversion*, 1st ed. (Boston: Allyn and Bacon, Inc., 1965).

28. H. Shimotake and E. J. Cairns, "A Lithium/Tin Cell with an Immobilized Fused-Salt Electrolyte: Cell Performance and Thermal Regeneration Analysis," *Intersociety Energy Conversion Engineering Conference 1968 Record*, Publication 68 C-21 Energy (New York: Institute of Electrical and Electronics Engineers, 1968).

29. R. A. Wynveen and F. H. Schubert, "A Regenerative Fuel Cell System for Modular Space Station Integrated Electrical Power," *8th Intersociety Energy Conversion Engineering Conference*, 1973 Proceedings (New York: American Institute of Aeronautics and Astronautics, 1973).

30. J. M. King and S. H. Folstad, "Electricity for Developing Areas via Fuel Cell Power Plants," *8th Intersociety Energy Conversion Engineering Conference*, 1973 Proceedings (New York: American Institute of Aeronautics and Astronautics, 1973).

31. W. R. Menetrey and J. Chrisney, *Energy Conversion Systems Reference Handbook*, Vol. VI—*Chemical Systems*, AD 257 358 (Washington, D.C.: Office of Technical Services, U.S. Department of Commerce, 1960.)

9 Other Modes of Direct Energy Conversion

9.1 INTRODUCTION

In this chapter we will discuss some other modes of converting thermal, mechanical, or radiation energy to electrical energy. The methods discussed in this chapter for one reason or another have not shown as much promise as the methods discussed in the earlier chapters. We will point out the advantages, the disadvantages, and the status of work for each of the modes discussed.

This chapter does not constitute a complete catalog of other means of converting thermal, mechanical, or radiation energy directly to electricity. Such a catalog, to our knowledge, does not exist and if it did, it would soon be out of date. Furthermore, we have arbitrarily excluded discussion of techniques for which at least one good scholarly reference could not be provided.

For the purpose of classification we have divided these modes into three broad groups—those which convert thermal energy into electrical energy, those which convert mechanical energy into electrical energy, and those which convert radiation energy into electrical energy.

9.2 OTHER MODES OF CONVERTING HEAT TO ELECTRICITY

In this section we will consider several less developed methods of effecting the direct conversion of heat to electricity. While at present these methods are not well exploited, breakthroughs in materials or techniques could cause one or more of them to come into prominence.

9.2.1 Nernst effect generator.

Considerable theoretical effort has been devoted to an effect that depends on the presence of crossed magnetic and thermal fields to generate a voltage. Harman and Honig [1], Angrist [2], and Riddiford and Krumhansl [3], among others, have contributed to the knowledge concerning the possibility of utilizing the Nernst effect, one of the thermomagnetic effects [4], as a means of direct energy conversion. In Section D.2.3 we discussed the Nernst effect device as an odd class, coupled energy converter. In that section we gave the definition of the Nernst effect and of the Ettingshausen effect that we will use in this analysis.

The Nernst generator, like the thermoelectric generator, would appear to perform most favorably if the working element is made of a semiconductor or semimetal. In conducting our analysis of this type of generator (illustrated in Fig. 9-1), we will make assumptions similar to those made for the analysis of a thermoelectric generator with the following additions and modifications:

(1) The generator consists of a single leg of either n- or p-type material, as it has been shown [1] that the use of arms of two different physical properties depresses the figure of merit below that obtained with the arm possessing the higher figure of merit.

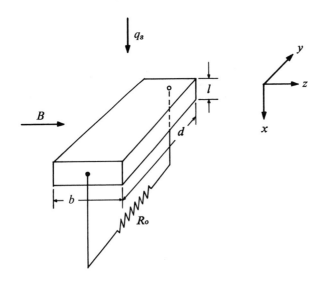

FIG. 9-1. A Nernst effect generator.

(2) The generator is assumed to rest in the air gap of a permanent magnet experiencing a uniform and constant magnetic flux density B.

An energy balance at the hot junction yields

$$q_s = K \Delta T - q_E - q_j, \tag{9-1}$$

where q_s is the heat input to the hot junction per unit time, $K \Delta T$ is the heat transferred by conduction due to the applied temperature difference, q_E the heat rejected to the source by the Ettingshausen effect, and q_j the Joule heat returned to the source.

Unlike the Peltier heat, which is absorbed at the source in a thermoelectric generator, the Ettingshausen effect causes a rejection of heat to the source, that is, a net reduction in heat transfer due to the applied temperature difference. This situation may be most easily understood from the point of view of irreversible thermodynamics, as explained in Section 2.2.3.

The heat transfer by conduction is

$$K \Delta T = (\lambda bd/l) \Delta T, \tag{9-2}$$

where λ is the thermal conductivity and b, d, and l are the dimensions of the device as shown in Fig. 9-1.

The energy rejected by the Ettingshausen effect q_E may be calculated by considering the temperature difference that the Ettingshausen effect would produce in the absence of an applied temperature difference,

$$q_E = \lambda bd \, \Delta T_E / l, \tag{9-3}$$

but by definition the Ettingshausen temperature difference is simply

$$\Delta T_E = P' BI / b, \tag{9-4}$$

where P' is the Ettingshausen coefficient. Substituting Eq. 9-4 into Eq. 9-3 yields

$$q_E = (\lambda P' d/l) BI. \tag{9-5}$$

The Bridgman equation defines the relationship between the Nernst coefficient and the Ettingshausen coefficient as follows:

$$P'\lambda = Q'T. \tag{9-6}$$

Applying Eq. 9-6 to Eq. 9-5 yields

$$q_E = (Q'd/l)T_c BI = \epsilon_E I, \tag{9-7}$$

where ϵ_E is a quantity analogous to the Peltier coefficient.

The Joule heat, half of which is returned to the source, may be calculated as

$$q_j = \tfrac{1}{2}I^2[\rho_{el}d/(bl)] = \tfrac{1}{2}I^2 R. \tag{9-8}$$

Now Eq. 9-1 can be written as

$$q_s = K \Delta T - \epsilon_E I - \tfrac{1}{2}I^2 R. \tag{9-9}$$

The electrical power output is

$$P_o = I^2 R_o,$$ (9-10)

where R_o is the external load resistance.

The thermal efficiency is the output power divided by the heat supplied:

$$\eta_t = \frac{I^2 R_o}{K \, \Delta T - \epsilon_E I - \frac{1}{2} I^2 R}.$$ (9-11)

The Nernst voltage is obtained from the definition of the Nernst effect to be

$$\Delta V_y = BQ' \, \Delta T d / l = \phi \, \Delta T,$$ (9-12)

where ϕ is a quantity analogous to the Seebeck coefficient.

By calling the ratio of the load resistance to the internal resistance m', the current may be written as

$$I = \frac{\phi \, \Delta T}{R(m' + 1)}.$$ (9-13)

Thus the power output P_o in terms of m' and ϕ becomes

$$P_o = \frac{\phi^2 \, \Delta T^2 m'}{R(m' + 1)^2}.$$ (9-14)

By substituting Eqs. 9-13 and 9-14 into Eq. 9-11 and rearranging, the efficiency is given as

$$\eta_t = \frac{m' \eta_{ca}}{\dfrac{KR}{\phi^2} \dfrac{(1 + m')^2}{T_H} - \dfrac{T_C}{T_H}(1 + m') - \frac{1}{2}\eta_{ca}},$$ (9-15)

where η_{ca} is the Carnot efficiency.

We observe that for a single material the quantity ϕ^2/KR denoted henceforth as θ becomes

$$\theta = \frac{\phi^2}{KR} = \frac{Q'^2 B^2}{\lambda \rho_{el}}.$$ (9-16)

We follow the practice of thermoelectrics and call this the figure of merit of a Nernst effect generator. Unlike the thermoelectric figure of merit, the Nernst effect figure of merit is not a pure material parameter as it involves the magnetic flux density B. The flux density must be included because the electrical resistivity ρ_{el} of the material is not independent of the magnetic field due to the magnetoresistance effect. The magnetoresistance effect is the increase in electrical resistance that occurs in a conductor when it is placed in a magnetic field. The Nernst coefficient and thermal conductivity under certain conditions are also field dependent.

The resistance ratio m', which maximizes the thermal efficiency, may be found by setting the derivative of Eq. 9-15 with respect to m' equal to zero, giving

$$m'_{opt} = (1 - \theta T_{av})^{1/2},$$ (9-17)

where the subscript opt denotes the optimum value of m' and T_{av} is the mean temperature.

The maximum thermal efficiency can now be obtained by substituting Eq. 9-17 into Eq. 9-15 to yield, upon simplification

$$\eta_{max} = \eta_{ca} \frac{1 - m'_{opt}}{1 + (T_C/T_H)m'_{opt}}. \tag{9-18}$$

It is interesting to note that a theoretical upper bound of unity has been placed on the dimensionless quantity θT_{av}. The solid state implications of such a bound have been explored by Angrist [5]. In Fig. 9-2 the thermal

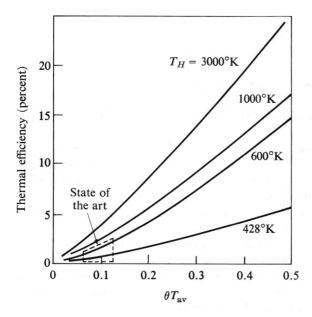

FIG. 9-2. The thermal efficiency of a Nernst effect generator as a function of the dimensionless figure of merit θT_{av} with the source temperature as a parameter. The sink temperature is assumed to be 300°K. After Ref. [2].

efficiency is given as a function of θT_{av} and T_H. The sink temperature has been assumed to be 300°K.

Colwell *et al.* [6] have performed quantitative calculations and experimental work on various materials. They found that a useful criterion to apply to a material that would be suitable for use in a Nernst generator is to require that the Hall coefficient be zero over a large temperature range. Such materials are those with $n = p$ (semimetals or intrinsic semiconductors) with equal mobilities. For a simple model of graphite they found that the

θT product would be about 0.08 or less, but for the simple model semimetal, theory indicates that θT product might reach 0.4.

The conclusions concerning material for a Nernst effect device are: conduction should be by both electrons and holes; and, furthermore, the effective mass of the two carriers should be about equal. The efficiency as a function of magnetic field is expected to increase, approximately, as the square of the field for[†] $\mu B < 1$, to increase less slowly if $1 < \mu B < 10$ and to increase very little, if at all, for $\mu B > 10$. The lattice thermal conductivity should be small.

These material requirements are met in semimetals and also, except for a large thermal conductivity, in single-crystal and pyrolytic graphite. The usual semiconductors (Ge, GaAs, Si, PbTe, and even InSb) do not meet these requirements because their band gap is so large that the intrinsic materials do not contain a sufficient number of carriers.

As a practical generator material, pyrolytic graphite was found by Colwell *et al.* [6] to be the most promising material studied. Assuming that nothing happens to its figure of merit at temperatures higher than 400°C, the engineering possibilities of this material are encouraging. The best θT product that was measured was 0.045 for this material at 400°C in a field of 34 kilogauss; the product was increasing with temperature and magnetic field. Extrapolation of this work indicated that the θT product would continue to increase until it would level off at a value of 0.133 when the field reached about 100 kilogauss.

Assuming the availability of magnetic fields of unlimited strength, research workers feel that Nernst effect generators might attain an effectiveness (that is, an efficiency not including the Carnot efficiency) of 15 to 25 percent; this limit appears to be imposed by the lattice thermal conductivity. Most workers in this area feel that while it would be impractical to build such a generator at this time, the initial results are encouraging enough to make further materials research worth doing.

9.2.2 Ferroelectric and thermomagnetic energy converters. The dielectric constant of certain materials varies rapidly in the neighborhood of their Curie point.[‡] We call these materials ferroelectric. This property can be used to construct a device that will convert heat directly to electricity provided we can find a way to heat-cycle a ferroelectric through its Curie temperature. Several different devices have been analyzed in the literature but we will consider an analysis of the simplest type of device, following the work of

---

† Where μ is the carrier mobility.

‡ The *Curie point* or *Curie temperature* is defined as that temperature above which a substance possesses a spontaneous magnetic moment even in the absence of an applied magnetic field.

Clingman and Moore [7]. At the end of this discussion we will also mention similar converters analyzed by Elliott [8] in the case of thermomagnetic devices and Chester [9] for superconducting thermomagnetic converters. Childress [10] has also presented an analysis of the ferroelectric converter.

A schematic of the circuit we will consider in our analysis is shown in Fig. 9-3. The capacitor in this circuit is a parallel-plate type whose dielectric

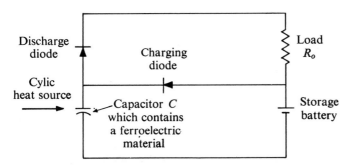

FIG. 9-3. A ferroelectric energy converter. After Ref. [7] with permission.

material is a ferroelectric ceramic. The diodes merely insure that the current flows in the correct direction during the charging and discharging portions of the cycle.

The cycle, for which we shall present a simplified analysis, is shown in Fig. 9-4. All the changes of state we discuss take place at constant volume of the dielectric. In the initial state (state 0) both the charge on the capacitor Q and the potential across the capacitor are zero, and the capacitor is in contact with the heat sink at temperature T_C, which is some initial temperature equal to or greater than the Curie temperature. The condenser is charged isothermally by the battery through the charging diode to $Q = Q_C$. The charge on the capacitor is given as the product of the static capacity $\mathcal{C}$ of the capacitor at the Curie temperature, and the voltage of the storage battery V_B.

The temperature of the capacitor is then raised to some higher temperature T_H, whereupon the dielectric constant of the ferroelectric material drops to a value $\mathcal{K}_H$; a typical plot of dielectric constant as a function of temperature is shown in Fig. 9-5. The corresponding drop in capacitance is given by

$$\mathcal{C}_H = (\mathcal{K}_H/\mathcal{K}_C)\mathcal{C}_C, \tag{9-19}$$

where $\mathcal{C}_H$ denotes the capacitance at temperature T_H, and $\mathcal{K}_C$ and $\mathcal{K}_H$ the dielectric constant at the Curie point and T_H respectively. Since no charge has been removed from the capacitor, the voltage is correspondingly in-

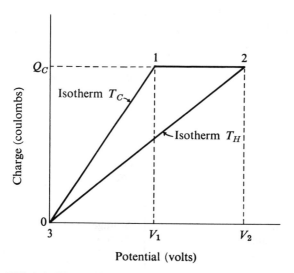

FIG. 9-4. Thermodynamic cycle that a ferroelectric energy converter might follow. After Ref. [7] with permission.

creased by a similar ratio. This increase in voltage without a loss of charge results in an increase in the electrical energy available.

With the condenser in thermal contact with the heat source, the condenser is discharged completely, bringing the system isothermally to state 3 with $T = T_H$, $Q = 0$, $V = 0$. During this process the battery is recharged, causing zero consumption of electrical energy from it. The increase in electrical energy results solely from the direct conversion of heat energy extracted from the source; heat is extracted during two processes of the cycle, in the raising of the temperature of the dielectric and during the isothermal discharge of the capacitor.

Now with zero charge on the capacitor, it is cooled from T_H to T_C, returning the capacitor to its initial state. The states of the ferroelectric cycle are given in Table 9-1.

TABLE 9-1. THE STATES OF THE FERROELECTRIC CYCLE ENERGY CONVERTER

State	Temperature	Charge	Voltage
0	T_C	0	0
1	T_C	Q_C	V_C
2	T_H	Q_C	V_H
3	T_H	0	0

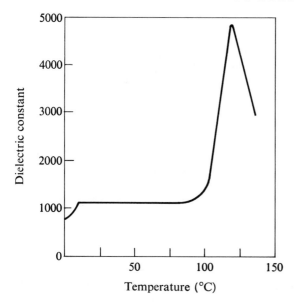

FIG. 9-5. The temperature dependence of the dielectric constant of barium titanate measured at 400 kilocycles and zero bias. After S. Roberts, *Physical Review*, 71 (1947), p. 890; with permission.

The isothermal processes of the cycle are thermodynamically reversible, that is, the entropy change during the charging of the capacitor from state 0 to state 1 is exactly the same as the entropy change that occurs during the discharging of the capacitor in going from state 2 to state 3, but of opposite sign. There is finite entropy production, of course, during the heating and cooling of the dielectric, thus preventing the cycle from obtaining the Carnot efficiency.

When an electric field passes through a polarizable medium,† the resulting polarization alters the effect of the applied field; we thus find it convenient to define a new quantity called the *dielectric displacement, D,* such that

$$D = \epsilon E, \tag{9-20}$$

where ϵ is called the *permittivity of the material*. In an isotropic homogeneous material ϵ is a constant, that is, a characteristic of the material. Insertion of a dielectric material in a parallel-plate capacitor that has a permittivity ϵ greater than that of a vacuum, ϵ_0, increases the capacitance and decreases

---

† Polarization of a medium takes place when an electric field is applied to the substance and the center of positive charge is slightly displaced in the direction of the applied field and the center of negative charge is slightly displaced in the opposite direction. This produces local dipoles throughout the medium; the process of inducing such dipoles in the crystal is called *polarization*.

the potential difference required to maintain the same charge, Q. When all the space between the two plates is filled by the dielectric material, the increase in the capacitance is measured by the *dielectric constant* of the material $\mathcal{K}$. This factor measures the ratio of the permittivity of the material to that of empty space, so that

$$\mathcal{K} = \epsilon/\epsilon_0. \tag{9-21}$$

In our analysis of the ferroelectric converter we consider ϵ, the permittivity, to be a function of temperature T and the displacement D. This is done for reasons of convenience and of the availability of data in these terms for barium titanate and barium strontium titanate, two materials that appear to be potentially useful in this type of energy converter.

In the discharge portion of the cycle—that is, the process from state 2 to state 3—the electrical work done by the capacitor† is

$$W_{2-3} = \int_0^{Qc} V\, dQ. \tag{9-22}$$

The voltage may be written in terms of D, the distance between the plates l, and the permittivity ϵ, which is a function of D and T. Thus from Eq. 9-20 we write the voltage as

$$V = \left[\frac{1}{\epsilon(D, T)} \right] Dl. \tag{9-23}$$

If the area of the plates is A, and the volume of the dielectric material is Ω, then the charge on the capacitor is given by the product of the area A of the plates and the displacement; thus $Q = AD = \Omega D/l$. Now Eq. 9-22 can be written in terms of Eq. 9-23 as

$$W_{2-3} = \int_0^{Qc} V\, dQ = \Omega \int_0^{Dc} D \left[\frac{1}{\epsilon(D, T_H)} \right] dD. \tag{9-24}$$

In charging the condenser from state 0 to state 1, the electrical work done on the capacitor is equal to

$$W_{0-1} = \Omega \int_0^{Dc} D \left[\frac{1}{\epsilon(D, T_C)} \right] dD. \tag{9-25}$$

The net electrical work, therefore, is simply

$$W_{\text{net}} = \Omega \int_0^{Dc} D \left\{ \left[\frac{1}{\epsilon(D, T_H)} \right] - \left[\frac{1}{\epsilon(D, T_C)} \right] \right\} dD. \tag{9-26}$$

If we assume that the permittivity is independent of the displacement, then we may integrate this equation directly to obtain

$$W_{\text{net}} = \frac{\Omega}{2} \epsilon_C E_C^2 \left[\frac{\epsilon_C}{\epsilon_H} - 1 \right]. \tag{9-27}$$

† Where the integral of $V\, dQ$ gives the work done in charging a capacitor. By reversing the limits of integration, we obtain the work done when the capacitor is discharged.

Since the charge on the capacitor can always be written as $Q = \epsilon A V / l$, then $\Omega \epsilon_C E_C^2 = Q_C V_C$ and Eq. 9-27 becomes

$$W_{\text{net}} = \tfrac{1}{2} Q_C V_C \left[\frac{\epsilon_C}{\epsilon_H} - 1 \right]. \tag{9-28}$$

The heat supplied, $\bar{Q}_s$, may be calculated by application of the first law of thermodynamics

$$\bar{Q}_s = \bar{Q}_r + W_{\text{net}}, \tag{9-29}$$

where $\bar{Q}_r$ is the heat rejected. If we assume that the heat rejection takes place as the capacitor is cooled from T_H to T_C under zero charge as the system goes from state 3 to the initial state, then

$$\bar{Q}_r = \Omega \int_{T_C}^{T_H} C_v(D, T) \, dT, \tag{9-30}$$

where $C_v(D, T)$ is the constant volume heat capacity (joule/°K-m³) of the dielectric, that is

$$C_v(D, T) = \frac{1}{\Omega} \left(\frac{\partial \mathcal{E}_{\text{int}}}{\partial T} \right)_{\Omega, D}, \tag{9-31}$$

where $\mathcal{E}_{\text{int}}$ is the internal energy of the dielectric as a function of displacement, temperature, and volume. If we assume that the specific heat is independent of temperature, then Eq. 9-30 can be integrated immediately and the heat supplied becomes

$$\bar{Q}_s = \Omega [C_v(T_H - T_C) + \tfrac{1}{2} \epsilon_C E_C^2(\epsilon_C / \epsilon_H - 1)]. \tag{9-32}$$

The thermal efficiency is simply the ratio of the net work (Eq. 9-27) to the heat supplied (Eq. 9-32); thus

$$\eta_t = \left[1 + \frac{2 C_v(T_H - T_C)}{\epsilon_C E_C^2(\epsilon_C / \epsilon_H - 1)} \right]^{-1}. \tag{9-33}$$

Calculations made for a capacitor filled with barium titanate do not show particular promise; the results of these calculations as presented in Ref. [7] are shown in Fig. 9-6. Ferroelectric energy converters may find future use in certain applications that require simple lightweight devices operating from a cyclic heat source. Such a heat source might arise in a spinning space vehicle in which a given point on the surface of the vehicle experiences a cyclic heating and cooling as a result of the periodic exposure to solar heat. In general, it is felt that ferroelectric converters will find rather limited application due to the unusual heat source requirements. Before closing we might add, however, that Childress [10] in his analysis predicts a theoretical power density of about 410 watts per lb compared to power handling capacities in the range of 10 to 100 watts per lb for other energy conversion devices. The major problem is one of getting the heat into and out of the dielectric.

Elliott [8] presents an analysis of a similar converter, which he calls a

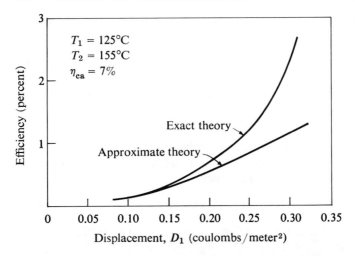

FIG. 9-6. Efficiency of a ferroelectric converter as a function of the displacement in a device that uses barium titanate. Calculations are shown for both the exact theory and the approximate theory followed in the text. These results follow Clingman and Moore [7]; with permission.

thermomagnetic generator, that uses a ferromagnetic material to complete the magnetic circuit of a permanent magnet as is shown in Fig. 9-7. The ferromagnetic shunt is heat cycled through its Curie point causing the flux in the coil to rise and fall as the magnetic circuit is alternately opened and

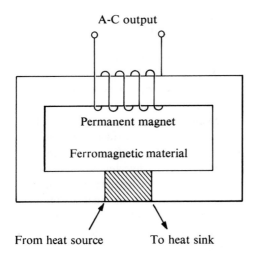

FIG. 9-7. A schematic representation of a generator that uses a ferromagnetic material.

closed. Particular attention is paid to the use of the ferromagnetic element gadolinium, which has a Curie point near room temperature. Such a material would allow the extraction of electrical power from low temperature heat sources—a task not easily accomplished at present. Elliott's calculations indicate that such devices would not have efficiencies greater than 1 percent and power densities less than 5 watts per lb. This device also suffers the disadvantage of being dependent on a cyclic heat source for its operation. At present it does not appear as a very promising mode of energy conversion.

Chester [9] has analyzed a similar device, except that the shunt is made of superconducting material instead of a ferromagnetic material such as gadolinium. The permanent magnet produces a field that is alternately accepted and rejected by the superconductor core. The alternation is produced by thermally changing the state of the core from normal to superconducting. When in a superconducting state, the core becomes perfectly diamagnetic, expelling the magnetic field by virtue of the Meissner effect. In the normal state, which is induced by raising the temperature of the core above its critical temperature, the field is able to penetrate the core. With each change in flux a current is induced in the pickup coil. The disadvantage of this system, in addition to the requirement of a cyclic heat source, is that the heat rejection temperature must be low enough to permit the superconducting phase to exhibit itself; this usually requires a temperature not much greater than that of liquid helium. Chester has calculated that for a niobium core maintained at 8°K during the heat rejection portion of the cycle an ideal device efficiency of 44 percent could be obtained. The realization of this device in the laboratory has not yet been achieved.

9.2.3 Thermo-photo-voltaic energy converters.

In both thermoelectric and thermionic energy converters, the electron gas, which acts as the working fluid in the conversion process, is heated through an energy exchange with the crystal lattice. The thermal contact between the lattice and the electrons is very good; the relaxation times that determine the energy transfer process between the electrons and the lattice are on the order of 10^{-11} sec. This causes electrons and lattice to be at the same very high temperature after the desired electronic excitation has taken place; the usual high temperature problems associated with all the other previously discussed modes of heat-to-electricity conversion processes must then be solved.

The generation of electron-hole pairs by light in a semiconductor is associated with relaxation times at least six orders of magnitude larger than the relaxation times of conduction processes. This means that electrons travel on the order of 10^{-6} to 10^{-3} sec instead of 10^{-11} sec between collisions with the lattice; thus it is possible to produce electronic excitation that is relatively weakly coupled to the lattice and, therefore, to "heat" the electron system by photons while still keeping the lattice "cool." This brings us to the possibility of building a converter in which heat is converted to light by way of incandescence, which in turn is converted to electrical energy by a photovoltaic converter. White *et al.* [11] and Wedlock [12] have described such converters in the literature.

In contrast to solar energy converters, the power level as well as the spectral characteristics of the radiation input to a thermo-photo-voltaic (TPV) converter may be controlled. The spectrum of the input radiation can be controlled by both the temperature and emissivity of the radiation source coupled with highly efficient thin film optical filters. For example, in germanium the radiation wavelength that leads to maximum energy conversion efficiency is approximately 1.5 to 1.6 microns (15,000 to 16,000 A); this is actually near infrared radiation rather than visible light. According to Wien's displacement law, a blackbody would produce this maximum wavelength in the range of 1810°K to 1930°K, a temperature not difficult to achieve with many heat sources.

This type of converter has another advantage: by utilizing suitable geometrical arrangements, reflection losses may be minimized by directing the energy that is not absorbed on initial impact to another converter surface. One example of such an arrangement is a coaxial system with an energy source at the center and the energy converters forming an inner surface at some appropriate radius, as is shown in Fig. 9-8. In this situation radiation

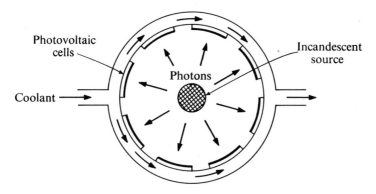

FIG. 9-8. A TPV converter that utilizes a coaxial geometry to maximize the collection of photons. After Ref. [12] with permission.

that is reflected is either accepted by a second converter or returned to the source.

It is desirable when considering the incident spectrum to work with photons that have energies near the energy gap of the semiconductor in order to minimize the excess photon energy. Excess photon energy is the energy that the photon has that exceeds the forbidden zone energy of the semiconductor; the excess photon energy does not contribute to the electrical output of the device but only heats the lattice, thus degrading the output of the device.

In Ch. 5 it was shown that the series resistance plays an important role in determining the efficiency at which a cell operates. The depth of the diffused layer on the surface of a solar cell controls the series resistance of the cell as well as its collection efficiency. In the TPV converter the depth of this junction can be several orders of magnitude larger because the diffusion lengths are longer in many of the materials of interest (especially germanium). A diffused layer of high conductivity may be placed on the face of the converter that accepts the input radiation to lower the series resistance of the converter. A schematic of this arrangement is shown in Fig. 9-9.

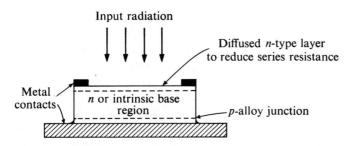

FIG. 9-9. Cross section of a TPV converter diode. After Ref. [12] with permission.

It has been shown [11], [12] that if the wavelength of the monochromatic illumination used to illuminate the TPV converter is made equal to the wavelength corresponding to the gap energy, the converter will have an efficiency given by

$$\eta_t = \{\eta_{ca} - (kT/\mathcal{E}_g) \ln [1/(1 - \eta_{co})]\} \eta_{co}, \qquad (9\text{-}34)$$

where η_{ca} is the Carnot efficiency defined by the temperature of the source and the temperature of the cell T, η_{co} is the collection efficiency†—that is, the fraction of generated electron-hole pairs that reach the junction. The source temperature is assumed to be high enough to deliver appreciable radiation at the desired wavelength. The radiation that is not absorbed initially is assumed to be reflected back to the source. To a good approximation Eq. 9-34 may be written as

$$\eta \approx \eta_{ca}\eta_{co}, \qquad (9\text{-}35)$$

since $kT \ll \mathcal{E}_g$ and the variation of η_{co} occurs under the logarithm. This

† See Ch. 5 for a more complete discussion of this parameter.

approximate efficiency expression does not include two additional factors that will also affect the operating efficiency of a TPV converter. They are (1) the small absorption coefficient at the wavelengths corresponding to the energy gap of the material, and (2) the reflection loss at the incident surface. We will discuss these two factors briefly.

As we pointed out in Section 5.4.2, a small absorption coefficient such as the one that corresponds to the energy gap of germanium will cause electron-hole pairs to be generated in a region far from the neighborhood of the junction. For this reason it is not possible to attain high collection efficiencies with radiation of the gap wavelength. In a practical device, therefore, wavelengths shorter than the gap wavelength must be employed to increase the absorption coefficient. This causes a further reduction in the overall efficiency since the only fraction of the total photon energy ε that can be extracted is $\varepsilon_g/\varepsilon$.

Reflection losses are of no consequence in a bank of cells that have been oriented into an array as previously suggested; however, in a single cell this loss can be of considerable consequence. This loss may be taken into account by an additional factor of $(1 - r_l)^2$, where r_l is the reflectivity, which further reduces the efficiency expression. We may take both the absorption and reflectivity losses into account in a new efficiency expression of the form

$$\eta_t = \eta_{ca}\eta_{co}(1 - r_l)^2\lambda'/\lambda_g', \qquad (9\text{-}36)$$

where we have used the wavelengths of the incident radiation, λ', and the wavelength of the radiation that corresponds to the energy gap of the material, λ_g', instead of the energies themselves. (Recall that the wavelength is inversely proportional to the energy.) It is interesting to observe how these various factors affect the efficiency of such a converter; this is done in Fig. 9-10, which clearly shows the importance of surface treatment to minimize reflection losses. The upper curve that bounds the region of operation is for a cell with zero reflectivity while the lower curve is for reflection from an untreated surface. It is also clearly evident from the drawing that optimization of the overall efficiency is largely dependent on successful optimization of the collection efficiency.

Experimental work carried out by Wedlock [12] showed that p-intrinsic-n-type structures were superior to the p–n converter by providing the maximum possible output voltage. Under wide-band infrared radiation a maximum efficiency of 4.23 percent was obtained with an input power density of 282 milliwatts per cm². Since efficiency is a steadily increasing function of intensity, obeying a predicted increase of 6 percent per decade, workers in the area predict that the efficiency will continue to increase with intensity up to the range of 10 to 16 percent with power inputs of 3 to 30 watts per cm².

Furthermore, it is felt that these estimates are conservative because the

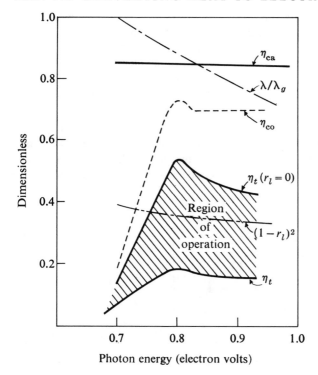

FIG. 9-10. Factors that affect the theoretical efficiency of a TPV converter. The region of operation (shown shaded) is bounded on the top by a zero reflectivity curve and on the bottom by a curve that has reflection from an untreated surface. After Ref. [12] with permission.

highest collection efficiency that was observed in the experiments was 67 percent; since it is possible to achieve nearly 100 percent collection efficiency over a wide range of absorption coefficients, this factor alone would cause the efficiency to increase by three-halves. In the experimental work carried out to date no attention has been paid to the reflection loss, which can be greatly reduced by use of antireflection coatings on the face of the converter. These two considerations led Wedlock to believe that efficiencies of 30 percent from power inputs of 10 watts per cm² are not overly optimistic.

In conclusion it might be noted that other workers have made a similar attack on this problem; Watts, Oestrich, and Robinson [13] suggest using beta particles from a radioisotope source to irradiate a luminescent material which emits a number of low energy photons, instead of heating a source to incandescence and then proceeding with photovoltaic conversion; the photons are then converted to electrical energy by a photovoltaic device.

The chief disadvantage of this mode of conversion was the damage inflicted on the *p–n* junctions by the radiation and the rapid decrease in efficiency of silicon *solar* cells (which were used in the experimental work) at the low illumination intensities of beta-excited phosphor. Until solutions to these two problems are found, this particular mode of energy conversion does not appear particularly promising.

9.2.4   Electron convection converters. S. R. Hoh and W. L. Harries [14] have reported a new method of converting thermal to electrical power based on the forced convection of electrons. A diagram of such a converter is given in Fig. 9-11, which shows a truncated cone enclosing a pool of liquid alkali

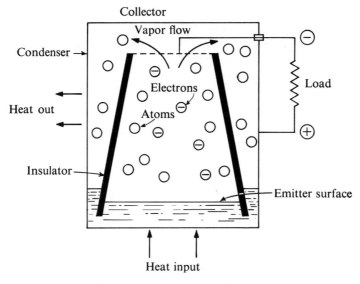

FIG. 9-11. Schematic diagram of an electron convection converter. After Ref. [14].

metal. Electrons are boiled out of the liquid emitter together with neutral atoms, which transport the electrons to a collector. The conversion takes place because the electrons transported with the metal vapor flow build up a charge difference between emitter and collector; the voltage thus established creates an electric field that opposes further electron flow. Work has to be done to raise the electrons to the energy level of the collector. A portion of this work is available as the output of the converter.

This type of converter is in some respects similar to a thermionic converter, but unlike a thermionic converter the space charge problem is overcome by the forced convection of the electrons; the output voltage is not

limited by the energy of emitted electrons, thus enabling much higher voltages to be achieved. In addition, this type of converter can operate with low
work function emitters, and consequently lower emitter temperatures.

We will consider a brief analysis of one mode of operation of this type
converter in order to highlight some of the characteristics of devices of this
nature.

A schematic of the device we will treat is shown in Fig. 9-12. The

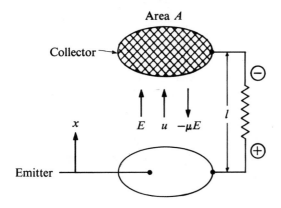

FIG. 9-12. Elements in the model of an electron convection converter.
After Ref. [14].

velocity of the neutral gas is denoted by u. Electrons that are driven toward
the collector through collisions with the neutral atoms charge the collector
negatively to $-V$. The voltage between the emitter and collector creates an
electric field E, which opposes the electron flow; in fact, this E field gives the
electrons a drift velocity u_d, which is in the opposite direction of the velocity
of the neutral atoms. Thus the gas must do work on the electrons to transport them to the collector; it is part of this work that we may release as
electrical power. Furthermore, the body force induced by the electric field
creates a pressure gradient which opposes the motion of the charge carriers.
The motion of an electron drifting through a stationary neutral gas with a
drift velocity u_d being subjected to an electric field may be represented by

$$m_e \frac{du_d}{dt} - K_v u_d = eE, \tag{9-37}$$

where m_e is the electron mass, K_v a viscous friction coefficient, and e the
electronic charge. If it is assumed that the electron reaches a limiting velocity
in a few collisions, then the first term becomes zero and

$$u_d = -eE/K_v. \tag{9-38}$$

This drift velocity can also be expressed in terms of the mobility μ, when it is recalled that the mobility is defined as the velocity per unit electric field, or

$$u_d = -\mu E. \tag{9-39}$$

The minus sign is used to denote direction only in this case. Comparison of Eqs. 9-38 and 9-39 shows that the frictional constant K_v is inversely proportional to the mobility.

Compared to ions, electrons have much higher mobilities, and therefore experience much lower frictional forces. Because of the high mobility, the electric field has a tendency to give the electrons a high velocity opposite in direction to the neutral gas. This is probably the main factor limiting the output of this type converter. However, it is encouraging to note that alkali metals such as cesium, rubidium, and potassium have the highest probability of collision with electrons in the gaseous phase. For example, for electrons in equilibrium with a gas at 900°K at a pressure of 1000 mm mercury, the mobility of electrons is about 300 cm² per volt-sec. It has been found that the mobility is inversely proportional to the pressure and directly proportional to the square root of the absolute temperature.

In Fig. 9-12, where the electric field is assumed parallel to the x direction, the net velocity of the electrons u_n equals the neutral gas velocity reduced by the drift velocity

$$u_n = u - u_d = u - \mu E \tag{9-40}$$

and the current density is just the product of the electron velocity (centimeters per second) times the space charge, ρ, in units of coulombs per cubic centimeter, thus

$$j = (u - \mu E)\rho. \tag{9-41}$$

In our simple analysis we assume the current density and gas velocity to be constant for all values of x. The potential V, electric field E, and space charge ρ, are functions of x, and we assume them to be related by Poisson's equation

$$\frac{d^2V}{dx^2} = -\frac{dE}{dx} = -\rho/\epsilon, \tag{9-42}$$

where ϵ is the permittivity of the medium. The only analysis we will carry out is the case of negligible space charge that occurs for very low electron emission rates; we treat it here because it is simple and brings out the important characteristics of this converter. We begin by using the usual relationship between voltage and E field, namely

$$E = V/l \tag{9-43}$$

and thus the current for an area A is

$$I = A\rho(u - \mu V/l). \tag{9-44}$$

In this equation the small space charge is assumed to be an independent variable which is a function of the emitter temperature alone; for a given E field and gas velocity, ρ is then a constant.

The maximum current occurs under short circuit conditions and can be found by setting $V = 0$ in Eq. 9-44 to obtain

$$I_{max} = A\rho u. \tag{9-45}$$

Thus Eq. 9-44 can be rewritten as

$$I = I_{max} - V/R, \tag{9-46}$$

since $l/(A\rho\mu)$ is the resistance of the gas, R. The power output of the device can be obtained by multiplying the voltage times the current as given by Eq. 9-46

$$P_o = I_{max}V - V^2/R. \tag{9-47}$$

The power can be maximized in the usual way by taking the derivative of it with respect to the voltage and equating the results to zero. The voltage that maximizes the power is simply half the open circuit voltage. The maximum power is then

$$P_{o(max)} = Al\rho u^2/(4\mu). \tag{9-48}$$

It is observed that the maximum power is proportional to the volume of the converter Al, the density of the emitted electrons as measured by the space charge, and the square of the gas velocity. As μ is inversely proportional to the neutral gas pressure, the maximum power is proportional to the neutral gas pressure. The external load that maximizes the power output is simply one with a resistance equal to the internal gas resistance. The case of intermediate space charge and dominant space charge is considered in Ref. [14].

One of the simplest measures of efficiency of this type of device is the ratio of the electron velocity to the gas velocity. That is

$$\eta = \frac{u_n}{u} = \frac{u - \mu E}{u} = 1 - \frac{\mu E}{u}. \tag{9-49}$$

Thus efficiency is seen to be greatly dependent on the mobility, neutral gas velocity, and electric field.

Hoh and Harries built several working models of electron convection generators charged with cesium as the working fluid. Open circuit voltages of as high as 18 volts with emitter temperatures as low as 540°C and short circuit currents near the limiting currents of the emitters (0.002 to 0.1 ma) were obtained. The efficiency is limited mainly by electron drift and mobility, which indicates that high operating pressures would have a favorable effect on performance. While the mobility increases as the square root of the absolute temperature, thus causing a decrease in the output of a converter, the emission current density goes up approximately as the square of the absolute temperature.† Considerable research must still be done in this area

---

† According to the Richardson-Dushman equation discussed in Ch. 6.

to determine the optimum pressure and temperature for this type of device's operation.

9.3 OTHER MODES OF CONVERTING MECHANICAL ENERGY TO ELECTRICITY

In this section we will consider briefly three methods that are capable of converting mechanical energy to electrical energy. Each of these methods is rather specialized in the power needs that it could fill.

9.3.1 Electrohydrodynamic energy converters. The energy converters described in this section are in many respects similar to the electron convection generator described in the previous section except that the fluid in an EHD converter is mechanically pumped instead of thermally driven. In 1867 Lord Kelvin [15] set up a demonstration that produced electrostatic high voltages from drops of falling water. In 1974 O'Byrne [16] carried out a more systematic study of this phenomenon by utilizing the device illustrated in Fig. 9-13. Water is introduced at a low flow rate into a small tube, where it

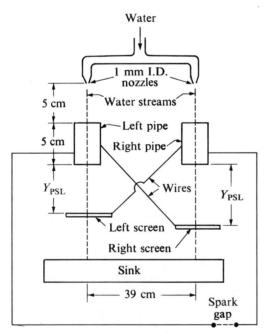

FIG. 9-13. Schematic of the arrangement used to produce an electrostatic voltage. After Ref. [16] with permission.

is split by a tree into two separate streams, each passing through a small nozzle. Each stream flows through an open-ended metallic pipe from which it emerges, charged relative to the pipe. Thus the "left-hand" stream assumes, say, a positive charge relative to the negative charge on the left-hand pipe. The opposite is true for the other stream, in that the "right-hand" stream assumes a negative charge relative to the right-hand pipe. The two streams continue to fall, eventually giving up their charge to screens. The left-hand pipe and the right-hand screen, having the same charge, are wired together to magnify the charge. The induced electrostatic voltage is measured across a spark gap. Figure 9-14 shows the relationship between the peak voltage and the Reynolds number of the falling stream.

In 1899 A. P. Chattock [17] described how electrical energy can be converted into mechanical energy. Until recently this so-called corona wind had received relatively little attention in the literature. Within the past 15 years, however, Stuetzer and others have proposed ion drag pumps [18], high voltage regulators, switches, d-c transformers [19], and high voltage generators [20]. These fluid high voltage generators offer several advantages over the conventional Van de Graaff generator, in which electric charge is mechanically transported to a high potential by means of a belt or disc. The chief advantages of using a fluid to do the ion transport is that the resulting machines are compact, rugged, and easily serviceable designs in which there are no critical mechanical alignments or tolerances. On the other hand, the machines are of low efficiency and high weight. For the most part the devices

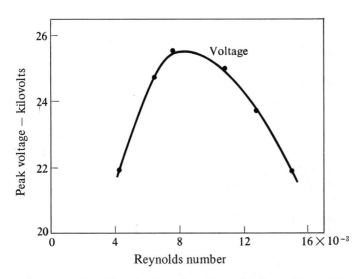

FIG. 9-14. The peak voltage generated as a function of Reynolds number in an electrostatic water voltage generation experiment. After Ref. [16].

have been considered only as high voltage sources and not as power sources; this fact is easily explained when it is realized that their current output is generally in the microampere range. Stuetzer [20], whose work we will follow, handles the case where the charge transport is carried out by a poorly conducting incompressible fluid while Smith [21] treats the case of the compressible fluid.

We will present here a brief outline of the analysis given by Stuetzer; details may be found in Ref. [20] and those cited above. The arrangement that we will analyze is illustrated in Fig. 9-15 and consists of a cylindrical tube with radius $r = r_1$, which for our purposes is assumed to be an ideal insulator. In it we assume that a poorly conducting fluid of permittivity ϵ moves with an average velocity u and a flow rate $i = \pi r_1^2 u$, both of which are assumed constant. At the location $x = 0$ positive ions with a mobility of μ are injected; at $x = x_1$ a collector removes them again. The charges cause a space charge of density ρ and their movement creates a current density of magnitude $J = I/\pi r_1^2$. The collector will assume a potential of V_1 which depends on I and the conductance C of the outside load; furthermore, an electric field E is created within the system.

Space charge density, electric field, current density, and (except for the fully developed flow situation) fluid velocity are functions of x and r. In transport systems that are much longer than they are wide ($x \gg r_1$), such

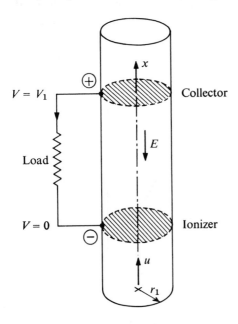

FIG. 9-15. Schematic arrangement of an ion transport high voltage generator. After Ref. [20] with permission.

as those we are going to consider, the radial dependence of the foregoing quantities constitutes second-order effects only; hence, we shall neglect radial variation.

In our one-dimensional problem the current density is constant over the whole transport system and is given by

$$J = (u + \mu E)\rho, \qquad (9\text{-}50)$$

where E and ρ are functions of x alone. The quantity in parentheses constitutes the ion velocity with respect to the electrodes where we have neglected diffusion currents. The field is related to the potential through Poisson's equation

$$\frac{d^2V}{dx^2} = -\frac{dE}{dx} = -\frac{\rho}{\epsilon}. \qquad (9\text{-}51)$$

The boundary conditions on this differential equation are that for $x = 0$ the space charge has a value ρ_e, which is determined by the ionizer. The electric field in our case opposes the flow of charge carriers and gives rise to an ion drag pressure p_i. This pressure drop must be added to the hydrodynamic losses in the system; it may be calculated from

$$\text{grad } p_i = dp_i/dx = \rho E. \qquad (9\text{-}52)$$

In our analysis we shall treat the mean velocity of the liquid u as an independent variable. Substituting ρ from Eq. 9-51 into the current density equation (Eq. 9-50) and integrating yields immediately the field strength in the system

$$E = \left[\frac{2Jx}{\epsilon\mu} + (E_e + u/\mu)^2\right]^{1/2} - u/\mu, \qquad (9\text{-}53)$$

where E_e is the integration constant representing the field strength at the emitter. The longitudinal distribution of charge may now be obtained by differentiating Eq. 9-53 with respect to x and multiplying the result by ϵ to obtain

$$\rho = \frac{J/\mu}{[(2Jx/\epsilon\mu) + (E_e + u/\mu)^2]^{1/2}}. \qquad (9\text{-}54)$$

Assuming that our emitter is a good supplier of ions, the field strength E_e at the emitter is small. We now consider the limiting case of $E_e = 0$ where we have arbitrarily set the voltage at the emitter equal to zero. Stuetzer [18] has shown that the operation of the generator can be divided into two regimes of operation, depending on whether the current density is limited by the opposing field or by the performance of the ionizer. Some simple calculations show that the first regime always has a higher output than the second. Under these assumptions the generated voltage V_1 is then found to be

$$V_1 \approx \frac{ux_1}{\mu} - \left[\frac{8Jx_1^3}{9\epsilon\mu}\right]^{1/2}. \qquad (9\text{-}55)$$

The power delivered to the load is simply IV_1 and thus

$$P_o \approx \pi r_1^2 J \left\{ \frac{ux_1}{\mu} - \left[\frac{8Jx_1^3}{9\epsilon\mu} \right]^{1/2} \right\}. \tag{9-56}$$

This expression is maximized by

$$I_{max} \approx \pi r_1^2 \epsilon u^2 / 2\mu x_1 \tag{9-57}$$

and

$$V_{1(max)} \approx ux_1/3\mu, \tag{9-58}$$

which yields a maximum power of

$$P_{o(max)} \approx \pi r_1^2 \epsilon u^3 / 6\mu^2 \tag{9-59}$$

into a matched external load of

$$R_o = 2x_1^2 / (3\pi r_1^2 \epsilon u). \tag{9-60}$$

Because of the small values of the mobility ($\sim 2 \times 10^{-7}$ m² per volt-sec) substantial voltages may easily be built up over small distances. Currents will typically be small (microamperes) and load resistances high because of the smallness of the dielectric constant ϵ ($\sim 2 \times 10^{-11}$ coulomb per volt-meter) of the carrier fluid.

The efficiency of this type of converter may be found by assuming that the input is the power required for the flow rate i to overcome the hydro-dynamic pressure loss p_h in the system plus the ion drag counter-pressure, p_{i1}. Thus

$$\eta = \frac{IV_1}{(p_{i1} + p_h)i}. \tag{9-61}$$

It may be shown [20] that for maximum power out this may be approximated by

$$\eta_{max} = \frac{1/3}{1 + a^2(x_1/r_1)}, \tag{9-62}$$

with $a^2 = \mu^2\delta/\gamma^2\epsilon$ where δ is the fluid density and γ is a correction factor that depends logarithmically on the Reynold's number of the flow. For very clean insulating fluids a approaches unity. The limiting efficiency is 33 percent for the case of μ equal to zero.

The only satisfactory method that has been found for the generation of carrier ions in a liquid is by use of the unipolar regime of a corona discharge. For a slowly moving fluid the charge density in the unipolar region is roughly proportional to the applied voltage and inversely proportional to the square root of the electrode distance. Experiments have shown that in line with this argument efficient corona point ionizers have to be built with close electrode spacings and operated near breakdown field strengths. If we wish to avoid rapid deterioration of the corona points in a stationary fluid, maximum ionizer currents must be limited to a few microamperes. For fast-moving fluids these currents can be increased by a factor of two or three. In those generators that use a liquid for the working fluid, the electrical power used to ionize the liquid has been found to be less than 1 percent of the hydrodynamic power input. However, Smith [22] found in his early experimental work that the electrical power input to the ionizer exceeded the electrical power output in his generator, which operated with high-pressure air.

Stuetzer [20] carried out a large number of measurements on a variety of devices. Output voltages ranged from 4000 to 500,000 volts; currents from 10^{-8} to 10^{-4} amp. Kerosene, transformer oil, and, in a few experiments, air were used as the transport fluids. Four hundred kilovolts with a current slightly higher than 20 microamperes yielded the highest power output. The optimum power output for operation in the space-charge-limited regime was measured with kerosene ($\mu \approx 2 \times 10^{-7}$ m² per volt-sec, $\delta = 750$ kg per m³). The efficiency in this case was about 10 percent, which compares favorably with the theoretical value; it was largely independent of flow rate and output voltage as long as a reasonably well-matched load was supplied. The efficiency with air, Stuetzer found, was less than 0.1 percent.

Admittedly, the efficiency of EHD converters is low with presently available insulating fluids; this factor, however, is not of prime importance in devices designed for high voltage generation. In addition to the advantages listed at the beginning of this section, experiments have also shown that with some loss in performance the generator may be made self-exciting—that is, not requiring an external power supply for the ionization voltage.

Extensive experimental work has been carried out by Lawson, *et al.* [23] using air as the working fluid. They have reported a law of similitude for electrical discharges that suggests that the product of the gas density and channel dimensions be kept constant, resulting in constant electrical performance but increasing efficiency at high pressure levels. Experimental results are presented which verify this scaling approach and in which they achieve a conversion efficiency of 12 percent of the kinetic energy of a Mach-1 flow into electrical energy. Unlike Stuetzer, they believe that conversion efficiencies can approach 50 percent. Figure 9-16 gives the experimental results they achieved using a primary flow at Mach 1.2.

9.3.2 Electrokinetic converters. When a pressure gradient that induces a flow is impressed on certain types of fluids confined in a fine capillary tube and no electrical current is permitted, an electrical potential difference will appear between the ends of the capillary. This situation is pictured in Fig. 9-17 for a bank of capillary tubes. Conversely, when an electric field is impressed on the fluid in a fine capillary tube and no flow is permitted, a pressure differential appears between the ends of the tube. These are the electrokinetic effects first studied by H. F. H. Helmholtz in 1879. If an electric current is permitted to flow in the first effect described above, pumping

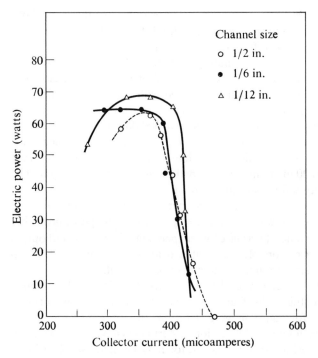

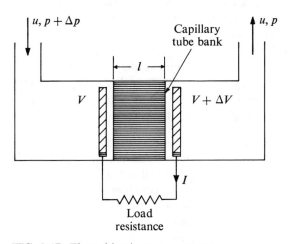

FIG. 9-16. The power output from an electrofluid/dynamic channel as a function of collector current and channel size. The inlet Mach number was 1.2 in this case. After Ref. [23].

FIG. 9-17. Electrokinetic energy converter.

power will be directly converted into electrical power; in the second effect, electrical power is directly converted into pumping power.

One of the theories used to explain the electrokinetic effects in a fluid electrolyte states they are caused by selective ion absorption on the tube wall which results in a net charge density in the bulk fluid. The theory is more complicated in other fluids (such as petroleum products, alcohol, acetone, liquid hydrogen, and mercury) where the effects have been observed. In liquid metals the effects are believed to be the result of diffuse electron scattering in the fluid at the walls rather than of ion absorption. In the pumping mode the electric field acting on this net charge develops a body force that gives rise to the pressure differential and, conversely, the applied pressure differential in the generator mode induces an electric field in the net charge of the fluid.

Osterle [24] has analyzed an electrokinetic energy converter that utilizes a fluid electrolyte in which the charge distribution and electrical potential were assumed to be related by Poisson's equation. McLennan and Osterle [25] extended the work of Ref. [24] by analyzing such a converter for any fluid without specifying the mechanism that maintains the charge distribution or assuming a relation between the charge and potential.

In both of the references previously cited, the analyses were begun by integrating the momentum equation of the fluid, including electric body forces. In Osterle's [24] less general but more direct approach three coefficients were found which could be used to describe the performance of the device. The three coefficients of interest are the electrical conductance of the fluid, the resistance to fluid flow, and the coupling coefficient α, which in the case of a pump is merely the pressure rise per unit voltage resulting from the interaction of the electrical and fluid effects.

The first of these coefficients, the electrical conductance, measured under zero flow conditions was found to be

$$C = \frac{\sigma A}{l}\left[1 + \frac{2\sigma_w}{r_1\sigma}\right], \tag{9-63}$$

where σ is the electrical conductivity of the bulk fluid, σ_w the surface conductivity of the tube walls, A the open cross-sectional area of the tube bank, l the length of the tube bank, and r_1 the tube radius.

The resistance to the fluid flow is

$$R_f = 8\zeta l/(r_1^2 A), \tag{9-64}$$

which will be recognized as the ordinary Poiseuille resistance; in this equation ζ is the fluid viscosity.

The coupling coefficient α was found by an application of the Onsager relation, under the assumption that the charge density and potential are related by Poisson's equation, to yield

$$\alpha = \frac{16\epsilon}{r_1^4}\left\{\int_0^{r_o} r\psi\, dr - \frac{\psi_w r_1^2}{2}\right\}, \tag{9-65}$$

where ϵ is the fluid permittivity, ψ the component of the voltage as defined by

$$V = \frac{l - x}{l}\Delta V + \psi(r) \tag{9-66}$$

and ψ_w is simply the value of ψ found on the tube walls. We will now examine the role these three coefficients play in the operation of the device.

In the Appendix we classify devices as either even or odd, coupled or uncoupled. An even class device is one in which the output force is induced by the input force, whereas an odd class device is one in which the output force is induced by the input flux. We now define the electrokinetic energy converter as an even class coupled device—that is, the output voltage is induced by an input force of a pressure differential; the pressure differential and voltage rise are, of course, coupled through the interaction of the fluid and electrical effects. Equations 2-36 and 2-37 describe such a device

$$X_o = \alpha_1 X_i - R_1 J_o, \tag{2-36}$$

$$J_i = C_1 X_i + \alpha_1 J_o. \tag{2-37}$$

Osterle found the coefficients that describe the electrokinetic energy converter in terms of C, R_f, and α, as given by Eqs. 9-63, 9-64, and 9-65, to be

$$\Delta V = \frac{\beta}{\alpha(1 + \beta)}\Delta p - \frac{1}{C(1 + \beta)}I, \tag{9-67}$$

$$i = \frac{1}{R_f(1 + \beta)}\Delta p + \frac{\beta}{\alpha(1 + \beta)}I, \tag{9-68}$$

where

$$\beta = \frac{\alpha^2}{R_f C}, \tag{9-69}$$

a quantity in some respects analogous to the figure of merit of a thermoelectric generator.

The coefficient of Δp in Eq. 9-67 is recognized as the so-called streaming potential S. Its classical value, as implied by Helmholtz, is given by

$$S = \frac{\epsilon(-\psi_w)}{\zeta\sigma}, \tag{9-70}$$

with ψ_w negative for a positive charge density in the fluid. Oldham et al. [26] have shown this to be a valid equation in capillaries of radii down to about 10^{-5} m. Tubes finer than this would be all but impossible to fabricate. Equation 9-70 can also be derived from the defining equations presented earlier and the definition of β, the so-called figure of merit.

We now consider the simplification of the descriptive Eqs. 9-67 and 9-68. We do this in several steps. First we assume that ψ is very nearly zero everywhere but quite near the tube wall, so that Eq. 9-65 becomes

$$\alpha = \frac{8\epsilon(-\psi_w)}{r_1^2}. \qquad (9\text{-}71)$$

If we neglect the contribution of surface conductance to C (as a consequence of r_1 being not too small), Eqs. 9-71, 9-63, and 9-64 inserted into Eq. 9-69 yield

$$\beta = \frac{8\epsilon^2\psi_w^2}{\zeta\sigma r_1^2}. \qquad (9\text{-}72)$$

Finally, we assume that β is much less than unity (this will be verified later); the streaming potential becomes β/α which from Eqs. 9-71 and 9-72 is the same as the value given by Eq. 9-70. We will consider that the validation afforded Eq. 9-70 by experiments justifies the assumptions we have just made to derive it. Therefore, we will continue to use these assumptions in the derivation which follows.

Equations 9-67 and 9-68, which govern the generation mode, now become

$$\Delta V = S\,\Delta p - (1/C)I, \qquad (9\text{-}73)$$

$$i = (1/R_f)\,\Delta p + SI. \qquad (9\text{-}74)$$

For a fixed Δp, the flow rate has a minimum value when $I = 0$ and a maximum value when $\Delta V = 0$. The ratio of the maximum value to the minimum value is easily shown to be $1 + \beta$. Thus by our assumption that β is much less than unity, the flow rate is essentially independent of the current, and Eq. 9-74 reduces to

$$i = \Delta p/R_f. \qquad (9\text{-}75)$$

The equations describing the operation of the generator may now be written as

$$\Delta V = \frac{\epsilon(-\psi_w)}{\zeta\sigma}\Delta p - \frac{l}{\sigma A}I, \qquad (9\text{-}76)$$

$$i = \frac{Ar_1^2}{8\zeta l}\,\Delta p. \qquad (9\text{-}77)$$

We may summarize some of the converter's operating characteristics for a fixed applied pressure difference as follows:

$$\text{zero-current voltage} = \frac{\epsilon(-\psi_w)}{\zeta\sigma}\Delta p,$$

$$\text{zero-voltage current} = \frac{A\epsilon(-\psi_w)}{\zeta l}\Delta p.$$

Because of the linearity between the voltage and current, the maximum power output of the converter occurs when the voltage is one-half the zero-current voltage and consequently the current is one-half the zero-voltage current. It is given by the product of this current and voltage:

$$\text{Maximum power generated} = \frac{A\epsilon^2\psi_w^2}{4\zeta^2\sigma l}(\Delta p)^2.$$

The maximum generating efficiency is found by dividing the above power by the product of the assumed pressure difference times the resulting flow rate:

$$\text{Maximum generating efficiency} = \frac{2\epsilon^2\psi_w^2}{\zeta\sigma r_1^2}.$$

To obtain numerical values for the pump and generator characteristics it is necessary to specify the working fluid. In Table 9-2 we tabulate some

TABLE 9-2. PROPERTIES OF MATERIALS SUITABLE FOR USE IN ELECTROKINETIC CONVERTERS[†]

Fluid	ζ (nt-sec/m²)	σ [(ohm-m)$^{-1}$]	ψ_w (volts)	β
Water	1×10^{-3}	1×10^{-4}	-0.20	1.57×10^{-2}
Methyl alcohol	5.97×10^{-4}	7×10^{-4}	-0.123	2.7×10^{-4}
Ethyl alcohol	1.2×10^{-3}	3.3×10^{-4}	-0.170	2.6×10^{-4}
Acetone	3.26×10^{-4}	5×10^{-8}	-0.230	8.7×10^{-2}
n-propyl alcohol	2.26×10^{-3}	4×10^{-8}	-0.139	4.8×10^{-3}
Mercury	1.5×10^{-3}	$9.8 \times 10^{+3}$	$-$[‡]	7.6×10^{-12}

† Refs. [24] and [25].
‡ No data available.

experimental data from the literature, Refs. [24], [25]. The value ψ_w for water is from [24], where it is indicated that ψ_w can approach -0.20 volts for pure water in equilibrium with atmospheric carbon dioxide where the ions are believed to be H^+ and HCO_3^- and is somewhat less for aqueous solutions. If salts are present in the water, they tend to decrease ϵ and increase the conductivity and viscosity, resulting in pure water having the highest efficiency when compared with water that has been contaminated. For pure water the permittivity ϵ has a value of about 7×10^{-10} coulomb per volt-m.

As an illustrative example we might consider a converter made up of tubes with an inside radius of 10^{-5} m, an open cross-sectional area $A = 10^{-2}$ m², and length $l = 10^{-2}$ m, which operates with water as the working fluid. If we apply a pressure difference of 10^5 newtons per m² (about 1 atm) the generator will have the following characteristics:

Zero-current voltage:	140 volts
Zero-voltage current:	0.014 amp
Maximum electrical power:	0.49 watt
Fluid flow rate:	1.25 liters/sec
Pumping power input:	125 watts
Maximum efficiency:	0.392 percent.

Thus the performance of this type of converter is seen to be far from outstanding; prospects for improvement in performance do not appear particularly bright.

9.3.3 Piezoelectric converters. The Greek-derived word *piezoelectricity* (pronounced pie-ease-oh-electricity) meaning "pressure electricity" describes an effect that was discovered in 1880 by the brothers Pierre and Jacques Curie. This effect can convert mechanical energy to electrical energy and, conversely, electrical energy to mechanical energy in some types of crystals [27].

The Curie brothers, who had long been interested in crystallography, noticed that certain crystals, such as rock salt, were highly symmetrical, whereas others showed a low order of symmetry. They believed that some types of asymmetrical crystals might, when compressed in particular directions, liberate electric charges, positive on one side, negative on the other; that is, such crystals would become electrically polarized when compressed. They verified their prediction on a great many substances and found the effect most pronounced in materials such as quartz, tourmaline, and Rochelle salt. More recently, certain ceramic materials, such as barium titanate and lead zirconate–lead titanate, have been found to yield very high piezoelectric outputs; these materials, moreover, can be easily molded or pressed into a variety of shapes previously unattainable with single crystals.

Piezoelectricity is observed only in asymmetrical crystals because in noncrystalline materials and in the more symmetrical types of crystals the charges tend to be displaced in opposite directions; therefore, pressure produces no external electrical effect in them. Crystals of low symmetry, however, have a tendency for their valence electrons to be squeezed in one direction. Of the thirty-two classes of crystals known to crystallographers, twenty lack enough symmetry to be piezoelectric.

The piezoelectric energy converter usually consists of a ceramic disc to which external energy is applied in the form of a force moving through a distance. The equivalent circuit illustrated in Fig. 9-18 shows the stressed crystal replaced by a generator, an internal capacitance C, and a resistance R; the generator has an output voltage V. The load capacitance is C_o and has a resistance R_o with a voltage V_o across it. Because of the nature of this type of generator the resistance R and R_o must be very high (greater than 10^{12}

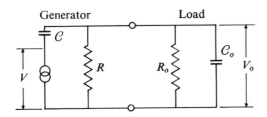

FIG. 9-18. Equivalent circuit of a piezoelectric generator and its load.

ohms) and thus the time constant in the R-$\mathcal{C}$ circuit is very long; for this reason the effect of the resistances can be neglected in the analysis.

The index that measures how well the crystal converts mechanical energy to electrical energy is the electromechanical coupling coefficient† k_{33}. It is defined as

$$k_{33}^2 = \frac{W_{\text{out}}}{W_{\text{in}}} = \frac{\text{electrical energy stored}}{\text{mechanical energy applied}}. \tag{9-78}$$

The mechanical energy applied may be calculated by taking the product of the force applied times the average distance that the crystal is displaced:

$$W_{\text{in}} = \tfrac{1}{2} F \, \Delta l. \tag{9-79}$$

Multiplying both sides of Eq. 9-79 by the product FA^2l and solving for W_{in} we obtain

$$W_{\text{in}} = \frac{1}{2} \times \frac{F^2/A^2}{\dfrac{F/A}{\Delta l/l}} \times Al.$$

F/A is just the stress s, and the stress divided by the strain $\Delta l/l$ is Young's modulus Y, and Al is the volume of the crystal Ω, so we may write the above equation as

$$W_{\text{in}} = \frac{1}{2} \frac{s^2}{Y} \Omega. \tag{9-80}$$

We may also write Eq. 9-80 as

$$W_{\text{in}} = \frac{1}{2} \frac{F^2 l}{YA}. \tag{9-81}$$

The electrical energy stored in the capacitance is simply the integral of the voltage-charge product,

$$\int dW = \int V \, dQ.$$

† The piezoelectric constants are generally written as tensor components with the usual double subscript. Thus d_{33}, g_{33}, k_{33} measure the electrical effects in the longitudinal or z direction caused by a stress in the same direction. In a direct energy conversion device the longitudinal direction is used, so we will concern ourselves only with these coefficients.

The voltage is related to the charge through the capacitance

$$V = \frac{Q}{\mathcal{C}}$$

and so

$$\int dW = \frac{1}{\mathcal{C}} \int_0^Q Q \, dQ,$$

which yields immediately upon integration

$$W_{\text{out}} = \tfrac{1}{2} Q^2 / \mathcal{C}. \tag{9-82}$$

Substituting Eqs. 9-81 and 9-82 into Eq. 9-78 yields

$$\tfrac{1}{2} Q^2 / \mathcal{C} = \tfrac{1}{2} k_{33}^2 F^2 l / (YA). \tag{9-83}$$

The capacity of a parallel plate capacitor is given by

$$\mathcal{C} = \epsilon_0 \mathcal{K} A / l, \tag{9-84}$$

where ϵ_0 is the permittivity of free space and $\mathcal{K}$ is the dielectric constant. Substitution of Eq. 9-84 into Eq. 9-83 yields the net charge displaced per unit force

$$Q/F = d_{33} = [k_{33}^2 \mathcal{K} \epsilon_0 / Y]^{1/2} \tag{9-85}$$

or

$$Q = d_{33} F. \tag{9-86}$$

The generator voltage is found by using the relationship between charge, capacitance, and voltage to obtain

$$V = d_{33} F / \mathcal{C} \tag{9-87}$$

or

$$V = d_{33} F l / (\epsilon_0 \mathcal{K} A). \tag{9-88}$$

The piezoelectric constant g_{33} measures the electric field produced by a given stress and is found by combining Eqs. 9-85 and 9-88 to yield

$$g_{33} = [k_{33}^2 / (\epsilon_0 \mathcal{K} Y)]^{1/2}. \tag{9-89}$$

Thus g_{33} and d_{33} are related through the dielectric constant of the material

$$g_{33} = d_{33} / (\epsilon_0 \mathcal{K}). \tag{9-90}$$

Upon combining Eqs. 9-88 and 9-90 we obtain the generator voltage

$$V = g_{33} l s. \tag{9-91}$$

From the equivalent circuit the output voltage across the load may be shown to be

$$V_o = \frac{V \mathcal{C}}{\mathcal{C}_o + \mathcal{C}}. \tag{9-92}$$

Some properties of interest for different ceramic materials are given in Table 9-3. These data, as well as the form of the preceding derivation, are taken from Ref. [28].

TABLE 9-3. PROPERTIES OF PIEZOELECTRIC CERAMICS†

Constant	Ceramic "B"	PZT-4	PZT-5
k_{33} (dimensionless)	0.48	0.70	0.71
d_{33} (coulomb/newton)	149×10^{-12}	285×10^{-12}	374×10^{-12}
g_{33} (volt-m/newton)	14.0×10^{-3}	24.9×10^{-3}	24.8×10^{-3}
Y_{33} (newton/m²)	11.1×10^{10}	6.6×10^{10}	5.3×10^{10}
$\mathcal{K}_{33}$ (dimensionless)	1200	1300	1700

† From Ref. [28].

With these constants it is possible to calculate the theoretical output of a piezoelectric generator. In Fig. 9-19 we give experimental results taken from Ref. [28] that show the effect of load capacitance on output voltage at low stress. Voltage and force are seen to be linearly related just as was

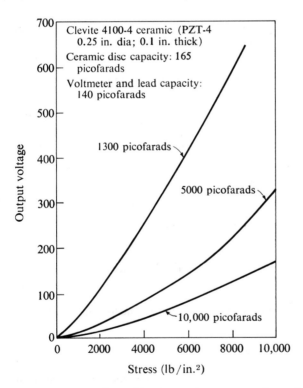

FIG. 9-19. The effect of load capacitance on output voltage as a function of the applied stress. After Ref. [28].

predicted in our derivation. The chief limitation to the use of piezoelectric converters is the charge that is displaced in a single application of a force. Using the data from Fig. 9-19 and the relationship $Q = eV$ we find the quantity of charge stored shown in Fig. 9-20; it is seen to be no more than 20×10^{-7} coulombs.

As a generator, the piezoelectric effect is useful at low power levels for measurement of force or pressure; however, at very low frequencies and power levels, current drawn by the measuring circuit and leakage in the circuit can neutralize the voltage generated by the element. For this reason piezoelectric elements have not been widely used for measuring forces that change slowly. It has distinct advantages, however, for the measurement of dynamic pressures such as those generated in measuring surface irregularities, accelerations, forces, and blast pressures. Details of applications, electrical characteristics, and relevant crystallography theory are presented in Cady [29].

Like the other methods of producing high voltages previously discussed, piezoelectric devices do not yield high currents. However, the theoretical output of a 1-cu in. spark pump type device such as might be used in an engine ignition system is about 30 watts with an applied stress of 15,000 lb per sq in. at 60 cycles per sec. Power capacity increases with frequency but this is limited by the capability of the mechanical driving system. An ideal mechanical design could yield at least 120 watts per cu in. of element.

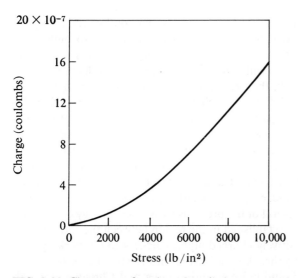

FIG. 9-20. Charge as a function of applied stress calculated from $Q = CV$ from the data of Fig. 9-19. After Ref. [28].

Reference [28] describes the design of a hand-operated generator that is to be used to charge a radiation detection device called a dosimeter. Because the unit is designed to be used under disaster conditions after a long storage period, no external power supply was considered permissible. The final design has an external case volume of about 32 cu in. and yields a maximum charge output of 8×10^{-7} coulombs between 0 and 200 volts direct current with a torque input of 10 in.-lb. The volume of the working element is about 0.005 cu in.

The piezoelectric effect has also found use in a device that converts electrical energy to mechanical motion in implantable hearts and heart-assist devices. In endurance tests these devices have run well over a billion cycles without failure or degradation of properties. Overall efficiency of these devices are on the order of 35 to 40 percent [30].

9.4 CONVERSION OF RADIATION ENERGY TO ELECTRICITY

This section contains brief discussions of several methods of converting radiation energy to electricity. We have divided these methods into two classes: (1) direct charging devices used primarily for power production purposes, and (2) secondary particle collection devices used primarily in nuclear instrumentation work.

9.4.1 Direct charging devices. In this section we will outline the principles of operation of devices that utilize fission particles directly to build up a potential. They appear to have several advantages—the chief one being their inherent simplicity. We will consider four types: the alpha particle triode, the fission electric cell, the beta battery, and the gamma battery.

Plummer and Anno [31] have published results that indicate that the kinetic energy of an alpha particle might be converted directly into a high electrical potential. Their device is called a triode because it consists of an emitter, a grid, and a collector. A schematic of the arrangement used is shown in Fig. 9-21. A source material such as polonium 210 or other high-energy alpha emitter, is distributed in a thin layer over the surface of the cathode. The collector surface where a positive potential will be built up is called the anode. As in several of the previously discussed energy converters, an electric field is quickly established in the region between the cathode and anode, requiring the positively charged alpha particles to do work against this field, thus converting their kinetic energy into electrical energy.

Mosely [32] in 1913, and more recently Linder and Christian [33] real-

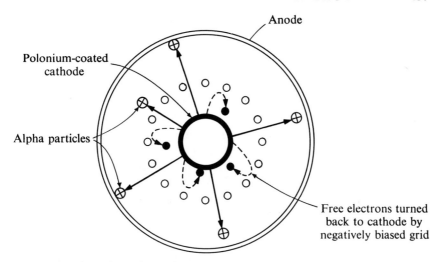

FIG. 9-21. Plan view of a cylindrical alpha particle energy converter.

ized that the emission of charged particles can build up a voltage on a properly insulated electrode. One of the problems that held back these earlier investigators was that along with the alpha particles, secondary electrons, which carry an opposite charge, are also emitted. These low-energy electrons (97 percent have energy less than 100 eV) are produced in such abundance that their total negative charge more than offsets the positive charge buildup. Under passive conditions a low-energy net negative charge rather than the desired high-energy positive charge is emitted from the cathode. To overcome this problem Plummer and Anno have suggested the insertion of a grid that can be biased negatively, thus repelling the secondary electrons back to the cathode. The grid can be so designed that it intercepts only a small fraction of the alpha particles emitted from the cathode.

Some of the problems that must be overcome before this type of converter becomes practical include: (1) electron escape from the grid to the anode; (2) attenuation of the charge and energy of the alpha particles as they leave the emitter surface; (3) ionization of the residual gas between electrodes; (4) loss of alpha-emitter material as the alpha particles emerge from the surface; (5) attaining and maintaining high voltages in the presence of alpha particle bombardment, and (6) the safety and containment requirements associated with kilocurie quantities of alpha emitters.

Hoped-for performance for this type of device includes operation at an average potential of 10^6 volts with charging currents of about 10^{-7} amp per cm^2 yielding a power output of 0.1 watt per cm^2 of cathode area. Experimental work carried out to date has shown that a potential of 50,000 volts could be obtained with a grid potential of -800 volts. While the early experimental work proves the principle of operation, the numerous practical problems that remain to be solved place formidable obstacles in the path of alpha particle kinetic energy conversion.

Another type of direct conversion device that is similar to the alpha triode is the fission electric cell, which has been described by Heindl, Krieve, and Meghreblian [34]. This type of device has been considered for use as a source of high voltage for electric propulsion systems in space vehicles.

A fission electric cell configuration closely resembles the configuration of an alpha triode. When bombarded with neutrons, the thin fissionable layer of material that covers the inner cylinder cathode of the two concentric tubes yields fission fragments, some of which penetrate the fuel layer, cross the vacuum gap, and strike the anode collector. Each fission fragment carries, on the average, about twenty positive charges with a mean kinetic energy of 80 MeV. Ideally, continued open circuit operation should yield an electrical potential of about a million volts. It is well to keep in mind the distinction between this type of cell and the alpha triode; the fission fragment cell must be located where it may be subjected to neutron bombardment to cause fission fragment ejection from the fuel layer.

Some of the requirements and problems of this type of converter will now be given. The fuel layer must be thin enough to allow the heavy highly charged fission fragments to escape. The vacuum between cathode and anode must be sufficient to insure that ionization of residual gas by fission fragments or electrons liberated by the fission fragments do not create a significant neutralizing current. Suppression of this current may be attained by biased grids or magnetic fields. Cells must be constructed that can sustain operation at high fuel-burnup levels without suffering damage to the fuel layer or the electrodes. None of the cells yet constructed has generated voltages near the design value; each succeeding experimental refinement, however, has been rewarded with an increased voltage buildup. It is believed that useful cells can be constructed provided that solutions to the problems discussed in the previous paragraph can be obtained.

Advantage has also been taken of the beta decay of krypton 85 to produce what is called a beta battery [35]. This source of high-energy electrons is confined in a glass sphere in which an electrode has been inserted. On the outside of the thin glass walls of the sphere is another concentric sphere—this is made of metal and serves as the collector electrode.

Krypton 85 was chosen as the energy source because of safety considerations: the gas is not metabolized by the body, it diffuses and is rapidly diluted in the atmosphere. Further, the gas can provide electrons with sufficient energy to pass through the glass dielectric walls. It has a half-life of 10.4 yr, is inexpensive, and easily handled.

Since krypton 85 produces a constant current, this current may be used to charge a capacitor, thus storing a relatively large amount of energy. Equilibrium potentials of 10,000 volts can be attained by the battery, but in practice they usually are operated at 1000 volts at currents near 10^{-9} amp.

These batteries, now produced commercially, are especially useful in making simple and reliable timing circuits. In order to maintain a power supply voltage at the selected value, a cold cathode diode and resistor may be connected in parallel with a capacitor as shown in Fig. 9-22. Such a power supply is a pulse-source of electrical energy for firing detonators or for impulse-counting devices or pulse-operation of relays. Length of time between discharges may be calculated from the familiar relationship between voltage, current, capacitance, and time.

$$V = It/\mathcal{C}. \tag{9-93}$$

The primary source of inaccuracy in the length of a timing period is the predictable decrease in battery current with decay of the radioactive isotope. The temperature coefficient of the capacitor and variation in diode breakdown voltage also affect accuracy, but to a lesser extent. This decrease in battery current can be compensated for by introducing a constant current component, such as an ion chamber, in the circuit.

Recently, renewed interest has been shown in the beta cell [36]. The newer devices utilize one or two slabs of promethium oxide in contact with the surface or surfaces of a slicon n/p diode. The device studied in Ref. [36] is illustrated in Fig. 9-23. The n-type region of the diode is a shallow, diffused layer about 0.8×10^{-6} m thick of highly doped material—on the order of 10^{20} atoms/cm^3. The reason for using n-on-p instead of p-on-n

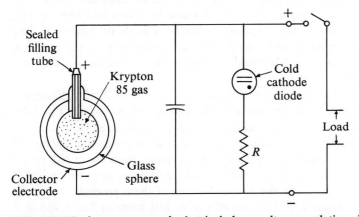

FIG. 9-22. Nuclear power supply that includes a voltage regulation circuit consisting of a cold cathode diode and resistor. When the switch is closed, a pulse is delivered to the load. Time required to recharge the supply depends on the value of the capacitance, the voltage across the capacitor, and the current supplied by the nuclear battery.

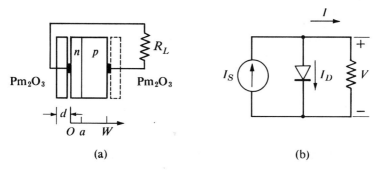

FIG. 9-23. (a) A beta-voltaic cell showing its physical arrangement with slabs of promethium oxide on either one side or both sides of the *p-n* junction. (b) The equivalent circuit of the beta-voltaic cell. After Ref. [36].

diodes is to make use of the higher minority (electron) lifetimes and diffusion coefficient in the *p*-type silicon substrate where most of the carriers are generated. The optimum substrate resistivity was found to be around 0.3 ohm-cm. Cell efficiencies of between 0.5 and 2.5 percent were found when source activity was on the order of 1.5 curie/cm².

Progress made in the design and construction of nuclear-powered or activated sources for special applications has been good; these devices will, no doubt, find wide application where simple, long-lived, low level energy pulses are required.

The last type of direct charging device we will discuss is the gamma battery, which has been proposed for the shield of megawatt reactors in space. The gamma battery has been discussed by Gross and Murphy [37] and the proposal for space application has been made by Raab [38]. The space application has been based on the assumption that a large radiation shield that does nothing but shield is a luxury that cannot be tolerated in a space situation.

The basic converter unit would consist of an assembly of high-atomic-number (Z) and low-atomic-number materials stacked as shown in Fig. 9-24. Gamma rays in Compton collisions (see Ch. 3 for an extended discussion of collisions between photons and electrons) would interact with the high-Z anode causing electrons to be ejected, which move from the anode to the cathode. Fast neutrons, on the other hand, produce protons in the low-Z cathodes, which travel to the anode. Neither of these processes results in significant attenuation of the gamma-ray or fast neutron fluxes within a single cell: thus many cells would have to be stacked and connected in parallel electrically to produce appreciable shielding or power output. The third component of radiation, slow neutrons, will be converted to high-energy electrons by being absorbed in a material that transmutes to a beta-decaying isotope with a short half-life. These electrons accumulate on the cathode.

Theoretical calculations indicate that in the SNAP 2 system, which is

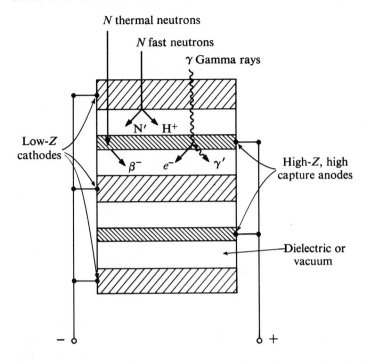

FIG. 9-24. Reactor radiation shown interacting with an active shield to create a potential across the parallel-connected anode and cathode.

expected to develop about 3 kW of electric power from 50 kW of thermal power, 100 lb of active shield could produce about 35 watts of electrical power (more than enough power, for example, to operate small transmitters and recording equipment).

9.4.2 Secondary particle collection devices. In this section we will consider briefly some energy conversion devices that are used almost exlcusively in instrumentation. They are included here simply because in many cases in the past instrumentation devices have evolved into power-producing devices; thermoelectric and thermionic equipment are two cases where this statement has proved true.

The first device we will consider is an ionization chamber [39] that can be used to detect secondary particles; these are particles created by primary radiation in the walls of the chamber, or primary radiation such as would occur if an alpha particle emitter were placed in the chamber. In essence, an ionization chamber is a gas-filled container such that, after it has been exposed to radiation, the degree of ionization in the gas can be measured by collecting the charge produced. Figure 9-25 gives a schematic for such a device.

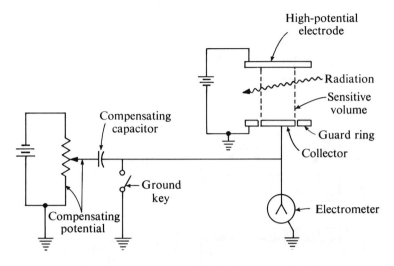

FIG. 9-25. Typical ionization chamber consists of a collector, guard ring, and accelerating electrode.

Since ions are formed by radiation in the sensitive volume between the collector and the high potential electrode, the half of them that have a sign opposite to that of the potential applied to the electrode are accelerated toward the collector. The result is a current that flows from the high-potential electrode to the collector by means of the ions. This current is generally in the range of 10^{-12} to 10^{-14} amp.

The current is measured by opening the ground key which displaces the electrometer from its zero position. By adjusting the compensating potential the electrometer may be returned to the zero position and kept there. The plate of the compensating capacitor acquires the charge falling on the collector. The collector remains at ground potential and the electrometer remains at zero. The magnitude of the current is determined from the time required for the compensating potential to advance to a value V, and the capacitance of the compensating capacitor $\mathcal{C}$. These quantities are all related through Eq. 9-93. The guard ring is to help define precisely the volume from which ions are collected and to isolate the collector from the potential applied to the high-potential electrode so that leakage across insulators does not add to the ionization current flowing to the electrometer.

Another secondary particle device is the p–n junction. We have in Ch. 5, treated extensively the subject of power production from p–n junctions exposed to visible light. It should also be noted, however, that alpha, beta, or gamma radiation will produce hole-electron pairs in semi-conductors; if the pairs are produced in the neighborhood of a junction, they may be collected for use in an external circuit just as are those produced by optical excitation.

One of the chief advantages of atomic-powered batteries is that they will produce power even if the sun is not available.

Pure beta emitters appear well suited as to range and energy, not requiring heavy external shielding. This type of radiation is strongly absorbed, the range for 0.5-MeV betas in germanium being 0.03 cm; a few emitters of this type have reasonably high energy, activity, and half-life. Gamma rays, by various processes, give rise to betas, which in turn produce electron-hole pairs. Even though gammas are not strongly absorbed, their use in combination with other beta and gamma emitters appears feasible for certain applications. Alpha particles can produce electron-hole pairs, and a few sheets of paper will provide adequate shielding; however, their use may be less desirable because of the damage they inflict on the lattice. Selective filtering of higher energy alpha particles may reduce radiation damage at a cost of reduced efficiency.

While beta radiation of high energy is desirable from the viewpoints of power and efficiency, a limit is imposed by the threshold energy for radiation damage. One way out of this dilemma is to use beta emitters that have maximum energy less than the threshold energy. Annealing the cells after they have incurred radiation damage can also be used to restore most of their original performance characteristics. Design of p–n junction converters powered by radioactive sources is similar to that described previously for the solar converter, once the radiation protection problems for humans and semiconductor materials have been solved.

Wide application has now been made of p–n junction devices as detectors for charged particles. In fact, this is now one of their most common uses. Taylor [40] gives an excellent review and survey of semiconductor particle detectors. A schematic of a p–n junction detector circuit is given in Fig. 9-26.

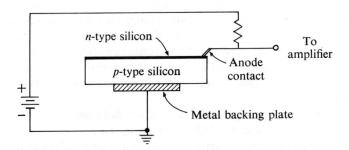

FIG. 9-26. A silicon *p-n* junction charged particle detector. The junction is operated under reverse bias; the *n*-type surface is heavily doped so that the face layer is of relatively low resistance.

The production of an electron-hole pair in silicon requires about 3.6 eV. A 10-MeV particle creates about 2.8×10^6 electron-hole pairs, which are initially distributed along the track of the particle and then move under the influence of the applied field. The number of carriers produced is closely proportional to the energy lost and is independent of the nature of the particle; this type of detector, therefore, can give excellent linearity with energy provided that all of the carriers are collected. Junction detectors are, of course, photosensitive and thus their faces must be kept in darkness. While the manufacture of these detectors is relatively staightforward, there are certain precautions and techniques that must be used in their production. These are clearly set forth in the previously cited Ref. [40].

The last type of secondary particle device we will mention is the bulk conductivity detector. These devices, which usually employ semiconductors, are described in Refs. [40] and [41]. Junction devices, which were described in the preceding paragraphs, are generally unsatisfactory for detecting gamma rays, both single photons and fluxes. A better device is the bulk photoconductivity detector, which consists of a homogeneous semiconductor material that is relatively thick.

In this type device, an ionizing particle is absorbed in a material such as silicon in 10^{-12} to 10^{-11} sec and its energy is almost entirely dissipated. Since the mean energy required to produce an electron-hole pair is almost independent of incident-particle energy, the current pulse size is a direct measure of the energy lost (assuming the charge can be separated and collected). If the particle is completely stopped, pulse size is directly proportional to total particle energy.

9.5 FUSION POWER

The problem of obtaining controlled power from the hydrogen bomb reaction is under intensive study in many parts of the world. Because every other source of energy in use today that produces substantial amounts of power is exhaustible, including fission, the solution to the problem of harnessing nuclear fusion could well be the most significant research problem that man has faced. In addition to using an unlimited source of fuel (deuterium, which is as inexhaustible as the oceans), it produces no appreciable amounts of radioactive by-products.

Nuclear fusion is not a new phenomenon: it has been generating the power of the sun and other stars for billions of years. To generate a sustained, controlled fusion reaction on earth, however, is a problem of a totally different order from that of harnessing the fission reaction.

Physicists in the twenties and thirties, working with particle accelerators, found that by accelerating protons (hydrogen nuclei) and other light nuclei to very high energies (many thousands of electron volts) they could break through the nuclear electrical repulsion forces and cause the projectiles to fuse with light nuclei in the target. This fusion releases energy because part of the mass of the fusing nuclei is transformed into energy according to Einstein's famous equation ε = mass $\times$ (velocity of light)^2. To cause a few nuclei to fuse requires a great deal of energy and there can be no net energy yield unless the reaction is made self-sustaining.

To obtain a continuing fusion reaction requires the same three conditions required in a chemical fuel reaction: (1) the fuel must be raised to its ignition point; (2) there must be enough of it to sustain a continuing reaction; (3) the energy released must be tapped in a controlled manner. The great difference between a fusion reaction and a chemical fuel reaction is that the ignition point is rather high—hundreds of millions of degrees Kelvin.

Currently the most promising reaction for harnessing fusion is the deuterium-tritium reaction. A deuterium atom reacts with a tritium atom to form a charged particle, He^4, with a kinetic energy of 3.5 MeV and a neutron with a kinetic energy of 14.1 MeV:

$$D + T = He^4(3.5 \text{ MeV}) + n(14.1 \text{ MeV}). \qquad (9\text{-}94)$$

The high energy neutron is slowed in a blanket which surrounds the plasma, and its kinetic energy is turned into heat. Depending on the design scheme used the charged particle's kinetic energy may be either utilized in a direct energy conversion device, for plasma heating or for blanket wall heating. Figure 9-27 illustrates the basic features of a fusion reactor.

Because tritium does not occur naturally it is necessary in the deuterium-tritium reaction to breed tritium in the blanket. The lithium reactions that can occur in the blanket are:

$$n + Li^6 \rightarrow T + He^4 + 4.6 \text{ MeV} \qquad (9\text{-}95)$$

$$n + Li^7 \rightarrow n^1 + T + He^4 - 2.47 \text{ MeV} \qquad (9\text{-}96)$$

The blanket must contain lithium and integrate three principal functions of a D-T system:

(1) The regeneration of tritium;

(2) The conversion of the neutron's kinetic energy to thermal energy and then making this energy available by fluid flow or other means to a power plant;

(3) The structure must be consistent with good neutron economy and high tritium breeding that will serve at the same time as an adequate enclosure for the heat transfer fluid. This last requirement of containment has proved to be the most difficult of all.

If the particles in the plasma are allowed to bounce off the walls of a

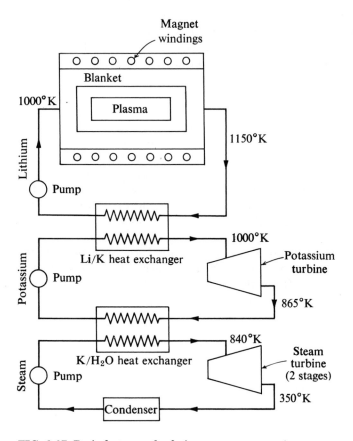

FIG. 9-27. Basic features of a fusion reactor power plant.

confining vessel two things happen that will automatically stop the fusion reaction. First, the plasma particles will be cooled immediately and quench the reaction and secondly, the particle impact on the walls will sputter off wall material which would increase plasma radiation loss and further accelerate plasma cooling. The problem of the quenching walls led to the concept of confining the plasma by the use of a magnetic field. That is, the lines of force of a magnetic field can be used to hold the hot, ionized plasma in a magnetic bottle. References [42], [43], [44], and [45] give good summaries of the numerous ingenious plans which have been proposed to trap the plasma.

Power could be extracted from the plasma generated in a fusion reactor in several ways. One system that has been proposed to utilize the deuterium-tritium reaction is one that turns the kinetic energy of the neutrons released into thermal energy by slowing them down and then transferring that thermal energy to a working fluid of an ordinary power plant. Some design parameters and cost estimates are presented in Refs. [43], [44], and [45].

Total world expenditure on controlled fusion research is still relatively small, but growing. The trend to higher budget allocations is partly due to the recent work of the Russians with their Tokamak machines. They have achieved plasma densities of 5×10^{13} particles/cm^3, temperatures of 10^{7}°K and confinement times of 20 milliseconds. These numbers may be placed in perspective by considering the goals that Werner *et al.* in Ref. [45] declare must be attained to achieve controlled fusion:

(1) Ion temperature must be at least 10^{8}°K.

(2) The particle density must be on the order of 10^{15} ions/cm^3.

(3) Confinement time with these densities must be in the range of a few tenths of a second. If greater densities are achieved confinement times can be correspondingly smaller.

The motivation for pursuing controlled fusion is not only technological and economic but is also social and environmental. The problem is simply how best to satisfy the rapidly growing worldwide demand for power. Ultimately some source of power must be found to replace our dwindling fossil fuel reserves and our not inexhaustible supply of fission fuels.

However there are a number of problem areas that must receive considerable attention before controlled fusion power will be a reality. In addition to containment these include: large complex magnet structures and their associated refrigeration systems; the injection and recovery of large amounts of high energy charged particles at high efficiency and low cost; the efficient generation and recovery of tritium and helium fuels; and the effective and efficient shielding of sensitive organisms and structures from very high energy radiation.

It is encouraging that at present none of these areas appears to pose problems that cannot be solved, given sufficient resources. Very significant progress has been made and much more can be accomplished by the application of developments now under way. In view of the immense benefits which would be derived from controlled fusion—in particular the important social, environmental and economic advantages which would be realized in its achievement—it is not only appropriate but essential that research toward this achievement be continued and intensified.

NOTATION

a	$= \mu^2 \delta / \gamma^2 \epsilon$, dimensionless
A	= area, m^2
b	= dimension, meters
B	= magnetic flux density, gauss
C	= conductance, (ohms)$^{-1}$

C_v	=	constant volume specific heat, joule/°K-m³
$\mathcal{C}$	=	capacitance, farad
d	=	dimension, meters
d_{33}	=	charge displaced per unit force, coulomb/newton
D	=	dielectric displacement, coulomb/m²
e	=	electronic charge, coulombs
E	=	electric field, volt/meter or volt/cm
$\mathcal{E}$	=	energy, electron volts, or joules
F	=	force, newtons
g_{33}	=	electric field per unit stress, volt-m/newton
i	=	flow rate, m³/sec
I	=	current, amp
J	=	current density, amp/m²
k	=	Boltzmann's constant, joule/°K
k_{33}	=	electromechanical coupling coefficient, dimensionless
K	=	thermal conductance, watts/°K
$\mathcal{K}$	=	dielectric constant, dimensionless
K_v	=	viscous friction coefficient, kg/sec
l	=	dimension, meters
m_e	=	electron mass, kg
m'	=	R_o/R, dimensionless
p	=	pressure, newton/m²
P_o	=	power output, watts
P'	=	Ettingshausen coefficient, °K-m/gauss-amp
q_E	=	Ettingshausen heat rate, watts
q_j	=	Joule heat rate, watts
q	=	heat rate, watts
Q'	=	Nernst coefficient, volt/gauss-°K
Q	=	charge on a capacitor, coulombs
$\bar{Q}$	=	heat, joules
r	=	radius, meters
r_l	=	reflectivity, dimensionless
R	=	electrical resistance, ohms
R_f	=	viscous resistance of fluid, newton-sec/m⁵
R_o	=	external load resistance, ohms
s	=	stress, newtons/m² or lb/in²
S	=	streaming potential, volts-m²/newton
t	=	time, sec
T	=	absolute temperature, °K
ΔT	=	temperature difference, K°
u	=	velocity, meter/sec
V	=	electrical potential, volts
W	=	work, joules
x	=	coordinate, meters
y	=	coordinate, meters
Y	=	Young's modulus, newton/m²
z	=	coordinate, meters
Z	=	atomic number
α	=	coupling coefficient defined by Eq. 9-65, coulomb/m³
β	=	figure of merit defined by Eq. 9-69, dimensionless
γ	=	correction factor
δ	=	fluid density, kg/m³

ϵ	= permittivity, farad/meter
ϵ_0	= permittivity of free space, farad/meter
ϵ_E	= defined by Eq. 9-7, volts
ζ	= viscosity, nt-sec/m²
η	= efficiency, dimensionless
η_{ca}	= Carnot efficiency, dimensionless
η_t	= thermal efficiency, dimensionless
θ	= Nernst generator figure of merit defined by Eq. 9-16, (°K)⁻¹
λ	= thermal conductivity, watt/m-°K
λ'	= wavelength, meters
μ	= mobility, m²/volt-sec or cm²/volt-sec
π	= 3.1416···
ρ	= space charge density, coulomb/m³
ρ_{el}	= electrical resistance, ohm-meter
σ	= electrical conductivity, (ohm-m)⁻¹
ϕ	= defined by Eq. 9-12, volts/°K
ψ	= voltage component defined by Eq. 9-66, volts
Ω	= volume, m³

Subscripts

av	= mean
B	= storage battery
C	= cold
d	= drift
e	= emitter
E	= Ettingshausen
g	= energy gap
h	= hydrodynamic
H	= hot
i	= ion
int	= internal
n	= electron
o	= load
opt	= optimum
p	= holes
r	= rejected
s	= supplied
w	= wall
y	= direction
1, 2, 3···	= states or position

PROBLEMS

9-1. Derive Eq. 9-15, which describes the thermal efficiency of the Nernst generator. For the maximum power case and fixed values of θ and T_C, plot the thermal efficiency as a function of T_C/T_H.

9-2. A Nernst generator operates between a sink temperature of 300°K and a source temperature of 600°K in the poles of a permanent magnet with a magnetic flux density of 10 kilogauss. The device's dimensions ratio is $l/d = 0.25$ while $b = 0.005$ meter. At the mean temperature the element made of InSb has the following properties: $Q' = 1.82 \times 10^{-8}$ volt per gauss-°K, $\rho_{el} = 1.33 \times 10^{-5}$ ohm-m, $\lambda = 11.5$ watt per m-°C. Find the value of the resistance ratio which maximizes the thermal efficiency, the corresponding external load resistance, and the power output, as well as the maximum thermal efficiency.

Answer: $P_o = 1.11$ watts; $\eta_t = 1.69$ percent.

9-3. Analyze the same device as described in Problem 9-2 for the case of maximum power output.

Answer: Wxz $= 735$ joules; $\eta_t = 1.57$ percent.

9-4. Derive an equation that corresponds to Eq. 9-18 for maximum power output.

9-5. Derive the net work of a ferroelectric energy converter, filling in the steps omitted in the text to obtain Eq. 9-28.

9-6. Consider a ferroelectric energy converter with a volume of 0.001 m³ operating between a temperature of 120°C and 140°C. The material of which it is made is barium titanate with the following properties: density, 5.5 gm per cm³; heat capacity, 0.1 cal per gm-°C. The low temperature dielectric displacement D is 0.25 coulomb per m². Find the net work (assuming the permittivity is independent of the displacement) and the thermal efficiency.

Answer: $W_{net} = 735$ joules; $\eta t = 1.57$ percent.

9-7. A TPV converter maintained at 50°C is made of germanium which is irradiated by a source at 2000°K. If the collection efficiency is 75 percent, what is this device's efficiency?

9-8. An electron in an electron convection converter has a mobility of 0.0300 m² per volt-sec in an electric field of 100 volt per meter. What is the viscous drag coefficient if the electron has reached terminal velocity? What is the electron's drift velocity?

9-9. If the gas in the electron convection converter of Problem 9-8 has a velocity of 5 meters per sec, what is this converter's efficiency as defined by Eq. 9-49? If this converter has a current density of 0.1 amp per cm² and an effective length l of 2 cm, what is the space charge and power density per square centimeter of emitter area?

9-10. What is the ion drag pressure gradient created in an EHD generator if it generates an electric field of 75,000 volts per cm with a uniform space charge of 0.1 coulomb per m³? If the fluid has a dielectric constant of 2.0, what is the gradient of the electric field?

Answer: $dE/dx = 5.66 \times 10^9$ volt/m².

9-11. Derive Eqs. 9-53 and 9-54.

9-12. In a certain EHD generator fluid is pumped at the rate of 2×10^{-2} m³ per sec in a pipe 2 cm in diameter; the fluid is silicone oil with a dielectric constant of 2.8, a mobility of 35×10^{-7} m² per volt-sec; we ignore the electric field at the ionizer. What is the electric field generated if the converter is 1 cm long and the current drawn is 10 microamp? What is the space charge density?

9-13. A liquid nitrogen ($\mathcal{K} = 1.5$, $\mu = 10^{-6}$ m² per volt-sec) EHD converter 0.2 cm long has fluid pumped through it at a velocity of 6 m per sec. What is the maximum current, voltage, and power output?

Answer: $P_{o(max)} = 480$ watts/m².

9-14. Assuming the insulating oil in the converter described in Problem 9-12 is very clean, what is the maximum efficiency possible from such a converter?

9-15. Consider the electrokinetic generator example solved in Section 9.3.2 with an applied pressure differential of 2 atm. How does this affect the performance characteristics of the generator?

9-16. For each of the fluids listed in Table 9-2, calculate the maximum generating power and efficiency if the tubes are 10^{-3} m long, the open cross-sectional area is 10^{-3} m², and the applied pressure differential is 5 atm. What is the magnitude of the coupling coefficient for each of these fluids if the tube radius is 10^{-5} m?

9-17. For each of the materials listed in Table 9-3, calculate the generator voltage for an applied stress of 7500 psi on an element 0.05 in. thick, 0.5 in. in diameter. Calculate the open circuit load voltage for these materials with a load capacity of 3000 picofarads and a generator capacity of 500 picofarads.

Answer: Load voltage (PZT-4) = 230 V.

9-18. For each generator analyzed in Problem 9-17 calculate the power output and current if the generators can be loaded at a rate of 120 cycles per sec. What is the power input to these generators?

Answer: P_o (PZT-4) = 7.8×10^{-2} watts.

9-19. Derive the descriptive equations of a piezoelectric generator as given by Eqs. 9-85, 9-88, 9-89, and 9-92.

9-20. The capacitance of the human body is roughly 3×10^{-11} farads. If the voltage between your fingers and a metal door knob is 750 volts, what is the energy released when a spark jumps the gap between your fingers and the knob?

Answer: 8×10^{-6} joules.

REFERENCES

1. T. C. Harman and J. M. Honig, "Theory of Galvano-Thermomagnetic Energy Conversion Devices. I. Generators," *Journal of Applied Physics*, 33 (1962), 3178–3188.

2. S. W. Angrist, "A Nernst Effect Power Generator," *Journal of Heat Transfer, Transactions of the ASME*, 85 (1963), Series C, 41–47.

3. A. W. Riddiford and J. A. Krumhansl, "A Model for a Diffusive Magnetothermoelectric Generator," *Journal of Applied Physics*, 34 (1963), 3572–3580.

4. S. W. Angrist, "Galvanomagnetic and Thermomagnetic Effects," *Scientific American*, 205 (1961), 124–136.

5. S. W. Angrist, "On the Boundedness of the Dimensionless Index of Performance of a Nernst Effect Generator," *Journal of Applied Mechanics, Transactions of the ASME*, 30 (1963), Series E, 291–294.

6. J. Colwell, G. Guthrie, and R. Palmer, *Static Energy Conversion Studies*, AD 411285 (Washington, D.C.: Office of Technical Services, U.S. Department of Commerce, 1963).

7. W. H. Clingman and R. G. Moore, Jr., "Application of Ferroelectricity to Energy Conversion Processes," *Journal of Applied Physics*, 32 (1961), 675–681.

8. J. F. Elliott, "Thermomagnetic Generator," *Journal of Applied Physics*, 30 (1959), 1774–1777.

9. Marvin Chester, "Thermodynamics of a Superconducting Energy Converter," *Journal of Applied Physics*, 33 (1962), 643–647.

10. J. D. Childress, "Application of a Ferroelectric Material in an Energy Conversion Device," *Journal of Applied Physics*, 33 (1962), 1793–1798.

11. D. C. White, B. D. Wedlock, and J. Blair, "Recent Advances in Thermal Energy Conversion," in *Proceedings 15th Annual Power Sources Conference* (Red Bank, New Jersey: PSC Publication Committee, 1962), pp. 125–132.

12. B. D. Wedlock, "Thermo-Photo-Voltaic Energy Conversion," *Proceedings of the IEEE*, 51 (1963), 694–698.

13. H. V. Watts, M. D. Oestreich, and R. J. Robinson, "A Nuclear Photon Energy Conversion Study," *Armour Research Foundation Quarterly Technical Report* ARF 1214-TR-2; 1 July 1962 to 30 September 1962; AD 286024.

14. S. R. Hoh and W. L. Harries, *Power Conversion by Electron Convection*, Technical Documentary Report No. ASD-TDR-62-693 (AD 291683), Washington, D.C.: Office of Technical Services, U.S. Department of Commerce, 1962).

15. Thomson, Sir William, "On a Self-Acting Apparatus for Multiplying and Maintaining Electric Charges, with Applications to Illustrate the Voltaic Theory," *Proceedings of the Royal Society*, June 20, 1867.

16. Joseph M. O'Byrne, "Electrostatic Voltage Generation From Flowing Water," *9th Intersociety Energy Conversion Engineering Conference*, 1974 Proceedings (New York: American Society of Mechanical Engineers, 1974).

17. A. P. Chattock, "On the Velocity and Mass of the Ions in the Electric Wind in Air," *Philosophical Magazine*, 48 (1899), 401–420.

18. O. M. Stuetzer, "Ion Drag Pumps," *Journal of Applied Physics*, 31 (1960), 136–146.

19. O. M. Stuetzer, "Electrohydrodynamic Components," *IRE Transactions on Component Parts*, CP-8 (1961), 57–64.

20. O. M. Stuetzer, "Ion Transport High Voltage Generators," *Review of Scientific Instruments*, 32 (1961), 16–22.

21. J. M. Smith, *Theoretical Study of the Electrohydrodynamic Generator*, General Electric TIS Report R61SD192 (1961).

22. J. M. Smith, *Electrohydrodynamic Power Generation-Experimental Studies*, General Electric TIS Report R62SD27 (1962).

23. M. O. Lawson, E. F. Fretter, and R. W. Griffith, "Report on Progress in Achieving Direct Conversion of a Major Fraction of Sonic Flow Kinetic Power into Electrical Power by Electrofluid Dynamic (EFD) Processes," *9th Intersociety Energy Conversion Engineering Conference*, 1974 Proceedings (New York: American Society of Mechanical Engineers, 1974).

24. J. F. Osterle, "Electrokinetic Energy Conversion," *Journal of Applied Mechanics, Transactions of the ASME*, 31 (1964), Series E, 161–164.

25. G. A. McLennan and J. F. Osterle, "Unconventional Methods for Influencing Fluid Flow, Part II, Electrokinetic Pumping," *Carnegie Institute of Technology Technical Report* No. AF APL-TR-64-143.

26. I. B. Oldham, F. J. Young, and J. F. Osterle, "Streaming Potential in Small Capillaries," *Journal of Colloid Science*, 18 (1963), 328–336.

27. Walter G. Cady, "Crystals and Electricity," *Scientific American*, 193 No. 12 (1949), 47–51.

28. R. Lehman and John Stirnkob, "Piezoelectric Charger CD V-751X," *Final Report Contract No. OCD-OS-62-83*, July, 1963; AD 412337.

29. Walter G. Cady, *Piezoelectricity* (New York: McGraw-Hill Book Company, Inc., 1946).

30. P. Smiley and C. G. O'Neill, "Development of an Implantable, Low Frequency Piezoelectric Driver for an Artificial Heart," *7th Intersociety Energy Conversion Engineering Conference*, 1972 Proceedings (Washington, D.C.: American Chemical Society, 1972).

31. A. M. Plummer and J. N. Anno, "Conversion of Alpha Particle Kinetic Energy into Electricity," in *AMU-ANL Conference on Direct Energy Conversion*, November 4-5, 1963 (Washington 25, D.C.: Office of Technical Services, U.S. Department of Commerce, 1964), pp. 170-180.

32. H. G. J. Moseley, "The Attainment of High Potentials by the Use of Radium," *Proceedings of the Royal Society*, 88 (1913), 471-476.

33. E. G. Linder and S. M. Christian, "The Use of Radioactive Material for the Generation of High Voltage," *Journal of Applied Physics*, 23 (1952), 1213-1216.

34. C. J. Heindl, W. F. Krieve, and R. V. Meghreblian, "Fission Fragment Conversion Reactors for Space," *Nucleonics*, 21, No. 4 (1963), pp. 80-85.

35. R. Perdreaux, "Nuclear Battery Applications," *Electro-Technology*, 69, No. 4 (1962), 152-154.

36. L. S. Wei, "Optimization of the Beta-Voltaic Cell," *9th Intersociety Energy Conversion Engineering Conference*, 1974 Proceedings (New York: American Society of Mechanical Engineers, 1974).

37. B. Gross and P. V. Murphy, "Currents from Gammas Make Detectors and Batteries," *Nucleonics*, 19, No. 3 (1961), 86-89.

38. B. Raab, "Power-Producing Shield for Space Reactors," *Nucleonics*, 21, No. 2 (1963), 46-47.

39. B. B. Rossi and H. H. Staub, *Ionization Chambers and Counters* (New York: McGraw-Hill Book Company, Inc., 1949).

40. J. M. Taylor, *Semiconductor Particle Detectors* (Washington, D.C.: Butterworths, Inc., 1963).

41. C. G. Clayton and J. B. Whittaker, "Bulk Conductivity Detectors Suitable for Gamma Radiation," *Nucleonics*, 21, No. 4 (1963), 60-64.

42. G. E. Boster, D. J. Dudziak, and W. R. Ellis, "A Preliminary Appraisal of Fusion/Fission (Hybrid) Reactor Based on the Linear Theta Pinch," *9th Intersociety Energy Conversion Engineering Conference*, 1974 Proceedings (New York: American Society of Mechanical Engineers, 1974).

43. R. G. Mills, "Economic and Environmental Aspects of a First Generation Fusion Power Plant," *9th Intersociety Energy Conversion Engineering Conference*, 1974 Proceedings (New York: American Society of Mechanical Engineers, 1974).

44. A. P. Fraas, "Conceptual Design of a Series of Laser-Fusion Power Plants of 100 to 3000 mW(e)," *9th Intersociety Energy Conversion Engineering Conference*, 1974 Proceedings (New York: American Society of Mechanical Engineers, 1974).

45. R. W. Werner, B. Myers, J. D. Lee and P. B. Mohr, "Controlled Thermonuclear Power," *Proceedings of the Fourth Intersociety Energy Conversion Engineering Conference* (New York: American Institute of Chemical Engineers, 1969).

APPENDIX A: PHYSICAL CONSTANTS†

Notation	Constant	Value
$\Re$	Universal gas constant	$= 8.314 \times 10^3$ joules/(kg-mole °K)
		$= 1.986$ kcal/(kg-mole °K)
		$= 0.08205$ liter-atm/(gm-mole °K)
		$= 8.314 \times 10^7$ ergs/(gm-mole °K)
N_o	Avogadro's number	$= 6.0230 \times 10^{26}$ per kg-mole
		$= 6.0230 \times 10^{23}$ per gm-mole
k	Boltzmann's constant	$= 1.38049 \times 10^{-23}$ joule/°K
		$= 1.38049 \times 10^{-16}$ erg/°K
		$= 8.6168 \times 10^{-5}$ eV/°K
σ	Stefan Boltzmann constant (for energy in watts/cm²)	$= 5.67 \times 10^{-12}$ watts/(cm²-°K⁴)
e	electronic charge	$= 1.60209 \times 10^{-19}$ coulombs
m	rest mass of electron	$= 9.1086 \times 10^{-31}$ kg
		$= 9.1086 \times 10^{-28}$ gm
h	Planck's constant	$= 6.6254 \times 10^{-34}$ joule-sec
		$= 6.6254 \times 10^{-27}$ erg-sec
m_p/m	ratio of proton to electron mass	$= 1836.09$
c	speed of light	$= 2.997928 \times 10^8$ m/sec
		$= 2.997928 \times 10^{10}$ cm/sec
$\mathcal{F}$	Faraday's constant	$= 96{,}493$ coulombs per chemical equivalent
		$= 23{,}060$ cal/(volt-mole of electrons)
ϵ_0	permittivity of free space	$= 8.85417 \times 10^{-12}$ farad/meter
	1 standard atmosphere	$= 1.013 \times 10^5$ newton/m²
		$= 760$ mm Hg
		$= 14.696$ lbf/in.
g	standard gravitational acceleration	$= 9.806$ meter/sec²
		$= 980.6$ cm/sec²

† From various sources, but mainly S. L. Soo, *Analytical Thermodynamics* (Englewood Cliffs, New Jersey: Prentice-Hall, Inc., 1962).

APPENDIX B: CONVERSION FACTORS

1 coulomb $= 1$ amp-sec

1 electron-
      volt $= 1.602 \times 10^{-19}$ joule
           $= 1.602 \times 10^{-12}$ erg

1 farad $\quad = 1$ coulomb/volt

1 joule $\quad = 10^7$ ergs
           $= 1$ newton-meter
           $= 2.389 \times 10^{-4}$ kcal
           $= 1$ watt-sec
           $= 0.7376$ ft-lb$_f$

1 kcal $\quad = 1000$ cal
           $= 4184$ joules
           $= 41.311$ liter-atm
           $= 3.969$ Btu

1 meter $\quad = 10^2$ cm
           $= 10^6$ microns
           $= 10^{10}$ angstroms
           $= 3.28$ ft

1 newton $\quad = 10^5$ dynes
           $= 1$ kg-m/sec^2
           $= 1$ volt-coulomb/meter
           $= 0.2248$ lb$_f$

1 ohm $\quad = 1$ volt/amp

1 volt $\quad = 1$ joule/coulomb

1 watt $\quad = 10^7$ ergs/sec
           $=$ joule/sec
           $= 1.341 \times 10^{-3}$ hp

1 weber $\quad = 1$ volt-sec
           $=$ joule/amp

1 weber/m$^2 = 10^4$ gauss
           $=$ newton/amp-meter
           $= 1$ tesla

APPENDIX C: THERMOELECTRIC PROPERTIES OF FOUR SEMICONDUCTORS

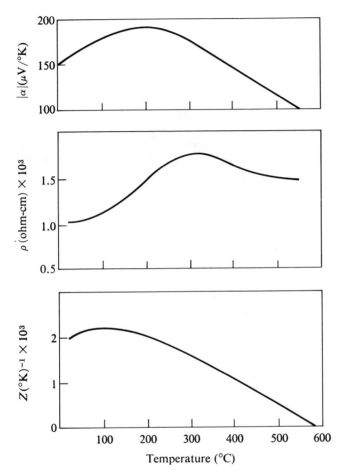

FIG. C-1. The Seebeck coefficient, electrical resistivity, and figure of merit of an n-type alloy: 75% Bi_2Te_3, 25% Bi_2Se_3. After F. D. Rosi, E. F. Hockings, and N. E. Lindenblad, "Semiconducting Power Generation," *RCA Review*, XXII (1961), p. 96; with permission.

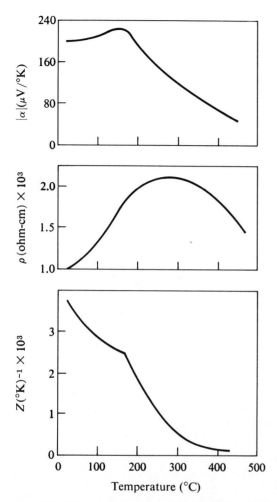

FIG. C-2. The Seebeck coefficient, electrical resistivity, and figure of merit of a p-type alloy: 25 % Bi_2Te_3, 75 % Sb_2Te_3 (1.75 % Se). After F. D. Rosi, E. F. Hockings, and N. E. Lindenblad, "Semiconducting Power Generation," *RCA Review*, XXII (1961), p. 99; with permission.

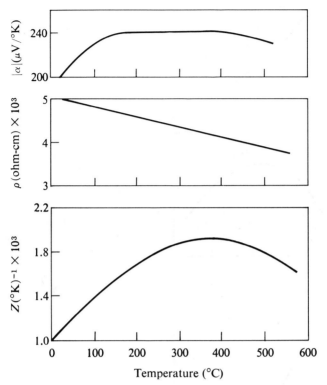

FIG. C-3. The Seebeck coefficient, electrical resistivity, and figure of merit of a p-type alloy: $AgSbTe_2$. After F. D. Rosi, E. F. Hockings, and N. E. Lindenblad, "Semiconducting Power Generation," *RCA Review*, XXII (1961), p. 103; with permission.

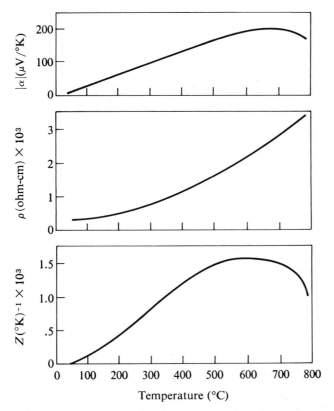

FIG. C-4. The Seebeck coefficient, electrical resistivity, and figure of merit of an *n*-type alloy: 75% PbTe, 25% SnTe. After F. D. Rosi, E. F. Hockings, and N. E. Lindenblad, "Semiconducting Power Generation," *RCA Review*, XXII (1961), p. 111; with permission.

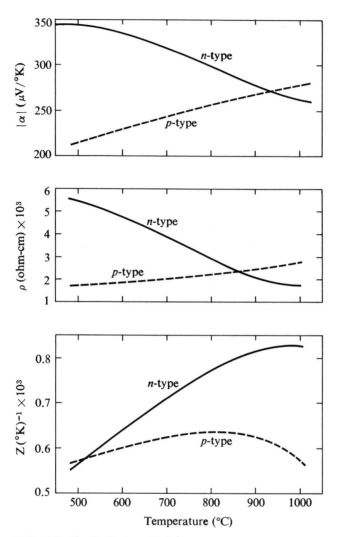

FIG. C-5. The Seebeck coefficient, electrical resistivity, and figure of merit of an *n*- and *p*-type alloy of SiGe. Data courtesy RCA Corporation.

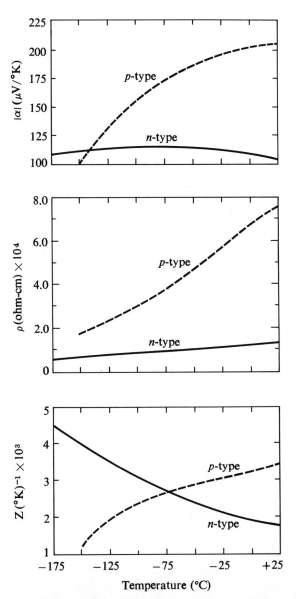

FIG. C-6. The Seebeck coefficient, electrical resistivity and figure of merit of a *p*-type alloy of 75 % Sb₂Te₃, 25 % Bi₂Te₃ and an *n*-type alloy of 95 % Bi, 5 % Sb. The *p*-type data are from Von Joachim Rupprecht, "Thermo-elektrische Eigenschaften einer *p*- und einer *n*- Leitenden Bi₂Te₃-Legierung im Temperaturbereich 100 bis 300°K," *Zeitschrift Für Angewandte Physik*, Band 16 (1963), Heft 5, p. 304–307. The *n*-type data are from G. E. Smith and R. Wolfe, "Thermoelectric Properties of Bismuth-Antimony Alloys," *Journal of Applied Physics*, Vol. 33 (1962), pp. 841–846.

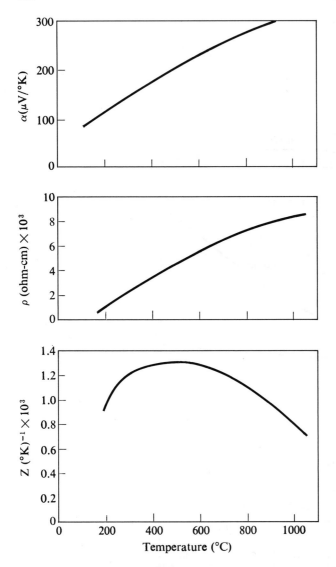

FIG. C-7. The Seebeck coefficient, electrical resistivity, and figure of merit of 3M Corporation's p-type alloy TPM-217 (composition A) which chemically resembles $Cu_{1.97}Ag_{0.31}Se_{1.0081}$. After E. F. Hampl, Jr., R. B. Ericson, W. C. Mitchell, and R. S. Reylek, *7th Intersociety Energy Conversion Conference, 1972 Proceedings* (Washington, D.C.: American Chemical Society, 1972).

APPENDIX D: PRINCIPLES OF ENERGY CONVERSION

Before we begin our discussion of specific modes of energy conversion, we will set forth a theory that will enable us to classify energy converters and to set bounds on their efficiency. This theory of steady-state energy conversion was developed by J. F. Osterle [1] at Carnegie-Mellon University. Osterle's theory rests on the principles of irreversible thermodynamics, on the assumption that deviations from equilibrium are small enough to permit the use of linear phenomenological equations such as Ohm's law and Fourier's law of heat conduction. Before we consider the development of a unified theory of energy conversion, we will outline briefly the relevant principles of irreversible thermodynamics, following the method of Denbigh [2] for our presentation. Other modes of development of this topic may be found in the standard references [3], [4].

D.1 IRREVERSIBLE THERMODYNAMICS

In the study of particle dynamics a general procedure is to consider velocities and forces. Onsager, one of the founders of irreversible thermodynamics, analogously regarded the processes of diffusion, heat conduction, and the flow of electricity as being describable in terms of a "velocity" together with a thermodynamic "force," the latter being a quantity that measures the extent to which a system is displaced from equilibrium. For example, in the case of heat transfer the velocity is the vector flow of energy and the force is proportional to the temperature gradient. Similarly, in the case of electricity the velocity term is proportional to the current and the force is simply the voltage gradient. In both examples the force may be regarded as being the cause of the flow.

For most processes of interest it is observed that the flow is directly proportional to the corresponding force that drives it. This fact is recognized in the empirical laws of Ohm and Fourier; for example,

$$J \text{ is proportional to } \text{grad } V,$$
$$q \text{ is proportional to } \text{grad } T,$$

where J and grad V are the electric current density and voltage gradient respectively, and where q and grad T are the heat flux and gradient of the temperature respectively. The abbreviation "grad" is used in the usual mathematical sense to mean the gradient of a scalar field, s',

$$\text{grad } s' = \nabla s' = \frac{\partial s'}{\partial x} i + \frac{\partial s'}{\partial y} j + \frac{\partial s'}{\partial z} k, \tag{D-1}$$

where i, j, and k are the unit vectors in the x, y, and z directions. Thus if J is taken to be the rate of flow and X the driving force, there is generally an empirical relationship of the form:

$$J = LX, \tag{D-2}$$

where L is a scalar quantity of the nature of a conductance (the reciprocal of a resistance).

We now consider the case where two or more transport processes take place simultaneously in the same molecular system. The rate of each process is still assumed to be linearly dependent on the corresponding force, but is supposed, in addition, to be dependent on the other forces as well. Clearly, this is a more general procedure than to suppose that each of the flows depends on only *one* of the forces. Onsager [5] has suggested a set of general linear equations, sometimes called the *thermodynamic equations of motion*, to represent the transport processes at the steady state of a system. His theory suggests that, in the absence of evidence to the contrary, each of the flows in the system is a function of all the forces operating on the system. Thus in a three-flow system, retaining the assumption of linearity, the flow rates may be expressed as

$$\begin{aligned} J_1 &= L_{11}X_1 + L_{12}X_2 + L_{13}X_3, \\ J_2 &= L_{21}X_1 + L_{22}X_2 + L_{23}X_3, \\ J_3 &= L_{31}X_1 + L_{32}X_2 + L_{33}X_3. \end{aligned} \tag{D-3}$$

These equations might be used to describe, for example, thermal conduction in a nonisotropic body where the J's are now heat flows along the three axes. The L's with identical subscripts, such as L_{11}, L_{22}, etc., connect the flows to their corresponding forces and are proportional to (though not necessarily identical to) the ordinary thermal conductivity, electrical conductivity, diffusion coefficient, and so forth. The L's with nonidentical subscripts, such as L_{12}, L_{23}, etc., represent possible coupling between a given flow and the various other forces. An example would be heat transfer in the y direction due to temperature differences in the x and z directions.

The most general set of linear equations is of the form

$$J_i = \sum_j L_{ij}X_j. \tag{D-4}$$

The equations are generally referred to as phenomenological relations and simply represent formal relations describing the rates of flow as a linear function of the forces; it remains to be seen whether the coupling coefficients, L_{ij}, $i \neq j$, are zero or not. Equation 2-4 may be applied to any system in which there is coupling among the various processes and in which the flows may be assumed to be linearly dependent on the forces. The equations, however, are of little use unless more is known about the forces X_j and the coefficients L_{ij}.

There is a good deal of latitude in the selection of the forces X. For example, in heat conduction as described by Fourier's law, the flow of heat is proportional to the temperature gradient. At a point in the body where the temperature is T, the thermal driving force may be chosen as $-\text{grad }T$ or $-(1/T)\text{ grad }T$ where the negative sign is used to indicate that the heat flow is in the opposite direction to the temperature gradient. In trying to determine how one should go about choosing the forces and coefficients, Onsager suggested that the forces should be selected so that when each flow J_i is multiplied by the appropriate force X_i, the sum of these products is equal to the rate of creation of entropy per unit volume of the system multiplied by the absolute temperature. In our work we will find it more convenient to compute the entropy creation per unit time. Thus, we choose to call the product of the time rate of entropy creation θ times the temperature T, the dissipation† and denote it by the symbol D,

$$D = T\theta = J_1 \cdot X_1 + J_2 \cdot X_2 + \cdots = \sum_i J_i \cdot X_i. \qquad \text{(D-5)}$$

Dissipation accompanies all irreversible processes, such as I^2R heating of a system, heat transfer due to a finite temperature difference, and so forth.

The concept of entropy creation may be more clearly understood by considering the simple example of a one-dimensional‡ heat flow along a laterally insulated bar as shown in Fig. D-1. The bar is placed between two reservoirs, one at a high temperature T_H and one at a low temperature T_C. After steady state is achieved the temperature gradient at each section of the

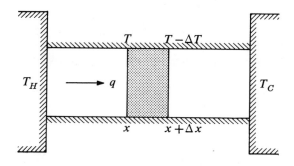

FIG. D-1. One-dimensional heat flow along a laterally insulated rod.

---

† Because the dissipation is a scalar, we must multiply the force and flux by the dot product method.

‡ Since we are considering a one-dimensional example, we drop the vector notation as superfluous.

bar is constant and therefore the entropy of the bar is a constant. However, it may be a function, at any point, of the local temperature and density. We now imagine that we cut out a small volume element of the bar of length Δx—whose dimensions are small compared with the dimensions of the system, but large enough to avoid fluctuations on a molecular scale. This method of obtaining a temperature "at a point" corresponds to drilling a very small hole in the rod and inserting a fine thermocouple in the hole. We stress this point to remind the reader that in classical thermodynamics the entropy of a body is considered to have a value only during a state of equilibrium.

We now inventory the energy and entropy of our element. The element is bounded by a plane at $x + \Delta x$. No work is done on the element, which has a heat flow into it of q (watts). Since there is no energy storage, q flows out the right-hand face of the element.

The state of the element remains unchanged if we assume that it is in contact with heat reservoirs maintained at temperatures T and $T - \Delta T$. The rate of heat flowing out of the reservoir at temperature T is q while the entropy flow rate§ is simply q/T. Since the left face of the element is also at T we consider this to be the rate of flow of entropy into the element at the left face. Thus we say there is an entropy current J_S at the left face given by

$$J_{S(x)} = \frac{q}{T} \tag{D-6}$$

and at the right face of the element the entropy current is

$$J_{S(x+\Delta x)} = \frac{q}{T - \Delta T}. \tag{D-7}$$

Since $T - \Delta T$ is less than T, the rate of flow of entropy out the right face exceeds that which flows in at the left face. The entropy creation in the element equals the difference between the rates of outflow and inflow, thus

$$\theta = J_{S(x+\Delta x)} - J_{S(x)} = \frac{q}{T - \Delta T} - \frac{q}{T} = q \frac{\Delta T}{T(T - \Delta T)} \tag{D-8}$$

and we may discard ΔT if it is assumed small in comparison with T to obtain

$$\theta = \frac{q \, \Delta T}{T^2} = J_S \frac{\Delta T}{T}. \tag{D-9}$$

We associate this entropy production with the irreversible process of heat conduction down the bar. For each flow and flux we may calculate the associated entropy production to use in Eq. D-5.

---

§ It should be recognized that entropy, being a state function, cannot correctly be said to flow; however, there is an entropy flux vector which may be shown to satisfy an equation of continuity, so that in some ways J_S accurately reflects the physical situation.

We may find the units of Eq. D-9 in the following way. The quantity θ is the entropy creation per unit time and we have already defined q to be in watts. If our bar has a length Δx and a cross-sectional area A which gives a volume Ω, we may rewrite Eq. D-9 as

$$\theta = \left[\frac{1}{T^2}\frac{\Delta T}{\Delta x}\frac{q}{A}\right]\Omega \qquad [\text{watts}/^\circ\text{K}]. \qquad \textbf{(D-10)}$$

In the limit $\Delta T/\Delta x$ approaches dT/dx, which is the x component of the temperature gradient. Since we have chosen A to be the cross-sectional area of the bar in the x direction, then q/A is the x component of the heat flow vector q, or more exactly its negative, since it is conventional to take the vector as being in the direction of increasing x and increasing T. Thus Eq. D-10 is just the special case of the more general relation which refers to a three-dimensional heat flow:

$$\theta = -q\cdot[(\text{grad } T)/T^2]\Omega \qquad [\text{watts}/^\circ\text{K}]$$

or

$$D = T\theta = -q\cdot[(\text{grad } T)/T]\Omega \qquad [\text{watts}]. \qquad \textbf{(D-11)}$$

We consider one more example to demonstrate the method of calculating the entropy production. A metal rod is assumed to carry an electric current between two reservoirs maintained at a potential difference of ΔV. Work is then done on the rod at the rate $I\,\Delta V$. We further assume that a heat reservoir at temperature T is in contact with the rod along its entire length and that the rate of heat flow out of the element into the reservoir is equal to the rate at which electrical work is being done on the element. All the properties of the rod, such as temperature, entropy, and internal energy, remain constant with time.

The heat leaving the element in time dt is $d\bar{Q}$, which just equals the work $I\,\Delta V\,dt$ in this isothermal system. The entropy flow into the reservoir is then equal to the heat transfer divided by the temperature, $d\bar{Q}/T$. Since the state of the system does not change, the energy balance is just maintained by the heat transfer and electrical work; however, there is a flow of entropy out of the system but no flow into it. We thus conclude that entropy is created or produced within the system due to the irreversible electrical work being done on the system. The rate of this production is

$$\theta = \frac{d\bar{Q}}{T}\frac{1}{dt} = \frac{I\,\Delta V}{T}. \qquad \textbf{(D-12)}$$

We may express Eq. D-12 a little differently by substituting the current density $J_I = I/A$ (amp/cm^2) for the current I and multiplying both numerator and denominator by Δx to obtain

$$\theta = \frac{1}{T}J_I\left[\frac{\Delta V}{\Delta x}\right]\Omega \qquad [\text{watts}/^\circ\text{K}], \qquad \textbf{(D-13)}$$

or on passing to the limit $\Delta V/\Delta x$ approaches dV/dx so that more generally we write

$$D = T\theta = -J_I \cdot [\text{grad } V]\,\Omega. \tag{D-14}$$

We may now apply the principle of superposition, which means we add Eqs. D-11 and D-14 after we have divided them by T, to find the entropy created per unit time in a rod carrying both a heat flux and an electric current

$$\theta = \left[-q \cdot \frac{\text{grad } T}{T^2} - J_I \cdot \frac{\text{grad } V}{T} \right] \Omega \tag{D-15}$$

or, for the one-dimensional case where we replace $-\text{grad } T$ and $-\text{grad } V$ by the positive quantities $\Delta T/\Delta x$ and $\Delta V/\Delta x$, to obtain

$$\theta = \left[\frac{1}{T^2} \frac{\Delta T}{\Delta x} \frac{q}{A} + \frac{1}{T} \frac{\Delta V}{\Delta x} \frac{I}{A} \right] \Omega \qquad [\text{watts}/{}^\circ\text{K}]$$

or

$$D = T\theta = \left[q\left(\frac{\Delta T}{T}\right) + I\,\Delta V \right] \quad [\text{watts}]. \tag{D-16}$$

It should be noted that the thermodynamic forces that are used in Eq. D-5 depend on the flow selected. For example, if we desire to use the entropy flow instead of the heat flux in Eq. D-5, then the force becomes $\Delta T/T$ instead of $\Delta T/T^2$.

After the forces and fluxes have been chosen to satisfy Eq. D-5, Onsager's theory then states that there is an equality among certain of the coefficients in Eq. D-4—the thermodynamic equations of motion. This equality for the magnetic-field-free case is simply

$$L_{ij} = L_{ji}, \tag{D-17}$$

which implies a symmetry in the coupling of the various processes. Onsager developed this theory on the assumption that the thermodynamic equations of motion also hold for fluctuations within the equilibrium state. Application of the principle of microscopic reversibility to these fluctuations led Onsager to Eq. D-17.

Under the circumstances of an external magnetic field acting on a system, the symmetry indicated by Eq. D-17 no longer holds. The coupling between forces becomes antisymmetrical, that is,

$$L_{ij}(\mathbf{B}) = L_{ji}(-\mathbf{B}), \tag{D-18}$$

where $\mathbf{B}$ is the magnetic flux density vector. This change in sign can be reasoned from the physical picture of what happens when a charged particle is made to retrace its motion in a magnetic field. If the velocity of a particle traveling in a magnetic field is reversed, the magnetic field must also be reversed in order that the Lorentz force will act on it in the same direction as it did in the initial pass through the field.

It should be stressed that the Onsager theory makes no statement as to the correctness of the thermodynamic equations of motion. In any case, we must rely on experimental verification to tell us whether or not the equations of motion are a good approximation to the physical situation. In particular it has to be shown that the forces X that satisfy Eq. D-4 are proportional to the flows. A large number of coupled flows have been verified experimentally, and these results have been summarized by Miller [6]. The Onsager theory is concerned with the reciprocal relations between the coefficients when these equations are a satisfactory approximation in describing the phenomena.

Some restrictions on the Onsager method have been formalized in a statement known as Curie's theorem, attributed to P. Curie. Briefly, it says that *quantities whose tensorial characters† differ by an odd integer cannot interact in an isotropic system.* Consider as an example the possibility of a velocity *change* inducing heat transfer. Curie's theorem forbids this, as the divergence of the velocity vector is a scalar;

$$\nabla \cdot u = \left(\frac{\partial}{\partial x} i + \frac{\partial}{\partial y} j + \frac{\partial}{\partial z} k \right) \cdot (u_x i + u_y j + u_z k)$$

$$= \frac{\partial u_x}{\partial x} + \frac{\partial u_y}{\partial y} + \frac{\partial u_z}{\partial z}, \tag{D-19}$$

the heat transfer is a vector;

$$q = q_x i + q_y j + q_z k \tag{D-20}$$

and their tensorial characters differ by one.

However, a temperature gradient (the gradient of a scalar field) with a tensorial character of 1 (according to Eq. D-1) can induce a mass flow (a vector); this phenomenon is known as the *Soret effect.* Similarly, a concentration gradient can induce an energy flux, as both quantities are vectors.

Before closing this section we summarize the Onsager procedures for the case of simultaneous flows:

(1) If two or more flows are present, coupling *may* be present.

(2) Linear equations can be assumed for each flow, relating the flow to the primary force and to the coupling forces.

(3) When the forces and fluxes are selected with due regard for dimensional homogeneity, the coupling coefficients are related by the Onsager equation as stated by Eq. D-13. This reduces the number of unknown coefficients.

(4) The unknown coefficients can be found if a number of experimental relations equal to the number of unknown coefficients determined in step 3 can be found. Obviously, a number of experimental relations equal to the number of flows are available or else step 2 could not be carried out. Thus

---

† The tensorial character of a scalar is 0; of a vector, 1; and of a dyadic, 2.

we need one additional experimental relationship for each independent cross-coupling coefficient that must be evaluated.

D.2   A UNIFIED THEORY OF ENERGY CONVERTERS

In this section we will present a theory, first developed by Osterle [1], that attempts to unify the theory of energy converters, allowing them to be classified according to some fundamental differences. It will be shown that energy converters may be divided into two classes, depending on whether it is the input force or the input flux that induces the output force. In each class two types of converters are found, one in which a conversion efficiency of unity is approachable by configurational adjustments and the other in which it is not. We will also develop a maximum conversion efficiency formula applicable to either class or type of device.

D.2.1   Basic equations. We will analyze a generalized energy conversion device contained within a thermodynamic control volume as shown in Fig. D-2 in which all properties are time independent. To simplify our presentation we will assume that the control volume exchanges heat with no more than two external infinite heat reservoirs and with only one external work reservoir through no more than a single shaft and a single electrical current. It is further assumed that only one mass flow stream passes through the control volume. The analysis could be extended to more external heat and work reservoirs and mass flow streams in a straightforward manner but is not necessary for the purpose of illustrating this method of analyzing energy converters.

The first law of thermodynamics applied to the control volume illustrated in Fig. D-2 is

$$q_s + q_r - P_o = m\left[h + \frac{u^2}{2g_c} + z\frac{g}{g_c}\right]_{\text{exit}} - m\left[h + \frac{u^2}{2g_c} + z\frac{g}{g_c}\right]_{\text{inlet}}, \quad \textbf{(D-21)}$$

where q_s is the heat flux to the device, q_r (a negative quantity) is the heat flux to the atmosphere, P_o is the rate at which external work is delivered by the device to the work reservoir, and m is the mass flow rate. The terms in brackets are enthalpy, kinetic energy, and potential energy of the mass flow stream. Because the control volume is at the steady state there is neither an accumulation of energy nor of mass within the device.

In the control volume the entropy is increased because the mass that crosses the boundary of the control volume has entropy and, similarly, entropy is carried out of the system by the mass that leaves the control volume. Because the control volume is at the steady state, the entropy of

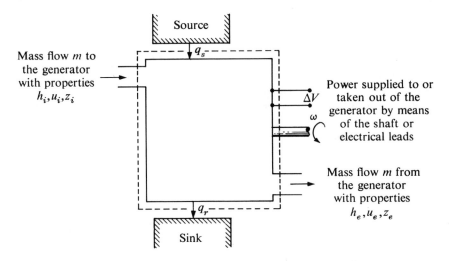

FIG. D-2. A generalized energy converter enclosed by a control volume.

the control volume does not change and the second law of thermodynamics demands that the net change of entropy for the mass stream be equal to or greater than integral of dq/T, thus

$$ms_e - ms_i \geq q_s/T_H + q_r/T_C, \qquad \text{(D-22)}$$

where the equality sign holds only during a reversible process. T_C and T_H are the temperatures of the two heat reservoirs, T_C being the temperature of the atmosphere, and s_e and s_i the entropy of the mass stream leaving and entering.

Combining Eqs. D-22 and D-21 to eliminate q_r and solving for P_o we obtain

$$P_o \leq q_s(1 - T_C/T_H)$$
$$- m\left[(h_e - h_i) + \frac{u_e^2 - u_i^2}{2g_c} + (z_e - z_i)g/g_c - T_C(s_e - s_i) \right], \qquad \text{(D-23)}$$

where we may rewrite Eq. D-23 with a Δ notation, to mean "carry out the subtraction of the initial quantity from the final quantity," thus:

$$P_o \leq q_s(1 - T_C/T_H) - m\Delta[h + u^2/2g_c + z(g/g_c) - T_C s]. \qquad \text{(D-24)}$$

The maximum work that our generalized energy conversion device can yield is given by Eq. D-24 when the equality sign is employed. Since every actual process has irreversibilities associated with it, the work will always be something less than that predicted by Eq. D-24. The difference between the maximum possible work rate and the actual work rate is defined as the *dissipation* (sometimes called the *irreversibility*). The dissipation can also be represented as the product of the entropy generation times the absolute temperature, thus

$$T\theta = D = P_{o(\text{max})} - P_o. \tag{D-25}$$

We might also note that we found another expression for the dissipation by a different method when we developed Eq. D-5. The quantity $P_{o(\text{max})}$ is obtained from Eq. D-24 by use of the equality sign; further examination of Eq. D-24 reveals that it can be written as the sum of the products of flux and force terms, namely,

$$P_{o(\text{max})} + J_1X_1 + J_2X_2,$$

with

$$
\begin{aligned}
J_1 &= q_s \quad \text{and} \quad X_1 = 1 - T_C/T_H \\
J_2 &= m \qquad\qquad\ X_2 = -\Delta[h + u^2/2g_c + z(g/g_c) - T_Cs]. \tag{D-26}
\end{aligned}
$$

The actual work rate P_o is, in general, the sum of a shaft power and an electrical power which can also be written as the sum of products of fluxes and forces. Thus

$$-P_o = J_3X_3 + J_4X_4, \tag{D-27}$$

with

$$
\begin{aligned}
J_3 &= \omega, &&\text{the angular velocity;} \\
X_3 &= \tau, &&\text{the external torque on the shaft in the direction of } \omega
\end{aligned}
$$

and

$$
\begin{aligned}
J_4 &= I, &&\text{the electrical current through the device;} \\
X_4 &= \Delta V, &&\text{the potential drop through the device in the direction of } I.
\end{aligned}
$$

We may now write Eq. D-25 as

$$D = J_1X_1 + J_2X_2 + J_3X_3 + J_4X_4. \tag{D-28}$$

If we restrict ourselves to small deviations from equilibrium within the control volume (small driving forces), the thermodynamic equations of motion for the generalized energy converter become

$$
\begin{aligned}
J_1 &= L_{11}X_1 + L_{12}X_2 + L_{13}X_3 + L_{14}X_4, \\
J_2 &= L_{21}X_1 + L_{22}X_2 + L_{23}X_3 + L_{24}X_4, \\
J_3 &= L_{31}X_1 + L_{32}X_2 + L_{33}X_3 + L_{34}X_4, \\
J_4 &= L_{41}X_1 + L_{42}X_2 + L_{43}X_3 + L_{44}X_4. \tag{D-29}
\end{aligned}
$$

The L's are the phenomenological coefficients related to each other by Onsager's theorem as represented by Eq. D-17 or Eq. D-18, depending on whether or not a magnetic field is present.

D.2.2   Classification of devices. The simplest type of energy converter that Eq. D-28 can describe would be one that could be represented by only one term. It would have to be the second term in Eq. D-28, the one that represents a mass flux. An example of such a device would be an adiabatic nozzle or diffuser that converts enthalpy into kinetic energy or vice versa. The next level of complication, the one on which we will concentrate in the balance of this appendix, is a converter that can be described by two terms in Eq. D-29. Of the two terms in the dissipation rate equation that describe the converter we will find it convenient to treat one as an input, denoted by the subscript i, and one as an output, denoted by the subscript o. Thus Eq. D-28 becomes

$$D = J_i X_i - J_o X_o, \tag{D-30}$$

where X_o is the negative of the force it corresponds to in Eq. D-28. We define conversion efficiency in the usual thermodynamic sense as output divided by input:

$$\eta = \frac{J_o X_o}{J_i X_i}. \tag{D-31}$$

Under the new restrictions of two forces and two corresponding fluxes, Eq. D-29 reduces to

$$J_i = L_{ii} X_i + L_{io}(-X_o), \tag{D-32}$$
$$J_o = L_{oi} X_i + L_{oo}(-X_o). \tag{D-33}$$

If the output power is to result from the input power, there must be an interaction or coupling between the fluxes and forces representing the input and output. That is, L_{io} and L_{oi} cannot both be zero.

We now distinguish two classes of energy converters based on our preceding work:

Even: The *output force* is induced by the *input force*.

Odd: The *output force* is induced by the *input flux*.

We first consider the even class converter, rewriting Eqs. D-32 and D-33 in a form that represents the kind of intereaction specified. Upon solving Eq. D-33 for X_o we obtain:

$$X_o = (L_{oi}/L_{oo}) X_i - (1/L_{oo}) J_o. \tag{D-34}$$

Substituting it into Eq. D-32 and rearranging yields

$$J_i = [(L_{oo} L_{ii} - L_{io} L_{oi})/L_{oo}] X_i + [L_{io}/L_{oo}] J_o. \tag{D-35}$$

We may now define the following quantities:

$\alpha_1' = L_{oi}/L_{oo},$ an interaction coefficient;
$R_1 = 1/L_{oo},$ a resistance coefficient;
$\alpha_1'' = L_{io}/L_{oo},$ an interaction coefficient;
$C_1 = (L_{oo} L_{ii} - L_{io} L_{oi})/L_{oo},$ a conductance coefficient.

By applying Onsager's theorem to the interaction coefficients α' and α'' listed above, the prime notation can be dropped—that is, $L_{oi} = L_{io}$, provided that the even class conversion devices are not magnetic field dependent. Thus we may write Eqs. D-34 and D-35 as

$$X_o = \alpha_1 X_i - R_1 J_o, \tag{D-36}$$
$$J_i = C_1 X_i + \alpha_1 J_o. \tag{D-37}$$

Upon substituting Eqs. D-36 and D-37 into Eq. D-30 we obtain

$$D = C_1 X_i^2 + R_1 J_o^2. \tag{D-38}$$

We may now consider the odd class of energy converters, in which the output force is induced by the input flux. We first solve Eq. D-32 for X_i and Eq. D-33 for X_o which yields

$$X_i = (1/L_{ii})J_i + (L_{io}/L_{ii})X_o, \tag{D-39}$$
$$X_o = (-1/L_{oo})J_o + (L_{oi}/L_{oo})X_i. \tag{D-40}$$

The result of eliminating X_i from X_o by combining Eq. D-39 with Eq. D-40 and rearranging is

$$X_o = [L_{ii}/(L_{oi}L_{io} - L_{ii}L_{oo})]J_o + [-L_{oi}/(L_{oi}L_{io} - L_{ii}L_{oo})]J_i. \tag{D-41}$$

We now eliminate the output force from Eq. D-39 by substituting Eq. D-41 into it:

$$X_i = [-L_{oo}/(L_{oi}L_{io} - L_{ii}L_{oo})]J_i + [L_{io}/(L_{oi}L_{io} - L_{ii}L_{oo})]J_o \tag{D-42}$$

We now define the following quantities:

$\alpha_2' = -L_{oi}/(L_{oi}L_{io} - L_{ii}L_{oo})$,   an interaction coefficient;

$R_2 = -L_{ii}/(L_{oi}L_{io} - L_{ii}L_{oo})$,   a resistance coefficient;

$\alpha_2'' = L_{io}/(L_{oi}L_{io} - L_{ii}L_{oo})$,   an interaction coefficient;

$C_2 = -L_{oo}/(L_{oi}L_{io} - L_{ii}L_{oo})$,   a conductance coefficient.

Application of Onsager's theorem to the interaction coefficients establishes the identity of the coupling coefficients provided that the odd class conversion devices are magnetic field dependent and the α's are magnetic field dependent—that is, $\alpha'(\boldsymbol{B}) = \alpha''(-\boldsymbol{B})$. Thus Eqs. D-41 and D-42 may be written

$$X_o = \alpha_2 J_i - R_2 J_o, \tag{D-43}$$
$$X_i = C_2 J_i + \alpha_2 J_o. \tag{D-44}$$

Equations D-43 and D-44 may be substituted into Eq. D-30 to produce a dissipation rate equation for odd class devices of

$$D = C_2 J_i^2 + R_2 J_o^2. \tag{D-45}$$

Note that Eqs. D-45 and D-38 are not identical.

We may further divide energy converters into *coupled* and *uncoupled* types. *Uncoupled* type energy converters have independent conductance and resistance coefficients. Such converters permit configurational adjustments that allow the R and C coefficients to become vanishingly small. When R and C have been made zero, conversion is said to be ideal. Ideal conversion is reversible since it is obvious from inspection of Eqs. D-38 and D-45 that it would be free from dissipation.

In *coupled* conversion devices the reduction of C causes an increase in

R thus excluding the possibility of simultaneously making them both zero. A coupled conversion device will always have a finite dissipation rate associated with it. Table D-1 presents a classification of a representative sample of the devices studied in this book.

TABLE D-1. CLASSIFICATION OF SOME DIRECT ENERGY CONVERSION DEVICES

Device name	Even	Odd	Coupled	Uncoupled
Thermoelectric	X		X	
Photovoltaic	X			X
Thermionic	X		X	
Magnetohydrodynamic		X	X	
Fuel cell	X			X
Nernst effect		X	X	
Electrokinetic	X		X	

D.2.3 Illustrative examples. Irreversible thermodynamics has been applied to a large number of different kinds of energy conversion devices [6], [7], [8], [9]. However, in this section we will apply the principles set down in the previous section to only four typical devices. We will examine, for purposes of clarification, one of each class and type of converter.

Even class, uncoupled type. We will consider as a first example a positive displacement hydraulic engine and reservoir system. We assume that in our control volume, illustrated in Fig. D-3, the energy delivered at the shaft is due only to the presence of the hydrostatic head across the turbine. The water at entrance and exit to the control volume is at zero velocity and atmospheric pressure. Under such assumptions we retain only the second and third terms in Eq. D-28 for the dissipation rate. From Eqs. D-26 and D-27, recalling the assumption of small forces, the associated fluxes and forces are:

$J_2 = m$ (the mass flow rate) $\qquad X_2 = +\Delta z(g/g_c)$ (the elevation drop across the control volume);

$J_3 = \omega$ (the angular speed) $\qquad X_3 = -\tau$ (the external torque on the shaft in the direction opposite to ω).

The dissipation rate—the difference between the theoretical power output and the actual power output—is found by substituting the above values into Eq. D-28:

$$D = J_2 X_2 + J_3 X_3 \qquad \text{(D-28)}$$
$$= m\,\Delta z(g/g_c) - \omega\tau \qquad \text{(D-46)}$$
$$= [\text{theoretically available}] - [\text{actually delivered}].$$

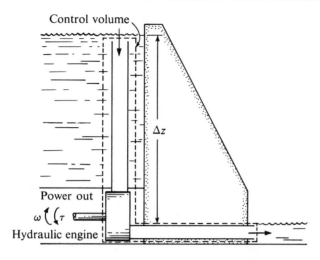

FIG. D-3. An energy converter that uses a positive displacement hydraulic engine shown enclosed in a control volume that eliminates pressure and velocity differences across the engine.

We now relate the above definitions to the thermodynamic equations of motion as set forth by Eqs. D-36 and D-37 where $J_i = m$, $X_i = \Delta z(g/g_c)$, $J_o = \omega$, and $X_o = \tau$. We insert mks units to make the example more meaningful:

$$\tau[\text{nt-m}] = \alpha_1[\text{kg}]\, \Delta z(g/g_c)[\text{nt-m/kg}] - R_1[\text{nt-m-sec}]\omega[\text{radians/sec}],$$
(D-47)

$$m[\text{kg/sec}] = C_1[\text{kg}^2/(\text{nt-m-sec})]\, \Delta z(g/g_c)[\text{nt-m/kg}] + \alpha_1[\text{kg}]\omega[\text{radians/sec}].$$
(D-48)

Dividing the angular velocity ω by 2π converts it to units of revolutions per second (rps); therefore it is evident that $2\pi\alpha_1$ in this case is the mass displaced by the engine in each revolution of the engine. C_1 is a measure of the leakage past the rotating element of the engine, and though it contributes to the mass flow of the device, it does not contribute to the torque or power output. R_1 is a measure of the friction in the device and is proportional to ω; the term that contains it subtracts from the output torque of the engine.

It is evident from the preceding discussion that R_1 and C_1 are independent of each other and thus by proper configurational adjustments could be made to approach zero. Thus ideal conversion is approachable in this example. The dissipation rate as given by Eq. D-38 is

$$D = C_1[\Delta z(g/g_c)]^2 + R_1(\omega)^2 \quad [\text{watts}].$$
(D-49)

Even class, coupled type. An example of this type of converter is a thermoelectric generator. In a thermoelectric generator a heat flux induces

a potential difference across a junction of dissimilar materials. This effect
was first analyzed by William Thomson (Lord Kelvin). Thomson applied
reversible thermodynamics to a situation that was obviously irreversible
due to heat conduction and Joule heating. His method of approach, while
successful, could not be justified from the physical point of view. Recently,
several workers [1]–[4] have shown the usefulness of irreversible thermodynamics in analyzing the thermoelectric phenomena.

Figure D-4 is a schematic of the thermoelectric engine that we will
examine from the point of view of coupled flows. We will treat the thermoelectric effects in more detail in Chs. 3 and 4, but for now we will concern
ourselves with the analysis of the coupling phenomenon in an engine that
converts heat directly to electricity.

Since we have defined a thermoelectric generator as a device that
converts a heat flux to an electric potential from which electric power can
be drawn, we need only retain the first and fourth terms in Eq. D-28. That
is, the dissipation rate for a device in which the temperature difference is
assumed to remain small is given by

$$D = q(\Delta T/T) - I\,\Delta V \qquad \text{(D-50)}$$
$$= [\text{theoretically available}] - [\text{actually delivered}],$$

where ΔT is the temperature drop through the device in the direction of the
heat flux q, and ΔV is the potential rise through the device in the direction
of I. From Eqs. D-36 and D-37 we may now write the output voltage and
input heat flux as

$$\Delta V = \alpha_1(\Delta T/T) - R_1(I), \qquad \text{(D-51)}$$
$$q = C_1(\Delta T/T) + \alpha_1(I). \qquad \text{(D-52)}$$

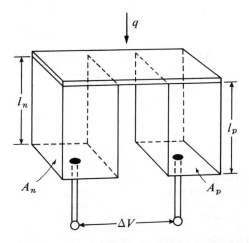

FIG. D-4. A thermoelectric generator utilizing one element with a negative
Seebeck coefficient and one element with a positive Seebeck coefficient.

We may now interpret the coefficients that appear in these equations. The first equation indicates that the voltage difference measured across the terminals of the device is proportional to the internal resistance and to the temperature difference applied to the generator. In the second equation we see that the heat flux is proportional to the temperature difference and to the current through the device. Thus, under open circuit conditions with zero current the product C_1/T represents the internal thermal conductance† of the generator‡ K:

$$K = C_1/T = (\lambda_n A_n/l_n + \lambda_p A_p/l_p) \quad \text{[watt/°K]} \quad \text{(D-53)}$$

and R_1 is the internal electrical resistance§

$$R_1 = (\rho_n l_n/A_n + \rho_p l_p/A_p) \quad \text{[ohms].} \quad \text{(D-54)}$$

In addition, we define α_1 to be the *Peltier coefficient*, π_T, the heat transfer per unit current for the particular combination of materials that makes up the generator

$$\pi_T = \pi_{T(n)} + \pi_{T(p)} \quad \text{[watts/amp],} \quad \text{(D-55)}$$

while α_1/T is defined as the *Seebeck coefficient*, α, the voltage rise per unit of temperature for the particular combination of materials for the device

$$\alpha_1/T = \alpha = (\alpha_n + \alpha_p)/T \quad \text{[volts/degree],} \quad \text{(D-56)}$$

where we have taken the absolute values of the Seebeck coefficients and added them because the voltage rises across the *n*- and *p*-type legs causing them to act like batteries in series. This will be explained more fully in Ch. 3.

Comparing the definition of the Seebeck coefficient and the Peltier coefficient given in the preceding paragraph we observe the following interrelationship:

$$\pi_T = \alpha T. \quad \text{(D-57)}$$

This is called *Kelvin's second relation*. Kelvin found this by the method of artificially separating the reversible effects from the irreversible effects. It has been verified experimentally many times [6].

Examination of Eqs. D-53 and D-54 reveals that R_1 and C_1 are not independent of each other. As A gets larger, thus reducing the electrical

---

† The thermal conductivity λ, which is used in the calculation of the thermal conductance, is the property that indicates how well a material will conduct heat. It may be defined from Eq. D-52 under a zero current condition as $\lambda = ql/(A \, \Delta T)$.

‡ We denote the properties of the two legs of the generator by subscripts *n* and *p*, which indicate whether an electric current is carried by electrons (*n*) or holes (*p*). The sign of the current carrier tells whether the Seebeck coefficient is positive or negative relative to some reference material. This subject is discussed more fully in Chs. 3 and 4.

§ The electrical resistivity, which is used in the calculation of the electrical resistance, is the property that indicates how well a material will conduct electricity. It may be defined from Eq. D-51 under isothermal conditions where the current flows minus to plus across the device as $\rho = A \, \Delta V/(lI)$.

resistance, the thermal conductance C_1 increases at the same rate. Thus R_1 and C_1 cannot both be made to vanish by adjusting the configuration of the device, and ideal conversion cannot be approached. The dissipation for this type of device is given by Eq. D-38 as

$$D = C_1(\Delta T/T)^2 + R_1(I)^2 \qquad \text{[watts]}. \qquad \text{(D-58)}$$

Odd class, uncoupled type. We next consider a device in which the output force is induced by the input flux while configurational adjustments permit an approach to ideal conversion. The direct-current generator is a device satisfying these criteria. We illustrate such a generator schematically in Fig. D-5. The dissipation is found by retaining the third and fourth terms in Eq. D-28:

$$D = \omega\tau - I\,\Delta V \qquad\qquad\qquad \text{(D-59)}$$
$$= \text{[theoretically available]} - \text{[actually delivered]},$$

where ω is the angular velocity in the direction of the externally applied torque τ and ΔV is the potential rise across the generator in the direction of I.

Equations D-43 and D-44 provide a phenomenological description of an odd class, magnetic field dependent device such as a d-c generator:

$$\Delta V = \alpha_2\omega - R_2 I \qquad\qquad \text{(D-60)}$$
$$\tau = C_2\omega + \alpha_2 I. \qquad\qquad \text{(D-61)}$$

We may note that R_2 is the internal electrical resistance of the machine

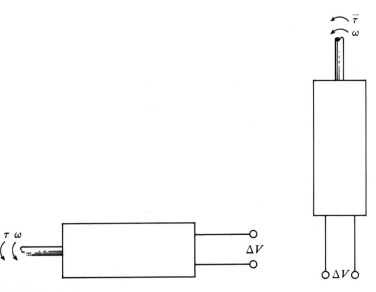

FIG. D-5. A d-c generator.

which reduces the output voltage by R_2I. The quantity C_2 is a drag coefficient, which accounts for bearing friction and windage; it has units of joule-seconds (newton-meter-seconds). These equations also illustrate the well-known electromagnetic relations for d-c machines according to which the voltage is proportional to the product of the field strength and the speed, while the torque is proportional to the product of the field strength and the current. The constant α_2 reflects these interrelationships and has units of volt-seconds. Note that $\alpha_2\omega$ represents the generated voltage which must have the IR drop subtracted from it to obtain the output voltage of the machine.

Here, as in the case of the positive displacement hydraulic engine, R_2 and C_2 are independent of each other and thus ideal conversion is approachable. The dissipation rate for the machine is given by Eq. D-45:

$$D = C_2\omega^2 + R_2I^2 \quad \text{[watts]}. \tag{D-62}$$

Odd class, coupled type. We now consider a device that is magnetic field dependent and cannot approach 100 percent conversion efficiency, the Nernst generator. We will discuss the operating characteristics of such a generator in Ch. 9. A Nernst generator may be thought of as a rectangular slab of material that has a heat flux applied to it in one direction while a perpendicular magnetic field is also applied. A voltage appears in a direction perpendicular to both the applied field and the heat flux. A schematic of such a device is shown in Fig. D-6.

We assume that the generator lies in the x-y plane while the magnetic field is in the z direction. We further assume that the heat flow is confined to the x direction and the current flow to the y direction. Under these assumptions the dissipation rate is given by the first and fourth terms of Eq. D-28. Thus

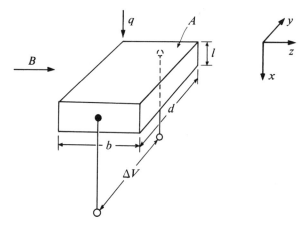

FIG. D-6. A Nernst effect generator.

$$D = q(\Delta T/T) - I\,\Delta V \qquad\qquad \text{(D-63)}$$
$$= \text{[theoretically available]} - \text{[actually delivered]},$$

where ΔT is the temperature drop through the converter in the direction of q; ΔV is the potential rise through the device in the direction of I. The thermodynamic equations of motion for this device are given by Eqs. D-43 and D-44, where we identify the input flux as q and the input force as $\Delta T/T$. Thus

$$\Delta V = \alpha_2 q - R_2 I \qquad\qquad \text{(D-64)}$$
$$\Delta T/T = C_2 q + \alpha_2 I. \qquad\qquad \text{(D-65)}$$

We now identify the coefficients in the above equations: R_2 is the internal electrical resistance,

$$R_2 = \rho d/(bl) \qquad \text{[ohms]}, \qquad\qquad \text{(D-66)}$$

while the reciprocal of $C_2 T$ is the internal thermal conductance

$$K = 1/C_2 T = \lambda A/l = \lambda bd/l \qquad \text{[watts/}^\circ\text{K]}. \qquad \text{(D-67)}$$

It is evident from Eqs. D-66 and D-67 that both $C_2 T$ and R_2 cannot be made to vanish simultaneously. Thus coupling in this device is clearly established.

The voltage rise that a temperature difference and magnetic field will produce in a material is measured by its Nernst coefficient, defined as

$$Q' = \frac{\Delta V\, l}{B\, \Delta T\, d} \qquad \text{[volts/gauss-}^\circ\text{K]}. \qquad\qquad \text{(D-68)}$$

Under zero current conditions the voltage rise that a heat flux will produce in a material in a magnetic field is measured by α_2 according to Eq. D-64:

$$\alpha_2 = \Delta V/q \qquad \text{[volts/watt]}. \qquad\qquad \text{(D-69)}$$

We may express the heat flux across the device in terms of the applied temperature difference and thermal conductivity as

$$q = \frac{\lambda\, \Delta T(bd)}{l} \qquad \text{[watts]}. \qquad\qquad \text{(D-70)}$$

Combining Eqs. D-70 and D-69 to eliminate the heat flux we obtain

$$\alpha_2 = \frac{\Delta V\, l}{\Delta T\lambda(bd)}. \qquad\qquad \text{(D-71)}$$

We may now eliminate $\Delta V/\Delta T$ from Eq. D-71 by means of Eq. D-68 to obtain

$$\alpha_2 = \frac{BQ'}{b\lambda}, \qquad\qquad \text{(D-72)}$$

which is clearly magnetic field dependent.

If a current from an external source is passed through the device, a temperature difference will be produced in the x direction proportional to the magnetic field and the current. The magnitude of this effect in a material is measured by its Ettingshausen coefficient, defined as

$$P' = \frac{\Delta T\, b}{BI}. \tag{D-73}$$

By perfectly insulating the surfaces of the device that lie in the y-z plane ($q = 0$), the extent of this temperature difference may be found from Eq. D-65 as

$$\alpha_2 = \frac{\Delta T}{TI}. \tag{D-74}$$

Combining Eqs. D-74 and D-73 to eliminate ΔT we obtain

$$\alpha_2 = \frac{BP'}{bT}. \tag{D-75}$$

We have now defined α_2 in terms of two different sets of parameters as given by Eqs. D-72 and D-75, which we may now equate to obtain an equation known in the thermodynamics of solid state generators as the *Bridgman relation:*

$$P'\lambda = Q'T. \tag{D-76}$$

The dissipation rate for this device is obtained from Eq. 2-45 as

$$D = C_2 q^2 + R_2 I^2. \tag{D-77}$$

D.2.4   Calculation of the conversion efficiency. Equation D-31 defined the thermodynamic conversion efficiency as

$$\eta = \frac{J_o X_o}{J_i X_i}. \tag{D-31}$$

This relationship, in some cases, is more accurately termed an *effectiveness.* That is, it is the fraction delivered of that which is theoretically available. For example, in the thermoelectric case it is the percent of the Carnot efficiency (the maximum efficiency for any heat engine) at which the device operates. Since in Section D.2.1 we established that the fluxes and forces are related in two different ways, depending on whether or not conversion is of the even or odd class, we will establish the efficiency of each class separately.

Even class conversion. Equations D-36 and D-37 are the thermodynamic equations of motion, which we substitute into Eq. D-31 to obtain the even class efficiency expression

$$\eta = \frac{J_o(\alpha_1 X_i - R_1 J_o)}{(C_1 X_i + \alpha_1 J_o) X_i}. \tag{D-78}$$

Assuming that X_i is fixed (for example, the change in elevation across the device or its Carnot efficiency $\Delta T/T$), we may take the derivative of the efficiency equation (Eq. D-78) with respect to the output flux and set the result equal to zero to find the output flux which maximizes the efficiency

$$(J_o)_{\mathrm{opt}} = [C_1 X_i/\alpha_1][(1 + \beta_1)^{1/2} - 1], \tag{D-79}$$

where

$$\beta_1 = \alpha_1^2/(R_1 C_1). \tag{D-80}$$

Substituting the optimum current expression (Eq. D-79) into Eq. D-78 yields a maximum efficiency of

$$\eta_{\max} = \frac{(1 + \beta_1)^{1/2} - 1}{(1 + \beta_1)^{1/2} + 1}. \tag{D-81}$$

Again we remind the reader that this result is valid only for the case of a small input force.

In working with generators that produce an electrical output it is more useful to find the optimum resistance ratio R_o/R—that is, the ratio of external load resistance to internal device resistance that maximizes the efficiency. For even class devices this ratio is

$$(m)_{\text{opt}} = R_o/R = (1 + \beta_1)^{1/2}, \tag{D-82}$$

which in the case of a thermoelectric generator is

$$\beta_1 = \frac{\alpha^2 T}{\rho\lambda} = Z_1 T, \tag{D-83}$$

where Z_1 is generally called the figure of merit for a thermoelectric generator.

Odd class conversion. The conversion efficiency for odd class devices may be found by substituting the expressions for the output force and input force given by Eqs. D-43 and D-44 into Eq. D-31:

$$\eta = \frac{J_o(\alpha_2 J_i - R_2 J_o)}{J_i(C_2 J_i + \alpha_2 J_o)}. \tag{D-84}$$

Assuming that J_i is fixed (for example, the angular velocity of the generator shaft or the heat flux to a Nernst generator), we may take the derivative of Eq. D-84 with respect to the output flux J_o and set the results equal to zero to obtain the output flux which maximizes the efficiency

$$(J_o)_{\text{opt}} = [C_2 J_i/\alpha_2][(1 + \beta_2)^{1/2} - 1], \tag{D-85}$$

where

$$\beta_2 = \alpha_2^2/(R_2 C_2). \tag{D-86}$$

Upon substituting Eq. D-85 into Eq. D-84, we find that the maximum efficiency expression for odd class conversion devices is the same† as for even class conversion devices with β_1 replaced by β_2 in Eq. D-81.

Thus we have derived a general expression for efficiency that applies to both odd and even class devices which may be coupled or uncoupled. The expression for efficiency given by Eq. D-81 merely requires that we utilize the appropriate coefficients in calculating the dimensionless β factor. In addition, the work in Section D.2 has allowed us to classify devices according to whether the output force is induced by an input force or by an input flux. Furthermore, we found that all converters could be classified into groups in which ideal no-loss conversion was possible (uncoupled type) and into groups in which no-loss conversion was impossible (coupled type). We were able to accomplish this classification by means of irreversible thermodynamics. Although the results of this work are not startling in themselves, we are certainly better prepared to examine the various modes of energy conversion because of the perspective we now have on the energy conversion process.

NOTATION

A	= area, m^2	
b	= length, meters	
B	= magnetic flux density, gauss	
$\boldsymbol{B}$	= magnetic flux density vector, gauss	
C	= conductance coefficient	
d	= length, meters	
D	= dissipation, watts	
g	= acceleration of gravity, m/sec^2	
g_c	= conversion factor, $m\text{-}kg/(nt\text{-}sec^2)$	
grad	= gradient of a scalar field as defined by Eq. 2-1	
h	= specific enthalpy, joules/kg	
i	= unit vector in the x direction	
I	= electric current, amperes	
j	= unit vector in the y direction	
J	= generalized rate of flow	
$\boldsymbol{J}$	= generalized rate of flow vector	
k	= unit vector in the z direction	
K	= thermal conductance, watts/°K	
l	= length, meters	
L	= scalar coefficient	
m	= mass rate of flow, kg/sec	
P'	= Ettingshausen coefficient, °K-cm/(gauss-amp)	
P_o	= power output, watts	
q	= rate of heat flow, watts	
$\boldsymbol{q}$	= rate of heat flow vector, watts/m^2	
Q	= heat, joules	
Q'	= Nernst coefficient, volts/(gauss-°K)	
R	= resistance coefficient	
R_o	= external load resistance, ohms	
s	= specific entropy, joules/kg-°K	

† Osterle and Angrist [11] have shown that this is true only if the dependent variables are chosen so that the dissipation rate is given by a two-term expression. They have termed this choice "natural" coordinates. If the dependent variables are chosen in a slightly different way, a three-term dissipation rate is obtained and these coordinates have been termed "unnatural." Unnatural coordinates lead to an efficiency expression different in several significant ways from Eq. D-81.

s'	= scalar quantity
T	= temperature, °K
u	= velocity, m/sec
$\mathbf{u}$	= velocity vector, m/sec
V	= electrical potential, volts
X	= generalized driving force
$\mathbf{X}$	= generalized driving force vector
x, y, z	= coordinates
$\alpha, \alpha', \alpha''$	= interaction coefficients
β	= figure of merit, dimensionless
η	= efficiency as defined by Eq. 2-31, dimensionless
θ	= rate of entropy creation, watts/°K
λ	= thermal conductivity, watt/m-°K
π	$= 3.141\cdots$
π_T	= Peltier coefficient, watts/amp
ρ	= electrical resistivity, ohm-cm
τ	= external torque, newton-meter
ω	= angular velocity, radians/sec
Ω	= volume, m³

Subscripts

C	= cold
e	= exit
H	= hot
i	= inlet or input
I	= current
io, oi	= interaction
n	= electrons
o	= output
p	= holes
r	= rejected
s	= supplied
S	= entropy
x, y, z	= coordinate directions
$1, 2$	= classes

PROBLEMS

D-1. Using the principle of increasing entropy and the first law of thermodynamics, find the rate of increase of entropy as a function of the Gibbs function ($G = H - TS$) for a constant pressure and constant temperature chemical reaction.

D-2. Find the heat flux in a rod with a mean temperature of 0°C with a dissipation rate of 105 watts that has Joule heating of 25 watts and an applied temperature difference of 10°K.

D-3. Discuss the possibility of a temperature gradient inducing a momentum flux.

D-4. Discuss the possibility of a concentration gradient inducing a mass flux.

D-5. A 100-ohm resistor carrying a current of 15 amp is maintained at a constant temperature of 300°K by forced convection. In 1 sec, what is the change in entropy of the resistor? What is the universe's change in entropy?

D-6. A thermally insulated 100-ohm resistor carries a current of 15 amp for 1 sec. The initial temperature of the resistor is 0°C; it has a mass of 7 gm, and its heat capacity is 900 joules per kg-°K. What is the resistor's change of entropy and the entropy change of the universe?

D-7. A hydraulic turbine in a new power plant delivers 100,000 kW with an efficiency of 92 percent to an electric generator. The drop across the turbines is 350 ft, and the turbine runs at 900 rpm. Find the mass rate of flow through the turbine. If the mass displaced in each revolution of the turbine is 100 kg, find the leakage and friction coefficients for the turbine.

Answers: $C_1 = 9.8 \times 10$ kg²/(nt-m-sec); $R_1 = 1.11 \times 10^4$ nt-m-sec.

D-8. A thermoelectric generator operates between 600°K and 300°K with the following properties for both the materials that make up the generator: Seebeck coefficient 500×10^{-6} volts per °K; resistance 0.05 ohm; thermal conductance 0.01 watt per °K. When a current of 0.5 amp is drawn from the device, what is its thermal efficiency and the rate of dissipation?

Answers: $\eta = 1.98$ percent; $D = 1.51$ watts.

D-9. A d-c generator has an output of 220 volts while running at 3600 rpm. The dissipation is 2000 watts when the current drawn is 100 amps. At this operating point the internal IR drop across the generator is 10 volts. What is the magnitude of the drag coefficient that accounts for friction and windage? What is the generator efficiency?

Answers: $C_2 = 7.1 \times 10^{-3}$ joule-sec; $\eta = 91.5$ percent.

D-10. Derive Eq. D-79, the expression for the optimum output flux, and Eq. D-81, the efficiency equation.

D-11. What is the optimum resistance ratio for the thermoelectric generator of Problem D-8?

D-12. Assume that conversion in the even class device were to proceed in the opposite direction (that is, the input becomes the output and the output becomes the input). Is the maximum efficiency still given by an expression like Eq. D-81, with a new coefficient β_1' defined? Justify your answer. How is β_1' related to β_1?

D-13. Consider, for odd class devices, the same situation as discussed in the preceding problem. What is the form of the reversed conversion efficiency expression?

D-14. If a thermionic converter is considered to be an even class device of the coupled type, identify J_i, X_i, J_o, and X_o for such a converter. Write the expressions for output force and input flux for the thermionic converter in terms of the coefficients α_1, R_1 and C_1. Evaluate the coefficients α_1 and C_1 for a thermionic converter.

D-15. Given a thermionic converter operating under the following conditions: emitter temperature = 2000°K; collector temperature = 800°K; internal resistance, $R_1 = 0.25$ ohm; collector work function = 1.6 volts; space charge barrier, $\delta = 0.80$ volt; thermal conductance, K = 0.01 watt/°K. Determine the optimum current that will be obtained and the power produced.

REFERENCES

1. J. F. Osterle, "A Unified Treatment of the Thermodynamics of Steady-State Energy Conversion," *Applied Scientific Research*, Section A, 12 (1964), 425–434.

2. K. B. Denbigh, *The Thermodynamics of the Steady State* (New York: John Wiley & Sons, Inc., 1951).

3. S. R. deGroot and P. Mazur, *Non-Equilibrium Thermodynamics* (New York: Interscience Publishers, Inc., 1962).

4. I. Prigogine, *Introduction to Thermodynamics of Irreversible Processes*. 3rd ed. (New York: Interscience Publishers, Inc., 1968).

5. L. Onsager, "Reciprocal Relations in Irreversible Processes, I," *Physical Review*, 37 (1931), 405–426.

6. D. G. Miller, "Thermodynamics of Irreversible Processes: The Experimental Verification of the Onsager Reciprocal Relations," *Chemical Reviews*, 60 (1960), 15–37.

7. F. A. Morrison and J. F. Osterle, "Electrokinetic Energy Conversion in Ultrafine Capillaries," *Journal of Chemical Physics*, 43 (1965), 2111–2115.

8. G. McLennan and J. F. Osterle, "Thermomolecular Energy Converters: Part I, Engine Cycles; Part II, Heat Pumps and Zero-Work Refrigerators," *Advanced Energy Conversion*, 6 (1966), 1–24.

9. F. A. Morrison and J. F. Osterle, "A Unified Treatment of the Thermodynamics of Sinusoidal Steady-State Energy Conversion," *Advanced Energy Conversion*, 9 (1969), 7–12.

10. M. A. Weinstein, "Irreversible Thermodynamics of Photoluminescence," *General Electric Lighting Research Laboratory Report No. 130–518*, August, 1965. Available from Lamp Division, General Electric Co., Cleveland, Ohio, 44112.

11. J. F. Osterle and S. W. Angrist, "On the Choice of Coordinates Used to Describe Thermoelectric and Thermomagnetic Generators," *Journal of Applied Mechanics, Transactions of the ASME*, 30 (1963), 426–429.

Additional basic references on irreversible thermodynamics

C. A. Domenicali, "Irreversible Thermodynamics of Thermoelectricity," *Reviews of Modern Physics*, 26 (1954), 237–275.

H. B. Callen, *Thermodynamics* (New York: John Wiley & Sons, Inc., 1960).

Name Index

Adams, W. G., 6, 192
Adler, R. B., 127
Allen, J. W., 68
Altenkirch, E., 7, 130
Anderson, K. E., 68
Angrist, S. W., 92, 418, 420, 423, 471, 504, 507
Amend, W. E., 345, 352
Anno, J. N., 456, 457, 473
Arntzen, J. D., 68
Austin, L. G., 383, 391, 418
Azaroff, L. V., 69, 127, 128, 196, 247

Bacon, F. T., 8, 356
Baker, B. S., 396, 400, 417
Bardeen, J., 8
Barnett, C. V., 351
Bartholme, L. G., 68
Bates, H. E., 155, 189
Baurle, J. E., 190
Becquerel, E., 6, 191, 249
Bell, A. G., 7
Berganini, D. F., 190
Berger, C., 417
Bergman, P. D., 338, 352, 356
Berl, W. G., 356
Bienstock, D. L., 338, 352
Bitterbeck, W. J., 247
Blackman, V. H., 351
Blair, J., 472
Blanchard, C. H., 190, 208, 247
Böhm, H., 401, 418
Boltzmann, L., 83, 84, 104
Bose, J. C., 7
Boster, G. E., 473
Brake, J. M., 418
Brattain, W. H., 8
Braun, F., 670
Breitwieser, R., 288, 297
Brink, W., 402–18
Brittain, W. M., 190
Brogan, T. R., 351
Brown, J. T., 68
Bube, R. H., 192, 246
Burnett, C. R., 190, 247
Burns, J. D., 352
Bush, J. B., Jr., 68

Cady, W. G., 455, 472, 473
Cahn, J. H., 127
Cairns, E. J., 417, 418
Callen, H. B., 7, 507
Cambel, A. B., 300, 302, 306, 351
Camp, R. N., 400, 417
Cassano, A. J., 289, 297
Chapin, D. M., 225, 226, 227, 228, 247

Chattock, A. P., 441, 472
Cherry, W. R., 241, 248
Chester, M., 425, 431, 472
Childress, J. D., 425, 429, 472
Chrisney, J., 418
Christenberry, S. T., 190
Christian, S. M., 456, 473
Clayton, C. G., 473
Clement, J. D., 352
Clingman, W. H., 425, 430, 471
Cobine, J. D., 351
Collins, M. F., 402, 418
Colwell, J., 423, 424, 471
Compton, A. H., 74
Cool, R., 247
Corliss, W. H., 190
Cotter, T. P., 297
Crabtree, L. W., 248
Cronin, J. H., 68
Crookes, W., 6, 299
Crossley, P. A., 247
Curie, J., 451
Curie, P., 451, 489
Curtin, D. J., 247
Cutting, J. C., 345, 352

Davison, E., 247
Davy, H., 5, 350
Day, R. E., 5, 6, 192
de Broglie, L., 71, 79
DeCorso, S. M., 351
DeGroot, S. R., 507
Demeter, J. J., 338, 352
Demitriades, A., 351
Denbigh, K. B., 483, 507
DeSteese, J. G., 291, 297
Dicks, J. B., 351
Dingwall, A. G. F., 190
Dirac, P. A. M., 83
Domenicali, C. A., 507
Douglas, R. W., 170, 190
Dowdell, R. B., 289, 297
Dudziak, D. J., 473
DuFay, C., 6, 249

Edison, T. A., 7, 250
Egli, P. H., 128, 190
Einstein, A., 73
Eisberg, R. M., 70, 127
Eisenberg, M., 388, 417
Eisenhower, D. D., 13
Elliott, J. F., 425, 429, 431, 471
Ellis, W. R., 473
Elsner, N. B., 190
Elster, J., 5, 7, 249
Engdahl, R. E., 289, 297
Erickson, G. F., 297
Ericson, R. B., 482
Erway, D. D., 247, 352
Evans, W. H., 417

Faraday, M., 5, 6, 69, 299
Fermi, E., 82–84, 85, 93, 94, 100, 101, 171
Fleming, J. A., 250
Folstad, S. H., 418
Fraas, A. P., 473
Franseen, R. E., 190
Freeman, D. C., 352
Fretter, E. F., 472
Frysinger, G. R., 417

Gains, L., 68
Gasper, K. A., 291, 297
Gay, E. G., 68
Geitel, F., 7, 249
Gerber, A., 36
Giacoletto, L. J., 31, 36
Gietzen, A. J., 297
Goldsmid, H. J., 8, 170, 190
Gore, D. C., 351
Griffith, R. W., 472
Grondahl, L. O., 192
Gross, B., 460, 473
Gross, S., 53, 67
Grove, W., 6, 354, 355, 382
Grover, G. M., 288, 297
Guthrie, G., 471

Hall, E. H., 6
Hampl, E. F., 482
Hand, R., 247
Hansen, C. F., 303, 351
Harman, T. C., 113, 127, 151, 189, 420, 471
Harries, W. L., 436, 439, 472
Harris, L. P., 351
Harrowell, R. V., 351
Harvey, D. L., 190
Hatsopoulos, G. N., 8, 250, 296
Heikes, R. R., 109, 127, 153, 154, 155, 156, 166, 170, 171, 189
Heindl, C. J., 458, 473
Heisenberg, W., 71, 74, 75
Helmholtz, H. F. H., 358, 445, 448
Henne, R., 285, 297
Hepler, L. G., 372, 417
Hernquist, K. G., 268, 272, 296
Hockings, E. F., 476, 477, 478, 479
Hodgman, C. D., 351
Hoffman, G. A., 67, 68
Hoh, S. R., 436, 439, 472
Hohmeyer, W. G., 297
Holden, A., 117, 128
Honig, J. M., 420, 471
Hottel, H. C., 56, 58, 68
Houston, J. M., 259, 265, 282, 296

Subject Index

510

Resistance ratio: maximum efficiency, 145, 503; maximum power, 147
Resistivity, electrical, 104, 167 (*see also* Conductivity, electrical) definition of, 104, 498
Resonance ionization, 268, 272 (*see also* Surface ionization)
Reverse bias, 200
Reversible cell potential, 362
Reynolds number, 386, 391, 441
Richardson-Dushman equation, 258
Rochelle salt, 451

Saha equation, 307
Sapphire covers, 237
Saturation current: in *p-n* junctions, 200–202 (*see also* Dark current); in thermionic converters, 258, 281 (*see also* Richardson-Dushman equation)
Scattering, 105–7, 112, 169
Scattering centers, 107
Scattering collision, 107, 108
Scattering constant, 109
Schmidt number, 386, 391–92
Schrödinger equation, 76–83
Second law of thermodynamics (*see* Thermodynamics)
Secondary particle collection devices, 461–64
Seebeck coefficient: absolute value of, 135–36; as a function of carrier concentration, 168; combined for two materials, 143, 158; definition of, 498; as an index to sign of semiconductors, 139; in metals, 166; in semiconductors, 138–39, 169; which maximizes the figure of merit, 171
Seebeck effect, early history of, 5–8
Seebeck voltage, 131–32
Seeding, 309
Segmented arm generators, 153–56, 173
Segregation constant, 119, 126
Selenium, 6, 7
Semiconductors: compensated, 115; concentration of carriers in, 101, 102; contacts to, 172–75; diffusion length, 206; dopants, 91; early history of, 5–8, 69–70; energy bands in, 91–103; excitation in, 91; extrinsic, 91, 92, 96–103; holes in, 91; intrinsic, 91, 93; lifetime in, 197; maximization of figure of merit in, 168–72; mechanical properties of, 172–75; *n*-type, 91, 92, 97–100; *p*-type, 91, 92, 97–103; optical effects in, 194–204; production techniques, 117–22
Sheaths, 271–72, 274, 276
Sign convention: electrochemical cells, 360; Latimer, 369
Silicon, 96–98; Debye temperature of, 113; Fermi level variation (*drawing*), 103; properties of (*table*), 214
Silicon germanium alloys, 173–75; properties of, 480
Silicon solar cell, 214, 221–26; fabrication of, 229–30; maximum efficiency of, 210
Silver antimony telluride, properties of, 478

Simple band approximation, 168–72
Simple harmonic oscillator, 78
Skylab space station, 232, 239
SNAP, 32, 181, 460
Sodium, energy levels in, 87–89
Sodium-sulfur battery, 50
Solar cell power systems (*see also* Photovoltaic generators) in large arrays, 238–39; reliability, 234
Solar energy, availability of, 226–27, 241
Solar farms, 242
Solar spectrum, as a function of absorption conditions (*table*), 194
Sonic velocity, 317
Soret effect, 489
Space, power requirements for, 28–32
Space charge, 260 (*see also* Retarding potential barrier)
Space charge control, 266–84
Specific heat, 255–56; ratio of, 317, 324 (*see also* Heat capacities; Constant pressure and Constant volume specific heat)
Spectral distribution, 193–95
Spectroscopic designation of electron states, 82–83
Speed, mean, in a Maxwellian distribution, 257, 270
Stagnation state, definition of, 317
Standard cell potential, 364
Standard emf (*see* Standard cell potential)
Standard free energy change (*see* Gibbs free energy)
Standard state, 362
State: definition of, 87; electron letter designation of, 87; localized, 99; stagnation, 317; standard, 362; static, 317
Statistics: Boltzmann, 202; classical, 110; Fermi-Dirac, 83–84; Maxwell-Boltzmann, 257
Stefan-Boltzmann law, 263, 474
Stopping potential, 71–73
Storage, energy (*see* Energy, storage)
Sun, energy production of, 17–18
Sunlight: hour of full, 226–27; spectral distribution of, 193–95
Superconducting magnet (*see* Magnet)
Superposition, principle of, 488
Surface ionization, 306
Surface recombination velocity, 209
Surface work, 253 (*see also* Work function)

Tafel equation, 380–81
Teledyne Corp., 180, 181, 182
Temperature distribution, in thermoelectric generators, 141–44
Tennessee Valley Authority, 289
Thermal conductance, 144, 498
Thermal conductivity, 111–13; cesium vapor, 282; contributors to, 112; definition of, 111, 498; electronic portion, 112, 164; from figure of merit, 167, 168; lattice portion, 112, 167, 170; measurement of, 113
Thermal efficiency, definition of, 144
Thermal energy storage, 56–59
Thermal excitation, 91
Thermal ionization, 300–303, 305

Volt, definition of, 35
Voltage factor, 219

Wave equation, 76-83
Wave function, 76-78
Wave theory of light, 73
Weather factor, 226-27
Westinghouse Electric Corporation, 275
Wiedemann-Franz-Lorenz law, 112, 166-67, 170, 283
Wien's displacement law, 432
Work: definition of, 35; done in charging a capacitor, 452-53; electrical, 362; maximum, 356-59, 362; maximum useful, 359, 362, 366, 368, 374;

Work (*cont.*)
reversible, 358-59
Work function, 251-54, 257; collector, 285; definition of, 73, 257; emitter, 284; neutralization (*table*), 267
World, energy consumption of, 9, 10, 15

Young's modulus, 452

Zinc-air battery, 49
Zinc-bromine battery, 45
Zinc-chlorine battery, 47
Zirconia, 333-34
Zirconium, 335
Zone refining, 119-20